Fiji

Justine Vaisutis

Mark Dapin, Claire Waddell, Virginia Jealous

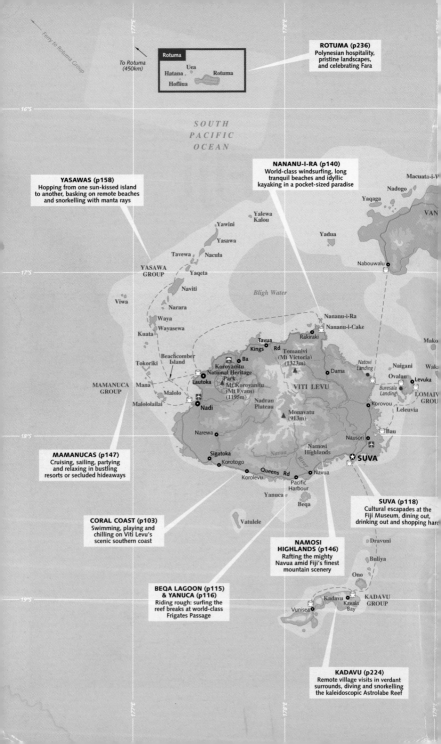

Ferry to Rotuma Group

To Rotuma
(450km)

Rotuma
Uea
Hatana   Rotuma
Hofliua

ROTUMA (p236)
Polynesian hospitality,
pristine landscapes,
and celebrating Fara

*SOUTH
PACIFIC
OCEAN*

Macuata-i-V

Nadogo

Yaqaga

VAN

NANANU-I-RA (p140)
World-class windsurfing, long
tranquil beaches and idyllic
kayaking in a pocket-sized paradise

YASAWAS (p158)
Hopping from one sun-kissed island
to another, basking on remote beaches
and snorkelling with manta rays

Yalewa
Kalou

Yawini

Yasawa

Yadua

Tavewa   Nacula

Nabouwalu

YASAWA
GROUP   Yaqeta

Naviti   *Bligh Water*

Viwa   Narara

Waya
Kuata Wayasewa   Nananu-i-Ra
                          Nananu-i-Cake   Mako
Tokoriki Beachcomber   Rakiraki
         Island   Tavua
                    Kings Rd
MAMANUCA   Ba   Tomanivi   Natovi   Naigani   Waka
GROUP   Mana Koroyanitu   (Mt Victoria)   Landing   Ovalau Levuka
        Malolo National Heritage (1323m)   Dama   LOMAIV
Malololailai   Park   VITI LEVU   Buresala GROU
             Mt Koroyanitu   Landing
       Nadi   (Mt Evans)   Leleuvia
             (1195m)   Monavatu
       Narewa   Nadrau   (913m)   Korovou
             Plateau   Namosi   Bau
                          Highlands Nausori
      Sigatoka   SUVA
  Korotogo
    Queens Rd
   Korolevu   Navua
         Pacific
  Yanuca   Harbour   **SUVA (p118)**
                    Cultural escapades at the
        Beqa   Fiji Museum, dining out,
                    drinking out and shopping hard

MAMANUCAS (p147)
Cruising, sailing, partying
and relaxing in bustling
resorts or secluded hideaways

Vatulele

CORAL COAST (p103)
Swimming, playing and
chilling on Viti Levu's
scenic southern coast

Dravuni

**NAMOSI
HIGHLANDS (p146)**
Rafting the mighty
Navua amid Fiji's finest
mountain scenery

Buliya

Ono

**BEQA LAGOON (p115)
& YANUCA (p116)**
Riding rough: surfing the
reef breaks at world-class
Frigates Passage

Kadavu   KADAVU
       Kavala   GROUP
Vunisea   Bay

KADAVU (p224)
Remote village visits in verdant
surrounds, diving and snorkelling
the kaleidoscopic Astrolabe Reef

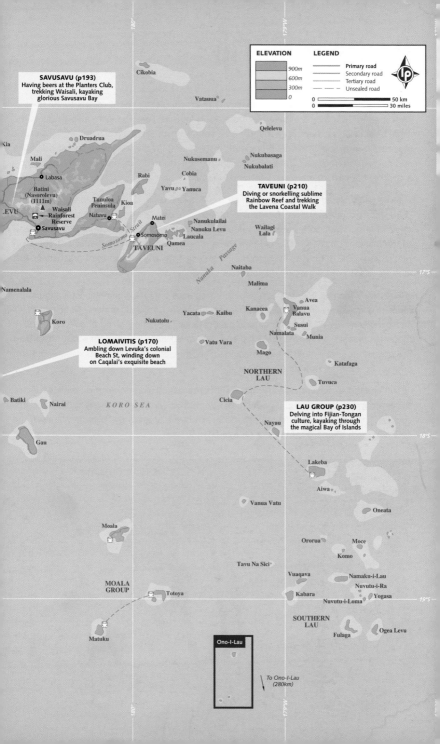

ELEVATION

900m
600m
300m
0

LEGEND

Primary road
Secondary road
Tertiary road
Unsealed road

0 _____ 50 km
0 _____ 30 miles

Cikobia

Vatauua

Qelelevu

SAVUSAVU (p193)
Having beers at the Planters Club, trekking Waisali, kayaking glorious Savusavu Bay

Druadrua

xia

Mali

Labasa

Batini (Nasorolevu) (1111m)

LEVU

Rabi

Nukusemanu

Nukubasaga
Nukubalati

Cobia

Yavu Yanuca

Tunuloa Peninsula

Kioa

Natuvu

Matei

Nanukulailai
Nanuku Levu
Laucala

Wailagi Lala

Waisali Rainforest Reserve

Savusavu

Somosomo

Qamea

TAVEUNI (p210)
Diving or snorkelling sublime Rainbow Reef and trekking the Lavena Coastal Walk

TAVEUNI

Somosomo Strait

Namuka Passage

Naitaba

Malima

Namenalala

Koro

Nukutolu

Yacata Kaibu

Kanacea

Avea

Vanua Balavu

Susui

Namalata

Munia

LOMAIVITIS (p170)
Ambling down Levuka's colonial Beach St, winding down on Caqalai's exquisite beach

Vatu Vara

Mago

Katafaga

NORTHERN LAU

Tuvuca

Batiki Nairai

KORO SEA

Cicia

LAU GROUP (p230)
Delving into Fijian-Tongan culture, kayaking through the magical Bay of Islands

Gau

Nayau

Lakeba

Aiwa

Vanua Vatu

Oneata

Moala

Ororua

Moce

Komo

Tavu Na Sici

Vuaqava

Namaku-i-Lau

Nuvutu-i-Ra

MOALA GROUP

Totoya

Kabara

Nuvutu-i-Loma

Yogasa

SOUTHERN LAU

Matuku

Fulaga

Ogea Levu

Ono-I-Lau

To Ono-I-Lau (280km)

Destination Fiji

Bula! Burn this word into your vocabulary. The brochures tell you it means Hello! Cheers! Welcome! But the only thing warmer than a sun-induced coma beneath a Fijian sky is the smile from locals as they cast a friendly *bula* your way. It's Fiji in a (coco)nut shell – beauty, grace, relaxation and charm. Its therapeutic resonance shifts the weight from your shoulders and the tension from your bones. Even 'Fiji time' adheres to the *bula* philosophy, occupying a concept somewhere between GMT and infinity.

Most visitors head here for the sublime sun and sea. Lapped by cerulean waters, this archipelago encompasses over 300 islands, so notions of cocktails on an alabaster beach aren't mere whimsy. Swim, surf, snorkel, kayak or simply wallow in the tepid Yasawa waters. Head to the Mamanucas for a family fling or find a remote hideaway in the Kadavu or Lomaiviti isles. Things only get hectic beneath the ocean's surface, where schools of psychedelic fish (and the odd diver) flutter amid kilometres of vivid coral.

But here's the real windfall: that superb coastline is only the perimeter. Fiji's rugged interior is a mass of emerald hills peppered with extinct volcanic craters, giant waterfalls and panoramic views. Amid the natural beauty lies a fascinating blend of cultures. Explore mountain villages, archaeological sites and colourful Hindu temples, then fast-forward to the present in Suva's multicultural melange. Shop for saris and *sulu* (skirts or sarongs) and dine on fiery curries or fragrant seafood.

Still looking for incentives? Try this – Fiji is the easiest country in the South Pacific to travel around and the friendly population adopts you on arrival. It caters to backpackers, couples, families, retirees, adventurers and beach bums. So grab the boardies, farewell the pets and ditch the daily grind for a slice of Eden.

RICHARD I'AN

Highlights

SIMON CHARLES ROWE

The relaxing, tropical grounds of a resort, Kadavu island (p224)

DAVID WALL

A short wade from a palm-fringed beach reveals an inviting rock pool, Korolevu (p110), Viti Levu

Village girl admires the highland scenery, Bukuya (p145), Viti Levu

DANIEL BOAG

CASEY & ASTRID WITTE MAHANEY

Hard-coral formations seem to reach for the sun, Great Astrolabe Reef (p62), Kadavu island

Snorkeller glides through crystal-clear water, Mamanuca Group (p147)

CASEY & ASTRID WITTE MAHANEY

CASEY & ASTRID WITTE MAHANEY

Diver admires the profusion of soft coral, Motualevu Atoll (p62), Taveuni island

Opposite: Scissor-tail sergeants swim amid a patch of cabbage coral, Nigali Passage (p60), Lomaiviti Group

CASEY & ASTRID WITTE MAHANEY

The aromas of an Indo-Fijian sweet shop attracts regular customers, Suva (p118), Viti Levu

A woman wears a traditional garland of pandanus in the Suva Curio & Handicraft Centre (p134), Suva, Viti Levu

An Indo-Fijian stall vendor waits patiently beside his wares, Nadi (p75), Viti Levu

CASEY & ASTRID WITTE MAHANEY

Villagers prepare for a *kava* (narcotic drink) offering in Fiji's highlands (p142), Viti Levu

Fijian man examines produce at an open-air market, Savusavu (p193), Vanua Levu

ROBYN JONES

PHILIP GAME

Spices at a market tempt the taste buds, Lautoka (p90), Viti Levu

ROBYN JONES

The impressive Sigatoka Sand Dunes (p105) rise up to 60m, Viti Levu

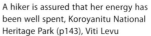

A hiker is assured that her energy has been well spent, Koroyanitu National Heritage Park (p143), Viti Levu

SCOTT DARSNEY

ROBYN JONES

The cloud-covered Sabeto Mountains form a backdrop to an Indo-Fijian school, Nadi (p75), Viti Levu

CASEY & ASTRID WITTE MAHANEY

Colourful kayaks line the beach at Musket Cove Marina (p155), Malololailai, Mamanuca Group

DAVID WALL

A waterfall graces the senses, Biausevu (p110), Viti Levu

ROBYN JONES

Local girls smile for the photographer, Vunisea (p225), Kadavu island

LIZ THOMPSON

Cannibal forks, fans and *masi* (bark cloth) on view at Suva Curio & Handicraft Centre (p134), Suva, Viti Levu

OTHER HIGHLIGHTS

- Surfing off the Mamanuca islands (p117) or at Frigates Passage (p117), Beqa Lagoon
- Swimming or relaxing at the Blue Lagoon (p167) or Oarsman's Bay (p168), Yasawa Group
- Easing into the laid-back life at colonial-era Levuka (p174), Lomaiviti Group

Model of a tribal chief with face paint (p40), Suva, Viti Levu

RICHARD I'ANSON

Artefacts of cannibalism evoke a bygone era at the Fiji Museum (p121), Suva, Viti Levu

SCOTT DARSNEY

Contents

The Authors 15

Getting Started 17

Itineraries 21

Snapshot 26

History 27

The Culture 35

Indo-Fijian History & Culture 44

Environment 51

Diving 57

Food & Drink 66

Viti Levu 71

NADI & THE WEST 75
Nadi 75
Around Nadi 87
Lautoka 90
Momi Bay 101
Robinson Crusoe Island 102
Natadola Beach 102
Yanuca & Around 103
CORAL COAST 103
Sigatoka 103
Around Sigatoka 105
Korotogo & Around 107
Korolevu & Around 110
Pacific Harbour & Navua 112
Offshore Islands 115
SUVA 118
History 118
Orientation 119
Information 120
Dangers & Annoyances 121

Sights 121
Activities 125
Walking Tour 126
Tours 128
Sleeping 128
Eating 130
Drinking 133
Entertainment 134
Shopping 134
Getting There & Away 135
Getting Around 135
KINGS ROAD 136
Nausori & the Rewa Delta 136
Korovou to Dama 137
Naiserelagi Catholic Mission 138
Rakiraki & Around 138
Nananu-i-Ra 140
Tavua & Ba 142
VITI LEVU HIGHLANDS 142
Koroyanitu National Heritage Park 143
Nausori Highlands 143
Nadarivatu, Navai & Koro-ni-O 145
Upper Sigatoka Valley 145
Namosi Highlands 146

Mamanuca Group 147
Bounty Island 150
South Sea Island 150
Beachcomber Island 151
Treasure Island 151
Vomo 151
Navini 151
Mana 152
Matamanoa 153
Tokoriki 154
Castaway Island 154
Wadigi 154
Malolo 154
Malololailai 155
Namotu 157
Tavarua 157

Yasawa Group 158
Kuata 162
Wayasewa 162
Waya 163
Naviti & Around 164
Tavewa 166

Nanuya Lailai 167
Matacawalevu 168
Nacula 168
Nanuya Levu
(Turtle Island) 169
Sawa-i-Lau 169
Yasawa 169

Lomaiviti Group 170

OVALAU **173**
Levuka & Around 174
Lovoni 176
Rukuruku 176
Arovudi (Silana) 177
Sleeping 177
Eating 178
Drinking & Entertainment 179
Getting There & Around 179
OTHER LOMAIVITI
ISLANDS **180**
Yanuca Lailai 180
Moturiki 180
Caqalai 180
Leleuvia 189
Wakaya 189
Koro 189
Naigani 190
Namenalala 190

Vanua Levu 191

Savusavu 193
North of Savusavu 202
Tunuloa Peninsula 202

Offshore Islands 203
Labasa 204
Around Labasa 207
Nabouwalu & Around 208
Wainunu Bay 209

Taveuni 210

Waiyevo, Somosomo
& Around 214
Southern Taveuni 216
Matei 218
Eastern Taveuni 221
Offshore Islands 222

Kadavu Group 224

Orientation 225
Information 225
Activities 225
Sleeping 226
Eating 228
Getting There & Away 228
Getting Around 229

Lau & Moala Groups 230

NORTHERN LAU **232**
Vanua Balavu 232
Kaibu 233
SOUTHERN LAU **234**
Lakeba 234
MOALA GROUP **235**
Moala 235

Rotuma 236

History 237
Information 237
Sights & Activities 237
Sleeping & Eating 237
Shopping 238
Getting There & Away 238

Directory 239

Transport 254

Health 266

Language 272

Glossary 278

Behind the Scenes 280

Index 285

World Time Zones 291

Map Legend 292

ROTUMA
p237

VANUA LEVU
pp192–3

YASAWA
GROUP
p159

TAVEUNI
p211

MAMANUCA
GROUP
p148

LOMAIVITI
GROUP
p172

VITI LEVU
pp72–3

LAU & MOALA
GROUPS
p231

KADAVU
GROUP
p226

The Authors

JUSTINE VAISUTIS   Coordinating Author, Viti Levu, Yasawa Group, Kadavu Group, Lau & Moala Groups, Rotuma, Directory, Transport

Justine has selflessly researched many a beach for Lonely Planet, having contributed to seven guides including *Queensland & the Great Barrier Reef* and *Australia*. Accordingly, she journeyed to Fiji with the cocky gait of a seasoned beach bum and found that her know-how had nothing on her know-now. Tireless diving and snorkelling expeditions, village visits, *kava* drinking, cultivating a 'Fiji Bitter' beer belly, highland treks – and scrutinising 40-odd beaches – instilled in her a great love for all things Fijian. Justine resides in Melbourne, where she is just as selflessly devoted to pub crawls, cricket and escaping to the beach.

The Coordinating Author's Favourite Trip

To be honest my favourite trip would last 12 months – six on the beach and six on the road. Of course 'the road' consists of mountains, islands, reefs…and roads. I'm a water baby and a sucker for those utopian Yasawas (p158). As a novice diver I go giddy in the coral here but I'd be cheating myself if I skipped the Astrolabe (p62) and Rainbow Reef (p61). To avoid becoming thoroughly waterlogged, I'd head to Suva (p118) for a 'bitter' and a curry with the locals before working the pins in the Namosi Highlands (p146). The picturesque town of Levuka (p174) would be the next port of call before wrapping things up on a beach at Caqalai (p180). Sure you could do it in a fortnight…but I'm using indulgent license.

MARK DAPIN   Mamanuca Group, Lomaiviti Group, Vanua Levu, Taveuni

Fiji will always have a special place in Mark's heart, as it was there he failed his first driving test. Mark is a features writer for *Good Weekend* magazine in the *Sydney Morning Herald* and the Melbourne *Age*. He began life in England, where he squandered every opportunity offered, before reinventing himself in Australia at the age of 26. He has travelled to more than 60 countries, and written travel stories for many newspapers and magazines including the *Guardian* and the *Times*. He was once an editor-in-chief of a group of men's magazines and – all too briefly – *Harness Racing News*. He is the author of *Sex & Money* – ostensibly about men's magazines – but actually about him. Mark lives in Sydney.

LONELY PLANET AUTHORS

Why is our travel information the best in the world? It's simple: our authors are independent, dedicated travellers. They don't research using just the Internet or phone, and they don't take freebies in exchange for positive coverage. They travel widely, to all the popular spots and off the beaten track. They personally visit thousands of hotels, restaurants, cafés, bars, galleries, palaces, museums and more – and they take pride in getting all the details right, and telling it how it is. For more, see the authors section on www.lonelyplanet.com.

CLAIRE WADDELL

Mamanuca Group, Lomaiviti Group, Vanua Levu, Taveuni

While Mark did all the glory work, Claire drew the maps, checked the facts, looked after the baby and walked all over the place carrying a blue clipboard. Born in Sydney, Claire took an Arts degree at Sydney University then a Diploma of Journalism at MacLeay College. She has worked as a magazine subeditor at Fairfax and Australian Consolidated Press. She has travelled throughout Europe, Central and South America, and parts of Asia. She is Mark's partner and Ben's mum.

VIRGINIA JEALOUS

Snapshot, History, The Culture, Environment, Food & Drink

Virginia has previously roamed bits of the Philippines, East Timor, Indonesia, Vietnam and Australia for Lonely Planet. Between 2004 and 2006 she took off her LP hat to work full-time with a Pacific regional nongovernmental organisation, based in Suva. A growing relationship with *dalo* (taro plant) and a variety of root vegetables – as well as some other, possibly more useful, Fiji-specific experiences – led her to reviewing and rewriting five of the introductory chapters for this guide.

CONTRIBUTING AUTHORS

Jean-Bernard Carillet wrote the Diving chapter. Born with restless feet and fins, his journeys have led him to the best dive destinations in the world, including French Polynesia, New Caledonia, the Red Sea, the Caribbean and, lately, Fiji and Vanuatu. As a dive instructor and incorrigible traveller, Jean-Bernard has written widely for various French publications, including *Plongeurs International* magazine. He has also coordinated and co-authored two Lonely Planet diving guides: *Tahiti & French Polynesia* and *The Red Sea*.

Clement Paligaru is an Indo-Fijian who came to Australia in 1984. An Asia-Pacific specialist, he has worked as a radio journalist and producer for the Australian Broadcasting Corporation for over 10 years. Clement currently produces Radio Australia's daily *In the Loop* programme, which profiles the cultures and societies of Oceania. Clement wrote the Indo-Fijian History & Culture chapter.

Michael Sorokin wrote the Health chapter. Dr Sorokin has extensive experience as a physician and GP in South Africa, the UK, the Pacific Islands and rural South Australia. He has special interests in rheumatology, infectious diseases and preventative medicine. Dr Sorokin was recently awarded the Order of Fiji in recognition of his services to health care in Fiji. He is partly responsible for the maintenance of the Traveller's Medical & Vaccination Centre (TMVC) database and helps with reference material for the continuing education of TMVC medical staff.

Getting Started

Blessed with some of the warmest people on the planet and a genuine zest for tourism, Fiji lends itself to all genres of travel. Honeymooners, divers, backpackers, families, bird-watchers, adventurers, independent travellers and tour groups all flock here to make the most of the stunning landscape and abundant sunshine. Luxury beachside resorts and private transport cater to tourists looking for pure R&R with minimum effort. But it's also easy to get off the tourist trail and explore the archipelago independently, regardless of your age or budget. Travellers in this camp can make the most of good transport networks and plenty of accommodation in popular destinations, with minimum preplanning. Peak-season travel will require more thought, as will reaching remote areas such as the Lau, Moala and Rotuma islands.

Fiji is an archipelago of over 300 islands, covering a total area of more than 1.3 million sq km, with a land area of 18,300 sq km and a population of only 836,000.

Fiji is also one of the South Pacific's major transit hubs. Even if you're just stopping over for a day or two, it's worth getting out and seeing something. Better yet, extend your stay (most airlines will allow you up to three months for a stopover) and really experience the country. Those visiting Fiji on a package tour should consider exploring Fiji for a week or two; many agents will allow you to extend your stay on either side of your accommodation package when you book.

Whatever your preferred approach to travel, bear in mind that Fiji is not a 'budget' destination per se and caters better to midrange wallets. That said, plenty of backpackers head here and travel comfortably enough without spending a ransom.

See Climate Charts (p246) for more information.

WHEN TO GO

The best time to visit is during the so-called 'Fijian winter' or 'dry season', from May to October. This time of year is more pleasant with lower rainfall and humidity, milder temperatures and less risk of meteorological hazards such as cyclones. Consequently these six months make up the high season, when airfare and accommodation costs are at their highest. Expect costs to peak in June and July.

DON'T LEAVE HOME WITHOUT...

- Insect repellent, which is sold in city pharmacies but needed most elsewhere.
- Plenty to read – bookshops are only found in cities.
- Reef shoes to protect yourself and the reefs that surround most of Fiji's islands.
- A Zen-like patience to cope with 'Fiji time', which is more official than GMT.
- Wedding rings if you're here to get hitched (p241).
- Your own snorkel and mask as they'll probably get a daily workout.
- Checking the current visa situation (p253).
- Keeping abreast of the current political climate – Fiji likes to coup.
- A waterproof camera to capture your marine encounters and make your friends jealous.
- Sunscreen and a raincoat to combat tropical climate conditions.
- Seasickness tablets if you don't have sea legs – with over 300 islands, there are a lotta boats in Fiji!

Fiji's 'wet season' is from November to April, with the heaviest rains falling from December to mid-April. This is when tropical cyclones, or hurricanes, are most likely to occur. Strong, destructive cyclones are, however, a fairly rare phenomenon in Fiji. The country has been hit by an average of 10 to 12 cyclones per decade, with only two or three of these being very severe.

If you're travelling during the wet season it's best to head to drier regions such as the Mamanuca and Yasawa island groups. That said, December and January are also busy months as they coincide with school holidays in both Australia and New Zealand, and Fijians visiting relatives. In February and March, and even November, however, Fiji sees fewer tourists and you're more likely to get bargains on your accommodation. The temperature during these months is also fairly appealing so you get the best of both worlds. The Diwali Festival (p248) is held in late October or early November and can be a fun, if manic time to be in Fiji.

Fijian school holidays can have an impact on accommodation availability. They generally last for two weeks from late April to early to mid-May and mid-August to early September. Summer holidays run from early December to late January.

COSTS & MONEY

Although cheaper than many Pacific countries, Fiji doesn't provide travellers with the same value as, say, Southeast Asia. Many backpackers are surprised to discover that Fiji is not a US$20-a-day destination.

Regardless of your budget, accommodation will easily be your greatest expense. Restaurants, transport and shops can be extremely good value, particularly in more remote areas; however, anything geared for tourists is far more expensive. On average, budget travellers can expect to pay about $60 to $90 per day for food, transport and accommodation. If you stay in dorms and dine on corned beef, you can do it for a little less. Island-hopping is generally fairly pricey: if you're planning to move around a lot, expenses will go up. It's good to plan your route to avoid backtracking.

Solo midrange travellers can expect to pay around $180 per day, and couples can expect to pay around $120 per person per day. These costs are based on transport, comfortable accommodation and eating out three times a day. Abundant self-catering options enable travellers in this price bracket to reduce their overall costs significantly; shopping at local markets for fruit and veggies is cheap. Families benefit the most from self-contained units as children are often charged either heavily discounted rates or nothing at all. Other tips to reduce daily costs include always looking for a 'return' boat, on its way back to base, and asking for walk-in rates at hotels – they can be a fraction of the advertised rate.

Resorts usually include all meals and plenty of activities in their tariffs, and hover around $200 to $300 per night for a single or double room, and $300 to $400 for a family. They can be especially good value for the latter, particularly as many offer free kids clubs. Moreover, some of the activities kids most enjoy, such as swimming, are free. Top-end options can cost anywhere up to $2000 a night for accommodation, food, alcohol and activities.

Most budget and midrange accommodation includes Fiji's 12.5% VAT (value-added tax) in the advertised rates, but this is not always the case with top-end options, so check before you book. All rates quoted in this book are peak season rates, which tend to be 10% to 20% higher than low season rates. See p239 and p66 for more information.

HOW MUCH?

Taxi in Nadi or Suva $4-10

Snorkel hire $5-10

Local bus ride $0.65

Coffee $2

Cocktail $6

See also Lonely Planet Index, inside front cover.

TOP TENS

Festivals & Events

Fijians love to celebrate and barely need a reason to do so. The country's festivals calendar is enhanced by two distinct cultures and the following are 10 reasons to get stuck into it. See p248 for more details.

- Hindu Holi (Festival of Colours; nationwide) February or March
- Ram Naumi (Birth of Lord Rama; Suva) March or April
- Bula Festival (Nadi) July
- Hibiscus Festival (Suva) August
- Hindu Ritual Fire Walking (nationwide) August
- Fiji Regatta Week (Musket Cove) September
- Lautoka's Sugar Festival (Lautoka) September
- Ram Leela (Play of Rama; Labasa) October
- Diwali Festival (Festival of Lights; nationwide) Late October or early to mid-November
- South Pacific World Music Festival (Savusavu) November

Must-See Flicks

Stoke your enthusiasm for a trip by getting an eyeful of the scenery and a mindset of the culture. Although Fiji hasn't exactly been the target of many films, the following were filmed, if not also set here. They range from the outstanding, award-winning *The Land Has Eyes*, to the swashbuckling, tacky iconic and plain ridiculous. See p40 for reviews of some of them.

- *The Land Has Eyes* (2004) directed by Vilsoni Hereniko
- *Coral Reef Adventure* (2002) distributed by Macgillivray Freeman
- *Flynn* (1993) directed by Frank Howson
- *Cast Away* (2000) directed by Robert Zemeckis
- *Mr Robinson Crusoe* (1932) directed by Edward Sutherland
- *The Blue Lagoon* (1979) directed by Randal Kleiser
- *The Dove* (1974) directed by Charles Jarrott
- *Savage Islands* (1983) directed by Ferdinand Fairfax
- *His Majesty's O'Keefe* (1953) directed by Byron Haskin
- *Anacondas: The Hunt for the Blood Orchid* (2004) directed by Dwight Little

DIY Cultural Experiences

Plenty of travellers come to Fiji on package holidays to avoid having to think too hard about how to enjoy what the country has to offer. But delving into the real Fiji on your own is so easy it requires minimal effort and brain cells. Below are some of the best cultural experiences to be had in this archipelago; all are unmissable.

- visiting a village (p245)
- watching a *meke* (dance; p41)
- drinking *kava* (p67)
- witnessing fire walking (p109)
- eating at a *lovo* (feast cooked in a pit oven; p67)
- rafting on a *bilibili* (bamboo raft; p243)
- offering *sevusevu* (presentation of a gift; p35)
- appreciating a Hindu temple (p77)
- catching a rugby match (p38)
- shopping for souvenirs and saris (p251)

TRAVEL LITERATURE

Sticking your head in a good book is a great way to get a feel for Fiji. Your local bookshop or library is best placed to advise you on the availability of the following recommendations. Many of the books listed below can also be ordered online through the **USP Book Centre** (Map p119; ☎ 321 2500; www.uspbookcentre.com; University of the South Pacific, Suva) or bought on the campus. Other books can be purchased at the Fiji Museum in Suva.

Fiji's national rugby team has won the Rugby World Cup Sevens twice – first in 1997 and then again in 2005.

On Fiji Islands by Ronald Wright is an oldie but a goody. It's a great read to get your head around the history, culture and flavour of the country, complimented by personal anecdotes of the author's travels.

Also good for a beautifully humanistic impression of the country is *Footprints in Fiji* by Geoff Raymond – an endearing and humorous memoir of an Australian family that moved to Fiji in the mid-80s to run a resort abandoned by its previous owners.

The Heart's Wild Surf by Stephanie Johnson is a bodice ripper set in 1918 about a colonial family on Taveuni coping with the cultural and social differences of their surrounding environment.

Kava in the Blood by Peter Thomson is a strong, evocative autobiography of a white Fijian who became a senior civil servant and was imprisoned by Rabuka during the 1987 coup.

Happy Isles of Oceania by Paul Theroux is an account of this legendary travel writer's journey through the Pacific in a collapsible kayak. He provides a frank personal impression of the politics, culture and aesthetics of the countries he visits.

Two excellent photographic books are *Children of the Sun* by Glen Craig, which gets under the skin of the country by capturing its diverse population, and *Fiji: The Uncharted Sea* by Federico Busonero, which is a visual celebration of the archipelago's exquisite marine life and beaches.

INTERNET RESOURCES

The Web is an absolute goldmine for travellers. Before leaving home you can research your trip, hunt down bargain airfares, book hotels, check on weather conditions or chat with locals and other travellers about where to go...and where to steer clear of.

Try the following websites for useful information on Fiji.

Fiji Times (www.fijitimes.com.fj) Fiji's daily newspaper online.

Fiji Village (www.fijivillage.com) Excellent site updated with daily news and links to local events, including music, movies and sport.

Fiji Visitors Bureau (www.bulafiji.com) Fiji's official tourist site, offering information on accommodation, activities and getting around, with links and an email directory.

Lonely Planet (www.lonelyplanet.com) Get started on your Fiji planning with snapshots of the country, travel links, postcards from other travellers, and the Thorn Tree travel forum.

Smart Traveller (www.smartraveller.gov.au) The Australian Department of Foreign Affairs & Trade's official travel advisory site.

South Pacific Tourism Organisation (www.spto.org) Useful travel directory with info on South Pacific countries.

Itineraries

CLASSIC ROUTES

WELL TRODDEN, WELL DESERVED Two Weeks / Western Isles & Coral Coast

Begin your fling in **Nadi** (p75), taking a day to acclimatise. Then get off the mainland and onto a boat heading to the **Mamanucas** (p147) and what you really came for – sea and sun. Revel in romance at **Tokoriki** (p154) or **Matamanoa** (p153), party at **Beachcomber island** (p151) or **Mana** (p152), or entertain the family at **Treasure** (p151) or **Castaway** (p154) island. But don't stop here: board the *Yasawa Flyer* for some island-hopping through the **Yasawas** (p158) to get into or away from it as much as you like. Bliss out on a post-card-perfect beach on **Waya** (p163), **Nacula** (p168) or **Nanuya Lailai** (p167), where you can paddle in the Blue Lagoon. Once you've had your South Seas fix, head back to the mainland to see what else Fiji has to offer.

From Nadi, take a trip along the Coral Coast. Picnic on **Natadola Beach** (p102) and chug into the verdant interior on the **Coral Coast Scenic Railway** (p103). Don the sneakers and trek the **Sigatoka Sand Dunes** (p105) or marvel at wildlife in **Kula Eco Park** (p107). Rest up at a resort at **Korolevu** (p110) and spend a couple of days inside, outside, poolside and barside. Amble into **Pacific Harbour** (p112) and spend a day diving **Beqa Lagoon** (p115) or rafting the mighty **Navua River** (p113). Finish your trip in **Suva** (p118).

Fabulous beaches and a dose of the mainland dominate this route. Enjoying parties in the Mamanucas, seclusion in the Yasawas and urban culture on the mainland will take about a fortnight but you could take three weeks. All up you'll cover 550km.

VANUA VENTURE
Nine Days / Suva to Vanua Levu

Beginning in **Suva** (p118), spend a morning at the excellent Fiji Museum and then feast on some fabulous fare, have a drink with a local and stock up on souvenirs. After exhausting Suva's urban comforts, flee the mainland on a flight to **Vanua Levu** (p191) and land yourself in **Labasa** (p204), 'India Town', where you can fuel up on some of the finest curries in Fiji. Visit the Wasavula Ceremonial Site and take a side-trip to the mystifying **Cobra Rock** (p207) inside the Naag Mandir Temple.

Continue your Vanua Levu adventure by jumping on a bus and heading south to **Savusavu** (p193). This scenic journey is a highlight in itself. Spend a day taking in Savusavu's sights; do the touristy thing at Copra Shed Marina and save enough stamina for a beer at the atmospheric Savusavu Yacht Club or Planters' Club. Take a day trip to the rich and colourful **Waisali Rainforest Reserve** (p202) and then spend a couple of days **hiking** or **kayaking** (p195), exploring the lesser-travelled Vanua Levu.

Time to head to gorgeous **Taveuni** (p210). If you've got sea legs catch a ferry, but the flight provides some spectacular views. **Somosomo** (p214) is a good base from which to explore the surrounding area. First on the itinerary should be a day snorkelling or diving magnificent **Rainbow Reef** (p61). Back on dry land, you'll want to marvel at the **Wairiki Catholic Mission** (p215), scare yourself silly on the **Waitavala Water Slide** (p215) and climb to the top of the world…well to the top of **Des Voeux Peak** (p215), which is just as good.

This route takes in Fiji's other 'mainland' – Vanua Levu. Trek, shop, eat and drink here before hopping over to neighbouring Taveuni with its spectacular snorkelling, diving, mountains and water slides. In total this trip covers about 420km.

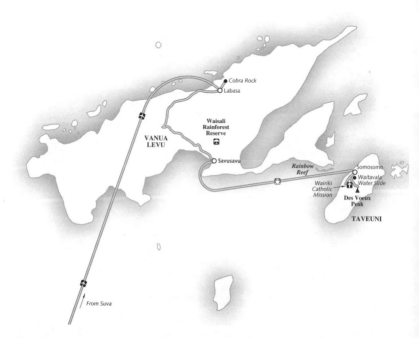

ROADS LESS TRAVELLED

MIDDLE OF NOWHERE   One Week / Lomaiviti Group

If you prefer to get off the beaten track and you're happy to put in a little effort, the following should be just the ticket. From Suva head to **Lomaiviti Group** (p170). The easiest way is to fly, but if the adventurous can take the ferry from Natovi Landing. Start your travels in Ovalau island, home to one of Fiji's most picturesque towns and original capital, **Levuka** (p174). Littered with colonial buildings and boasting a harmonious, multicultural population, this town and its surrounds deserve three days or so. Travel by bike or make the most of the sights by travelling on foot, including revisiting the town's rich history at the branch of the Fiji Museum here. Spend a day in the village of **Lovoni** (p176), nestled into a crater in the centre of Ovalau, and in **Arovudi** (Silana; p177) with its remarkable church.

Once you've had your urban fix head to the beach. From Levuka, book a passage to the coral island of **Caqalai** (p180) and leave consumer crutches behind. Take a day or two to circumnavigate this tiny island (it only takes 15 minutes). Make the most of its dazzling beaches and dabble in some excellent snorkelling and diving. Finish up the week with a flutter on some of the less frequented islands of **Yanuca Lailai** (p180) or **Leleuvia** (p189). Boasting chilled-out budget resorts and pocket-size beaches, both are a quick trip from Levuka, or catch a weekly service between Caqalai and Leleuvia. From Caqalai and Leleuvia you can also catch a boat to the mainland and make the whole jaunt a round trip.

Heading into the middle of nowhere will plant you in the unhurried Lomaiviti islands. Exploring colonial heritage and Fijian history in Levuka plus a round of hopping across coral islands and remote beaches will cover about 200km.

NORTHERN PASSAGE   One to Two Weeks / Northern Viti Levu & the Highlands

Starting in Nadi, turn your eyes away from the water and plant them firmly on the hilly climb into Viti Levu's imposing interior. The **Nausori Highlands** (p143) are an easy day-trip from tourist central and feature some of Fiji's most verdant scenery. Hire a 4WD or take a tour to **Navala** (p144), one of the most photogenic villages in the Pacific. Spend another three days exploring the nearby interior on a trek through **Koroyanitu National Heritage Park** (p143).

Next on the itinerary is to head north from Nadi. You can do this route in a 4WD but regular buses are easy and fun. First stop is **Lautoka** (p90), an Indo-Fijian centre and Fiji's second-largest city. Spend a couple of days soaking in the city's relaxed atmosphere and dose up on curries and Bollywood. Continue your coastal journey along the rugged **Kings Road** (p136) and head to petite and pretty **Nananu-i-Ra** (p140). Exhaust yourself windsurfing, swimming, snorkelling, diving or doing nothing at all.

Back on the mainland navigate your way south into Viti Levu's dramatic eastern interior, visiting the distinctly Fijian stop at **Naiserelagi** (p138) and the humbling **Wailotua Snake God Cave** (p138). End the day in **Suva** (p118) and indulge in some cosmopolitan hospitality.

The final leg of your itinerary can be a three-day escape to Fiji's remote far east. Book a flight to **Vanua Balavu** (p232) in the Lau island group. Explore exquisite coves, beaches and inland walks ignored by most tourists. Delve into the island's Tongan influence then kayak and snorkel the spectacular **Bay of Islands** (p232).

This route takes you into Viti Levu's dramatic highlands and Lautoka. You'll then visit petite Nananu-i-Ra before traversing eastern Viti Levu on the lush Kings Road. Top it off by fleeing tourism altogether on the remote Lau islands. The journey covers around 620km.

TAILORED TRIPS

IN PURSUIT OF THE PERFECT BEACH

It's no accident that Fiji is synonymous with sun, sand and sea. Boasting over 300 islands, the archipelago offers copious versions of the perfect beach. The Mamanucas are a good place to start, with wide sandy beaches populated by partygoing backpackers at **Beachcomber Island** (p151) or families indulging in innumerable water sports at **Treasure Island** (p151). If you're looking for something more exclusive, the intimate beaches at **Matamanoa** (p153) and **Tokoriki** (p154) should be just the ticket.

The Yasawa islands are home to two of Fiji's finest: Oarsman's Bay's sublime beach on **Nacula** (p168) and the exquisite beach of the Blue Lagoon in **Nanuya Lailai** (p167). On **Waya** (p163), the Sunset Beach Resort sits on a beautifully thick curve of beach and Botaira Beach Resort on **Naviti** (p164) is planted on a long stretch of soft, white sand.

Glorious **Natadola Beach** (p102) is Viti Levu's best stretch of shoreline and **Levukalailai** (p203) on Vanua Levu hugs 5.5km of superb coast.

Miniscule **Caqalai** (p180) in the Lomaivitis is a coral island renowned for its perimeter of lovely beach. Other prime beaches nearby lie on **Leleuvia** (p189) and **Naigani** (p190).

Taveuni has world-class diving and divine beaches at **Matagi** (p222) and **Qamea** (p223), and on **Kadavu** (p224) you'll find gorgeous swimming beaches at Dive Kadavu Resort and Nagigia Island Resort.

HIKERS' DELIGHTS

Many of Fiji's islands are thick with mountainous terrain, providing plenty of opportunity to work the pins in splendid surrounds.

Viti Levu's interior is a vast area of forested land with some great treks. Close to Nadi and Lautoka, **Koroyanitu National Heritage Park** (p143) is a must for hikers, with a four-hour trail to the summit of Castle Rock as well as a full-day trek through the park. There are also trekking tours in the **Nausori Highlands** (p143) and the rainforests of the steamy **Namosi Highlands** (p146).

On Vanua Levu, the **Waisali Rainforest Reserve** (p202) features a short but spectacular descent to a waterfall. Hilly **Waya** (p163), in the Yasawas, is crisscrossed with hiking trails leading to the Yalobi Hills, which offer 360-degree views of the entire chain of islands on a clear day.

Head to **Taveuni** (p210) for the stunning Lavena Coastal Walk – a 5km trail though forests, beaches and villages. Elsewhere on the island you can climb Des Voeux Peak for panoramic views and the chance to see Fiji's orange dove. Bouma National Heritage Park has challenging tracks with three waterfalls to reward your effort. Inside the park you can also tackle the shaman-guided Vidawa Rainforest Hike.

Snapshot

Picture-postcard perfect, Fiji comprises classic tropical islands of white sand and coconut palms, and steamy green hills and forests. Unfailingly hospitable, Fijians will gladden the hearts of visitors.

Beyond the scenery and warm welcomes is a dynamic cultural landscape. It's a heady mix of indigenous Fijian traditions that sit colourfully – if not always comfortably – alongside the more recent influences of British colonisers, Indian indentured labourers, Chinese traders and other Pacific islanders. Visitors with time to scratch below the surface will be enthralled by the country's variety of cultural celebrations, contrasts and subtle conflicts.

FAST FACTS

Population: 836,000

GDP: US$1.8 billion

GDP per capita: US$2151

Annual inflation rate: 4.2%

Land area: 18,270 sq km

Length of coastline: 1129km

Length of sugar-cane railway: 597km

Number of phone land lines: 102,000

Number of airports: 28; 3 with sealed runways

Year women given the right to vote: 1963

A vibrant civil society includes church groups, unions and nongovernmental organisations that campaign loudly and vigorously in the media and on the streets. Some of the current issues on the agenda are the ending of 99-year Indo-Fijian land leases, environmental concerns ranging from forestry to fishing to municipal waste disposal (see p55), and the rights of women and minority groups. Last but by no means least, there is the opposition to (and, in a few cases, support of) the controversial Promotion of Reconciliation, Tolerance and Unity (PRTU) Bill, intended to resolve ongoing effects of the most recent coup in 2000. This active local scene provides a context for the work of Fiji's community of visual artists, writers and – most recently – film makers, with Fiji's first locally made movie, *The Land Has Eyes*, entered in the Foreign Language section of Hollywood's 2005 Academy Awards (see p41).

Fiji, independent since 1970, is a parliamentary democracy. Since 1987 it has experienced three coups that unseated elected governments. These coups articulated a usually covert tension between many indigenous Fijians and Indo-Fijians. Related issues currently on the political agenda include land rights (with a number of Indo-Fijians being forced off their leased land and either migrating or drifting to squatter settlements) and more equitable inclusion of Indo-Fijians in the political process (see p31). Despite the separation of powers between state, church and military, the Methodist Church is highly influential in public affairs, and the Fiji military remains a force to be reckoned with politically, with its commander publicly criticising the PRTU Bill's clause to grant amnesty to the participants of the 2000 coup.

A small but growing source of income is the remittances sent home by Fijians living and working overseas, particularly soldiers employed by the British Army and by security companies in trouble spots such as Kuwait and Iraq. The major sources of foreign exchange continue to be sugar exports and tourism. Sugar processing makes up one-third of industrial activity, but this may be affected by the expiration of Indo-Fijian sugar-farmers' land leases. Tourism has bounced back after the 2000 coup, and the lack of hotel rooms, rather than the lack of tourists, is a current preoccupation. In a post-9/11 world, Fiji and the Pacific is still seen as a safe and, well, pacific, destination.

History

VITIAN HISTORY

Shaped over 35 centuries, Fiji's precolonial history is a complex blend of influences by Polynesian, Melanesian and, to a lesser extent, Micronesian peoples who came and either left or stayed.

The original inhabitants of Fiji called their home Viti. These were Lapita people, probably from Vanuatu, who arrived about 1220 BC and stayed for only a short while before disappearing from the archaeological record. Their descendants, who became assimilated with people who arrived from Melanesia, were coastal dwellers, who initially relied on fishing and seem to have lived in relative peace. Around 500 BC a shift towards agriculture occurred along with an expansion of population – probably due to further incursions from other parts of Melanesia – that led to an increase in intertribal feuding. Cannibalism became common and in times of war, villages moved to ring-ditched fortified sites. By around AD 1000 Tongan invasions had started and continued sporadically until the arrival of Europeans.

There's a widespread legend that the first Fijians arrived from Tanganyika, East Africa in the ancestral canoe *Kaunitoni*.

Eventually the islands became known to Europeans as Fiji. The story goes that Captain Cook asked the Tongans what the name of the islands to their west was. He heard 'Feegee', the Tongan pronunciation of Viti: so 'Fiji' came from an Englishman's mishearing of a Tongan's mispronunciation!

While there were extended periods of peace, Fiji was undergoing intense social upheaval at the time of the first European settlement in the early 19th century, and these regular tribal skirmishes lead Europeans to believe that it was in a constant state of war.

Lapita pottery found at the Sigatoka Sand Dunes – now open to visitors – suggest this was one of the earliest settlements in Viti.

EUROPEAN EXPLORERS & TRADERS

The goal of Europeans who sailed the Pacific during the 17th and 18th centuries was to find *terra australis incognita*, the great 'unknown southern land' later called Australia. Some of them bumped into Fiji on the way.

Abel Tasman became the first European to sail past the Fiji islands in 1643, and his descriptions of treacherous reef systems kept mariners away for the next 130 years. The English navigator James Cook visited uneventfully, stopping on Vatoa in the southern Lau Group in 1774. After the famous mutiny on the *Bounty* in 1789, Captain Bligh and his castaway companions passed between Vanua Levu and Viti Levu, through a channel now known as Bligh Water.

Crimson ceremonial *kula* feathers come from the common collared lory, a chunky, multicoloured, acrobatic parrot that hangs out in small flocks.

Tongans had long traded colourful *kula* feathers, *masi* (printed bark cloth) and weapons with the eastern Fiji islands. From the early 19th century, European whalers, and traders of sandalwood and *bêche-de-mer* (sea cucumber), tackled their fears of reefs and cannibals and also began to visit.

Fragrant sandalwood was highly valued in Europe and Southeast Asia. Tongans initially controlled the trade, obtaining sandalwood from the chiefs of Bau Bay on Vanua Levu, and then selling it to the Europeans. However, when Oliver Slater – a survivor of the shipwrecked *Argo* – discovered the

TIMELINE

1220 BC	500 BC
Lapita people arrive, probably from Vanuatu, and settle on the coasts	Melanesians from elsewhere in the Pacific arrive and begin permanent settlement

Life in Feejee: Five Years Among the Cannibals by a Lady (whaler's wife Lady Mary Wallis) provides an alarmingly frank and often funny read. Look for David Routledge's edition of her 1840s journals.

location of the supply, he spread the news of its whereabouts and in 1805 Europeans began to trade directly with Fijians, bartering metal tools, tobacco, cloth, muskets and gunpowder. By 1813 the accessible supply of sandalwood was exhausted, but the introduction of firearms and the resulting increase in violent tribal warfare were lasting consequences of the trade.

Considered a tasty delicacy in Asian markets, *bêche-de-mer* was another lucrative commodity. The intensive harvesting and drying process required hundreds of workers for a single *bêche-de-mer* station. Chiefs who sent their villagers to work boosted their own wealth and power, and it's estimated that 5000 muskets were traded during this period. It, too, was a short-lived trade, lasting from 1830 to 1850.

Expanding Chiefdoms & Tongan Influence

By 1829 the chiefdom of Bau, in eastern Viti Levu where trade with Europeans had been most intense, had accumulated great power. Bauan chief Cakobau, known to foreigners as Tui Viti (King of Fiji), was at the height of his influence by 1850 despite having no real claim over most of Fiji. But in 1848, Tongan noble Enele Ma'afu had led an armada of war canoes to capture Vanua Balavu in northern Lau. He became governor of all Tongans in Lau and by 1854 he was a serious threat to Cakobau's power. By the late 1850s, the Tongans were the controlling force in eastern Fiji.

Contact with the firearms – and diseases – of Europeans had a marked impact on Fiji's ethnic population, which only recently regained its 18th-century level.

EUROPEAN SETTLEMENT
Missionaries

In the 1830s London Missionary Society pastors and Wesleyan Methodist missionaries arrived in Southern Lau to find converts and to preach against cannibalism.

Progress was slow until the chiefs started to convert. Powerful Cakobau somewhat reluctantly adopted Christianity in 1854. This was a triumph for the Methodist Church, who later sent Reverend Baker out to spread the gospel in the western highlands of Viti Levu. In 1867, unfortunately

---

GOING NATIVE

Trade was often helped along by beachcombers. Generally regarded as 'white savages', these were mainly deserting or shipwrecked sailors, or escaped convicts from the recently established penal colony of Australia. Sensible beachcombers increased their chances of survival by making themselves useful to chiefs, serving as interpreters and go-betweens with the Europeans, and as carpenters and marksmen.

Charles Savage was especially influential. After being shipwrecked on the *Eliza* in 1808, the Swede retrieved muskets and ammunition from the wreck and helped Bau to become one of the most powerful chiefdoms in Fiji. In return for war service he received a privileged position and many wives, and survived for about five years before being killed in battle. His skull was preserved as a *kava* bowl.

First marooned in Tonga, Harry Danford made his way to Fiji's Namosi Highlands in 1846. He repaired muskets, acted as a doctor, and advised Chief Kuruduadua in his dealings with European settlers. Harry guided several expeditions into the interior of Viti Levu: his knowledge of the language and culture – not to mention his survival for a decade in previously 'unknown' territory – made him a legendary figure.

AD 1000	1774
Tongan and Samoan warriors begin a series of incursions into Vitian territory	Captain Cook hears 'Viti' pronounced as 'Fiji', and thus names the country

for him, he was killed and eaten by locals who resented his manner and the imposition of ideas associated with Bau (see p120).

Christianity became accepted for its similarity to the existing beliefs of *tabu* (sacred prohibitions) and *mana* (spiritual power), and most Fijians adopted it alongside their traditional spirituality. Many villagers continue to worship their ancestral gods through such practices as *kava* ceremony, *tabu* areas and codes of conduct, and the symbolic *tabua* (whales' teeth; see below).

The Nabutautau villagers, whose ancestors ate Reverend Baker in 1867, apologised to his descendants in a public ceremony in the village in 2003.

Commercial Settlers

By the 1830s a small whaling settlement had been established at Levuka, on Ovalau, which became one of the main ports of call in the South Pacific for traders and warships. In 1840 Commandant Charles Wilkes led a US expedition to Fiji that produced the first reasonably complete chart of the Fijian islands. He also negotiated a port-regulation treaty whereby the chiefdom of Bau was paid for the protection of foreign ships and the supply of provisions.

This mutually beneficial relationship was fraught with tension. Relations began to deteriorate in 1841 when Levuka was razed by fires, which the settlers suspected Cakobau of instigating. Later, during the 1849 US Independence Day celebrations, the Nukulau island home of US consul John Brown Williams was destroyed by fire and locals helped themselves to his possessions. Williams held Cakobau (as nominal King of Fiji) responsible for the actions of his people and sent him a substantial damages bill.

Missionaries developed written Fijian language – called Bauan – from the dialect spoken in the powerful chiefdom of Bau during the 1830s.

Cakobau came under increasing pressure and in 1862, still claiming to have power over all Fiji, he proposed to Britain's consul that he would cede the islands to Queen Victoria in return for the payment of his debts. The consul declined, but the rumours caused a large influx of settlers to Levuka who bickered among themselves, and disputes erupted with Fijians over land ownership. The town became a lawless and greedy outpost, on the verge of anarchy and racial war. Cakobau's huge debt was not cleared until 1868 when the Australian Polynesia Company agreed to pay it in exchange for land (see p118).

Blackbirding

The worldwide cotton shortage prompted by the American Civil War resulted in a cotton boom in Fiji that indirectly stimulated blackbirding – the

---

TABUA

Tabua, carefully polished and shaped whales' teeth, were believed to be shrines for the ancestor spirits. They were, and still are, highly valued items and essential to diplomacy. Used as a powerful *sevusevu* – a gift presented as a token of esteem or atonement – the acceptance of *tabua* binds a chief to the gift-giver. Traditionally, a chief's body was accompanied to the grave by a *tabua*.

Originally *tabua* were rare, obtained only from washed-up sperm whales or through trade with Tonga. However, European traders introduced thousands of whale teeth and replicas made of whalebone, elephant tusk and walrus tusk. These negotiation tools became concentrated in the hands of a few dominant chiefdoms, increasing their power.

1789	1830
Captain William Bligh makes rough navigation charts while drifting between the Vitian islands after the *Bounty* mutiny	The first London Missionary Society pastors arrive and begin to devise a written language

trade in labourers. Europeans brought other Pacific Islanders to labour on the Fijian cotton (and copra and sugar) plantations.

Most were islanders from the southwest Pacific Islands, especially the Solomon islands and New Hebrides (now Vanuatu). Initially, people were coaxed into agreeing to work for three years in return for minimal wages, food, clothing and return passage. Later, chiefs were bribed and men and women were traded for ammunition. By the 1860s and 1870s the practice had developed into an organised system of kidnapping, and stories of atrocities and abuses by recruiters resulted in pressure on Britain to stop the trade. In 1872 the Imperial Kidnapping Act was passed, but it was little more than a gesture as Britain had no power to enforce it.

For a clear, concise and readable overview of Fijian and regional history, dip into *Worlds Apart: A History of the Pacific Islands* by IC Campbell.

THE COLONIAL PERIOD

With the end of the American Civil War in 1865 came a slump in the world cotton market. In the following years, epidemics swept the country: an outbreak of measles wiped out about one-third of the indigenous Fijian population. Social unrest was on the rise.

Nevertheless, by 1873 Britain was interested in annexing Fiji, citing the need to abolish blackbirding as justification. On the grounds of Cakobau's earlier offer, Fiji was pronounced a British crown colony on 10 October 1874 at Levuka.

If the chiefs could be persuaded to collaborate with the colonisers, then Fiji would likely be more easily, cheaply and peacefully governed, so the colonial government protected Fijian land rights by forbidding sales to foreigners. This successfully retained land rights for the indigenous owners, and 83% of the land is still owned by indigenous Fijian communities. Give or take a dissenting chief or two, it also helped to maintain peace.

Levuka's geography hindered expansion, so the administrative capital was officially moved to Suva in 1882.

Indentured Labour

In a further attempt to maintain good relations with its subjects, the colonial government prohibited the employment of indigenous Fijians as plantation labourers. Fijians were increasingly reluctant to take full-time work for wages, preferring traditional subsistence work that satisfied their village obligations and was less regimented.

Plantation crops such as cotton, copra and sugar cane had the potential to make the Fiji economy self-sufficient, but demanded large pools of cheap labour. Indentured labour seemed the perfect solution. In 1878 negotiations were made with the Indian colonial government for labourers to come to Fiji on five-year contracts, after which time the labourers, or *girmitiyas*, were free to return to India, though free passage for the return trip was only available under certain conditions. They began arriving in Fiji at a rate of about 2000 per year.

About 80% of the labourers were Hindu, 14% Muslim, and the remainder mostly Sikhs and Christians. Overcrowded accommodation gave little privacy, people of different caste and religion were forced to mix, and social and religious structures crumbled. Despite the hardship, the vast majority of *girmitiyas* decided to stay in Fiji once they had served their

1867	1874
Methodist minister Reverend William Baker is eaten by villagers in the Western Highlands	Fiji cedes to Britain on 10 October in a ceremony at Levuka

contract and many brought their families across from India to join them. For more information on Indo-Fijian history and culture, see p44.

By the early 1900s India's colonial government was being pressured by antislavery groups in Britain to abolish the indenture system. In 1916 recruitment stopped and indenture ended officially in January 1919. By this time, 60,537 indentured labourers were in Fiji.

Power Plays & the World Wars

Fiji's colonial government discouraged interaction between Indians and Fijians. Indians, restricted from buying Fijian land, moved instead into small business, or took out long-term leases as independent farmers.

The 1920s saw the first major struggle for better conditions for Indians and increasing labour unrest. By siding with the Fijians, Europeans diverted attention from their own monopoly on freehold land and their power and influence in the civil service. It was convenient to blame all problems on the Indian community and to exacerbate fears that the size of the Indian population would surpass that of indigenous Fijians.

Fiji had only a minor involvement in WWI: about 700 of Fiji's European residents and about 100 Fijians were sent to serve in Europe. The conflict in the Pacific during WWII was much closer to home. Around 8000 Fijians were recruited into the Fiji Military Force (FMF) and from 1942 to 1943 fought against the Japanese in the Solomon Islands.

For daily news, views and sports information check out the *Fiji Times*, established in 1869 and currently owned by the Murdoch media empire, at www.fijitimes.com.

INDEPENDENCE & INCREASING ETHNIC TENSION

The 1960s saw a movement towards Fijian self-government and, after 96 years of colonial administration, Fiji became independent on 10 October 1970. In the rush towards independence, important problems such as land ownership and leases, and how to protect the interests of a racially divided country, were not resolved. Fiji's first postindependence election was won by the indigenous Fijian Alliance Party (FAP). But despite an economic boom in the immediate postindependence years, by the early 1980s there was a decline in the price of sugar and the reality of the country's accumulating foreign debt began to hit home.

Ethnic tensions became apparent as the economy worsened. In Fiji most shops and transport services were (and still are) run by Indo-Fijian families. A racial stereotype developed portraying Indo-Fijians as obsessed with making money despite the fact that, like indigenous Fijians, the vast majority belonged to poorer working classes and – unlike indigenous Fijians – would never secure land tenure on their farming leases.

The FAP was perceived to be failing indigenous Fijians in their hopes for economic advancement. Greater unity among workers led to the formation of the Fiji Labour Party (FLP) and in April 1987 an FLP government was elected in coalition with the National Federation Party (NFP). Despite having an indigenous Fijian prime minister, Timoci Bavadra, and a cabinet comprising an indigenous Fijian majority, the new government was labelled 'Indian dominated' as the majority of its MPs were Indo-Fijian.

Military Coups of the 1980s

The victory of the coalition immediately raised racial tensions in the country. The extremist Taukei movement played on Fijian fears of losing their

1879	1951
The first group of Indian indentured labourers, *girmitiyas*, arrives to work in the sugarcane fields	Fiji Airways, now Air Pacific, is founded

---

GREAT COUNCIL OF CHIEFS

The basic unit of Fijian administration is the *koro* (village) headed by the *turaga-ni-koro* (a heredi-tary chief), who is appointed by the village elders. Several *koro* are linked as a *tikina*, and several *tikina* form a *yasana* or province. Fiji is divided into 14 *yasana,* and each has a high chief.

The Great Council of Chiefs was created by British colonisers to strengthen the position of the cooperating, ruling Fijian elite, and it gained great power after the military coups of the 1980s and the introduction of the 1990 constitution. The council appoints the president, who in turn is responsible for appointing judges, in consultation with the Judicial & Legal Services Commis-sion. It also has authority over any legislation related to land ownership and common rights. The council supported the 2000 coup, as well as the controversial 2005 Promotion of Reconciliation, Tolerance and Unity Bill, which seeks to offer amnesty to the perpetrators of the coup.

---

land rights and of Indo-Fijian political and economic domination. On 14 May 1987, only a month after the elections, Lieutenant Colonel Sitiveni Rabuka took over from the elected government in a bloodless coup and formed a civil interim government supported by the Great Council of Chiefs.

In September 1987, Rabuka again intervened with military force. The 1970 constitution was invalidated, Fiji was declared a republic and Rabuka proclaimed himself head of state. The following month, Fiji was dismissed from the Commonwealth of Nations.

The coups, which were supposed to benefit all indigenous Fijians, in fact caused immense hardship and benefited only an elite minority. When the Indo-Fijians were effectively removed from the political proc-ess, tensions within the indigenous Fijian community were exposed. These included conflicts between chiefs from eastern and western Fiji; between high chiefs and village chiefs; between urban and rural dwellers; and within the church and trade-union movement.

The economic consequences of the coups were drastic. The economy's two main sources of income, tourism and sugar, were severely affected. Development aid was suspended and from 1987 to 1992 about 50,000 people – mostly Indo-Fijian skilled tradespeople and professionals – emigrated.

Fiji's first coup took place 108 years to the day after the arrival of the *Leonidas* carrying the first group of Indian indentured labourers.

Tipping the Scales

On 25 July 1990 a new constitution was proclaimed. It greatly increased the political power of the Great Council of Chiefs and of the military while diminishing the position of Indo-Fijians in government. Indo-Fijian political leaders immediately opposed the constitution, claiming it was racist and undemocratic. As the 1992 elections approached, the Great Council of Chiefs disbanded the multicultural FAP and in its place formed the Soqosoqo-ni-Vakavulewa-ni Taukei (SVT; Party of Policy Makers for Indigenous Fijians). Rabuka returned to the scene as interim prime minister and party leader of the SVT. Changing his hardline ap-proach, he was twice elected, in 1992 and 1994.

The 1997 Constitution

In 1995, a Constitutional Review Commission (CRC) presented its find-ings. It called for a return to a multiethnic democracy and, while accepting

1970   **1979**

Fiji becomes independent on 10 October after 96 years of colonial rule | A remake of *The Blue Lagoon* in the Yasawas catapults Brooke Shields to teenage stardom

that the position of president be reserved for an indigenous Fijian, proposed no provision of ethnicity for the prime minister. The government acted on most of the CRC's recommendations and a new constitution was declared in 1997.

In the same year, Rabuka apologised to Queen Elizabeth for the 1987 military coups, presented her with a whale's tooth *tabua* as a gesture of atonement and the following month Fiji was readmitted to the Commonwealth.

The May 2000 Coup

In the May 1999 elections, voters rejected Rabuka's SVT and its coalition partners. The FLP won the majority of seats and its leader Mahendra Chaudhry became Fiji's first Indo-Fijian prime minister.

Many indigenous Fijians were far from pleased. Convinced that their traditional land rights were at stake, protests increased and many refused to renew expiring 99-year land leases to Indo-Fijian farmers. On 19 May 2000, armed men entered the parliamentary compound in Suva and took 30 hostages, including Prime Minister Chaudhry. Failed businessman George Speight quickly became the face of the coup, claiming to represent indigenous Fijians. He demanded the resignation of both Chaudhry and President Ratu Sir Kamisese Mara and that the 1997 multiethnic constitution be abandoned.

Support for Speight's group was widespread and Indo-Fijians suffered such harassment that many fled the country. Chaudhry, despite having suffered broken ribs during a beating by his captors, refused to resign. Finally, in an attempt to bring the situation to an end, President Ratu Mara unwillingly announced that he was removing Chaudhry from power. Speight's group demanded Mara's resignation as well and, with lawlessness increasing and the country divided over his role, Ratu Mara relinquished power. The head of Fiji's military, Commander Frank Bainimarama, announced martial law. After long negotiations between Speight's rebels and Bainimarama's military, and after eight weeks in captivity, the hostages were released and the 1997 constitution was revoked.

International disapproval for the coup was meted out as trade sanctions and sporting boycotts. Travellers were given warnings to steer clear of Fiji. The economy, particularly the tourism sector, was hit hard and many businesses folded.

In March 2001, the appeal court decided to uphold the 1997 constitution and ruled that Fiji be taken to the polls in order to restore democracy. Lasenia Qarase, heading the Fijian People's Party (SLD), won 32 of the 71 parliamentary seats in the August 2001 elections. Claiming that a multiparty cabinet in the current circumstances would be unworkable, Qarase proceeded to defy the spirit of the constitution by including no FLP members in his 18-strong cabinet.

In the meantime, Speight pleaded guilty to treason. He was given a death sentence that was quickly commuted to life imprisonment, likely out of fear of further protests and rioting. Ironically, Speight is serving out this sentence on the small island of Nukulau off Suva. This is the island where, in 1849, the looting of the US consul's house acted

The 2000 coup is described from the inside by one of the hostages, and from the outside by one of the journalists on the scene, in *Speight of Violence*, by Michael Field, Tupeni Baba & Unaisi Nabobo-Baba.

as an impetus for cession of Fiji to Britain; one of the major products of cession was the coming of the first indentured labourers, the presence of whose descendants sufficiently enraged Speight to instigate the 2000 coup.

Borrowing a line from Quentin Tarantino, opponents of the 2005 Promotion of Reconciliation Tolerance and Unity Bill sported 'Kill Bill' stickers.

TO BE CONTINUED...

With a general election due in 2006, it will be interesting to see what the future holds. While the economy slowly struggles to its feet after 2000, and tourists return to Fiji, in many places racial issues continue to simmer. There are notable exceptions: in the west of Viti Levu, for example, Indians and Fijians have lived amicably for decades under leadership that has encouraged racial tolerance and collaborative development.

The Qarase government's draft Promotion of Reconciliation, Tolerance and Unity (PRTU) Bill divided the country during 2004 and 2005. Supporters say it will start to heal the wounds left by the last coup; opponents say that its amnesty provisions will allow those involved in the coup to disown responsibility for their actions. In early 2006 tension between the military (who are opposed to the bill) and the government rose again and rumours of an impending coup hit the airwaves. As this book goes to press, though, negotiation rather than confrontation seems to be the method of resolution.

2000

Businessman George Speight heads the May 19 coup; 30 hostages are held in parliament for eight weeks; Speight is jailed

2005

The draft Promotion of Reconciliation, Tolerance and Unity Bill offers possible amnesty to the 2000 coup perpetrators

The Culture

THE NATIONAL PSYCHE

In Fiji, a smile goes a long way. Fijians welcome *kaivalagi* – foreigners, literally 'people from far away' – by going out of their way to assist visitors, or to chat in shops and cafés, and this makes for comfortable travelling. Not wishing to disappoint, a Fijian 'yes' might mean 'maybe' or 'no'; this can be disconcerting for visitors.

Despite its recent history of internal conflict, face-to-face confrontation is rare in Fiji and is discouraged. Impersonal forms of dissent and argument are common, though, as a look at the letters page of any Fijian newspaper will show. The presence of Indo-Fijians (descendants of indentured workers) remains both one of the great strengths of, and challenges to, a sense of national identity in the country; see p47.

The UN's Human Development Report provides detailed information annually about Fiji's position in the world development rankings. Link to Fiji on their website http://hdr.undp.org/statistics.

LIFESTYLE

Food is relatively plentiful and easy to grow in Fiji's tropical climate, and many people live well and live long; the average life expectancy is 69 years. Unemployment is around 8%, with almost half of all households living below the poverty line. The negative effects of these are mitigated by extended family networks, whose village members often support the town-dwellers with food; the town-dwellers in turn support villagers who come to town for schooling, medical treatment or work.

In rural areas, many aspects of an interdependent way of life remain strong. Indigenous Fijian villagers live in land-owning *mataqali* (extended family groups) under a hereditary chief who allocates land to each family for farming. Clans gather for births, deaths, marriages, *meke* (traditional dances) and *lovo* (feasts). *Yaqona,* or *kava,* drinking is still an important social ceremony; see the boxed text p67. Communal obligations have to be met, including farming for the chief, preparing for special ceremonies and feasts, and village maintenance.

Village life is also conservative: independent thinking is not encouraged and being too different or too ambitious is seen as a threat. Concepts such as *kerekere* and *sevusevu* are still strong, especially in remote areas. *Kerekere* is unconditional giving based on the concept that time and property is communal; this can prove difficult, for example, for anyone attempting to start up a village shop. *Sevusevu* is the presentation of a gift such as *kava* for, say, permission to visit a village or, more powerfully, a *tabua* (whale's tooth) as a token of reconciliation or as a wedding gift.

Fijians are usually happy to have their photo taken (or are too polite to say no) but always ask first. Consider sending photos as a thank-you present.

Fiji is becoming increasingly urbanised, and traditional values and the wisdom of elders are often less respected in towns and cities. Many young people travel to the cities for education, employment or to escape the restrictions of village life, but the increased freedom comes with competition for jobs and a less supportive social structure. Television's mostly imported programmes present different values and contradictory messages to the ones associated with village life.

The population drift to urban centres is becoming a challenge for Fiji, with squatter-settlements on the edges of many towns; see p128 for more details. As everywhere, high levels of deprivation have lead to an obvious presence of beggars and street kids, and to the increased use of alcohol and drugs, and accompanying crime.

For those in work, disposable income is almost nonexistent. With wages for government workers around $150 a week – and just $50 for

HOME & HOSTED: VILLAGE ETIQUETTE

If you visit a village uninvited, ask to see the headman at once; it's not proper just to turn up and look around. Never wander around unaccompanied: beaches, reefs and gardens are all someone's private realm. Complex codes of behaviour are in operation; do as you're asked, and discretely find out why later.

- Dress modestly; sleeves and *sulu* or sarongs are fine for both men and women. You will rarely see adult Fijians swimming and when they do they cover up with a T-shirt and *sulu*. Wear slip-on shoes: they're easier to take off when entering houses or temples.

- Take off your hat and sunglasses, and carry bags in your hands, not over your shoulder; it's considered rude to do otherwise.

- It is rare to see public displays of affection between men and women so curtail your passions in public to avoid embarrassing or offending locals.

- Bring *yaqona (kava)* with you. This is for your *sevusevu*, requesting permission to visit the village from the *turaga-ni-koro* (hereditary chief) and, in effect, the ancestral gods. He will welcome you in a small ceremony likely to develop into a *talanoa* (gossip session) around the *tanoa* (*yaqona* bowl) so be prepared to recount your life story. The custom throughout Fiji is to finish drinking *yaqona* before dining. Be warned – this can result in some very late meals!

- Check with your host if you can take photos and wait until after the *sevusevu* to start snapping.

- Stoop when entering a *bure* (thatched dwelling) and quietly sit cross-legged on the pandanus mat. It is polite to keep your head at a lower level than your host's. Fijians regard the head as sacred – never ever touch a person's head.

- If you're staying overnight, and had planned to camp but are offered a bed, accept it; it may embarrass your hosts if they think their *bure* is not good enough. If you'll be bathing in the river or at a shared tap, wear a *sulu* while you wash.

- The custom of *kerekere* means that people may ask you for things. If you don't want to give an item away, just say that you can't do without it; but be sensitive to people's lack of material goods, and take minimum gear on village visits.

- Travel with thank-you gifts of tea, tinned meat, or sugar, or contribute some cash to cover costs.

- Sunday is for church and family so avoid visiting then.

---

unskilled workers – paying the rent is often hard enough. There are exceptions of course, and the salaries of some executives are on a par with the Western world. Spacious houses with big gardens reflect this affluence, but most homes are modest and often crowded.

About 25% of the population is of school-age. Education is heavily subsidised by the government; almost all children attend primary school, and most complete lower secondary education. While not officially segregated, many schools are run by the major religions; Indo-Fijian children tend to go to Hindu or Muslim schools and indigenous Fijians tend to go to Christian schools. There's also a Chinese-Fijian school in Suva.

> English is the official language of Fiji, literacy stands at 97%, and Fiji is regarded as the educational centre of the Pacific.

The University of the South Pacific (USP) was established in 1968 as a Pacific regional university, with its main campus in Suva. The Fiji School of Medicine (FSM) and the Fiji Institute of Technology (FIT) are also in Suva.

POPULATION

Fiji's population is guestimated to be around 836,000. Population growth has almost halved in the last 30 years or so, with Fijians opting to have smaller families, and about 30% of Fijians are aged under 15. About 60% of Fijians are urban dwellers, which is high given that urban centres are few.

The government categorises people by their racial origins, as you'll notice on the immigration arrival card. 'Fijian' means indigenous Fijian, and while many Indo-Fijians have lived in Fiji for several generations, they are referred to as 'Indian', just as Chinese-Fijians are 'Chinese'. Fijians of other Pacific Island descent are referred to by the nationality of their ancestors. Australians, Americans, New Zealanders – and Europeans – are 'Europeans'. Mixed Western and Fijian heritage makes a person officially 'part-European'. There is relatively little intermarriage.

Several thousand people from the island of Rotuma have moved to 'mainland' Fiji to pursue a level of education and work that their remote northern island can't offer. I-Kiribati from Banaba island and Tuvaluans from Vaitupu island have resettled on Rabi and Kaio islands off Vanua Levu.

MULTICULTURALISM

One of Fiji's hot topics, the almost equal number of Fijians and Indo-Fijians has shaped the country's culture for both the better and the worse. From colonial days the notion of racial integration and sense of one national identity has been discouraged, and the legacy has been maintained by successive Fiji administrations. There is ongoing tension between land-owning ethnic Fijians, and entrepreneurial Indo-Fijians – in simplified terms, this is tension between those who have power but little capital, and those with capital but little power. Visitors, though, will rarely sense this tension, and the upside of Fiji's cultural heritage is a heady mix of laid-back Melanesian lifestyle and Indian commercial street scenes. See p44 for more information on Indo-Fijian culture.

Islanders from Banaba (Ocean Island), Kiribati, were resettled on Rabi, Vanua Levu after their homeland had been stripped bare by phosphate mining.

MEDIA

Newspapers are printed in English, Fijian, Hindi and Chinese and are lively forums for the controversial issues – such as race – that people rarely discuss face-to-face. A weekly newspaper, *Kaila,* is aimed at teenagers. Great attention is paid to local and human interest stories, and political journalism treads warily around government sensibilities – in 2004 a New Zealand journalist was blacklisted for his unfavourable reportage in 2000.

There are several Fiji radio stations, mostly of the music, chat and sports variety, and BBC World Service and Radio Australia can be heard on local FM stations. femTALK's 'radio-in-a-suitcase' broadcasts community radio geared towards women's issues.

Television arrived in Fiji in 1991 when Television New Zealand relayed World Cup rugby matches. The one government-run local free-to-air station – called, sensibly, Fiji One – has been criticised for the lack of local content except for news, sport and game-shows: it broadcasts mostly foreign sitcoms and series in English. An exception is *The Pacific Way,* a monthly programme about development issues in the region, made by the media unit of the Secretariat of the Pacific Community (SPC) and usually shown around the third Sunday of the month. At about 10pm Fiji One switches over to the Australian Broadcasting Corporation's Asia-Pacific TV station for overnight viewing of ancient serials and documentaries. Fee-for-service satellite channels are available in most hotels and bars.

The International Press Institute's annual World Press Freedom Review is both broadly encouraging and constructively critical about Fiji's media at www.freemedia.at.

RELIGION

Traditional Fijian religion was based on ancestor worship whereby, for example, a good warrior became a war god after death, or an outstanding farmer became a god of plenty. Belief in an afterlife was strong, with priests mediating between people and the gods who required appeasement by initiation ceremonies, mutilation rituals and mourning sacrifices.

GROWING PAINS

In traditional Vitian society, growing up may well have been dreaded by young girls. Until the 20th century, a girl's initiation into adulthood was marked by the *veiqia* rite, the elaborate tattooing of the pubic area. Each village had a female *duabati* (hereditary tattoo specialist) who used a spiked pick, light mallet, bamboo slivers, sharp shells and soot to create the blue-black designs. Often a few girls were tattooed at once, taking turns to hold each other down. The ritual would stretch out over weeks or months and was carried out during the day when men were out, to conceal the screaming.

It was believed that untattooed women would be persecuted by the ancestor spirits in the afterlife – slashed about the pubic region or pounded to a pulp and fed to the gods – so girls were loath to defy the custom. Even after missionaries had suppressed what they saw as a pagan ritual, fake tattoos were sometimes painted on dead girls in an attempt to bluff the gods.

These practices appalled the first missionaries and from the 1830s onwards the old religion was gradually supplanted by Christianity, now enthusiastically practiced by most Fijians. About 52% of Fijians are Christians, the majority of whom (about 37% of the population) are Methodists, and the church is a powerful force in internal affairs. There's a Catholic minority of around 9%, and evangelical Christian churches are increasingly popular.

The arrival of Indian indentured labour brought other religions to Fiji. Hinduism is practised by 38% of the population, and Islam by about 8%. About 2% of the population follow other religions or none.

WOMEN IN FIJI

On paper, Fiji's working women are doing relatively well. Women received the right to vote and to stand for parliament in 1963, yet still hold only 6% of seats in parliament. While 51% of senior officials and managers are women, they earn only 36% of their male counterpart's salary.

There's an active Fiji Women's Rights Movement, which helped push the Family Law Bill through parliament in 2004; women now have the right to pursue issues around child custody, access and maintenance. Paid maternity leave, while rarely matching a full-time wage, makes it easier for working women to spend more time with their babies.

In much of Fiji, violence disguised as a cultural norm prevails. According to the Fiji Women's Crisis Centre, two-thirds of men in Fiji consider it acceptable to hit the women in their family, and incidents of random violence against women are common.

Everything you ever wanted to know about Fiji rugby union – including how the national women's team is doing – can be found at www.teivovo.com.

SPORT

Rugby, especially popular with indigenous Fijians, is the one sport that has continually put Fiji on the world sporting scene since the first match between Fijian and British soldiers was held in 1884. Under coach and captain Waisale Serevi, the national team took the Rugby World Cup Sevens title for the second time in 2005. The rugby season is from April to September and every village in Viti Levu seems to have its own rugby pitch.

Women's rugby, initially a source of some controversy in conservative villages, is gaining acceptance but has nowhere near the resources of the men's game – an invitation for the Fiji women's rugby union to tour South Africa in 2004 had to be declined because of lack of funds.

Soccer is popular with Indo-Fijians. Even if you're not a footy fan, it's worth going to a rugby or soccer match just to watch the crowd!

The British also brought the golfing habit to Fiji; one of the world's current top golfers, Vijay Singh, is Indo-Fijian (see p48 for more on Vijay). There are golf courses on Denarau island, at hotels along Viti Levu's Coral Coast and Suva. Basketball and netball are played widely, and there's a small local surfing circuit.

When the Pacific Games were held in Suva in 2003, new sporting facilities were built and existing ones upgraded. Many regional sporting events are now held in the capital. Check out the sports pages of the *Fiji Times* for venues and events.

News of the current Fiji arts and entertainment scene can be found at www.kulchavulcha.com or in the fortnightly *Kulcha Vulcha* newsletter available at Suva's coffee shops and elsewhere.

ARTS

Traditional arts and crafts such as wood carving and weaving, along with dancing and music, remain an integral part of life in many villages. These traditions have inspired much of the small but thriving Fijian contemporary arts scene, and Suva is the place to seek it out.

The Oceania Centre for Arts & Culture (p124), in the grounds of the USP, provides working space for artists, musicians and dancers. The Fiji Arts Club has an annual exhibition, usually in August or September, in Suva. Suva is also the hub for things literary in Fiji, including occasional readings by members of the Pacific Writing Forum, and performances of work by Fijian playwrights.

Writers from Fiji and the nearby region are well-represented in poetry and prose in two anthologies, *Nuanua: Pacific Writing in English since 1980* and *Niu Waves: Contemporary Writing from Oceania*.

Literature

There's still a strong oral storytelling tradition in Fiji, especially in rural areas where nights are long and electricity is limited or nonexistent. When stories are transcribed it's usually into English, and *Myths and Legends of Fiji & Rotuma*, by AW Reed and Inez Hames, gives a good selection.

Fiji has a small but strong community of poets and writers, whose work is often gritty and realist. Joseph C Veramu's 1996 novel *Moving Through*

A HAIRY SITUATION

For indigenous Fijians, the head is *tabu* (sacred) and, in reverence to its sanctity, precolonial Vitians spent entire days with the hairdresser.

Until initiation, boys were kept bald except for one or two upstanding tufts. A man's hair, on the other hand, was a symbol of his masculinity and social standing. Men sported flamboyant, extravagant and often massive hair-dos, ranging from the relatively conventional giant puffball to more original shaggy or geometric shapes. Styles were stiffened into place with burnt lime juice. Hair was dyed grey, sky blue, rust, orange, yellow and white, often striped or multicoloured.

Before initiation, girls wore a lavish cascade of bleached or reddened corkscrew ringlets which hung down to their hips. These ringlets, known as *tobe*, represented the prawns they were destined to fish in later life. Women, on the other hand, wore more conservative hair-dos – close-cropped with random tufts dyed rusty brown or yellow. A wife's hair could never outdo her husband's and a husband's could not outdo the chief's.

People slept on raised wooden pillows to keep their coiffure from being spoilt. The head was especially dressed for festive occasions with scalp scratchers (practical for lice), ornamental combs, scarlet feathers, wreaths of flowers, and perfumed with grated sandalwood.

Shaving one's head was a profound sacrifice for a man and was often done as a symbol of mourning or to appease a wrathful ancestral spirit. Women's *tobe* were popular war trophies.

Early Europeans were astonished by the variety of elaborate hair styles. Not long after a missionary measured one indigenous hair-do at 5m in circumference, the custom was deliberately suppressed as a 'flagrant symbol of paganism', not suitable for the 'neat and industrious Christian convert'.

A BRUSH WITH CULTURE

If you entered an indigenous Fijian village in the mid-19th century, there was enough make-up flying around to make you think you'd landed backstage of a Broadway show. Before the practice was stamped out by the missionaries, Fijians decked themselves out in face and body paint on a daily basis. They worked from a palette of yellow from ginger root or turmeric; black from burnt candlenut, charcoal or fungus spores; and blue and vermilion introduced by the traders. Vermilion became worth its weight in gold and was traded with the Europeans for baskets of *bêche-de-mer* (sea cucumber).

A typical day saw Fijians made-up in stripes, zigzags and spots. Ceremonies and war called for more specialised designs, often used to carry specific meanings.

Men mostly used red and black, associated with war and death, on their faces and sometimes chests. Young men were covered in turmeric for *buli yaca* (puberty) ceremonies, or renaming ceremonies to celebrate their first enemy kill.

Women favoured yellow, saffron, pink and red body paint, with fine black circles drawn around their eyes for beauty. In the first three months of pregnancy, women were painted with turmeric as, during pregnancy, a woman was under sexual *tabu*. (Males found smudged with turmeric paint were ridiculed.) After the birth, both mother and baby would be made-up again until the baby was weaned. The bodies of dead or dying women were adorned with turmeric or vermilion paint.

These days, there's not a stripe or a zigzag to be found among indigenous Fijians; however, in the Indo-Fijian society, body painting still remains an important and commonly practiced art. In a tradition brought from India, intricate henna (or *mehndi*) designs are most commonly painted on women's hands and feet for marriage ceremonies. Painting the bride is a ceremony in itself, seen as both therapeutic and spiritual, and most designs are linked to religious beliefs and practices. Hidden in the design will often be the initials of the husband. If the husband can find them, he will be the dominant partner; if he fails, his wife will rule the roost. The henna lasts anywhere from a few days to three weeks; as long as it does, the new bride is exempt from all housework.

As in the rest of the world, henna 'tattoos' are becoming trendy and you may spot young Indo-Fijian women painting them onto customers in the markets.

the Streets is an eye-opener about disaffected youth in Suva. Daryl Tarte's sweeping historical saga *Fiji*, and more recent novel *Stalker on the Beach*, both look at the influence of outsiders on the country.

Beyond Ceremony: An Anthology of Fiji Drama showcases Fiji's playwrights including Vilsoni Hereniko, Sudesh Mishra, Jo Nacola, Raymond Pillai and Larry Thomas; look out for occasional performances of their work in Suva.

Since the 1970s Indo-Fijian writers have increasingly worked in English. Writers of note include Subramani, Satendra Nandan, and poet Mohit Prasad who wrote *Eating Mangoes* (2001). The theme of the injustice of indenture – and, latterly, the experience of the coups – rates highly in Indo-Fijian literature.

Check out the latest literary offerings from and about Fiji and the Pacific online at the University of the South Pacific's bookshop www .uspbookcentre.com.

Collections of women writers' poetry include *Of Schizophrenic Voices* by Frances Koya and *Nei Nim Manoa* by Teresia Teaiwa.

Cinema

Fiji's gorgeous scenery has attracted filmmakers since the original *Blue Lagoon* was filmed in the Yasawas in 1948. It was remade there in 1979 starring Brooke Shields, and *Return to the Blue Lagoon* with Milla Jovovich was shot on Taveuni in 1991. In 2001 Tom Hanks filmed *Castaway* on Monuriki in the Mamanuca islands, where Jodie Foster's 'heaven' sequence in the sci-fi movie *Contact* was also filmed. The fantastically awful *Anacondas: The Hunt for the Blood Orchid*, released in 2004, was filmed in the waterways and hills around Pacific Harbour.

The Fiji Audio Visual Commission, formed in 2002, hopes to attract more filmmakers to the country by offering significant tax incentives. Yaqara Studio City, a huge and high-tech audiovisual complex, is in development in western Viti Levu.

Fiji's first home-grown feature film, *The Land Has Eyes*, is set during the last gasp of colonialism in 1960s Rotuma. Made in Rotuman language with English subtitles, and a mostly local (and nonprofessional) cast, it paints a wonderfully low-key picture of a community on the cusp of change.

Fiji's first indigenous film, The Land Has Eyes, filmed in Rotuma by Rotuman-born writer and filmmaker Vilsoni Hereniko, premiered to rave reviews in 2004 and was submitted for nomination in the 2005 Academy Awards

Music

For a taste of contemporary pop and rock music, check out popular local musicians Seru Serevi and Danny Costello, and bands including Delai Sea and Voqa ni Delai Dokidoki. The band Black Rose has become Fiji's most successful music export. Reggae has been influential and is very popular, and there are a couple of jazz bands in Suva. Sunday church services usually feature fantastic choir singing. The Oceania Centre produces CDs of Pacific music with a contemporary twist; listen to, for example, Sailasa Tora's album *Wasawasa*.

Indo-Fijian singer Aiysha is a big hit in India, and local Indo-Fijian band The Bad Boys play at venues around Fiji. Music from Bollywood films, and Indian dance and pop music is popular, as is classical *qawali*. Vocal, tabla (percussion) and sitar lessons are given at Indian cultural centres.

Dance

Visitors are often welcomed at resorts and hotels with *meke*, a dance performance that enacts local stories and legends. In the past, *meke* were accompanied by a chanting chorus or by 'spiritually possessed seers', as well as by rhythmic clapping, the thumping and stamping of bamboo clacking sticks and the beating of slit drums. The whole community participated in *meke*. In times of war, men performed the *cibi*, or death dance, and women the *dele* or *wate*, a dance in which they sexually humiliated enemy corpses and captives. Dancing often took place by moonlight or torchlight, with the performers in costume, and with bodies oiled, faces painted and combs and flowers decorating their hair.

Traditional Chinese dancing is also still practised in Fiji, and Indian classical dance, including Bharat Natyam and *kathak*, is taught at Indian cultural centres.

MELODIOUS MEASURES

Replaced with guitars and keyboards, traditional indigenous instruments are a rare find in Fiji these days. Yet once upon a time, nose flutes were all the rage. Made from a single piece of bamboo, some 70cm long, the flute would be intricately carved and played by your typical laid-back Fijian, reclined on a pandanus mat and resting his or her head on a bamboo pillow. Whether it was the music or the pose, flutes were believed to have the power to attract the opposite sex and were a favourite for serenading.

Other instruments had more practical purposes, such as shell trumpets and whistles which were used for communication. Portable war drums were used as warnings and for communicating tactics on the battlefield. One instrument you are still likely to see (and hear) is the *lali*, a large slit drum made of resonant timbers. Audible over large distances, its deep call continues to beckon people to the chief's *bure* or to church.

For a more contemporary dance experience, look out for performances by the Oceania Dance Theatre (p124) in Suva.

Architecture
TRADITIONAL
The most beautiful example of a traditional Fijian village is Navala (p144), nestled in the Viti Levu highlands. It is the only village remaining where every home is a *bure*. *Bure*-building is a skilled trade passed from father to son, although the whole community helps during construction and people know how to maintain its woven walls and thatched roof. Today, however, most villagers live in simple rectangular, pitched-roof houses made from industrialised materials requiring less maintenance. For more information on *bure,* see p81.

COLONIAL
The historic town of Levuka (p174), the former capital of Fiji, has been nominated for World Heritage Listing. A number of buildings here date from its boom period of the late 19th century, and the main streetscape is surprisingly intact, giving the impression that the town has been suspended in time.

The British influence on Suva is reflected in its many colonial buildings, including Government House, Suva City Library, and the elegantly decaying Grand Pacific Hotel, due for renovation in 2006.

Fiji's Treasured Culture (www.museum.vic .gov.au/fiji) is an online exhibition of fabulous artefacts held in Museum Victoria (in Melbourne) and Suva's Fiji Museum.

MODERN
Some of the country's modern architecture combines modern technology with traditional Fijian aesthetics, knowledge and materials. Notable buildings include the parliament complex, the USP campus in Suva, the *bure bose* (meeting house) at Somosomo on Taveuni and, begun in 2005, the Great Council of Chiefs complex in Suva.

Resorts with distinctive architecture include the upmarket Vatulele Island Resort, Koro Sun Resort near Savusavu and Raintree Lodge outside Suva.

Pottery
Pottery, first brought to Fiji by the Lapita people, has a 3000-year history in the islands, and some modern potters still use traditional techniques. Wooden paddles of various shapes and sizes beat the pots into shape, while the form is held from within using a pebble anvil. Coil and slab-building techniques are also used. Once dried, pots are fired outdoors in an open blaze on coconut husks, and often sealed with resin varnish taken from the *dakua* tree.

Two of Fiji's best-known pottery villages – Nakabuta, in the lower Sigatoka Valley, and Nasilai, on the Rewa River near Nausori – receive visitors. Pottery demonstrations take place every Tuesday and Thursday on the veranda of the Fiji Museum in Suva.

Wood Carving
Traditional woodcarving skills are largely kept alive by the tourist trade, providing a ready market for war clubs, spears and cannibal forks. *Tanoa* (drinking bowls) and *bilo* – *kava* cups of coconut shell – remain part of everyday life. *Tanoa* shaped like turtles are thought to have derived from turtle-shaped *ibuburau*, vessels used in indigenous Vitian *yaqona* rites.

The Fiji Museum is the best place to see authentic traditional woodcarvings, and there are usually carvings in progress at USP's Oceania

Centre in Suva. Be aware that many 'handmade' artefacts for sale at handicraft centres may have been mass-produced by a machine.

Bark Cloth

Masi, also known as *malo* or *tapa,* is bark cloth with black and rust-coloured printed designs. In Vitian culture, *masi* was invested with status and associated with celebrations and rituals. It was worn as a loincloth by men during initiation rituals, renaming ceremonies and as an adornment in dance, festivity and war. *Masi* was also an important exchange item, used in bonding ceremonies between related tribes. Chiefs were swathed in a huge puffball of *masi,* later given to members of the other tribe.

While men wore the *masi,* production has traditionally been a woman's role. Made from the inner white bark of the paper mulberry bush, which has been soaked in water and scraped clean, it's then beaten and felted for hours into sheets of a fine, even texture. Intricate designs are done by hand or stencil and often carry symbolic meaning. Rust-coloured paints are traditionally made from an infusion of candlenut and mangrove bark; pinker browns are made from red clays; and black from the soot of burnt *dakua* resin and charred candlenuts.

It is difficult to see *masi* being made, though you'll see the end product used for postcards, wall hangings and other decorative items. Textile designers have also begun incorporating traditional *masi* motifs in their fabrics.

Mat & Basket Weaving

Most indigenous Fijian homes use woven *voivoi* or pandanus-leaf to make baskets, floor coverings and fine sleeping mats. Traditionally, most girls living in villages learned to weave, and many still do. Pandanus leaves are cut and laid outdoors to cure, stripped of the spiny edges, and boiled and dried. The traditional method of blackening leaves for contrasting patterns is to bury them in mud for days and then boil them again. The dried leaves, made flexible by scraping with shells, are then split into strips of about 1cm to 2cm and woven. Mat borders are now often decorated in brightly coloured wools instead of parrot feathers.

'What's something creative to do while relaxing under a coconut palm?' you ask. For a user-friendly picture-by-picture guide to basket weaving and other crafts look for a copy of Mereisi Tabualeva's *Traditional Handicrafts of Fiji.*

Indo-Fijian History & Culture
Clement Paligaru

It would be hard to imagine Fiji without Indo-Fijians. With enterprise and resilience, they have forged a presence that permeates throughout the country. Despite mostly being the descendants of indentured labourers who arrived in the country up to 130 years ago, Indo-Fijians are still considered *vulagi* (visitors) by many indigenous Fijians. But this has never stopped them making the most of life on the islands, adding their own touch to the rich mosaic of Fiji's cultural traditions.

For a visitor, this Indo-Fijian presence is difficult to ignore. Fiji may well be best known for indigenous ceremonies, *lovo* (earth ovens), leis and crafts; however, Indo-Fijian culture provides another dimension – food, shopping, temples and festivals, as colourful as you would find in Rajasthan but with an undeniably Fijian character.

After decades of living the island life, Indo-Fijians have dispensed with many formalities they carried from India. Instead, a laid-back culture has evolved, forever changed by circumstance and liberal doses of the infectious Pacific way. It's one Indian lifestyle you're unlikely to encounter or enjoy anywhere else in the world.

> An Indo-Fijian, Clement Paligaru came to Australia in 1984. He has reported extensively on the Pacific region for the Australian Broadcasting Corporation.

COMINGS & GOINGS: A HISTORY
The earliest Indian arrivals in Fiji were indentured labourers brought by the British to work in the sugar industry in the 1870s. As the pioneers adapted to life as labourers, they also forged the foundations of a unique Indo-Fijian cultural identity, later bequeathed to generations that followed.

Very early on, it had dawned on most workers that the confines of plantation life were simply too tough and restrictive to accommodate the strict social and religious codes of India. Labourers began socialising, eating and marrying across caste and religious lines. That's not to say religious and cultural practices were abandoned. The new Indo-Fijians simply got rid of the social hang-ups. The 'subversive' practice of selecting only the Indian customs that suited life on the islands had begun.

> Today's Indo-Fijians are among some 10 million descendents of indentured Indian labourers who live outside India.

When the time came to return home after their labour contracts had expired, many Indians decided to remain in Fiji. For many this decision was made because they were not eligible for, or couldn't afford, the costly passage to India. Another reason was the possibility of being kicked out of their communities back home for breaking Indian mores. In any case, the idea of starting anew in Fiji was much more attractive for many Indian labourers. Little did they realize that the bountiful future would also be a fraught one.

By the time indentured labour was abolished in 1919, independent sugar-cane, cotton, tobacco and rice farms had been set up by Indo-Fijians on land mostly leased from indigenous Fijians. Other migrants ran small stores or became public servants and maids. The big move into commerce began in the 1930s, following the arrival of a second wave of business migrants from India. There was no doubt Indo-Fijians were hard working and becoming prosperous. Some indigenous Fijians found they didn't make bad friends either. But their success did not go down well with everyone.

As the new migrants set about laying the foundations for their future, many indigenous Fijians began to feel increasingly uneasy. The customs and ambitions of Indo-Fijians were deemed offensive. And some Fijians regarded the migrants as usurpers of their land. This was despite laws introduced in the late 1800s forbidding the sale of native land, and forever guaranteeing indigenous Fijians over 80% of land ownership. This, however, did not stop the Indio-Fijians from demanding rich arable land for lease. As the Indo-Fijian farmers and businesspeople became prosperous, many indigenous groups became wary of being eclipsed economically. The seeds were sown for decades of dispute, primarily over land leases, between the two ethnic groups.

By the mid-1900s the Indo-Fijians had became indispensable to the economy, dominating agriculture, business and the public service. They also outnumbered indigenous Fijians. But the lack of political power and land-ownership rights remained a source of insecurity for the Indo-Fijians. A previously fledgling campaign for political equality began gaining momentum despite facing stiff resistance from Europeans and Fijians.

When independence from Britain occurred in 1970 the campaign for equality had laid the foundations for race-based politics in the country. After much debate, the new constitution set out an electoral system arranged along racial lines. Indo-Fijians, like other races, would be allocated a set number of seats in parliament. The politics of ethnicity was now institutionalised. To win easy votes, political parties could play the race card.

After independence, Indo-Fijians felt fairly secure under the rule of Prime Minister Ratu Sir Kamisese Mara, whose Alliance Party promoted multiracialism. During this period, national celebrations showcasing Indo-Fijian culture alongside the indigenous became the norm. But some Fijians were troubled by this increased acceptance of Indo-Fijian culture. In the mid-1970s the Alliance Party's concessions to Indo-Fijians on issues such as land leases, combined with the lack of prosperity among indigenous Fijians, led to a backlash by nationalists. Warning of an Indo-Fijian takeover, they demanded that 'visitors' leave.

As the Alliance Party scrambled to introduce pro-indigenous policies in the mid-1980s, Indo-Fijian voters turned to the new Fiji Labour Party (FLP) and its platform of social reform. Labour, in coalition with an Indo-Fijian–dominated party won the elections in 1987. But, soon afterwards, it was overthrown in a military coup led by Lieutenant Colonel Sitiveni Rabuka. The reason? Although the government was lead by an indigenous Fijian, Dr Timoci Bavadra, the idea of an Indo-Fijian–dominated coalition was too much for the nationalists. To ensure the pendulum didn't ever swing back to favour Indo-Fijians, Rabuka introduced a racially biased constitution in 1990. Thousands of skilled and professional Indo-Fijians fled the country.

By the mid-1990s Rabuka, now prime minister, came under pressure internally and internationally to review the 1990 constitution. It was during this review that Fiji came closest to ending its long history of the politics of race. Calls were made to minimise the number of race-based parliamentary seats. A complex system of governance was recommended, which would force parties to cooperate across ethnic lines and 'share power'. The new constitution, declared in 1997, adopted some of these ideas. It was fairer to the Indo-Fijians, but it was not as progressive as some had hoped, and seats were still race based. Nevertheless, constitutional experts lauded the idea of political power sharing in government, which aimed to promote interethnic cooperation.

The word *girmit* is used to describe the indenture system. It entered the Indo-Fijian lexicon when the *girmitiyas* (early labourers) mispronounced the word agreement.

At least 15 Indo-Fijian religious and cultural associations exist around the country, through which communities maintain cultural and religious affiliations with India. One organisation established the new University of Fiji near Lautoka in 2005.

THE BOLLYWOOD BEAUTY

This 2005 book, by Shalini Akhil, tells the story of Kesh and her cousin, Rupa. Kesh is a feminist, loves pubs, swears a lot and was born and raised in Australia. Her Indo-Fijian cousin Rupa is the exact opposite. She diligently cooks curries, wears saris and is heading for an arranged marriage. When Rupa comes to live with Kesh in Melbourne, their worlds collide. Wicked humour and disarming honesty spice up this tale of culture clash, identity struggle and the Indo-Fijian way. For more information on the book, see www.kai-india.com.

In the 1999 elections, Rabuka was rejected and Fiji's first Indo-Fijian prime minister, FLP leader Mahendra Chaudhry, came to office. But within a year, Chaudhry's confrontational style and social-reform agenda proved unpalatable for the nationalists. In 2000 the Chaudhry government was overthrown, following a coup led by nationalists. Chief among Chaudhry's sins was his insistence on a fair outcome for thousands of Indo-Fijian farmers whose long-term land leases were expiring.

After a lengthy series of court battles regarding the coup, Fiji returned to the polls in 2001. The country elected Lasenia Qarase, a declared champion of the indigenous cause, as its leader.

Since Qarase's election, Indo-Fijians have again been leaving the country in droves. But many more have chosen to remain in Fiji, the country they call home, including those Indo-Fijians in the business community who hold Qarase in high regard. Despite acceptance from some Indo-Fijians, many are concerned about Qarase's pro-indigenous policies and his controversial campaign to pardon the jailed perpetrators of the 2000 coup.

THE FIJIAN IN INDO-FIJIAN

One of the most common observations made when Indo-Fijians are compared with Indians on the subcontinent is that they are very relaxed and friendly. There's no doubt that more than a century of living in the islands with laid-back indigenous Fijians who greet others warmly has had an effect. The distance from India and its strict mores has had a profound influence and Indo-Fijians have largely discarded the rigidities of India's caste and social structure. In Fiji, schools, higher-education institutions, the workplace and places of worship do not discriminate according to caste or class differences. As a result, the relative ease with which Indo-Fijians socialise and engage is arguably one of the characteristics that sets them apart from Indians – especially the middle classes in India. For example, in Fiji wedding invitations from economically disadvantaged or village-based relatives are seized upon by their well-to-do relatives as an opportunity to catch-up with family and indulge in feasting and celebration. Such disregard for social codes would be frowned upon in India. Although some traditions such as arranged marriages are still the norm, Hindu wedding practices have generally changed in Fiji. While still distinctly Indian,

Indo-Fijian muslims, Labasa, Vanua Levu
PHOTO BY TOM COCKREM

weddings in Fiji have largely been standardised and are an amalgam of various traditions. The nuptials are attended by family and friends, and last at least an hour. In some states in India, rituals last just a few minutes, and in other states, they are sometimes witnessed only by a handful of family members.

One of the more significant cultural departures from India has been the emergence of an unique Hindi dialect. Known as 'Fiji-Hindi', it is an amalgam of regional dialects spoken by the indentured labourers from India. Today it is used in all informal family and social settings. In India, it would be regarded as *toota-phoota*, or broken Hindi. But universal use among Indo-Fijians has contributed to its increasing acceptance as a legitimate dialect. For some useful words and phrases in Fiji-Hindi, see p275.

On special occasions, such as weddings and festivals, younger family members learn to make *mithai* (traditional sweets).

THE INDIAN IN INDO-FIJIAN

With some five generations of history in Fiji, the Indo-Fijian community has forged a strong identity in its adopted homeland. This identity is an unique blend of Fijian and Indian cultures. For an Indo-Fijian, being ethnic Indian as opposed to being indigenous Fijian is about a certain type of upbringing and way of life. The outlook and aspirations of Indo-Fijians emphasise the importance of education and hard work to ensure a secure future. Add thriftiness for good measure and you have the core of the Indo-Fijian package.

India remains an important cultural beacon for Indo-Fijians, influencing rituals, culinary traditions, dress and entertainment. Today these influences provide some of the more obvious signs of cultural distinction between Indo-Fijians and indigenous Fijians.

Most Indo-Fijians love homemade rotis (traditional breads) straight from the kitchen. Steaming curries are served with roti and rice, with condiments completing the meal. Many Indo-Fijians have a weakness for *mithai* (traditional sweets). Out of the home, the curry combo also finds its way to schools, the workplace and the outdoors.

Fiji remains a popular stopover for Bollywood stars and musicians on overseas tours. Check papers for events if you want a slice of Bollywood action.

Tradition, pride and identity have also ensured that saris, the colourful Indian dress worn by women, remain popular in Fiji. The Muslim- and Punjabi-influenced *salwaar-kameez* (flowing top, top and scarf outfit) is also standard. Most Indo-Fijians are practising Hindus, Muslims or Sikhs, and across the country, temples and mosques lend a particularly Indian feel to the landscape. The domes, minarets and red flags atop bamboo poles in backyards also serve as a reminder of the strength of Indo-Fijian adherence to the faiths of India. Hindus make up about 38% of Fiji's population and Muslims 8%.

Entertainment and recreation continue to have a decidedly subcontinental flavour for many Indo-Fijians, with the local cinemas providing a regular dose of Hindi-language Bollywood film and music. Indo-Fijian home-entertainment systems are often tuned to provide Bollywood on tap, as well as an endless supply of Hindi-pop music videos. Apart from the pure escapism value, Bollywood films also provide many with the only connection they have with India and subcontinental Hindi.

MILAAP – DISCOVER YOUR ROOTS

A small but growing number of Indo-Fijians are now retracing their ancestral roots in India. Sydney-based documentary maker Satish Rai has been making documentaries about his and others' experiences. Documentaries include *Milaap: Discover Your Indian Roots* (2001) and *Milaap: A Royal Discovery* (2003). Another film is in the pipeline.

Most Indo-Fijians will never visit India. Few now dream of going there. Those who do visit are motivated by a desire to explore their cultural heritage and ancestry, while others simply visit out of curiosity; however, few are compelled to take the journey as an affirmation of their identity; it is Fiji they turn to for that.

ETHNIC TENSIONS

Most aspects of Indo-Fijian lifestyle and culture have comfortably co-existed with the indigenous Fijian way of life for more than a century. A quick look around reveals that large numbers of Indo-Fijians and indigenous Fijians live side by side, work together and go to the same schools. But apart from attending some sports, entertainment and special occasions together, the two groups still tend not to engage socially. Their economic, educational, cultural and social priorities, including *tabu* (that which is forbidden or sacred), differ. These differences have proven rich fodder for political agitators seeking to exploit the insecurities of indigenous Fijians.

For example, the domination of a few Indo-Fijians in the economic sphere, as well as their high visibility in white-collar occupations, has often been used by nationalists to fan the coals of resentment. In reality, many Indo-Fijians remain economically disadvantaged. Yet the threat of 'eventual Indian domination' has been a recurring theme in Fiji politics.

Quite often, Indo-Fijian success, flamboyance (new cars, big houses and gold jewellery) and materialism have served as convenient reminders of what makes Indo-Fijians different as well as threatening. The perceived lack of Indo-Fijian respect for Fijian customs also serves to annoy many indigenous Fijians. For example, when people are sitting down at a meeting on the ground or floor, Fijian custom requires that you pass them in a crouching motion. The tendency for Indians to walk upright in such situations is seen as arrogant and disrespectful. One coup leader even referred to the way Indians 'look different and smell different' when justifying his actions to the international media.

The Indo-Fijian 'threat' has in fact often served as a perfect smoke-screen for other agendas. Since the 2000 coup, the media has been a forum for speculation about whether the coup was in the economic or political interests of the disenfranchised or whether it only benefited an elite group of indigenous and nonindigenous opportunists. Whether these allegations will reverse entrenched perceptions about Indo-Fijians is yet to be seen. Widespread opposition to Prime Minister Qarase's move to permit the release of jailed 2000 coup leaders indicates that many indigenous Fijians will not blindly follow their nationalist government. Even though the bill is said to be inspired by indigenous concepts of forgiveness, there is recognition that such appeals to indigenous loyalty will serve only to ridicule the law, placate nationalists and divide the races.

In the mid-1970s Indo-Fijians made up 49% of the country's population. It is estimated by some that, by 2022, Indo-Fijians may comprise just 20% of the population.

There are hundreds of small Hindu clubs called '*mandalis*' around the country. Once a week they recite the Indian epic of Ramayana and sing hymns as part of devotional rituals.

VIJAY SINGH

Indo-Fijian Vijay Singh is one of the world's most successful golfers and has won many of the world's prestigious events. When he was young, he used to climb over a fence and dart across the Nadi airport runway to practise on the only course in Fiji. After he left the country in search of his dream, he never thought he would return again. His relationship with Fiji remained on ice for decades but thawed in 2005 when he returned to oversee the planning of a new golf course.

COMING TOGETHER

Despite the differences between Indo-Fijians and indigenous Fijians, the way the two groups coexist and influence each other is testament to shared experiences for over a century. In many ways Fiji is already witnessing the synergy that has resulted from cooperation between these two communities. Many Indo-Fijians may be leaving the country in search of economic and political stability, yet this has not stalled the momentum of a mutual cultural exploration by Indo-Fijians and indigenous Fijians.

Increasing numbers from both communities speak each other's language. In Fiji's cane belts on the western side of Viti Levu and around Labasa on Vanua Levu, many indigenous cane farmers who work alongside Indo-Fijians speak Fiji-Hindi fluently, while their families immerse themselves in Bollywood films. Indo-Fijian music and songs have even been recorded and released commercially by indigenous Fijian artists. Elsewhere, Indo-Fijians in rural communities, including former Christian mission settlements, also speak Fijian.

In larger urban centres, fashion and popular culture are also breaking down barriers. Visit Fiji during the Hindu Diwali festival (held in October or November) and you will see many indigenous Fijian women wearing Indian fashion. More generally, indigenous women are now wearing Indian jewellery and using sari cloth for traditional outfits. Nightclubs are playing Bollywood DJ mixes and bars are serving bowls of curry with drinks the way Indo-Fijians do in their homes. Across the country, sport, in particular soccer, plays a role. Team members hold regular curry, beer and *kava* (a narcotic drink) nights and banter in Hindi or Fijian. Indo-Fijians are now even playing the indigenous Fijian–dominated rugby. When victorious national rugby sides return from overseas, Indian dancers greet them alongside the thousands of Fijian spectators.

Indo-Fijian mother and child, Labasa, Vanua Levu
PHOTO BY TOM COCKREM

Perhaps the most amazing transformation that has taken place is the elevation of Indian food in indigenous Fijian life. In many homes, almost every second meal is a curry. So be prepared: if you accept an invitation to an indigenous Fijian home, you may not be served Islander food.

Intermarriage, however, remains one area few are willing to explore. For many the cultural, religious and social differences remain insurmountable. Among Indo-Fijians, notions of cultural differences and religious purity have placed intermarriage firmly in the too-hard basket. Early colonial policy prohibiting racial intermingling has also been blamed for limiting interaction and understanding between the communities. There is a minuscule, but growing, number of intermarriages taking place; this is testament to the resolve of the few who are risking ostracism and breaking *tabu*.

Elsewhere, filmmakers, nongovernmental organisations and artists often push the boundaries of cross-cultural experimentation to promote national unity and understanding. Cultural groups such as the Shobna

A growing number of Fijian performers are fusing Indian and indigenous Fijian traditions in their music and choreography. They include popular band Black Rose, musician Karuna Gopalan and choreographer Shobna Chanel.

Chanel Dance Group fuse rhythms and traditions of Indo-Fijian and indigenous Fijian cultures at national and international events. Femlink-pacific, a community-based organisation produces radio programmes and video documentaries that reflect universal themes in Indian festivals. Indo-Fijian filmmaker James Bhagwan has even scored international prizes for his documentaries promoting freedom and tolerance using cross-cultural themes.

Temple etiquette must be followed. Wear modest clothes, remove footwear and abstain from non-vegetarian meals and alcohol on the day of your visit.

CULTURAL IMMERSION

The best way to experience Indo-Fijian culture is to share a meal at the home of an Indo-Fijian. To increase the chances of being invited, you can always meet sociable Indo-Fijians at some of their favourite celebrations, haunts, shops and cultural venues around urban centres. If you are lucky enough, you may meet someone who could take you to an Indo-Fijian settlement to witness rural life and be treated to real down-to-earth hospitality. That could mean anything from a glass of fresh country-style lemon juice to a village-style curry feast, complete with home-grown vegetables. Just remember to take some sweets with you as a gift for your hosts.

There are many fantastic eateries in cities and towns serving home-style meals. But try to also explore some of the places in smaller towns that cater for Indo-Fijians. They often serve seasonal vegetables such as *duruka* (Fijian asparagus), *katahar* (jackfruit) and *kerela* (bitter melon). Do not forget to ask for pickles and chutneys made from local fruits such as mangoes, *kumrakh* (star-apple) and tamarind. Remember even some of the locals do not know these places exist. So put some effort into asking around and you're likely to experience a culinary adventure you will never forget.

Annual festivals and events also offer the visitor a chance to experience Indo-Fijian culture. Diwali (Festival of Lights) takes place across the nation in October or November. You can join in the fun by wearing some traditional gear (or a *bindi* on the forehead) and sharing *mithai* and candles. Events include temple fairs where thousands of Indo-Fijians gather to watch rituals and enjoy folksy meals. In Suva, the South Indian firewalking festival, held during July or August, takes place at the **Mariamma Temple** (Map p119; Howell Rd, Samabula). In Vanua Levu, the Ram Leela festival is held at the Mariamman Temple in Vunivau (east of Labasa) around October. If you want to explore Hindu mysticism, try the Naag Mandir (Pathaar) temple north of Labasa, where a shrine is built around a large rock that devotees believe is growing in the shape of a cobra (p207). Other interesting events include the annual South Indian Sangam convention (www.sangamvillage.com), which takes place around Easter. During the rest of the year, visitors are welcome at Hindu and Sikh temples.

Fairground activities accompany Fiji's soccer season, which runs from February to October. Club soccer matches are played on weekends and culminate in the interdistrict tournament, held in a different location each year (www.fijifootball.com). On the sidelines there is fierce culinary competition under tin sheds, where *pulau* (aromatic fried rice), curry and roti are sold. Be prepared to eat with your fingers and put up with the distorted Bollywood and folk music blaring around you.

If you want to hear and watch authentic Bollywood, there are cinemas in all major towns and cities with regular sessions of Hindi films (without subtitles); newspapers carry screening details. Bollywood music tapes and CDs are usually available in duty-free shops, as well as at music stores such as **Procera Music Stores** (Map p122; ☎ 330 3365) in Suva. In major Indo-Fijian shopping areas, such as Toorak and Cumming Sts in Suva, there is a wide variety of stores selling Indian spices, saris and knick-knacks.

Environment

THE LAND

Fiji is south of the equator and north of the tropic of Capricorn. The country's territorial limits cover an enormous 1.3 million sq km, but only about 18,300 sq km of this – less than 1.5% – is dry land. The 180-degree meridian cuts across the group at Taveuni island, but the International Date Line has been doglegged eastward so all islands fall within the same time zone – 12 hours ahead of GMT.

The more than 300 islands vary from tiny patches of land a few metres in diameter, to the main island, Viti Levu, which is 10,390 sq km. Tomanivi (also called Mt Victoria), Fiji's highest at 1323m, is near the northern end of a range that separates eastern and western Viti Levu. The mountain range also acts as a weather barrier, with Suva, the country's capital, on the island's wetter side. Both Nadi, home to the country's main international airport, and Lautoka, the second most important port after Suva, are on the drier western side of the island.

Vanua Levu, the second-largest island 60km northeast of Viti Levu, is also mountainous, with many bays of various shapes and sizes. Taveuni, the third-largest, is rugged and, with rich volcanic soil, is known as the 'Garden Island'. Kadavu, south of Viti Levu, is formed by three irregularly shaped land masses linked by isthmuses, with beautiful reef lagoons, mountains, waterfalls and dense vegetation.

The remainder of Fiji's islands are relatively small.

Writer Umberto Eco is captivated by the time-shifting possibilities of the 180-degree meridian that bisects Taveuni island, and by its fabulous orange dove, in his wonderfully strange novel *The Island of the Day Before*.

WILDLIFE

Like many isolated oceanic islands, Fiji's native wildlife includes a few gems but is otherwise relatively sparse. Many plants and animals are related to those of Indonesia and Malaysia, and probably drifted in on the winds and tides.

Animals

Fiji's main wildlife attraction is its birdlife, but bird-watching in the wet season (roughly November to April) is hard work.

More than 3500 years ago, the first settlers introduced poultry, Polynesian rats, dogs and pigs to Fiji. This was good for the people but not so good for native animals; two big-footed mound-building birds and a giant flightless pigeon immediately became extinct.

NATIVE MAMMALS

Six species of bat are the only native terrestrial mammals; you'll almost certainly see large fruit bats – *beka* or flying foxes – flying out to feed around sunset or roosting during the day in colonies in tall trees. Two species of insectivorous bats are cave dwellers and seldom seen.

Dolphins and whales are found in Fijian waters, with several other species passing by on their annual migration. *Tabua*, the teeth of sperm whales, have special ceremonial value for indigenous Fijians (see p29).

INTRODUCED MAMMALS

All other land-dwelling mammals have been introduced. The common Indian mongoose was introduced in 1883 to control rats in the sugar-cane plantations. Unfortunately, the rats are still there as the mongoose mostly chose to eat Fiji's native snakes, frogs, birds and birds' eggs instead.

FIJI'S ISLANDS & REEFS

Wondering what lies beneath? The majority of Fijian islands are volcanic in origin, but you'll also encounter coral and limestone islands. Fiji's reefs take three different forms: fringing, barrier and atoll.

Volcanic Islands

Volcanic islands generally have a series of conical hills rising to a central summit. Pinnacles indicate the sites of old volcanoes, with crystallised lava flows reaching the coast as ridges, forming cliffs or bluffs. Between these ridges are green valleys, with the only flat land to be found along the river basins of larger islands. The coasts are lined with beaches and mangroves, and the wetter sides of the islands – facing the prevailing winds – support thriving forests. The leeward hills are home to grasslands with only a sparse covering of trees.

There are no active volcanoes in Fiji but there is plenty of geothermal activity on Vanua Levu; in Savusavu some locals use the hot springs to do their cooking! Viti Levu and Kadavu are also volcanic islands.

Limestone Islands

These are characteristically rocky land masses that have risen from the sea, with cliffs undercut by the sea, and topped by shrubs and trees. Generally, a central depression forms a basin, with fertile undulating hills, and volcanic materials thrust up through the limestone. Vanua Balavu in the Lau Group is a limestone island.

Coral Islands

If you're looking for somewhere to swim or snorkel, head to one of Fiji's coral islands. Small and low, they are generally found in areas protected by barrier reefs, with surface levels at the height at which waves and winds can deposit sand and coral fragments. Their coasts have bright, white-sand beaches, and mangroves are found in the lagoon shallows. Examples of coral islands are Beachcomber and Treasure Islands in the Mamanucas, and Leleuvia and Caqalai in the Lomaivitis.

Fringing Reefs

Narrow fringing reefs link to the shore of an island and stretch seaward; during low tide the reefs are exposed. Often the bigger fringing reefs have higher sections at the open-sea edge and drainage channels on the inside, which remain water-filled and navigable by small boats. Where rivers and streams break the reefs, fresh water prevents coral growth. The Coral Coast on southern Viti Levu is an extensive fringing reef.

Barrier Reefs

Large strips of continuous reef, barrier reefs are broken only by occasional channels some distance from the coastline. Fiji's Great Sea Reef extends about 500km from the coast of southwestern Viti Levu to the northernmost point of Vanua Levu. A section of this is unbroken for more than 150km, lying between 15km and 30km off the coast of Vanua Levu. Smaller barrier reefs encircle Beqa, and the Astrolabe Reef circles Kadavu.

Atolls

Atolls are small rings of coral reef with land and vegetation on top, just above sea level and enclosing a lagoon. Despite their idyllic representation in tales of the South Pacific, most have inhospitable environments. The porous soil derived from dead coral, sand and driftwood retains little water, and is often subject to droughts. The vegetation is hardy pandanus, coconut palms, shrubs and coarse grasses. Of Fiji's few atolls the best-known is Wailagi Lala, in the Lau Group.

Domestic animals turned feral include pigs, introduced by the Polynesian settlers, and goats, brought by missionaries.

In the 19th century, Europeans inadvertently but inevitably brought with them the brown-and-black rat and the house mouse.

BIRDS

Of the 57 birds that breed in Fiji, 26 are endemic. Despite the fairly short distances between islands, some birds, such as the orange dove of Taveuni and the cardinal honeyeater of Rotuma are found on one or two islands only.

In urban areas you're likely to see the chunky collared lory – a common parrot – and the brilliant emerald red-headed parrotfinch. Aggressive introduced species, such as Indian mynahs, have forced many native birds into the forest, where you'll hear barking pigeons and giant forest honeyeaters. Some 23 tropical sea birds are also seen in Fiji. Fiji's rarest bird, the Fiji petrel or *kacau* (seen on the back of the $50 note), is only known on Gau in the Lomaiviti Group.

Taveuni and Kadavu islands, and Colo-i-Suva Forest Park outside Suva, are good bird-watching spots.

> Birders will want copies of two essential illustrated pocket guides, *Birds of the Fiji Bush*, by Fergus Clunie, and Dick Watling's *Birds of Fiji – Sea & Shore Birds*.

REPTILES & AMPHIBIANS

Fiji's 27 species of reptiles are mostly lizards. The endemic crested iguana, only identified in 1979, is found on the Yasawas and, mostly, on Yadua Taba, off the west coast of Vanua Levu; its ancestors are thought to have floated to Fiji on vegetation from, unusually, South America. The banded iguana is also found in Fiji.

Two native terrestrial snakes are found in Fiji. There's a small (and nonpoisonous) Pacific boa, and the Fiji burrowing snake. Both are rarely seen. Of the four sea snakes in Fiji you may see the *dadakulaci,* or banded sea krait; occasionally they also enter freshwater inlets to mate and lay eggs on land. They are placid, but while they can't open their jaws wide enough to bite humans, don't risk it: the venom is highly poisonous.

> Check out the (mostly) encouraging results of Birdlife International's 'Important Bird Areas in Fiji' project online at www.birdlife.org and link to Fiji.

Five turtle species are found in Fijian waters: the hawksbill, loggerhead, green (named after the colour of its fat), Pacific Ridley, and leatherback. As in many other parts of the world, turtle meat and eggs are considered a delicacy in Fiji, although the taking of eggs and the capture of adults with shells under 46cm, is banned. As most turtles only reach breeding age at a size much larger than this, the ban isn't really effective.

The cane toad was introduced from Hawaii in 1936 to control insects in the cane plantations. It's now become a pest itself, competing with the native ground frog in coastal and lowland regions. The native tree frog and ground frog have retreated deep into the forests and are rarely seen.

MARINE LIFE

Fiji's richest animal life is underwater. There are hundreds of species of hard and soft coral, sea fans and sponges, often intensely colourful and fantastically shaped.

As coral needs sunlight and oxygen to survive, it's restricted to depths of less than 50m. Wave-breaks on shallow reefs are a major source of oxygen and corals on a reef-break are generally densely packed and able to resist the force of the surf. Fragile corals such as staghorn grow in lagoons, where the water is quieter.

Fiji's tropical fish are exquisite. Among many you're likely to see are yellow-and-black butterflyfish, coral-chomping blue-green parrotfish, wraithlike needlefish, and tiny territorial black-and-white clownfish guarding their anemone home. Fat-fingered blue starfish and delicate feathered starfish are common. Some marine creatures, such as fire corals, scorpionfish and lionfish, are highly venomous; if in doubt, don't touch! And watch where you put your bare feet.

Small black- and white-tipped reef sharks cruise along channels and the edges of reefs. The open sea and deeper waters are the haunt of larger fish, including tuna, swordfish, and rays.

Plants

Most of Fiji is lush with fragrant flowers and giant, leafy plants and trees. There are 1596 identified plant species here, and about 60% of these are endemic. Many are used for food, medicine, implements and building materials.

Can't tell a batfish from a butterflyfish? *Tropical Reef Life – a Getting to Know You & Identification Guide*, by Michael Aw, gives an informally detailed overview of underwater life, plus photographic tips.

RAINFOREST PLANTS

Forest giants include valuable timbers such as *dakua* (Fijian kauri). It's a hard, durable timber with a beautiful grain, used for furniture making. Of many different fern species in Fiji, a number are edible and known as *ota*. *Balabala* (tree ferns) are similar to those in Australia and New Zealand; once used on the gable ends of *bure* (traditional thatched dwellings), they are now commonly seen as carved garden warriors – the counterpart to the Western gnome. The Pacific Islands are famous for their palm trees and Fiji has 31 species that reside in the rainforest and on the coasts.

You'll see *noni* products – cordials and soaps – for sale. *Noni* is an evergreen that produces a warty, foul-smelling, bitter-tasting fruit. Despite this, it's gaining credibility worldwide for its ability to help relieve complaints including arthritis, chronic fatigue, high blood pressure, rheumatism, and digestive disorders.

Fiji's national flower is the *tagimaucia*, with white petals and bright red branches (see the boxed text, p215). It only grows at high altitudes on the island of Taveuni and on one mountain of Vanua Levu.

Orchids are abundant. Vanilla is a common orchid and there's a renewed commercial interest in its cultivation for use as a natural food flavouring.

COASTAL & RIVER PLANTS

Mangroves are the most distinctive plant communities along the coast. They provide important protection for seashores against erosion, and are

---

CORAL WARNING: GLOBAL WARMING

One of the most obvious effects of global warming is the melting of polar icecaps and consequential rise in sea level – estimated at 0.5m to 1m in the next 100 years. Rising sea levels will eventually cause devastating flooding and coastal erosion in many low-lying Pacific countries; the island of Gau, in Fiji's Lomaiviti group, has already lost 200m of coast. As well as the loss of land, the rising seawater table will poison crops and reduce the available fresh groundwater.

To date, Fiji's greatest warning of global warming has been coral bleaching. When physiologically stressed by raised water temperatures, coral loses the symbiotic algae that provide its colour and nutrition. If water temperatures return to normal, coral can recover; however, with repetitive bleaching entire reefs can be degraded and die. In 2001 and 2002, Fiji's reefs experienced huge amounts of bleaching, affecting 65% of reefs and killing 15%. As one of the most productive ecosystems on earth, reefs provide habitat and food for 25% of marine species; they also protect Fiji's smaller islands, provide food for local people and are a major source of income through tourism. As the bleaching occurs in shallow waters it has so far had no effect on Fiji's dive-tourism industry, but continued degradation could quickly spell disaster. In recognition of this, Fiji signed the Kyoto Protocol on Climate Change in 1998.

breeding grounds for prawns and crabs. Mangrove hardwood is used for firewood and for building houses, which has led to the destruction of many mangrove areas.

Casuarina, also known as ironwood or *nokonoko,* grows on sandy beaches and atolls. As its name suggests, the timber is heavy and strong and was used to make war clubs and parts of canoes.

An icon of the tropics, the coconut palm continues to support human settlement. Coconuts provide food and drink, shells are used for making cups and charcoal, leaves are used for baskets and mats, and oil is used for cooking, lighting and as body and hair lotion.

Several species of pandanus are cultivated around villages; the leaves provide raw material for roof thatching and weaving baskets and mats.

Other common coastal plants include the beach morning glory, with its dawn-blooming purple flowers, and beach hibiscus with its large yellow flowers and light wood once used for canoe building. The *vutu* tree flowers only at night; its highly scented blooms are white and pink with a distinctive fringe, and were traditionally used as fish-poison.

Suva's beautiful (but under-resourced) public gardens opened in 1913, named after botanist JB Thurston, who introduced many ornamental plants to Fiji.

GARDEN PLANTS

Botanist John Bates Thurston brought many plants to Fiji in the 19th century. Introduced African hibiscus is Fiji's most common garden plant, and is used for decoration, food and dye, and a medicine for treating stomach pains can be distilled from the leaves and fruit. Bougainvillea and yellow allemanda are also common, both introduced from Brazil. *Bua,* or frangipani, with its strongly scented flowers, is often used in soaps and perfumes, or tucked into people's hair.

NATIONAL PARKS & RESERVES

Fiji has several protected conservation areas, though lack of resources means that conservation is hard to ensure. Bouma National Heritage Park and Ravilevu Nature Reserve now protects over 40% of Taveuni's land area and contains several well-maintained walking tracks. Koroyanitu National Heritage Park, near Lautoka in the highlands of Viti Levu, is also well established.

Other significant sites include the Sigatoka Sand Dunes on Viti Levu's Coral Coast, Colo-i-Suva Park and Garrick Reserve near Suva, and Tunuloa Silktail Reserve near Navua on Vanua Levu; the respective chapters have more information. For permits to go the Yadua Taba (home to the crested iguana), Garrick Reserve, and several other sites of ecological and historical importance you will need to contact the **National Trust for Fiji** (Map p122; ☎ 330 1807; nationaltrust@is.com.fj; 3 Maafu St) in Suva.

Fiji's first piece of national environmental protection legislation, the Environment Management Act, came into force in 2005.

ENVIRONMENTAL ISSUES

Ecotourism is a buzzword in Fiji, as elsewhere. In areas of intense tourism, it has become trendy for resorts and tours to tack an 'eco' onto their name; some are more environmentally aware than others. However, while remote villages can benefit from the income brought by low-impact tourism, it also brings additional pollution and rapid cultural change.

Greenpeace and the World Wildlife Fund have offices in Suva, and campaign regionally on issues including ocean fisheries and climate change.

Find out what climate change means for the Pacific at the World Wildlife Fund's website at www .wwfpacific.org.fj or see how Greenpeace's Pacific fisheries campaign is going at www.greenpeace.org .au/oceans.

Air Pollution

Out of town, air quality is generally good, though there's often a smoke haze from burning domestic rubbish. In towns, lack of maintenance means

RESPECT & PROTECT

Many of Fiji's endangered animals and plants are protected by the Convention on International Trade in Endangered Species (Cites). Others are protected by national legislation. If you buy a souvenir made from protected or endangered species, and don't get a permit, you're breaking the law and chances are that customs will confiscate it at your overseas destination. In particular, remember:

- *Tabua* are *tabu* (sacred) – whale's teeth are protected.
- Turtle shell looks best on live turtles.
- Leave seashells on the seashore; protected species include giant clams and helmet shells, trochus, and tritons.
- Tread lightly. Stepping on live coral is like stepping on a live budgie; you'll kill it.
- Many plants including most orchids are protected.

Trash & Carry
Your litter will become someone else's problem, especially on small islands; where possible, recycle or remove your own.

Don't Rush to Flush
Fresh water is precious everywhere, especially on small islands; take short showers, and drink boiled or rain water, rather than buy another plastic bottle.

---

that many vehicles emit thick exhaust; local authority spot-checks and fines are an attempt to address this. In 2005 a deep toxic fire burned for days in the Suva municipal rubbish tip, provoking debate on the problem of solid waste management for island states.

Erosion & Deforestation

Burning of forests and land-clearing for agriculture has resulted in the erosion of fertile topsoil. Sugar-cane and other steep-slope farming have increased erosion even further. Pine plantations (though they have drawbacks in other ways) and the reintroduction of sustainable agricultural practices are ongoing attempts to restore soil quality, quantity and jobs.

For encouraging and creative examples of how communities can manage their own resources, check out the Communities and Coasts web page of www.fspi.org.fj.

Water Pollution

About 59% of the population has access to a sustainable water source. In urban centres water quality is generally good but not everywhere; Lautoka residents, for example, boil their water before drinking.

The sea around the busy ports of Suva and Lautoka is polluted with sewage seepage, oil spills and litter dumping. Destructive fishing techniques, such as the use of explosives, are still used without much control, and coral harvesting for the aquarium industry can be a problem. The use of drift nets for fishing is illegal. These and other issues are being addressed by local and international nongovernmental organisations (NGOs), which work with local people on community-based coastal management, aiming both to improve community livelihoods and protect biodiversity.

Diving
Jean-Bernard Carillet

Diving in Fiji is truly amazing, offering innumerable underwater glimpses that will make even the most world-weary diver dewy-eyed. The water is warm, clear, and teeming with life. You'll see a myriad of multihued fish, canyonlike terrain and vertigo-inducing walls festooned with exquisite soft and hard corals resembling a lush flower garden in full bloom. You can also have heart-pounding experiences such as drifting with the current in Somosomo Strait or going nose-to-nose with massive bull sharks in Beqa Lagoon. Whatever your level of expertise and your inclinations, you'll find your slice of underwater heaven.

A dive instructor and incorrigible traveller, Jean-Bernard Carillet has written widely for various French publications and has also coordinated and co-authored Lonely Planet diving guides.

Diving conditions
Although Fiji is diveable year-round, the best season is from April to October. November to March tends to see the most rainfall, which can obscure visibility off the main islands with river runoff.

Keep in mind that many dives are subject to currents, which vary from barely perceptible to powerful. Visibility varies a lot, from a low of 10m at certain sites up to 40m at others.

Water temperatures range from 23°C in August to 29°C in January. You won't need anything more than a thin neoprene or a 3mm wetsuit.

DIVE SITES
For well-informed divers, Fiji equals soft corals, and justifiably so. Dive Somosomo Strait off Taveuni and you'll know what we mean. But soft corals and drift dives are not the only raison d'être of the diving in Fiji. You'll also find majestic reefs ablaze with technicoloured critters and a spectacular underwater topography. The only weak point is the dearth of impressive wrecks. But the dive repertoire is endless, with diving on offer on all islands. In fact, it's hard for divers to decide where to go: there are so many fabulous dive sites. Just as the individual islands have their distinct flavours, so too do the dive sites have their own hallmark. Just take your pick!

Fiji is dubbed 'the soft coral capital of the world', and rightly so.

FIJI'S TOP DIVE SITES

For Beginners
Shark Reef (Beqa Lagoon, Viti Levu) Bull sharks galore – a once-in-a-lifetime experience.
Gotham City (Mamanuca Group) Reef species aplenty and excellent coral.
Dreadlocks (Vanua Levu) An aquariumlike setting, with a host of kaleidoscopic tropicals.
Yellow Wall (Kadavu) An atmospheric site resembling a fairytale castle.
Lekima's Ledge (Yasawa Group) An underwater cliff and a feast for the eyes.

For Experienced Divers
Great White Wall (Taveuni) Possibly the best soft-coral dive in Fiji.
Nigali Passage (Shark Alley, Lomaiviti Group) An exhilarating drift dive spiced up with regular sightings of grey sharks.
Nasonisoni Passage (Vanua Levu) Another rip-roaring drift dive in a narrow passage.
Split Rock (Kadavu) A maze of faults, canyons and tunnels.
E6 (Bligh Water, Lomaiviti Group) A phenomenal seamount that brushes the surface; a magnet for pelagics.

Viti Levu

Viti Levu is normally the visiting diver's first glimpse of Fiji. Although less charismatic than Taveuni or Kadavu, it boasts a fair share of underwater wonders and deserves attention for its variety of sites. The best diving is found off Nananu-i-Ra island to the north and in Beqa Lagoon to the south, but there are also some interesting options off Toberua island to the east and in Navula Passage to the west. Most dive sites are suitable for all skill levels.

But what sets it apart is the diving at Shark Reef in Beqa Lagoon, where you can witness a phenomenal shark-feeding session (see the boxed text, below). Here you're almost certain to go nose-to-nose with massive predators.

Of course there are much less intimidating sites around Viti Levu. In Beqa Lagoon, the quality of the corals is not the strong point but you'll

The site rundown in this chapter is by no means exhaustive. For more information see Lonely Planet's *Diving & Snorkeling Fiji*. It details 74 dive sites, with full-colour photos throughout.

UP CLOSE & PERSONAL WITH THE OCEAN'S MOST FEARED CREATURES

We've done it, and we won't forget it. Believe us: you'll experience the adrenaline thrill of a lifetime. A few kilometres off the Viti Levu coast near Pacific Harbour lies Shark Reef. For once, you won't come here to marvel at soft or hard corals. Instead, this spot is home to a phenomenal shark-feeding session three times a week – an exclusivity of **Beqa Adventure Divers** (☎ 345 0911; www.fiji-sharks.com).

In other parts of the world, shark feeding usually involves grey reef sharks and, if you're lucky, lemon sharks and nurse sharks. Here, up to eight different types of sharks turn up: tawny nurse sharks, white-tip, black-tip and grey reef sharks, sicklefin lemon sharks, silvertips and the star performers, massive bull sharks (up to 25 individuals at a time) and even the heavyweight of them all – tiger sharks! Handfeeding these monsters would seem suicidal. However, the two feeders from Beqa island have become experts in 'taming' the predators. They claim they are protected by traditional magic. Apparently, this protection is effective as no incident has ever been recorded in their more than six years of diving.

There are two distinct dives. The first one is at 30m. On a coral rubble patch, the divers form a line, behind a purpose-built small coral wall, a few metres away from the feeders. The feeder dips into a huge bin and pulls out hunks of dead fish. He is soon in the middle of a maelstrom. For several minutes at a time it may be hard to work out what is happening in the swirl of tails and fins as one shark after another materialises, ripping and tearing at the bait. It's definitely (in)tense, but there's no frenzy to speak of. The sharks approach in surprisingly orderly fashion, even the more ponderous-looking bull sharks. Being within touching distance of these predators is absolutely awesome, but you'll also be enthralled by the other fish species that are invited to this free meal, including schools of giant trevally, snapper, grouper and surgeonfish.

The second dive takes you down to 17m. Again, you sit on a clear arena behind a small wall. Now, the hefty bull sharks and the lemon sharks are more inquisitive and come even closer to the feeder. But wait! The adrenaline level has not reached its maximum. If the arena suddenly clears, then you know that a four-metre tiger shark is going to make its appearance. When it takes the bait from the feeder, you can see its cavernous maw...

Let's put it frankly. This is more a show than a dive. Fish feeding is a controversial subject among diving operators all over the world. On the one hand, these artificial encounters undeniably disrupt natural behaviour patterns. Sharks that grow dependent on 'free lunches' may unlearn vital survival skills. Some have developed dangerous Pavlovian responses to the sound of revving boat motors. On the other hand, some experts think that these shows have educational virtue and raise awareness among divers; a diver who has viewed these often misunderstood creatures up close becomes an instant shark-lover with a positive image of these feared denizens of the deep.

Whatever your stance on the issue, these dives are conducted in a very professional way. There's a comprehensive briefing prior to the dive and divers are watched over by divemasters with large poles. At no time do you feel a sense of threat.

Take note that bull sharks leave the spot from October to January to mate.

like the underwater scenery at Caesar's Rock, which has a multitude of pinnacles riddled with tunnels and caves. A long-standing favourite, Side Streets features a collection of small coral pillars scattered in a reef passage. ET features a vast tunnel more than 30m long and 5m in diameter. The sides of the tunnel are densely blanketed with sea fans and soft corals. Carpet Cove (also known as Seven Sisters) is a good spot, with the wreck of a Japanese trawler that was scuttled in 1994, at about 25m.

Diving along the northern shore of Viti Levu is focused on the offshore islands and reefs near Rakiraki, including Nananu-i-Ra. This area is a diver's treat, with a good balance of scenic seascapes, elaborate reef structures and dense marine life. Dream Maker ranks among the best sites in the area. You'll enjoy weaving your way among large coral heads lavishly blanketed in a bright mosaic of sea fans and gorgonians – a typical Fiji dive. Breath Taker is famous for its dense concentration of colourful tropicals and the quality of the corals. To the northwest, off Charybdis Reef, Spud Dome Spud Dome is renowned for its dramatic scenery while Heartbreak Ridge offers a chance at spotting pelagics.

Mamanuca Group

Due to their proximity to Nadi and Lautoka on Viti Levu, the Mamanuca islands are very popular among divers and can easily be reached from these two towns by boat. You can also base yourself on Malolo island. Most dive sites are scattered along the Malolo barrier reef or off the nearby islets. Diving is probably less spectacular than in other areas of Fiji but it's still rewarding, with diverse marine life, good visibility and a varied topography, as well as a glut of easy sites that will appeal to novice divers.

A well-regarded site, The Supermarket is famed for shark encounters but we found the site pretty barren the day we were there. Divemasters occasionally feed the predators at this site. Inside the barrier reef lagoon, Gotham City comprises several coral heads surrounded by a smorgasbord of reef fish in less than 20m. Other sites to look for include Namotu Reef, The Big Ws (where you'll see some big fish) and Bird Rock. Wreck buffs will explore the *Salamanda*, a 36m vessel that was sunk as an artificial reef. She rests upright on a rubble seafloor in the 20m range and is partly encrusted with a variety of glowing soft corals and anemones. There's usually abundant fish life hanging around.

Diving lesson,
Mana island
PHOTO BY PHIL WEYMOUTH

Yasawa Group

No crowds and very few dive boats: this is diving in the Yasawas. This chain of ancient volcanic islands offers excellent corals, pristine reefs and good visibility – not to mention superb topside backdrops. Check out Lekima's Ledge, a stunning underwater cliff off Vawa island, suitable for novice divers, and Paradise Wall, another recommended wall dive off the western side of Yasawa island. There are also interesting caves to explore off Sawa-i-Lau island, including Blue Lagoon Caves.

Lomaiviti Group & Bligh Water

Central Fiji roughly covers the area between the country's two main landmasses – it extends from Bligh Water in the east to Namena and the Lomaiviti Group in the west. Most sites in this 'golden triangle' can only be accessed by live-aboards (see p65) and remain largely untouched. One of the most spectacular dive regions in Fiji, it boasts a unique configuration, which consists of an intricate maze of vast barrier reefs surrounding large lagoons and islands, all exposed to both nutrient-rich runoff and clean ocean water. This constant interplay of ecosystems ensures prolific marine life and reefs abloom with corals.

E6 is consistently rated as one of the best sites in Fiji. This seamount in Vatu-i-Ra Channel rises from 1000m to the surface and acts as a magnet for pelagics in search of easy pickings. You might come across schooling barracuda, hammerheads and eagle rays. On the leeside you'll marvel at soft corals and fans in full blossom. A huge swim-through in the seamount, called the Cathedral, creates a magical atmosphere, especially when beams of sunlight filter through the cracks in the ceiling.

Another spectacular seamount reaching from 1000m to just below the surface, Mount Mutiny is sheer delight, with a colourful collection of throbbing coral communities adorning the wall. Keep an eye out for cruising pelagics.

In the mood for an adrenaline rush? Off Gau island, Nigali Passage (also known as Shark Alley) is the right place. A drift dive by essence, this narrow channel is one of the most active in this region. The site's biggest claim to fame is the almost ever-present squadron of grey sharks (up to 20 individuals) that haunt the passage, as well as schooling trevally, barracuda, snapper and the occasional rays. A less challenging site on the northwest side of Gau's barrier reef, Jim's Alley features a collection of coral boulders that bottom out at 24m.

TAKE THE PLUNGE!

You've always fancied venturing underwater on a scuba dive? Now's your chance. Fiji is a perfect starting point for new divers, as the warm water in the shallow lagoons is a forgiving training environment. Most resorts offer courses for beginners and employ experienced instructors, most of them competent in English.

Just about anyone in reasonably good health can sign up for an introductory dive, including children aged eight years and over. There are various programmes on offer, including Discover Scuba, which takes place in a pool, and Discover Scuba Diving, which is a guided dive in open water.

If you choose to enrol in an Open Water Course while in Fiji, count on it taking about three days, including classroom lectures and training. Another option is to complete the classroom and pool sessions in your home country and perform the required open water dives in a PADI- or SSI-affiliated dive centre in Fiji. Once you're certified, your C-card is valid permanently and recognised all over the world.

For some top dives for beginners, see the boxed text on p57.

Off the southeastern coast of Vanua Levu, Namena island is another hotspot, with several breathtaking sites, including Chimneys, in less than 25m. As the name suggests, you'll see several towering coral pillars, all coated with soft corals, sea fans and crinoids. Numerous reef species hide in the undercuts. Finish your dive in the shallows atop the pinnacles, where constellations of basslets and blennies flit about the coral structures. Some instructors also swear by North-Save-a-Tack, located in a current-swept passage renowned for its copious fish life and healthy corals.

Off Wakaya island, make a beeline for Blue Ridge. This site derives its name from the abundance of bright-blue ribbon eels. Although they lead the show, many other species will vie for your attention, including dartfish, gobies and leaf fish and, if you're lucky, hammerheads and manta rays.

Vanua Levu

Fiji's second-largest island, Vanua Levu is a true gem with numerous untouched sites for those willing to venture away from the tourist areas. Most dive sites are in or around Savusavu Bay. The underwater scenery is striking, the walls are precipitous and the fish population (which includes pelagics) is diverse.

Experienced divers won't miss Nasonisoni Passage, a rip-roaring drift dive in a narrow, current-swept channel. During tidal exchange, divers are sucked into the passage and propelled through the funnel by the forceful current.

Do you like tiny critters? Dreadlocks, right in the middle of Savusavu Bay, is an enchanting site that will appeal to all levels. A jumble of coral pinnacles in less than 20m harbours numerous kaleidoscopic tropicals, including harlequin filefish, lionfish, butterflyfish, gobies, nudibranchs, sweetlips…

As the name suggests, Barracuda Point is famed for schooling barracuda that can be spotted at about 25m. Batfish are also regularly seen here. Healthy staghorn corals and gorgonians complete the picture.

Dreamhouse refers to a small seamount that seems to attract a wealth of pelagics, including grey reef sharks, jacks and tuna. If the current is not running, all you do is spiral up around the coral mound and marvel at the luxuriant setting.

Taveuni

Blessed with lush rainforests, cascading waterfalls and a profusion of tropical plants and flowers, Taveuni is called 'The Garden Island'. It's more or less the same story below the waterline. The Somosomo Strait, a narrow stretch of ocean that is funnelled between Taveuni and Vanua Levu, has achieved Shangri-la status in the diving community, and for good reason. Strong tidal currents push the deep water back and forth through the passage, providing nutrients for the soft corals and sea fans that form a vivid and sensual tapestry on the reefs. This area is often described as Rainbow Reef. As if it wasn't enough, vertical walls add a touch of drama.

Start with the aptly named Purple Wall. And what a wall: it is suffused with a dense layer of purple soft-coral trees, whip corals and sea fans wafting in the current. Numerous overhangs and arches harbour soldierfish and squirrelfish. At the entrance of Somosomo Strait, Great White Wall is one of Fiji's signature dives. It's an awesome wall and drift dive, with a phenomenal concentration of white soft coral (it's actually pale lavender), resembling a snow-covered ski slope. When the current is running, soft-coral trees unfurl from the wall to feed and feature an almost heavenly glow – a truly ethereal sight. In the same area, don't miss

The only downside in Somosomo Strait is the average visibility. It does not exceed 15m to 20m when the currents flow.

FREE THRILLING RIDES

Drift diving is an integral part of Fiji diving. As the tide rises and falls, enormous volumes of water flow in and out of the channels, across the reefs and along the walls, forming bottle-necks and creating strong currents. The current becomes a great buddy, helping propel you through the water with amazing ease. All you do is immerse yourself in the ocean and let yourself be sucked through the channel, until the effects of the current weaken. Because the distance covered during the drift dive is huge, a boat follows divers' progression by tracking their bubbles. At the end of the dive, the instructor inflates a brightly coloured marker buoy to signal the exact position of the group, and the boats picks up the divers.

Drift diving is very exciting because you feel as though you're flying or gliding through the channels. But it's an advanced activity that requires specific skills, including a perfect control of buoyancy. Such dives are more suitable for intermediate or advanced divers. Local dive centres usually check divers out before taking them to these sites.

Rainbow Passage. Once again a photogenic spot, it features a large, sub-merged reef offering a wealth of marine life and spectacular bouquets of soft corals. A number of pinnacles protruding from the reef are wreathed with luxuriant soft-coral trees in every colour of the rainbow. Look closely for the rich resident fish and invertebrate population, including nudibranchs, Christmas tree worms, crinoids and clown fish.

In the middle of Somosomo Strait, Annie's Bommies is an explosion of colour, with several big boulders liberally draped with soft corals and surrounded by swirling basslets. Unlike other sites, it's not a wall dive, so you can leisurely weave your way among the boulders and stare at coral exuberance. Other sites include Cabbage Patch, Blue Ribbon Eel Reef, the Ledge, the Pinnacle, Yellow Grotto and the Zoo.

Currents bring life to the reef. They constantly channel nutrients in and out with the tides, attracting all forms of sealife along the food chain. When the current flows, the corals bloom into flowerlike beauty. When it's absent, the corals withdraw into their spicules.

But there's more to Somosomo Strait than coral splendour and vertigo-inducing walls. The nutrient-rich water also produces pelagic sightings. It's not uncommon to encounter manta rays, white-tip reef sharks, king-fish, barracuda and, with a bit of luck, even leopard sharks.

There are also superb dive sites around neighbouring Matagi, Qamea and Laucala islands and at Motualevu Atoll, some 30km east of Taveuni. Check the Edge, off Motualevu Atoll. This breathtaking drop-off is adorned with a wide variety of soft and hard corals and carved by nu-merous overhangs and windows at various depths. Another renowned site, Noel's Wall, is a feast for the eyes. The wall is showered in soft-coral bushes covering the whole colour spectrum. Due to the isolation of the site, you've got a reasonable chance to spot bronze whalers, tuna, bar-racuda, jacks and manta rays.

Kadavu

Kadavu's main claim to fame is the Great Astrolabe Reef, a barrier reef that hugs the south and east coasts of the island for about 100km. For divers, this is a gem of a reef, with a vibrant assemblage of exquisite hard and soft-coral formations and breathtaking walls beginning as shallow as 10m. The dramatic seascape is another highlight, with a network of passages, swim-throughs and crevices sheltering a stunning variety of reef species. You can't get bored here. Unlike Taveuni, currents are pro-bably easier to handle in this area, but be prepared for rough seas and reduced visibility when it's raining or when the winds blow, especially from November to April.

On the western side of the Great Astrolabe, recommended dive sites include Broken Stone, Split Rock and Vouwa. They more or less share the same characteristics, with a mind-boggling combination of twisting canyons, tunnels, caverns and arches. If you like scenic underwater sea-scapes, you'll be in seventh heaven here.

In the mood for an adrenaline-pumping ride? Try Naiqoro Passage, just off the east coast of Kadavu. This narrow channel is frequently swept by strong tidal currents and offers rewarding drift dives along steep walls.

Mystical cavern at Broken Stone, Kadavu Group
PHOTO BY CASEY & ASTRID WITTE MAHANEY

The northwestern side of Kadavu is a bit overshadowed by the Great Astrolabe but it also features superb dives in their own right. Novice divers in particular will feel comfortable here – the dive conditions are less challenging than anywhere else in Kadavu but still offer excellent fish action. If you want a relaxed dive, Mellow Reef does the trick. It consists of several boulders, in less than 20m. It's an ideal site to refresh your skills before taking on deeper dives. Another easy dive, Yellow Wall is a very atmospheric site in the 20m range, featuring several pinnacles graced with yellow soft corals. Wend your way around these rocks and marvel at the colourful fauna fluttering about. Once you've had your fill of soft corals and drift dives, you might want to explore the *Pacific Voyager*, a 63m-long tanker that was intentionally sunk in 1994 as an artificial reef in 30m of water. It's nothing spectacular but it makes for a welcome change.

DIVE CENTRES

Dive centres are open year-round, most of them every day. Many are attached to a hotel and typically offer two-tank dive trips. Try to book at least a day in advance. Operators offer a whole range of services, such as introductory dives (for children aged eight years and over, and adults), night dives, exploratory dives, and certification programs. Most dive centres are PADI- or SSI-affiliated, two agencies that are recognised internationally.

Diving in Fiji is rather good value, especially if you compare it to other South Pacific destinations. If you plan to do many dives on one island, consider buying a multidive package, which comes out much cheaper. Generally, prices don't include equipment rental, so it's not a bad idea to bring all your gear. Most dive shops offer free pick-ups from your accommodation and accept credit cards.

There's one recompression chamber in Suva (p120).

Go to www.divefiji.com and the diving page at www.bulafiji.com for more information on diving in Fiji.

DIVING & FLYING

Most divers get to Fiji by plane. While it's fine to dive soon *after* flying, it's important to remember that your last dive should be completed at least 12 hours (some experts advise 24 hours) *before* your flight, to minimise the risk of residual nitrogen in the blood that can cause decompression. Careful attention to flight times is necessary in Fiji because so much of the interisland transportation is by air.

Hard-coral garden,
Lau Group

PHOTO BY CASEY & ASTRID WITTE
MAHANEY

Documents

If you're a certified diver, bring your C-card; it's a good idea to have your dive logbook with you as well. Centres welcome certification from any training agency (CMAS, PADI, NAUI etc), but may ask you to do a dive to assess your skills.

Choosing a Dive Centre

There are at least 30 professional dive centres in Fiji. All of them are affiliated with one or more internationally recognised certifying agencies, usually PADI or NAUI. In general, you can expect well-maintained equipment, good facilities and knowledgeable staff, but standards may vary from one centre to another. On islands with several operators, do your research and opt for the one that best suits your expectations. The list that follows is by no means exhaustive. More dive centres are detailed in the destination chapters. For information on diving in the Lau Group, see p232.

Viti Levu

AquaBlue (☎ 672 6111; www.aquabluefiji.com) At Wailoaloa Beach, near Nadi; see p78 for more details.

Aqua-Trek Beqa (☎ 325 0324; www.aquatrek.com) At Pacific Harbour; p113.

Beqa Adventure Divers (☎ 345 0911; www.fiji-sharks.com) At Pacific Harbour; p58.

HOW MUCH?

Introductory dive: about $150

Two-tank dive: about $190, including equipment rental

Open Water certification course: about $820

RESPONSIBLE DIVING

The Fiji islands are ecologically vulnerable. By following these guidelines while diving, you can help preserve the ecology and beauty of the reefs:

- Encourage dive operators to establish permanent moorings at appropriate dive sites.
- Practice and maintain proper buoyancy control.
- Avoid touching living marine organisms with your body and equipment.
- Take great care in underwater caves, as your air bubbles can damage fragile organisms.
- Minimise your disturbance of marine animals.
- Take home all your trash and any other litter you may find.
- Never stand on corals, even if they look solid and robust.

LIVE-ABOARDS

A couple of live-aboards ply the Fiji waters, with usually week-long itineraries. A live-aboard dive trip is recommended for those looking to experience unchartered and uncrowded dive sites beyond the reach of land-based dive operations, especially the sites in Bligh Water and off the Lomaiviti Group.

Fiji Aggressor (www.fijiaggressor.com)
Nai'a (☎ 345 0382; www.naia.com.fj)
Sere-ni-Wai (☎ 336 1171; www.sere.com.fj)

Beqa Divers Fiji (☎ 336 1088; www.beqadivers.com) At Pacific Harbour and Suva; p126.
Crystal Divers (☎ 669 4747; www.crystaldivers.com) At Rakiraki and Nananu-i-Ra.
Dive Tropex (☎ 675 0944; www.divetropex.com) At Sheraton Fiji Resort, Sheraton Royal Denarau; p78.
Ra Divers (☎ 669 4511; www.radivers.com) At Rakiraki and Nananu-i-Ra; p141.
Scuba Bula (☎ 651 0116; www.scubabula.com) At Seashell Surf & Dive Resort, Momi Bay; p102.
Toberua Island Resort (☎ 347 2777; www.toberua.com) On Toberua island; p137.
Vatulele Island Resort (☎ 672 0300; www.vatulele.com) On Vatulele island; p118.

Bring a light to appreciate the wealth of colours below the surface.

Mamanuca Group
Castaway Dive Centre (☎ 666 1233; www.castawayfiji.com) At Castaway Island Resort; p154.
Dive Tropex (☎ 675 0944; www.divetropex.com) At Tokoriki Island Resort; p78.
Subsurface (☎ 666 6738; www.fijidive.com) At Beachcomber Island Resort, Musket Cove Resort, Malolo Island Resort, Treasure Island Resort, Navini Island Resort, Tavarua Island Resort and Wadigi Island Resort; p149.

Yasawa Group
Dive Trek Wayasewa (☎ 666 9715; www.bbr.ca/wayalailai) At Wayalailai Eco Haven Resort on Wayasewa island; p163.
Yasawa Island Resort (☎ 672 2266; www.diveyasawa.com) On Yasawa island; p169.

Lomaiviti Group
Moody's Namena (☎ 881 3764; www.moodysnamenafiji.com) On Namenalala island, just south of Vanua Levu; p190.

Vanua Levu
Dive Namale (☎ 885 0435; www.namalefiji.com) At Namale Resort; p199.
L'Aventure Jean-Michel Cousteau Fiji (☎ 885 0188; www.fijiresort.com) See p199.

Taveuni
Aqua-Trek Taveuni (☎ 888 0286; www.aquatrek.com) See p212.
Dive Taveuni/Vunibokoi (☎ 888 0060; http://divingwithtyrone.tripod.com) At Tovu Tovu Resort, led by experienced Tyrone Valentine; p212.
Pro-dive (☎ 888 0125; www.prodive.com) See p212.
Swiss Fiji Divers (☎ 888 0586; www.swissfijidivers.com) See p212.
Taveuni Estates Dives (☎ 888 0063; www.taveunidive.com) See p212.

Kadavu Group
Dive Kadavu (☎ 333 7780; www.divekadavu.com) See p225.
Matava Resort (☎ 333 6098, 330 5222; www.matava.com) See p226.
Waisalima Beach Resort Dive Centre (☎ 333 7281; www.waisalimafiji.com) See p227.

Food & Drink

Fiji's food reflects the country's location as the multicultural hub of the Pacific, with its blend of indigenous Fijian, Polynesian, Indian, Chinese and Western tastes. Starchy carbohydrates play a big part in Pacific diets, but a spending spree at a fabulous local fruit and veggie market will increase your intake of the other food groups.

The ubiquitous corned beef became easier to preserve (and serve) after the 1875 invention, in Chicago, of the tapered corned beef can.

STAPLES & SPECIALITIES

Traditional Fijian foods include *tavioka* (cassava) and *dalo* (taro) roots, boiled or baked fish, and seafood in *lolo* (coconut cream). Meat is fried and accompanied with *dalo* and *rourou* (boiled *dalo* leaves in *lolo*), though you'll often find the colossally popular corned beef substituting for the real thing. *Kokoda* is a popular dish made of raw fish marinated in *lolo* and lime juice, with a spicy kick. See also p68 for details on popular local snacks.

Indo-Fijian dishes are usually spicy, and a typical meal is meat (but never beef or pork), fish or veggie curry with rice, *dahl* (lentil soup) and *roti* (a type of Indian flat bread). Chinese food is generally a Western-style takeaway affair with stir-fries, fried rice, chop suey, chow mein and noodle soups.

DRINKS
Nonalcoholic Drinks

Ask locally if the tap water's OK to drink – in some places it is, in others it's not and will need to be boiled – but local and imported mineral water and soft drinks are available. Most milk is long-life or powdered. Fresh local fruit juices and smoothies are great, but 'juice' on a menu often means sickly sweet cordial. The chilled water from green coconuts is refreshing.

Legend has it that the plant that *kava* is made from sprung from the grave of a Tongan princess who died of a broken heart.

Alcoholic Drinks

A variety of local and imported spirits and beer is available in bottle shops, most restaurants, and some supermarkets. Fiji Bitter and Fiji Gold are locally brewed beers, and the Malt House Brewery in Suva brews its own. Most wine is from Australia or New Zealand, and decent enough bottles start around $15. You can expect to pay about $4 for a beer in a bar, more at upmarket resorts. A 750mL bottle of Fiji Rum is about $30.

TRAVEL YOUR TASTEBUDS

A wander through a busy Saturday market is a must – you'll have some fun encounters asking stallholders what they're selling, and how to cook it.

Follow your nose to the seafood. That bright-green mini bubble-wrap is actually *nama*, a seaweed that becomes a cold salad to accompany fish; the yellow bird-nesty mass is *lumi*, another seaweed that gets cooked into a sort of jelly. Plates of scary-looking raw peeled shellfish are sold with a squeeze of lime and fresh chilli, and the less said about the rubbery *bêche-de-mer* the better. Don't know if you'll recognise *bêches-de-mer*? They're also known as sea cucumber, and that's just what they look like.

If you prefer something sweet, look for stalls with piles of things wrapped in banana-leaf. Try teeth-jarringly sweet *vakalolo*, made of cassava. It may look as though it's been passed through the digestive system of a large animal, but it's actually delicious.

KAVA

Kava, also called *yaqona* or grog, is as much a part of Fiji as beaches and *bure* (traditional thatched dwellings). It is mildly narcotic, looks like muddy water and makes your tongue go furry. You won't escape trying it!

Yaqona is an infusion prepared from *Piper methysticum,* a type of pepper plant. It holds a place of prominence in Fijian culture – in the time of the 'old religion' it was used ceremonially by chiefs and priests only, but today *kava* is a part of daily life, across the country and across the races. 'Having a grog' is used for welcoming and bonding with visitors, for storytelling sessions or merely for passing time. When visiting a village you will usually be welcomed with a short *sevusevu* ceremony (whereupon you'll present a gift to a village chief), where you will be initiated into *kava*-culture (see p36).

There are certain protocols to be followed at a *kava* ceremony. Sit cross-legged, facing the chief and the *tanoa*, or large wooden bowl. Women usually sit behind the men. Never walk across the circle of participants, turn your back to or point your feet at the *tanoa*, or step over the cord – if there is one – that leads from the *tanoa* to a white cowrie shell (it represents a link with the spirits).

The dried and powdered root, wrapped in a piece of cloth, is mixed with water in the *tanoa* and squeezed out; you will be offered a drink of the resulting concoction from a *bilo* (half a coconut shell). Clap once, accept the *bilo*, say *'bula'* (meaning 'cheers' or, literally, 'life'), and drink it down in one go. Clap three times in gratification. The drink will be shared until the *tanoa* is empty. You are not obliged to drink every *bilo* offered to you, but it is polite to drink at least the first. Despite rumours, it doesn't taste that awful (kind of like a murky medicine) and the most you're likely to feel from one *bilo* is a furry tongue. After a few drinks you may feel a slight numbness of the lips. Long sessions with stronger mixes can make you very drowsy, and some heavy drinkers develop *kanikani*, or scaly skin.

Kava is a mild narcotic and has been used as a diuretic and stress reliever for pharmaceutical purposes. It has properties that combat depression, reduce anxiety, and lower blood pressure – news that spread like wildfire through health-obsessed Western countries in the 1990s. When trade in *kava* peaked in 1998, Fiji and neighbouring Vanuatu were exporting US$25 million worth of *kava* each year. But the good times didn't last. A German study done in 2001 indicated that *kava* potentially caused liver damage, and in late 2002 most of Europe as well as Canada and the USA had either banned or put warnings and restrictions on *kava*.

After further research and lobbying, in 2005 the World Health Organization gave its support for reviving *kava* sales, and the Fiji Kava Council is hopeful that the ban will be lifted.

CELEBRATIONS

Fijians love food. The communal selection, preparation, cooking, and eating of enormous multiple servings all play a central role in ceremonies and celebrations.

Lovo are traditional indigenous Fijian banquets in which food is prepared in an underground oven. A hole is dug in the ground and stones are put inside and heated by an open fire. The food – whole chickens, legs of pork, fragrant stuffed *palusami* (meat or corned beef, onions and *lolo*) or *dalo* – is wrapped in banana leaves and slowly half-baked and half-steamed on top of the hot stones. Delicious! Traditionally, *lovo* is served for family get-togethers and for more formal occasions such as church festivals and funerals.

If you're fortunate enough to be around Indo-Fijian Hindus during Diwali (Festival of Lights; p248), you'll be served fabulous vegetarian food during the three-day celebratory period, plus an astonishing array

You'll find some neat Fiji food and folklore stories by following the 'restaurant' link at www.fijilive.com /fijimagic.

of sweets such as *gulab jamun* (deep-fried dough served in a sugar syrup) and *barfi* (Indian confectionery made from milk and sugar) on the day itself.

Lunar New Year is celebrated by Fiji's Chinese community with multi-course banquets accompanied by lion dancers and drummers.

WHERE TO EAT & DRINK

Nadi and Suva have a good variety of eateries ranging from cheap cafés in town to fine dining on the waterfront. Most places serve a combination of adapted Chinese, Fijian, Indian and Western dishes, and Japanese and Korean speciality restaurants are increasingly popular. Cheap restaurants and food halls charge between $4 and $8 for main meals; in decent city restaurants and resorts expect to pay upwards of $20 for a dish. Locals don't often linger over the dinner table and restaurants close early; you won't find many places open after 9pm.

One of Fiji's efforts to combat obesity was an import ban in 2000 of high-fat 'lamb flaps' (don't ask) from New Zealand.

Quick Eats

Fijians, like many peoples of the world, are forgoing traditional foods for readily available fast foods, but interesting (and often nutritionally better) local snack foods can be found at street stalls and in the markets.

You haven't truly eaten locally until you've had a roti parcel. Easy food for travelling and breakfast, it's Indian flat bread wrapped around a serve of some sort of curried meat or spicy vegetable; most food stalls sell it.

In the markets you'll see all manner of anonymous cooked foods wrapped in banana-leaf packages. These will almost certainly be something starchy, probably *tavioka,* which has been grated and mixed with coconut, slightly sweetened, then baked or steamed. They're filling, with the ultimate biodegradable packing.

Around town you'll see Indian *mithai la gaadi* – sweet stalls that also sell cheap snacks such as roasted salted peas or cassava chips. They're often stationed around school entrances.

Test your culinary skills and enjoy fabulous food photos from a Fijian kitchen at www.fijibure .com/namatakula/food .htm.

Be sensible about what you try. It's not a good idea to scoff down cooked meat that's been sitting around for a while, but if it comes from an icebox and is cooked in front of you – like the street barbecues that spring up at night – it's probably fine.

Self-Catering

Every large town in Fiji has a fresh fruit-and-vegetable market and at least one supermarket where you can buy basic groceries. Most villages have a small shop but, as villagers grow their own fresh produce, stock is often limited to tinned fish, corned beef, and packets of instant noodles.

FIJI'S TOP FIVE

- Raffles Floating Restaurant (Tradewinds; p131), a floating restaurant at the Raffles Tradewinds in Lami – just outside Suva – has a lunchtime view to die for and great fish burgers.
- Capital Palace (p132), a Chinese restaurant in Suva, has chaotically loud, busy and fun yum cha sessions on weekend mornings; the food's good, too.
- Daikoku in Nadi (p85) and Suva (p132) sizzles up superlative teppanyaki and serves some of the finest sushi and sashimi in the Pacific.
- Gopal's (p206) in Labasa serves scrumptious, filling and dirt-cheap Hare Krishna food and thalis.
- Bula Re Café (p200) puts an inventive slant on traditional Fijian fare with alfresco dining.

DOS & DON'TS

■ Don't start serving yourself or eating until asked to do so by your host – there may be prayers said beforehand.

■ Do have a snack before joining a *kava* session; you won't eat until it's finished – and this may take some time.

■ Tipping is not expected but is, of course, welcome; 10% of the bill is sufficient if you feel so inclined.

If your accommodation has cooking facilities, it will generally sell (very) basic supplies; but you'll be better off to stock up in town.

VEGETARIANS & VEGANS

Being vegetarian in Fiji is pretty easy, especially if you're partial to Indian food. Many Indo-Fijians are strict vegetarians, so most Indo-Fijian restaurants have lots of veggie options and there are Govinda's or Hare Krishna vegetarian restaurants in most sizeable towns. Most resorts and tourist restaurants have at least one token veggie meal on the menu.

The only time a person's vegetarian-ness can prove tricky is on visits to indigenous Fijian villages. If you are planning to go on a tour, be sure to tell the tour operator of your eating preferences when you book as your hosts may find it strange – and perhaps offensive – that you'd refuse meat that they may not easily be able to afford. Communicating that your religious beliefs or your health won't allow you to eat meat are probably the most acceptable explanations.

Can't tell a mango from a mangosteen? You will once you've savoured *A Taste of the Pacific*, a regional food guide and recipe book by Susan Parkinson, Peggy Stacy & Adrian Mattinson.

EATING WITH KIDS

You'll have no problem feeding children in resorts, where kids' menus are on offer. Food halls in Suva are good value with a variety of food styles, and most will hold back on the chilli or cook up a special request out the back.

For fussy eaters, there's always the standby of a bunch of fresh bananas and fresh bread from Fiji's many hot bakeries. There's Western-style fast food in Suva and Nadi. Baby food is available in supermarkets, and it's probably wise to use boiled or bottled water for infants. See also p245.

HABITS & CUSTOMS

People rise at first light in Fiji, so breakfast – of fresh bread, or roti – is taken early. Fijians snack regularly in the gaps between eating a big lunch and a big, early dinner. Many people prefer to eat with their hands, and most restaurants have hand-washing basins available. In villages or in homes people often eat seated on a mat on the floor; men generally eat first, along with any visitors. As a guest, you'll be served the best food available; if it's not to your taste, accept and eat it graciously.

Fiji's flag illustrates three of the country's main food crops – sugar, bananas and coconuts.

The fasting month of Ramadan is observed by Muslim Fijians, who don't eat during daylight hours. It doesn't make much difference to eating options for visitors, but your taxi driver or tour guide might be less energetic than normal during this period.

Public eating places are often theoretically nonsmoking, though this is rarely enforced. In the larger towns, bars and nightclubs are open until the early hours of the morning, and the party animals only get going after 10pm.

EAT YOUR WORDS

If you thought *kokoda* was a WWII walking trail in Papua New Guinea, think again. For a better taste of the language, see the pronunciation guidelines, p272.

Useful Phrases

breakfast – *katalau*
lunch – *vakasigalevu*
dinner – *vakayakavi*

Food Glossary

achar – Indian pickles
baigan – eggplant
barfi – Indian confectionery made from milk and sugar
bêche-de-mer – sea cucumber
bele – green leafy vegetable, served boiled
bhaji – spinach, or any leafy green vegetable
bhindi – okra
bu – green coconut
bulumakau – beef
čã – tea (Fiji-Hindi)
dalo – taro, a starchy root served boiled or baked
dhaniya – coriander
gulab jamun – deep-fried dough served in a sugar syrup; an Indian dessert
ika – fish
jalebi – Indian sweet
jira – cumin
kava/yaqona – narcotic drink prepared from the roots of a *Piper methysticum* shrub
kokoda – raw fish marinated in lime juice and *lolo,* served with chilli and onion…yum
lolo – coconut cream
lovo – food cooked on hot stones in an underground oven
lumi – a seaweed that is commonly cooked into a jelly
masala – curry powder
mithai – Indian sweets
nama – a seaweed commonly served as an accompaniment to fish…not so yum
palusami – corned beef (or meat), onions and *lolo* wrapped in *dalo* leaves and baked in *lolo*
puri – deep-fried, flat Indian bread
roti – Indian flat bread
rourou – boiled *dalo* leaves in *lolo*
seo – Indian savoury snack
tavioka – cassava
thali – Indian dish with several vegetarian dishes
toa – chicken
ura – freshwater prawns
uto – breadfruit, usually boiled or baked in a *lovo*
vakalolo – a sweet made from cassava

Viti Levu

Frequently referred to as 'the mainland' Viti Levu is that hub of a place where commerce, industry and the small matter of running a country supersedes the idyllic holiday business 'offshore'. Around three-quarters of the population resides here, many in the three biggest cities; Suva, Lautoka and Nadi. That said, don't forget that we are talking about Fiji, so while Viti Levu may be all the above to the local population, for visitors it's an opportunity to discover a Fiji you never imagined.

With the exception of Natadola, Viti Levu's beaches run a poor second to the sublime shorelines on the outer islands; but the island's best features lie elsewhere. Turn your attention from the coast and plant it firmly in the cooler climbs of the interior's dramatic highlands. Trek through national parks, freshen up under a waterfall or 10 and visit a local village without the gimmicky hype. Marvel in the views and history of hill forts or get caught up in the heady hype of a local festival. Don your culture vulture hat and delve well beyond the brochures in Fiji's sultry capital. Sporting the country's most diverse population, cuisine, cultural attractions and nightspots, Suva is the best spot to simmer in the local culture.

Quite simply Viti Levu is all things Fijian that an idyllic beach is not. But, if you're still yearning for a slice of the coast, escape to enigmatic Nananu-i-Ra island in the north, renowned for its windsurfing and diving, or pick and choose from the smorgasbord of resorts along the Coral Coast.

HIGHLIGHTS

- Take a southern road trip along the scenic **Coral Coast** (p103)

- Trek the spectacular mountains of **Koroyanitu National Heritage Park** (p143)

- Savour some urban culture in **Suva's bars** (p133) and **restaurants** (p130)

- Explore Fijian culture at the **Fiji Museum** (p121) and **Ka Levu Cultural Centre** (p103)

- Kayak or raft the mighty **Navua River** (p113) in the rugged Namosi Highlands

- Dive at **Beqa Lagoon** (p115) and **Nananu-i-Ra's** (p140) vivid reefs

- Tackle the surf or soak up the sun at **Natadola Beach** (p102)

- Ride the waves – surf **Frigates Passage** (p116) or windsurf **Nananu-i-Ra** (p140)

■ POPULATION: 581,000   ■ AREA: 10,400 SQ KM

VITI LEVU

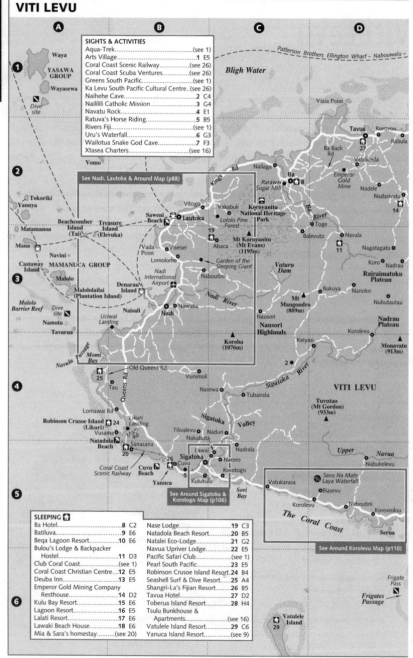

SIGHTS & ACTIVITIES
Aqua-Trek	(see 1)
Arts Village	1 E5
Coral Coast Scenic Railway	(see 26)
Coral Coast Scuba Ventures	(see 26)
Greens South Pacific	(see 1)
Ka Levu South Pacific Cultural Centre	(see 26)
Naihehe Cave	2 C4
Naililili Catholic Mission	3 G4
Navatu Rock	4 E1
Ratuva's Horse Riding	5 B5
Rivers Fiji	(see 1)
Uru's Waterfall	6 G3
Wailotua Snake God Cave	7 F3
Xtasea Charters	(see 16)

SLEEPING
Ba Hotel	8 C2	Nase Lodge	19 C3
Batiluva	9 E6	Natadola Beach Resort	20 B5
Beqa Lagoon Resort	10 E6	Natalei Eco-Lodge	21 G2
Bulou's Lodge & Backpacker		Navua Upriver Lodge	22 E5
Hostel	11 D3	Pacific Safari Club	(see 1)
Club Coral Coast	(see 1)	Pearl South Pacific	23 E5
Coral Coast Christian Centre	12 E5	Robinson Crusoe Island Resort	24 B4
Deuba Inn	13 E5	Seashell Surf & Dive Resort	25 A4
Emperor Gold Mining Company		Shangri-La's Fijian Resort	26 B5
Resthouse	14 D2	Tavua Hotel	27 D2
Kulu Bay Resort	15 E6	Toberua Island Resort	28 H4
Lagoon Resort	16 E5	Tsulu Bunkhouse &	
Lalati Resort	17 E6	Apartments	(see 16)
Lawaki Beach House	18 E6	Vatulele Island Resort	29 C6
Mia & Sara's homestay	(see 20)	Yanuca Island Resort	(see 9)

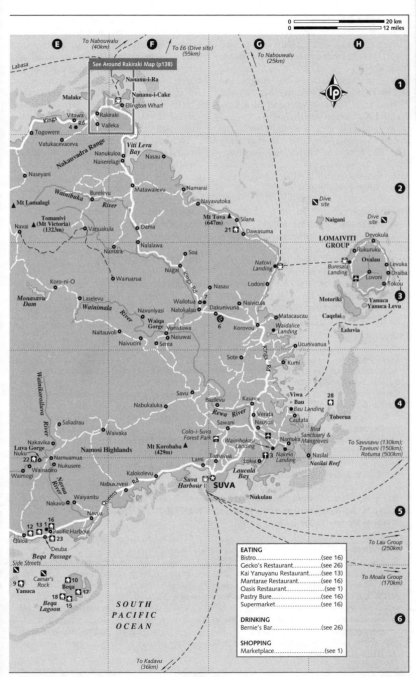

0 _____ 20 km
0 _____ 12 miles

To Nabouwalu
(40km)

To E6 (Dive site)
(55km)

To Nabouwalu
(25km)

E **F** **G** **H**

Labasa

See Around Rakiraki Map (p138)

Nananu-i-Ra

Malake

Nananu-i-Cake

Vitawa Rakiraki Ellington Wharf
Kings Rd
Togowere 4 Vaileka

Vatukacevaceva

Viti Levu
Bay

Nakauvadra Range

Nanukuloa Nasau
Naiserelagi

Naseyani

Matawailevu Namarai

Wainibuka Burelevu

Mt Lomalagi River Nayavutoka

Mt Tova Silana
Tomanivi (647m)
(Mt Victoria) Vanuakula Dama 21 Dawasuma
(1323m)
Navai Nalalawa

Naigani

Dive
site

Dive
site

LOMAIVITI
GROUP

Devokula

Rukuruku

Namara Soa Natovi
Landing Buresala Levuka
Landing Lovoni Draiba
Koro-ni-O Nagai Kings Rd Nasau Tokou
Wairuarua

Ovalau

Laslevu Wailotua 7 Naivicula Motoriki Yanuca
Monasavu Wainimala Natokalau Dakunivuna Yanuca Levu
Dam River Navuniyasi 6 Matacaucau Caqelai
Waiqa Vunidawa Korovou Waidalice Leluvia
Naitauvoli Gorge Naiuwai Landing
Naivucini Serea Ucunivanua

Sote Kumi

Savu Kasavu Viwa 28
Nabukaluka Bailevu Bau
Rewa River Verata Bau Landing
Saliadrau Waivaka Sawani Nausori Cautata Toberua
Colo-i-Suva Bird
Nakavika Forest Park Wainibokasi Namuka Sanctuary &
Luva Gorge Mt Korobaba ▲ Landing Nakelo Mangroves
Nuku Namosi Highlands (429m) Lami Tamavua Lokia 3 Landing Nasilai
22 Namuamua Kalokolevu Laucala Nasilai Reef
Waimogi Nukusere Nabukavesi Bay
Waimadiro Nakavu Suva SUVA
Navua River Waiyanitu Queens Rd Harbour Nukulau

To Savusavu (130km);
Taveuni (150km);
Rotuma (500km)

16 Navua
12 13 1
Qaloa Pacific Harbour
23
Deuba
Beqa Passage
Side Streets
9 Caesar's 10
Rock Beqa 17
Yanuca 18
Beqa 15
Lagoon

SOUTH
PACIFIC
OCEAN

To Kadavu
(36km)

To Lau Group
(250km)

To Moala Group
(170km)

EATING
Bistro....................................(see 16)
Gecko's Restaurant................(see 26)
Kai Yanuyanu Restaurant.......(see 13)
Mantarae Restaurant.............(see 16)
Oasis Restaurant....................(see 1)
Pastry Bure...........................(see 16)
Supermarket.........................(see 16)

DRINKING
Bernie's Bar..........................(see 26)

SHOPPING
Marketplace..........................(see 1)

VITI LEVU

Geography & Geology

At 10,400 sq km, Viti Levu (Great Fiji) is Fiji's largest island. The roughly oval-shaped island (146km from east to west and 106km from north to south) has a mountainous interior scattered with remote villages. The highest Fijian peak, Tomanivi (Mt Victoria; 1323m) is at the northern end of a high backbone running north–south. Rugged ranges and hills slope steeply down to the low-lying coast. Viti Levu has four large rivers: the Rewa and the Navua Rivers form fertile delta regions near Suva; the Sigatoka River flows south to the Coral Coast; and the Ba River flows north.

Orientation

Suva, the country's capital, largest city and main port, is in the southeast. Most travellers, however, arrive in the west at Nadi International Airport, which is 9km north of central Nadi and 24km south of Lautoka.

Nadi and Suva are linked by the sealed Queens Road along the 221km southern perimeter of Viti Levu, which contains a scattering of villages and resorts known as the Coral Coast. Many minor roads lead off this road to isolated coastal areas and into the highlands. Most are unsealed and often too rough for non-4WD vehicles. Between the wetter months of November and April, some roads can become impassable. The fertile Sigatoka Valley, formed by Fiji's second-largest river, extends far into the highlands.

Heading north from Suva, the Kings Road is mostly sealed and travels for 265km through Nausori (where Suva's airport is located), the eastern highlands, Rakiraki and Ba on the north coast, and on to Lautoka.

There are three roads leading up from the coast to the Nausori Highland villages of Navala and Bukuya (beginning at Ba, Nadi and Sigatoka).

Getting There & Away

Most travellers arrive in Fiji at Nadi International Airport (although some do arrive at Suva's Nausori airport). See p254 for contact details of airline offices. Nadi is

---

VITI LEVU IN...

Four Days

Acclimatise yourself by dabbling in Nadi's souvenir shops and markets (p86) and gaping at the vivid **Sri Siva Subramaniya Swami Temple** (p77). Test your tastebuds with a curry lunch at **Saffron the Corner** (p85) or **Tata's** (p86) or save your appetite for a beer at **Ed's Bar** (p86) and a teppanyaki feast at **Daikoku** (p85).

On day two head south and spend the morning chilling out amid the spectacular orchids at the **Garden of the Sleeping Giant** (p89) then take your first ocean dip at **Natadola Beach** (p102). Picnic on the beach or dig into a seafood lunch at **Natadola Beach Resort** (p102).

Spend day three traversing the **Sigatoka Sand Dunes** (p105) or for something less energetic, mingle with the wildlife at **Kula Eco Park** (p107). Check into a Coral Coast resort in **Korotogo** (p107) or **Korolevu** (p111) and laze the afternoon away poolside.

On day four head further east to Pacific Harbour. Kayak or raft up the **Navua River** (p113) or take a day trip out to **Beqa Lagoon** (p115) and snorkel or dive in one of Fiji's finest reefs. Treat yourself to an indulgent night at the **Pearl South Pacific** (p114) or immerse yourself in a village at **Navua Upriver Lodge** (p114).

One Week

After your four-day meander through the Coral Coast head to Suva and a return to urban life. Dose up on culture at the **Fiji Museum** (p121), fuel up on a curry or Fijian speciality at the **Old Mill Cottage** (p131), savour a Fiji Bitter and some Suva hospitality at **Traps Bar** (p133) and then escape the crowds with a night at the **Raintree Lodge** (p128).

On day six start early and head north along the Kings Road to Ellington Wharf. Jump across to **Nananu-i-Ra** (p140) and spend a couple of days snorkelling, diving, windsurfing, kayaking or doing nothing at all. If you want to escape the coast make your way to **Lautoka** (p90) and soak up the balmy atmosphere of Fiji's second-largest city or head into the interior for a tour of the **Nausori Highlands** (p143).

also a main domestic transport hub. From here there are flights to many of the other larger islands and reliable boat services and cruises to offshore islands. See p259 and individual island chapters for information on interisland flights and boat services.

Getting Around

For those in a hurry or after a scenic flight, there are cheap, regular light plane flights between Nadi and Suva for around $160.

Viti Levu has a regular and cheap bus network. Express buses operated by Pacific Transport and Sunbeam Transport link the main centres of Lautoka, Nadi and Suva, along both the Queens and Kings Roads. Most will pick up or drop off at hotels and resorts along these highways. Look for timetables at their offices in Lautoka. Slower, local buses also operate throughout the island and even remote inland villages have regular (though less frequent) services. These trips might take awhile as they stop frequently along the way. Before heading to an isolated area, check that there is a return bus so that you don't get stranded without any accommodation – sometimes the last bus of the day stays at the final village.

Companies and services available:

Coral Sun Fiji (☎ 672 3105) Runs comfortable, air-conditioned coaches between Nadi and Suva ($20, four hours, once daily), stopping at resorts on the Coral Coast.

Feejee Experience (☎ 672 0097; www.feejeeexperience .com) Offers hop-on-and-hop-off coach and accommodation deals. See p265 for more information.

Pacific Transport Limited Lautoka (☎ 666 0499; Yasawa St) Nadi (☎ 670 0044) Sigatoka (☎ 650 0088) Suva (☎ 330 4366) About six express buses run daily between Lautoka and Suva ($12.50, five/six hours for express/regular) via the Coral Coast. Generally it's OK to turn up at the bus station, but you can book in advance for an extra $0.50.

Sunbeam Transport Limited Lautoka (☎ 666 2822; Yasawa St) Nadi (☎ 927 2121) Suva (☎ 338 2122/2704) Around four Lautoka–Suva express services go daily via the Queens Road ($12, five hours). Also around six services daily travel via the Kings Road.

United Touring Fiji (☎ 672 2811; www.atspacific .com/fiji/; Nadi Airport) Has two daily air-conditioned services between Nadi and Suva ($25, 4½ hours) departing 7.30am and 1pm, dropping off at Coral Coast resorts along the way. Nadi to Korolevu is $18.

Minibuses and carriers (small trucks) also shuttle locals along the Queens Road. Taxis are plentiful, but drivers don't always use meters, so confirm the price in advance. Viti Levu is also easy to explore by car or motorbike, although for the unsealed highland roads you'll generally need a 4WD. See p263 for rental details.

NADI & THE WEST

NADI

pop 30,900

Something of a perennial adolescent, Fiji's third-largest city Nadi (pronounced *nan*-di) seems to be in a constant pursuit of identity. Not sure whether it's a city, tourist junction or business hub, it seems to have settled on urban centre for the time being. The population resides in several villages strung out along and just off the Queens Road, and the northern horizon is dominated by the Nausori Highlands, which loom hazily over town.

For visitors most action takes place in busy, dusty 'downtown' where Main St provides 1km or so of shopping, eating and other commercial options. In the back streets small businesses cater to everything from auto needs to sunburn. Most visitors use Nadi as a stopover to acclimatise and make the most of the infrastructure before heading out to more picturesque locales. If you're looking for something quieter Lautoka with its more authentic atmosphere is a better option. There is also accommodation between the two towns at Vuda Point and near the Sabeto Mountain Range. Nadi makes no bones about the fact that it's no idyllic snapshot of Fiji, but once you've got your head around this you're likely to enjoy the place more. As one wise traveller said, 'It is what it is'.

Orientation

From Nadi airport the Queens Road heads north to Lautoka and 9km south to downtown Nadi. Nadi's Main St extends southward from the Nadi River for about 800m to the T-junction at the large Swami temple. From here the Queens Road continues right to Suva, while Nadi Back Rd bypasses the busy centre and rejoins the Queens Road back near the airport. The road to the Nausori Highlands leads off into the mountains from Nadi Back Rd.

VITI LEVU

The market, bus station and post office are downtown just east of Main St.

Just north of downtown, between the mosque and the Nadi River, Narewa Rd leads west for 6km to Denarau island, where you'll find Nadi's most upmarket resorts, and Denarau Marina, where boats depart for Mamanucas and Yasawas.

Near Martintar village, Wailoaloa Rd also turns west off the Queens Road and after 1.8km hits Wailoaloa Beach. To reach New Town Beach, turn right off Wailoaloa Rd after 1.3km and continue for another 1.3km. You can also get to Wailoaloa Beach along Enamanu Rd, which extends south from the coast.

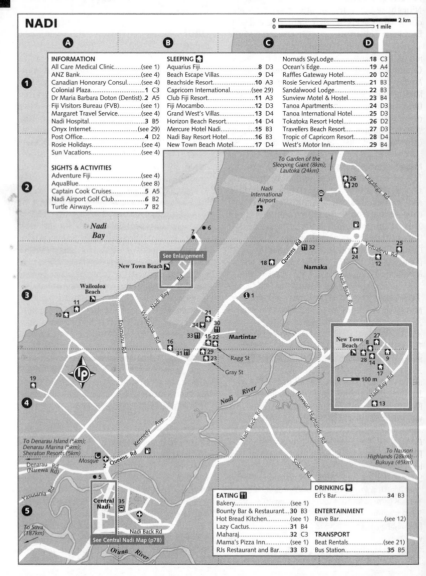

NADI

0 — 2 km
0 — 1 mile

INFORMATION
All Care Medical Clinic..............(see 1)
ANZ Bank..................................(see 4)
Canadian Honorary Consul......(see 4)
Colonial Plaza.............................**1** C3
Dr Maria Barbara Doton (Dentist)..**2** A5
Fiji Visitors Bureau (FVB)..........(see 1)
Margaret Travel Service............(see 4)
Nadi Hospital.............................**3** B5
Onyx Internet.........................(see 29)
Post Office.................................**4** D2
Rosie Holidays...........................(see 4)
Sun Vacations...........................(see 4)

SIGHTS & ACTIVITIES
Adventure Fiji..........................(see 4)
AquaBlue..................................(see 8)
Captain Cook Cruises..................**5** A5
Nadi Airport Golf Club.................**6** B2
Turtle Airways............................**7** B2

SLEEPING
Aquarius Fiji...............................**8** D3
Beach Escape Villas......................**9** D4
Beachside Resort........................**10** A3
Capricorn International............(see 29)
Club Fiji Resort...........................**11** A3
Fiji Mocambo.............................**12** D3
Grand West's Villas.....................**13** D4
Horizon Beach Resort.................**14** D4
Mercure Hotel Nadi....................**15** B3
Nadi Bay Resort Hotel.................**16** B3
New Town Beach Motel..............**17** D4

Nomads SkyLodge.....................**18** C3
Ocean's Edge.............................**19** A4
Raffles Gateway Hotel................**20** D2
Rosie Serviced Apartments.........**21** B3
Sandalwood Lodge......................**22** B3
Sunview Motel & Hostel..............**23** B4
Tanoa Apartments......................**24** D3
Tanoa International Hotel............**25** D3
Tokatoka Resort Hotel................**26** D2
Travellers Beach Resort...............**27** D3
Tropic of Capricorn Resort..........**28** D3
West's Motor Inn........................**29** B4

To Garden of the Sleeping Giant (8km); Lautoka (24km)

Nadi International Airport

Nadi Bay

New Town Beach

Wailoaloa Beach

Namaka

Martintar

Ragg St

Gray St

Nadi River

To Denarau Island (5km); Denarau Marina (5km); Sheraton Resorts (5km)

Denarau Rd (Narewa Rd)

Mosque

Queens Rd

Yavusania Rd

To Suva (187km)

Central Nadi

Nadi Back Rd

See Central Nadi Map (p78)

Oruna River

To Nausori Highlands (28km); Bukuya (45km)

Nawson Highlands Rd

Solovi Rd

Kennedy Ave

Vatualevu Rd

Lolulevu Rd

Nadi Back Rd

Nadi Bay Rd

New Town Beach
0 — 100 m

EATING
Bakery.......................................(see 1)
Bounty Bar & Restaurant...........**30** B3
Hot Bread Kitchen....................(see 1)
Lazy Cactus...............................**31** B4
Maharaj.....................................**32** C3
Mama's Pizza Inn......................(see 1)
RJs Restaurant and Bar..............**33** B3

DRINKING
Ed's Bar....................................**34** B3

ENTERTAINMENT
Rave Bar.................................(see 12)

TRANSPORT
Beat Rentals...........................(see 21)
Bus Station...............................**35** B5

Information

EMERGENCY
Ambulance (☎ 911)
Fire (☎ 911)
Police (Map p78; ☎ 911/670 0222) On Koroivolu Ave.

INTERNET ACCESS
Internet access is easy to find in downtown Nadi and costs around $0.10 per minute. Most backpacker lodges also offer Internet connection.

Bula Internet Cafe (Map p78; Main St, Nadi; per hr $3; ☺ 8am-8pm) Also has a fax service, digital photo scanning and CD burning.

Connect Cafe (Map p78; ☎ 670 7365; Shop 6, Connect Arcade, Lot 7, Queens Rd, Nadi; per hr $5; ☺ 8am-8pm Mon-Fri, 9am-6pm Sat, 10am-4pm Sun) Fast and reliable.

Onyx Internet (Map p76; ☎ 672 0088; Rm 201, Capricorn International Hotel, Martintar; per hr $6; ☺ approx 9am-5pm) You can also download images from digital cameras onto CD.

MEDICAL SERVICES
For medical treatment, contact any of the following.

All Care Medical Clinic (Map p76; ☎ 6720 960; Colonial Plaza, Queens Rd, Namaka; ☺ 8am-1pm & 2-5pm Mon-Fri)

Dr Maria Barbara Doton (Map p76; ☎ 6700 899; Queens Rd, Nadi; ☺ 9am-5pm Tue, Thu & alternate Sat) Dentist.

Nadi Hospital (Map p76; ☎ 670 1128; Market Rd, Nadi; ☺ 8am-4.30pm Mon-Thu, till 4pm Fri, till noon Sat)

MONEY
At the airport arrivals concourse there is an ANZ bank (open for all international flights). Elsewhere banks usually give a slightly better rate. Downtown, on Main St, ANZ, Westpac and Colonial National Bank all have ATMs and exchange money.

Just Exchange (Map p78; ☎ 670 5477; Ground fl, Prouds Bldg, Main St, Nadi) Foreign currency exchange with no commission.

POST
Post office Airport (Map p76; ☎ 6722 045; Nadi International Airport) Downtown (Map p78; ☎ 670 0001; Sahu Kahn Rd, Nadi)

TOURIST INFORMATION
Many hotels have their own travel desks.
Fiji Visitors Bureau (FVB; Map p76; ☎ 672 2433; www.bulafiji.com; Suite 107, Colonial Plaza, Namaka; ☺ 8am-4.30pm Mon-Thu, to 4pm Fri) Fiji's official tourism bureau is excellent. Friendly and helpful staff provides accurate information.

TRAVEL AGENCIES
Many of Nadi's numerous travel agencies are at the Nadi International Airport arrivals area on the ground and 1st floors. Domestic plane tickets can be bought directly from the Air Fiji and Sun Air offices at the arrivals concourse.

Some travel agencies specialise in budget accommodation and offer good deals, particularly for the islands. Be mindful though that you're not receiving independent advice, as it's largely based on the commission the agencies earn, not the best value for your dollar. For budget accommodation, both the resort and you will be better off financially if you book directly.

See p239 for information on booking accommodation, particularly offshore budget options.

Some agencies:
Argo Travel & Foreign Exchange (Map p78; ☎ 670 1645; argotravel@connect.com.fj; 267-269 Main St, Nadi)
Awesome Adventures Fiji (Map p78; ☎ 675 0499; www.awesomefiji.com; 2/534 Main St, Nadi; ☺ 8am-6pm Mon-Sat, 10am-3pm Sun) Operates the *Yasawa Flyer* to the Yasawa and Mamanuca islands as well as arranging budget-accommodation packages for these islands.
Margaret Travel Service (Map p76; ☎ 672 1988; fax 672 1992; 1st fl, Nadi airport concourse)
Rosie Holidays (Map p76; ☎ 672 2755; www.rosiefiji .com; Nadi airport concourse) Organises road tours, cruises, treks, accommodation, and is an agent for Thrifty Car Rental.
Sun Vacations (Map p76; ☎ 672 4273; www.sun vacationsfiji.com; Nadi airport concourse)

Dangers & Annoyances
Downtown you may be pestered by swordsellers and overly keen souvenir vendors. While Fiji is a relatively safe place to travel, there are occasional muggings and thefts in the Nadi area, not limited to lone travellers. Avoid wandering with valuables or packs along the beach or quiet roads such as Wailoaloa Rd or along Wailoaloa and New Town Beaches, especially at night.

✴Sri Siva Subramaniya Swami Temple
At the base of Main St, away from the commercial hype, this peaceful Hindu temple (Map p78; ☎ 670 0016; admission $3.50; ☺ 5am-8pm) strikes a vibrant pose against a dramatic mountain backdrop. The prolific wooden

carvings of Hindu deities travelled all the way from India, as did the artists who dressed the temple in its colourful coat and impressive ceiling frescos. You can wander around the main temple to see Lord Shiva's various forms, all incarnations being manifestations of the One Supreme Lord. This is a Murugan temple and worship of Lord Murugan is equivalent to the worship of nature. He is the guardian deity of the seasonal rains.

Nadi's Festivals such as Karthingai Puja (held monthly), Panguni Uthiram Thiru-naal (in April) and Thai Pusam (January) attract devotees from around the world. Devotees circle around the temple where they offer banana, smash a coconut, burn some camphor and receive blessing from the priest.

Visitors are welcome as long as they wear neat and modest dress, and haven't consumed alcohol or nonvegetarian food that day. It is fine to take photos in the grounds but not inside the temple. The grounds themselves are a tranquil spot to reflect and distance yourself from Nadi's boisterous main drag.

Activities
DIVING

There are two good diving outfits in Nadi, both of which cover a range of sites in the Mamanucas and come with excellent reputations for equipment, safety and instruction.

AquaBlue (Map p76; ☎ 672 6111; www.aquabluefiji.com; Lot 33, Wasawasa Rd, New Town Beach) A no-frills, small diving operation offering one-/two-tank dives ($120/160) and PADI Open Water Course ($500).

Dive Tropex (Map p88; ☎ 675 0944; www.divetropex.com; Sheraton Fiji Resort, Denarau) One-/two-tank dives ($120/185) and PADI Open Water Course ($670).

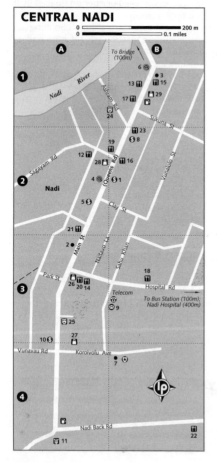

INFORMATION

ANZ Bank	**1** B2
Argo Travel & Foreign Exchange	**2** A3
Awesome Adventures Fiji	**3** B1
Bula Internet Café	**4** A2
Colonial National Bank	**5** A2
Connect Café	**6** B1
Divisional Registrar	**7** B4
Just Exchange	**8** B2
Post Office	**9** B3
Westpac Bank	**10** A3

SIGHTS & ACTIVITIES

Sri Siva Subramaniya Swami Temple	**11** A4

EATING 🍴

Chefs the Edge	(see 12)
Chefs, the Restaurant	**12** A2
Continental Cakes & Pizza	**13** B1
Curry House	**14** A3
Daikoku	**15** B1
Hot Bread Kitchen	**16** B2
Mama's Pizza	**17** B1
Market	**18** B3
Saffron The Corner	**19** B2
Seafood Garden Bar Restaurant	**20** A3
Sentai Seafood Restaurant	**21** A2
Supermarket	(see 16)
Tata's	**22** B4
Zigzag Café	**23** B2

ENTERTAINMENT 🎬

Galaxy 2 Cinema	**24** B1
Novelty Cinema	**25** A3

SHOPPING 🛍

Fiji Surf	**26** A3
Handicraft Market	**27** A3
Jack's Handicrafts	**28** A2
Nad's Handicrafts	**29** B1

HINDU SYMBOLIC RITES

Around 35% of Fijians practise Hinduism, and the distinctive and sometimes flamboyant temples and shrines in which they worship are dotted liberally around Viti Levu. Sculptured deities and colourful frescoes pose photogenically against a tropical or mountain background; taking a reverent five minutes to pay your respects can be a cathartic experience regardless of your religious persuasion. The most celebrated of Fiji's Hindu temples is the Sri Siva Subramaniya Swami Temple in Nadi, which was constructed and decorated in part by craftsmen flown in from India.

A Hindu temple symbolises the body, the residence of the soul. Union with God can be achieved through prayer and by ridding the body of impurities (meat cannot be eaten on the day of entering the temple).

Water and fire are used for blessings. Water carried in a pot with flowers is symbolic of the Great Mother (the personification of nature), while burning camphor symbolises the light of knowledge and understanding. A trident is used to represent fire, the protector and the three flames of purity, light and knowledge.

Hindus also believe that the body should be enslaved to the spirit and denied all comforts. Consequently fire walking is practised in order to become one with the Great Mother. Hindus believe life is like walking on fire and that a disciplined approach, like the one required in the ceremony, helps them to achieve balance, self-acceptance and to see good in everything.

Before entering a Hindu temple always ask permission and remove your shoes. Photography outside the temple is generally OK but considered offensive inside.

HIKING

There are hiking possibilities, including trekking tours, in the Koroyanitu National Heritage Park (see p143) and the Nausori Highlands (p143and p81).

RIVER RAFTING & KAYAKING

Several companies operate exciting river-rafting and kayaking trips to the superb Namosi Highlands and will pick-up/drop-off from Nadi.

Discover Fiji Tours (☎ 345 0180; www.discoverfiji tours.com) See p113 for more information.

Rivers Fiji (☎ 345 0147; www.riversfiji.com; Pacific Harbour) See p113.

Wilderness Ethnic Adventure Fiji (☎ 331 5730; www.wildernessfiji.com.fj) See p128.

MOUNTAIN BIKING

Based at Stoney Creek Resort, **Wacking Stick Adventure Tours** (Map p88; ☎ 672 4673, 995 3003; www.wackingstickadventures.com) rents good mountain bikes for $25 per day and sends you off with a map to explore the cane fields and the foothills of the Sabeto Mountains and Valley.

It also offers good half- and full-day tours, including the Sleeping Giant Bike and Hike tour (per adult/child $135/110, Monday, Wednesday, Friday and Saturday), which includes a visit to the Garden of the Sleeping Giant and a hot spring, a bike ride around the Sabeto area, and a hike to a cave and a waterfall through jungle. There are also half-day and sunset tours (from $120 per person) and for the really energetic, three- or five-day tours (from $1500 per person), which include all meals and accommodation.

GOLF & TENNIS

The **Denarau Golf & Racquet Club** (see p87), on Denarau island, offers tennis and has an 18-hole golf course.

Nadi Airport Golf Club (Map p76; ☎ 672 2148; 18 holes $15), at New Town Beach, is a much cheaper golf option. Clubs and pull-cart are an extra $30.

JET-BOAT TRIPS

For those in need of an adrenalin rush **Jet Fiji** (☎ 675 0400; reservations@jetfiji.com.fj; per adult/child $85/40; 30min) has a roaring, hair-raising tear around the Nadi River mangroves. It departs from Denarau Marina and there's a courtesy minibus for transfers from Nadi hotels.

Tours

Most tour companies will pick up guests from their hotels.

VITI LEVU

VITI LEVU FOR KIDS

Fiji's main island has plenty to offer families with young tackers in tow. If you're staying in the Nadi area try a day cruise to one of the **Mamanuca** or **Yasawa islands** (below).

A day on the **Coral Coast Scenic Railway** (p103) is a fun way for kids to gain an appreciation of Fiji's landscape and the barbecue lunch is a family-oriented affair. Nearby, the **Ka Levu South Pacific Cultural Centre** (p103) showcases Fijian singing, dancing and ceremonies that will entertain children. A little more kitsch and flashy are the demonstrations, boat tours and mock battles at the **Arts Village** (p113) in Pacific Harbour.

The Coral Coast is home to a number of attractions that will appeal to kids. Take them horse riding at **Natadola Beach** (p102) or along a private stretch of coast at the **Beachhouse** (p111). Show them Fiji's less-domesticated wildlife at the excellent **Kula Eco Park** (p107).

The **Fiji Museum** (p121) is choc-full of cultural and historical exhibits (including cannibal utensils – eeeewwwww) that will capture inquisitive young minds. You can also take them for a dip with local families at the **Suva Olympic Pool** (p126) and then a swing on the monkey bars at the family-infested **Umaria Park** (p127). The picnic tables at this esplanade playground make it perfect for a lunch pit stop.

Off the northern coast, **Nananu-i-Ra** (p140) is only a short hop from the mainland and offers calm swimming and snorkelling seas, and self-catering accommodation. Kids can also partake in kayaking and windsurfing here.

Many of the resorts have abundant activities to occupy the kids. Some kid-friendly resorts:

Shangri-La's Fijian Resort (p103)
Hideaway Resort (p112)
Sonaisili Island Resort (p90)
Sheraton Denarau Villas (p87)
Naviti Resort (p111)

OFFSHORE ISLANDS

You'll need to head out of Nadi to dabble in the dreamy beaches synonymous with Fiji, and the Mamanuca islands are close enough for an easy day trip.

Organised trips to Robinson Crusoe Island (p102) just offshore from Viti Levu and south of Nadi are also an easy and fun day excursion.

The following companies offer tours to the Mamanucas and some also go to the Yasawas. Most of these trips depart from Denarau Marina. Blue Lagoon Cruises and Beachcomber Cruises depart from Lautoka.

Beachcomber Cruises (☎ 672 3828/666 1500; www.beachcomberfiji.com; day tour per adult/child $80/40) Runs day trips to Beachcomber Island where there are lots of water sports on offer. Included in the price are lunch, coral viewing and fish feeding.

Blue Lagoon Cruises (☎ 666 1622; www.bluelagoon cruises.com) Has floating-hotel cruises to the Yasawas. Cruises are generally prebooked, although sometimes trips are last-minute deals. See p160 for more details.

Captain Cook Cruises (Map p76; ☎ 670 1823; www .captaincook.com.au; 15 Narewa Rd, Nadi) Has a day trip to Tivua island aboard the magnificent *Ra Marama*, a tall ship.

See p149 for more information. It also runs floating-hotel trips to the Yasawas (see p160).

Coral Cats (☎ 651 3475; sailfiji@connect.com.fj; per person $130) Offers day cruises around the Mamanucas on a 13m high-speed catamaran, with a stop at Malololailai. Snorkelling gear and a barbecue lunch are included in the price. This is a good option if you're looking for a smaller group tour.

Fun Cruises Fiji (☎ 670 2433; funcruises@connect .com.fj; Port Denarau) Offers day trips to uninhabited Malamala island. See p149 for more details.

MV Sundancer (☎ 672 0786; www.sundancerfiji.net; per day $1750) If you've got the cash and you're looking for something more intimate, charter this 13m yacht for day trips including fishing and snorkelling gear and lunch. It can accommodate up to six people, all of whom will be thoroughly pampered.

Oceanic Schooner Company (☎ 672 2455; fun cruises@connect.com.fj; Port Denarau) Has sailing trips from Port Denarau to the Mamanucas. See p149 for more information.

South Sea Cruises (☎ 675 0500; www.ssc.com.fj; ☺ departs Denarau Marina 9am) Offers sailing tours to several of the Mamanuca islands; see p149for more destinations and prices. It also runs day tours to the Yasawas (see p160). Most of these include lunch and resort facilities but check for any hidden extras.

SCENIC FLIGHTS

Most domestic flights are scenic, especially on a sunny day. It takes only 10 minutes to fly from Nadi to the Mamanucas and the islands, coral reefs and depths of blues and greens are gorgeous when seen from above – snorkellers and divers will drool at the sight. **Sun Air** (☎ 672 3016; www.fiji.to) flies to Mana and Malololailai (see p150 for more information). Confirm in advance if you wish to use a resort's facilities.

Joy flights over the Nausori Highlands and the patchwork farmland of the Sigatoka Valley are also spectacular. For details of **Turtle Airways** (Map p76; ☎ 672 1888, www.turtleair ways.com) and **Island Hoppers** (☎ 672 0410; www .helicopters.com.fj) services, see p260.

THE HIGHLANDS

Organised tours are the easiest way to see the high country and visit interior villages.

The highland village of Abaca in the Koroyanitu National Heritage Park is an easy day trip from Nadi or Lautoka; **Mount Batilamu Trek** (☎ 664 5747, 927 3592) has trips to this region; see p143.

Adventures in Paradise (☎ 652 0833; www.adven turesinparadisefiji.com) offers Cannibal Cave and Waterfall day tours on the Coral Coast, where it is based, and will collect guests from Nadi hotels. See p107 for more details.

Adventure Fiji (bookings through Rosie Holidays; Map p76; ☎ 672 2755; www.rosiefiji.com; Nadi International Airport) can organise four- or six-day 50km highland treks (per person $485/670) through the province of Ra. By bus, boat train and foot, you'll follow a route used by missionaries since 1849. Accommodation and meals are in villages. The trek is run from May to October with a maximum of 15 people aged 12 to 60 years. Pick-ups from Nadi hotels can be arranged.

TRADITIONAL BURE

Before the age of concrete and brick, Fijian villagers resided in traditional thatched dwellings known as *bure*. Travellers to Fiji will become familiar with the term almost immediately as it is virtually synonymous with the concept of accommodation at every price range.

In the past, these homes were dark and smoky inside, with no windows, usually only one low door, and with hearth pits where the women would cook. The packed-earth floor was covered with grass or fern leaves and then finely woven pandanus leaf or coarse coconut-leaf mats. Sleeping compartments were at one end, behind a bark-cloth curtain, where people slept on woven mats and with wooden headrests.

Traditional *bure* are usually rectangular in plan, with timber poles and hipped or gabled roof structure lashed together with coconut-fibre string. Thatch, woven coconut leaves or split bamboo is used as wall cladding, and roofs are thatched with grass or coconut leaves. *Bure* are cheap, relatively quick to build and withstand the elements well. Communities band together to finish a *bure* in a few weeks and re-thatch every couple of years. Most villages still have some traditional-style *bure* but, as the traditional structure of village life breaks down and natural materials become scarcer, most Fijians now find it easier and cheaper to use concrete block, corrugated iron and even flattened oil drums.

The *bure* advertised on your resort brochure is likely to be a long stretch from its forbearer. Although budget resorts offer rustic and Spartan constructs, most *bure* at resorts are mock structures to provide travellers with a dose of indigenous Fijian culture without losing the creature comforts they so crave.

Bure Kalou

In the days of the old religion, every village had a temple, or *bure kalou*, also used as a meeting house for the men. These buildings had a high-pitched roof and usually stood on terraced foundations. The *bete*, or priest, who was an intermediary between the villagers and the spirits, lived in the temple and performed various rituals, including feasting on slain enemies and burying important people. A strip of white *masi* (bark cloth) was usually hung from the ceiling, serving as a connection to the spirits. The construction of such a temple required that a strong man be buried alive in each of the corner post holes.

See p143 for more on organised tours and visiting the mountains independently.

Sleeping

Regardless of what the websites or brochures promise there are no appealing beaches in the Nadi area. That said, the resorts located at the grey-sand New Town or Wailoaloa Beaches are fairly isolated and peaceful, while those in Martintar and along the Queens Road are conveniently placed on the main bus route.

On arrival at Nadi International Airport you will be bombarded with a huge range of accommodation options. Most hotels have free transfer vehicles awaiting international flights, so it is best to already have some idea of where to go for the first night.

BUDGET
Along the Queens Road

Sandalwood Lodge (Map p76; ☎ 672 2044; sandal wood@connect.com.fj; Ragg St, Martintar; s $75-95, d/tw $85-105; ❄ 🖳 ♣) This hotel offers perky, self-contained rooms with blindingly colourful décor, small kitchenettes and TVs. They're neat and great value for self-caterers and families, plus the location off the main road promises a good night's sleep. Garden Wing rooms on the ground floor have patio doors leading to the pool, while the Orchid Wing rooms upstairs have balconies and more modern and spacious interiors.

Nadi Bay Resort Hotel (Map p76; ☎ 672 3599; www.fijinadibayhotel.com; Wailoaloa Rd, Martintar; dm $21-25, s/d without bathroom from $60/80, s/d/tr with bathroom $85/100/110, 2-bedroom ste $120; ❄ ❄ 🖳 ♣) One of Nadi's best-equipped budget resorts, the Nadi Bay buzzes perennially with the tank-top, cargo-clad 18- to 35-year-old set. It has the ambience of a shopping mall and is best suited to social animals, but the tide of facilities includes two excellent restaurants (mains $10 to $20), two bars, a palm-fringed pool, laundry service, luggage storage and tour desk. Dorms range in price from crowded, fan-cooled options to spacious, modern, air-conditioned rooms devoid of bunks. The single and double rooms and the suites are comfortable and clean.

Nomads SkyLodge (Map p76; ☎ 672 2200; www .nomadsskylodge.com.fj; Queens Rd, Namaka; 8-/6-/4-bed dm $22/24/26, tw & d $35-120; ❄ ❄ 🖳 ♣) Reposed over sloping green grounds with oceans of room and tree coverage, this sizeable property has plenty of options including neat and plain dorms, standard, Spartan twins and rooms with air-con, bathrooms, phone, TV, fridge and towels. It's a little like a school camp for grown ups; groups ply in to take advantage of the basketball and volleyball courts, games room, and space.

Sunview Motel & Hostel (Map p76; ☎ 672 4933; sunviewmotel@connect.com.fj; 14 Gray St, Martintar; dm from $20, d/tw/f $50/55/90; ❄ ❄ 🖳) A find for backpacking baby boomers, this pristine hostel has squeaky-clean dorms, compact rooms, polished wooden floors, spacious communal areas and extremely friendly hosts. Leave party plans at the gate; this is a modest and quiet option.

New Town Beach

A haul from downtown and the main road, New Town Beach offers budget travellers a cluster of backpacker resorts amid a smattering of wealthy residential properties. It's a peaceful area with great views of the Sabeto Mountain Range across the water.

Aquarius Fiji (Map p76; ☎ 672 6000; www .aquarius.com.fj; 17 Wasawasa Rd; dm $25-28, r $80-90; ❄ 🖳 ♣) Aquarius swims in South Pacific kitsch and warm vibes. The restaurant and pool area stretch languidly onto the beach where hammocks provide hangover respite to the beer-weary. All dorms and rooms have bathrooms and are stocked with cheerful décor. 'Oceanview' rooms upstairs have balconies overlooking the beach. The facilities are good and it's a professional setup.

Tropic of Capricorn (Map p76; ☎ 672 3089; chopkins@bigpond.net.au; 11 Wasawasa Rd; dm $15, s/d $30/40; ❄ ♣) This small and homely option is run by the ebullient 'Mama' who's warmer than a hot choccy on an arctic night. The main building sits on a patch of beach and contains spotless dorms and a central dining area. Roomy singles and doubles are located in a two-storey house around the corner with shared bathrooms and a kitchen. Travellers return here for the home-away-from-home vibes.

New Town Beach Motel (Map p76; ☎ 672 3339; new townbeach@connect.com.fj; r/f $40/50; ❄ ♣) Small and unassuming, this unpretentious motel hides behind a panel of foliage and is good for travellers beating a retreat from the hollering crowds. The fan-cooled rooms are neat, petite, and lovely. A wee restaurant (mains $10) on-site serves simple and filling fare.

THE AUTHOR'S CHOICE

Tanoa Apartments (Map p76; ☎ 672 3685; www.tanoahotels.com; off Votualevu Rd, Namaka; r/ste $170/215; ✗ ❄ 🖳) Perched above the city, this lofty option is one of Nadi's best. The superb apartments have sophisticated décor, stone walls and heavy wooden doors to imbue a touch of the Mediterranean. The cool interiors contain floor-to-ceiling timber wardrobes, modern kitchens and cushioned window benches with sweeping views of the highlands. Each apartment is doused in natural light and there's more than enough space to spread out and make yourself at home. The more expensive penthouse suites have a mezzanine level with single beds.

Travellers Beach Resort (Map p76; ☎ 672 3322; beachvilla@connect.com.fj; Wasawasa Rd; dm $15, s $33-40, d $40-70; ✗ ❄ 🖳 🖳) The digs at this commodious and long-standing resort are adequate without being outstanding but the sociable atmosphere is the main drawcard. There's a poolside bar and restaurant (mains $13 to $20) and facilities include laundry service, tour desk and Internet access.

More budget options:

Horizon Beach Resort (Map p76; ☎ 672 2832; www .horizonbeachfiji.com; 10 Wasawasa Rd; dm without/with air-con $10/17.50, s/d/f with fan $35/40/55, s/d/f with air-con from $40/55/75; ✗ ❄ 🖳 🖳) Good range of rooms plus a restaurant and bar. Popular with a young backpacker crowd.

Beach Escape Villas (Map p76; ☎ 672 4442; www .beachescapefiji.com; off Wasawasa Rd; dm without/with air-con $18/22, d & tw $40-65; ✗ ❄ 🖳 🖳) Pleasant timber villas with verandas but the maintenance is lackadaisical.

MIDRANGE

Most of the midrange hotels are located along the Queens Road between downtown Nadi and the airport. Rooms generally have air-con, TV, phone and fridge, and most hotels have tour desks, luggage storage, courtesy airport transfers and restaurants open for breakfast, lunch and dinner.

Along the Queens Road

Raffles Gateway Hotel (Map p76; ☎ 672 2444; www .rafflesgateway.com; Namaka; r $70-130; ✗ ❄ 🖳 🖳) Raffles lays on a spread of charm from the mock colonial entrance to the central pagoda topped with a fine head of bougainvillea. Cheaper standard rooms are pinchy but cool and crisp while the superior rooms are a leap in value with their lounge settings, TVs and private patios. There's also a poolside restaurant (mains $20 to $30) and a grassed central courtyard with sun lounges. Kids will love the waterslide.

Capricorn International (Map p76; ☎ 672 0088; www.capricorn-hotels-fiji.com; Queens Rd, Martinar; r incl continental breakfast $85-110, f $160; ✗ ❄ 🖳 🖳) The Capricorn's colourful and pleasant rooms are a tad dated but all have mod-cons and gargantuan beds. Pricier deluxe models come with a balcony. The two-bedroom family suite is good value for a small army and the property includes a spacious restaurant (mains $10 to $25), laundry service, salon and small shop.

Mercure Hotel Nadi (Map p76; ☎ 672 2438/2255; reservations@mercurenadi.com.fj; Queens Rd, Martinar; r $135; ✗ ❄ 🖳) The former Grand Melanesian has been renovated into a flashy haven of creature comforts. All rooms have a bar fridge, TV, phone and glossy bathrooms. The 'deluxe' rooms come with a king-size bed and are larger than the 'superior' rooms but the latter are more modern. The extensive grounds encompass a sprawling alfresco restaurant (mains $20) and family-pleasers such as table tennis, trampolines and a large pool.

Rosie Serviced Apartments (Map p76; ☎ 672 2755; reservations@rosie.com.fj; Queens Rd, Martinar; r $70-115; ✗ ❄) The block's a bit of an ugly duckling and the décor hasn't had a makeover in a while, but these studio, one- and two-bedroom apartments are meticulously maintained and great value for self-caterers. There's enough room in even the studios to accommodate a small nation and each apartment comes with a balcony and semi-modern, fully equipped kitchen.

West's Motor Inn (Map p76; ☎ 672 0044; wests motorin@connect.com.fj; Queens Rd, Martinar; r $55-85; ❄ 🖳 🖳) Circumnavigating a central pool, this hotel offers colourful, tiled deluxe rooms with TVs and pool views or older standard rooms. The poolside bar-restaurant (dinner $14 to $19.50) offers OK meals.

New Town Beach & Wailoaloa Beach

Grand West's Villas (Map p76; ☎ 672 4833; grand westvillas@connect.com.fj; Nadi Bay Rd, New Town Beach;

r $95-160; 🏊 🖲) It looks a little lonely, planted on the road to New Town Beach, but this condominium-style complex has white and bright studios, villas and one-bedroom apartments. The latter are fully self-contained and can accommodate four people. It's a good option if you've got wheels.

Wailoaloa Beach, about 1.5km southwest of New Town Beach, is quiet, isolated and a world away from downtown Nadi. The drawback is a lack of transport.

Beachside Resort (Map p76; ☎ 670 3488; www .beachsideresortfiji.com; Wailoaloa Beach Rd; r $60-90, f $125; 🍽 🏊 🖳 🖲) The moniker's a tad misleading, but this compact and personal resort (away from the beach) has stylish and immaculate rooms dressed in timber and Fijian prints. Cheaper rooms are tucked behind the main complex, while the pricier ocean view suites have balconies overlooking the central pool. The trendy Coriander Cafe (mains $12 to $24) dishes up inventive fare along the lines of Thai chicken pizza or coconut fish bites. The Beachside has friendly and professional staff.

Club Fiji Resort (Map p76; ☎ 670 20150; www .clubfiji-resort.com; Wailoaloa Beach Rd; d $100-165; 🍽 🏊 🖲) One for the comfort-needy looking to avoid the big resorts, this lively property has classy, Mediterranean-style villas decked out in mahogany and Italian tiles, plus smaller, timber and thatched *bure*. Oceanview *bure* are more expensive again ($180 to $300). The restaurant (mains $12 to $30) hosts Mexican, Mongolian and Fijian theme nights and live entertainment.

Ocean's Edge (Map p76; ☎ 651 1560; www.oceans edge.org; Fantasy Forest Park, Nadi; r $150; 🍽 🖲) Tucked away in a slowly progressing residential estate, this health and fitness complex has four trendy units with timber decks, edgy-urban interiors and extras such as fridges and individual libraries. Access to the pristine pool and gym are included in the price but you'll need a car to reach anywhere else.

TOP END

Tokatoka Resort Hotel (Map p76; ☎ 672 0222; tokatokaresort@connect.com.fj; Queens Rd, Namaka; r $175-230; 🍽 🏊 🖳 🖲) This low-rise, upscale resort carpets itself over a lush tropical setting and lays out semidetached, private villas, the most expensive of which are one-bedroom and self-contained. All digs are fresh and polished and facilities include a restaurant

(mains $15 to $30), health spa, and glorious swimming pool with water slide. It is access-friendly to disabled people.

Fiji Mocambo (Map p76; ☎ 672 2000; mbo@shangri -la.com; Namaka; s/d from $180/210; 🍽 🏊 🖳 🖲) Like an anchored *Love Boat* this capacious resort keeps coach tours and fussy guests happy with boutiques, a business centre, nine-hole golf course, spa, nightclub, restaurant and pool. The superior rooms are like upgraded motel rooms with generic décor, but a small jump in price will get you a classy, renovated 'deluxe'. Most rooms have beautiful highland views.

Tanoa International Hotel (Map p76; ☎ 672 0277; www.tanoahotels.com/international; d from $195; 🍽 🏊 🖳 🖲) Another flashy, self-contained resort, this hotel is loaded with facilities and distractions, making it popular with package pool addicts and families from Australia, New Zealand and the USA. Rooms are sassy and Westernised and guests won't need to lift a finger for anything.

See p87 for details of the Sheraton hotels on Denarau island.

Eating

Nadi is a tourist town catering well for a variety of tastes and budgets. Most places serve a mixture of traditional Fijian, Indian, Chinese and Western dishes, and there are lots of cheap lunch-time eateries downtown. Some of the resorts have special *lovo* nights, where food is cooked in a pit oven.

RESTAURANTS
Central Nadi

Chefs, the Restaurant (Map p78; ☎ 670 3131/3322; Sagayam Rd; mains $30-45; 🕑 lunch & dinner Mon-Sat; 🍽) One of Nadi's finest; this swanky restaurant is perfect for a splurge on taste and atmosphere. Meals match the refined surrounds with a truly global menu offering roasted duckling ravioli, Afghan chicken and excellent seafood dishes.

Chefs, the Edge (Map p78; ☎ 670 3131; Sagayam Rd; mains $16-30; 🕑 lunch & dinner Mon-Sat; 🍽 🏊) The café version of the main event upstairs has a roomy and relaxed interior and serves Indian and Thai curries as well as pizza, pasta, salads and burgers. The air-con will allow you to enjoy the vindaloo even in summer.

Seafood Garden Bar Restaurant (Map p78; ☎ 670 1302; Hospital Rd, Nadi; mains $15-30; 🕑 breakfast, lunch & dinner; 🍽) A jack-of-all-trades, this breezy

THE AUTHOR'S CHOICE

Daikoku (Map p78; ☎ 670 3622; Main St, Nadi; mains $20-30; ☻ lunch & dinner Tue-Sun) Behind a fortress of ornate timber doors, Daikoku is about having as much fun as you can filling your belly. Patrons sit around large square hotplates while their individual chef performs the sometimes gentle, sometimes energetic, always entertaining art of teppanyaki. Also gracing the menu is delicate sushi and sashimi as well as traditional pickles and Japanese beer to whet the palate. The atmosphere is intimate, the service flawless and the food utterly sublime.

restaurant dishes up good fish and chips, Indian curries and traditional *lolo* (coconut cream) in duck, chicken, beef, crab, fish and lobster versions. The crowd is touristy and the fare tame but it hits the spot.

Sentai Seafood Restaurant (Map p78; ☎ 670 0928; Main St, Nadi; mains $12-25; ☻ lunch & dinner Mon-Sat, dinner Sun) The décor may be shambolic but Sentai's Asian infusion menu knows exactly what it's doing. There's a heavy emphasis on seafood and adventurous souls can tuck into a *bêche-de-mer* (sea cucumber) combination hotpot. There's always beef in black-bean sauce or prawns with lemon and ginger for the meek.

Mama's Pizza (Map p78; ☎ 670 0221; Main St, Nadi; mains $8-20; ☻ lunch & dinner; ✗) It serves traditional crowd-pleasers as well as woodfired gourmet treats including garlic-glazed chicken, smoked *walu* (butter fish) or eggplant and sun-dried tomato pizzas. Pastas and salads are also up for grabs. Mama's downtown outlet is cool, dark and inviting.

Other Locations

Lazy Cactus (Map p76; ☎ 672 6890; Queens Rd, Martintar; mains $12-20; ☻ lunch & dinner) This snappy little cantina oozes a warm atmosphere and delicious smells. The food is Mexican and the cooks mean business – burritos, enchiladas and a kicking *camarones en mojo de ajo* (shrimp with garlic, chillies and butter). You can dine inside or in the pleasant courtyard.

Bounty Bar & Restaurant (Map p76; ☎ 672 0840; 79 Queens Rd, Martintar; lunch $10-20, dinner $20-45; ☻ lunch & dinner; ✗) This convivial restaurant-cum-bar boasts seafaring décor, expats at the bar and a constant, happy buzz. The menu is a

who's who of seafood, steak and meaty grills, with the odd curry and stir-fry thrown in.

Maharaj (Map p76; ☎ 672 2962; Queens Rd, Namaka; dishes $6-15; ☻ dinner) The spicy curries served at this long-standing Indian eatery are generally considered to be Nadi's finest. They can be hit and miss, but when the chef's on a roll the food is hot enough to induce a sweaty coma.

Mama's Pizza (Map p76; ☎ 672 0922; Colonial Plaza, Queens Rd, Namaka; mains $8-20; ☻ lunch & dinner; ✗) Another outlet of this Nadi institution (see left), the Namaka restaurant has diner-style booths.

RJs Restaurant & Bar (Map p76; ☎ 672 2900; Queens Rd, Martintar; mains $20-30; ☻ dinner Tue-Sun) A carnivore's delight, RJs sizzles up prime fillet steaks, veal masala, char-grilled ribs and plenty of seafood options. There's a Hungarian goulash for the left-of-centre palates and all servings are hearty. The wine list is suitably impressive.

The restaurants at a number of hotels welcome nonguests. Inventive fare at reasonable prices is cooked up at the Nadi Bay Resort Hotel (p82) and Beachside Resort (opposite). In New Town Beach, Travellers Beach, Aquarius Fiji and Horizon Beach resorts (p82) boast lively bars and restaurants.

Nonguests are also welcome at the finedining restaurants at the Sheraton resorts on Denarau (p87).

CAFÉS

Continental Cakes & Pizza (Map p78; ☎ 670 3595; Main St, Nadi; meals $6-16; ☻ 8am-6pm; ✗) This long, narrow café lures locals and visitors with fresh, deli-style sandwiches, subs and rolls, and pizzas. Sponge cakes, slices, pies and other sweet goodies flaunt themselves under a glass cabinet and the coffee here is good.

Saffron the Corner (Map p78; ☎ 670 1233; Main St, Nadi; mains $8; ☻ breakfast & lunch; ✗) Delicious curries served in one-meal-a-day portions display themselves under the counter at this corner diner. The ambience is a tad fast-food chain and you'll need to contend with Hindu tunes butchered by a drum machine, but it's a good spot for a mountainous feed.

Curry House (Map p78; ☎ 670 0798; Hospital Rd, Nadi; mains $8-18; ☻ breakfast, lunch & dinner) Popular with travellers, this atmospheric curry joint is busy but deservedly so. Traditional Indian curries and side dishes are vacuumed at an alarming rate. You can dine air-con or alfresco, although the outside seating is right next to a busy intersection.

Zigzag Cafe (Map p78; ☎ 670 5442; Ground fl, Prouds Bldg, Main St, Nadi; snacks $3-8; ⊗ breakfast & lunch; ⊠) Fresh fruit smoothies, club sandwiches and bakery goods cater to an almost exclusively tourist clientele at this Western-style café, but the coffee is strong and the crisp interior provides cool respite from the heat.

The kiosk at Domestic Departures at the airport has good-quality local food at local prices, while the one at International Departures is priced for tourists. If you have a bit of time to kill before a flight try the poolside bar at Raffles Gateway Hotel, opposite the airport entrance.

QUICK EATS

The bottom end of Main St in downtown Nadi has a number of cheap curry houses, all of which expend far more energy on the cheap nosh than on the dim surrounds. You can lunch for around $4.

Tata's (Map p78; ☎ 670 0520; Nadi Back Rd, Nadi; meals $4; ⊗ breakfast, lunch & dinner Mon-Fri, till 5pm Sat) You won't find this unadorned little curry house on any of the tourist brochures and its location ain't exactly salubrious, but Tata's serves some of the best, and hottest curry in the country. It's legendary among the locals.

Hot Bread Kitchen Downtown (Map p78; Main St, Nadi) Namaka (Map p76; Colonial Plaza, Queens Rd, Namaka) This chain bakery has two outlets in Nadi, both of which are good for lunches and snacks on the run. Tasty sausage rolls and pies go for under $1 and there's a steady stream of fresh bread and sweet rolls.

SELF-CATERING

Nadi has a large produce **market** (Map p78; Hospital Rd, Nadi), which sells lots of fresh fruit and vegetables. Good-quality meat, however, is not so easy to come by. There are several large supermarkets and bakeries downtown as well as along the Queens Road at the Colonial Plaza and at Namaka.

Drinking

Ed's Bar (Map p76; ☎ 672 4650; Lot 51, Queens Rd, Martintar) Nadi's best watering hole draws local and visiting social animals and keeps them happy with cheap beer and friendly staff. There's a small dining section inside but the bar is the main event, where stool seating,

pool tables and live bands dominate. Tables outside catch the breeze but they generally fill by late afternoon so you'll have to strap your beer boots on earlyish to nab one.

Bounty Bar & Restaurant (79 Queens Rd, Martintar; see p85) Another favourite with those in the know, the Bounty hosts a solid drinking phase somewhere between dinner and the live music. Things get loud, beery and fun as the night draws on. You're sure to meet your new best mate here.

The bars at the Aquarius Fiji (p82), Travellers Resort (p83) and Nadi Bay Resort Hotel (p82) are also atmospheric options for a beer or cocktail. Also, check out Rave Bar (see following) or the Planters Club and Planters Lounge (p88).

Entertainment

Rave Bar (☎ 672 2000) A nightclub at the Fiji Mocambo (p84) has live bands, karaoke and rave music. There is a cover charge and a dress code (no flip-flops or shorts) and the crowd is unsurprisingly touristy.

The Sheraton Royal has a disco Thursday to Saturday, nightly live Fijian music, and fire-walking and *meke* (Fijian dance) nights (see p88).

Two cinemas downtown that show a mix of Hollywood and Indian Bollywood movies are **Galaxy 2 Cinema** (Map p78; ☎ 670 0176; 5 Ashram Rd, Nadi) and **Novelty Cinema** (Map p78; ☎ 670 0155; Upstairs Nadi Civic Centre, Main St, Nadi). Admission is around $4.

Shopping

Nadi's Main St is largely devoted to souvenir and duty-free shops. Popular souvenirs include printed designs on *masi* and *tanoa* (bowls for drinking *kava*, a narcotic Fijian drink). See p251 for general information.

Jack's Handicrafts (Map p78; ☎ 670 0744; Main St, Nadi) Unashamedly aimed at the tourist wallet, this outlet of Jack's is colossal in size and contents. Crafts, clothing, jewellery and house items are sold at reasonable prices but it's all fairly mass-produced and you're unlikely to find anything truly unique here.

Nad's Handicrafts (Map p78; ☎ 670 3588; Main St, Nadi) Competing fiercely with Jack's, Nad's has the same stock for the same prices and lures shoppers with a 'Fijian warrior' at the gates promising the best deals in Nadi.

Handicraft Market (Map p78; Koroivulu Ave) You may pick up something more authentic at the handicraft market but check out the prices in the shops beforehand to ensure you really are getting a bargain. Be aware that wooden items are unlikely to have been treated and may be quarantined once you get home.

High-quality handicrafts are sold at the Pacific Art Shop in the Sheraton Fiji Resort, Denarau (see right).

Fiji Surf (Map p78; ☎ 670 5960; cnr Main St & Hospital Rd, Nadi) This little surf shop sells trendy surf wear, boards and equipment. It also repairs and rents boards and can be a good source of information for general surf conditions.

Getting There & Around

Nadi International Airport is 9km north of downtown Nadi and there are frequent local buses from just outside the airport that travel along the Queens Road to town ($0.65); otherwise a taxi is $10. Most of the hotels have free transfer vehicles awaiting international flights. From Nadi bus station (in downtown Nadi) there are buses to Lautoka and Suva; nonexpress buses can be picked up at regular bus stops along the Queens Road. For details of domestic flights from Nadi, see p259.

Buses depart from New Town Beach for downtown Nadi ($0.64, 15 minutes, six services Monday to Saturday). A taxi costs $4/6/10 to the Queens Road/downtown/airport.

For details on ferries to the Mamanuca islands and Yasawa islands, see p150 and p161, respectively. Most boat companies and organised tours will pick up guests from Nadi's hotels. You can get to Denarau island independently: **West Bus Transport** (☎ 675 0777) has six buses Monday to Saturday (fewer on Sunday) from Nadi bus station to Denarau island. The first is at 8.30am and the last at 5pm ($0.65, 30 minutes).

Taxi drivers are always on the lookout for business. They don't use meters so confirm prices in advance. Remember if they are returning to base, you pay less. See p263 for a list of car- and motorbike-hire companies.

AROUND NADI
Denarau Island

Developing at the speed of light, this upmarket island (2.55 sq km) is laden with fancy resorts, with even fancier extensions on the way. Although it's only 6km west of Nadi town, the disparity couldn't be starker. Everything here is manicured to perfection and if you're looking to splash some cash, enjoy a

dose of pampering and avoid Nadi altogether the island's got your name stamped all over it. Denarau is a reclaimed mangrove area and the beach has dark-grey sand, however the pools are heavenly and the Sheraton Resorts take day-trippers to a private offshore island with white-sand beaches.

Pacific Art Shop (☎ 675 0677; Sheraton Fiji Resort) is pricier than the downtown Nadi options but this upmarket handicrafts shop sells high-quality arts goods.

ACTIVITIES

Many trips to nearby islands (see p80) depart from Denarau Marina.

Dive Tropex (p78) is located in the Sheraton Fiji Resort.

Jet Fiji (☎ 675 0400; reservations@jetfiji.com.fj; per adult/child $85/40; 30min) tears around the Nadi River mangroves in a jet-boat.

The **Denarau Golf & Racquet Club** (☎ 675 9711; info@denaraugolf.com.fj) caters mainly to guests of the Sheraton hotels. It has an immaculately groomed 18-hole golf course with bunkers in the shape of sea creatures. Green fees are $110 for 18 holes and $70 for nine holes. Equipment hire is an additional $16/32 per nine/18 holes. A game of tennis will set you back $20/25 per hour on a synthetic/grass court. Racquet hire is $12 per person.

SLEEPING

Sheraton Royal Denarau Resort (☎ 675 0000; fax 675 0818; sheratondenarau@sheraton.com; r incl breakfast from $630; ✗ ⊗ ▣) The oldest of the Sheraton establishments at Denarau is still one of the most handsome hotels in Fiji and certainly the most Fijian flavoured of the group. The hotel rooms are casually splendid and come with all wonders of modern technology. The resort itself is tucked into a beautifully maintained tropical garden.

Sheraton Fiji Resort (☎ 675 0777; www.sheraton .com/fiji; r incl breakfast from $540; ✗ ⊗ ▣) The middle of the Sheraton sisters is uberchic and laid out in Mediterranean splendour. Low-rise condos, separated by gulfs of thick grass and multihued flora have ocean views and all the five-star perks. There are seasonal price variations and most patrons arrange some sort of package deal or discount.

Sheraton Denarau Villas (☎ 675 0777; www .sheraton.com/denarauvillas; r incl breakfast from $640, ste incl breakfast from $870; ✗ ⊗ ▣) The classiest of the lot, the Sheraton Villas are a series of modern one-, two- and three-bedroom bungalows with opulent interiors and small kitchens. The 'infinity' pool is unbearably blue, you can pamper yourself in the 'Mandara Spa' and staff wait on you hand and foot.

The hotels run a baby-sitting service. In addition there are some 18 restaurants, and just about any activity you can conjure on offer.

ENTERTAINMENT
The Sheraton hotels host a plethora of bars. The Planters Club at the Sheraton Royal is a mock-traditional pub that converts to a disco Thursday to Saturday. Also here is Planters Lounge, a sweeping cocktail bar with live Fijian music nightly. On Wednesday night you

can catch fire walking, and a *meke* is held every Saturday night ($50/25 per adult/child over 12 including a *lovo* dinner).

Young families are well catered for at the Sheratons with a daily entertainment programme for children.

GETTING THERE & AWAY
There are local bus services from Nadi to Denarau island (see p87; a taxi from Nadi town costs $12 and from the airport $24.

Foothills of the Sabeto Mountains
The undulating countryside between Nadi and Lautoka offers isolated accommodation with soaring mountain backdrops or ocean views. It's a lovely area to explore by local

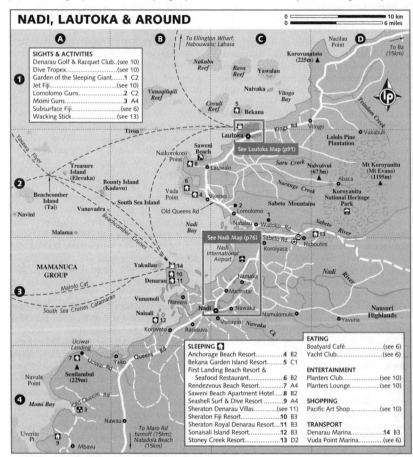

NADI, LAUTOKA & AROUND

SIGHTS & ACTIVITIES
Denarau Golf & Racquet Club..(see 10)
Dive Tropex.....................................(see 10)
Garden of the Sleeping Giant......**1** C2
Jet Fiji...(see 10)
Lomolomo Guns............................**2** C2
Momi Guns.....................................**3** A4
Subsurface Fiji................................(see 6)
Wacking Stick................................(see 13)

SLEEPING
Anchorage Beach Resort................**4** B2
Bekana Garden Island Resort........**5** C1
First Landing Beach Resort &
　Seafood Restaurant....................**6** B2
Rendezvous Beach Resort..............**7** A4
Saweni Beach Apartment Hotel.....**8** B2
Seashell Surf & Dive Resort...........**9** A4
Sheraton Denarau Villas.............(see 11)
Sheraton Fiji Resort.....................**10** B3
Sheraton Royal Denarau Resort...**11** B3
Sonaisali Island Resort.................**12** B3
Stoney Creek Resort.....................**13** D2

EATING
Boatyard Café.................................(see 6)
Yacht Club......................................(see 6)

ENTERTAINMENT
Planters Club................................(see 10)
Planters Lounge............................(see 10)

SHOPPING
Pacific Art Shop............................(see 10)

TRANSPORT
Denarau Marina...........................**14** B3
Vuda Point Marina........................(see 6)

bus, mountain bike, motorbike, hire car, taxi or organised tour. One tour company that rents mountain bikes and organises trips here is Wacking Stick (see p79).

The **Garden of the Sleeping Giant** (☎ 672 2701; Wailoko Rd; adult/child/family $12/6/30; ♥ 9am-5pm Mon-Sat, 9am-noon Sun), at the foothills of the Sabeto (Sleeping Giant) Mountain Range, is a peaceful place for a picnic or to spend a few hours strolling around the lily ponds and forested tracks. The garden is awash with Fiji's largest collection of orchids as well as vivid indigenous flora. About 6km north of Nadi airport turn inland off the Queens Road along Wailoko Rd for about 2km. A taxi from Nadi will cost around $13.

Further north along the Queens Road visit **Lomolomo Guns** for a short walk and a great view. The abandoned WWII battery, built to protect Nadi Bay, is on a rise at the foot of the Sabeto Mountains. The turn-off is 400m north of Lomolomo police station and about 8.5km north of the airport. Follow the dirt road for about 300m, turn left and follow the road up and around for about 400m.

SLEEPING & EATING

Stoney Creek Resort (☎ 672 2206; www.stoneycreekfiji .net; Sabeto Rd; dm $20, s/d without bathroom $30/45, d/tr with bathroom $55/75; 💻 🖴) It's a little bit 'wild west', a little bit Mountain Momma and a lotta bit of Fiji. This retreat, hidden at the base of the highlands, is a superb budget option. Dorms are reminiscent of train carriages and share an open communal area. *Bure* are kitsch and cosy and come with breakfast, privacy and sweeping mountain views. On site is a saloon-style bar and a restaurant (meals $6 to $10; open breakfast, lunch and dinner), which serves pastas, burgers and grills. Activities include mountain biking ($25 per person per day), horse riding and kayaking.

The resort provides a free airport shuttle; otherwise a taxi costs $10/14 from the airport/downtown. There are also regular 'Sabeto' buses from Nadi bus station, which can also be picked up at the Sabeto Rd/ Queens Road junction ($1, 12 buses between 8am and 5.30pm).

Viseisei & Vuda Point

About 12km north of Nadi airport the Queens Road bypasses the village of Viseisei, which receives tourists on organised tours. Viseisei was the home of the late Dr Timoci Bavadra, whose government was deposed by Fiji's first coup in 1987. The *mataqali* (extended family or landowning group) here own and lease several of the Mamanuca islands to resorts. Local buses between Nadi and Lautoka go past the village.

About 1km north of Viseisei there is a turn-off from the Old Queens Road to Vuda Point peninsula, which juts out towards the Mamanucas between Nadi and Lautoka. According to local legend the first Melanesians arrived in Fiji at this spot circa 1500. Today it's mostly farmland interrupted by two resorts, which are pleasant alternatives to staying in Nadi. Also here is the **Vuda Point Marina** (☎ 666 8214; vudamarina@connect.com.fj), a thriving boaties lure.

There is a good dive operation at the First Landing Resort, **Subsurface Fiji** (☎ 666 6738; www.subsurfacefiji.com), which runs diving trips to the Mamanucas and southern Yasawas reefs. A two-tank/PADI Open Water Course costs $190/560.

SLEEPING & EATING

First Landing Resort (☎ 666 6171; www.firstlanding fiji.com; r incl breakfast $145-220; 2-bedroom villa incl breakfast $440-520; 🗶 😄 🖴) Perched on the water's edge and dripping in palms and colourful foliage, this resort is a made-to-order brochure-retreat and the package-holiday guests who fill its rooms are not disappointed. Nestled into the thick gardens, the *bure* and villas are like cheerful hotel rooms, with bright, tiled bathrooms and bedrooms, and mosquito-screened verandas. Although the beach had fallen victim to energetic renovations at the time of writing, the lagoon-style pool proved adequate compensation.

Anchorage Beach Resort (☎ 666 2099; www .anchoragefiji.com; r $95-200; 🗶 😄 🖴) On a great hilltop site with panoramic views of Nadi Bay and the Mamanucas, this middling resort fits somewhere between idiosyncratic and generic. The rooms and villas are a little weary, yet the whole place is less premeditated than many of the other resorts in the area, so it's a good option for unfussy families and couples. The beach is a five-minute walk down the hill and there is a small pool but no organised activities.

First Landing Seafood Restaurant (mains $16-30; ♥ lunch & dinner) Serves excellent seafood alongside fairly timid pastas, burgers and other resort-style food. The outdoor seating is particularly pleasant and offers uninterrupted views of the closer Mamanucas.

Yacht Club (mains $8-17; ☿ lunch & dinner) It screams 'members only' from a sign out the front but that's all bravado and travellers are more than welcome. Dinner mains consist of Cajun steak, curries and stir-fries and the beach-shack structure makes for breezy dinner surrounds.

At Vuda Point marina, the **Boatyard Café** (snacks $4-10; ☿ breakfast & lunch) dishes up breakfasts, muffins, sandwiches, cakes and roti wraps to tables with water views. The marina also has a good **store** (☿ 7.30am-7pm), laundry and other services for yachties.

Naisali Island

Like Denarau, Naisali (42 hectares) is on the edge of the mangroves. This long, flat island is just 300m off the mainland, and about 12km southwest of Nadi. The resort is on a dark-sand beach with quick access and great views to the Mamanucas.

The large luxury **Sonaisali Island Resort** (☎ 670 6011; www.sonaisali.com; r incl breakfast $420, ste incl breakfast from $580; ✗ ✗ ☐ ☐) is a self-contained dose of fancy Fiji. Hotel rooms in the double-storey building have sea views and plenty of added extras and there are capacious, thatched *bure* with high ceilings and elevated verandas. The resort's facilities include a beauty spa, sunken bar and poolside, beachfront restaurant (meal package per adult/child $65/35), free kids club, and more activities than you could possibly exhaust.

Naisali is a 25-minute drive followed by a three-minute boat shuttle from Nadi airport. Turn off the Queens Road at Nacobi Rd and drive for a couple of kilometres by sealed road to the resort landing and taxi stand. A taxi here will cost about $20.

Uciwai Landing

Uciwai Landing, used by surfers to access the Mamanuca breaks and island resorts on Namotu and Tavarua, is 18km southwest of Nadi. Surfing is really the only reason to head here – it's accessed by a dirt road

The lingo and 'tude hang thickly in the air at **Rendezvous Beach Resort** (☎ 651 0571; www.surfdivefiji.com; camping per person $35, dm incl meals $55, s/d incl meals from $75/140; ☐ ☐) where an unfussy target market mill about the simple lodgings with the languid gait of seasoned surfers. Quick access to the Mamanuca surf

breaks and dive sites are the attraction and the idea is to spend as much time away from the resort as possible. Accommodation is in minimal bungalows and there's plenty of grass to pitch a tent. Renovations were under way at the time of writing.

Surfing boat fees per day are $50, which includes a packed lunch. A two-tank dive/ PADI Open Water Course costs $150/500.

Resort transfers from Nadi airport are $40, or there are local buses to Uciwai from Nadi bus station ($1.50) departing at 8am, 1.30pm and 5.30pm weekdays, and 7am, 1pm and 5pm Saturday.

LAUTOKA
pop 43,270

Fiji's second-largest city creeps up on you like a delicious noontime nap. Wide streets steeped in foliage create a permanently relaxed ambience and the backdrop of the Koroyanitu (Mt Evans) Range acts as a reminder that the urban reaches are well and truly finite. At the waterfront, a picturesque esplanade stems the low-rise construction, and yachts and cruise ships hang languidly and unobtrusively offshore. Lautoka's downtown grid teems with the ambling saris of a strong Indo-Fijian presence, and the shops, services and large market here provide a pleasant commercial alternative to Nadi.

The Lautoka Sugar Mill has been operating here since 1903 and the local economy still relies heavily on the diminishing sugar industry. In the latter half of the year little sugar trains putt along the main street, which is lined with royal palms. There is also the smell of woodchips in the air.

Information
EMERGENCY
Ambulance (☎ 911)
Police (☎ 911/666 0222; Drasa Ave)

INTERNET ACCESS
Compuland (☎ 666 6457; 1st fl, 145 Vitogo Pde; per hr $5; ☿ 8am-8pm)
Internet Café (cnr Narara Pde & Tavewa Ave; per hr $5; ☿ 8am-5pm Mon-Fri, till noon Sat)

MEDICAL SERVICES
Lautoka Hospital (☎ 666 0399; Thomson Cres) South of the Botanical Gardens.
Vakabale St Medical Centre (☎ 665 2955, 995 2369; 47 Drasa Ave)

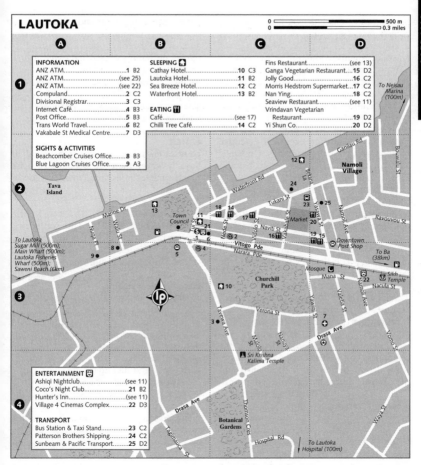

LAUTOKA

0 ————— 500 m
0 ————— 0.3 miles

INFORMATION
ANZ ATM...**1** B2
ANZ ATM.....................................(see 25)
ANZ ATM.....................................(see 22)
Compuland...................................**2** C2
Divisional Registrar........................**3** C3
Internet Café.................................**4** B3
Post Office....................................**5** B3
Trans World Travel.........................**6** B2
Vakabale St Medical Centre............**7** D3

SIGHTS & ACTIVITIES
Beachcomber Cruises Office...........**8** B3
Blue Lagoon Cruises Office............**9** A3

SLEEPING
Cathay Hotel...............................**10** C3
Lautoka Hotel..............................**11** B2
Sea Breeze Hotel..........................**12** C2
Waterfront Hotel..........................**13** B2

EATING
Café..(see 17)
Chilli Tree Café.............................**14** C2

Fins Restaurant...........................(see 13)
Ganga Vegetarian Restaurant......**15** D2
Jolly Good...................................**16** C2
Morris Hedstrom Supermarket......**17** C2
Nan Ying....................................**18** C2
Seaview Restaurant.....................(see 11)
Vrindavan Vegetarian
  Restaurant...............................**19** D2
Yi Shun Co.................................**20** D2

ENTERTAINMENT
Ashiqi Nightclub.........................(see 11)
Coco's Night Club........................**21** B2
Hunter's Inn..............................(see 11)
Village 4 Cinemas Complex...........**22** D3

TRANSPORT
Bus Station & Taxi Stand..............**23** C2
Patterson Brothers Shipping.........**24** C2
Sunbeam & Pacific Transport........**25** D2

To Neisau Marina (100m)

Namoli Village

Tava Island

To Lautoka Sugar Mill (500m); Main Wharf (500m); Lautoka Fisheries Wharf (500m); Saweni Beach (6km)

Town Council

Market

Downtown Post Shop

To Ba (38km)

Churchill Park

Mosque

Sikh Temple

Botanical Gardens

Sri Krishna Kalima Temple

To Lautoka Hospital (100m)

MONEY
There are several banks downtown that will change money and travellers cheques. There are ANZ bank ATMs on Vitogo Pde, Yasawa St and near the cinema on Namoli Ave.

POST
Post office (cnr Vitogo Pde & Tavewa Ave) Has public phones.

TRAVEL AGENCIES
Trans World Travel (☎ 665 1566, 666 5466; 138 Vitogo Pde) Can handle all tour and travel needs.

Sights & Activities
Koroyanitu National Heritage Park is a fantastic place for hiking (see p143).

Saweni Beach is fairly unappealing but popular with locals for weekend picnics. It is 2km off the Queens Road and the turn-off is 6km south of Lautoka.

Cruises are offered by:
Beachcomber Cruises/Resort office (☎ 666 1500; www.beachcomberfiji.com; 1 Walu St)
Blue Lagoon Cruises (☎ 666 1622; www.bluelagoon cruises.com; 183 Vitogo Pde)

Sleeping
Lautoka Hotel (☎ 666 0388; ltkhotel@connect.com.fj; 2-12 Naviti St; dm $15, r $35-65; ⊠ ⊠) Aged like a vintage beer, this hotel has lost some of its kick but it still puts a smile on your face. Rooms are cosy and welcoming and the more expensive versions have air-con,

private bathrooms and TVs. The corner balcony provides sweeping views of the street below and the whole place is charming in a faded, distinguished kind of way.

Waterfront Hotel (☎ 666 4777; waterfront@connect .com.fj; Marine Dr; r $120-140; ✗ ✗ ⚑) Lautoka's top hotel has a breezy waterfront location and the ambience and trimmings of a midrange US hotel chain. Spacious rooms have generic, cheerful décor plus air-con, balcony and TV. The more expensive executive rooms also have lounge settings. On site is a gym, small children's playground, bar and Fins Restaurant (see p101).

Sea Breeze Hotel (☎ 666 0717; fax 666 6080; Bekana Lane; s $35-50, d $40-55; ✗ ✗ ⚑) Tucked down an alley near the city centre, the Sea Breeze has piously austere rooms (the dominating embellishment is the bedside bible), which provide spotless and tranquil sanctuary to noise-weary travellers. Cheapest are the fan-cooled digs, but the more expensive, seaview rooms with air-con are the nicest. There's also a TV lounge, a bar and a restaurant serving breakfast ($4 to $10).

Cathay Hotel (☎ 666 0566; www.fiji4less.com; Tavewa Ave; dm/r from $14/40; ✗ ⚑) The Cathay's spacious rooms have nifty 1970s décor but the cleanliness of a 1920s Paris boarding house. It's a decent option for a cheap doss and the compact dorms have private bathrooms. There's also a loud TV lounge attached to a bar and restaurant (meals $10; open for breakfast and dinner), which serves filling but stodgy omelettes, burgers and curries.

Saweni Beach Apartment Hotel (☎ 666 1777; www.fiji4less.com; dm $17, ste $80-100; ✗ ✗ ⚑) The neat bungalow-style apartments at the Saweni, 8km south of town, have modern kitchens, cheerful décor and oodles of room in the lounge and bedrooms. It's a great option for families, self-caterers and those looking for a base to explore the nearby highlands, but you'll want your own wheels and imagination – there's little to do at the resort but paddle in the pool. Splurgers should take advantage of the opulent Beach House ($375), which has two-bedrooms, polished floors, TV, DVD, stereo and five-star class.

Bekana Garden Island Resort (☎ 664 0180; www .bekanaislandfiji.com.fj; d $125-280; ✗ ✗ ⚑ ⚑) This sassy, family-friendly resort occupies a small island close to Lautoka and is a good escape from the urban crowds. There are three types of smart *bure*, the largest of which is split

level, right on the water and can accommodate a family of four. On site are a restaurant and bar and the resort offers a plethora of activities, including waterskiing, windsurfing, snorkelling, kayaking and more. The beach itself isn't spectacular but there's a pool and the resort is a fun spot to spend a few days. The resort runs a regular shuttle service from Lautoka Fisheries Wharf.

Eating

Lautoka has fewer restaurants than Nadi or Suva; however, there are lots of inexpensive lunch-time eateries frequented by locals. They usually offer Indian, Chinese and traditional Fijian fare.

Chilli Tree Café (☎ 665 1824; 3 Tukani St; meals $6-12; ❧ breakfast & lunch; ✗) This corner café satiates fussy palates with fabulous muffins, focaccias, quiches, wraps, cakes and great coffee. The interior is more nanna than nouveau but the 180-degree windows make for great people watching.

Jolly Good (cnr Naviti & Vakabale Sts; meals $3.50-5.50; ❧ breakfast, lunch & dinner) Tasty takeaway including chop suey, curries and chicken and chips fill the hot counter at this outdoor restaurant. The seating is shaded and enclosed and it's a great place to mingle with locals and fuel up on the cheap.

Seaview Restaurant (☎ 666 0388; cnr Naviti & Tui Sts; mains $10-20; ❧ lunch & dinner) Beneath the Lautoka Hotel, the Seaview has an extensive menu boasting fresh seafood, Fijian dishes, triple-decker club sandwiches, salads, roasts, curries and more. The cool interior has low lighting and lacklustre furniture but the convivial vibes and excellent food more than compensate.

Vrindavan Vegetarian Restaurant (☎ 666 2990; 88 Naviti St; meals $4-7.50; ❧ 7.30am-6pm Mon-Wed, till 6.30pm Thu & Fri, till 5pm Sat; ✗) This clean and bright Indian eatery serves good vegetarian curries and thalis as well as colourful and delicious Indian sweets. The spacious interior is laid out like a diner and you choose your meals from the front counter.

Nan Ying (☎ 665 2668; Nede St; mains $12-20; ❧ lunch & dinner Mon-Sat, dinner Sun; ✗) Diminutive and commonplace from the outside, this Asian restaurant simmers in delicious smells and sizzles up some of the finest seafood dishes in Fiji – coconut crab, baked

(Continued on page 101)

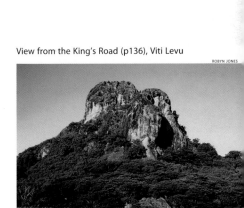

View from the King's Road (p136), Viti Levu

PETER HENDRIE

Sugar-cane farm, Sabeto Mountains (p88), Viti Levu

ROBYN JONES

Sri Siva Subramaniya Swami Temple (p77), Nadi, Viti Levu

ROBYN JONES

An anemone provides shelter for a shrimp,
Savusavu Bay (p61), Vanua Levu

CASEY & ASTRID WITTE MAHANEY

CASEY & ASTRID WITTE MAHANEY

School of barracudas, Savusavu
Bay (p61), Vanua Levu

Diving at a hard-coral garden, Naigani island (p190), Lomaiviti Group

CASEY & ASTRID WITTE

ROBYN JONES

Picturesque Navala village (p144), Nausori Highlands, Viti Levu

TOM COCKREM

Fijian girl adorned with hibiscus flower, Suva (p118), Viti Levu

Tourist shuttle boat at sunset, Denarau island (p87), Viti Levu

PETER HENDRIE

PETER HENDRIE

Women singing with gusto, Yasawa island (p169),
Yasawa Group

Lovo (feast prepared in a pit
oven), Wakaya island (p189),
Lomaiviti Group

JOHN BORTHWICK

Performers at a *meke* (traditional dance), Denarau island (p87), Viti Levu

PETER HENDRIE

PETER HENDRIE

Musicians playing on the cruise boat *Whale's Tale* (p149), Mamanuca Group

Windsurfer glides past the beach, Malololailai (p155), Mamanuca Group

PETER HENDRIE

Seaplane near Sawa-i-Lau island (p169), Yasawa Group

MARK DAFFEY

ROCCO FASANO

Harvesting bananas, Yasawa island (p169), Yasawa Group

Opposite: Passenger ferry heading for the islands, Mamanuca Group (p147)
DAVID WALL

Cooling off in the shallows, Sawa-i-Lau island (p169), Yasawa Group
MARK DAFFEY

Local boys at the seaside, Yasawa island (p169), Yasawa Group

Beach football, Yasawa island
(p169), Yasawa Group

Taking a dip, Yasawa island (p169), Yasawa Group

(Continued from page 92)

lobster or salt and pepper fried prawns to name a few. Fragrant poultry and noodle dishes also grace the menu.

Also recommended:

Ganga Vegetarian Restaurant (cnr Naviti & Yasawa Sts; meals $2-5; ☼ breakfast & lunch) Popular Hare Krishna restaurant serving good vegetarian meals.

Fins Restaurant (☎ 666 4777; Marine Dr; mains $12-25; ☼ breakfast, lunch & dinner) Cosmopolitan dining at the Waterfront Hotel.

The **café** (Naviti St; meals $3-5; ☼ breakfast & lunch) at the Morris Hedstrom supermarket also has good-value fast food. Adventurous self-caterers can stock up on Chinese groceries at **Yi Shun Co** (☎ 666 4615; Sugar City Mall, Yasawa St) and everyone else will be happy with Lautoka's produce market.

Entertainment

Lautoka has a small number of pubs and clubs, which are generally on the seedy side.

Coco's Night Club (☎ 666 8989; 151 Vitogo Pde) Probably the most welcoming club in town, Coco's puts on live music most Friday and Saturday nights as well as happy hours nightly (5pm to 9pm). The crowd is generally relaxed and mixed.

Seaview Restaurant (cnr Naviti & Tui Sts) The small bar at this restaurant is frequented by expats talking business or more sociable topics. It's a nice spot to grab a table and enjoy a few beers before dinner.

Village 4 cinema complex (Namoli Ave) Hollywood and Bollywood screen in harmony at Lautoka's main cinema. Tickets are $4, except on Tuesday when they're $3.50.

More clubs:

Ashiqi Nightclub (Lautoka Hotel; Tui St) Bollywood hits at alarming decibels.

Hunter's Inn (☎ 666 0388; Lautoka Hotel, Tui St) Popular with a Fijian crowd.

Getting There & Around

Lautoka is 33km north of Nadi and 24km north of Nadi airport. Local buses shuttle between the two towns every 15 minutes during the day ($2) and less frequently in the evening. There are also regular express buses along the Kings and Queens Roads, as well as carriers (small trucks) and mini-buses to Suva. Sunbeam Transport and Pacific Transport have offices in Yasawa St

opposite the market and both have frequent services to/from Nadi ($2.80, 1½ hours) and Suva ($13, six hours).

Local buses connect Lautoka with Saweni Beach ($1, 45 minutes, six daily) Alternatively any local bus to Nadi will drop you at the turn-off, from where it is an easy walk along 2km of unsealed road. A taxi will cost approximately $8/25 from Saweni to Lautoka/Nadi airport.

Beachcomber Cruises (☎ 666 1500; www.beachcomberfiji.com; 1 Walu St) runs ferries twice daily to Beachcomber and Treasure Islands. **Patterson Brothers Shipping** (☎ 666 1173; 15 Tukani St) runs interisland ferries to Vanua Levu.

Lautoka is easy to get around on foot. Taxis are plentiful and short rides are cheap.

MOMI BAY

South of Nadi the Queens Road winds through cane fields; the first interesting detour is to Momi Bay and along the coast on Old Queens Road The turn-off is about 18km south of Nadi (27km from the airport). Some local buses take this dusty unsealed route, but if you jump off you will have to wait a while for the next one. The 29km of unsealed road back to the Queens Road takes you through beautiful farmland, cane fields and pine plantations. There are lots of small temples and mosques in the area.

The **Momi Guns** (adult/child/family $3/1/6; ☼ 9am-5pm) is an evocative WWII battery on a hilltop about 6km from the Queens Road turn-off, coming from Nadi. The position of the battery was crucial as it overlooks the single entry into Western Fiji for large ships – the Navula Passage. The restored bunkers and fine collection of photos provide a tangible sense of the site's activity when in service. Take your camera – the views to the Navula Passage, Malolo Barrier Reef and Mamanuca islands are quite breathtaking.

Sleeping & Eating

Seashell Surf & Dive Resort (☎ 670 6100; www.seashellresort.com; camping $10, dm incl meals $60, s/d/tr $40/65/75, ste $150-220; ✕ ✕ 🖵 🖳) Something between a shack and the Shangri-La Fijian, this isolated resort has an undiscovered air about it. The grassy grounds encompass simple dorms, unadorned but comfortable lodge rooms and classier *bure* and suites. Lodge room 1 will get you ocean views. Also on site are a tennis court, children's playground, restaurant (meals $10 to $20; open for breakfast, lunch and dinner) and enough palm trees for a whole island. The *bure* are self contained.

There are plenty of activities on offer from Scuba Bula including diving (a two-tank dive/PADI Open Water Course costs $170/550) and surfing in the Mamanucas at Wilkes Passage, Mini Clouds and Desperations.

Getting There & Away

The resort is about 30km from Nadi. From Nadi, travel about 11km along Old Queens Road, then turn right and continue for another 1.5km. Airport transfers by resort minibus are $15 each way and taxis cost $50 (45 minutes). Local buses depart from Nadi bus station ($2, one hour, three daily). There is also a daily 1.30pm local bus from Sigatoka ($3, one hour) and taxis charge $40.

ROBINSON CRUSOE ISLAND

This small coral island, also known as Likuri, is near the passage into Likuri Harbour just offshore of Natadola Beach.

There are day trips here from Nadi and Coral Coast hotels on Tuesday, Thursday and Sunday ($90 per person), but staying overnight is much better value. The resort also offers a four-night sailing adventure to the Yasawa islands on the 15m yacht *Pelorus Jack* (per person $500), which includes all meals and accommodation on the boat.

Like bees to Bacardi, budget travellers in the 18- to 30-year-old bracket swarm on **Robinson Crusoe Island Resort** (☎ 651 0100; www.robinsoncrusoeislandfiji.com; dm/s/d incl meals from $70/90/170; ⬚) for dizzy fun packaged in a cultural wrapping. The accommodation is basic and comfortable; small thatched private *bure* or bunk beds in the large dorm share communal bathrooms and showers are by bucket and hand-pump. It has a gorgeous white-sand beachfront with sunsets Hollywood would pay for. Buffet meals are served in a large horseshoe-shaped shelter with a sandy central area for performances. The entertainment programme is intense and some will undoubtedly find it a little tacky – your boat is 'attacked by cannibals' on your arrival. But if you go into the whole affair without expecting the height of cultural experiences you'll have a blast.

Activities on offer include windsurfing, snorkelling, volleyball and the use of paddle boards. Nautilus Divers offers two-tank dives/PADI Open Water Courses for $120/450.

The resort operates a bus/boat return transfer to/from Nadi ($70).

NATADOLA BEACH

Gorgeous Natadola Beach is Viti Levu's best. Its vast bank of white sand slides into a cobalt sea, providing good swimming regardless of the tide level. If you want to snorkel, surf or windsurf, take your own gear. Natadola's strong currents often defy the brochures so instead of glassy, still conditions you may find sufficient churn for good body surfing. Take care; the varying conditions and undertow have caught out even experienced surf swimmers and readers have reported injuries. For nonswimmers Natadola is an utterly photogenic spot to zone out but watch your valuables as there have been reports of theft.

Local villagers offer horse riding along the beach ($10) and sell green coconuts for drinking, and necklaces; unfortunately they can be pretty pushy. If you don't want to take them up on their offer issue a firm but polite 'no thank you' and put some distance between you and the car park.

Sleeping & Eating

Natadola Beach Resort (☎ 651 1251; www.natadola .com; r incl breakfast $250; ⬚) A pretty splash of Spain, this resort shuns mod cons and opts for privacy and class instead. Plump sofa chairs and beds, cool wooden interiors and private courtyards make for idyllic rooms. The restaurant-bar (mains $10 to $25; open for breakfast, lunch and dinner) serves great seafood and is open to nonguests. The resort is small, intimate and isolated and a couple of days should satiate all those urges you'd had to escape civilisation.

Mia and Sara are a married couple in the nearby village of Sanasana who offer warm and hospitable **homestay accommodation** (incl meals $35-40). To contact them call the only phone in the village on ☎ 651 0926 between 10am and 1pm and ask for Mia or Sara. Then call back in 10 minutes to speak to them.

InterContinental were constructing a lavish five-star resort at Natadola at the time of research. For information click onto www .natadolafiji.com.

Getting There & Away

Natadola Beach is fairly isolated and makes a good day escape from Nadi. The Maro Rd turn-off heads south to Natadola off the Queens Road, 36km from Nadi (45km from the airport) just past the police post. The beach is signposted.

Paradise Transport buses head to Natadola from Sigatoka ($2.50, one hour, four daily on weekdays). The Coral Coast Scenic Railway runs tours to this beach (see below). Keen walkers could follow the track between Yanuca and Natadola Beach. It is a pleasant 3½-hour walk. You can catch the train or a bus back.

YANUCA & AROUND

Past the turn-off to Natadola, the Queens Road continues southeast, winding through hills and down to the coast at Cuvu Bay and Yanuca, about 50km from Nadi. Yanuca itself is a blink of a village but it's home to a couple of good attractions.

The station for the **Coral Coast Scenic Railway** (☎ 652 8731; Queens Rd) is at the causeway entrance to the Shangri-La Fijian Resort. It offers scenic rides along the coast on an old, diesel sugar train, past villages, forests and sugar plantations, to beautiful Natadola Beach. The railway was once used for transporting cane and passengers to the Lautoka Mill. The 14km trip takes about 1¼ hours, leaving at 10am and returning at 4pm ($80 including barbecue lunch). It is a popular trip with families and guests of the Fijian Resort suffering hangovers or sunburn.

Ka Levu South Pacific Cultural Centre (☎ 652 0200; http://fijiculturalcentre.com; admission 1-hr/day $25/100; dm incl meals $65, d & tw $75, r $90-135) is a purpose-built centre featuring cultural dancing, *kava* ceremonies, handicrafts and cooking in a faux-Fijian village. It's well set-up and best for a cultural insight rather than handicrafts. You can overnight in neat dorms and doubles with shared bathrooms, crisp hotel rooms with funky décor or capacious self-contained units. All rates include tours of the centre. Bernie's Bar is on site.

At the cultural centre, **Gecko's Restaurant** (mains $15-30; ☯ breakfast, lunch & dinner) cooks up great steaks and fish curries.

The sprawling five-star **Shangri-La's Fijian Resort** (☎ 652 0155; www.shangri-la.com; r incl breakfast from $490; ☒ ☒ ☒) occupies the entire island of Yanuca (43 hectares) and is perfect for

families seeking pure R&R and indulgence. You can while the hours away by one of the three palm-skirted pools or work off a cocktail or 10 with a bout of golf, tennis, jet-skiing, parasailing, snorkelling, water-skiing, fishing or even cycling. Coral Coast Scuba Ventures (p107) is based here. Two children can share a room with parents for free and then be shunted (lovingly) into the child care centre. The squeals of delight indicate they won't mind a bit. Yanuca island is just offshore and linked to the mainland by a causeway.

Getting There & Away

The Fijian Resort is about a 45-minute drive from Nadi and 11km west of Sigatoka. There are regular express buses, minibuses and carriers travelling along the Queens Road. A taxi to Nadi airport is about $70 and the Coral Sun Fiji coach costs $15.

CORAL COAST

A wide bank of coral offshore gives this stretch of coast between Korotogo and Pacific Harbour its name. Flanked by waves of richly vegetated hills and a fringing reef that drops off dramatically into the deep blue of the South Pacific Ocean, it's the most scenic slice of the Queens Road and resorts of all standard exploit the views. The scenery peaks around Korolevu. This said, the Coral Coast's beaches are poor cousins to those on Fiji's smaller islands and most swimming is done in hotel pools. Travellers are better off focussing on highlights such as the Sigatoka Sand Dunes, Tavuni Hill Fortification, Sigatoka Valley and, near Pacific Harbour, river trips in the Namosi Highlands and diving in the Beqa Lagoon. Lounging in a resort is also a prime pursuit in these parts.

The Queens Road is sealed and largely hugs the coast; unsealed roads head inland off the highway and up into the highlands. Both Sunbeam Transport and Pacific Transport have regular buses along the Queens Road.

SIGATOKA

pop 8000

Sigatoka (pronounced sing-a-*to*ka) is an industrious and compact town perched next to a fertile swathe of the Sigatoka River, Fiji's second-largest river. Surrounded by small villages and inhabited by farming communities, it also acts as a service town for the Coral Coast region. There is a produce market in the heart of town, a few souvenir shops, a large mosque and a fantasy-style, privately owned mansion on the hill behind the town. For visitors it's really a place to stock up on travel needs; a couple of hours will exhaust your souvenir cravings.

Information

Westpac and ANZ have banks in town.
Gerona Medical & Surgical Clinic (☎ 652 0128; Sigatoka Valley Rd)
TWicks Internet Café (☎ 652 0928; 50 Sigatoka Valley Rd; per hr $6) Internet access.

Sleeping & Eating

Sigatoka doesn't offer any outstanding accommodation options and unless you're stuck, you're much better off heading to nearby Korotogo (p107).

River View Restaurant (☎ 650 1530/1520; jrms traveltours@connect.com.fj; Queens Rd; mains $16-30; ☽ lunch & dinner; ☒ ☒ ▣) This elevated restaurant has lovely river views and serves

great seafood in a cavernous dancehall-like interior. The space is absorbed by happy chatter when it's occupied and there's a modicum of clean, white and bright rooms attached (dorms $20; rooms $45 to $65). All except the dorms include a private bathroom and fridge.

Hotel Riverview (☎ 652 0544; s/d $35/45; ☒) Across the roundabout from the Sigatoka Club, the Riverview has weary but tidy rooms that are fair value for the price. The beds are more than a tad saggy but the balconies offer decent views.

Sigatoka Club (☎ 650 0026; mains $8-20; ☽ lunch & dinner) Downstairs from the River View Restaurant, this club is the best drinking hole in town with waterfront booths, oceans of sunlight and decent pub nosh.

Vilisite's Seafood Restaurant (☎ 650 1030; Queens Rd; mains $8-20; ☽ breakfast, lunch & dinner; ☒) Spectacular seafood dishes are served in kitschy tropicana surrounds at this deservedly popular Fijian eatery. The menu is extensive and also includes curries and Chinese options but you'd be nuts to bypass the shellfish. Takeaway is also available.

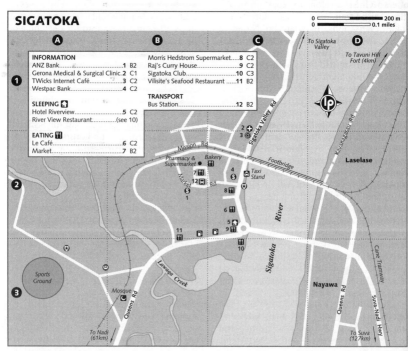

SIGATOKA

0 — 200 m
0 — 0.1 miles

INFORMATION	
ANZ Bank	1 B2
Gerona Medical & Surgical Clinic	2 C1
TWicks Internet Café	3 C2
Westpac Bank	4 C2

SLEEPING ⌂	
Hotel Riverview	5 C2
River View Restaurant	(see 10)

EATING ⍾	
Le Café	6 C2
Market	7 B2

Morris Hedstrom Supermarket	8 C2
Raj's Curry House	9 C2
Sigatoka Club	10 C3
Vilisite's Seafood Restaurant	11 B2

TRANSPORT	
Bus Station	12 B2

To Sigatoka Valley

To Tavuni Hill Fort (4km)

Sigatoka Valley Rd

Kavanagasau Rd

Laselase

Mission Rd

Footbridge

Pharmacy & Supermarket

Bakery

Market Rd

Taxi Stand

River

Sigatoka

Cane Tramway

Sports Ground

Lawaqa Creek

Mosque

Queens Rd

Nayawa

Queens Rd

Suva–Nadi Hwy

To Nadi (61km)

To Suva (127km)

Le Café (☎ 652 0668/877; 28 Queens Rd; meals $10-15; ☯ breakfast & lunch; ✗ ⊑) The only café-style eatery in Sigatoka dishes up tame but tasty burgers, sandwiches, curries, snacks and utterly perfect omelettes. The surrounds are pleasant and tables are given plenty of space. It's Sigatoka's nicest spot for brekkie.

Raj's Curry House (☎ 650 1470; Queens Rd; mains $7-12; ☯ lunch & dinner) The setup may be a little on the shadowy side but Raj's lives up to its name with curries that make your tastebuds dance. Vegetarians are well catered for and locals test their mettle here on a regular basis.

Self-caterers can stock up at the market and the Morris Hedstrom supermarket.

Getting There & Around
Pacific Transport and Sunbeam Transport run several express buses a day between Nadi and Sigatoka ($4, 1¼ hours) and between Sigatoka and Suva ($8, 2¾ hours). Add about an hour for nonexpress buses.

There are also carriers, minibuses and taxis along the Queens Road.

AROUND SIGATOKA
Sigatoka Sand Dunes
One of Fiji's natural highlights, these impressive **dunes** (adult/child/family $8/3/20; ☯ 8am-6pm) are a ripple of peppery monoliths skirting the shoreline near the mouth of the Sigatoka River. Windblown and rugged, they stand 5km long, up to 1km wide and on average about 20m high, rising to about 60m at the western end. Do not expect golden Sahara-like dunes, as the fine sand is a grey-brown colour and largely covered with vines and shrubs. The dunes have been forming over millions of years and archaeological excavations here have uncovered pottery more than 2600 years old and one of the largest burial sites in the Pacific. A mahogany forest was planted in the 1960s to halt the dunes' expedition onto the Queens Road and the state-owned part of the area was declared a national park in 1989.

The dunes are quite spectacular and a great place for a walk. On a hot day visit before 11am or after 3pm. Enter through the Sigatoka Sand Dunes visitors centre at the western end of the dunes, 4.5km southwest of Sigatoka on the Queens Road. From here there are trails to the dunes; avoid eroding the fragile dunes and stick to the trails.

Allow about one hour for the round-trip walking tour and take plenty of water and sunscreen.

Lower Sigatoka Valley
The Sigatoka River's tributaries originate as far away as Tomanivi (Mt Victoria) and the Monasavu Dam. The river has long provided a line of communication between mountain peoples and coast dwellers, and the fertile river flats are productive agricultural land. Almost 200 archaeological, cultural or historically significant sites have been found in and around the valley; sadly, many of the sites are being taken over by farmland or housing.

This fertile river valley is known as Fiji's 'salad bowl'. Cereals, vegetables, fruits, peanuts and sugar cane are grown here, mostly on small-scale farms. The Sigatoka Valley Rural Development Project (SVRDP) coordinates cropping programmes and provides training for farmers on up-to-date techniques and irrigation systems. Much of the produce ends up at the municipal markets, and vegetables such as eggplant, chilli, okra and root crops such as *dalo* (taro), *tavioka* (cassava) and yams are exported to Canada, Australia, New Zealand and the USA. It's a great landscape to fly over, with the mountains, the patchwork valley, the muddy brown river flowing into the blue ocean, and the Coral Coast's vast fringing reef.

Two valley villages are known for their **pottery**: Lawai and Nakabuta. The latter is home to one of Fiji's best potters, Diana Tugea. Visitors are welcome at both villages. If turning up unannounced, you should ask the first person you meet to guide you. They will take you to a pottery *bure* with various works on display. Large, smooth cooking pots are the traditional pots from this area, but small items such as pottery pigs and *bure* are also sold to tourists who visit the area.

SURFING
The Sigatoka area has Fiji's only beach-break. Most other areas have fringing reefs but here the fresh water has prevented their formation. The break is over a large, submerged rock platform covered in sand. Surfing is at the point-break at the mouth of the Sigatoka River and beach-breaks pound the shore. You need your own transport to get here.

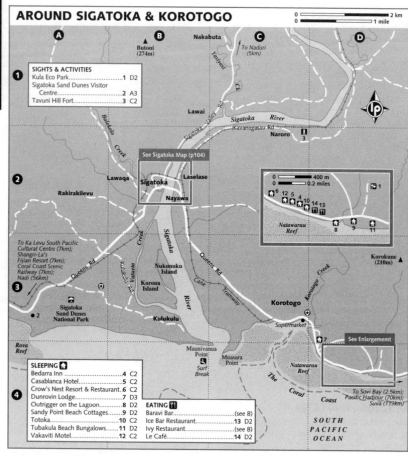

AROUND SIGATOKA & KOROTOGO

SIGHTS & ACTIVITIES
Kula Eco Park.....................................1 D2
Sigatoka Sand Dunes Visitor
  Centre..2 A3
Tavuni Hill Fort.................................3 C2

SLEEPING
Bedarra Inn 4 C2
Casablanca Hotel.............................5 C2
Crow's Nest Resort & Restaurant..6 C2
Dunrovin Lodge................................7 D3
Outrigger on the Lagoon................8 D2
Sandy Point Beach Cottages..........9 D2
Totoka...10 C2
Tubakula Beach Bungalows.........11 D2
Vakaviti Motel................................12 C2

EATING
Baravi Bar................................(see 8)
Ice Bar Restaurant.....................13 D2
Ivy Restaurant...........................(see 8)
Le Café..14 D2

GETTING THERE & AWAY

You can visit Lawai and Nakabuta by just
hopping on a local bus. Paradise Valley buses
travel up the Sigatoka Valley on the western
side of the river. Lawai is about 2.5km north
of Sigatoka. Nakabuta is twice as far ($5 by
taxi, $0.60 by bus, or a 10-minute drive).
There are regular buses to Naduri, which
pass Lawai and Nakabuta (every one to two
hours from about 6.30am to 7.30pm). On
weekends services are less frequent. Heading inland by local bus offers beautiful scenery. Try a ride to Keiyasi village about 55km
upriver ($5, about four hours return). The
morning buses generally return (check with
the bus driver), while the afternoon buses
stay in the village overnight.

Tavuni Hill Fort

Built in the 18th century by Tongan chief
Maile Latumai, this **fort** (adult/child/family $12/3/30;
8am-5pm Mon-Fri, 8.30am-1.30pm Sat) was a de-
fensive site used in times of war and is one
of Fiji's most interesting historical sights. It
provides an excellent insight into the strong
precolonial links between Tonga and Fiji and
although there are many like it scattered all
over Fiji, this is the most accessible for visitors. The site has been restored and has an
information centre. The centre was set up
in a combined effort between the Ministry
of Tourism and the people of Naroro, and
received funding from the European Union
(EU). It now provides income to the local
villagers whose ancestors lived in the fort.

Chief Maile Latemai and his clan fled Tonga to escape a dispute during an era of political and social upheaval. He and his entourage of servants sailed all the way in a double-hulled canoe and arrived in the Sigatoka area in about 1788. They originally set up in Korotogo but were kept on the move by constant tribal warfare. Eventually the local tribes accepted the newcomers, and the chief was given some land and a local wife.

The steep limestone ridge, about 90m high at the edge of a bend in the Sigatoka River, was an obvious strategic location for a fortification. From this position the surrounding area could easily be surveyed, both upstream and downstream and the views are spectacular. Substantial earthworks were carried out to form *yavu* (bases for houses) and terraces for barricade fencing. There are also a number of grave sites, a *rara* (ceremonial ground), a *vatu ni bokola* (head-chopping stone), and some beautiful curtain figs and an *ivi* (Polynesian chestnut tree) on the site.

Tavuni fort is about 4km northeast of Sigatoka on the eastern side of the river, above Naroro village. There are regular local buses that pass Tavuni Hill (about $0.60). They leave Sigatoka bus station and travel along Kavanagasau Rd heading for Mavua (seven times on weekdays between about 7am and 5.30pm). A taxi to the fort is about $5 one-way.

KOROTOGO & AROUND

The start of the Coral Coast begins in earnest at this condensed group of hotels flanking the water. Korotogo itself is a small village but travellers will find themselves outside of its confines. When sunny, the region is pretty, sparkling and pleasant. When overcast, the menacing skies provide an atmospheric respite if only for a couple of days. Korotogo is the best area to lodge when exploring the sights around Sigatoka.

On most parts of the coast the beach is tidal and, except for some lagoons, is only suitable for swimming and snorkelling at high tide. Sovi Bay, 2.5km east of Korotogo is OK for swimming; however, be careful of the strong channel currents.

Sights & Activities
KULA ECO PARK
This **wildlife sanctuary** (☎ 650 0505; www.fijiwild .com; adult/child $15/7.50; ☺ 10am-4.30pm) is a must

for fans of the furred, feathered and scaled. Supported by the National Trust for Fiji and several international parks and conservation bodies, the park showcases some of the country's magnificent wildlife, including hawksbill sea turtles (hand fed at 11am, 1pm and 3.30pm daily), musk parrots, collared parrots (the kula bird), goshawks, peregrine falcons, honeyeaters, fruit bats, raptors and owls. It also acts as an educational facility for schools and runs invaluable breeding programmes with success stories for the Pacific black duck (Fiji's only remaining duck species), and the crested and banded iguana.

All of this aside, ambling down the wooden walkway amid indigenous flora and fauna is a thoroughly enjoyable tourist excursion. A stream runs throughout the park in the wet season with plenty of bridge crossings.

DIVING
Coral Coast Scuba Ventures (☎ 652 8793; www.coral coastscuba.com), based at Shangri-La's Fijian Resort, takes dive trips to some of the Coral Coast reefs and passages around the area. A two-tank dive/PADI Open Water Course costs $230/670.

Tours
Adventures in Paradise (☎ 652 0833; www.adventures inparadisefiji.com; tours per person from Coral Coast/Nadi $100/120) Offers day trips to the Naihehe cave (see p145), and tours to the village of Biausevu and the Savu Na Mate Laya waterfall near Korolevu. Tours include a village visit, *kava* ceremony, lunch and transport. Its office is in a small group of shops just west of Outrigger on the Lagoon.
Rivers Fiji (☎ 345 0147) Offers great rafting trips up the Navua River and pick up from Coral Coast resorts. See p113 for more details.

Sleeping
BUDGET
Vakaviti (☎ 0800 650 0526, 650 0526; www.vakaviti .com; dm $15-20, r $70-80; ☒) Tumbling down a steep and densely vegetated embankment overlooking the water, Vakaviti is a small resort with a good variety of accommodation. Bright and modern motel rooms open onto a lovely pool area with wooden decking and a barbecue, and there are generous *bure* tucked amid the jungle, closer to the road. The dorms are spick and Spartan.

Casablanca Hotel (☎ 652 0600; fax 652 0616; s/d $45/64; ☒) This mock-Moroccan mansion run by the exuberant Mostafa offers self-contained rooms of varying size and quality. The interiors are a little dated and haphazard but comfortable nonetheless and each room has splendid views. The commodious family room has the most modern interior and a fabulous balcony. It's great value but ask to see a few rooms before you choose.

More budget options:

Dunrovin Lodge (☎ /fax 652 0235; dm/s/d $20/40/50) Small lodge with kitchen, TV room and laundry.

Crow's Nest Resort (right; dm $25) This midrange option also has a clean eight-bed dorm.

MIDRANGE

Tubakula Beach Bungalows (☎ 650 0097; www.fiji4less.com; dm $17.50, s/tw without bathroom $40/45, ste $80-120; ☒ ☎) If it weren't for the palm trees, swimming pool and waterfront setting, this low-key resort would be right at home in the mountains. Simple dorms, singles and doubles have shared facilities and the excellent A-frame chalets have strapping timber frames, modern kitchens and verandas with slouchy wooden seats. It's perfect for self-driving, self-catering, self-sufficient travellers, although there's a restaurant (p110) attached.

Sandy Point Beach Cottages (☎ 650 0125; cbcom@connect.com.fj; ste from $90; ☎) Tucked off the roadside and nestled into a tree-littered patch of the seaside, Sandy Point has five quaint and comfy self-contained cottages. The tropical setting is overshadowed somewhat by the proliferation of satellite dishes but these provide satellite TV. It's a peaceful setting and a favourite with in-the-know Suvanites.

Bedarra Inn (☎ 650 0476; www.bedarrafiji.com; r $110-155; ☒ ☎) This large white hotel offers spiffy rooms with tiled floors, spotless interiors and plenty of natural light. Budget rooms are fan-cooled, two-bedroom, self-contained and sleep up to four. The lofty deluxe rooms don't have kitchens but include balconies and air-con, although unless it's stifling the budget rooms are better value. There's also a restaurant (right) and small lounge bar with TV. It's a good option for those after a more intimate atmosphere than the larger resorts.

Totoka (☎ /fax 650 1083; d $100) This wee B&B has one charming double room with polished timber furnishings and plenty of character. It can accommodate a family of

four with an adjoining room and there's a lived-in central TV room and kitchen. It's quiet and homely.

Crow's Nest Resort (☎ 650 0230; www.crowsnestfiji.com; dm $25, r $135-145; ☒ ☎ ☐ ☎) This well-ordered resort offers split-level timber bungalows with lovely balconies and views but slightly tired and mismatched interiors. Each is self-contained and large enough to sleep a family but some of the kitchens look precolonial. There's a restaurant (see p110) and there are Fijian dancing shows every Saturday night.

TOP END

Outrigger on the Lagoon (☎ 650 0044; www.outrigger.com/fiji; r from $590; ☒ ☎ ☐ ☎) Huge, five-star and sassy, the Outrigger has stylish rooms in the four-storey main building with balconies or verandas, and superb views over the resort grounds and coral reef. Fanned out amid the lush beachfront gardens are fabulous *bure* (from $1020), which have high ceilings lined with hand-painted *masi* cloth. Facilities include three restaurants, bars, a nightclub and child-minding. There is a Fijian fire-walking show (per person $20) every Tuesday night (nonguests welcome).

Eating

Bedarra Inn Restaurant (☎ 650 0476; Bedarra Inn; mains $15-30; ☺ lunch & dinner) This hotel restaurant serves the best food in the area. Inventive steak, chicken and stir-fry dishes are on the menu as well as perfectly cooked, fresh seafood. You can dine in the atmospheric restaurant or at the poolside tables, which offer great ocean views.

Ice Bar Restaurant (☎ 650 1513; Queens Rd; mains $10-20; ☺ breakfast, lunch & dinner) Delicious seafood and Indian curries are served in this open-air eatery with wooden bench tables and seating. It's attached to a small supermarket and while the setting is utterly unsophisticated, the food is excellent.

Le Café (☎ 652 0877; Queens Rd; mains $10-15; ☺ breakfast, lunch & dinner) Just west of the shops; Le Café has a Swiss chef Jean Pierre, who cooks European-style food, although tasty pizzas are the speciality. There's also a nightly happy hour from 5pm to 7pm.

Outrigger on the Lagoon (above) has several dining options including the **Baravi Bar** (☎ meals $15-25; ☺ lunch & dinner), which serves a Mongolian barbecue for lunch and pasta at

FIRE WALKING

Of all Fiji's cultural rituals, the extraordinary art of fire walking is perhaps the most impressive. Watching men display the poise of a lead ballerina while they traverse a pit of blazing embers without combusting is truly baffling. Even more mystifying is the fact that, originally, this ritual was practised in Fiji only on the tiny island of Beqa, and by two neighbouring and disparate cultures for completely different reasons. Perhaps there's simply something in the water.

Fijian

Indigenous Fijian fire walking is known as *vilavilairevo* (literally 'jumping into the oven'). The ability to walk barefoot on white-hot stones without being burned was, according to local legend, granted to a local chief by the leader of the *veli*, a group of little gods. Now the direct descendants of the chief *(tui qalita)* serve as the *bete* (priests) who instruct in the ritual of fire walking.

Preparations for fire walking used to occupy a whole village for nearly a month. Firewood and appropriate stones had to be selected, costumes made and various ceremonies performed. Fire walkers had to abstain from sex and refrain from eating any coconut for up to a month before the ritual. None of the fire walkers' wives could be pregnant, or it was believed the whole group would receive burns.

Traditionally *vilavilairevo* was only performed on special occasions in the village of Navakaisese. Today, though, it's performed only for commercial purposes and has little religious meaning. There are regular performances at the Pacific Harbour Arts Village, at the larger resort hotels, and at Suva's annual Hibiscus Festival.

Hindu

The Hindu fire walking is part of an annual religious festival coinciding with a full moon in July or August and lasts 10 days. It takes place at many temples in Fiji, including the Mariamma Temple (Map p119) in Suva.

Preparations for the ceremony are overseen by a priest and take three to 10 days, with the fire walking the climax of the ritual. During this period participants isolate themselves, abstain from sex and eating meat, and meditate to worship the goddess Maha Devi.

The participants rise early, pray until late at night, survive on little food or sleep and dress in red and yellow, which symbolises the cleansing of physical and spiritual impurity. Yellow turmeric is smeared on the face as a symbol of prosperity and power over diseases.

On the final day the participants at the Mariamma Temple bathe in the sea. The priests pierce the tongues, cheeks and bodies of the fire walkers with three-pronged skewers. The fire walkers then dance into an ecstatic trance for about 2km back to the temple for the fire walking; their altered state enabling them to perform the feat.

Devotees' bodies are whipped before and during the ceremony. If fire walkers are focused on the divine Mother they should not feel pain.

A decorated statue of the goddess is placed facing the pit for her to watch and bless the ceremony. It only takes about five seconds to walk along the pit, which is filled with charred wood raked over glowing coals, and the walk is repeated about five times to chanting and drumming.

Hindu fire walking is a religious sacrament performed mostly by descendants of southern Indians. They believe life is like walking on fire; discipline helps them to achieve a balanced life, self-acceptance and to see good in everything.

night; and the elegant **Ivy Restaurant** (mains $20-35; ☽ dinner), which caters only to adults and serves exquisite and contemporary fare.

More hotel restaurants:

Tubakula Beach Bungalows (☎ 650 0097; meals $8-17; ☽ breakfast, lunch & dinner) Burgers, steaks and sandwiches.

Crow's Nest Resort (☎ 650 0230; mains $15-30; ☽ lunch & dinner) Serves good, if overpriced food from a cosmopolitan menu.

Getting There & Around

Pacific Transport and Sunbeam Transport run regular buses along the Queens Road, stopping at resorts along the way (about $5 from Nadi, 1½ hours). Coral Sun Fiji has air-conditioned coaches that also stop outside resorts ($8 from Nadi, 1½ hours). There are also local buses that are slightly cheaper but take longer. A taxi from Korotogo to Siga-toka is $5, and around $45 to Nadi.

KOROLEVU & AROUND

Further east, the section of the Queens Road between Korotogo and Korolevu is the most beautiful. The road winds along the shore, with scenic bays, beaches, coral reefs and mountains; photo opportunities beg around every bend. It's an especially spectacular trip at sunrise or sunset. A good range of places to stay pepper the coast, each pocketed within their own private cove.

In the village of Vatukarasa, west of Korolevu, **Baravi Handicrafts** (☎ 652 0364; ☽ 7.30am-6pm Mon-Sat, 8.30am-5pm Sun) is a souvenir shop that sells local crafts, clothes and jewellery.

East of Korolevu, the Queens Road turns away from the shore and climbs over the southern end of Viti Levu's dividing mountain range. To the east of this range the road improves and the scenery changes to lush rainforest as the road winds its way past wider bays.

Activities

Take care while swimming; currents can be dangerous and there have been drownings near here. At Hideaway Resort (see p112) there is a right-hand **surfing** break for experienced surfers at the passage about 100m from the shore – the best chances of good surf are between January and May. It is also possible to surf offshore from Waidroka Bay Resort (opposite) and at Frigates Passage in the Beqa Lagoon.

The turn-off to the village of **Biausevu** is about a 15-minute drive east of Hideaway Resort. The village is 2.5km inland, and a waterfall is an easy 15- to 30-minute walk from the village. See p36 for information on village etiquette.

Adventures in Paradise (☎ 652 0833) has trips into the interior, including to Biausevu, from Korolevu; see p107.

Rivers Fiji (☎ 345 0147) offers great rafting trips; see p113 for details.

The Coral Coast offers some spectacular **diving** within close distance to the shore and it's a good place to learn. Votua Reef is home to some notable sites including Morgan's Wall, which is popular with barracuda,

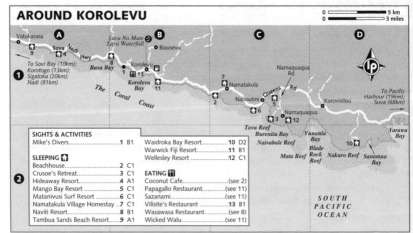

AROUND KOROLEVU

0 —— 5 km
0 —— 3 miles

Vatukarasa · Ⓐ
Savu Na Mate ☽ Ⓑ
Lava Waterfall ○ Biausevu
Ⓒ
Ⓓ

Suva Nadi Hwy
9
4
8
To Sovi Bay (10km);
Korotogo (13km);
Sigatoka (20km);
Nadi (81km)
Busa Bay
Korolevu ⓐ
1 ⓕ 13
Korolevu ⓐ
Bay 11
7
Namatakula ⓕ
Namaquaqua
Rd
Namaquaqua Rd
To Pacific
Harbour (19km);
Suva (68km)

Ⓛ Ⓟ

The Coral Coast
Naboutini ○
Queens Rd
2 ⓕ
5
Korovisilou
12
3 ⓕ
Namaquaqua
6 ⓕ

Tovu Reef
Burenitu Bay
Naivabale Reef
Vunaniu
Bay
10 ⓕ
Yarawa
Bay
Blade
Mata Reef Rock Nakuro Reef Sanamua
Reef
Bay

SOUTH
PACIFIC
OCEAN

SIGHTS & ACTIVITIES	
Mike's Divers	1 B1

SLEEPING ⓕ	
Beachhouse	2 C1
Crusoe's Retreat	3 C1
Hideaway Resort	4 A1
Mango Bay Resort	5 C1
Matanivusi Surf Resort	6 C1
Namatakula Village Homestay	7 C1
Naviti Resort	8 B1
Tambua Sands Beach Resort	9 A1

Waidroka Bay Resort	10 D2
Warwick Fiji Resort	11 B1
Wellesley Resort	12 C1

EATING ⓕ	
Coconut Cafe	(see 2)
Papagallo Restaurant	(see 11)
Sazanami	(see 11)
Vilisite's Restaurant	13 B1
Wasawasa Restaurant	(see 8)
Wicked Walu	(see 11)

sea fans and lionfish. **Mike's Divers** (☎ 653 0222; www.dive-fiji.com) is based in the area and offers a two-tank/PADI Open Water Course for $150/600. It picks up from most places around Korolevu.

Sleeping
BUDGET

Beachhouse (☎ 0800 653 0530, 653 0500; www .fijibeachouse.com; camping per person $16, 4-/3-/2-bed dm $25/28/30, d $80; ✗) A mammoth budget spread, this place welcomes backpackers with simple digs and heady social activity. Dorms are in two-storey houses and the doubles are colourful duplex bungalows. All facilities are shared. Activities include horse riding ($15 per hour) and a recommended waterfall trek ($5), for which sandals are a must. Travellers lounge under coconut trees on the pleasant beachfront area and move to a small deck close to the water to sit and drink at sunset or night. The Coconut Cafe (p112) serves good lunches.

Namatakula Village Homestay (www.fijibure.com /namatakula/index.htm; per adult/child incl meals $70/35) This village homestay is about as close as you'll get to the real deal. Simon and Judith Batibasaga welcome travellers into their home and afford them an insight into village life. The accommodation is simple and the meals generous but the real payoff is the opportunity to visit the school, attend a mass and immerse yourself in a traditional village.

Waidroka Bay Resort (☎ 330 4605; www.waid roka.com; dm $22, d $100-155) This resort has seen more owners than a New York penny in recent years and the dorms and atmosphere could use a little TLC, but the majority of clientele are surfers and they don't seem to mind. The fan-cooled oceanfront *bure* are comfortable, though, and each has a veranda facing the water. There's a communal TV lounge and restaurant (meals about $10; open for lunch and dinner) serving hearty meals. It's best suited to avid divers – Waidroka has its own dive setup (1-/2-tank dive $105/175) – bird-watchers and surfers, although the latter will need to pay $60 per day for transfers out to Frigate Passage.

Transfers for up to four people cost $15/ 110/100 from either Korovisilou village/ Nadi/Suva.

MIDRANGE

Tambua Sands Beach Resort (☎ 650 0399; www .tambuasandsfiji.com; d $155-170; ✆) Smeared across a pretty slice of coast, this friendly resort will suit intrepid travellers looking to indulge. *Bure* are beachside or oceanview; the latter are pricier but dressed up like chic holiday flats and better value. All *bure* have plenty of window space to let the breeze in. The manicured lawns are littered with sun lounges and there of plenty of activities on offer. The restaurant (mains $15 to $30; open for breakfast, lunch and dinner) has a good à-la-carte menu.

Mango Bay Resort (☎ 650 1565; www.mangobay resortfiji.com; dm $40, r $150-220; ✆) This resort was in the making at the time of research. It promises a seven-bed dorm, safari tents that can sleep up to three and Fijian *bure* with atrium showers and verandas. It seeks to target the 18- to 35-year-old set with full moon parties, cocktails and sunset bonfires and will probably do quite a good job of it.

Waidroka Bay Resort (d/tr bure $100/140) There are comfortable, fan-cooled, oceanfront *bure* at this budget resort (see left).

TOP END

Crusoe's Retreat (☎ 650 0185; www.crusoesretreat .com; r incl breakfast $240-280; ✆) Blessed with one of the Coral Coast's most sublime locations, this small resort is hidden by a lush plummet of hills and boasts a white, secluded beach. Scattered around the colourful grounds are 28 spacious and fan-cooled *bure* with polished Fijian interiors. There's a tennis court and a restaurant (mains $15 to $25; open for breakfast, lunch and dinner) serving classy fare. **Dive Crusoes** (www.divecrusoes.com) charges $210/680 for a two-tank dive/PADI Open Water Course. Return transfers to the resort from Nadi or Suva cost $75/150 one-way/ return.

Naviti Resort (☎ 653 0444; www.navitiresort.com .fj; r $320-340, ste $570; ✗ ✆ ✆) Heavy on the greenery and light on the concrete, the colossal Naviti is about as pretty as large-scale resorts go. Like all five-star joints the rooms are packed with amenities and very comfortable, but it's the health spa, nine-hole golf course, kids' club, copious activities and excellent service that distinguish it from the rest. It has good access for the disabled.

Warwick Fiji Resort (☎ 653 0555; www.warwick fiji.com; s & d incl breakfast $350-550, ste incl breakfast

$740; ⊠ ⊠ ⊠) This five-star and suitably fabulous resort has panoramic views, glossy rooms, five restaurants and bars, two pools, a nightclub and gym, and free kayaking, snorkelling and windsurfing. It's family friendly and you won't need to think about a thing.

Hideaway Resort (☎ 650 0177; www.hideaway fiji.com; d/tr $320-510; ⊠ ⊠ ⊠ ⊠) A package-holidayers' stomping ground, this expansive resort teems with American, Australian and New Zealand families and couples. Accommodation ranges in size and price from tidy and classy 'frangipani *bure*' to cavernous two-bedroom villas. The meticulous grounds include man-made sand alcoves and plenty of grassy sunbaking plots, and there's a superfluity of cruise ship–like entertainment and activities to slake stimulus junkies. The three-course meal plan is $75 per person per day and this place is super child-friendly.

Wellesley Resort (☎ 650 0807; www.wellesley resort.com.fj; Man Friday Rd; d incl meals from $280; ⊠ ⊠ ⊠) This brand new boutique resort has 15 lavish suites, world-class cuisine and a stunning location. It's definitely one for the couples.

Matanivusi Surf Resort (☎ 992 3230; www.surfing fiji.com; d per person incl meals $400; ⊠) Another new five-star option in the making, Matanivusi is planted right on a lagoon and should be an opulent ecoretreat for avid surfers and divers. It has access to three right-hand breaks that are about a 10-minute boat ride into the lagoon, and surfers can also be taken to Frigates Passage. Nonwater babies will be just as welcome and pampered. Rates will include all meals, transfers, surfing and snorkelling.

Eating

Vilisite's Restaurant (☎ 653 0054; Queens Rd; mains $20-45; ☯ breakfast, lunch & dinner) Dripping in tropical garb in front of sweeping ocean views, Vilisite's is the nicest restaurant in the area outside of the flashy resorts. Plentiful quantities of fresh seafood dishes including king prawns, lobster, octopus and seafood curries are dished up in large quantities by uberfriendly staff.

Coconut Cafe (☎ 653 0500; meals $4-9; ☯ breakfast, lunch & dinner) Based at the Beachhouse (p111), this casual restaurant serves a set dinner each night plus fresh and tasty pitas, rolls and smoothies for lunch. It's a nice place to stop for a lunch or snack break but

dinner is essentially a guest-only affair and needs to be ordered by 4pm.

Visitors are welcome at the larger resorts' restaurants. The first three below are at the Warwick Fiji Resort, see p111.

Papagallo Restaurant (mains $15-25; ☯ dinner) Good pizza and pasta.

Sazanami (mains $15-30; ☯ dinner) Japanese cuisine including teppanyaki grills.

Wicked Walu (mains $25-35; ☯ dinner) Excellent steaks and seafood; reservations recommended.

Wasawasa Restaurant (Naviti Resort, p111; meals $35; ☯ dinner) International themed buffet nights.

Getting There & Around

There are plenty of buses shuttling along the Queens Road (getting to Suva or Nadi costs about $6) and drivers will pick up and drop off at resort gates. The Warwick and the Naviti have a free shuttle bus for guests going between the resorts and Nadi International Airport. Taxis to the airport cost about $85/95 one way/return for the 1½-hour ride, or $20 for the 20-minute drive to Sigatoka.

PACIFIC HARBOUR & NAVUA

Leaving the glorious vegetation and hilly passes of Korolevu in your wake and entering Pacific Harbour is a bit like dipping your toes into the Twilight Zone. The widely spread cul-de-sac streets, flawless lawns and ordered river setting are more 'soccer mum and bridge parties' than anything Fijian. The town started as a planned, upmarket housing and tourism development, and although the large grassy blocks are brochure-perfect, many are still waiting to be filled with the anticipated boom. For visitors the attraction lies outside the sleepy town. Offshore, Beqa (pronounced *ben*-ga) Lagoon has world-class diving and an awesome surf break and inland are the spectacular Namosi Highlands (p146) with opportunities for kayaking and white-water rafting.

The small but lively town of Navua, on the banks of the wide Navua River, is 39km west (a 20-minute drive) from Suva and 143km from Nadi. Early in the 20th century, sugar cane was planted here and a sugar mill built, but this activity ceased as the drier western region proved more productive. Farmers of the delta region then turned to dairy farming, cattle grazing, rice and other crops. Many of the old buildings in the town date from the beginning of the 20th century.

Sights & Activities

ARTS VILLAGE

This faux **village** (☎ 345 0065; www.artsvillage.com; tours per adult/child from $35/18; ⏱ 9am-4pm Mon-Sat) is unashamedly 'Fiji in a theme park', but it still draws the tour buses in by the convoy. Within the Disneylike confines are a temple, chief's *bure*, cooking area with utensils and weaving hut. Fijian actors dressed in traditional costumes carry out a mock battle. Tours include an Island Boat Tour (one for the kids), Island Temple Tour and Arts Village Show. There's also a fire-walking and *meke* show every Thursday (per adult/child $45/25; 11am). It's good fun for families but a far cry from authentic village life.

MARKETPLACE

Attached to the Arts Village, the Marketplace is a modern congregation of eateries and souvenir shops selling Fiji-style resort wear and some very good but pricey handicrafts. New shops are springing around this area all the time; at the time of research a shop renting scooters and mountain bikes was being touted. It's a pleasant spot to mill about for an hour or so.

For superb views of Beqa Lagoon take a sunset or sunrise walk up to the hilltop.

GOLF

Greens South Pacific (☎ 345 0022; 9-/18-holes $20/40) is a gorgeous, 18-hole golf course designed by Robert Trent Jones Jr, who has designed more than 200 courses around the world. The proliferation of bunkers and canals is a challenge for avid golfers. Club rental is $15/20 per nine-/18-holes.

DIVING

There are more than 20 dive sites near Pacific Harbour, mostly within Beqa Lagoon. Based at the Pearl South Pacific (p114), **Aqua-Trek Beqa** (☎ 325 0324; www.aquatrek.com) is one of the best diving operations in the area. A two-tank dive/PADI Open Water Course costs $170/700. Keen divers can take advantage of 10 dives for $750. Aqua-Trek also operates shark-feeding dives ($200 for two dives), which get rave reviews from readers.

Beqa Adventure Divers (☎ 345 0911; www.fiji-sharks.com) also has shark-feeding dives (see p58 for details). The **Pacific Safari Club** (River Dr; see p114) has a small diving outfit. A two-tank dive costs $95.

FISHING

Xtasea Charters (☎ 345 0280; www.xtaseacharters .com) operates fishing charters on a cruiser for up to six people including gear and tackle for $1540. The vessel can also be charted for day cruises (price on inquiry).

SURFING & SWIMMING

There is first-class surfing at Frigate Passage and surf camps on Yanuca island (p116). The beach at Deuba is reasonable for swimming.

VILLAGE VISITS

There are market boats and local buses to/from Namuamua and Nukusere villages about 20km up the Navua River. The trip can take up to two hours, depending on the river's water level and general conditions. Before visiting a village, see the boxed text, p36.

Tours

Based at Pacific Harbour, **Rivers Fiji** (☎ 345 0147; www.riversfiji.com) offers excellent kayaking and white-water rafting trips into the Namosi Highlands (p146) north of Pacific Harbour. It is well organised and has excellent equipment.

The day trip to Wainikoroiluva (Luva Gorge) is highly recommended – fine for novices and those of average fitness. The scenery is well worth the two-hour bumpy trip by carrier up the hills to the Namosi Valley. At Nakavika village the chief and his family welcome you to their home for a chat, *kava* and a *sevusevu* (ceremony whereupon a gift is presented to the village chief). From here you paddle downstream (four hours) by inflatable kayak over stretches of gentle rapids and past waterfalls. At Namuamua village, where the river joins the Upper Navua to become the Navua River, you take a motorised longboat (1½ hours) to Nakavu or Navua. Food, drinks and equipment are included in the price (per person $190).

For gorgeous gorges and more advanced rapids try the day trip to the Upper Navua River (per person $260). It is more physically demanding and spends seven hours on the water. The one-hour road trip to Nabukelevu village is as rough as it is scenic, then it's all aboard an inflatable raft down to Wainadiro or Waimogi.

Discover Fiji Tours (☎ 345 0180; www.discoverfiji tours.com), based in Navua, has several tours

VITI LEVU

to the Navua River area. Tours include waterfall visits, 4WD trips, trekking, kayaking and white-water rafting and cost from $130/145 including transfers from Pacific Harbour/Suva. All tours last 10 to 12 hours and include lunch. Some also include *bilibili* (bamboo rafting). It also offers one- to three-day guided treks across the Namosi Highlands, camping overnight in villages.

Wilderness Ethnic Adventure Fiji (☎ 331 5730; www.wildernessfiji.com.fj) offers canoe tours to the Navua River, picking up passengers from Pacific Harbour as well as from Suva hotels.

Sleeping
BUDGET
Pacific Safari Club (☎ 0800 3450 498, 345 0498; www .pacificsafari.com; River Dr, Pacific Harbour; dm/d/f $20/55/65; ✕ ✿) This compact resort has a single-storey block of excellent self-contained flats with tidy, floral interiors and spotless kitchens. Some also have TVs. It's all fairly Westernised and is located in a convenient spot on the canal. There were expansion plans at the time of research.

Deuba Inn (☎ 345 0544; theislander@connect.com .fj; Queens Rd, Deuba; s/d without bathroom $20/35, r $55-65) Behind the outstanding Kai Yanuyanu restaurant (right) this inn has two self-contained units which are slightly shabby but roomy. One is significantly more comfortable so ask to see both if you can. Singles and doubles are in basic, portable-style units that are far more welcoming on the inside than the outside.

Coral Coast Christian Centre (☎ 345 0178; coral coastcc@connect.com.fj; Queens Rd, Deuba; s/tw from $12/21, d $45) It's frugal and strict (no alcohol on the grounds thanks very much) but this school camp–like setup has medicinally clean accommodation in simple cabins with shared bathrooms and kitchens or self-contained motel units. There are also a children's playground and laundry facilities on-site.

Tsulu Bunkhouse & Apartments (☎ 345 0065; www.artsvillage.com; dm $26-30, d $68-98, 1-/2-/3-bedroom apt $150/300/600; ✿ 🖳 ✿) Attached to the Arts Village, the Tsulu had not opened its doors at the time of research but promises to be a place worth checking out. Its décor is island style, right down to the unique swimming pool and its swim-up bar. The doubles have air-con and shared kitchens; the more expensive ones also have

en suites and a balcony. The apartments have air-con, kitchen, room entertainment and balconies.

Navua Upriver Lodge (☎ 334 2549; navrest05@ yahoo.com; Nuku Village; dm/d incl meals $45/65) Situated about 25km north of Navua town, this Fijian-run lodge offers travellers a genuine river-village experience. Accommodation and food is simple and the surrounding environment is simply stunning. Call the lodge from Navua and they'll arrange a *bilibili* transfer (per person $15). The 1½-hour ride up the Navua passes some 20 waterfalls.

MIDRANGE & TOP END
Club Coral Coast (☎ 345 0421; clubcoralcoast@connect .com.fj; Lot 12 Belo Circle, Pacific Harbour; r without/with bathroom $40/90, f $120; ✕ ✿ ✿) Occupying it's own bend in the river, this petite resort has a series of split-level rooms with wicker furniture, sunny décor, kitchenettes and patios. Rooms with shared facilities are cosy and neat. Immersed in the leafy grounds are a small pool and tennis court.

Pearl South Pacific (☎ 345 0022; www.thepearl southpacific.com; Queens Rd, Pacific Harbour; r $300-360, ste $640; ✕ ✿ 🖳 ✿) Revamped and reworked with industrial-strength botox this is now one of Fiji's finest hotels. No expense is spared in the Fijian-Asian fusion rooms, which contain TV, phone, marble bathrooms, low-slung beds and private decked alcoves with cushioned sun lounges. The rest of the resort is littered with sueded box couches, oriental-style booths, vast open-air terraces, restaurants and bars backed by mirrored water features. Style gurus will overdose here.

Lagoon Resort (☎ 345 0100; www.lagoonresort .com; Fairway Pl, Pacific Harbour; r $160-260, ste $300; ✕ ✿ ✿) This grandiose hotel presides over the river like an engorged colonial estate. Pristine white, it has stately rooms with river views, balconies, TVs, fridges, phones and sumptuous marble bathrooms. The whole place is polished and elegant and staff are extremely friendly.

Eating
Kai Yanuyanu Restaurant (☎ 345 0544; Deuba Inn; Queens Rd, Deuba; mains $14-30; ⏲ breakfast & dinner) This humble dark horse serves outstanding seafood alongside curries, chicken and steaks. The interior is decked out with soft

lighting and chic beach-house décor. The fruit crushes are thick enough to make your straw stand on end.

Pastry Bure (☎ 345 0126; Arts Village Marketplace; meals $4-10; ☺ breakfast & lunch; ☒ ▣) The place to be for breakfast, this nifty little café cooks up delectable pancakes, sandwiches, quiches, muffins, croissants and other baked goodies with a fat side of happy vibes. Coffee addicts will appreciate the hot and strong brews here.

Lagoon Resort Restaurant (☎ 345 0100; Fairway Pl, Pacific Harbour; lunch mains $8-15, dinner mains $20-30; ☺ lunch & dinner) The Lagoon's regal restaurant serves hearty sandwiches and curries for lunch and fancy dinner mains such as char-grilled *mahi mahi* (a local fish), beef tornadoes, and angel-hair pasta with prawns. Seating is at high-backed chairs and the floor-to-ceiling windows provide ample vistas of the green lawns.

Oasis Restaurant (☎ 345 0617; Arts Village Marketplace; mains $10-30; ☺ lunch & dinner; ☒ ▣) Burgers, sandwiches, tortillas, curries and a whole lotta seafood is served at this atmospheric restaurant. Darkened wood tables and seating adorn the cool interior and there are bookshelves of second-hand books to pass the waiting time.

Fine dining options at the Pearl South Pacific (opposite):

Mantarae Restaurant (mains $25-35; ☺ dinner) Sophisticated cuisine and wine list.

Bistro (mains $15-25; ☺ lunch) Casual atmosphere and fare.

Self-caterers can stock up at the **supermarket** (Arts Village Marketplace).

Getting There & Around

Pacific Harbour is about an hour's express bus ride from Suva and around three hours from Nadi. There are frequent Pacific Transport and Sunbeam Transport buses travelling the Queens Road between Lautoka and Suva, as well as vans and carriers. The first bus from Pacific Harbour to Lautoka ($9.70, four hours) leaves at about 7.50am and the last at around 7pm. The first bus to Suva ($3.20, one hour) leaves at 10.35am and the last is at 10pm. A taxi to Suva costs $35; call **Ratan's Taxi** (☎ 346 0329). Ratan provides excellent commentary and manages to make friends out of every fare. Taxis to Nadi cost about $110.

The regular express buses along the Queens Road stop at Navua, 10km east of Pacific Harbour. They take about 50 minutes from Suva and about 3¼ hours from Nadi.

OFFSHORE ISLANDS

Offshore from Pacific Harbour, a 64km-long reef encloses the 360-sq-km **Beqa Lagoon** and the islands of Beqa and Yanuca. The lagoon has many famous dive sites: Side Streets (soft corals, coral heads and gorgonian fans); Frigate Pass (a 48m wall with large pelagic fish, including white-tip reef sharks); and Caesar's Rocks (coral heads and swim-throughs). See p58 for more details. Surfing is first-class at **Frigate Passage**, also known as **Kavu Kavu Reef**, southwest of Yanuca island. It has left-hand waves, which can get really big. The break has three sections, which join up under the right conditions: the outside take-off, a long, walled speed section with a possibility of stand-up tubes; and an inside section breaking over the shallow reef and finishing in deep water.

Beqa

The high island of Beqa (area 36 sq km), about 7.5km south of Pacific Harbour, is visible from the Queens Road and even from Suva. The island is about 7km in diameter with a deeply indented coastline and a rugged interior with ridges averaging 250m and sloping steeply down to the coast. The surrounding coral reef is famous for its dive sites. Beqa has two upmarket resorts, one budget resort and eight villages. The villagers of Rukua, Naceva and Dakuibeqa are known for their tradition of fire walking.

Formerly the Marlin Bay, **Beqa Lagoon Resort** (☎ 330 4042; www.beqalagoonresort.com; 4-/5-/ 7-nights per person from $1710/2050/2340; ☒ ▣) no longer appeals to the adult-only crowd and a change in mood comes courtesy of new two-bedroom *bure* designed specifically for families. Couples will still love the opulent bathrooms and interiors of the double *bure* though and the surrounding landscape and sea still lends itself to excellent snorkelling, kayaking, unlimited shore diving, hiking to waterfalls and village visits. There's a large restaurant-lounge *bure* serving fabulous food and a pool on a nice coconut tree–fringed beach. They resort charges $160 for a two-tank dive or two half-day surf lessons. Rates include all transfers from Nadi

THE AUTHOR'S CHOICE

Lawaki Beach House (☎ 992 1621; www
.lawakibeachhouse.com; camping $50, dm/s/d
$65/95/160) Aptly named, this small resort
sits in front of an isolated beach on the
southwestern side of Beqa island at Lawaki.
Comprising of two double *bure* with en
suites and verandas and a six-bed dorm,
the unobtrusive and cosy set-up blends
well with the surrounding environment.
Guests mingle together in the communal
TV lounge soaking up the relaxed mood.
There is good snorkelling off the secluded
pristine white-sand beach, as well as visits
to the nearby village and gorgeous sunsets.
Rates include three meals, and children
under 12 pay 15% less. The hospitality here
is legendary.

The resort offers transfers from Pacific
Harbour on a covered, aluminium boat
(one-way per person $130), which has its
own radio and life jackets. Alternatively
you can catch the small public ferry from
the Navua Jetty. The ferry usually leaves at
noon and 2.30pm on weekdays, and costs
$50 per person one way. You should call
the resort first to confirm one will be there.
Be aware that the ferry trip can be rough,
and depending on the weather, it may be
unsafe as they normally do not carry life
vests or a radio.

as well as meals and children are charged no
more than 50% of the adult rate, depending
on the package.

Two more five-star options:

Lalati Resort (☎ 347 2033; www.lalati-fiji.com;
7-night package per person from $2920; ✕ ⚑ ⚑) Intimate
and lavish – worth the splash. Rates include all transfers
and meals.

Kulu Bay Resort (www.kulubay.com; d 7-nights $2000;
✕) A five-star romantic hideaway. Rates include all
meals and most activities. Boat transfer from Pacific
Harbour is $65 per person.

Yanuca Island

Tiny Yanuca is a hilly speck inside Beqa
Lagoon, about 9km west of Beqa. It has
comely beaches, good snorkelling and is
close to the humbling breaks of **Frigates Passage**. Unsurprisingly it lures avid surfers,
many of whom come for a week, slip into
the lifestyle, and stay for a month. If living

in your swimmers 24/7 is your idea of bliss
then you've found utopia. The island has
two surf camps and one small village.

Batiluva (☎ 345 1019, 992 0019; www.batiluva
.com; dm/d incl meals $150/300) This long-standing
camp is the stuff of surfers' dreams. The
sturdy accommodation structure houses
three spotless and airy dorms as well as two
double rooms. Guests are ensured plenty of
space and comfort and the owners are extremely hospitable. 'Gourmet jungle meals'
are included in the tariffs and the food is
superlative. If any of the guests are successful in their fishing expedition their catch
is seared up for dinner or prepared into
perfect sushi. The beach here is quite pretty,
but for a good snorkel you need to go on a
short boat trip (free of charge). Daily boat
trips to the surf break are also included in
the price. Transfers from Pacific Harbour
are $50 return per person.

Yanuca Island Resort (☎ 336 1281, 997 8958; www
.frigatesreef.com; dm/s/d $40/70/120). Were Robin-
son Crusoe a surfer he'd bless his surf booties if he stumbled across this place. Run by
the softly spoken Wise, this simple camp is
etched into a protected, grassy groove of the
island. Guests here focus on surfing rather
than partying but the atmosphere is utterly
warm and friendly. The camp is staffed by
locals and financial gains provide a source
of income for the neighbouring village –
Yanuca. There is one dorm with solid timber
bunks and mosquito nets plus two cabins
with private bathrooms attached. Meals,
which are plentiful, tasty affairs (breakfast/
lunch/dinner $10/15/15), are served in an
open-air dining area. Snorkelling straight
off the tiny beach is good but most guests
head out to the reef on a daily basis. Boat
transfers to Frigates Passage cost $50 and
return transfers from Pacific Harbour are
$80 per person.

Vatulele
pop 950

The beautiful island of Vatulele (31 sq km)
is 32km south of Korolevu, off Viti Levu's
southern coast and west of Beqa Lagoon. It is
13km long and mostly flat, the highest point
being just 33m above sea level, with scrub
and palm vegetation. The western coast is
a long escarpment broken by vertical cliffs
formed by fracturing and uplifts. A barrier
reef up to 3km offshore forms a lagoon on

A SURFER'S GUIDE AT A GLANCE *Andrew Bock*

Aquamarine water and curling, coral-reef waves surround the Fijian islands. Fijian villages own the reefs and often lease surfing rights to select resorts. Individuals who want to surf without staying at these resorts need to observe Fijian custom, buy *kava*, and approach village chiefs for permission to surf. But, if you're so inclined, exploring will pay off in Fiji – there are many unsurfed waves. At these places, too, you will need to buy *kava*.

Most surf pitches over outer reefs, in passages, and is for intermediate to advanced surfers only. For these reefs, you need boats and guides. Marine safety can be lax so ask for oars, life jackets and drinking water, if not radio service, on board.

Southerly swells are consistent from May to October but there is surf year-round. The trade winds are southeast and off-shore at famous breaks. Northerlies, from November to April, are off-shore on the Coral Coast.

Booties are wise, sunscreen and rashies (wetsuits) essential and a compass helps. Good boards are scarce but **Fiji Surf** (☎ 670 5960; cnr Main St & Hospital Rd) in Nadi has everything – advice, lessons, tours and equipment.

See the relevant sections for more information on the major surfing locations below.

Viti Levu – Coral Coast
Beachhouse, Korolevu (p111) Has average rights.
Hideaway Resort (p112) A hollow, high-tide right.
Matanivusi Surf Resort (p112) Has exclusive access to several rights and all-day access to Frigates Pass.
Natadola Beach (p102) Beginner beach breaks and an outside left.
Sigatoka (p105) Has good beach breaks.
Waidroka Bay Resort (p111) Has access to Frigates Pass but only go out at high tide.

Viti Levu – Frigates Pass (Kavu Kavu Reef)
This reef has a world-class left, rarely crowded, 15km off Yanuca island. Some resorts on the mainland have access to Frigates (see above); from Beqa Lagoon access is from:
Batiluva resort (opposite)
Yanuca Island Resort (opposite)
Beqa Lagoon Resort (p115)
Waidroka Bay Resort (p111)

Mamanuca Islands
Breaks shared by budget mainland resorts such as Seashell Surf & Dive Resort (p101) and Rendezvous Beach Resort (p90) include Wilkes Passage – a fast, long right – Mini Clouds and Desperations. These breaks can get crowded. Other options:
Tavarua Island Resort (p157) Exclusive access to world-famous Cloudbreak and Restaurants. Approach Tavarua well in advance to join a public session on Saturday but it can be a lottery.
Namotu Island Resort (p157) Has Namotu Lefts and Swimming Pools.

Yasawas & Vanua Levu
Northerly swells are common from November to March, and hit reefs outside the northern Yasawas and Vanua Levu. Apart from the Great Sea Reef near Kia island, these regions remain unexplored.

Kadavu
King Kong lefts are exclusive to Nagigia Island Resort (p228). Surfable gaps in the Great Astrolabe Reef include Vesi, Naiqoro and Sosi Passages. Access is via Albert's Sunrise Resort or Matava Resort (p226).

Southern Lau group
Kabara island and many others have breaks, but there are no surf resorts and access is strictly by village permission.

the eastern and northern ends with two navigable passages at the northern end.

Vatulele has four villages and one exclusive resort. The villagers live mostly off subsistence farming and fishing and are one of Fiji's two main producers of *masi*. Vatulele has **archaeological sites**, including ancient rock paintings of faces and stencilled hands, and unusual geological formations, including limestone caves and pools inhabited by red prawns that are considered sacred.

Vatulele Island Resort (☎ 672 0300; www.vatulele .com; s/d from $1170/1740), an exclusive intimate-scale place, is definitely one of Fiji's best top-end resorts and with a price to match. The location is idyllic and the architecture stunning – a mix of thick, Santa Fe–style rendered walls with the lofty thatched roofs of traditional Fijian *bure*. The 18 open-plan, split-level villas are well spaced for privacy, each with an outdoor terrace and its own stretch of white-sand beach and turquoise lagoon. There are no excuses if you can't relax here! Gourmet meals, alcohol and most activities are included in the rate; dive packages and game fishing are available.

GETTING THERE & AWAY

Unless you are a resort guest or charter a boat, you are unlikely to visit this beautiful island. There is an airstrip and return transfers are by resort charter plane to Nadi ($700 per person return, 25 minutes).

SUVA

pop 358,500

If you've only come to Fiji for the islands and beaches then you best join the people on package tours and avoid Suva (pronounced *soo*-va) altogether. Nestled into a yawning harbour, this city is sticky with sweat and industry but it's Fiji's most concentrated confluence of ethnicities and cultures. Swimming in the urban milieu you'll discover the influence of every island and background.

Downtown is a jigsaw of colonial buildings, modern shopping plazas, abundant eateries and a breezy esplanade. Small passages transport you to a city somewhere in India with curry houses, sari shops and bric-a-brac traders. Dribbled along the hilly ascent behind the central business district are Suva's suburbs, some of which have the best urban views in the country. When the sun is out the city is relaxed and ambient and you can easily fill a couple of days visiting the sights and shopping.

Suva is Fiji's political and administrative capital and home to almost half of the country's population. It's also the largest city in the South Pacific and has become an important regional centre; students from the Pacific region and a growing expat community make up a significant chunk of the population. As with most cities, crime and poverty are factors to be aware of (see p121) and around half of Suva's inhabitants are crowded into settlements on land that has no title.

On a less serious but equally grey note, clouds tend to hover over Suva and frequently dump rain on the city (around 300mm each year). You may, however, find this a welcome relief to the heat and humidity that often cloak the city.

HISTORY

Suva's contemporary history has its roots in the fickle mismanagement of Chief Cakobau of Bau, who, with the help of King George of Tonga, proclaimed himself Tui Viti, or King of Fiji in the 1850s. Cakobau promptly took it upon himself to give away bits and pieces of Fiji to foreign settlers, while concurrently acquiring giant debts with American immigrants. By 1862 his inability to pay the debts off became apparent when he attempted to cede Fiji to Britain in exchange for debt clearance.

Up until this time, the only Europeans in the Suva area had come from Melbourne, seeking new sources of fortune after the decline of the gold rushes and subsequent downturn in the Australian economy. In 1868 the opportunistic Aussies formed the Australian Polynesia Company and agreed to clear Cakobau's debts with the Americans in return for the right to trade in Fiji and also a large chunk of land, 90 sq km of which covered the Suva Peninsula.

While it was not his land to trade, the powerful Chief Cakobau had the Suva villagers relocated and welcomed new Australian settlers to the area in 1870. The settlers cleared dense reed from what is now downtown Suva and attempted, unsuccessfully, to grow cotton and sugar cane. In an effort to increase land values, two Melbourne merchants, Thomson and Renwick, encouraged the government to relocate the capital from Levuka to Suva with incentives in the form of land grants. As Levuka had little room for expansion the government officially moved to Suva in 1882. In the 1880s Suva was a township of about a dozen buildings but by the 1920s it was a flourishing colonial centre.

In May 2000 Suva's Parliament Buildings became the site of a hostage drama when George Speight and his militia held 36 government officials captive for almost two months (see p33).

ORIENTATION

Suva is on a peninsula about 3km wide by 5km long, with Laucala Bay to the east and Suva Harbour to the west. Most of the

peninsula is hilly apart from the narrow strip of land on the western edge of the city where you'll find Suva's main drag, Victoria Pde, as well as the market and wharf.

The suburb of Toorak tumbles up onto the hill east of Suva Market. Originally Suva's posh neighbourhood (named after Melbourne's exclusive suburb), it has fallen from grandeur. In this area, Waimanu Rd passes the hospital in the northeast and then rolls down into town, becoming Renwick Rd at Nubukalou Creek and then Victoria Pde.

Victoria Pde holds many of the city's restaurants, shops and clubs. Heading south, it continues past the Government Buildings, Albert Park and to Thurston Gardens

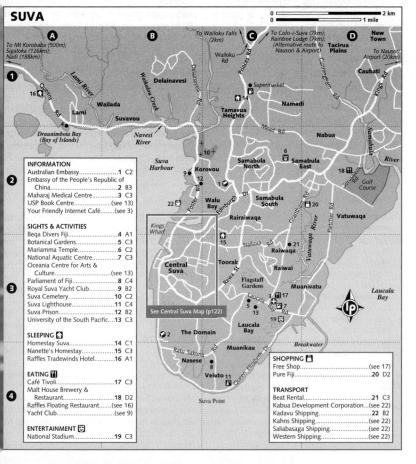

SUVA

INFORMATION
Australian Embassy.....................**1** C2
Embassy of the People's Republic of
China.....................................**2** B3
Maharaj Medical Centre.............**3** C3
USP Book Centre...................(see 13)
Your Friendly Internet Café.......(see 3)

SIGHTS & ACTIVITIES
Beqa Divers Fiji...........................**4** A1
Botanical Gardens.......................**5** C3
Mariamma Temple......................**6** C2
National Aquatic Centre..............**7** C3
Oceania Centre for Arts &
Culture.................................(see 13)
Parliament of Fiji.......................**8** C4
Royal Suva Yacht Club.................**9** B2
Suva Cemetery..........................**10** C3
Suva Lighthouse........................**11** C4
Suva Prison...............................**12** B2
University of the South Pacific...**13** C3

SLEEPING
Homestay Suva..........................**14** C1
Nanette's Homestay...................**15** C3
Raffles Tradewinds Hotel...........**16** A1

EATING
Café Tivoli.................................**17** C3
Malt House Brewery &
Restaurant.............................**18** D2
Raffles Floating Restaurant.......(see 16)
Yacht Club................................(see 9)

ENTERTAINMENT
National Stadium......................**19** C3

SHOPPING
Free Shop.................................(see 17)
Pure Fiji..................................**20** D2

TRANSPORT
Beat Rental..............................**21** C3
Kabua Development Corporation...(see 22)
Kadavu Shipping.......................**22** B2
Kahns Shipping.........................(see 22)
Saliabasaga Shipping.................(see 22)
Western Shipping......................(see 22)

See Central Suva Map (p122)

(and the museum). Beyond Albert Park, the road is renamed Queen Elizabeth Dr and heads out past Suva Point and around to the University of the South Pacific (USP) and National Stadium on the eastern side of the peninsula.

Drivers may find central Suva's one-way streets, angled intersections and contorted loops a bit challenging at first. There are three major roads in and out of the city: the Queens Road from Nadi; Princes Rd to the north (the scenic route to Nausori); and the Kings Road from Nausori and the international airport. The Kings Road meets Princes Rd closer to Suva, where it turns into Edinburgh Dr. Edinburgh Dr and the Queens Road converge at Walu Bay roundabout; if you're heading downtown, head south from here onto Rodwell Rd, which you can follow past the bus station and market, across Nubukalou Creek and into central Suva.

Maps

The **Fiji Visitors Bureau** (FVB; Map p122; cnr Thomson & Scott Sts) can provide a basic, photocopied map of Suva. For something more detailed, head around the back of the Government Buildings to the **Map Shop** (Map p122; ☎ 321 1395; Rm 10, Department of Lands & Surveys; ⊗ 8am-1pm & 2-3.30pm Mon-Thu, till 3pm Fri). It stocks a good map of Suva and the surrounding areas, as well as large survey maps of the rest of Fiji.

INFORMATION
Bookshops
Bookmasters (Map p122; ☎ 331 888; 173 Victoria Pde) Good range of guidebooks, paperbacks and more.

Fiji Museum (Map p122; ☎ 331 5944; www.fijimuseum .org.fj; Thurston Gardens; ⊗ 9.30am-4.30pm Mon-Sat) The gift shop stocks a good selection of Fijian books on history, cooking and birds.

Republic of Cappuccino (ROC; Map p122; Renwick Rd) A good café that has a book exchange.

Suva Bookstore (Map p122; ☎ 331 1355; Greig St) Children's books and Fijian and Indo-Fijian cookbooks.

USP Book Centre (Map p119; ☎ 321 2500; www.usp bookcentre.com; USP) Excellent selection of local and international novels, Lonely Planet guides, and Pacific nonfiction. Pricey but you can order online and it delivers.

Emergency
Ambulance (☎ 911)

Fiji Recompression Chamber Facility (Map p122; ☎ 999 3506, 885 0630; cnr Amy & Brewster Sts)

Police (Map p122; ☎ 911/331 1222; Pratt St)

Internet Access
Internet access is cheap and abundant in Suva.

Alpha Computer (Map p122; ☎ 330 0211; 181 Victoria Pde; per hr $6; ⊗ 8am-7pm Mon-Fri, 8am-4pm Sat, 10am-3pm Sun) Internet access and digital camera downloads to CD.

Connect Internet Café (Map p122; ☎ 330 0777; Post Office Bldg, 10 Thomson St; per hr $5; ⊗ 8.30am-8pm Mon-Fri, 9am-8pm Sat) Broadband access.

THE HEADSTRONG REVEREND BAKER

Thomas Baker, a Wesleyan Methodist missionary, was killed on 21 July 1867 by the Vatusila people of Nabutautau village (also known as Navatusila), deep in the isolated Nausori Highlands. A few years earlier Baker had been given the task of converting the people of the interior of Viti Levu to Christianity. Baker's predecessors had been able to convert many groups peacefully (and without becoming dinner), and he was advised to keep to these areas. But out of impatience, martyrdom, foolhardiness or the urge for success, he ignored the advice and with it crucial cultural know-how.

The highlanders associated conversion to Christianity with subservience to the chiefdom of Bau. As they were opposed to any kind of extended authority, knocking off the reverend may well have been a political manoeuvre. However, a second and more widely believed theory maintains that it was Baker's own behaviour that brought about his nasty end. Apparently, the local chief had borrowed Baker's comb to festoon his voluptuous hairdo. Insensitive or forgetful of the fact that the chief's head was considered sacred, Baker grabbed the comb from the chief's hair. Villagers were furious at the missionary for committing this sacrilege and killed and ate him in disgust. According to one local, his ancestors ate everything, 'even tried to eat his shoes', but one is now exhibited in the Fiji Museum.

In 2003, believing they had suffered a curse of bad luck as a result of their ancestors' culinary habits, the people of Nabutautau held a tribal ceremony to apologise to the descendants of the missionary. Around 600 people attended, including Thomas Baker's great-great-grandson and Prime Minister Lasenia Qarase.

Cyberzone (Map p122; ☎ 331 6967; Upstairs, 107 Victoria Pde; per hr $4.80; ☽ 24 hr) Slow access but always open.
Fintel (Map p122; ☎ 331 2933; 158 Victoria Pde; per hr $5; ☽ 8am-8pm Mon-Sat) Fast and reliable. Also sells telecards.
Your Friendly Internet Café (Map p119; ☎ 327 0166; Shop 7, Sports City Centre, Laucala Bay Rd, Laucala Bay; per hr $6; ☽ 8am-8pm Mon-Sat, 10am-6pm Sun)

Medical Services
Visits to general practitioners are usually $10 to $20.
Boulevard Central Pharmacy (Map p122; ☎ 330 3770; Shop 13, Downtown Boulevard Shopping Centre)
Boulevard Medical Centre (Map p122; ☎ 331 3355; dbmc@connect.com.fj; Downtown Boulevard Shopping Centre, 33 Ellery St) Excellent reputation.
Colonial War Memorial Hospital (Map p122; ☎ 331 3444; Waimanu Rd)
Fiji Recompression Chamber Facility (Map p122; ☎ 885 0630; recompression@connect.com.fj; cnr Amy & Brewster Sts)
Maharaj Medical Centre (Map p119; ☎ 327 0164; Sports City Centre, Laucala Bay Rd, Laucala Bay; ☽ 9am-1pm, 2-5pm & 6-9pm Mon-Fri, 9am-1pm Sat) Private medical centre.
Pharmacy Plus (Map p122; ☎ 330 5300; 190 Renwick Rd) Large and well-stocked pharmacy.

Money
ATMs are scattered along Victoria Pde. Some hotels provide foreign exchange but the rates are usually uncompetitive.
ANZ bank (Map p122; ☎ 132 411; 25 Victoria Pde) ATM and foreign exchange.
Money Exchange (Map p122; ☎ 330 3566; cnr Thomson & Pier Sts) Foreign exchange.
Westpac bank (Map p122; ☎ 132 032; 1 Thomson St) ATM and foreign exchange.

Post
Post office (Map p122; ☎ 330 2022; Thomson St)

Tourist Information
FVB (Map p122; ☎ 330 2433; www.bulafiji.com; cnr Thomson & Scott Sts) Friendly, knowledgeable and unbiased staff.
South Pacific Tourism Organisation (Map p122; ☎ 330 4177; www.spto.org; 3rd fl, Dolphin Plaza, cnr Loftus St & Victoria Pde) Promotes tourism in the region; the website has a travel directory.

Travel Agencies
See p261 for contact details of interisland ferry agencies and p135 for airline offices.
Hunts Travel (Map p122; ☎ 331 5288; fax 330 2212; 1st fl, Dominion House Arcade, Thomson St) Hunts can book domestic and international flights along with hotels and cars.

DANGERS & ANNOYANCES
Suva suffers many of the same dangers as most urbanised centres. Pickpockets roam; keep your valuables out of sight, particularly in crowded areas such as the market or on dance floors. Walking around during daylight hours is perfectly safe; however, as soon as night begins to descend it's a no go. From dusk onwards locals are smart enough to catch a taxi, even for a distance of 300m, so you should be as well. Taxis are metered, cheap and safe.

SIGHTS
Fiji Museum
In the heart of Thurston Gardens, this excellent **museum** (Map p122; ☎ 331 5944; www.fijimuseum .org.fj; Ratu Cakobau Rd; adult/child $7/5; ☽ 9.30am-4pm Mon-Sat) captivates visitors with a journey into Fiji's archaeological, political, cultural and linguistic evolution. Original examples of musical instruments, cooking apparatus, jewellery – including chiefs' whale-tooth necklaces, and a daunting array of Fijian war clubs and cannibal utensils imbue a vivid insight into traditional life. The growing influence of other South Pacific and European cultures on the Fijian islands is also demonstrated through exhibits on pottery, fishing methods and trade; while descriptions throughout bestow a heightened understanding and awareness of the country's customs and people.

Taking centre stage is the massive Ratu Finau (1913); Fiji's last *waqa tabus* (double-hulled canoe), which measures 13.43m in length and includes an enclosed deck for inclement weather. It's a spectacular feat of design and engineering.

The ground floor also contains a good book and souvenir and shop and upstairs, the small **Indo-Fijian Gallery** features magnificent works by the country's finest contemporary artists.

The museum continually undertakes archaeological research and collects and preserves oral traditions. Many of these are published in *Domodomo*, a quarterly journal on history, language, culture, art and natural history that is available in the museum's gift shop. It also organises craft demonstrations; contact the museum for times.

VITI LEVU

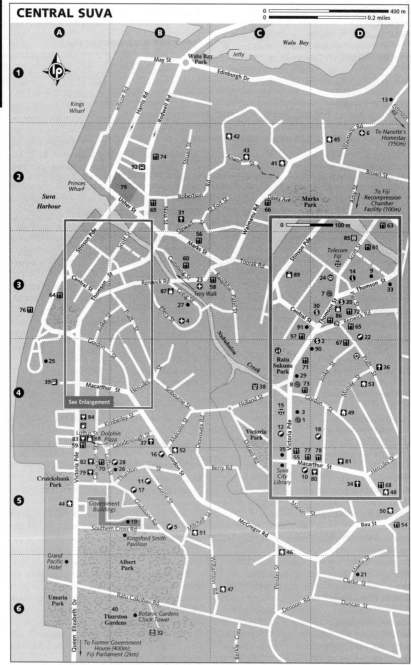

CENTRAL SUVA

INFORMATION
Alpha Computer.......................... **1** C4
ANZ Bank................................... **2** D4
Bookmasters............................... **3** C4
Boulevard Central Pharmacy.....(see 4)
Boulevard Medical Centre.......... **4** B3
British Consulate........................ **5** B5
Colonial War Memorial Hospital.. **6** D2
Connect Internet Café................ **7** D3
Cyberzone.................................. **8** C4
Dominion House Arcade............ **9** D3
Embassy of Nauru..................... **10** C5
Embassy of Tuvalu..................... **11** B5
European Union
    Representative...................... **12** C4
Fiji Disabled People's
    Association........................... **13** D1
Fiji Visitors Bureau (FVB).......... **14** D3
Fintel (Fiji International
    Telecommunications)............ **15** C4
French Embassy........................(see 9)
High Commission of Papua New
    Guinea................................. **16** B5
High Commission of Tuvalu...... **17** B5
Hunts Travel............................(see 9)
Japanese Embassy...................(see 9)
Korean Embassy......................(see 29)
Malaysian Embassy................... **18** D4
Map Shop.................................. **19** B5
Money Exchange....................... **20** D3
National Trust for Fiji **21** D6
New Zealand Embassy............... **22** D3
Pharmacy Plus.......................... **23** B3
Post Office................................ **24** D3
Registrar General's office.......... **25** A4
Representative of the Federated
    States of Micronesia............. **26** B5
South Pacific Tourism
    Organisation.......................(see 88)
Suva Bookstore......................... **27** B3
US Embassy............................... **28** B5
Vanua Arcade........................... **29** C4
Westpac Bank........................... **30** D3

SIGHTS & ACTIVITIES
Centenary Methodist Church.... **31** B2
Fiji Museum.............................. **32** B6

Garrick Hotel............................ **33** D3
Holy Trinity Cathedral.............. **34** D5
Old Town Hall........................... **35** C5
Roman Catholic Cathedral........ **36** D4
St Andrew's Church................... **37** B4
Shree Laxmi Narayan Temple... **38** C4
Suva Olympic Pool.................... **39** A4
Thurston Gardens...................... **40** B6

SLEEPING
Annandale Apartments............. **41** C2
Capricorn Apartment Hotel...... **42** C2
Colonial Lodge......................... **43** C2
Holiday Inn.............................. **44** A5
Motel 6.................................... **45** D2
Peninsula International Hotel.... **46** C5
South Seas Private Hotel........... **47** C6
Southern Cross Hotel................ **48** D5
Sunset Apartment Motel........... **49** D4
Suva Apartments...................... **50** D5
Suva Motor Inn......................... **51** B5
Tanoa Plaza Hotel..................... **52** B5
Town House Apartment
    Hotel................................... **53** D4

EATING
Aberdeen Grill.......................... **54** D5
Ashiyana...............................(see 35)
Bad Dog Cafe........................... **55** C5
Cakes 2000............................... **56** B3
Capital Palace........................... **57** C3
Curry House.............................. **58** C3
Daikoku Restaurant.................. **59** A4
Dolphin Plaza Food Court........(see 88)
Downtown Boulevard
    Shopping Centre................(see 4)
Focaccia Café........................(see 29)
Govinda's Vegetarian
    Restaurant........................... **60** B3
Harbour Centre......................... **61** D3
Headworks................................ **62** D3
Hot Bread Kitchen.................... **63** D2
Jardin..................................(see 3)
JJ's on the Park......................... **64** A3
Kahawa.................................... **65** D3
Korea House.............................. **66** C2
Lantern Palace.......................... **67** D4

L'Opera.................................... **68** D5
Morris Hedstrom Supermarket.. **69** B2
Old Mill Cottage....................... **70** A5
Palm Court................................ **71** C4
Pizza Hut...............................(see 77)
Republic of Cappuccino............ **72** D3
Republic of Cappuccino..........(see 88)
Sichuan Pavillion Restaurant...(see 33)
Singh's Curry House................. **73** C4
Supermarket............................. **74** B2
Suva Municipal Market............. **75** B2
Tiko's Floating Restaurant........ **76** A3
Victoria Wines & Spirits........... **77** C5
Zen Restaurant......................... **78** D5

DRINKING
Barn....................................... **79** A5
Birdland R&B Club................... **80** D5
O'Reilly's.............................(see 77)
Purple Haze Nighclub............... **81** D5
Shooters Tavern........................ **82** A5
Signals Night Club................... **83** A4
Traps Bar................................. **84** A4

ENTERTAINMENT
Village 6 Cinema Complex....... **85** D3

SHOPPING
Bob's Hook Line & Sinker........(see 61)
Boom Box..............................(see 4)
Government Crafts Centre........(see 10)
Jack's Handicrafts..................... **86** D3
Procera Music Shop.................. **87** B3
ROC Market.............................. **88** A4
Suva Curio & Handicraft
    Centre.................................. **89** C3
Wai Tui Surf..........................(see 71)

TRANSPORT
Air Fiji..................................(see 77)
Air New Zealand....................... **90** D4
Air Pacific................................ **91** C3
Bus Station............................... **92** B2
Consort Shipping Line.............(see 9)
Qantas..................................(see 91)
Sun Air..................................(see 71)
Taxi Stand............................(see 92)

Thurston Gardens

After visiting the museum, ponder on your new found knowledge with a wander through these compact but beautiful gardens (Map p122). The dense conglomeration of native flora and surrounding lawns are less manicured and more scattered haphazardly but heavy landscaping would detract from the tropical element. The colourful vegetation will generate appreciative murmurs from the casual visitor and much of the vegetation is also labelled for the benefit of avid horticulturalists. Crisscrossing walking trails traverse the park, and bench seating provides sensory-fatigue relief. It's a lovely spot for a picnic, particularly if you camp yourself under one of the grand and stately fig trees.

Parliament of Fiji

Opened in June 1992, the **parliament complex** (Map p119; ☎ 330 5811; www.parliament.gov.fj; Battery Rd; admission free) must be one of the world's most striking political hubs. Designed in post-1987-atmosphere, the aim of maintaining indigenous-Fijian values is apparent through the open-air corridors, traditional arts and structures and *masi* cloths throughout. The main building, *vale ne bose lawa* (parliament house), takes its form from the traditional *vale* (family house) and has a ceremonial access from Ratu Sukuna Rd. The complex is 5km south of the city centre. It's easiest to reach by taxi; however, you can hop on a bus along Queen Elizabeth Dr and walk along Ratu Sukuna Rd for 1km.

WINGING IT

Charles Kingsford Smith was the first aviator to cross the Pacific, flying in his little Fokker trimotor, *The Southern Cross*, from California to Australia. The longest leg of the flight was the 34-hour trip from Hawaii to Fiji. Suva's Albert Park, with its hill at one end and the Grand Pacific Hotel at the other, was made into a makeshift landing strip for his arrival. Trees were still being cleared after Smith had already left Hawaii. Kingsford Smith and his crew arrived on 6 June 1928, and were welcomed by a crowd of thousands, including colonial dignitaries who had gathered at the Grand Pacific Hotel to witness and celebrate this major event. Because the park was too short to take-off with a heavy load of fuel, Smith had to unload, fly to Nasilai Beach and re-load for take-off to Brisbane and Sydney. Kingsford Smith and his crew were presented with a ceremonial *tabua* (whale's tooth) as a token of great respect.

It's advisable to call ahead if you want to tour the grounds, but you can also obtain a visitor's pass from the guard at the main entrance. It's also possible to sit in on a parliamentary session by phoning in advance.

University of the South Pacific

With beautiful lawns and excellent facilities, the USP's **Laucala Campus** (Map p122; ☎ 331 3900; fax 330 1305) offers some picturesque strolling and fascinating people watching. This is the biggest of USP's campuses, and with more than 11,000 students it attracts attendees and staff from all over the South Pacific as well as the USA, New Zealand and Australia. Mingling among Fijian students you're likely to see young academics from the Cook Islands, Kiribati, Tonga, Vanuatu and Western Samoa. The university itself is jointly owned by the governments of 12 Pacific countries and is a fee-paying institution. Many students rely on scholarships for which the competition is fierce.

The campus is on the site of a New Zealand seaplane base and inside the northwestern entrance, on the right, is a small **botanical garden** with peaceful trails winding around Pacific trees and plants. You can also visit the **Oceania Centre for Arts & Culture**

where you can see temporary exhibits of paintings and carvings and sometimes even catch an artist at work. The Oceania Dance Theatre and other performance groups use the centre and you can usually catch a free rehearsal on weekday mornings. The centre also produces CDs of Fijian music with a modern twist.

The university's main entrance, off Laucala Bay Rd, is a 10- to 15-minute drive from downtown Suva. There are frequent buses to the USP: the Vatuwaqa bus departs opposite the Dominion House Arcade in Thomson St, near the FVB or you can hop on a Raiwaga bus from Victoria Pde. The taxi fare from the city is about $4.

Colo-i-Suva Forest Park

This lush rainforest **park** (☎ 332 0211; adult/child $5/1; ✆ 8am-4pm Mon-Sun), pronounced tholo-ee-*soo*-va, is a 2.5-sq-km oasis teeming with vivid and melodic birdlife and tropical flora. The 6.5km of walking trails navigate clear natural pools and gorgeous vistas, with just a touch of Indiana Jones in the rope swings over water and stone steps across streams. Sitting at an altitude of 120m to 180m, it's a cool and peaceful respite from Suva's urban hubbub.

Flowing through the forest is the Waisila Creek, which makes its way down to the Waimanu River and is the water catchment for the Nausori/Nasinu areas. The creek gives rise to natural swimming holes, and there are picnic tables, shelters and change rooms as well as a superb lookout. Dense patches of mahogany distinguish themselves from the native vegetation. Planted after a period of aggressive logging in the 1940s and '50s, they have stabilised the topsoil without impinging on the indigenous vegetation.

Among the wildlife are 14 different bird species, including scarlet robins, spotted fantails, Fiji goshawks, sulphur-breasted musk parrots, Fiji warblers, golden doves and barking pigeons.

Colo-i-Suva Forest Park is located 11km north of Suva on Princes Rd. The visitor information centre is on the left side of the road as you approach from Suva; buy your ticket here and then head to the entrance booth on the other side of the road. Before entering ask the guards about the security situation within the park. In recent years there have been some distressing attacks

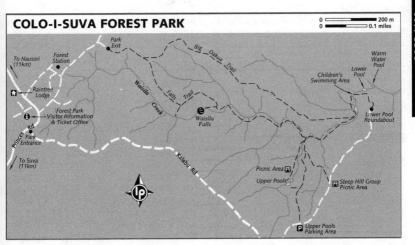

COLO-I-SUVA FOREST PARK

and as the park is open to the public, it's difficult to monitor who goes in and out. You can pay an additional fee (on asking) to have a guard accompany you and if travelling alone this is definitely recommended.

The park receives an annual rainfall of 420cm, with showers about four days each week. The trails can be extremely slippery so be sure to wear good footwear. If you drive out to the park, leave any valuables at the visitor information centre.

The Sawani bus leaves Suva bus station every half-hour ($0.65, 20 minutes). If driving, take Princes Rd out of Suva, past Tamavua and Tacirua villages.

Churches & Temples

Despite their cosmopolitan lifestyle, the majority of Suva's Indo-Fijians and indigenous Fijians are still very religious and dash off to temple or church on a regular basis. While few of these buildings are interesting in themselves, a couple are worth a gander if you're in the neighbourhood.

Just east of downtown, the bright orange-and-blue **Shree Laxmi Narayan Temple** (Map p122; Holland St) generally has a caretaker around to let you in for a look. The South Indian firewalking festival is held during July or August at the **Mariamma Temple** (Map p119; Howell Rd, Samabula). See p109 for details of this ceremony.

Holy Trinity Cathedral (Map p122; cnr Macarthur & Gordon Sts), with its unique boat-shaped interior, interesting Fijian tapestries and wood-beamed ceiling is a peaceful retreat.

The gigantic tree in front of the church is a showcase of Pacific plants with cacti and ferns making themselves at home in its branches. The 1902 **Roman Catholic Cathedral** (Map p122), at the corner of Murray and Pratt Sts is built of sandstone imported from Sydney and is one of Suva's most prominent landmarks; unfortunately, it's most often locked. For a rousing chorus of song on a Sunday morning, head to the **Centenary Methodist Church** (Map p122; Stewart St); the pitch is more invigorating than dulcet and it often fills the surrounding streets.

If you entered town via the Queens Road, you likely passed **Suva cemetery** (Map p119). Graves are dug by the inmates from the 1913 prison just down the road, and then decorated with bright cloth.

ACTIVITIES

Suva all but closes down on a Sunday so try to organise activities in advance or attend a Fijian church service to hear some uplifting, boisterous singing.

Trekking

Colo-i-Suva Forest Park is an easy place for bushwalking close to Suva (see opposite for details). You can also hike to Mt Korobaba, about a one- to two-hour walk from the cement factory near Lami. Joske's Thumb is an enticing spectacle for serious climbers; check with FVB about getting permission. A climb to this peak was featured in the film *Journey to the Dawning of the Day*.

Keen trekkers should contact the Rucksack Club for weekly walking adventures either inland or to other islands. Ask the FVB for the latest contact number because the membership changes regularly, as most of the 80 to 100 members are expats on contract in Fiji. The club hosts fortnightly meetings on Wednesday nights at St Andrew's Church (on Gordon St) in appreciation of Fiji's beauty and culture, with guest speakers and performers.

Swimming

The **National Aquatic Centre** (Map p119; ☎ 331 8185; Laucala Bay Rd, Laucala Bay; admission $3; ✆ 6am-8pm Mon-Sat year-round, 9am-6pm Sun Oct-Jun, 10am-6pm Sun Jul-Sep) was built for the 2003 South Pacific Games and includes a 50m and 25m pool. It's the best spot in Suva if you're looking to do some laps rather than just cool off.

Seldom crowded, the giant, outdoor **Suva Olympic Swimming Pool** (Map p122; 224 Victoria Pde; adult/child $1.65/0.80; ✆ 10am-6pm Mon-Fri, 8am-6pm Sat Apr-Sep; 9am-7pm Mon-Fri, 7am-7pm Sat Oct-Mar) is an oasis on a hot day. Entry is fantastically cheap; child entry is for age 13 and under. There is a kiddies' play area, lap lanes and change cubicles ($2 deposit). Keen lap swimmers can also attend the **USP's 25m pool** (Map p119; admission $2; ✆ 7am-6pm).

Between Suva and Colo-i-Suva, **Wailoku Falls** is not a good place for a dip as muggings are a *very* common occurrence.

The nearest decent beach is at Deuba, close to Pacific Harbour. It is a 50-minute drive from Suva, although by local bus it can take much longer. Alternatively, there are the freshwater pools at Colo-i-Suva Forest Park (p124).

Diving

Beqa Divers Fiji (Map p119; ☎ 336 1088; www.beqa divers.com; 75 Marine Dr, Lami) is about a 10-minute drive from Suva. It offers two-tank dives/PADI Open Water Courses to Beqa Lagoon for $145/550. This outfit also offers overnight trips including accommodation from $255, which includes return airport transfers, twin or double-share accommodation, two-tank dives and a picnic lunch.

The **Holiday Inn** (Map p122; ☎ 330 1600; Victoria Pde) can organise dive trips to Beqa Lagoon with Aqua-Trek (p113), based at Pacific Harbour.

Surfing

There is a surf-break near Suva lighthouse, accessible by boat; the **Fiji Surf Association** (☎ 999 7719) may be able to give some advice on how to get out there and on local conditions.

Sailing

Visiting yachties can get membership at the **Royal Suva Yacht Club** (Map p119; ☎ 331 2921; rsyc@connect.com.fj; ✆ office 8am-5pm Mon-Fri, 9am-1pm Sat). Mooring fees for a small yacht start at $40 per day. Prices for larger yachts depend on the size of the boat and length of stay. The club has bathrooms with hot water, and a laundry, which are open 24 hours a day. There's also a restaurant, an ATM and also a kid's playground. The **bar** (✆ 8am-10pm Mon-Thu, till midnight Fri & Sat) here is a popular watering hole for yachties and locals and has great views of the Bay of Islands and the mountains, including Joske's Thumb. Even without a yacht, overseas visitors are welcome and can be signed in. The notice board in the clubhouse is a good place to find boats looking for crew.

WALKING TOUR

Downtown Suva has a scattering of colonial buildings and places of interest in between the shops and office blocks, making it a pleasant place to wander around. Give yourself several hours for this tour, taking lunch and other pit stops into consideration.

Start your pedestrian journey on Stinson Pde at the **Suva Curio & Handicraft Centre** (**1**; p134). Have a good look around but don't make any purchases yet – there are a few more shops on the itinerary. Cross to the opposite side of the street and follow the esplanade south, taking in the gorgeous views of Suva Harbour and Joske's Thumb. Once you reach **Tiko's Floating Restaurant** (**2**; p131), one of Suva's finest eateries, cross the road and amble through the tree-lined **Ratu Sukuna Park** (**3**) to Thomson St. Continue south down Victoria Pde, past the pale, colonial 1926 **Fintel building** (**4**) and the 1904 **old town hall** (**5**). Now home to several restaurants, the old town hall building was once used for dances, bazaars and performances. The **Suva Olympic Pool** (**6**) is set back between this building and the 1909 **Suva City Library** (**7**).

Continue down Victoria Pde. On your left hand side are the stately **Government Buildings**

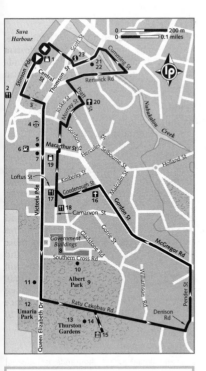

WALK FACTS

Start Stinson Pde
Finish Stinson Pde
Distance 3.5km
Duration two to four hours

(8), built between 1939 and 1967. Presiding over the manicured green lawns are statues of Ratu Cakobau and Ratu Sukuna. In the block south of the Government Buildings is **Albert Park (9)**, a large sporting field where you can often catch rugby union teams in action or training. The park is named after Queen Victoria's husband and was given to the Fijian Government by the Australian Polynesia Company as an incentive for moving the capital to Suva. Towards the back of the park are a cricket ground and tennis courts. The **Kingsford Smith Pavilion (10)**, named after the famous aviator who landed here is on Southern Cross Rd. On the seaside opposite the park is the glorious old **Grand Pacific Hotel (11)**. Built in 1914 by the Union Steamship Company, its ship-style architecture is remi-

niscent of the luxury liners that once plied the seas. The splendid white façade hints at the hotel's former glory but it has remained abandoned and in a continuing state of decay since closure in 1992. A string of redevelopment plans and backers have failed to prove fruitful but in 2005 a joint venture by the Fiji National Provident Fund and the Fiji Investments Corporation promised to restore the Grand Pacific to its former position of top billing among Suva's hotels.

Just past Ratu Cakobau Rd you'll stumble across **Umaria Park (12)** where you can take a breather. If you've got kids in tow they'll enjoy scrambling over the colourful monkey bars and playground. A scattering of concrete picnic tables and benches make this a popular spot for picnicking families on the weekend.

Cross the road at the corner of Ratu Cakobau Rd and Queen Elizabeth Dr and enter **Thurston Gardens (13**; p123). Meander through this colourful and balmy park, which was built in 1913 and named after Sir John Bates Thurston, an amateur botanist who introduced many ornamental plant species to Fiji. Within the grounds is the **Botanic Gardens Clock Tower (14)** and the **Fiji Museum (15**; p121).

Keep walking east along Ratu Cakobau Rd and climb into the escalating inner suburbs. Turn left at Pender St and left again at McGregor Rd. Amid the tranquil residential streets you'll find sweeping views of the city below. Continue along McGregor Rd, which turns into Gordon St and leads back to the city centre. Turn left at Goodenough St, with **St Andrew's Church (16)** on the corner. Follow Goodenough St and dog-leg onto Carnarvon St. If you need a pick-me-up drop into **Republic of Cappuccino (17**; p133) or head to the **Old Mill Cottage (18**; p131) for a traditional Fijian feast.

Stroll north past the bars and clubs of this little back road and duck into the **Government Crafts Centre (19**; p134) on Macarthur St. This small outlet sells some of the finest crafts in Fiji. Continue walking north along Carnarvon St, crossing Gordon St to Murray St. At the corner of Murray and Pratt Sts is the sandstone **Roman Catholic Cathedral (20**; p125), one of Suva's most prominent landmarks.

Turn left onto Pratt St and then right onto Renwick Rd. Window shop your way to Cumming St. Turn left to immerse yourself in Suva's little India, with curry houses, sari sellers, souvenir shops and the scent of incense thick in the air. In the 1920s this street was known for its *kava (yaqona)* saloons and 'dens of iniquity'.

Turn left onto Thomson St and make your way past the stately old **Garrick Hotel (21)**. Built in 1914, it's now home to shops and the **Sichuan Pavilion Restaurant (22**; p132). Make a right at the 1912 **FVB building (23)** and head towards the water and your starting point at the Curio & Handicraft Centre. If you've got any energy left spend it on a bout of souvenir shopping.

TOURS

Wilderness Ethnic Adventure Fiji (☎ 359 3230; www .wildernessfiji.com.fj) Offers several tours on the Navua River that pick up from Suva hotels. There are rafting and canoeing tours (per person $115), half- and full-day tours to Nasilai village (per person $60/85) and city tours of Suva that take in the Fiji Museum and bushwalking in Colo-i-Suva Forest Park (per person $70).

Discover Fiji Tours (☎ 345 0180; www.discoverfiji tours.com) Based in Navua, this outfit also offers canoe trips along the Navua River to a waterfall (see p113).

SLEEPING

Suva has some excellent budget accommodation, some good midrange motels and self-contained apartments and a couple of quality top-end options. There are also several dodgy places along the northern stretch of Robertson Rd that are the haunts of prostitutes and their clients; if you notice no other travellers and a lot of traffic, you may want to move on.

Budget

Raintree Lodge (Map p125; ☎ 332 0562; www .raintreelodge@connect.com.fj; Princes Rd, Colo-i-Suva; camping per person $12.50, dm $18-20, d $60-110; ⊠ ⚏ ⚏) Immersed in a lush rainforest with glassy lakes and prolific birdlife, this tranquil retreat has tidy bunk dorms in timber cottages and a two-storey cabin containing cosy doubles with ceiling fans, plump beds and a chunk of balcony with water views. A few stylish and intimate *bure* sleep four; all rooms have shared facilities. Activities on offer are abundant and there's a beautiful open bar and restaurant (p130).

HOME AWAY FROM HOME

On the outskirts of Suva, away from the flashy shops and colonial homes, thousands of people are living in settlements of tiny, corrugated-iron huts. These dilapidated settlements have little sanitation and often no water supply. In April 2002, more than 60,000 Fijians were landless and squatting, a number that is continuously climbing with the country's unsolved land issues.

Indigenous Fijians have traditional ownership rights to over 80% of the country's landmass, large tracts of which they've leased to Indo-Fijian farmers for the past century. However, with these leases coming to an end and ethnic friction heightened by recent political events, many indigenous landowners are turfing Indo-Fijian farmers off property where their families have lived for generations. Most Indo-Fijians are fleeing to the cities for safety. Unfortunately, with their livelihood gone, many families are ending up in suburban squatter settlements.

These impromptu, crowded towns are not strictly Indo-Fijian. The substantial pay cuts and rise in unemployment that have followed the country's coups have left many urban indigenous Fijians unable to pay the rent. Their only means of survival is also to head for the squatter settlements.

In 1994 the government of the day approved a policy to upgrade squatter settlements. Since then, many landless families have been promised resettlement, particularly evicted Indo-Fijians. However, the constant juggling of politics and politicians in Fiji has left many families squatting for more than a decade. Some have turned to begging and others attempt to sell crafts to tourists.

The Government does acknowledge the severe impact this issue has made on Fiji's social and economic fabric and between 2000 and 2005 around $11.3 million was spent on squatter resettlement, mostly in the form of estates (primarily around Lautoka) and new housing developments. Unfortunately, the proportion of squatters continues to outgrow the solution; a survey conducted by the Fijian Government's Squatter Resettlement Unit in 2005 concluded that some 90,000 people in Suva would be living as squatters by 2006. For the majority of these families, the immediate future continues to look dim.

The Tacirua Transport bus to Sawani passes the Raintree Lodge ($1, 20 minutes, half-hourly to hourly). Expect to pay about $12 for a taxi ride here from Nausori airport.

South Seas Private Hotel (Map p122; ☎ 331 2296; www.fiji4less.com; 6 Williamson Rd; dm $14, s/d/f $25/35/40; ✗) The sweeping interior veranda, classic white exterior and symposium of trees at this glorious old hotel will work the smile lines of any Pacific romantic. Clad in a sea of polished timber, the interior is reminiscent of a 1920s ocean liner and houses neat, simple and spacious rooms. Dorms have large steel bunks and all but one room has shared facilities. It doesn't see a huge amount of human traffic, which may be a plus or minus depending on your preference.

Colonial Lodge (Map p122; ☎ 330 0655; colonial lodge@connect.com.fj; 19 Anand St; dm $30, s $65, d without/with bathroom $80/90) Run by a friendly and boisterous family, this budget homestay is housed in a restored colonial bungalow with cheerful doubles upstairs, a large and airy dorm downstairs and a voluminous room with bathroom. Breakfast is included in the tariff and dinner is also available on request. There's a veranda where you can lounge in a hammock and it's close to the city centre.

Suva Apartments (Map p122; ☎ 330 4280; fasa noc@fasanoc.org.fj; 17 Bau St; s/d/tr from $45/60/75; ✗ ✗) Originally built to accommodate Fijian Olympians, this apartment block contains 20 modern and spotless units with fully equipped kitchens. You certainly get value for money and it's an excellent option for long stays, though the abundance of concrete and steel creates a slightly clinical ambience. It fills up quickly so bookings are advised.

Two good and central options with dated, but accommodating apartments:

Sunset Apartment Motel (Map p122; ☎ 330 1799; fax 330 3446; cnr Gordon & Murray Sts; dm/s/d from $12/45/55; ✗)

Town House Apartment Hotel (Map p122; ☎ 330 0055; townhouse@connect.com.fj; 3 Foster St; s/d $55/70; ✗)

Midrange

Suva Motor Inn (Map p122; ☎ 331 3973; www.hexagon fiji.com; cnr Mitchell & Gorrie Sts; d 110-175; ✗) Fab for families, the Suva Motor Inn is a little humble with its title. Smart and fresh studio and two-bedroom apartments contain sunny furnishings, modern kitchens (including microwaves) and enough room to accommodate a wee troupe. All rooms have balconies (ask for one with Albert Park views) and the water slide attached to the central pool is a kid-magnet.

Nanette's Homestay (Map p119; ☎ 331 6316; www.nanettes.com.fj; 56 Extension St; r $90-100; ✗ ✗) Housed in the upper echelons of a large residence near the hospital, this B&B is so friendly you'll want to pack the staff in your suitcase. The four upstairs rooms with bathroom vary in size and some have deliciously large tubs. There's also a communal TV lounge and kitchen. Downstairs are three schmick apartments ($135 to $150) with modern kitchens. You'll feel well looked after here.

Motel 6 (Map p122; ☎ 330 7477; fax 330 7133; 1 Walu St; r/f $70/95) This complex is perched at the end of a cul-de-sac off Waimanu Rd with boggling harbour views. It offers well-maintained motel rooms with TV, fridge and tea and coffee facilities, and also one-bedroom family rooms with small basic kitchenettes. It's spotless, friendly and very secure and the out-of-the-way location makes for a contented night's sleep.

Capricorn Apartment Hotel (Map p122; ☎ 330 3732; www.capricorn-hotels-fiji.com; 7 St Fort St; r $100-130; ✗ ✗) Cool, inviting, secure and friendly, this block of apartments sits high on Toorak hill and buzzes with a happy, personable air. Mix-and-match décor fills the self-contained units and not a cushion is out of place. The well-equipped kitchens contain microwaves and some of the balconies have addictive city and harbour views.

Holiday Inn (Map p122; ☎ 330 1600; reservations@holi dayinnsuva.com.fj; Victoria Pde; r $120-200; ✗ ✗ ✗ ✗) This inn occupies a great location on the harbour shore, across from the Government Buildings and near the museum. Rooms are generically spacious, cool and comfortable and will please picky travellers. The inn patently appeals to business travellers and those on coach tours and it has the facilities to match. However, the staff is a tad apathetic and there's a dearth of atmosphere.

Peninsula International Hotel (Map p122; ☎ 331 3711; www.peninsula.com.fj; cnr McGregor & Pender Sts; s/d $75/90; ✗ ✗ ✗) Pleasantly situated in a leafy residential area, the Peninsula is a little confused and tired but does its best to provide reasonable value. Behind a large cream façade are several floors of snug single rooms and roomy, well-lit doubles. All come with TV, tea and coffee and phone. There is also a restaurant and bar on-site.

THE AUTHOR'S CHOICE

Homestay Suva (Map p119; ☎ 337 0395; home staysuva@connect.com.fj; 265 Princes Rd, Tamavua; d incl breakfast $165-195; ☒ ☒) The pool deck alone looks like a photo shoot for *Vogue*, and the interior follows suit. Suva's finest location to rest the head is a gorgeous colonial house with indulgent rooms containing classy décor and plush bathrooms. The beds are so comfortable you'll forget all about the sightseeing, and the common living areas are littered with sophisticated furnishings. Cheapest are the rooms downstairs in the house; those upstairs are a tad pricier ($180) and top of the line are the capacious and modern studio rooms, which have balconies, TVs and kitchenettes. All rooms come with a bathroom.

Guests are treated like royalty but children aren't welcome. An excellent breakfast is served on the terrace overlooking the pool and bay, while home-cooked dinners (per person $35) are available on request. Definitely book in advance.

Also recommended:

Southern Cross Hotel (Map p122; ☎ 331 4233; southerncross@connect.com.fj; 63 Gordon St; r $100-135; ☒ ☒) Smart rooms, popular with business travellers.

Annandale Apartments (Map p122; ☎ 330 9766; annandalefiji@hotmail.com; 265 Waimanu Rd; r $50-90; ☒ ☒) Friendly joint with a good range of rooms, including two-bedroom apartments.

Top End

Tanoa Plaza Hotel (Map p122; ☎ 331 2300; www .tanoahotels.com; cnr Gordon & Malcolm Sts; r $185-200; ste $410; ☒ ☒ ☐ ☒) Opened in 2003, this sleek and sophisticated hotel caters to comfort-needy creatures with capacious beds, chic interiors, fully-equipped minibars and pamper products in the bathrooms. It's the most stylish of Suva's hotels and views from floors 5 and up are simply dazzling. The suites on floors 8 and 9 are heavenly.

Raffles Tradewinds Hotel (Map p119; ☎ 336 2450; www.rafflestradewinds.com; Queens Rd, Lami; d/tr/f from $130/170/270, ste $280; ☒ ☒ ☐ ☒) This one-time starlet has let herself go in recent years, but she's still snazzy enough to turn heads. Accommodating rooms have a touch of the flashy airport lobby about them, but with TV, phone, bathtub, fridge, hairdryers

and balconies no-one's really complaining. Rooms come in studio, one-bedroom and two-bedroom configurations. Raffles' best feature is its superb waterfront location; the hotel is frequently used as a conference centre.

EATING

For a compact city Suva offers a relatively diverse and multicultural array of eateries. It's the best place in Fiji to try authentic Fijian and Indo-Fijian food but there are plenty of Western-style options on offer if your tummy and palate are timid.

Restaurants
WESTERN

JJ's on the Park (Map p122; ☎ 330 5005; Stinson Pde; mains $15-25; ☺ lunch & dinner) Dishing up good Western-style food and blessed with terrific harbour views from the 180-degree glass frontage, JJ's is an atmospheric place to dine. Salads, burgers, enchiladas, steak and fresh seafood dishes are served in generous quantities and the wine list is impressive. The surrounds are glossy and polished, service is attentive and a Fijian Belafonte often taps the ivory in the background.

Malt House Brewery & Restaurant (Map p119; ☎ 337 1515; 88 Jerusalem Rd, Vatu; mains $15-30; ☺ lunch & dinner) Never short of a happy crowd, this bar-restaurant entertains patrons with delicious home-brew and even better food. Wood-fired pizzas go down well with the ales and lagers made on the premises but you can also treat your tastebuds to some of the most refined and creative seafood and meat dishes in Fiji. It's a bit of a trek from the centre (a taxi should cost about $6) and often filled with a boisterous din, but leaving Suva without a night here would be a crime.

L'Opera (Map p122; ☎ 331 8602; 59 Gordon St; mains $20-35; ☺ lunch & dinner Mon-Fri, dinner Sat, brunch Sun; ☒) Decadent to the extreme, L'Opera is a luscious slice of Italy from the ornate fabrics gracing the walls and high-backed chairs to the lovingly made gnocchi and ravioli. Authentic tuna, veal and lobster dishes are also on offer and the antipasto and wine list are excellent. Pure romance.

Raintree Lodge (see p128; mains $12-23; ☺ breakfast, lunch & dinner) Suva's most tranquil restaurant sits on an open-air veranda above a peaceful lake. Dappled sunlight filters through the surrounding rainforest and bird calls

THE AUTHOR'S CHOICE

Old Mill Cottage (Map p122; ☎ 331 2134; 49 Carnarvon St; dishes $6-12; 🕑 7am-6pm Mon-Fri, till 5pm Sat) Housed (as the name suggests) in a gracious old timber cottage, this Suva institution is the city's best spot for adventurous gastronomes to dabble in authentic Fijian fare. Exotic dishes including *palusami* (meat, onion and *lolo* wrapped in *dalo* leaves and baked in a *lovo*), curried shellfish, and seaweed or fish stewed in *lolo* assemble themselves underneath the front counter alongside Indian curries and vegetarian dishes. You can also dig into a traditional roast. Addicted office workers cram into the joint for lunch, parking themselves at tables on the front veranda or at the large booth seating inside. The spacious interior is filled with a pleasant cross-breeze (which may be of assistance with some of the curries) thanks to open doors at both ends and ceiling fans. Helpings are huge and $10 will easily buy your main meal of the day.

accompany your meal. Traditional Fijian fare, inventive vegetations options and fragrant curries are served and the pancakes at breakfast are legendary.

Tiko's Floating Restaurant (Map p122; ☎ 331 3626; off Stinson Pde; mains $20-35; 🕑 lunch & dinner Mon-Fri, dinner Sat) Elegant and devoid of pretension, Tiko's serves excellent surf-and-turf fare, including New Zealand steak and fresh local fish (*walu* and *pakapaka*), on board a gracious cruising vessel. The wine list includes Grange Hermitage and the windowed walls bathe the place in amber at sunset. It's best enjoyed on calm nights.

Bad Dog Cafe (Map p122; ☎ 330 4662; cnr Macarthur St & Victoria Pde; mains $15-25; 🕑 lunch & dinner Mon-Sat) This trendy drinking hole serves tasty bar snacks and crowd-pleasing mains. Cajun chicken, Thai curries, burgers, squid rings and potato wedges accompany your beverage of choice and you can scoff it at a booth or window table.

Raffles Floating Restaurant (Map p119; ☎ 336 2450; Queens Rd, Lami; mains $15-30; 🕑 lunch & dinner) The floating restaurant attached to Raffles Tradewinds hotel is one of the most scenic spots in Suva to dine. Lunch is the best time to enjoy the harbour views, when the glass windows surrounding the interior flood the room with light. Seafood and classy steak

dishes feature highly on the dinner menu, but lunch is a cheaper and more relaxed affair. The burgers here are legendary.

Aberdeen Grill (Map p122; ☎ 330 0384; 16 Bau St, Flagstaff; mains $20-35; 🕑 lunch & dinner) This stately restaurant has the interior of an old boys' club; plenty of dark wood, brass, mock antique seating and wide bay windows. The food is similarly conservative, but it's done well. European-influenced chicken, seafood and steak are the predominant stars of the carnivorous menu. Lunch is a three-course set menu ($25).

Also recommended:

Pizza Hut (Map p122; ☎ 331 1825; Victoria Pde; mains $9-25; 🕑 lunch & dinner Mon-Sat, dinner Sun) Inventive pizzas served in huge quantities. Takeaway is available.

Suva Yacht Club (Map p119; ☎ 331 2921; mains $12-20; 🕑 lunch & dinner) Global menu with indoor and outdoor seating.

INDO-FIJIAN

There are enough hole-in-the-wall curry houses in Suva to set your head spinning and your mouth watering. This is where those on tight budgets can eat like kings.

Curry House (Map p122; ☎ 331 3756; 44 Waimanu Rd; meals $4-10; 🕑 9am-5pm Mon-Fri, till 2.30pm Sat; ⊠) This industrious curry house serves excellent lamb, chicken, fish and vegetarian curries in a canteen-style setting. The pakoras, samosas and other sides are hefty and fresh and a good option if you're on the run. It gets busy so the earlier you eat lunch the shorter the table wait.

Singh's Curry House (Map p122; ☎ 359 1019; Gordon St; meals $4-10; 🕑 lunch & dinner; ⊠) Owner Mamaji runs a tight ship at this great little curry joint, where a delectable array of mostly South Indian curries tempts diners from the front counter. Seating is at booths or you can take away. It's one of the few places open on a Sunday and a great option for vegetarians.

Ashiyana (Map p122; ☎ 331 3000; Old Town Hall Bldg, Victoria Pde; mains $10-15; 🕑 lunch & dinner Tue-Sat, dinner Sun) For an Indian feast in more refined surrounds, Ashiyana is a step up in atmosphere and style from the curry houses and serves good thali and tandoori dishes. The spicy curries here are legendary – even the taxi drivers consider them hot.

Govinda's Vegetarian Restaurant (Map p122; ☎ 330 9587; 93 Cumming St; meals $5-7.50; 🕑 9am-5pm Mon-Fri, till 2pm Sat; ⊠) Saris and families dominate the patronage at this vegetarian restaurant, which is a good indication of the authenticity of the food. The array of thalis is impressive but you should definitely leave room for the delicious Indian sweets on display. Indian tunes fill the background.

CHINESE

Capital Palace (Map p122; ☎ 331 6088; 64 Victoria Pde; mains $10; ☒ lunch & dinner; ☒) It seems half of Suva converges here for the excellent Sunday yum cha but the regular menu also sites authentic delights including shark-fin soup and fried squid with chilli plus infusions such as sesame chicken with *dalo*. Mouth-watering smells and a happy din surround diners.

Lantern Palace (Map p122; ☎ 331 4795; 10 Pratt St; mains $7.50-10; ☒ lunch & dinner Mon-Sat) Dimly lit and suitably oriental in its décor, this long-standing institution offers a fairly predictable Chinese-Western menu with a few left-field gems thrown in such as garlic *bêche-de-mer* in chilli sauce. The banquets here are good value.

Sichuan Pavilion Restaurant (Map p122; ☎ 331 5194; 6 Thomson St; mains $13-18; ☒ lunch & dinner Mon-Sat, dinner Sun) Occupying a 1st-floor corner of the Garrick Hotel, this elegant restaurant serves a refreshing alternative to the ubiquitous chow-mien and chop-suey menu, with Sichuan dishes the speciality. On balmy days the alfresco seating on the balcony induces long and lazy lunches.

JAPANESE & KOREAN

Daikoku Restaurant (Map p122; ☎ 330 8968; Victoria Pde; mains $15-20; ☒ lunch & dinner Mon-Sat) The acrobatic culinary skills of Daikoku's chefs are reason enough to spend an evening here, and the seafood, chicken and beef seared on the sizzling teppanyaki plates would hold up to any Tokyo restaurant. Sushi and sashimi is also on the menu and a happy chatter fills the room. Bookings are recommended – it's one of Suva's finest and is often full.

Zen Restaurant (Map p122; ☎ 330 6314; Level 1, Pacific House, Butt St; mains $15-22; ☒ lunch & dinner Mon-Fri, lunch Sat) This small and intimate restaurant serves delicately presented sushi, tempura, *udon* (wheat noodles) and *soba* (buckwheat noodles) dishes as well as a modicum of Korean meals. The graceful décor features Japanese screens, and soft Japanese tunes play in the background. The menu provides helpful pictures for the uninitiated.

Korea House (Map p122; ☎ 331 1711; 178 Waimanu Rd; mains $12-17; ☒ lunch & dinner) The interior of this restaurant may lose its oomph once you pass the grand entrance flanked by a Korean mural does not. Pungent *kimchi* (pickled vegetables) and sticky Korean barbecue dishes are served as well as authentic squid, pork, tofu, prawn and chicken. There's a $10 lunch special and many dishes attract a 10% discount at night.

Cafés & Quick Eats

Cafe Tivoli (Map p119; ☎ 338 5407; Garden City Complex, Grantham Rd, Raiwai; meals $6-13; ☒ breakfast & lunch) The café of the moment, Tivoli serves salsa-and-cheese stuffed croissants, mammoth bagels and toasted focaccias, eggs any style you like and dense quiches. Tables are scattered beneath a breezy outdoor pagoda and there are delicious sweet treats if you still have room.

Focaccia Café (Map p122; ☎ 330 9117; Vanua Arcade, Victoria Pde; meals $5; ☒ breakfast & lunch Mon-Sat) This bustling city eatery serves fresh burgers, wraps, rolls, kebabs and focaccias at counter-seating or tables in the arcade lobby (it sounds incongruous but it works). The breakfasts are hot and filling and staff supremely friendly.

Palm Court (Map p122; ☎ 330 4662; Queensland Insurance Bldg, Victoria Pde; meals $4-8; ☒ breakfast & lunch Mon-Fri) Another popular city café, Palm Court keeps tourists and office workers full and happy with tasty cooked breakfasts, toasted sandwiches, curries and chicken and chips. Plastic tables are arranged beneath umbrellas to shield the sun and meals are dirt cheap.

Cakes 2000 (Map p122; ☎ 330 8994; 113 Marks St; meals $5-7; ☒ 7.30am-4pm; ☒) This café-cum-bakery-cum-cake shop dishes up hearty breakfasts and the best sausage rolls and pies in town. Tuck into overstuffed sandwiches or Fijian faves such as *palusami* stuffed with fish and roast lamb neck for lunch, or just gorge on a tiramisu and baileys or choc-orange-chip cheesecake.

Headworks (Map p122; ☎ 330 9449; Upstairs, cnr Renwick & Thomson Sts; dishes $4; ☒ breakfast & lunch Mon-Sat) Overlooking Suva's main drag, this is a great pit stop if the hustle is tiring you. The wicker seating on the balcony catches plenty of breeze and although the lunch options (omelettes, sandwiches and rolls) are limited, the smoothies are a meal unto themselves.

Both outlets of **Republic of Cappuccino** (ROC; ⏲ breakfast, lunch & dinner Mon-Sat, 10am-7pm Sun; ✗) Dolphin Arcade (Map p122; ☎ 330 0333; Dolphin Arcade, Victoria Pde); Downtown (Map p122; ☎ 330 0828; Renwick Rd) serve good coffee, juices, smoothies and snacks in air-conditioned surrounds.

For the coffee addicts:

Kahawa (Map p122; ☎ 330 9671; 1st fl, Suva Central, Renwick Rd; snacks $3-6; ⏲ breakfast & lunch Mon-Sat) Hot and iced coffees plus wraps and sandwiches.

Jardin (Map p122; ☎ 331 8588; Shop 25, Downtown Boulevard Shopping Centre, Victoria Pde; snacks $4-7; ⏲ breakfast, lunch & dinner Mon-Sat; ✗) Great coffee and cake.

Suva has a few food courts: one at **Downtown Boulevard Shopping Centre** (Map p122; Ellery St), another upstairs in **Harbour Centre** (Map p122; Scott St) and one at **Dolphin Plaza** (Map p122; cnr Loftus St & Victoria Pde). All have a variety of takeaway-food outlets, including pizza, pasta, Chinese, curries and Fijian dishes for around $5.

Self-Catering

Suva Municipal Market (Map p122; Usher St) is the best place for fish, fruit and vegetables. There are a couple of supermarkets on Rodwell Rd, facing the market and bus station. At the

Hot Bread Kitchen (Map p122; ☎ 331 3919; Scott St; ⏲ 5.30am-7pm Mon-Fri, till 1pm Sat) you can pick up fresh cheese-and-onion loaves and coconut rolls. For something to wash it all down with, try **Victoria Wines & Spirits** (Map p122; ☎ 331 2884; Victoria Pde; ⏲ 11am-9pm Mon-Fri, till 2pm Sat).

DRINKING

Suva has a good mix of drinking and dancing dens and Friday and Saturday nights see Victoria Pde swarming with clubbers and bar-hoppers. Check out the *Fiji Times* entertainment section for upcoming events and what's on at nightclubs. You don't need to get completely dolled up but if you're wearing shorts or flip-flops you'll be turned away. Watch out for pickpockets on the dance floor and always take a taxi after dark, even if you're in a group – walking home is dangerous.

Traps Bar (Map p122; ☎ 331 2922; Victoria Pde) Something of a subterranean saloon bar, Traps is one of Suva's best drinking holes. Take a seat in the publike pool room with wide-screen TV (yes with sports) or join the happy din at the main bar, which also features a vibrant dance floor. The crowd is generally young and trendy, but not pretentious. Live music is frequent as are Bob Marley sing-alongs.

MOVING TO THE BEAT OF A DIFFERENT DRUM

Dancers pay homage to the steady beat of the drums, seemingly oblivious to the spectators. The poorly lit room is crowded with both tourists and locals yelling *'bula'* to one another over the din. As a big, indigenous Fijian man – who should be playing the chief in this scene – approaches with a flower behind his ear and a pitcher of beer on his tray; you don't need any reminding that this is no *meke*. This is Saturday night in Suva, when the country's urban youth let down their hair and pole dance to pop music.

Fiji's urban youth face many of the same difficulties as young people around the globe: teenage parenting, crime, drugs and skyrocketing unemployment (only one in eight school leavers finds a job). However, these youths also find themselves straddling two opposing worlds – the traditional, conservative society of the villages many have left behind, where life was filled with cultural protocols; and on the other hand, the liberal, individualistic lifestyle of the modern and increasingly Westernised city. With 90% of its airtime devoted to Western sitcoms and serials, young people watch television filled with an irrelevant and often unattainable world. On the positive side, the rising club and café culture is bringing together youths from indigenous and Indo-Fijian backgrounds, in the midst of a city filled with ethnic tension. On the negative side, many face the near impossibility of surviving unemployment in the city; returning 'home' to a village sporting dreadlocks and skin-tight jeans isn't much easier. Youth have little room to voice their own opinions and it's not entirely surprising that many look for routes out of the country.

This is not the Fiji of postcards, of grass skirts and beachside *lovo*; however, it's well worth grabbing a cappuccino or putting on your dancing shoes to check out Fiji's rising urban youth culture. It's an unexpected eye-opener.

THE AUTHOR'S CHOICE

O'Reillys (Map p122; ☎ 331 2968; 5 Macarthur St) O'Reillys kicks the evening off in relatively subdued fashion – relaxed punters playing pool or watching sport on the numerous TVs. But it brews quite a party as the hours tick by and come 11ish the place is generally throbbing with a gleeful crowd of locals and travellers. There's no distinct age code – backpackers, foreign contractors, locals and expats fill the dance floor, shaking their bits to Europop, soft metal, techno, peppy country and western…basically anything that keeps the crowd moving. Forget warm pints of Guinness; the only Irish quality about O'Reillys (aside from the name) is that it's enough fun to knock your socks off.

Bad Dog Cafe (Map p122; ☎ 330 4662; cnr Macarthur St & Victoria Pde) Despite the name, this is one of Suva's stylish bars and heady cocktails and imported beers are served to chilled beats. The atmosphere is dark and swanky and you can grab a booth or prop yourself beneath the funky lighting at the bar.

Birdland R&B Club (Map p122; ☎ 330 3833; 6 Carnarvon St) This underground bar looks like a jazz and blues den and the smoky air certainly adds the appropriate bouquet but the live music is mostly in the form of rock, played loudly on Friday, Saturday and Sunday nights.

Barn (Map p122; ☎ 330 7845; Carnarvon St) It's a rugged, country-and-western bar with live music nightly except Sunday and Monday. Music is country with a bit of pop and reggae thrown in for good measure. The cowboy crowd is a little older.

Purple Haze Nightclub (Map p122; ☎ 330 3092; McArthur St) Inflatable aliens, neon planets and a wall mural suggesting 'Purple Haze is the best nightclub in the universe' fit in quite nicely at this eccentric club. Fijian and Hindi pop and R'n'B pump out of the speakers at intergalactic decibels; it's gay-friendly.

JJ's on the Park (Map p122; ☎ 330 5005; Stinson Pde) This classy eatery also has a long bar, which is a nice place to sip a cocktail or glass of red. The atmosphere is refined and relaxed and caters to an older crowd. A piano player often provides the background music.

Alternatives:

Shooters Tavern (Map p122; Carnarvon St) Good for a beer buzz and rock soundtrack.

Signals Night Club (Map p122; ☎ 331 3590; 255 Victoria Pde) Gay-friendly nightclub playing decent dance tracks.

ENTERTAINMENT
Cinemas
Village 6 Cinema Complex (Map p122; ☎ 330 6006; Scott St; admission $6) Suva's flashy commercial cinema complex shows recently released Hollywood and Bollywood films.

Check out the *Fiji Times* entertainment section for cinema listings.

Sport
Fijians are fanatical about their rugby and, even if you aren't that keen on the game, it's worth going to a match. The season lasts from April to September and teams tough it out at the **National Stadium** (Map p119; Laucala Bay Rd, Laucala). The atmosphere is huge. Ask at the FVB if there will be a match during your stay.

You can also catch players training hard at Albert Park during the week.

SHOPPING
Suva is bursting at the seams with shops; whether you're looking for souvenirs, a new swimsuit or some new music, you've come to the right place.

Souvenirs & Handicrafts
Government Crafts Centre (Map p122; ☎ 331 5869; Macarthur St) Although its goods are generally more expensive than elsewhere, this craft shop sells high-quality work by local artisans so it's a better place to head for a unique piece. Moreover, it assists rural artisans in the process.

Free Shop (Fiji Retail Enterprise Engine; Map p119; ☎ 3593 201; 1st fl, Garden City, Raiwai) Supported by the UN Development Program, the Free Shop sells excellent jewellery, clothing and crafts by local artists. Each item is given a small write-up to provide background information on the piece. Prices are also reasonable.

Suva Curio & Handicraft Centre (Map p122; Stinson Pde) This crafts market has endless stalls and is an interesting place to wander through. It can offer some fantastic buys but be prepared to bargain! Not all artefacts are as genuine as the vendor would like you to believe; if you aren't an antique expert, only pay what the object is worth to you.

Jack's Handicrafts (Map p122; ☎ 330 8893; Thomson St) Jack's sells a good selection of crafts, souvenirs and Fiji-made clothes at reasonable prices.

Pure Fiji (Map p119; ☎ 338 3611; 52 Karsanji St; ☺ 10am-12.45pm Sat) This spot is actually a classy day spa, but every Saturday morning you can purchase their exquisite creams, soaps and scrubs made from coconut oil and other natural extracts at bargain prices.

ROC Market (Map p122; Victoria Pde; see p133) The Dolphin Arcade outlet of the Republic of Cappuccino holds a small but eclectic market on the third Sunday of every month. Stalls feature homemade food, arts and crafts at reasonable prices.

Music

Procera Music Shop (Map p122; ☎ 331 4911; Greig St) Procera sells hard-to-find Fijian and other South Pacific releases as well as plenty of Hindi pop.

Boom Box (Map p122; ☎ 330 8265; Downtown Boulevard Shopping Centre; Ellery St) This chain outlet is a good spot to head for recent and popular Western and Fijian releases. Most music is imported and fairly pricey.

Water Sports Gear

Wai Tui Surf (Map p122; ☎ 330 0287; Queensland Insurance Bldg, Victoria Pde) If you're looking for beachwear, daypacks, snorkel gear or surf boards, this place sells plenty of name brands.

Bob's Hook, Line & Sinker (Map p122; ☎ 330 1013; Harbour Centre, Thomson St) Bob's sells good snorkelling, diving and fishing gear.

GETTING THERE & AWAY

Suva is well connected to the rest of the country by air and interisland ferries, and to western Viti Levu by buses and carriers. Most international flights, however, arrive at Nadi International Airport.

Air

Nausori International Airport is around 23km northeast of central Suva. There are no direct local buses between Suva and the airport, but **Nausori Taxi & Bus Service** (☎ 331 2185, 330 4178) has regular buses between the airport and the Holiday Inn hotel in Suva ($3). Otherwise, a taxi from the airport to/from Suva costs a standard $20 (taxi drivers generally won't budge on this). Alternatively, cover the 3km to/from Nausori's bus stations by taxi (about $3), and catch one of the frequent local buses to Suva for about $1.65. Allow plenty of time, as some buses speed while others crawl.

See p259 for domestic flight routes.

Airline offices in Suva:

Air Fiji (Map p122; ☎ 331 3666; suvasales@airfiji.com.fj; 185 Victoria Pde)

Air New Zealand (Map p122; ☎ 331 3100; www.pacific islands.airnewzealand.com; Queensland Insurance Bldg, Victoria Pde)

Air Pacific (Map p122; ☎ 330 4388; www.airpacific.com.fj; Colonial Bldg, Victoria Pde)

Qantas (Map p122; ☎ 331 1833; fax 330 4795; Colonial Bldg, Victoria Pde)

Sun Air (Map p122; ☎ 330 8979; Victoria Pde)

Boat

From Suva there are regular ferry services to Vanua Levu and Taveuni with **Consort Shipping** (Map p122; ☎ 330 2877; fax 330 3389; Ground fl, Dominion House Arcade, Thomson St) and to Levuka (Ovalau) and Labasa (Vanua Levu) with **Patterson Brothers Shipping** (Map p122; ☎ 331 5644; fax 330 1652; Suites 1 & 2, Epworth Arcade, Nina St). See p261 for more information about ferry services.

Bus & Carrier

There are frequent buses operating along the Queens Road and Kings Road from Suva's **main bus station** (Map p122; Rodwell Rd). If you can cope with busy bus stations and sometimes crowded buses, they are more fun and better value than tourist buses and will stop at resorts along the way upon request.

Small trucks or carriers with tarpaulin-covered frames on the back also take passengers along the Queens Road. If you're travelling in a group, you can usually get a taxi for little more than the price of a bus.

GETTING AROUND

It is easy to get around central Suva on foot. Local buses are cheap and plentiful and depart from the main bus station. There are relatively few buses in the evening and barely any on Sundays.

Taxis are cheap for short trips ($3), and in Suva they actually use the meter! The city's one-way looping streets may make you think the taxi driver is taking you on a goose chase; drivers along Victoria Pde may get caught on a long run around the market and wharf area. Suva is *not* considered a safe place to wander about at night and you'd be nuts not to hop in a taxi. To order one call **Jason's Taxis** (☎ 337 2220), **Carnarvon Taxi** (☎ 331 5315), **Sanyo Cabs** (☎ 330 4541) or **Piccadilly Taxis** (☎ 330 4302; ◷ 24hr).

See p263 for car-rental companies in Suva.

KINGS ROAD

Carving a route partially through the interior of Viti Levu, the Kings Road is just as spectacular as the Queens Road but the absence of infrastructure and coastline adds a remote flavour to it. Distances between villages are greater and the ascent into the highlands produces humbling scenery. The road coils and extends for around 256km, linking Suva to Lautoka via the east and north of the island. It's a great trip either by bus or car, but the road is unsealed between Korovou and Dama. Promises to amend this have been in the pipeline for many years but work appears to be carried out at an excruciatingly cautious rate; nevertheless locals maintain an optimistic outlook. You may even be driving on tar when you read this.

NAUSORI & THE REWA DELTA
Nausori
pop 22,000

The township of Nausori is on the eastern bank of the Rewa River, about 19km northeast of downtown Suva. It has the country's second-largest airport and is a bustling service centre and transport hub for the largely agricultural and manufacturing industry workers. If you're passing through there are a few banks and inexpensive eateries near the market and bus stations.

Now a major rice-producing region, the town developed around the CSR sugar mill, which operated here for eight decades until 1959. Growing sugar cane proved more successful on the drier western side of Viti Levu.

There are many eroded ring-ditch fortifications in the Rewa Delta. About 10m wide with steep, battered sides and a strong fence on the inner bank, they were necessary for the survival of a village in times of war, protecting it against a surprise attack.

GETTING THERE & AROUND
The Kings Road from Suva to Nausori is the country's busiest and most congested stretch of highway; regular buses ($1.50, 30 minutes) travel this route. The Nausori bus station is in the main street. **Sunbeam Transport** (☎ 347 9353) has regular buses to Lautoka via the Kings Road ($9.90, 4½ hours, six daily between 6am and 5pm).

Nausori International Airport
The airport is about 3km southeast of Nausori, 22km from Suva. Qantas and Air Pacific have international flights here and Air Fiji and Sun Air have domestic flights (see p259 for details). The airport premises are small, with a newspaper stand (selling a few magazines, books and phonecards) and a snack counter. An ANZ bank opens for international flights only.

There are regular buses from Nausori airport to nearby boat landings: Bau Landing, Wainibokasi Landing (for Naisali village) and Nakelo Landing (for Toberua). From Nakelo Landing there are local village boats, which you may be able to join or hire to explore the area.

Nakelo Landing is on the Wainibokasi River, southeast of the airport. If driving from Nausori, turn left before the airport and then take the first right. Follow the road for 5km and turn right before Namuka.

Nasilai Village & Naililili Catholic Mission
Nasilai village is home to the well-known potter Taraivini Wati. Pottery is a major source of income for the village, and when large orders are placed, everyone participates in the process, helping to collect and prepare the clay and make the pots. When a baby girl is born in the village, a lump of clay is placed on her forehead. It's believed she will then automatically know how to carry on the pottery-making tradition.

Catholic missionaries from France built the Naililili Catholic Mission at the turn of the century. The stained-glass windows, imported from Europe, incorporate Fijian writing and imagery. The delta area on which the mission is built is a flood plain and so the priests no longer live here.

Wilderness Ethnic Adventure Fiji (☎ 331 5730; www.wildernessfiji.com.fj) runs tours of the Rewa Delta and Nasilai village, departing from Suva hotels (see p128).

There are regular buses to Wainibokasi Landing from the Nausori bus station. If driving from Nausori, head southeast for 6km on the road that runs parallel to the Rewa River. Pass the airport entrance and turn right at the T-junction. The landing is a further 1km before the bridge across the Wainibokasi River. There you can catch a boat to the Naililili Catholic Mission, which is almost opposite the landing, or take a short trip downriver to Nasilai village. Ask a local for permission to visit the village and take along some *kava* for a *sevusevu*.

Bau

If you fly over the island of Bau today it is bizarre to think that in the 19th century such a tiny speck of land was the power base of Cakobau and his father Tanoa (see p28). In the 1780s there were 30 *bure kalou* (ancient temples) on the small chiefly island, including the famous Na Vata ni Tawake, which stood on a huge *yavu* faced with large panels of flat rock. Also of interest are its **chiefly cemetery**, **old church** and a **sacrificial killing stone** on which enemies were slaughtered prior to being cooked and consumed.

To visit the island and possibly stay the night you must be invited by someone who lives there or have permission from the **Ministry of Fijian Affairs** (Map p122; ☎ 321 1458; Government Bldgs, Suva). Dress conservatively, take a large *waka* (bunch of *kava* roots) for presentation to the *turaga-ni-koro* (chief).

There are regular buses from Nausori bus station to Bau Landing, which is northeast of Nausori airport. If you are driving from Nausori, turn left before the airport and after about 4km turn left at the intersection and follow the road to its end. Boats cross to nearby Bau. Boats also leave from Bau Landing for the island of **Viwa**, where missionaries lived during Cakobau's time.

Toberua

This small island (2 hectares) is just off Kaba Point, the easternmost point of Viti Levu, about 30km from Suva.

Toberua Island Resort (☎ 347 2777; www.toberua .com; s/d from $380/420, child under 16 free; 🏊) is the perfect island hideaway for those seeking some South Pacific solitude. Originally built in 1968 as an American millionaire's hideaway, it's since reinvented itself to cater to unfussy couples and families. The 15 waterfront *bure* scattered along the beach have gloriously high roofs, minibars, sundecks and stylish bathrooms. The *bure* are large enough to house a family. Meal plans for adults/children are $110/50 per day and the cuisine is excellent. Toberua only receives about one-third of Suva's annual rainfall so the climate is balmy for most of the year. At low tide the beach is used for golf and there is snorkelling (you will probably see sea snakes), paddle boating, and tours to the nearby island bird sanctuary and mangroves. A two-tank dive/PADI Open Water Course costs $165/550. Transfers involve a taxi from Nausori airport/Suva to Nakelo Landing ($18/35) followed by a boat trip ($75/35 per adult/child, 40 minutes).

KOROVOU TO DAMA

While the Kings Road is mostly sealed, the 56km section between Korovou and Dama is not. Although locals tackle the route in 2WDs it's best traversed with a 4WD and a prayer to the god of suspension. After a downpour you can throw the complication of mud into the equation and some off-road experience is recommended. The reward is the untouched landscape, devoid of a coastline and commercial infrastructure. It's one of the most scenic road trips in the country and travelling by bus will afford the views without the hassle.

Korovou (one of many towns known literally as 'new village') is not much more than a transport intersection, about 50km north of Suva. There are a few shops near the bus stop, and a post office across the river near the roundabout. From here, the Kings Road continues to the northwest and over the hills. Another unsealed road follows the coast to Natovi Landing (see p138), a 20-minute drive from where there are bus/ferry services to Labasa (Vanua Levu) and Levuka (Ovalau). See p261 for details. Arranged boat pick-ups to resorts on Leluvia and Caqalai islands are from Waidalice Landing, southeast of Korovou.

About 14km from Korovou on the Kings Road you'll pass the beautiful **Uru's Waterfall**, which descends over a rocky slope on the northern side of the road and ends its journey in a serene pool surrounded by colourful foliage. It's possible to swim here – just ask one of the villagers for permission and assistance navigating the descent.

Wailotua Snake God Cave, 23km west of Korovou, is reputedly one of the largest caves in the world (no arguments from this quarter). The name derives from six glittering stalactites in the shape of snakes' heads. During times of war the village would pack up en-masse and seek shelter in the cave's pitch-black labyrinth, which culminates in a huge chamber inhabited by bats. To get here hop on one of the Suva–Lautoka buses and ask the driver to let you off at Wailotua village. Ask the first person you approach if you can visit the cave; they'll organise a couple of lads to guide you through it by lantern. This is the village's main source of income and a $15 donation is well worth the tour and commentary.

Between Korovou and Rakiraki the Kings Road crosses dairy-farming country (land given to returned soldiers after WWII), winds through hills and along the Wainibuka River, and passes many villages where you'll receive a friendly wave. Watch out for mad drivers and the odd timber truck that hurtle along the gravel, and expect delays at milking time when cows plod along the road. You may see the occasional *bilibili*.

Natovi Landing

There is a general store at Natovi Landing but little else. Patterson Brothers has a bus/ferry service ($45, Monday to Saturday); bus between Suva and Natovi and ferry to Nabouwalu on Vanua Levu. It also has a Suva–Natovi–Ovalau bus/ferry service ($24, daily except Sunday) to Buresala Landing, with a bus connection to Levuka.

It is possible to travel north by road and meet the Kings Road again further on, but the road deteriorates significantly as you approach Mt Tova.

Natalei Eco-Lodge (☎ 881 8220; dm/r incl meals $35/100), in Nataleira Village, offers travellers the opportunity to diverge right off the beaten track and into a cultural adventure. The double and dorm *bure* are frugal but exploring the surrounding landscape is the real appeal here. Close to Mt Tova, the area offers some excellent hiking and the Bligh Waters are renowned for snorkelling and diving. It's also a great opportunity to immerse yourself in a Fijian village. There are buses from Suva ($4, three hours) departing at 1.30pm, 2.30pm and 4.30pm daily and returning at 6am, 7am and 8am.

NAISERELAGI CATHOLIC MISSION

About 25km southeast of Rakiraki is this old mission (1917) overlooking Viti Levu Bay. The church is famous for its mural depicting a black Christ painted in 1962 by Jean Charlot. The three panels of biblical scenes depict Christ on the cross in a *masi sulu* (sarong) with a *tanoa* at his feet. Indigenous Fijians are shown offering mats and *tabua* (whale's tooth), and Indo-Fijians presenting flowers and oxen. Visitors are welcome and a small donation is appreciated.

From Vaileka or the Kings Road intersection, take the Flying Prince local bus ($2, 30 minutes, five to eight daily) ideally before 9am when buses are more regular. Otherwise it will cost $30 return by taxi. Naiserelagi is just south of Nanukuloa village, on the right past the school. The mission is on the hill, about 500m up a winding track.

RAKIRAKI & AROUND

The scenery is stunning along the Kings Road winding down from the mountains from Dama past Viti Levu Bay and to the beautiful region of Rakiraki, Viti Levu's northernmost

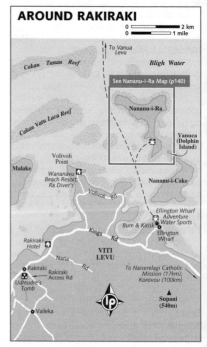

AROUND RAKIRAKI

0 — 2 km
0 — 1 mile

To Vanua Levu

Cakau Tanau Reef

Bligh Water

See Nananu-i-Ra Map (p140)

Nananu-i-Ra

Cakau Vatu Laca Reef

Yanuca (Dolphin Island)

Volivoli Point

Malake

Wananavu Beach Resort; Ra Diver's

Volivoli Rd

Nananu-i-Cake

Ellington Wharf Adventure Water Sports

Bure & Kiosk

Ellington Wharf

Rakiraki Hotel

Kings Rd

VITI LEVU

Naria

Rakiraki

To Naiserelagi Catholic Mission (17km); Korovou (100km)

Rakiraki Access Rd

Udreudre's Tomb

Supani (540m)

Vaileka

AN UNEARTHLY APPETITE

In 1849, some time after Ratu Udreudre's death, the Reverend Richard Lyth asked Udreudre's son Ratavu about the significance of a long line of stones. Each stone, he was told, represented one of the chief's victims, and amounted to a personal tally of at least 872 corpses. Ratavu went on to explain that his father consumed every piece of his victims of war, sharing none. He ate little else, and had an enormous appetite.

---

tip. The climate on the northern side of the **Nakauvadra Range** is similar to that of western Viti Levu, drier and suited for growing sugar cane. According to local legend, the imposing mountains are the home of the great snake-god Degei, creator of all the islands. The opening and closing of his eyes is the cause of night and day, and thunder is said to be Degei turning in his sleep.

The turn-off to **Ellington Wharf** is about 5km east of Rakiraki (at the 112.4km post from Lautoka), and the wharf is a further 1.5km by sealed road. Nananu-i-Ra (p140) is just a short boat ride offshore. Ferries also leave from the wharf for Nabouwalu on Vanua Levu (see p261); there are plans to build a large marina here.

West of Rakiraki, there is a turn-off that leads past the sugar mill to the small service town of **Vaileka** (about 2km inland from Rakiraki). Here there is a bus station, taxi stands, market, supermarket and a few cafés (one with Internet access). You can change travellers cheques at the Westpac bank (only open Tuesday and Thursday) or at the Colonial National Bank.

When heading west out of Rakiraki, keep your eyes peeled for **Udreudre's Tomb**, the resting place of Fiji's most notorious cannibal (see above). While it may be overgrown it is just by the roadside on the left, about 100m west of the Vaileka turn-off.

About 10km west of Rakiraki near Vitawa is a large outcrop known as **Navatu Rock**. There was once a fortified village on top of the rock and it was believed that from here spirits would depart for the afterlife.

Tours

Ellington Wharf Adventure Water Sports (☎ 669 3333; www.safarilodge.com.fj) offers lots of water-

based activities including: two-hour snorkelling trips around Nananu-i-Ra (from $25 per person) and windsurfing (from $70 per person per hour) plus sailing, fishing, kitesurfing and diving. Especially interesting are the sea kayaking safaris ($960/2200 for three/seven days), which include all meals, accommodation in villages and a qualified guide. These trips come highly recommended by travellers.

Sleeping & Eating

Rakiraki Hotel (☎ 669 4101; www.tanoahotels.com; Kings Rd; s/d $65/100; ✕ ⚛) Located 1.8km east of the Vaileka turn-off; this colonial lodge is nestled into spacious grounds dripping in bougainvillea and mango trees. Within two-storey blocks the hotel rooms are more 1970s than 1870s but each comes with firm beds, tea and coffee, TV and glorious garden vistas. There are cheaper, simple rooms ($40) in an annex with private bathrooms. The hotel has a pool with lovely wooden decking, half-size tennis court, lawn bowling and nine-hole golf course nearby. The restaurant-bar (meals $16 to $20; open for breakfast, lunch and dinner) open to visitors, has standard fare including curries, roasts, fried fish, grilled steak and vegetables.

Ellington Wharf (☎ 693 3333; dm/d $20/60) If you've made it to the wharf it's preferable to head to Nananu-i-Ra, but if you get stuck you can bunk down in a clean dorm or comfortable double here. The structures are thatched from the outside but tiled, polished and modern within and one of the doubles has a bathroom.

Wananavu Beach Resort (☎ 669 4433; www .wananavu.com; d from $290-320, f $480; ✕ ⚛) East of Rakiraki at the northernmost point of Viti Levu, this is a lovely midrange resort. The hillside position has beautiful views of Nananu-i-Ra island and the mainland's mountainous coastline. The comfortable *bure* have balconies, and at a pinch can accommodate up to four people. There are also three self-contained two-bed villas down near the water. Ask about walk-in deals. Visitors are welcome at the restaurant/bar (meals $10 to $35; open breakfast, lunch and dinner), which has gorgeous views and good food. The beach here is semi-man-made and requires some maintenance, but it's pleasant nonetheless. There's also a marina, tennis and volleyball courts,

VITI LEVU

and diving and snorkelling through either Ra Divers (opposite) or **Kaiviti Divers** (☎ 669 4522; www.kaivitidivers.com).

The turn-off to the resort from the Kings Road is about 3.5km east of the Vaileka turn-off. Follow the unsealed (sometimes muddy) road to the north for about 3km. Airport transfers from Nadi are $100 by taxi or $15 per person by minivan. A taxi to Vaileka from the resort will be $10.

Vaileka has a few cheap cafés near the bus station, and a cake shop at the Community Centre building. The **Coconut Cafe** (meals $4-10; ⏰ lunch & dinner) at Ellington Wharf serves delicious curries, fish, soups and snacks.

Getting There & Around

Sunbeam has regular express buses along the Kings Road from Suva and Nadi, which stop at Vaileka and the turn-off to Ellington Wharf. Flying Prince local buses also run between Vaileka or the Kings Road intersection and Naiserelagi ($2, 30 minutes, five to eight daily). To avoid lugging groceries and gear the 1.3km to the wharf, though, get off at Vaileka and catch a taxi for around $8. Sharing a taxi from Nadi is another option (about $90).

Nananu-i-Ra is just a 15-minute boat ride from Ellington Wharf. All the resorts on Nananu-i-Ra have their own boat transfers. Arrange your pick-up in advance (there is also a phone at Ellington Wharf). Boat transfers for the budget resorts are around $20 per person return.

From Ellington Wharf there is a Patterson Brothers ferry twice a week to Nabouwalu, southwest Vanua Levu (see p261).

NANANU-I-RA

This pocket-sized paradise is a must on any northern Viti Levu itinerary. Beautifully hilly, the 3.5-sq-km island is surrounded by scalloped bays, white-sand beaches and mangroves. Cattle grazing has cleared much of the dense vegetation and today rolling hills of grass inhabit the interior. It's only 3km north of Ellington Wharf, but the atypical landscape and small enclave of wealthy holiday homes exaggerate the distance.

Nananu-i-Ra is an excellent option for those who want an offshore-island experience but minimal boating and associated cost. It's also renowned for windsurfing and diving. The island has no roads and no

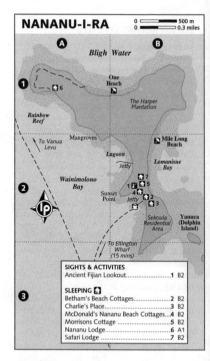

NANANU-I-RA

0 ——— 500 m
0 ——— 0.3 miles

Bligh Water

Ⓐ **Ⓑ**

① 🏠 6   One Beach 🏠

The Harper Plantation

Rainbow Reef

To Vanua Levu

Mangroves   🏠 Mile Long Beach

Lagoon
Jetty   Lomanisue Bay

② Wainimolono Bay   🏠 7
🏠 5
1 🏠 4 🏠 2
Sunset Point   Jetty   🏠 3

Sekoula Residential Area   Yanuca (Dolphin Island)

To Ellington Wharf (15 mins)

③

SIGHTS & ACTIVITIES	
Ancient Fijian Lookout.....................1	B2

SLEEPING 🏠	
Betham's Beach Cottages...................2	B2
Charlie's Place..............................3	B2
McDonald's Nananu Beach Cottages...4	B2
Morrisons Cottage..........................5	B2
Nananu Lodge...............................6	A1
Safari Lodge 7	B2

village – most of the residents are of European descent so there's not much contact with traditional culture here.

Activities
TREKKING

Great for trekking, the island has wonderful views to the mainland; a common sight from the southern side is billowing white clouds swallowing the volcanic Nakauvadra mountain range in the background. The grassy hilltops also provide bird's-eye views of the surrounding turquoise reefs. If your time it right with the tides you can walk around the island in about four to five hours and pass the mangroves at low tide. Part of the island is rocky so shoes are recommended.

KAYAKING

McDonald's Nananu Beach Cottages (p142) rent out kayaks. Weather permitting, kayaking around the island would take four to five hours.

Ellington Wharf Adventure Water Sports offers sea-kayaking tours on Nananu-i-Ra (see p139).

BOVINE BULLIES

Some of Nananu-i-Ra's long-term residents have become an unlikely menace to unaware tourists taking leisurely beach ambles or hilly strolls and the threat is enhanced somewhat by their harmless appearance. In the mid-1960s an American millionaire bought a sizeable chunk of the island and cleared it for cattle grazing. It proved to be a fruitful venture and cattle have become a permanent fixture of the Nananu-i-Ra's landscape. Unfortunately, an absence of management in recent years (the said millionaire passed away some years ago) has left some of the cows at a loose and uninhibited end. Consequently a group of bovine renegades now roam the island and these wild cows have been known to chase tourists up the beach, surprising them first with an (un)coordinated assault from the mangroves. Proposed land sales and development over the next few years may solve the problem once and for all but in the meantime keep a keen eye out for hoof prints in the sand and disturbances in the scrub.

DIVING & SNORKELLING

Snorkelling offshore you can expect to see some coral, abundant fish, and, on the north side of the island, many sea snakes. You can also go on snorkelling trips to the outer reefs with McDonald's Cottages (p142) and Ellington Wharf Adventures Water Sports (p139). The surrounding reefs and especially **Bligh Water** to the north have some amazing dive sites (see p59). The weather, though, can be tricky; while rainfall is relatively low it can be very windy.

Ra Divers (☎ 669 4511; www.radivers.com), based at Nananu-i-Ra will pick up from Wananavu Beach Resort, on the mainland, and from the budget resorts on Nananu-i-Ra. It charges $400 for a six-tank dive and $550 for a PADI Open Water Course.

Crystal Divers (☎ 669 4747; www.crystaldivers.com) also operates here.

FISHING

Ellington Wharf Adventure Water Sports (p139) offers three-/seven-day fishing tours in that cost $1000/2200 and include equipment for hand, sport and game fishing, accommodation and meals. A one-day excursion costs $100/400 for hand line/game fishing including lunch. There's a minimum of two people for the latter.

Ra Divers organises game fishing charters around Nananu-i-Ra. The boats are only small and can carry a maximum of four people; hats and sunscreen are recommended. A half-/full-day charter including all equipment and refreshments or lunch cost $350/650 for the boat.

WINDSURFING

The climate here is relatively dry (water supply is sometimes a problem on the island) and the island's exposure to the trade winds make it especially suited for windsurfing. Many windsurfers come here, especially from June to August when winds are generally 10 knots or more almost every day. Book ahead during this period. Ellington Wharf Adventure Water Sports hires out equipment (see p139).

Sleeping & Eating

It's a good idea to book accommodation in advance, especially if you want a cottage, as the island can get busy, particularly from June to August. Take cash and plenty of change, as not all places accept credit cards. All the budget places are well set up for self-caterers (linen and cutlery provided). Both Betham's and McDonald's Nananu Beach Cottages have an outdoor café open to outsiders.

Three of the budget places are close together facing the same bay – it's a narrow isthmus and there is another beach east that is generally more exposed to the wind (good for windsurfing or kitesurfing). Power is supplied by generator, which stops after about 10pm.

Safari Lodge (☎ 669 3333; www.safarilodge.com; dm/ d $25/80) This spanky new lodge is housed in a stylish two-storey house. There's a six-bed dorm with private bathroom downstairs and loft-style doubles up top. Plans to add a restaurant, three *bure* and another dorm were also afoot. A daily meal plan costs $45 and is well worth the dosh; the food is excellent. Served on the open-air veranda, guests tuck into chickpea and veggie curries, homemade samosas, marinated chicken and a host of other Fijian, Indian and Western dishes. The Australian owners are extremely considerate. Because one of Fiji's finest beaches sits at the doorstep, paddling, snorkelling, swimming, windsurfing and doing absolutely nothing are prime pursuits.

Betham's Beach Cottages (☎ 669 4132; www .bethams.com.fj; dm/r $20/110) This professionally run property accommodates guests in cottages akin to upmarket caravan cabins. Each is fully furnished and decked out with good kitchen⸱ ⸱⸱⸱⸱⸱⸱⸱ and has ⸱⸱⸱⸱ randa. ⸱ get a de café (ma and din⸱

McDon 4633; dm/⸱ tidy scat scaped ⸱ The cute containe⸱ up to fou⸱ The dor⸱ are ham⸱ rupted v⸱ restaurant (meals $10 to $20; open breakfast, lunch and dinner) serves pastas, chicken, *lovo* and curries. Snorkelling gear/kayaks are $6/8 per half-day. You can snorkel off the jetty (lots of colourful fish) or do day trips to the reefs at Bligh Water ($25 per person, minimum four people).

Charlie's Place (☎ 669 4676; dm/d $20/80) Run by Charlie and Louise, this place offers the most privacy. There are two self-contained cottages on the hill, each with well-equipped kitchens and laundry. The more spacious one is used as a dorm and has views to both bays. The other also has a lovely view and is good for families. There is also a cottage in the garden next door.

Also available:

Morrisons Cottage (☎ 669 4516; tipple@connect.com.fj; dm $25, d without/with bathroom $75/100) Simple bungalows on spacious grassy grounds. Closed November to May.

Nananu Lodge (☎ 669 4290; www.nananuislandlodge .com; camping per person $15, dm $20, d without/with bathroom $40/60, f $120) Well-established with good accommodation. Home to Feejee Experience (p265) when it hits the island.

Self-caterers can buy basic supplies from the shops at Betham's Beach Cottages and McDonald's Nananu Beach Cottages, but it's best to bring supplies over from the mainland, especially fruit and vegetables.

TAVUA & BA

Tavua is a small, quiet agricultural town with lots of temples, churches and mosques. The Emperor Gold Mining Company began mining here in the 1930s. Gold is Fiji's third-largest earner of foreign exchange. Most of the mine's 1500 workers live in **Vatukoula**, a purpose-built town of about ⸱⸱⸱⸱, 9km south of Tavua. Take ⸱⸱⸱⸱al bus to see the contrasting ⸱⸱⸱rkers and their bosses. From ⸱⸱ers may take the scenic back ⸱⸱ich passes cane farms and ⸱⸱nts.

⸱⸱son head up to the hill town ⸱⸱om where you can hike to ⸱⸱k Tomanivi (Mt Victoria) ⸱⸱See p145 for more details. ⸱⸱ the township of Ba, and ⸱⸱much reason for the aver⸱⸱y here, the bustling town ⸱⸱ople here are soccer mad. ⸱⸱ten wins national tour⸱⸱catch a match. Ba also boasts Fiji's best racecourse, and the town's horse-racing and bougainvillea festivals are in September. Local buses travel between Ba and picturesque Navala (p144).

If you want to break your journey you can overnight at the small and comely **Tavua Hotel** (☎ 668 0522; dm/s/d $18/45/70; 🐕) or at the **Ba Hotel** (☎ 667 4000; 110 Bank St; s/d from $40/60, ste $75; 🐕 🐕). Both hotels have reasonably priced restaurants and bars.

VITI LEVU HIGHLANDS

Climbing into the interior of Viti Levu will change all your perceptions of Fiji. This is the Fiji you never knew about. The sultry heat of the beach eases into a cooler clime and tracks snake their way through massive grassy moguls. Shifting green hues replace the dominant blue of the sea and the diversity of foliage and birdlife seems to increase tenfold.

There are small, largely self-sufficient villages and settlements scattered through the hills. Koroyanitu National Heritage Park and the Nausori Highlands have some fantastic trekking and opportunities to work the camera. That one jumper you packed may also get a workout; the mountainous inland areas can get chilly, particularly at night.

KOROYANITU NATIONAL HERITAGE PARK

If you are a keen walker or nature lover, the Koroyanitu National Heritage Park in the mountains about 10km southeast of Lautoka is definitely worth a visit. Contact Ms Kalesi Bose at the **Abaca Visitor Centre** (☎ 666 6644, after the beep dial 1234; admission $5) for more information. There are six villages within the park that cooperate as part of an ecotourism project. They maintain the landscape and tracks and subsequently earn tourist dollars through village stays and manning the office.

Abaca (pronounced am-b*arth*-a) village is at the base of **Mt Koroyanitu** (Mt Evans). The area has beautiful walks through native Dakua forests and grasslands, bird-watching, archaeological sites and waterfalls.

Trekking

Those who make the climb to the summit of **Castle Rock**, from Nase Lodge, will be rewarded with panoramic views of the Mamanucas and Yasawas. A marked track leads its way up; it takes about four hours (one way). There is also a two-hour hike that takes in a waterfall, the terraced gardens at Tunutunu and the Navuratu village site. A full-day hike to Mt Koroyanitu visits the remains of a fortified village.

Mount Batilamu Trek (☎ 664 5747, 927 3592; fax 664 5547) organises 2½-day tours up the Sabeto Valley. The tour starts with a 4WD up to the village of Navilawa for a *sevu-sevu*. After a night in the village community hall you will be taken on the walk up to Fiji's sleeping giant (Mt Batilamu, five to eight hours). There you'll be rewarded with gorgeous views of Nadi Bay and a bed in Fiji's highest *bure* at about 1150m. On the following day you head down to Abaca and are then transported back to Nadi or Lautoka. Everything will be organised for you, including meals, drinks and transport to and from Nadi/Lautoka hotels for $360. Trips depart Tuesday and Thursday from mid-April to mid-November.

Sleeping

You can experience highland village culture by staying with a family in Abaca. Village stays are $35 per night, including all meals and can be organised through the Abaca Visitor Centre (above).

Nase Lodge (camp sites per person $10, dm $25) is an old colonial lodge about 400m uphill from the village. It has 12 bunk beds, a living area, cooking facilities, a cold-water shower and toilet. You can order meals at the village for $5/7/10 to $15 for breakfast/lunch/dinner, but you should also take some groceries as there is only a small village shop. Make bookings at the Abaca Visitor Centre.

Getting There & Away

There are no buses to Abaca but you can contact **George Prasad** (☎ 664 5431, 991 6956; george_prasad@hotmail.com), who operates transfers from Nadi to the village ($25/50 one way/return).

If driving from Nadi, turn right off the Queens Road at Tavakubu Rd past the first roundabout after entering Lautoka. Continue for about 6.5km, past the police post and the cemetery, then turn right at Abaca Rd. It is a further 10km of gravel road up to the village, suitable for 4WDs only, and about one hour's drive from Lautoka.

NAUSORI HIGHLANDS

In stark contrast to the dense rainforests of the eastern highlands, the Nausori Highlands ascend into the interior in a panorama of grassy moguls. Massive folds of pale green tussle and tumble into the background as the coastline diminishes along the horizon. There are patchy areas of forest and small villages scattered in the hills; the more remote the more traditional the villagers are in their ways. Sunday is a day of rest, for church and spending time with the family, so visits to villages on this day may be disruptive and unappreciated. The villagers in Navala are Catholic, while in Bukuya they are Methodist.

If you have your own transport the loop from Nadi to Ba, going part of the way (to Bukuya) and then either back down to Nadi, or down via the Sigatoka Valley is a fun and usually easy day trip. You'll need a 4WD and you should check road conditions before heading off, especially during the wet season, as bridges occasionally wash out. Fill up on petrol before heading for the hills as there is nowhere to refill.

Tours

The following companies do pick-ups from Nadi and Lautoka.

Mountain View Tours (☎ 651 3620) Operates small-group sightseeing and trekking tours into the area. A Navala day tour costs $130 per person visiting both Navala and Bukuya, and including a picnic lunch and *kava* ceremony. It also offers a three-day/two-night trek through the area for $240 per person, which includes a guide, village-stay accommodation, all meals and transfers.

Rosie Holidays (☎ 672 2935; www.rosiefiji.com) Offers a one-day Nausori Highland Trek (per person $80), which includes transfers, a two-hour trek and lunch at Yavuna village.

Navala

pop 800

Nestled in the rugged grassy mountains is Navala, by far Fiji's most picturesque village. Navala's chief enforces strict town-planning rules: the dozens of traditional thatched *bure* are laid out neatly in avenues, with a central promenade sloping down banks of the Ba River. All of the houses here are built with local materials; the only concrete block and corrugated iron in sight is for the school and radio shed (housing the village's emergency radio telephone). The rectangular-plan houses have a timber-pole structure, sloping stone plinths, woven split-bamboo walls and thatched roofs. Kitchens are in separate *bure*, and toilets in *bure lailai* (little house).

Navala is a photographer's delight but you need to get permission to take shots, even from across the bridge. The *turaga-ni-koro*, Karoalo Vaisewa, allows tourists to visit and take photos but they must present a *sevusevu* and a donation of $15. If you arrive independently, ask the first person you meet to escort you to the chief.

SLEEPING & EATING

Bulou's Lodge & Backpacker Hostel (☎ 666 6644, after the beeps dial 2116; dm $45, bure per person $55) Located 1km past Navala village and on the right about 50m before a river crossing. It is run by a retired Fijian couple, Seresio and Bulou N Talili, and their son Tui. Activities include visiting the village, horse riding ($20 for a few hours), swimming, and trips up to the Talili's farm (a two-hour walk uphill), from where you can see the offshore islands in the distance. The home is on the

---

CANNIBALISM

Archaeological evidence from food-waste middens shows that cannibalism was practised in Viti Levu from 2500 years ago until the mid- to late-19th century, during which time it had become an ordinary, ritualised part of life. In a society founded on ancestor worship and belief in the afterlife, cannibalising an enemy was considered the ultimate revenge. A disrespectful death was a lasting insult to the enemy's family.

Bodies were either consumed on the battlefield or brought back to the village spirit house, offered to the local war god, then butchered, baked and eaten on the god's behalf. The triumph was celebrated with music and dance. Men performed the *cibi*, or death dance, and women the *dele* or *wate* an obscene dance in which they sexually humiliated corpses and captives. Torture included being thrown alive into ovens, being bled or dismembered, being forced to watch their own body parts being consumed or to have to eat some themselves!

Mementos were kept of the kill to prolong the victor's sense of vengeance. Necklaces, hairpins or ear-lobe ornaments were made from human bones, and the skull of a hated enemy was sometimes made into a *tanoa*. Meat was smoked and preserved for snacks, and war clubs were inlaid with teeth or marked with tally notches. To record a triumph in war, the highlanders of Viti Levu placed the bones of victims in branches of trees outside their spirit houses and men's houses, as trophies. The coastal dwellers had a practical use for the bones: leg bones were used to make sail needles and thatching knives. Sexual organs and foetuses were suspended in trees. Rows of stones were also used to tally the number of bodies eaten by the chief.

The growing influence of Christianity had the greatest impact on cannibalism and the practice began to wane in the mid 1800s. By all accounts it had ended by the turn of the century. Western fascination with the gruesome practice has remained alive and well, however, and souvenir cannibal forks are sold in abundant quantities. Traditionally chiefs used these to as it was forbidden for human flesh to touch their lips. Considered sacred relics, these forks were kept in the spirit house and were not to be touched by women or children. Today it would appear they make interesting wall features.

river's edge from where you can take *bilibili* trips in the dry season.

There is a traditional *bure* in the garden or you can stay in the 10-bed dorm attached to their house; they have cold-water showers and flush toilets but no electricity. All meals and *kava* are included in the nightly fee. Bulou's home cooking is good, with plenty of home-grown fruit and vegetables including local dishes such as *palusami*. It is best to ring in advance in case they have to stock up on food in town. Take some food as a present for them. Bulou sells her handicrafts (pandanus mats and printed *masi* cloth) for reasonable prices. Ring Bulou's Lodge in advance and they will pick you up from Navala.

GETTING THERE & AWAY
There are local buses from Ba to Navala ($4, 1½ hours, twice daily). There is one at 5.15pm, but the 12.15pm one is better to avoid arriving at the village when it's dark. Buses return to Ba at 6am and 8am. Carriers cost about $60 one way for the vehicle. The rough, gravel road has a few patches of bitumen on the really steep bits. While only about 26km away, Navala is about an hour's drive from Ba, past the Rarawai Sugar Mill, through beautiful rugged scenery.

If driving from Ba, there are a couple of turns to watch out for – at the police post take the left turn passing a shop on your right, and at the next fork in the road, keep left. The road is rough and rocky, but usually passable as long as the car has high clearance – but seek local advice on conditions before heading out. The Ba River floods occasionally and the concrete bridge just before the village becomes impassable.

Bukuya
pop 700
The village of Bukuya is at the intersection of the gravel roads from Sigatoka, Nadi and Ba. The drive from Sigatoka up the Sigatoka Valley is a stunning 1½ hours, as is the journey from Ba via Navala. From Nadi along the Nausori Highlands Rd it takes about 1½ to two hours.

Bukuya is a little more commercial than Navala, but still a worthy cultural experience. If you want to overnight here call **Moses** (☎ 651 1852) who lives in the village, but the easiest way to organise a village stay is on a tour. See p143.

GETTING THERE & AWAY
All roads to Bukuya are rough and unsealed, and are best suited to a 4WD or, if the weather is fine, at least a vehicle with high clearance. It's a bone-crunching ride in the back of a carrier, which will cost around $50 to/from Ba or $15 to/from Navala.

NADARIVATU, NAVAI & KORO-NI-O
The forestry settlement of Nadarivatu (30km southeast of Tavua) is a beautiful highland area. Hike up to Mt Lomalagi (meaning 'sky' or 'heaven' in Fijian) for great views (three hours return). The **Forestry Office** (☎ 668 9001) can arrange camping, dorm accommodation or a homestay with a local family (bring provisions and give money or groceries to cover costs). Alternatively, seek permission from the manager at **Vatukoula's Emperor Gold Mining Company** (☎ 668 0630) to stay at their resthouse. It is spacious and has an open fire.

Navai, 8km southeast of Nadarivatu is at the foot of Fiji's highest peak, **Tomanivi** (Adam and Eve's Place; 1323m), also known as Mt Victoria. Allow at least five hours return to hike from the village. Guides can be hired for $10. The last half of the climb is practically rock climbing and can be very slippery.

The Wainibuka and Wainimala Rivers (eventually merging to form the Rewa) originate around here, as does the Sigatoka River. Past Navai the road deteriorates, and is recommended for 4WD vehicles only. Koro-ni-O (meaning 'Village of the Clouds') and the **Monasavu Dam** are about 25km to the southeast. The Wailoa/Monasavu Hydroelectric Scheme here provides about 93% of Viti Levu's power needs.

Getting There & Away
The turn-off to the hills, crossing Fiji's highest mountain range and eventually ending up in Suva, is about 3km east of Tavua. The windy, rough gravel road climbs sharply, affording spectacular vistas of the coast and takes about 1½ hours by 4WD. Local bus services from Tavua ceased operating due to poor road conditions. The road from Navai to Suva is barely passable; avoid it unless you have a 4WD or are getting a lift in a carrier.

UPPER SIGATOKA VALLEY
Using local buses is an easy and cheap way of sightseeing. The **Naihehe cave**, about an hour's drive upriver from Sigatoka, was once

used as a fortress by hill tribes and has the remains of a ritual platform and cannibal oven. Adventures in Paradise (p107) offer guided tours of the area, departing Nadi and the Coral Coast.

NAMOSI HIGHLANDS

The steamy Namosi Highlands north of Pacific Harbour have Fiji's most spectacular mountain scenery (dense lush rainforests, steep ranges, deep river canyons and tall waterfalls). If you have your own wheels (preferably 4WD) take a detour as far inland as you can from Nabukavesi, east of Navua. If you intend to visit a village take along some *kava*. Sunday is observed as a day of rest.

Tour company **Rivers Fiji** (☎ 345 0147; www .riversfiji.com), offers trips to this beautiful area that travellers otherwise rarely see. It also offers kayaking and white-water rafting. See p113 for more information.

Discover Fiji Tours (see p113), and **Wilderness Ethnic Adventure Fiji** (p128) both offer tours into the Navua River area.

Mamanuca Group

The Mamanucas are movie stars, Fiji's glittering jet set, forever photographed and fêted, valued more for their natural beauty than any contribution they make to the national culture. Tiny, uninhabited Monuriki (and not, ironically, Castaway Island) played the island in the Tom Hanks movie, *Cast Away*. The reality TV show *Treasure Island* was shot in the Mamanucas (although not, on Treasure Island). The Resort Walu Beach on Malolo featured in *The Resort,* another reality TV show. *Survivor: Fiji* was made on Bounty Island.

There are about 20 islands in the group, basking in a large lagoon formed by the Malolo Barrier Reef and Viti Levu. Many of the islands take day-trippers from the mainland, who gorge themselves on buffets washed down with Fiji Bitter, and sunbake on white sand beneath coconut palms. The ocean around the islands has some excellent dive sites and Fiji's gnarliest surf spots. The snorkelling here is generally fantastic with the clear waters offering fascinating windows into the undersea world.

Most of the habitable islands support a tourist resort (on land leased from nearby villages and/or a Fijian community). If there is a resort but no village, it is usually because there is no natural source of water. Most resorts bring in their water from the mainland by barge. A few of the smaller islands, such as Monuriki, retain significant areas of forest with native birds and reptiles. You often see heavy rain clouds hanging over Nadi and Lautoka while the drier, magical Mamanucas remain unaffected.

HIGHLIGHTS

- Surf the wicked left-hander at **Cloudbreak** (p149), and the other fantastic breaks of the southern Mamanucas
- **Snorkel** (p149) in azure water straight from the beach, almost everywhere
- **Dive** (p59) among big fish and harmless sharks at amazing sites such as Gotham City and The Supermarket
- Enjoy a sunset drink with the yachties at the **Ratu Nemani Island Bar** (p156) on Malololailai
- Party the night away at **Beachcomber Island** (p151), then next morning parasail over the scene of the crime to clear your head
- Enjoy an intimate break with your partner on beautiful, peaceful **Navini** (p151)
- Treat yourself to tasteful luxury on **Tokoriki** (p154)
- Have a wild night on the *kava* (a narcotic Fijian drink) in one of **Mana's** (p152) confusingly interconnected backpacker resorts

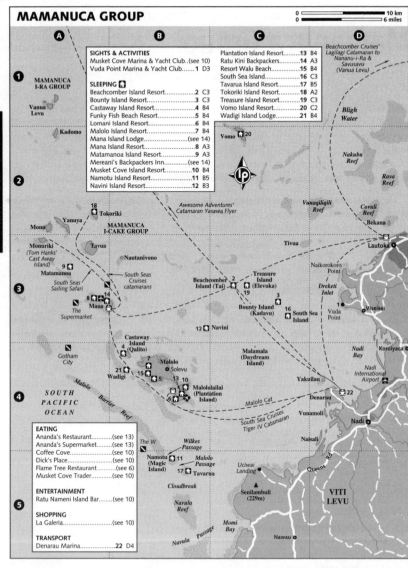

MAMANUCA GROUP

0 [=====] 10 km
0 [=====] 6 miles

SIGHTS & ACTIVITIES
Musket Cove Marina & Yacht Club..(see 10)
Vuda Point Marina & Yacht Club.......**1** D3

SLEEPING
Beachcomber Island Resort.................**2** C3
Bounty Island Resort...........................**3** C3
Castaway Island Resort........................**4** B4
Funky Fish Beach Resort......................**5** B4
Lomani Island Resort...........................**6** B4
Malolo Island Resort............................**7** B4
Mana Island Lodge.........................(see 14)
Mana Island Resort..............................**8** A3
Matamanoa Island Resort.....................**9** A3
Mereani's Backpackers Inn................(see 14)
Musket Cove Island Resort.................**10** B4
Namotu Island Resort.........................**11** B5
Navini Island Resort...........................**12** B3

Plantation Island Resort.........**13** B4
Ratu Kini Backpackers...........**14** A3
Resort Walu Beach.................**15** B4
South Sea Island....................**16** C3
Tavarua Island Resort............**17** B5
Tokoriki Island Resort...........**18** A2
Treasure Island Resort...........**19** C3
Vomo Island Resort................**20** C2
Wadigi Island Lodge.............**21** B4

EATING
Ananda's Restaurant.............(see 13)
Ananda's Supermarket.........(see 13)
Coffee Cove.........................(see 10)
Dick's Place.........................(see 10)
Flame Tree Restaurant...........(see 6)
Musket Cove Trader...............(see 10)

ENTERTAINMENT
Ratu Nameni Island Bar........(see 10)

SHOPPING
La Galeria.............................(see 10)

TRANSPORT
Denarau Marina..................**22** D4

*Beachcomber Cruises'
Lagilagi Catamaran to
Nananu-i-Ra &
Savusavu
(Vanua Levu)*

**MAMANUCA
I-RA GROUP**

Vanua
Levu

Kadomo

Vomo **20**

*Bligh
Water*

*Nakubu
Reef*

*Rava
Reef*

Tokoriki **18**

**MAMANUCA
I-CAKE GROUP**

Yanuya
Monu

*Vunaqiligili
Reef*

*Covuli
Reef*

Bekana

Tavua

Nautanivono

Monuriki
(Tom Hanks'
Cast Away
Island)

*Awesome Adventures'
Catamaran Yasawa Flyer*

Tivua

Lautoka

Matamanoa **9**

*South Seas
Cruises
catamarans*

Beachcomber
Island (Tai) **2**

Treasure
Island
(Elevuka) **19**

*Naikorokoro
Point*

*Dreketi
Inlet*

*South Seas
Sailing Safari*

8 14

Mana

Bounty Island
(Kadavu) **3**

16 South Sea
Island

Vuda
Point

Viseisei

The
Supermarket

12 Navini

Gotham
City

Castaway
Island
(Qalito) **4**

Malamala
(Daydream
Island)

*Nadi
Bay*

Koroiyaca

21
Wadigi

Malolo
7 Solevu

15 5

13 10

Malololailai
(Plantation
Island)

*Nadi
International
Airport*

Yakuilau

**SOUTH
PACIFIC
OCEAN**

Malolo Barrier Reef

6

Maolo Cat

Denarau

22

*South Sea Cruises
Tiger IV Catamaran*

Vunamoli

Nadi

The W

*Wilkes
Passage*

Namotu **11**
(Magic
Island)

*Malolo
Passage*

17 Tavarua

Naisali

Cloudbreak

Uciwai
Landing

Senilambuli
(229m)

**VITI
LEVU**

*Navula
Reef*

*Momi
Bay*

Nawau

Navula Passage

Activities

The Mamanucas are about water sports or extreme relaxation. Most activities are organised through resorts or tour groups.

DIVING

Mamanuca dive sites teem with fantastically gaudy fish circling psychedelic corals. The visibility here astounds first-time divers. You can see 30m to 40m under the sea. Major sites include Gotham City (named after the batfish), the Supermarket (where you can see many sharks) and The Big Ws. Other sites include the North Reef (the Circus), Fish Store, Driwas Dream, Yadua Island, Barrel Head and Camel Humps. The wall diving and pinnacle diving are peerless. See p59 for more information.

Many resorts have their own dive operations. **Subsurface** (☎ 666 6738; www.subsurfacefiji.com) is a well-respected operation with dive shops at Beachcomber Island, Malolo, Musket Cove and Treasure Island. It also offers diving with free pick-ups for guests at Bounty, Namotu, Navini, Tavarua, Wadigi and Resort Walu Beach. Half-price diving is usually offered in February and March for guests staying a minimum of five nights at Beachcomber, Bounty, Treasure, Musket Cove and Navini. A two-tank dive costs $190, an unlimited dive package $750 and the PADI Open Water Course $560. There are also diving classes for children eight years and older. **Aqua-Trek** (☎ 670 2413), based at Mana Island Resort and Matamanoa, is another good dive operation in the area. Backpackers on Mana and South Sea Island can use the excellent **Reef Safari** (☎ 675 0950). From Nadi you can dive the Mamanucas with **AquaBlue** (☎ 672 6111) or **Dive Tropex** (☎ 675 0944). See p78 for details on these two outfits.

The Fiji Recompression Chamber Facility in Suva is 45 minutes away from the Mamanucas by helicopter.

SNORKELLING

You can snorkel just about anywhere in the Mamanucas. There's even a lot of great snorkelling to be done right off the beach.

SURFING

For most of the week, the world-famous surf-breaks of Cloudbreak and Restaurants are the exclusive domain of Tavarua Island Resort. A popular public session is available on Saturday, though. Namotu Lefts and Swimming Pools are accessed from Namotu Island Resort.

Breaks shared by various resorts, including some from the mainland include Wilkes Passage – a fast, long right – Mini Clouds and Desperations. These breaks can get very crowded.

Tours & Cruises

All these companies do pick-ups from Nadi hotels.

Blue Lagoon Cruises (☎ 666 1622; www.bluelagooncruises.com) has combined cruises of the Mamanuca and Yasawa islands from Lautoka. For more details see p160.

Captain Cook Cruises (☎ 670 1823; www.captaincook.com.au) offers a day cruise from Denarau island to Tivua, a tiny coral island, on board the sailing ship *Ra Marama*, a 33m former governor's brigantine. The cost ($95/47.50 for adult/child) includes transfers from Nadi hotels, guided snorkelling, coral viewing in glass-bottom boats and a buffet lunch. Overnight stays at Tivua are also offered. The starlight dinner cruise ($99/49.50 per adult/child, three hours) includes a three-course meal. Captain Cook Cruises also has the popular three-day, two-night cruise/camping trip to the Mamanucas and the southern Yasawas (see p160).

Fun Cruises Fiji (☎ 670 2433; funcruises@connect.com.fj; Port Denarau) offers day trips to uninhabited Malamala for $75 per person (7.30am start) and $89 per person (10am start) daily. Children 10 to 15 years/under 10 are half-price/free. Included are a barbecue lunch and open bar, snorkelling and coral viewing.

Oceanic Schooner Company (☎ 672 2455; funcruises@connect.com.fj; Port Denarau) offers a five-island champagne day cruise ($165 per person) aboard the 30m schooner *Whale's Tale* including champagne, continental breakfast, buffet lunch, an open bar and snorkelling gear.

Apart from catamaran transfers (see p150), **South Sea Cruises** (☎ 675 0500; www.ssc.com.fj) has a full-day combination of a catamaran and sailing cruise aboard the famous *Seaspray*, a two-masted schooner that featured in the *Adventures of the Seaspray* TV series. You cruise by three uninhabited islands (including Monuriki), stop for snorkelling, barbecue lunch and a village visit ($165/89 per adult/child). South Sea Cruises also offers day cruises to Castaway Island ($125/85), Mana ($115/59), Malolo ($115/59), Treasure Island ($115/59) and South Sea Island ($99/49). Cruises include lunch (and unlimited beer and wine for the South Sea Island cruise), nonmotorised water sports, use of the resort facilities and pick-up from Nadi.

Other options from Nadi:

Beachcomber Cruises (☎ 672 3828, 666 1500; www.beachcomberfiji.com; day tour per adult/child $80/40) Runs day trips to Beachcomber Island.

Coral Cats (☎ 651 3475; sailfiji@connect.com.fj; per person $130) Offers day cruises around the Mamanucas on a 13m high-speed catamaran, with a stop at Malololailai.

Getting There & Around

The price of a light-plane ticket is comparable with catamaran prices, and the flight over tropical islands with white-sand beaches is more scenic and much quicker (no more than 15 minutes). **Sun Air** (☎ 672 3016; www .fiji.to) has daily flights (although sometimes flights are cancelled if there aren't enough passengers) from Nadi to Mana (adult/child $88/58 one way) and Malololailai (adult/ child $71/40). **Turtle Airways** (☎ 672 1888; www .turtleairways.com) and **Pacific Island Seaplanes** (☎ 672 5644; www.fijiseaplanes.com) offer more expensive seaplane flights to the Mamanuca resorts, as does helicopter outfit **Island Hoppers** (☎ 672 0410; www.helicopters.com.fj). For more information, see p260.

Awesome Adventures (☎ 675 0500; www.awe somefiji.com) runs the *Yasawa Flyer* (also known as the 'Yellow Boat'), which connects with South Sea Island and, on request, Bounty and Beachcomber Islands.

Beachcomber Island Cruises (☎ 666 1500; www .beachcomberfiji.com) operates transfers to Beachcomber and Treasure Islands twice daily from Port Denarau and most days from Lautoka (one-way/return $45/77, and half-price/free for children two to 16/under two), which includes pick-ups from Nadi. You can take a day trip to either island for the same price. Beachcomber also offers a water-taxi service for late flight arrivals and departures, for $117 one way per adult.

Malolo Cat I & II (☎ 666 6215) are fast and comfortable catamarans that make the 50-minute trip between Malololailai and Denarau Marina three times daily ($45/22.50 for an adult/child one way).

South Sea Cruises (☎ 675 0500; www.ssc.com.fj) operates two fast catamarans that run a loop from Denarau to most of the Mamanuca islands, including: Malolo and Castaway ($65 one way); Mana ($70); Treasure/Beachcomber ($55); Bounty ($50); South Sea Island ($30); and Matamanoa and Tokoriki ($100). Hopping between islands costs between $15 and $75 depending on how far you want to go. Prices include transfers from Nadi. Children aged five to 15 are half-price, and those aged under five are free. There are six departures daily.

It's easy to charter a boat. Try **Sea Fiji** (☎ 672 5961; www.seafiji.net; Port Denarau), which offers a convenient 24-hour water-taxi service that can be economical if you are in a group. For up to eight people, prices start at $375.

Fully crewed yachts are a fun way to explore the group and can be chartered at Musket Cove Marina on Malololailai (see p155).

BOUNTY ISLAND

Bounty Island, also known as Kadavu, is a 20-hectare coral island just 15km offshore from the mainland. It's one of the best options for budget travellers. The flat island is rimmed by a white-sand beach where endangered hawksbill turtles nest and the marine reserve has some pristine coral for snorkellers.

Bounty Island Resort (☎ 651 1271; www.fiji -bounty.com; dm/r/bure $46/143/234, child under 12 half price; 🕃) is a happy place. Many people come here as a stopover between the mainland and the Yasawas, but it is worth a few days' R&R by itself. There are 12 new double *bure* (traditional dwellings) with tiled floors, air-con, fridge and bathroom, while the older family *bure* (with two bunks and one double bed) have air-con, fridge and bathroom, too. All the *bure* have ocean views and hammocks. They are very clean, but there is no furniture apart from the beds. The eight family rooms sleep six and are bright and clean. They have sinks but hot-water facilities are shared. The two dorms are clean and fan-cooled, but perhaps a bit hot. Meal packages are $35 per person per day (children under 12 are half-price) and servings are generous. Nonmotorised sports equipment – including snorkels, canoes, kayaks, sailboards and trail bikes – is free. Diving can be arranged with Subsurface (see p149). Transfers are by South Sea Cruises or Awesome Adventures' *Yasawa Flyer* (see left).

SOUTH SEA ISLAND

Newly renamed South Sea Island is a tiny, flat, sandy island southeast of Bounty and Treasure Islands. You can just imagine the marketing geniuses brainstorming the new name. 'Hey, guys, we've got this, like, south sea island. How about we call it…'

In the middle of this fun, friendly island is **South Sea Island** (☎ 675 0499; www.awesomefiji .com; dm $75; 🕃), a double-storey *bure* with a restaurant and bar downstairs and a forest of beds (mostly bunks) upstairs. There are 32 beds in the main dorm, and two six-bed family dorms. The beach is good for swimming and OK for snorkelling, and there is a fresh-water swimming pool and lots of water-play equipment including free snorkelling gear, paddleboards, sailboards and a sailing catamaran. Prices include three good meals a day.

Diving is through **Reef Safari** (☎ 675 0950; www.reefsafari.com.fj). It offers two-tank dives ($170 including gear), night dives ($100), and dive courses from PADI Open Water Course ($530) to Divemaster ($1500).

This island is an easy stopover for trips to the Yasawas but it can get crowded with day-trippers. Transfers are by South Sea Cruises or the *Yasawa Flyer* (see opposite).

BEACHCOMBER ISLAND

Tiny Beachcomber Island (Tai) is 20km offshore from the mainland. It is circled by a beautiful beach and an invading army of holiday-makers, approaching as parasailers from the air, kayakers from the water, and snorkellers from the undersea world.

Beachcomber is a famous party island that is almost completely covered by **Beachcomber Island Resort** (☎ 666 1500; www.beachcomberfiji .com; dm $79, s/d $195/265, s/d bure from $295/345, extra child/adult in bure only $59/79; ✗ ☐ ☑), which caters for up to 250 energetic guests plus crowds of rowdy day-trippers. Entertainment includes live music and frenetic dancing on the sand dance floor in the big, lively bar.

Bunk upon bunk is crowded into the huge, dorm *bure*. Lockers are provided. The 16 modest twin lodge rooms with fridge and private bathroom are set some way from the beach. There are also 16 slightly rustic duplex *bure* and six premium beachfront *bure* – all with fridge and bathroom – although some of the bathrooms are outside. All accommodation is fan-cooled. The rates include surprisingly good meals.

Snorkelling equipment is free for house guests ($10 for day-trippers). Sailing and windsurfing lessons are also free of charge. Also on offer are waterskiing ($35), parasailing ($65), jet-skiing ($65 per 15 minutes), wakeboarding ($35) and fishing trips ($150 per hour for four people). Diving is through Subsurface (see p149).

A kids' club operates during the Australian and New Zealand school holidays.

Transfer is by the resort's catamaran service or South Sea Cruises (see opposite).

TREASURE ISLAND

Treasure Island (Elevuka) is a small coral island near Beachcomber Island.

Treasure Island Resort (☎ 666 6999; www.fiji -treasure.com; bure/duplex $525/1050; ✗ ☐ ☑) caters well for families and honeymooners. The landscaped tropical gardens cover the entire island, which is encircled by a beautiful white-sand beach. It has 67 comfortable air-conditioned beachfront *bure*, each taking up to three adults, or two adults and two children under 16 years. Optional meal packages cost $66/79 for two/three meals daily (half-price for kids under 12).

There is a pretty good gym and spa, a fun children's playground, and free Internet and guest laundry. Every *bure* (apart from the one facing the wedding chapel) is on the beach and has a hammock, and further down the beach are deckchairs and a beach umbrella. Many *bure* are semidetached, with an L-shaped living area. Some are divided into four apartments, enhancing the prevailing 1980s Queensland holiday-home feel.

There is nightly entertainment in the large, open dining room–bar, a games room and a freshwater pool. The resort has an excellent kids' club (for children aged three to 14) and babysitting is available for under threes ($5 per hour). Nonmotorised activities are included in the rate. Diving trips are organised with Subsurface p149).

The island is serviced by South Sea Cruises and Beachcomber Island Cruises (see opposite).

VOMO

This wedge-shaped, 90-hectare island rises to a magnificent high ridge and has lovely beaches, good snorkelling and diving.

Vomo Island Resort (☎ 666 7955; www.vomofiji .com; garden/beachfront villa $1590/1730; ✗ ☐ ☑) is a Sofitel luxury resort with a pool, a golf course and 'honeymoon island', Vomolailai, just offshore. The 29 very comfortable, air-conditioned villas each have a spa and a mosquito-proof deck. Rates include gourmet meals and nonmotorised activities. There is a three-night minimum stay. Most guests arrive by helicopter or seaplane (see p260).

NAVINI

From a distance, Navini looks like a round wafer biscuit topped with thick pesto. Up close, this small island is just as delicious.

MAMANUCA GROUP

It is surrounded by a white-sand beach and offshore reef. It's owned by the people of Solevu on Malolo, who used to fish here and hold meetings for their chiefs.

Navini Island Resort (☎ 666 2188; www.navini fiji.com.fj; 1-bedroom/premier/duplex/honeymoon bure $498/540/610/690; 🖥️) is a lovely Australian-run resort for a maximum of 30 guests (with 36 staff!). No day-trippers are allowed. Its 10 *bure* are all within 10m of the beach. One-bedroom *bure* are small but comfortable. Master bedrooms are at the back of the *bure*, through the sitting rooms. Duplex *bure* (sleeping five) have sitting rooms and the more spacious 'premier' *bure* (sleeping three) have verandas on two sides. The honeymoon *bure* have a private courtyard and spa. All guests usually eat at the same table. A three-meal plan costs $96/55/40/20 for adult/child six to 12/child two to five/child under two. Two-meal plans are also available. The food is good, especially the fresh fish.

Snorkelling is excellent just off the beach. Kayaking, windsurfing, use of coral-viewing boards and morning trips, including fishing and visiting other resorts or villages, are included in the price. Diving and other motorised sports can be arranged with Subsurface (see p149).

Navini guests are picked up from Nadi or Lautoka hotels, taken to Vuda Point Marina and then catch a speedboat. Return transfers cost $198/99/594 for adult/child/family.

MANA

The beautiful but divided island of Mana is about 30km northwest of Denarau. The upmarket Mana Island Resort stretches between the north and south beaches over 80 hectares of leased land. There are three budget resorts next to the village on the southeastern end. The northern beach and the western beach (known as Sunset Beach) are quite good for snorkelling with lots of tiny colourful fish. Also check out the south beach pier, where the fish go into a frenzy under the night lights. Hike up to the tallest hill for a good view over the surrounding reefs.

There are good dive sites at the main reef off the island. **Aqua-Trek** (☎ 670 2413; www.aqua trekdiving.com) caters for Mana Island Resort divers. A two-tank dive costs $186 including equipment, and a PADI Open Water Course costs $700. The excellent **Reef Safari** (☎ 675 0950; www.reefsafari.com.fj) services Mana's backpacker resorts. The diving and snorkelling sites are uncrowded and Reef Safari's reef talks inspiring. It offers two-tank dives ($170 including gear), night dives ($100), and dive courses from PADI Open Water ($450) to Divemaster ($1500).

Sleeping

You can use credit cards on Mana but you will need to bring some cash. Beware of theft on the beaches and in the dorms. Parts of Ratu Kini's and Mereani's are indistinguishable from the village (and, from each other).

DIVIDED LOYALTIES

Incredibly, a manned guard post and a high fence separate the upmarket Mana Island Resort from the three backpacker resorts on Mana. It is like a mini Berlin wall, dividing the wealthy west from the ragged poor in the east. Signs throughout Mana Island Resort warn 'nonguests' are not welcome in the restaurants, shops, even the toilets – nor can they use the beach shelters or deck chairs – but sick or injured backpackers are helped in the clinic.

The backpacker resorts are sewn into a ramshackle new Fijian village that grew up after local landowner Ratu Kini built a couple of demonstration *bure* to show the Japanese management of the Mana Island Resort how it was done. His relatives then moved into the *bure* and hooked up to the resort's electricity, causing a long-running court case. Ratu Kini and his brother both built small backpacker operations – Ratu Kini's and Mereani's. There is only a metre distance between the two resort bars, and Mereani's bar-reception area is wrapped inside Ratu Kini's, flanked on one side by its bar and on the other by its dining room, an enclave once again, like a mini former East Berlin. A third resort – Mana Island Lodge – was recently opened by another family member.

There is no longer a sense of aggressive competition between the resorts, since both the original brothers are dead. It's all a bit strange, though. That said, it won't spoil your holiday on Mana, which is very much a stop on the party circuit for British and Irish backpackers.

To reach the various backpacker resorts, get off at the ferry wharf, turn left, and walk through the village until you reach the guardhouse. Each backpacker resort offers diving through Reef Safari (see opposite).

Ratu Kini Backpackers (☎ 672 1959; www.ratu kini.com; camping per person $35, dm $45, s/d with shared bathroom $75/95, s/d/tr with bathroom $95/110/135) Most of the accommodation is set back from the beach in gardens among breadfruit trees, and it's almost indistinguishable from the village. Ask to see the newest rooms, which have big, very comfortable beds. The lively bar here is the centre of backpacker nightlife, since (a) it overlooks the beach and (b) there is a TV. You can use the bar wherever you stay, although Mana Island Resort guests may have to jump the fence (it happens!). The rates include huge meals. Activities include snorkelling trips ($10 per person, plus $10 snorkel hire), kayaking ($5 per hour), visits to the island where the movie *Cast Away* was shot ($50 per person including snorkel and lunch) and island hopping ($45 per person).

Mana Island Lodge (☎ 681 3436; manalodge2@ yahoo.com; dm/r $60/130, tw/d bure $150/200) The newest of the backpacker places, this lodge shows promise. At the time of writing, there was a restaurant here but no bar. All meals are included. The brand new fan-cooled *bure* have bathrooms but no cooking facilities. The eight-person dorm has its own bathroom and there is one private room nestled in the dorm. Snorkel hire costs $10 per person but snorkelling boat trips are free, island hopping is $45, fishing $30.

Mereani's Backpackers Inn (☎ 651 3359, 995 6446; www.manaislandbackpackers.com; dm/s/d/beachfront $45/75/95/200) Rates include three meals. All double rooms have a double bed, a single bed and a fan, apart from one room, which is air-conditioned. All facilities are shared. There is an eight-bed dorm, with two double rooms that can only be reached by walking through the dorm. The main, big, 20-bed, mixed dorm is in the village. Two bathrooms come off the dorm and there is another set outside for dorm users, just 3m away. The dorm will eventually be extended to meet the bathrooms. Activities include reef-fishing trips ($5), four-island sightseeing ($35), Tom Hanks picnic ($50), snorkelling, as well as nightly *kava*.

Mana Island Resort (☎ 666 1455; www.manafiji .com; garden/deluxe bure $336/504, ste $784, honeymoon bure $1064; ❌ ❌ 🖳 🖳) With 128 *bure* and 32 hotel rooms, this is one of Fiji's largest island resorts. It is owned by a Japanese company, and transport from the secluded honeymoon *bure* is by that most Japanese of vehicles, the golf buggy. The honeymoon *bure* have a very long deck (useful if you're taking a lot of people on your honeymoon) and overlook a secluded cove. Garden *bure* have room for up to four people, and deluxe oceanview, air-conditioned *bure* are spacious, elevated and have a porch.

Children aged under 12 years stay free and rates include breakfast and all non-motorised water sports. Snorkelling, fishing and island-hopping trips are also available. Diving is through Aqua-Trek (see opposite). Meal plans are available and there are two restaurants (lunch/five-course dinner $16/55) and three bars. The South Beach Restaurant (mains from $25) is a pleasant spot right on the beach. Resort facilities include a circular pool, a horizon pool and spa, tennis courts and a free kids' club for three to 12 year olds. Babysitting costs $5 an hour.

Getting There & Away
Flying with Sun Air is the quickest (12 minutes) and most scenic way to get to the island (see p150). Mana is serviced by South Sea Cruises catamarans (p150). Guests of Mereani's and Ratu Kini's can use the resorts' own *Mana Flyer* transfer boat ($80 return).

MATAMANOA
Matamanoa is a small, high island just to the north of Mana.

Matamanoa Island Resort (☎ 672 3620; www .matamanoa.com; d unit/bure incl breakfast $330/510; ❌ 🖳 🖳) has 20 *bure* overlooking a lovely beach. All *bure* have a veranda and beach views (half facing sunrise, half sunset). The 13 good-value air-conditioned units have garden views. The resort does not cater for children under 12 and is best suited to couples who want a relaxing holiday. Daily meal plans cost $49/74 for dinner/lunch and dinner. There is a three-night minimum stay.

Nonmotorised water sports are free. Other activities include a trip to the nearby pottery village on the island of Tavua. Diving is with Aqua-Trek (see opposite).

Most guests arrive via the South Sea Cruises catamarans (see p150).

MAMANUCA GROUP

THE AUTHOR'S CHOICE

Tokoriki Island Resort (☎ 666 1999; www
.tokoriki.com; d bure $825, extra person $150, d villa
$1100; ❄ 🖳 🖭) This gorgeous resort ca-
ters mainly for couples. No children under
12 are allowed. The tasteful and comfortable air-conditioned *bure* can sleep three
and are just a few steps from the beach.
The five new villas have private plunge
pools and large sandstones terraces. Lunch
is served in the pleasant terrace and pool
area while gourmet candle-lit, three-course
dinner ($45) is in the restaurant. Meal plans
cost $99 per day.

Nonmotorised sports are included in the
rate. Dive Tropex Tokoriki is equipped with
excellent boats and gear. It has an interesting giant clam–farming dive site nearby
and visits some pristine local sites. Many are
very close to the island. The only blue coral
in Fiji is located in the imaginatively named
Blue Coral Reef. A two-tank dive trip costs
$190, a night dive $100 and the PADI Open
Water Course $640.

Most guests take the South Sea Cruises'
catamaran (p150) or a flight on a seaplane
or helicopter from Nadi (see p260).

TOKORIKI

The small, hilly island of Tokoriki has a
beautiful, long fine-white-sand beach facing
west to the sunset. Near the northern end of
the Mamanucas, it has a special, remote feel.
The resort here is superb, see above.

CASTAWAY ISLAND

Reef-fringed, 70-hectare Castaway Island,
also known as Qalito, is 27km west of Denarau island.

Castaway Island Resort (☎ 666 1233; www.cast
awayfiji.com; garden/oceanview/beachfront/f bure $680/
790/890/1780; 🖳 🖭) covers about one-eighth
of the island. There are a lot of families here,
the majority from Australia and New Zealand. The simple fan-cooled *bure* are quite
spacious and sleep four. White brick walls
and thatched roofs give them an English-
country look, belied somewhat by the intricate *masi* (bark-cloth) lining the ceilings.
From the outside, it is as if a Cotswolds
village had been picked up by a cyclone and
deposited on a great beach. Inside, the *bure*
are a little shabby but are being gradually

renovated. There is a swimming-pool bar,
an open-air pizza bar with sea views, and
a great dining terrace (all-day casual meals
$15; dinner $42) overlooking the water. Alternatively pay $79/39 adult/child per day
for the unrestricted meal plan. The excellent kids' club will take three to 12 year olds
off your hands except for a lunch break.
Babysitting is also available.

All nonmotorised sports are free. Castaway Dive Centre charges $105 (includes gear)
for a one-tank dive and $685 for unlimited
dives. Open water courses are $710. Several
speciality diving courses are also offered.

Castaway Island Resort is serviced by
South Sea Cruises catamaran (p150), and
Pacific Island seaplane/Island Hoppers helicopter ($65/186/210 one way). For more
details see p260.

WADIGI

This cute, tiny, privately owned island (1.2
hectares) is just west of Malolo.

Wadigi Island Lodge (☎ 672 0901; www.wadigi
.com; island charter per day d $3595, extra person per day
$1155; 🖳 🖭) could be your own private is-
land. Guests charter the whole place and
nobody else is allowed to intrude. It caters
for a maximum of six people (no children
under 12). The luxury three-bedroom suite
is perched atop the single hill with gorgeous
sea views from the living areas and decks.
Included are all meals and drinks (prepared
by two gourmet chefs) as well as the use of
snorkelling gear, kayaks, windsurfers and a
4m aluminium boat. There is a three-night
minimum stay. Diving is available through
Subsurface (see p149). Transfers (round trip
from Nadi) can be via catamaran/seaplane/
helicopter for $114/308/368 per person.

MALOLO

Malolo is the largest of the Mamanuca islands with two villages, three resorts (with
one more under construction), mangroves
and coastal forest. The island's highest point
is **Uluisolo** (218m), which was used by locals
as a hill fortification and by the US forces
in 1942 as an observation point. From here
there are panoramic views of the Mamanuca
islands and the southern Yasawas.

Diving offered by the resorts is with Subsurface (see p149).

Funky Fish Beach Resort (☎ 651 3180; www
.funkyfishresort.com; dm/d $30/80, 1-bedroom bure $120,

2-bedroom bure $240, extra person $35; 🖭 💻) This is affable former rugby All Black Brad Johnston's stab at the surfer/backpacker party market. The bright, happy *bure* have outdoor showers and bright yellow interior walls. The sand-floor bar stocks good Australian wines and is home to perhaps Fiji's only garden gnome. The chef here punches several divisions above his weight. There's an à-la-carte menu as well as a three-meal menu plan (adult/child $40/20). Power is turned off at night, but it's a great little spot with good snorkelling and a swimming pool.

The best surf-breaks are accessible from here. On Saturday morning you can line-up for Cloudbreak when there is a changeover at Tavarua Resort, but you might not be let in. You can, however, surf Rourke's Passage, a tremendous right hander, and Desperation, which only works in certain weather conditions but also has a good right-hand break. Weather conditions are ideal for kitesurfing.

Resort Walu Beach (☎ 665 1777; www.walu beach.com; dm incl meals $90, 1-/2-/3-bedroom bure $450/580/690; ✗ 🖭 💻) Walu Beach was built for a reality TV show *The Resort,* and also consumed a local timeshare operation. A manager was brought in to turn it into a real hotel in two weeks, but he was still here after 18 months. Walu Beach still feels a bit generic, particularly in its furnishings, but the bar is great, the food is very good, and the rather Spartan dorm, which is divided into six-bed rooms with private lockers, is fantastic value. Essentially, you get all the facilities of an international-standard resort for the same cost as a backpacker place. Meal plans are $80 per person for those staying in *bure.*

There's a good beach, well-organised activities, and a real push to keep the party happening. Nonmotorised water sports are free.

Malolo Island Resort (☎ 672 4275; www.malolo island.com; oceanview/beachfront/f bure $542/632/1054; ✗ 🍴 🖭 💻) It's a reasonable resort on the western side of the island. As well as making use of the white-sand beach and the usual resort amenities, guests can go hiking. There is a pool and a kids' club and rates, including all Nonmotorised water activities, are for two adults and up up to two children. There is a hillside restaurant (mains $32) as well as a beachfront bar/restaurant (mains $26). Optional meal packages are adult/child $85/42.50 per day.

Getting There & Away

Sun Air ($70) flies to the airstrip on nearby Musket Cove, Malololailai. By seaplane it takes 10 minutes to Malolo. For more details see p150.

To get here by boat catch the *Malolo Cat* ($45) via Musket Cove or a South Sea Cruises catamaran ($65) and staff from your resort will pick you up from Malolo Island Resort. See p150 for more. The Resort Walu Beach runs the *Walu 6* speedboat from Denarau ($65 per person each way, 45 minutes).

MALOLOLAILAI

Tranquil Malololailai is approximately 20km west of Denarau island and, at 2.4 sq km, the second-largest island of the Mamanuca Group. Apart from the three resorts, there is a marina with bar, grocery and café, a dive shop, a restaurant near the airstrip, and on the hill above Musket Cove there's a kitschy art/gift shop, **La Galerie** (☎ 651 0050), with a small book exchange, too.

Musket Cove Marina

In September each year, the **Musket Cove Yacht Club** (☎ 666 2215; www.musketcovefiji.com) hosts Fiji Regatta Week and the Musket Cove to Port Vila yacht race. Traditional nautical sports such as wet T-shirt, hairy-chest and beer-drinking contests feature in the programme. Yachts can anchor at the marina for $10/60/220 per day/week/month. Berths start at $16 per day. Call on VHF 68 for reservations. You can stock up on fuel, water and provisions at the general store. Second-hand books and a treasure trove of magazines are available from the office. The marina also offers a choice of charter yachts ranging in size from 6m to 32m; charter rates vary depending on duration and extent of services required.

Surfing

There is no official transport from Malololailai to the excellent surf-breaks at Malolo and Wilkes Passage, but Jacob ('Scobie'), a local villager, can get you there. He has a boat with insurance and life jackets. Contact him through the dive shop or on ☎ 925 8778 (or through his mum, Viema, on ☎ 923 0828). If one/two to three/four to five people go, rates are $40/30/25 per person.

Sleeping

Musket Cove Island Resort (☎ 666 2215; www
.musketcovefiji.com; r $250; d garden/lagoon/beachfront
bure $460/460/535, q villa $660, extra person $30; ☒)
This is a lovely, serene resort overlooking
a lagoon. The yachties from Musket Cove
Yacht Club lend life to the bars – especially at
the Ratu Nemani Island Bar (where you can
barbecue your own food) – but this a place
to come for a quiet break. There are several
types of accommodation, from hotel rooms
to self-catering thatched *bure*. The newer
Armstrong Island villas – clustered on an
artificial island linked to the mainland by
a bridge – have over-water verandas and a
private pool, TVs and DVD players. The lagoon *bure*, configured so living rooms face
the lagoon, have a fridge and breakfast bar,
and are nicely decorated with *mangi mangi*
(traditional weavings) and bamboo. Villas
boast their own spa pools. Activities such
as windsurfing, canoeing, hand-line fishing
and snorkelling are included. Game fishing,
diving (through Subsurface, see p149) and
use of catamarans cost extra. Meal plans for
Dick's Place (see right) are available (two/
three meals per day $67/82 for adults and
$41/$33.50 for children under 12).

Lomani Island Resort (☎ 666 8212; www.lomani
island.com; deluxe r $575, honeymoon ste $625; ☒ ☒)
Lomani is a labour of love developed by the
children of the man who built Plantation
Island. It is an intimate, adults-only resort
with a huge pool, a classy Colonial-style bar
and a decent outdoor restaurant. Big, bright
rooms with huge balconies look out across
the beach to the ocean. They're equipped
with divan lounges, fridges and also DVD
players. Lomani is one of very few places
in Fiji where topless bathing is tolerated –
at the quiet end of the 4km white-sand
beach. Rates include breakfast and the usual
nonmotorised activities; diving is available
through Plantation Island's dive centre.

Plantation Island Resort (☎ 666 9333; www.plan
tationisland.com; d garden/beachfront $248/371, studio/2-
bedroom/beachfront bure $371/470/545, 2 children under 16
free, extra person $34; ☒ ☐ ☒) There are kids
spilling out everywhere here; they're in the
sea, in the pool, painting T-shirts, climbing
plaster cows, egg-and-spoon racing, watching
TV and eating chips. Most of them are with
the free Club Coconut, and look to be having a great time. There are three swimming
pools: one for kids (with water slide), one es-

sentially for adults, and one for all ages. The
two-bedroom garden *bure* are popular and
often booked out. They feature twin beds in
the front, a big lounge area with sinks and
the master bedroom at the back. There's a
big bathroom, but none of the walls reach
the ceiling. Rooms and *bure* accommodate
up to four adults and one child, except the
two-bedroom *bure,* which sleep up to eight.
The new Plantation Village double rooms
are bright and cheerful, with enclosed patios.
They flank a large swimming pool, a little
way from the beach. Staff here are friendly.

Meal packages are $39/59 for two/three
meals a day. Otherwise expect to spend from
$10 for lunch, $23 for dinner or $28 for a
seaside barbecue. There is a well-stocked
shop and you can enjoy rotis, samosas,
burgers and pies (all $8) at the Snack Bar
looking out over the water. The Sunset Bar
has cheap drinks from 2pm to 9pm.

The many activities include snorkelling
trips, canoeing, windsurfing, paragliding,
tennis and even lawn bowls. At Plantation
Divers, a two-tank dive is $142 (includes
gear), and unlimited diving is $640. PADI
certification and various advanced courses
are also available.

Eating

Coffee Cove (☎ 666 2215; lunch $12.50; ☒ 10am-6pm)
The bistro-style lunches overlooking a lagoon are good value, plus you can bring
your own alcohol. Order barbecue packs by
4.30pm for you to cook at the Ratu Nemani Island Bar at sunset. A choice of meats
comes with green salad, potatoes and garlic
bread ($16). Snacks, coffee and ice-creams
are also served.

Ananda's Restaurant (☎ 666 9333; mains $20;
kids' meals $9; ☒ lunch & dinner) Ananda's has a
menu so long it almost covers a wall. The
tables are outside, the food is good and
there is often live music.

Flame Tree Restaurant (☎ 666 8212; lunch/dinner
$16/35; ☒ lunch & dinner) This is an 'adults only'
restaurant, but not the sort of place where
you lick your dessert off a naked body. Flame
Tree is part of Lomani Resort, where no children are allowed. Dine quietly outside under
the boughs of a flame tree. It makes a pleasant change from the sometimes crowded
nights elsewhere.

Dick's Place (☎ 666 2215; breakfast from $17, lunch
$14, dinner mains $25, 3-course set menu $30; ☒ breakfast,

lunch & dinner) Musket Cove Resort's restaurant serves international cuisine with some Indian and Fijian dishes and weekly barbecues. Thursday night is *meke* (traditional dance) night, and the only food available is pig on a spit and an accompanying buffet.

Musket Cove Trader (General Store; ☎ 666 2215; ☻ 8am-7pm) This general store is probably the best stocked shop in the Mamanucas, but it doesn't sell alcohol. It does, however, have a bakery and a reasonable selection of fresh vegetables. Rotisserie chickens ($9.80) make a good picnic lunch. It's great for yachties.

Next door to Ananda's Restaurant, Ananda's Supermarket is smaller than the general store but still well stocked.

Getting There & Away

Sun Air has a shuttle service from Nadi to Malololailai ($140 return). It is a lovely 10-minute scenic flight. The *Malolo Cat* catamaran runs three times daily. Return fares from Denarau Marina cost $90/45 per adult/child and take 50 minutes.

NAMOTU

Namotu, a tiny (1.5 hectares) and pretty island next to Tavarua, is first and foremost a surfing resort, although game fishing is also popular here.

Namotu Island Resort (☎ 670 6439; www.namotu island.net; ✖ ☐ ☻) is a little bit of Bali in Fiji. If you're jetlagged, you might think you're in the wrong country – there are Balinese decorations everywhere. If you

don't surf – or at least fish – you might think you're on the wrong planet. Surfbreaks include Swimming Pool, one of Fiji's cleanest waves, and the consistently surfable Namotu Lefts (both exclusive to the resort) and Wilkes Passage. Diving can be arranged with Subsurface (see p149). Generally, guests are in groups and book in advance through **Waterways Surf Travel** (☎ in the USA 310-456-7744; fax 310-456-7755), but Namotu does occasionally take 'walk-ins' to fill out a group. No children under 12.

TAVARUA

This small coral island is at the southern edge of the Malolo Barrier Reef which encloses the southern Mamanucas. It is 12 hectares, rimmed by beautiful white-sand beaches and has great surf nearby at Cloudbreak and Restaurants.

Tavarua Island Resort (☎ 670 6513; www.tavarua .com; ✖ ✖ ☐ ☻) is American-run and most of the guests are American surfers on weeklong package deals. Accommodation is in simple elevated *bure* spaced along the beach. Rates include all meals, transfers from Nadi and boat trips to great surf breaks. Drinks are extra. Bookings are handled exclusively through **Tavarua Island Tours** (☎ in the USA 805-686-4551; fax 805-683-6696) in California. Reservations need to be made well in advance, although in the low season (December to February) the resort may accept 'walk-ins'.

Diving can be arranged with Subsurface (see p149).

MAMANUCA GROUP

Yasawa Group

Lacing their way up the west coast of Fiji, the Yasawas are a chain of 20 ancient islands famous for crystal blue lagoons, rugged volcanic landscapes, abundant sunshine and some of the Pacific's most ethereal beaches. They're the big sister of the Mamanucas; grander in size and stature, sparsely populated and just what the doctor ordered for leaving civilisation and its consternations behind. Most of the people live in small isolated villages and have their own distinct dialect, which is known as Vuda. Technology is an enigma and any stay will nudge you surreptitiously into the true meaning of 'Fiji time'.

Snorkelling, swimming and diving are avidly pursued owing to wide banks of coral around most of the islands. Ample peaks ranging from grassy hills to jungle climbs also provide spectacular hiking and views from some of the summits take in the whole chain from north to south.

After the famous mutiny on the *Bounty* in 1789, Captain William Bligh paddled through the island group on his way to Timor. His longboat was chased along by Fijian canoes.

Backpacker lodges have dominated accommodation options in the Yasawas for many years but a new wave of midrange and top-end options are making appearances, so families and couples looking for creature comforts and pampering are now well-catered for. You can prebook packages to the Yasawas but unless you're travelling in peak season or with kids in need of facilities it's not essential to have all your accommodation tied up before you head out. Many of the backpacker resorts go through ebbs and flows of quality and you'll get your best advice from travellers on the *Yasawa Flyer*.

HIGHLIGHTS

- Cool the skin and the senses – dip the bod into the **Blue Lagoon** (p167) on Nanuya Lailai
- Simmer on sun-soaked **Oarsman's Bay beach** (p168)
- Work the pins and hike across **Waya** (p163), **Nacula** (p168) and **Tavewa** (p166) for dramatic vistas
- **Cruise** (opposite), **kayak** (p160) or **sail** (p160) the indigo seas
- Meet the manta rays off **Manta Ray Island** (p165)
- Don a snorkel or tank and cavort with turtles, reef sharks and other vivid marine life around **Tavewa** (p166), **Nacula** (p168) or **Nanuya Lailai** (p167).
- Explore the dark chambers of **Sawa-i-Lau's caves** (p169)
- Suit up in the Sunday best for a **village church service** (p168) on Nacula

Sawa-i-Lau Caves
Oarsman's Bay Beach ★ ★Nacula
Tavewa ★
★Blue Lagoon (Nanuya Lailai)

Manta Ray Island ★

★Waya

■ POPULATION: 5000 | ■ AREA: 135 SQ KM

Geography & Geology

The Yasawas stretch for around 90km, beginning about 40km northwest of Viti Levu. The group forms a roughly straight line within the Great Sea Reef. The land is mostly hilly; four of the larger islands have summits close to 600m above sea level. While the relatively dry climate is a plus for visitors, the land is prone to drought, and Hurricane Gavin wrought havoc in early 1997.

Information

The Yasawas are still remote and there are no shops, banks, postal, medical or phone services. Radio-phones are not always reliable.

A dozen or so resorts in the Nacula Tikina (ie on Nacula, Tavewa, Nanuya Lailai

and Matacawalevu islands) have banded together and, with the help of Turtle Island Resort management, have formed the **NTTA** (Nacula Tikina Tourist Association; www.fijibudget.com) to promote their area. The website provides current and reliable information on accommodation, transport and activities for budget travellers.

Unless otherwise stated, all accommodation tariffs listed below include meals. For detailed information on diving in the Yasawas, see p60.

Tours

CRUISES

The floating hotel/cruise ships are an excellent mid- to top-range option for visiting

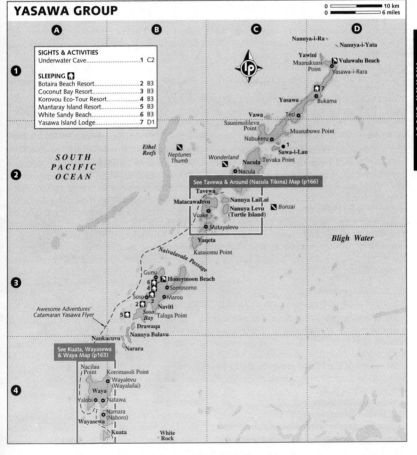

YASAWA GROUP

0   10 km
0   6 miles

SIGHTS & ACTIVITIES
Underwater Cave..............................1 C2

SLEEPING
Botaira Beach Resort..........................2 B3
Coconut Bay Resort............................3 B3
Korovou Eco-Tour Resort.....................4 B3
Mantaray Island Resort.......................5 B3
White Sandy Beach.............................6 B3
Yasawa Island Lodge..........................7 D1

SOUTH PACIFIC OCEAN

Ethel Reefs
Neptunes Thumb
Wonderland
Nacula

Nanuya-i-Ra
Nanuya-i-Yata
Yawini
Muanakuasi Point
Vulawalu Beach
Yasawa-i-Rara
Yasawa
Bukama
Vawa   Teci
Saunimolilevu Point
Muanabuwe Point
Nabukeru
Sawa-i-Lau
Tuvaka Point

See Tavewa & Around (Nacula Tikina) Map (p166)

Tavewa
Matacawalevu
Nanuya LaiLai
Nanuya Levu
(Turtle Island)
Vuake
Matayalevu
Bonzai

Yaqeta
Katasomu Point

Bligh Water

Naivalavala Passage

Gunu
Honeymoon Beach
Somosomo
Soso
Marou
Naviti
Soso Bay
Talaga Point
Drawaqa
Nanuya Balavu

Awesome Adventures'
Catamaran Yasawa Flyer

Naukacuvu
Narara

See Kuata, Wayasewa & Waya Map (p163)

Nacilau Point
Koromasoli Point
Wayalevu
(Wayalailai)
Waya
Yalobi   Natawa
Namara
(Naboro)
Wayasewa
Kuata
White Rock

the Yasawas. With good food and comfortable accommodation laid on, you can take it easy aboard your luxury vessel, pop overboard for excellent snorkelling and diving, drop in on beautiful white-sand beaches and stop to visit local villagers.

Captain Cook Cruises (☎ 670 1823; www.captaincook.com.au; 15 Narewa Rd, Nadi) offers a three-night Mamanuca and southern Yasawa cruise, a four-night Yasawa cruise, and a seven-night combination cruise onboard the MV *Reef Escape*. The 68m cruise boat has a swimming pool, bars, lounges and air-conditioned accommodation spread over three decks. Accommodation options include cabins with bunk beds, staterooms and deluxe staterooms. Prices per person, twin-share, for cabin/stateroom including all meals and activities (except diving) are $1260/1570 (three nights) or $2640/3310 (seven nights). Children under two years travel free of charge; those up to 15 years pay $350/770 for a three-/seven-day trip, regardless of the type of accommodation. Cruises depart from Denarau Marina on Denarau island, west of Nadi.

Blue Lagoon Cruises (☎ 666 1662; www.bluelagooncruises.com; 183 Vitogo Pde, Lautoka) offers three-, four-, or seven-day Club Cruises to the Yasawas aboard huge motor-yachts. Club Cruises cost from $1130/2480 for two/four nights per twin-share cabin. Seven-day Gold Club Cruises aboard the luxury MV *Mystique Princess* start at $4950 for a twin share cabin on saloon deck. Children under 15 pay 11% to 15% depending on the cruise and those aged under two are free. Transfers, cruise activities and food are included but drinks, snorkelling and diving are extra. Cruises depart from Lautoka's Queens Wharf on Viti Levu.

Blue Lagoon Cruises also has a seven-day Luxury Dive Cruise aboard the *Fijian Princess*. It includes all the activities (village visits, *kava* ceremonies, shore excursions, walks etc) and the comforts of a luxury cruise in addition to 15 dives. The dive sites are scattered from the south to the northernmost tip of the island group and take in some of the most pristine areas. Prices start at $5040 per person.

Awesome Adventures (☎ 675 0499; www.awesomefiji.com) offers three-night cruises on board their sister catamaran, the 27m *Wanna Taki*, for $330 per person in either a dorm or double room. Rates include all meals, transfers and activities. Berths are tight but clean and fresh seafood is sometimes on the menu. Although the boat looks snug, these trips are fun and relaxed – travellers rave about the opportunity to snorkel and swim offshore.

South Sea Cruises (☎ 675 0500; www.ssc.com.fj) also runs day tours from Denarau island to Botaira Beach Resort on Naviti island ($125/65 per adult/child) and Sunset Beach Resort on Waya island ($120/60 per adult/child).

SAILING

Captain Cook Cruises (☎ 670 1823; www.captaincook.com.au; 15 Narewa Rd, Nadi) has sailing trips to the southern Yasawas aboard the tall ship SV *Spirit of the Pacific*. Swimming, snorkelling, fishing, island treks, village visits, campfire barbecues and *lovo* (feasts cooked in a pit oven) are all part of the deal. Accommodation is in simple *bure* (traditional thatched dwellings) ashore, or aboard in fold-up canvas beds below the deck cabins. Prices per person, twin share, are $510/680 for a three-/four-day trip.

Yachts can also be chartered from Musket Cove Marina (p155), located on Malololailai in the Mamanucas.

KAYAKING

Australian-operated **Southern Sea Ventures** (☎ in Australia 02-8901 3287; www.southernseaventures.com) offers nine-day kayaking safaris along the Yasawa chain. The trips (May to October) cost A$1965 per person, for a maximum of 10 people per group. The price includes all meals, two-person fibreglass kayaks, safety and camping gear. The pace of the tour is dictated by the weather and the fitness of the group. There are six days of kayaking – you'll follow in Bligh's oar strokes, stopping along the way for snorkelling and village visits. Expect to paddle for three to four hours daily.

A Canadian company offering similar tours is **Ecomarine Ocean Kayak Centre** (☎ in Canada 604-689-5926; www.ecomarine.com). Tours cost around A$1920 and run from May to October. Accommodation is a combination of village stays and camping.

HIKING

Many resorts offer guided hiking trips, some of which visit local villages. Good places to hike include Waya, Nacula and Tavewa.

CORAL'S TRUE COLOUR

The Yasawa islands are home to some of the most vivid coral in the world and excellent visibility provides snorkellers and divers with plenty of opportunity to appreciate it. Although its flowery exterior appears plantlike, coral is actually an animal, and a hungry, carnivorous one at that.

Corals belong to the same class of animals as sea anemones and jellyfish. The true reef-building corals or *Scleractinia* are distinguished by their lime skeletons. This skeleton forms the reef and as new coral continually builds on old, dead coral the reef gradually builds up.

All coral formations are made up of polyps, the tiny tubelike, fleshy cylinders that look very like their close relation, the anemone. The top of the cylinder is open and ringed by waving tentacles, which sting and draw any passing prey into the polyp's stomach. This is why 'coral cuts' can be quite painful – when you graze your skin on coral you're actually receiving a sting. Although this is reason enough to avoid touching coral, it's more important to remember that coral is quite fragile, so if you break it you're essentially killing decades of growth and life.

Each polyp is an individual creature, but each can reproduce by splitting to form a coral colony of separate but closely related polyps. Although each polyp catches and digests its own food, the nutrition passes between the polyps to the whole colony. Most coral polyps only feed at night: during the daytime they withdraw into their hard limestone skeleton, so it is only at night that a coral reef can be seen in its full colourful glory.

Hard corals take many forms. One of the most common and easiest to recognise is the staghorn coral, which grows by budding off new branches from the tips. Brain corals are huge and round with a surface looking very much like a human brain. They grow by adding new base levels of skeletal matter and expanding outwards. Flat or sheet corals, such as plate coral, expand at their outer edges.

Like their reef-building relatives, soft coral is made up of individual polyps, but does not form a hard limestone skeleton. Without the skeleton that protects hard coral, it would seem likely that soft coral would fall prey to fish, but it seems to remain relatively immune either due to toxic substances in its tissues or to the presence of sharp limestone needles, which protect the polyps. Soft corals can move around and will sometimes engulf and kill hard coral.

When diving or snorkelling be careful to respect the underwater environment; admire but don't touch. If your expedition takes you to the ocean floor, look what's beneath you before touching the bottom. Corals may appear resilient and hardy but they are extremely vulnerable and preserving them ensures a healthy ecological balance for all marine life in the area.

Getting There & Around

Turtle Airways (☎ 672 1888; reservations@turtleairways .com) has seaplanes flying daily from Nadi (from Turtle Airways Base in New Town, 20 minutes drive west from Nadi International Airport) to Tavewa island. The flight takes about 35 minutes and costs $300 one way (a fraction of what the upmarket resort guests pay). It is a spectacular scenic flight and well worth it for at least one leg. The flight, on small vintage planes (Cessnas or the less noisy de Havilland Beaver), is a great experience itself.

Most people travelling to the Yasawas choose to go by the *Yasawa Flyer* (also called the 'Yellow Boat') operated by **Awesome Adventures Fiji** (☎ 675 0499; www.awesomefiji.com). The comfortable 25m high-speed catamaran has toilets, air-con and snack bar and departs 9.15am daily from Denarau Marina on Viti Levu. It takes about 1¾ hours to Kuata or Wayalailai ($75), two hours to Waya ($75), three hours to Naviti ($80) and 4½ hours to Tavewa ($95). Interisland fares are around $60, even for short distances.

If you want to linger in the islands without a prebooked itinerary then a 'Bula Pass' (seven/14/21 days $250/370/400) can be a good deal. The pass enables unlimited island-hopping within the time period but only one return trip to Denarau. Awesome Adventures also offers three-/seven-night stays (from $300/800 per person) on up to four islands including transport, accommodation, meals and activities. Be warned, however, your choice of accommodation is limited, usually to the lower end of the quality scale. So if you've got a firm idea of what you want from your holiday you're better off booking your own accommodation separately.

YASAWA GROUP

WARNING

Some of the budget resorts offer their own, cheaper boat transfers to the Yasawas; however, be aware that the trip is quite long, across an exposed stretch of water, and weather conditions can change quickly. Depending on the weather and your state of mind, these trips by small boat can be a fun adventure or uncomfortable, vomit-inducing and frightening! Exposure to rain or too much sun may also be a problem if the boat does not have a roof. In the past, passengers have been stranded for hours due to engine failure and in 1999 an overcrowded boat sank! Fortunately no one died but, as one survivor told us, it's worth checking beforehand if boats have sufficient life jackets, a marine radio and are licensed by the Fijian government. Furthermore, the resorts generally only undercut the *Yasawa Flyer* by around $10, which makes the *Flyer* an utter bargain for the comfort and security you get on the large catamaran. Transfers from the *Yasawa Flyer* to the resorts, while usually only a short distance, also involve the use of local boats.

Petrol is a limited resource here and travelling around by local boat can expose you to the risk of running out of petrol. The best way to avoid this is to give as much notice as possible to your resort if you plan to go island-hopping – it will enable them to plan for boat transfers.

At the time of writing there was rumour of another company commencing transfers to the Yasawas, departing from Lautoka.

KUATA

Petite Kuata is the first stop in the Yasawa string. It's quite spectacular with unusual volcanic rock formations, caves, coral cliffs on the southern end, and great snorkelling just offshore.

Well… **Kuata Natural Resort** (☎ 666 9020, 933 4508; sites per person/dm/d incl meals $45/55/130) is not a tower of condominiums, but that's about as far as the natural tag stretches. Sitting be-

TIPS FOR THE BACKPACKER

Many of the budget resorts within the Yasawas are identical in standard and price. Accommodation is in simple thatched *bure* with concrete bathrooms or bunk dorms with shared bathrooms. Mosquito nets are a given, although the cheaper the tariff the larger the holes. Cleanliness can also be an issue at some but properties tend to pick up their act if the grapevine gets noisy with complaints. Almost all offer an overwhelmingly friendly greeting, but the bigger the joint the less personal it will be. Activities such as village visits, snorkelling trips and hiking (all around $10 per person) are additional and snorkelling gear can be hired for $5 to $10 per day. Food is generally filling and stodgy but the target market tends to focus more on the beer and/or conversation.

hind a coarse sandy beach with Wayasewa hovering in the near distance, Kuata appeals to that unfussy backpacker with a taste for beer and raucous fun. The resort has a 20-bed and 10-bed dorm and many traditional style double *bure* with private bathrooms, tightly arranged around the gardens. The standards are pretty simple and the emphasis is on fun and activities, which include guided walks of the island ($8), though you can do this on your own, snorkelling trips ($10) and village visits ($14), which are both worthwhile. The other side of the island also has a nice beach and the best snorkelling.

Transfers to Kuata are by the *Yasawa Flyer* ($75 one way per person), plus a $10 transfer fee from the *Flyer* to the resort.

WAYASEWA

Also known as Wayalailai (Little Waya), Wayasewa greets visitors with Vatuvula; a humbling volcanic rock face that gazes out to Kuata from across the small passage of ocean between the two islands. Wayasewa has good beaches and coral reefs. The Fijian Government declared Namara village unsafe and had it moved to its present location in 1975 after a rockslide from the cliff damaged some of the buildings. The new **Namara**, also known as Naboro village, also has a spectacular setting. The high grassy hills to the south form a theatrical backdrop for *meke* (traditional dance) in the late afternoon light. Villagers welcome tourist groups and present *meke* and host *kava* ceremonies (see p67 for information

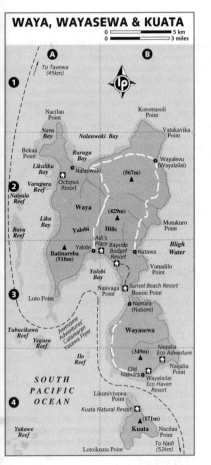

WAYA, WAYASEWA & KUATA

are also snug singles and doubles in the ageing former schoolhouse, although collective snoring can prove cacophonous. Snorkelling off the beach is reasonable at high tide, but the best place is off Kuata, a short boat ride away. There are shared cold-water showers and flush toilets but water supply can be restricted at times. Drinks and snacks can be bought at reasonable prices, and the restaurant-bar has a lovely raised deck overlooking the beach. A new restaurant was being built at the time of writing.

Dive Trek Wayasewa, based here, offers two-tank dives/PADI Open Water Courses for $110/350. The daily activities include a sunset cruise ($15 per person), half-day picnic ($10) and guided walks ($10), although obvious tracks enable you to do the latter yourself. The hike to the top of the cliff passes through high grass, trees and sharp rocks and from the hilltop you have excellent views of the whole Yasawa Group.

Naqalia Eco Adventure (☎ 666 1572, 932 3446; sites per person $35) Just around the corner from Wayalailai, this simple campground is operated by two of the clans on Wayasewa. It's utterly rudimentary and consequently a magnet for keen hikers and campers. It's also a much quieter option than its bigger neighbour.

Getting There & Away

Transfers to Wayasewa with the *Yasawa Flyer* cost $75 per person one way, plus a $5 transfer fee charged by the resorts. Wayalailai also offers transfers to Viti Levu in a small boat ($60 one way, about 1¾ hours, Monday to Saturday).

WAYA

Waya is exquisite on the eyes and promises travellers some postcard scenery. It has rugged hills, beautiful beaches and lagoons and a periphery that alternates between long, sandy beaches and rocky headland. There are four villages, a nursing station and a boarding school on the island. Resorts vary in quality and price and are spread out so the locations are generally isolated.

One for the walkers, Waya has a good network of **hiking trails** snaking through the tropical vegetation of its hilly centre. It's easy to hike to the top of Yalobi Hills, from where you can see the entire Yasawa islands chain. However, hiking across the island requires

on *yaqona* drinking). Many of the images in Glen Craig's beautiful photographic book *Children of the Sun* were taken on Wayasewa and Waya.

Sleeping & Eating

Wayalailai Eco Haven Resort (☎ 666 9715, 672 1377; www.bbcdi.ca/wayalailai; sites per person $30, dm/s $40/45, d $110-200) Owned and operated by the villagers of Wayasewa, this rustic budget resort has one of the most dramatic settings in the Yasawas. Tucked squarely at the base of Vatuvula's granite façade, the property is tiered over two levels above the beach and encompasses wooden bunked dorms and bamboo *bure* overlooking the ocean. The *bure* closest to the water are the best. There

---

THE AUTHOR'S CHOICE

Octopus Resort (☎ 666 6337; www.octopusresort.com; sites per tent $90, dm $80, d $145-200; ☒ ☒)
Sweet mercy, this chic resort is a far cry from the Yasawas' trademark thatched walls and cold
showers. Although it's one of the oldest properties in the island group, meticulous maintenance
and constant evolution have fashioned a Shangri-la façade. Visitors are greeted with the oasis-like
vision of a swanky bar-restaurant, which dishes up chilled tunes and fabulous food. The stylish
bure are tiled and fan cooled and some have two bunks to accommodate families. The spotless
bathrooms have roofless showers so you can stargaze while you wash. Prices escalate as you
get closer to the water, but all *bure* have plenty of garden and space surrounding them for
privacy. The dorm is the best in the Yasawas (if not all of Fiji!) and each solid bed comes with
its bedside table, fan and electricity outlet. Camping is in large domed tents provided by the
resort. All guests are treated to bath towels and generous beach towels, and the water's edge
is peppered with padded timber sun lounges.

The beach is wide at low tide and has good snorkelling and a secluded atmosphere. It's un-
nervingly easy to spend your entire day on the soft sandy bank but there are plenty of activities
on offer and nightly entertainment. Snorkelling gear costs $5 per person to rent, babysitting is
available and the one-hour massage at $15 a pop is the best value in the country. It also has
a good dive outfit that charges $150/480 for a two-tank dive/PADI Open Water Course.

---

more preparation as it is 10km each way
over the hills. It's best done with a guide but
if you want to head out on your own take
plenty of water. It's also advisable to avoid
going after heavy rains; the tracks are steep
in parts and navigating their slushy ascent
varies from difficult to impossible. At low
tide it's possible to walk from Wayasewa to
Waya on a sandbank so avid trekkers can
avoid transfers altogether.

A thick rim of coral follows the shoreline and provides great **snorkelling** just off
the beaches, particularly near Sunset Beach
Resort and Octopus Resort.

Sleeping & Eating

Sunset Beach Resort (☎ 666 6644; after the beep dial
6383; dm/d $55/140) In an exposed but beautiful
setting, this place welcomes guests with a
wide curve of beach and a semilandscaped
frontage. There's a basic, five-bed dorm and
five double *bure* with private bathroom. Accommodation is all thatched, as is the dining room, which has a sand floor and long
communal tables. It's small and quiet and
perfect for low-maintenance travellers in
search of no-frills serenity. The swimming
here is lovely and the tidal sandbar that
connects Waya and Wayasewa is on the
resort's doorstep. You can walk across at
low tide, and the snorkelling on the eastern
side of the point is good. Transfers from the
Yasawa Flyer are an additional $10.

There are two additional budget options
with more basic setups tucked into the ma-

jestic Yalobi Bay – the family-owned **Adi's
Place** (☎ 665 0573, 9926 377; sites per person $25, dm/
d $35/80) and the teeny **Bayside Budget Resort**
(☎ 666 6644, after the beep dial 6383; dm/d $40/100).
Both are rudimentary but utterly friendly.
The snorkelling at Adi's and Bayside is not
as good as that at Octopus Resort or Sunset
Beach Resort and you'll need to take a boat
to a nearby reef or walk to the eastern side
of Nativaga Point for the best spots.

Getting There & Away

The *Yasawa Flyer* comes past Yalobi Bay
daily ($75 per person each way). Octopus
Resort also operates its own transfers from
Lautoka and Nadi in a solid, covered boat
for $65/35 per adult/child one way.

NAVITI & AROUND

Roughly midway along the Yasawas, and
one of the largest (33 sq km) and highest of the group, Naviti has a rugged volcanic profile, up to 380m high. The island's
main attraction is an amazing snorkelling
site where you can swim with manta rays.
It's near the aptly named **Manta Ray Island**.
Korovou, Coconut Bay and White Sandy
Beach Resorts all share a protected, long
stretch of white sand, about halfway up the
west coast of the island. Unfortunately the
swimming is only just possible at high tide
here – low tide exposes a wide bank of dead
and ugly reef. Fortunately a short track
(around a 10-minute walk) next to White
Sandy Beach Resort crosses over a hill to

the pretty and secluded Honeymoon Beach. Visitors need to make a $1 donation to the village to visit this little cove but the pay off is calm and tranquil swimming waters and great snorkelling.

Sleeping & Eating

Botaira Beach Resort (☎ 675 0499; www.botaira .com; dm $70, d from $275) Definitely catering to the more discerning traveller, Botaira extends over a long patch of secluded beach thick with palm trees, offering guests plenty of privacy in spacious and stylish timber *bure*. High roofs, bright bathrooms and crisp white sheets are the order of the day here. The swimming and snorkelling are lovely and activities include guided walks and swimming with manta rays. Botaira has couples stamped all over it but it's devoid of pretension and caters to all age groups.

Coconut Bay Resort (☎ 666 6644, after the beep dial 1300; dm/d $45/120) The gracious staff at this warm and friendly resort are drawcards unto themselves. Dorms are roomy 12-bed affairs with sturdy timber bunks. Doubles are in spotless and simple duplex buildings and although the walls are thin, the clientele is generally quiet. Little touches such as couches on the veranda give the place a homely air. The food is excellent and if you're here for a curry night you've hit the jackpot. Coconut Bay is a good option for couples or travellers seeking a chilled-out retreat.

Mantaray Island Resort (☎ 664 0520; www .mantarayisland.com; sites per person $25, dm $35, d $100-150) One of the newest of the Yasawa resorts, Mantaray occupies its own wee island and has a lovely beach with wide ocean views. Its proximity to the manta rays' favoured stomping grounds is a huge plus, but the classy wooden dorm and beachfront *bure* are also a notch better than its average budget counterparts. The resort also has an eco-back and uses compost toilets. Meal plans are an additional $40 per person.

Korovou Eco-Tour Resort (☎ 666 6644, after the beep dial 2244; korovoultk@connect.com.fj; sites per person $35, dm $55, d $130-160) In stark contrast to its neighbour (Coconut Bay), Korovou can accommodate a small army and is frequently packed with young and social troops. The 32-bed dorms are a tad on the cramped side and can get stuffy in the heat. Cheaper

---

BEACH BUSINESS

All the resorts in the Yasawas are on the waterfront but not all can claim idyllic beaches. If white sand, turquoise depths and simmering in a sun-coma are what you came for then the following resorts should be just the ticket.

Oarsman's Bay Lodge (p168) It's on the best of the Yasawas' resort-based beaches. Protected from the trade winds, the water is still, clear and deep. A large bank of coral provides excellent snorkelling.

Nanuya Island Resort (p167) The resort occupies an enviable and isolated position on a quiet beach in front of the renowned Blue Lagoon.

Sunset Beach Resort (opposite) At the southern hook of Waya Island, Sunset Beach has a 270-degree bend of beach with plenty of sand. There's great snorkelling in the small passage between Waya and Wayasewa.

Octopus Resort (opposite) The beach in this protected cove is beautiful for swimming at high tide and great for sunbaking and wandering at low tide.

Botaira Beach Resort (left) Botaira's beach is a length of soft white sand with ample room to park a towel. The calm water has a good stretch of shallows before it drops into the deep.

---

doubles are in thatched *bure* or duplex-style rooms; the latter are much better value so ask to see your digs before you check in. There are also solid timber cabins with clean and cool interiors. Meals are served on a large open deck overlooking the water and there's a bar with Sky TV. Snorkelling is OK off the beach (only at high tide). Gear hire is $10 per day and a snorkelling trip costs $20 per person. A two-tank dive/PADI Open Water Dive Course costs $170/530.

White Sandy Beach (☎ 666 6644, after the beep dial 1360; dm/d $55/130) The sand somehow seems softer and the pace significantly slower at this personable budget resort. There are two comfortable *bure* (with two more in the making) and a clean and cosy dorm. Dining is a communal affair at picnic tables and the dive centre here offers two-tank dives for $170.

Getting There & Away

Boat transfers to all the resorts listed here are with the *Yasawa Flyer* ($80 each way).

YASAWA GROUP

TAVEWA

Tavewa is a small (3 sq km), low island right in the middle of the Yasawa Group but it houses some of the group's northern-most resorts. A pleasant beach unfurls itself on the southeastern coast of the island but it's often plagued by buffeting trade winds. You need to head west to the beach around the bend of Savutu Point to find relief from the gales and you're best off doing so at low tide. The snorkelling just offshore here is excellent. An ambling ascent to the top of the central crest affords photogenic views of the Yasawa chain and is particularly spectacular at sunset. The track joins the path connecting Coral View Resort and the southeastern beach.

All the resorts listed here offer boat trips to the Blue Lagoon and trips to Sawa-i-Lau caves (p169) for $10 and $25 per person, respectively. Volleyball, nightly music and *kava* sessions are also standard.

Based on the island, **Westside Watersports** (☎ 666 1462, 998 862; westside@divefiji.com) is an excellent, experienced dive operation. It caters to guests at resorts on nearby islands including the upmarket Turtle Island Resort,

as well as Blue Lagoon Cruise passengers. A two-tank dive/PADI Open Water Course costs $160/580 and the instructors and equipment are outstanding.

Sleeping & Eating

Otto & Fanny's (☎ 666 6481; dm/d $45/90) On a sprawling property, this homely place has just five *bure* with private bathrooms and a 12-bed dorm. The flat, grassy grounds are inundated with palm trees and offer plenty of wide open space. *Bure* nearest the beach catch more of the sea breeze. Two of the *bure* can fit three to four people, with one in a more secluded spot in the jungle and near the beach. Travellers talk up the meals here (meal packages per person $50) and the afternoon tea of banana cake, chocolate cake or scones (for only $1.50!) is legendary. This place has a real family feel to it and lures travellers of all ages. Otto and Fanny's is also closest to Tavewa's best patch of beach.

David's Place (☎ 672 1820, 665 2820; davidsplace resort@yahoo.com; sites per person $35, dm $60, d with/without bathroom $180/120) Also occupying capacious grounds but with a more structured feel and

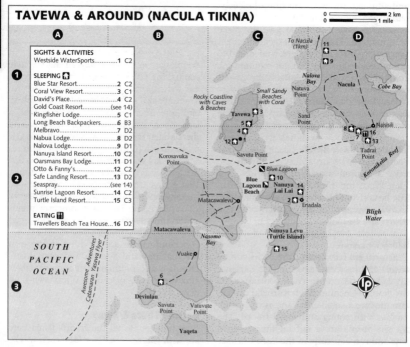

TAVEWA & AROUND (NACULA TIKINA)

0 ——————— 2 km
0 ——————— 1 mile

SIGHTS & ACTIVITIES
Westside WaterSports..............1 C2

SLEEPING
Blue Star Resort.....................2 C2
Coral View Resort.................3 C1
David's Place.......................4 C2
Gold Coast Resort..............(see 14)
Kingfisher Lodge...................5 C1
Long Beach Backpackers......6 B3
Melbravo............................7 D2
Nabua Lodge.......................8 D2
Nalova Lodge......................9 D1
Nanuya Island Resort..........10 D1
Oarsmans Bay Lodge...........11 D1
Otto & Fanny's...................12 C2
Safe Landing Resort............13 D2
Seaspray...........................(see 14)
Sunrise Lagoon Resort.........14 C2
Turtle Island Resort............15 C3

EATING
Travellers Beach Tea House...16 D2

SOUTH
PACIFIC
OCEAN

To Nacula
(1km)

Nalova
Bay

Natuva
Point

Nacula

Cobe Bay

Rocky Coastline
with Caves
& Beaches

Small Sandy
Beaches
with Coral

Tavewa

Sand
Point

Naisisili

Korosavuka
Point

Savutu Point

Tadrai
Point

Matacawalevu

Blue Lagoon

Blue
Lagoon
Beach

Nanuya
Lai Lai

Eriadala

Bligh
Water

Matacawalevu

Nasomo
Bay

Vuake

Nanuya Levu
(Turtle Island)

Deviulau

Savuta
Point

Vatuvute
Point

Yaqeta

fewer trees than Otto and Fanny's, this resort has an abundance of simple *bure* with double beds, lights and mosquito nets. The more expensive deluxe *bure* have private bathrooms and are a huge increase in style but there's only two so you'll need to book. The dorm contains a whopping 26 beds.

Coral View Resort (☎ 666 6644, after the beep dial 8876; coral@connect.com.fj; sites per person $35, dm $55, d $130-180) Nestled beneath a dense hilly backdrop, this ever-expanding resort is furnished with a constant buzz thanks to sparky staff and a range of accommodation options to suit everyone. The 16-bed concrete-floored dorm is comfortable with decent chunks of space and light. Standard *bure* are Spartan and a tad on the pricey side, but the swish new deluxe versions are the best on the island with classy bathrooms, mezzanines, bar fridges and private verandas. The dining room is like a big beachy dance hall with long communal tables and although the food is unadventurous, it's filling and you can get fresh coffee! Coral View's beach is virtually nonexistent and you'll need to cover the short distance to the southeast beach for a dose of sea and sand, but the resort offers plenty of activities.

Kingfisher Lodge (☎ 665 2830; s/d *bure* $130/160) Best suited to couples after a quiet time, Kingfisher Lodge has just one comfortable fan-cooled cottage in a jungle-like garden. You can order meals in advance or duck down the beach to Otto & Fanny's. This place is so quiet it sometimes has an abandoned air about it, which may be a plus or a minus depending on what you're looking for.

Getting There & Away

The *Yasawa Flyer* costs $95 per person each way and the seaplane $300 (see p161). Coral View has its own transfer boat to Lautoka (3¼ hours, organised on demand) costing $70/120 one way/return. Guests of other resorts can be included for a little extra.

NANUYA LAILAI

This is it folks, home to that celebrity of all the Yasawas' beaches – the Blue Lagoon. Crystalline and glossy, it doesn't disappoint the bevy of swimmers, snorkellers, divers, and people on cruise boats or yachts who dabble in its gorgeous depths. Actually it's not dissimilar to many of the lagoons scattered around the Yasawas, but the protected

beach *is* lovely and the water *is* achingly lucent. A narrow channel separates it from the larger Nanuya Levu (Turtle Island) to the south. Travellers are advised (by signs and enforced at times by security staff) to stay clear of Nanuya Levu as well as the section of Blue Lagoon beach used by Blue Lagoon Cruises. The settlement of **Enadala** and several budget resorts reside on the eastern side of Nanuya Lailai, where the beach is deep and choppy. Inland, the island is a mass of gently sloping hills and mangroves.

Sleeping & Eating

Nanuya Island Resort (☎ 666 7633; www.nanuyafiji .com; d $210-350) Swish and understated, this resort is the kind of place you picture when you dream of indulgence, cocktails and exquisite vistas. The *bure* are Fiji-nouveau; the roofs may be thatched but the interiors are chic and elegant. All are fan cooled and have their own bathroom. Your tariff includes breakfast, and the à-la-carte lunch and dinner menus are reasonable ($12 to $25) and inventive. And it's *right* on the Blue Lagoon.

Gold Coast Resort (☎ 666 6644, after the beep dial 9484; dm $40, d with/without bathroom $120/90) The private timber *bure* here have sand floors and simple surrounds but are the nicest along this beach. This resort is also a smallish affair and consequently a good place to escape the masses. Meals often feature catch of the day and are a refreshing departure from the starchy carb feasts at other budget resorts.

Sunrise Lagoon Resort (☎ 666 6644, after the beep dial 9484; dm/d $55/150) Something like a 'South Seas school camp' (particularly the food), this budget resort swarms with 18 to 25 year olds who delve into 'hi, my name is…' intro sessions, nightly *meke* and industrious socialising. The accommodation and bathrooms are a little on the sloppy side but the crowd is chatty and there's a warm atmosphere pervading the whole place.

More budget options:

Seaspray (☎ 666 8962; dm/d $45/95) Budget and basic with decent dorms.

Blue Star Resort (☎ 992 5825; info@bluestarfiji.com; s $80-120, d $90-150) Quiet option with lovely *bure*. Recommended by readers.

Getting There & Away

Transfers to Nanuya Lailai are with the *Yasawa Flyer* ($95). Turtle Airways (p161) has flights for $300 per person one way.

YASAWA GROUP

MATACAWALEVU

Matacawalevu is a 4km-long hilly volcanic island protected by the large Nasomo Bay on its eastern side. Nanuya Levu (Turtle Island) is to the east and to the south, across a protected lagoon which is used for seaweed farming, is Yaqeta. The island has two villages, Matacawalevu on its northeast end and Vuake in Nasomo Bay.

On a lovely long curved beach with a protected lagoon, **Long Beach Backpackers** (☎ 666 6644, after the beep dial 3032; dm/d $55/$90) has a stunning location. There is good snorkelling nearby, including an excellent reef drop off on the western side of the island. It has easy access to the small rocky island of Deviulau, home to local seabirds. Accommodation and facilities are pretty basic in Fijian style *bure*. It charges $10 per person for pick-ups from the *Yasawa Flyer* or $20 per person to meet the seaplane at Tavewa.

NACULA

Nacula, a hilly volcanic island, is the third-largest in the Yasawas. Blanketed with rugged hills and soft peaks, its interior is laced with well-trodden paths begging for mooching to villages and small coves. There are four villages here, including Nacula, home of Ratu Epeli Vuetibau, the high chief of Nacula Tikina. The *tikina* (group of villages) includes the islands of Nacula, Tavewa, Nanuya Levu, Nanuya Lailai and Matacawalevu, and is home to about 3500 people. Catching a church service in one of the villages is a real treat. Beach devotees will be ecstatic to know that Nacula also has some of the finest swimming and snorkelling in Fiji, particularly at Oarsman's Bay. A new, intimate resort is on its way to being built on the tiny island just north of Oarsman's Bay. It promises to be flash.

Sleeping & Eating

Oarsman's Bay Lodge (☎ 672 2921; nacula@hotmail .com; sites per person $22.50, dm/d/f $50/140/240; ✗) You'll hear murmurs about the beach at Oarsman's Bay much further afield than the *Yasawa Flyer* and for good reason. Its long swathe of powdery sand eases gently into a glassy, cerulean sea, offering impossibly clear views to the bottom well past wading height. The classy digs at the lodge do the beach justice and this is deservedly one of the most popular resorts in the Yasa-

was. Clean and crisp *bure* with bright hues, modern bathrooms and private verandas are strung out on either side of the resort. Several have interconnecting rooms for families. Above the central, open-air dining room is a 13-bed dorm, which has fairly close but atmospheric quarters and a lovely landing with views across the bay. The food here (additional compulsory meal plan per adult/child six to 16/child under six $50/25/11) is very good, particularly on buffet nights which occur at least twice a week. Activities include island-hopping, reef-hopping, village visits and hand-fishing (all $10), but the big attraction is the spectacular snorkelling right off the beach. Oarsman's has remained relatively small; even at full capacity there's enough space to make you feel like you're at an exclusive resort. Payment is by credit card only.

Safe Landing Resort (☎ 672 2921; nacula@hotmail .com; sites per person $12, dm $17-35, d without bathroom $45-85, d with bathroom $125-135) Although this neat little resort doesn't have quite the same style (or beach) as Oarsman's Bay, it's still one of the most comfortable resorts in the Yasawas. Timber *bure* are fan-cooled, tiled and compact with plenty of windows for sunlight. The more expensive deluxe dorms are housed in similar units and are quite a treat with only six beds and a private bathroom. Standard dorms are simpler affairs and the cheaper Fijian *bure* are thatched, basic huts. Both share rudimentary facilities. There's an ocean of flat grassy space behind the resort for camping (or just mucking around) and although the beach isn't huge, it's calm and private. The food (additional compulsory meal plan per adult/child six to 16/child under six $41/21/11) is quite good but drinks and snacks from the bar are expensive. Boat transfers from the *Yasawa Flyer* or the seaplane 'airport' in Tavewa cost $10 per person. The resort has free village visits, a couple of small paddleboats, snorkelling gear ($5 per day, snorkel trips $10 per person), island-hopping ($10 per person each way) and underwater cave trips ($25 per person). Payment is by credit card only.

Nalova Lodge (☎ 666 9055; d $195) Right next door to Oarsman's Bay Lodge this teeny resort has been in the making for years. There are three spacious and homey *bure* with a modicum of furniture, wallpapered floors and simple bathrooms. Breakfast and lunch

are served on your own *bure* porch and dinner is served in the small dining room. It
enjoys *that* fabulous beach, the food is fresh
and good and the staff are lovely.

Nabua Lodge (☎ 666 6644, after the beep dial 6369;
dm $50, d with/without bathroom $150/95) Just west of
Safe Landing on a nicely landscaped plot of
grass, this lodge has generous timber cottages
facing the ocean. Rooms have ceiling fans,
wooden furniture and endearing porches.
They're not the Ritz but are great value for
the price. Standard *bure* are also roomy but
the lack of fans may produce stuffy summer
nights. Dorms are plain and simple. Hammocks are placed strategically between shady
trees throughout the property and right out
front is a tidal white-sand beach fringed by
reefs. Nabua is a great place to switch to 'Fiji
time' and adopt the local lifestyle.

Melbravo (☎ 666 6644, after the beep dial 7472; dm
$50, d with/without shower $150/100) Also spread
out on a patch of lawn, Melbravo's accommodation could do with a touch of TLC.
Bure with private bathrooms, fans, electric
lights and a decent splash of space are the
best buy, but the standard *bure* and dorms
are a little on the dark and stuffy side.

Travellers Beach Tea House (☺ 8am-6pm) Based
in and out of a wee shack, this beachy tea
house serves tea, coffee and cake (all $1.50).
It's a lovely spot to survey the ocean and
chat with the friendly owners.

Getting There & Away
Transfers to all the resorts on Nacula are
by *Yasawa Flyer* ($95). Resorts charge an
additional $10 transfer fee.

NANUYA LEVU (TURTLE ISLAND)
Nanuya Levu is a privately owned island (2
sq km) with protected sandy beaches and
rugged volcanic cliffs. The 1980 film *The
Blue Lagoon*, starring Brooke Shields, was
partly filmed here, as was the original 1949
version starring Jean Simmons.

One of the world's finest and most fa-
mous resorts, **Turtle Island Resort** (☎ 672 2921;
www.turtlefiji.com; d $3400-4100) lures the celebri-
ties, romantics and flush from around the
world to its exclusive shores. The resort
is owned by American Richard Evanson,
who, after making his fortune in cable TV,
bought the island in 1972 for his own personal hideaway. The 14 two-room *bure* are
spaced along the beach. Rates include all
food, drinks and most activities and there
is a six-night minimum stay. Children are
allowed only during July and Christmas
holidays. Transfers are by Turtle Airways
seaplane charter ($1400 return per couple),
a 30-minute flight from Nadi.

SAWA-I-LAU
Sawa-i-Lau is the odd limestone island amid
a string of high volcanic islands. The underwater limestone is thought to have formed
a few hundred metres below the surface
and then were uplifted over time. Shafts of
daylight enter the great dome-shaped cave
(15m tall above the water surface) where you
can swim in the natural pool. With a guide,
a torch and a bit of courage, you can also
swim through an underwater passage into
an adjoining chamber. The limestone walls
have carvings, paintings and inscriptions
of unknown meaning. Similar inscriptions
also occur on Vanua Levu in the hills near
Vuinadi, Natewa Bay and near Dakuniba on
the Tunuloa (Cakaudrove) Peninsula.

Most Yasawa budget resorts offer trips to
the caves and the cruise ships call here.

YASAWA
Yasawa, the northernmost island of the
group, has six small villages and a fabulous,
five-star resort.

Remote **Yasawa Island Resort** (☎ 672 2266;
www.yasawa.com; s/d from $1490/1580; ✗ ☒) is set
on a gorgeous beach. The 16 air-conditioned
bure are spacious with separate living and
bedroom areas. Rates include lobster omelettes for breakfast and all à-la-carte meals
(drinks extra) and activities (except for diving, game fishing and massage). The resort
has its own dive shop and activities include
4WD safaris and picnics to deserted beaches.
Transfers are by charter flight from Nadi
($320 per person one way, 30 minutes).

YASAWA GROUP

Lomaiviti Group

Lomaiviti (Middle Fiji) is the heart of Fiji. It's the place where the Fijian nation came into being. The islands lie just off the east coast of Viti Levu, but they feel like another world in another time. They are rustic and peaceful, and travellers tend to stay here far longer than they intended.

Historic Ovalau is the closest island to Viti Levu. Its rugged volcanic landscape, sharp peaks and central crater have a prehistoric beauty. Picturesque Levuka, Ovalau's main town, was Fiji's earliest European settlement and the country's first capital. It is definitely worth a visit, as is Lovoni village, deep in the extinct caldera. There are plenty of opportunities for diving, snorkelling and island hopping – and even more for afternoon-napping, people-watching and drinking *kava* (a narcotic drink) – so you can easily spend a few days here.

The sea south of Ovalau is sprinkled with the tiny coral islands of Leleuvia, Yanuca Lailai and Caqalai. Each has beautiful white sandy beaches, good snorkelling and simple, budget resorts. Hawksbill turtles visit their beaches to lay eggs. To the north, wedge-shaped Koro rises abruptly from deep water. It has lush rainforest and great diving nearby. The resort island of Naigani is northwest of Ovalau.

The annual migration of a pod of humpback whales brings them along the east coast of Ovalau between May and September.

LOMAIVITI GROUP

HIGHLIGHTS

- Eat the breakfast that goes on forever at **Levuka Homestay** (p177)

- Drink in the atmosphere – and the cheap Fiji Bitter – at the **Ovalau Club** (p179), Levuka

- Hike around **Lovoni** (p176), the village in a fractured volcanic crater

- Wander Levuka's **colonial streets** (p174), bumping into the ghosts of the first colonists

- Snorkel around **Caqalai** (p180), the almost-perfect budget resort

- Exchange *bula* (a greeting) and fall into conversation with the locals in **Levuka** (p174)

- Dive the **Levuka Passage** (opposite), just minutes from the shore, if you're an experienced diver

- Watch for **whales** (p176) in Levuka's harbour, from May to September

Levuka ★ ★ Levuka Passage
Lovoni ★
★ Caqalai

- POPULATION: 15,000 | ■ AREA: 409 SQ KM

History

The town of Levuka in the 19th century was a bolthole where embittered sailors jumped ship, escaped convicts hid out, polygamous drunks took strings of island brides, and disputes were settled with the musket.

As early as 1806, European sandalwood traders stopped at Levuka in search of supplies, but they did not begin to settle here until the 1830s. They built schooners, traded for *bêche-de-mer* (sea cucumber), turtle shells and coconut oil and settled down with several Fijian women, explaining to the local people this was the custom where they came from.

The Lovoni people, warriors of the caldera in the centre of Ovalau, saw the settlers as interlopers, and repeatedly burned down their timber town. The whites lived under the protection of the chief of Levuka, who was murdered by raiding Lovoni in 1846.

Levuka grew and by the 1850s it had reputation for drunkenness, violence and immorality. It attracted beachcombers and freebooters, conmen and middlemen, dreamers and crooks. In the 1870s a flood of planters and other settlers came to Fiji, and the booming town reached a population of about 3000 Europeans, who drank in 52 hotels. The cotton boom was brief and its aftermath bitter. A short-lived Ku Klux Klan was formed in Levuka with the (quickly frustrated) aim of installing a white supremacist government.

In 1825 the coastal villagers ended their alliance with the chief of Verata (a village on Viti Levu's Rewa Delta), and gave allegiance to Ratu Seru Cakobau, the powerful chief of Bau (an island off the southeast coast of Viti Levu). Cakobau attempted unsuccessfully to form a national government in 1871, and in 1874 Great Britain acted on an earlier offer by Cakobau and Fiji was ceded to the Crown. Fiji thus became a British colony and Levuka was proclaimed its capital. (For more information see p29.) The government was officially moved to Suva in 1882. By the end of the 19th century, trade was also shifting to Suva, and with copra markets plummeting in the 1930s, Levuka declined further.

While the northern end of town was swept away in the hurricanes of 1888 and 1905, many of the boom-time buildings remain.

Climate

The climate of these islands is sunnier and drier than the east coast of Viti Levu, although Levukans say that if it doesn't rain for a week, it's almost a drought.

Information

All facilities for tourists in the Lomaiviti Group are in Levuka, Ovalau. Fast, cheap Internet is available at Ovalau Watersports, and the Royal Hotel also has a computer in its office where you can get online.

Dial ☎ 911 for the ambulance or police.

Colonial National Bank (Beach St, Levuka) Exchanges travellers cheques and currency.

Levuka Hospital (☎ 344 0221; Beach St, Levuka; ☺ outpatient treatment 8am-1pm & 2-4pm Mon-Fri, 8am-noon Sat, emergencies only after hr) A good, new hospital at the northern end of town. Efficient doctors will treat tourists for $5.

Ovalau Tourist Information Centre (☎ 330 0356; Community Centre, Morris Hedstrom Bldg, Levuka; ☺ 8am-1pm & 2-4.30pm Mon-Fri, Sat till 1pm) Features friendly staff who will do their best to help you hunt down any information you're after, or they'll bat you to Ovalau Watersports.

Ovalau Watersports (☎ 344 0166; www.owlfiji.com; Beach St, Levuka; ☺ 8.30am-5pm Mon-Fri, till 1pm Sat) A dive shop cum information centre cum Internet provider cum tour-booking office.

Police station (☎ 344 0222; Totoga Lane, Levuka)

Post office (Beach St, Levuka) Near Queen's Wharf at the southern end of town; there's a cardphone outside.

Westpac bank (Beach St, Levuka) Has the only ATM in Lomaiviti; also exchanges travellers cheques and foreign currency, and gives cash advances on Visa or MasterCard.

Activities

CYCLING

Cycling is a good way to explore Levuka and its surrounding area. The road to the south is fairly flat, and the north is OK until about Cawaci, after which it gets very hilly. It takes about a day to cycle around the island. Mountain bikes are available from Levuka's **Ovalau Watersports** (Beach St; half-/full day $10/15).

DIVING & SNORKELLING

The Lomaiviti waters offer some great dive sites where you can encounter manta rays, hammerheads, turtles, white-tip reef sharks and lion fish. There is stunning soft coral at Snake Island and Shark Reef in the Moturiki Channel, and excellent hard coral at Waitovu Passage (the best snorkelling spot – although most dives are suitable for snorkellers). The Pipeline, two minutes by boat from town at Levuka Passage, is for experienced divers only. Here, the fishy waste from

LOMAIVITI GROUP

LOMAIVITI GROUP

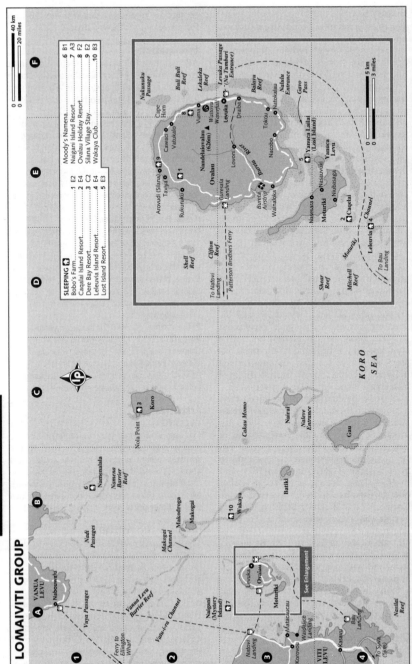

SLEEPING 🛏
Bobo's Farm..........................**1** E2
Caqalai Island Resort.............**2** E4
Dere Bay Resort....................**3** C2
Leleuvia Island Resort............**4** E4
Lost Island Resort.................**5** E3
Moody's Namena...................**6** B1
Naigani Island Resort.............**7** A3
Ovalau Holiday Resort............**8** F2
Silana Village Stay.................**9** E2
Wakaya Club........................**10** B3

0   40 km
0   20 miles

VANUA LEVU
Nabouwalu
Ferry to Ellington Wharf
Viya Passages
Vanua Levu Barrier Reef
Nadi Passages
Namenalala
Namena Barrier Reef
Moody's Namena 6

Nola Point
Koro 3
Dere Bay Resort

Makodroga
Makogai
Makogai Channel

Wakaya 10

KORO SEA

Vatu-i-ra Channel

Naigani (Mystery Island) 7
Levuka
Ovalau
Moturiki
See Enlargement

Natovi Landing
Korovou
Waidalice Landing
Matacaucau
Kasavu
Bau Landing
To Suva (5km)
Nasidai Reef
VITI LEVU

Batiki

Nairai
Nadeve Entrance

Gau

See Enlargement:
Nukunuku Passage
Cape Horn
Buli Buli Reef
Lekaleka Reef
Levuka Passage ('Na Tumburi Entrance)
Arovudi (Silana) 9
Tavaya
Rukuruku
Cawaci
Vatukalo
Nandelaiovalau (626m)
Ovalau 1
Levuka 8
Waitovu Waterfall
Draiba
Lovoni
Bureta Landing
Wainaloka
Bureta Airstrip
Nacobo
Tokou
Natokalau
Balavu Reef
Nalulu Entrance
Gavo Pass
Yanuca Lailai (Lost Island) 5
Yanuca Levu
Bureuta River
Nakesaka
Moturiki
Nasuvolo
Niubasaga
Caqelai 2
Lelewia 4
Lelewia Landing
Moturiki
Mitchell Reef
Shear Reef
To Bau Landing
Moturiki Channel
Shell Reef
Clifton Reef
To Natovi Landing
Patterson Brothers Ferry

0   5 km
0   3 miles

the Pafco tuna plant attracts giant groupers, eagle rays and bull sharks. **Ovalau Watersports** (☎ 344 0166; www.owlfiji.com; Beach St, Levuka) offers two-tank dives/PADI Open Water Course for $150/460, including gear (minimum of two divers). Instruction can be in English or German. Reef snorkelling trips, accompanying divers, cost $40 per person including equipment.

Tours

As a general rule, phone ahead to arrange pick-ups from your hotel.

Epi's Midland Tour (☎ 602 1103, 923 6011; epitours@hotmail.com; full-day per person $35, minimum 4; ☺ departs 10.30am-11.30am Mon-Sat) takes you into the crater of an extinct volcano, which sits in the centre of Ovalau like a giant, upturned, broken eggshell. This is the site of Lovoni village. The tour is run by Epi, a Lovoni married to an Englishwoman. It is very popular, because the scenery is stunning and Epi is a fantastic storyteller. Epi's version of the history of Fiji has the Lovoni as the prime movers in almost every epoch. He tells how they were the only Fijians undefeated in battle and the only Fijians sold as slaves. The one thing he says they didn't do is burn the Masonic Lodge in Levuka.

The tour is a combination of trekking and transport on local carrier. Epi will point out many medicinal plants during your trek. Once you've reached the village and presented your *sevusevu* (gift for the village chief) – assuming the chief is around – you can take a dip in the river. A delicious lunch is laid on in one of the village homes. You can book the tour through the Royal Hotel. Price includes transfers and lunch.

The next three are organised through **Ovalau Holiday Resort** (☎ 344 0329; ohrfiji@connect .com.fj).

Fishing trips (per hour $40) leave Ovalau Holiday Resort in search of rock cod, trevally and Spanish mackerel in Levuka Passage, Waitovu Passage and Toki Passage. The resort will barbecue your catch for free.

Round Island 4WD Tours (per person $35, minimum 4; ☺ departs 10am) takes in the entire island, including the major historical sites around Levuka, the village of Lovoni, and the Solomon Islanders' settlement at Wainaloka. You drop in for refreshments at Bobo's Farm in Rukuruku, hike out to a waterfall and swim in the Bureta River. The tour includes

a picnic lunch. You can also book through Ovalau Watersports.

A **Waitovu Tour** (per person $15) is also offered from time to time. Travellers hike to the peak of Gun Rock, through pine forests and *kava* plantations, then swim in Waitovu waterfall. It takes about 3½ hours.

The following three can be booked through **Ovalau Watersports** (☎ 344 0166; www .owlfiji.com; Beach St, Levuka).

Silana Village Tour (per person $30, minimum 6) runs every Wednesday and includes a *meke* (traditional dance), a *lovo* (feast cooked in a pit oven), and a chance to make your own handicrafts from coconut and pandanus leaves. Book at Ovalau Watersports or the Royal Hotel before 4pm Tuesday, but double check the situation by phone with Silana Village (see p178). The guide, Seru, will also take you around his village any time for $15 (including lunch). Before you set out, ascertain whether you're getting the full package or just a look around the fairly ordinary village.

Talanoa means 'have a chat', and with **Tea & Talanoa Tours** (per person $15) you can have a chat with Fijian grandmother Bubu Kara or long-term expat resident Duncan Chrichton ('Mr Duncan'). Bubu makes delicious scones, and Mr Duncan has a fabulous garden.

Town tours (per person $10) of Levuka are available from Nox, the personable gardener at Levuka Homestay. Nox also runs a Waitovu tour, similar to that described earlier ($15). There are also town tours ($8) that leave from Ovalau Tourist Information Centre at 9am and 2pm weekdays.

Wainaloka Tour (per person $30; ☺ departs 10.30am Sun) Attend an Anglican church service and tour this settlement of Solomon Islanders, the descendents of people blackbirded to work Ovalau's plantations. The tour can be booked with, and departs from, the Royal Hotel and includes transfers and lunch at Wainaloka.

Day trips to **Leleuvia** (p189) or **Caqalai** (p180), including lunch, cost $50 per person.

OVALAU

Ovalau is the largest island in the Lomaiviti Group. The capital, Levuka, is the only town, and the only place with significant shops and services.

The Bureta airstrip and Buresala ferry landing are on the western side of Ovalau,

LOMAIVITI GROUP

while Levuka is on the eastern coast. A gravel road winds around the perimeter of the island and another follows the Bureta River inland to Lovoni village.

LEVUKA & AROUND

pop 3750

Levuka is the most picturesque town in Fiji, and one of very few places in the South Pacific that still has a significant number of colonial buildings. Sandwiched between the sea and lush, green mountains, the timber pool halls, offices and stores downtown look like they've been lifted straight out of a John Ford western.

Indigenous Fijians, Indo-Fijians, Chinese Fijians, part-European Fijians and a smattering of sometimes eccentric expats live together in laid-back Levuka, but the racial tensions that run through the bigger islands are largely absent. Nearly everyone is welcoming to visitors, and if you stay for a week, you'll meet half the town.

The food is surprisingly good, Levuka is the only place on the island where you can buy a beer, and nobody is going to try to carve your name on a worthless piece if wood. When Levukans stop you in the street, they genuinely want to know who you are. Come and find out who they are. It's worth the effort.

Levuka has the Lomaiviti islands' only infrastructure (see p171). For details of tours around Levuka and Ovalau, see p173.

Orientation

Beach St is Levuka's main drag. Don't bother looking for the 'beach', because there isn't one. The north of town is marked by one of two boulders going by the name of Gun Rock and you can follow your nose to the Pafco tuna cannery at the southern end; it's the source of sudden wafts of ferociously fishy smells.

Sights

Start your walking tour at Nasova, about 10 minutes' stroll south of the Pafco cannery. The Deed of Cession, handing over Fiji to Britain, was signed here in 1874. **Cession Site**, a memorial commemorating the event, is a pair of anchors and a scattering of plaque-bearing stones.

Across the road is the nutritious-looking **Provincial Bure**, a bit like a loaf of wholemeal bread covered in straw, where Prince Charles

made his headquarters when he represented Her Majesty's Government during the transition to independence in 1970. Next door is faded **Nasova House**, once the governor's residence. The small building furthest south is where Prince Charles stayed.

The **tuna cannery** (Pafco), at the southern end of Levuka, employs about 800 people and gives the whole town its distinctive odour. It was occupied by Lovoni villagers during the 2000 coup, as part of a dispute about unloading cargo.

Head north along **Beach St** where the streetscape dates from the late 19th and early 20th centuries. Just in front of the post office is the site of the original **Pigeon Post**, marked by a nondescript drinking fountain in the centre of the road. From the timber loft that stood here, pigeons provided the first postal link between Levuka and Suva. The birds flew the distance in less than 30 minutes, and were considerably faster and more reliable than Post Fiji.

A few doors away stands the **former Morris Hedstrom trading store** (1868), the original and first MH store in Fiji. Behind its restored façade is the Levuka Community Centre, library and a branch of the **Fiji Museum** (admission $2; ⏰ 8am-1pm & 2-4.30pm Mon-Fri, 9am-1pm Sat), which offers a fascinating, if chaotically organised, glimpse of old Levuka, through its wonderfully atmospheric displays.

Sacred Heart Church (Beach St) dates from 1858. The clock strikes each hour twice, with a minute in between. Locals say the first strike is an alarm to warn people who are operating on 'Fiji time'. The light on the spire guides ships through Levuka Passage. From the church, head west along Totoga Lane to explore the backstreets.

The **Marist Convent School** (1882) was a girls' school opened by Catholic missionaries and run by Australian and French nuns. It is now a lively co-ed primary school. It was built largely of coral stone in an attempt to protect it from the hurricanes that have claimed so many buildings in town, and it remains an impressive monument against the mountain backdrop.

The little weatherboard building on the corner of Garner Jones Rd and Totoga Lane was Levuka's original **police station** (1874), and across Totoga Creek in Nasau Park you'll find Fiji's first private club – the colonial-style timber **Ovalau Club** (1904). It's well worth

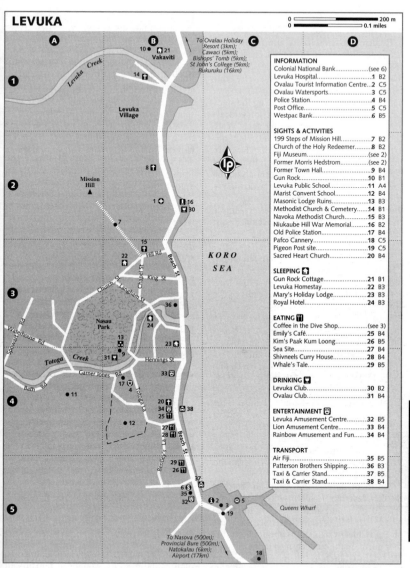

LEVUKA

INFORMATION
Colonial National Bank..................(see 6)
Levuka Hospital.............................**1** B2
Ovalau Tourist Information Centre..**2** C5
Ovalau Watersports......................**3** C5
Police Station...............................**4** B4
Post Office....................................**5** C5
Westpac Bank...............................**6** B5

SIGHTS & ACTIVITIES
199 Steps of Mission Hill................**7** B2
Church of the Holy Redeemer........**8** B2
Fiji Museum...............................(see 2)
Former Morris Hedstrom..............(see 2)
Former Town Hall..........................**9** B4
Gun Rock....................................**10** B1
Levuka Public School.....................**11** A4
Marist Convent School..................**12** B4
Masonic Lodge Ruins....................**13** B3
Methodist Church & Cemetery.....**14** B1
Navoka Methodist Church............**15** B3
Niukaube Hill War Memorial........**16** B2
Old Police Station.........................**17** B4
Pafco Cannery..............................**18** C5
Pigeon Post site............................**19** C5
Sacred Heart Church.....................**20** B4

SLEEPING
Gun Rock Cottage.........................**21** B1
Levuka Homestay..........................**22** B3
Mary's Holiday Lodge....................**23** B3
Royal Hotel..................................**24** B3

EATING
Coffee in the Dive Shop................(see 3)
Emily's Café.................................**25** B4
Kim's Paak Kum Loong..................**26** B5
Sea Site.......................................**27** B4
Shivneels Curry House..................**28** B4
Whale's Tale................................**29** B5

DRINKING
Levuka Club.................................**30** B2
Ovalau Club.................................**31** B4

ENTERTAINMENT
Levuka Amusement Centre............**32** B5
Lion Amusement Centre................**33** B4
Rainbow Amusement and Fun......**34** B4

TRANSPORT
Air Fiji..**35** B5
Patterson Brothers Shipping..........**36** B3
Taxi & Carrier Stand.....................**37** B5
Taxi & Carrier Stand.....................**38** B4

stopping in for a beer, if it's open. See p179 for more on this club and its famous letter. Next door to the Ovalau Club is the **former town hall** (1898), built in typical British colonial style in honour of Queen Victoria's silver jubilee.

Alongside this place, you'll find the stone shell of the South Pacific's first **Masonic lodge**;

Lodge Polynesia (1875) was once Levuka's only Romanesque building, but it was burnt to a husk in the 2000 coup by villagers egged on by their church leaders. Local Methodists had long alleged that Masons were in league with the devil and that tunnels led from beneath the lodge to Nasova House, the Royal Hotel, and through the centre of the world to

Masonic headquarters in Scotland. Surprisingly, this turned out not to be the case.

Return across the creek and follow Garner Jones Rd west to the **Levuka Public School** (1879). This was Fiji's first formal school and many of Fiji's prominent citizens were educated here including Percy Morris and Maynard Hedstrom. If you continue up the steps behind the school you can join some locals for a chat at a popular resting spot. Walk back down to Garner Jones Rd, turn left into Church St and pass Nasau Park. There are many old colonial homes on the hillsides and the romantically named **199 Steps of Mission Hill** are worth climbing for the fantastic view – although, if you count them, you might find there are closer to 185 steps. The very simple coral and stone Gothic-style **Navoka Methodist Church** (1864), near the foot of the steps, is one of the oldest churches in Fiji.

Head down Chapel St then left along Langham St. The **Royal Hotel** (1860s) is Fiji's oldest hotel, rebuilt in 1903. It is the lone survivor of the once-numerous pubs of the era. Originally it had an open veranda with lace balustrading, but this was built in to increase the size of the rooms. Check out the fantastic old snooker room, and play a game of hunt-the-Royal-Hotel-staff.

Back on Beach St, continue north to **Niukaube Hill**, on a point near the water. This was once the site of Ratu Cakobau's Supreme Court and Parliament House. This is also where the first indentured Indian labourers landed in Fiji after being forced to anchor offshore for several weeks in an attempt to control an outbreak of cholera. The site now has a memorial to locals who fought and died in WWI and WWII.

North of here is the Anglican **Church of the Holy Redeemer** (1904), with its colourful stained glass and altar of *yaka* and *dakua* wood. Tidy little **Levuka village**, once the home of Tui (Chief) Cakobau, is about 200m further north. In the **cemetery** next to the village's Methodist Church, is the grave of American consul JB Williams. It was his claims for financial compensation that led Cakobau to hand over Fiji to Britain.

With the chief's permission you can climb one of two local sites known as **Gun Rock** for a great view over Levuka. In 1849 Commodore Wilkes, of the US Exploring Expedition, pounded this peak from his ship with canon fire in an attempt to impress the chief of

Levuka. Commodore Goodenough repeated the 'entertainment' in 1874. You can still find canon ball scars on the rock. (The other Gun Rock is much smaller, and named for the canon mounted upon it in the 1850s.) Gun Rock might be a good place to spot **whales**; about 10 humpback whales swim past between May and September. In 2005 they spent days around Levuka's harbour.

Walk, cycle or take a taxi the 7km north to Cawaci, where you'll find the Gothic-style **Bishops' Tomb** (1922), with Latin inscriptions and spooky acoustics, where Fiji's first two Roman Catholic bishops are entombed on a point overlooking the sea. From here you can see the limestone and coral **St John's College** (1894), where the sons of Fijian chiefs were educated in English. These days, girls are educated here, too. The boys' and girls' dormitories are separated by a bridge that no student is allowed to cross after 6pm.

LOVONI

Lovoni village nestles among thick, prehistoric rainforest in a cracked but spectacular extinct volcano crater in the centre of Ovalau. It is the navel of the island and the heart of local indigenous culture. There's no accommodation for travellers here, but guided tours are available from Levuka (see p173). A hike around the caldera can be muddy and slippery – and the weather can change in an instant – so bring some hardy footwear. Your guide should provide a *sevusevu* for the chief (if he's around) and point out the **chief's burial site** opposite the church and **Korolevu hill fortification**, high on the crater rim, where villagers took refuge in times of war.

The villagers of Lovoni are extremely proud people. They believe that since Chief Cakobau was only able to defeat them with trickery, not by war, they are the strongest tribe in Fiji (see the boxed text, opposite). On 7 July each year, the enslavement of the Lovoni people is commemorated. People of all religions gather in the same church and the history is read out.

There is a Levuka–Lovoni truck leaving Levuka at 7am and 11am on Monday to Saturday, which returns at about 3pm.

RUKURUKU

The village of Rukuruku is a bumpy 17km drive north of Levuka. There are fantastic views across the sea on the way. Near the

---

WARRIORS IN CHAINS: FIJI'S ONLY SLAVES

The saddest exhibit in the Fiji Museum at Levuka is the photograph of a 'dwarf' priest and two Lovoni warriors who were sold by Tui Cakobau to the Barnum & Bailey circus in the USA. In 1870 and 1871 Cakobau fought battle after battle with the ferocious Lovoni highlanders, who regularly sacked the settlement of Levuka and did not accept Cakobau's claim to be king of all Fiji. After repeated attempts to penetrate their hill fort failed, Cakobau sent a Methodist missionary to subdue the people. The Lovoni put their trust in a 'dwarf priest' (actually just a short bloke) who had the ability to foresee the future. The priest was the first to notice the approaching missionary and, seeing a brightness emanating from him, believed he came in peace. The missionary read from the *Bible* in Bauan, referring to the Lovoni villagers as the lost sheep of Fiji. He then invited them to a reconciliation feast with Cakobau.

On 29 June 1871, the Lovoni people came down from the safety of their village to Levuka, and in good faith put aside their weapons. However, as they started their meal, Cakobau's warriors caught them off guard, quickly surrounding and capturing them.

Cakobau humiliated his captives horribly, then sold them as slaves for £3 a head. His takings helped him form his government. Families were separated as the villagers were dispersed as far as Kavala (in the Kadavu Group), Yavusania (near Nadi on Viti Levu), Lovoni-Ono (in the Lau Group) and Wailevu (on Vanua Levu). The Lovoni were the only Fijians ever to suffer this fate. When the British administration took over Fiji, it freed the Lovoni slaves, and the blackbirding of other Pacific Islanders began instead.

---

village is a black-sand beach with a view of Naigani island, and a small waterfall about 15 minutes' walk up the valley. It's best to arrange a day out there with Bobo (see p173) to avoid trespassing on village property. Schoolchildren might sing you a song and old people will share a bowl of *kava*. Tours are free to house guests at Bobo's Farm. There is a carrier to Rukuruku ($3) at about 12.30pm on Tuesday, Thursday and Saturday. On Monday, Wednesday and Friday, it only goes as far as Taviya, but give an extra $10 to the driver and he'll take you to Bobo's. A taxi will cost about $30 each way.

AROVUDI (SILANA)

There's a sweep of pretty pebble beach in Arovudi. About 70 people live in the village, but many houses are empty because the inhabitants, including the chief, are away working in Suva. The **Methodist village church** (1918) is made of coral cooked in a *lovo*. A *tabua* (whale's tooth) hangs by the side of the altar; it was presented to the village by the first missionaries who came here. A crypt of stones overlooking the beach was the grave site of a chief, but it frightened the children so the villagers moved the body to the hills where their other ancestors are buried. There is one place to stay, run by the enterprising Seru, who also organises regular tours from Levuka (see p173).

SLEEPING
Levuka
Levuka Homestay (☎ 344 0777; www.levukahomestay .com; Church St; s/d incl breakfast $120/140, extra person $40) Here you will stay at a lovely neocolonial-style house with great sea views from the deck, fantastic service, and four big, bright, tremendously clean rooms, each one set on its own level. The laid-back owners live on the highest level. You might want to ask for the room below theirs, which has a private deck. Breakfast never ends: delicious servings of fruit, cereal, toast, banana pancakes, muesli, and bacon and eggs keep flowing from the kitchen. There is a high chair and a cot here for babies.

Royal Hotel (☎ 344 0024; www.royallevuka.com; dm/s/d/tr $10/18/28/35, cottages $80; ✂ 🖳 🖳) It's a place to stay, it's a thing to see, it's an institution, but Fiji's first hotel is no longer a place to eat. The staff has given up the daily struggle to serve meals, and the only food on offer is an all-day breakfast. This proud timber building has been in the hands of the Ashley family since 1927, and the ghosts of plantation days haunt the bar more frequently than living customers. There is a small swimming pool, a well-equipped weights gym, slow Internet service, twirling ceiling fans, great views from private verandas, and a unique colonial atmosphere you could cut with a cane knife. This place is the real thing. The sometimes eccentric service may or may not be part of the charm, depending on whether you're hungry, thirsty, in a hurry etc.

Gun Rock Cottage (☎ 344 0166; d $65) There is some controversy over which bit of Levuka rock is actually Gun Rock. The owners of this fan-cooled one-bedroom cottage – also the owners of Ovalau Watersports – have plumped for the big, black crag that looms over this cabin. They live next door to the cabin, and ensure the place is kept clean and well maintained. There's a full kitchen, a washing machine and a hot-water shower. You can swim out from the sea wall in high tide, and snorkel around the rock under the beacon. Dolphins occasionally pass this way. It's about 1.6km north of town, $2 by taxi.

Mary's Holiday Lodge (☎ 344 0013; Beach St; dm/s/d with shared bathroom incl breakfast $15/20/35) Once the Old Capital Inn, this basic, friendly, slightly shabby old hotel has sea views from the veranda. It is a noisy, timber building with small rooms, fans, cold-water showers, thin walls and sometimes threadbare bed linen, but you can't argue with the price.

Around Ovalau

Ovalau Holiday Resort (☎ 344 0329; ohrfiji@connect .com.fj; camping per person $10, dm/s/d $12/15/$28, s/d self-contained bungalow $45/77, extra person $25; 🛋) Ovalau is not really the spot to come for a resort holiday, but the landscaped gardens of this resort make for a quiet, relaxing place to get away from it all (insofar as Levuka can be described as 'it all'). There is a very good restaurant (see right), a small swimming pool, a little white-sand beach across the road, and a cluster of comfortable bungalows. The two cabins with private facilities have kitchens and hot water, and are Levuka's most suitable accommodation for families. A taxi from Levuka will cost $5. A carrier (every half hour from town) costs $0.50.

Bobo's Farm (☎ 993 3632, 344 0166; www.owlfiji .com; Rukuruku; s/d $35/50) This tranquil retreat is as far away from urban life as you can get while remaining in the 21st century. Accommodation is in a two-bedroom cabin with a small kitchen in the gorgeous garden of Bobo's own home. If you intend to cook for yourself, you'll need to bring your ingredients with you, but the food here is highly praised (breakfast/lunch/dinner $7/8/12). You can use the fridge in the main house as well as the TV. The main house has a large deck where local villagers often gather for singing and *kava* drinking.

There's a freshwater stream where you can catch prawns or bathe in small, natural pools. About 15 minutes upstream is a waterfall and 15 minutes downstream is a black-sand beach. The village of Rukuruku is 15 minutes away, too. Bobo will gladly escort you to all of them. He can also arrange island hopping, snorkelling and fishing trips. Book ahead through Ovalau Watersports in Levuka. Bobo can pick you up by boat from Bureta airstrip ($13) or Buresala ferry landing ($20).

Silana Village (☎ 344 0166; silana@owlfiji.com; dm $18, bure per person $25) Close to the beach are two basic, wooden cabin *bure* (traditional thatched dwelling; sleeping four) with shared cold-water facilities, and one more traditional five-person dorm *bure*. The owners will cook lunch and dinner ($5), or you can self-cater from the kitchen. The fishing here is spectacular, and Seru will take you out on a boat to catch trevally, wahoo and skipjack for the price of the fuel. The carrier from Levuka takes about 40 minutes and costs $1.70.

EATING

All these options, apart from the Ovalau Holiday Resort, are on Beach St, Levuka.

Whale's Tale (☎ 344 0235; breakfast $6, lunch sandwiches $5, mains $9; 🕒 lunch & dinner Mon-Sat) The Whale's Tale offers Levuka's most tasteful dining experience, in a maritime-themed restaurant where the wine is blessedly reasonable ($10 a carafe) and standard dishes such as pasta, burgers and fish are far better than they ought to be. The Whale's Tale serves breakfast all day except, curiously, at breakfast time, when it is closed. It's licensed only for people who eat here.

Ovalau Holiday Resort (☎ 344 0329; meals $13; 🕒 breakfast, lunch & dinner) It is open all day, seven days, although it might be a good idea to ring ahead and warn them you are coming. The food here is a delicious take on the Indo-Fijian–Chinese–Western hybrid that has become local cuisine. Try it at least once when you are in Levuka.

Shivneels Curry House (☎ 344 0616; mains $3; 🕒 breakfast, lunch & dinner before 6pm Mon-Sat) Exhausted Chinese/Indian food lies collapsed all day in the *bain-marie,* but if you give the owners an hour's notice and $10, they will prepare you a delicious curry plate comprising a fish or chicken curry, *dahl* (lentil soup), vegetables, pappadums, rice and rotis, served with a cup of masala tea.

Kim's Paak Kum Loong (☎ 344 0059; mains $8; ☽ lunch & dinner) Pull up a chair on the balcony and watch Levuka go by (insofar as Levuka's somnambulant drift can be described as 'going by'). Kim's eclectic menu includes standard Chinese dishes, very hot Thai curries and tasty Fijian-style fish, all cooked with flair and care. The big, eclectic buffet ($13.50) is the best option in town on Sunday night, but don't be afraid to ask them to heat up your plate.

Emily's Café (☎ 344 0382; lunch $4, pizzas $7; ☽ breakfast, lunch & dinner Mon-Sat, dinner Sun) By day, it's an ordinary greasy café fronted by an ordinary Chinese hot-bread shop. By night, it's the surprisingly professional Ovalau Pizza, offering good, crispy, none-too-cheesy pizzas and a bicycle delivery service to local hotels. Delivery is free, but the pizza box costs $0.35!

Coffee in the Dive Shop (sandwiches $3.50; ☽ 9am-5pm Mon-Fri, 9am-1pm Sat) This is a Fijian-run café upstairs at Ovalau Watersports. Drop in for sandwiches or, er, a coffee at the dive shop.

Sea Site (☎ 344 0382; meals $4.50; ☽ lunch & dinner) Grab a tasty chicken curry roti from this otherwise unexciting locals' café.

Self-Catering

On Thursday, local villagers come to sell fresh fruit and vegetables alongside the waterfront roughly opposite Shivneels on Beach St. You can get most everything else at the numerous general stores on Beach St.

DRINKING & ENTERTAINMENT

Levuka's clubs are worth a night out, but don't expect bacchanalia.

Ovalau Club (☽ 4pm-9.30pm Mon-Thu, 2pm-midnight Fri, 10am-midnight Sat, 10am-9.30pm Sun) This was Fiji's first gentleman's club, and it's a sight in its own right. It's no longer a colonial club in any respect, but expats and part-Europeans gather for a drink at 6pm every Tuesday. Ask the bar staff to show you a letter written by Count Felix von Luckner during WWI, just before his capture on nearby Wakaya. Von Luckner cruised the South Seas in a German raider disguised as a Norwegian merchant ship, sinking Allied supply boats. When he lost his own ship, he tried to avoid arrest by disguising himself as an English writer on a sporting cruise. He signed the letter 'Max Pemberton'.

Levuka Club (☽ 5.30-9.30pm Mon-Thu, 5-11pm Fri, 10am-11pm Sat, 10am-9pm Sun) This place was founded by Indians who were excluded from the Ovalau Club, although now it is, of course, multiracial. Its busy night is Thursday, after payday at Pafco. The beer garden around the back looks out to the sea, Levuka town, and even Pafco.

There are a number of pool halls where locals pot balls to pop music. Those looking for amusement and fun can try **Rainbow Amusement & Fun** (Beach St; ☽ 10am-10pm Mon-Sat). Two similar places, the Lion Amusement Centre and Levuka Amusement Centre, offer amusement and the same opening hours without the fun.

GETTING THERE & AROUND

For flights head to the office of **Air Fiji** (☎ 344 0139; fax 344 0252; Beach St, Levuka; ☽ 8am-4pm Mon-Fri) next to Levuka Amusement Centre at the Pafco end of town. From Ovalau, Air Fiji flies to Suva (adult/child $65/32 one way; 12 minutes; twice-daily Monday to Saturday, once only on Sunday) but will book onward flights throughout Fiji. Credit cards are accepted. The airstrip is about 40 minutes' drive to/from Levuka. Minibuses to the airstrip ($5 per person) will pick you up from outside the Air Fiji office or from your hotel on request. A taxi costs about $25.

Patterson Brothers Shipping (☎ 344 0125; Beach St; ☽ 8.30am-4.30pm Mon-Fri, 8.30-noon Sat) has a bus/ferry/bus service from Levuka to Suva via Natovi Landing ($24, four hours, gather at 4.30am for 5am departure daily). You can also opt to stay on the boat at Natovi to Nabouwalu (on Vanua Levu) and then continue by bus to Labasa ($55), daily except Tuesday.

Levuka is a port of entry into Fiji for yachties. Authorities don't always answer on radio Channel 16, so anchor near Queen's Wharf and make your way ashore. Formalities are usually simpler here than in Suva.

Levuka is tiny and easy to get around on foot. There is a taxi stand opposite the Westpac bank, where carriers depart for Lovoni. Carriers to Rukuruku leave from a second taxi stand opposite Emily's Café. Mountain bikes can be hired in town (see p171).

LOMAIVITI GROUP

OTHER LOMAIVITI ISLANDS

Lomaiviti's smaller islands are beautiful and welcoming, although some are looked after better than others.

YANUCA LAILAI

Yanuca Lailai (Lost Island) is an island between Ovalau and Moturiki. It has a hill with a short, golden-sand beach, and the rest of the island is rocky. It is too shallow to swim at low tide but it is possible to snorkel.

Lost Island Resort (www.owlfiji.com/lostisland.htm; dm/bure incl meals per person $40/55) dropped off the map for a while, but luckily it has found itself again. The closest island resort to Levuka, only a short hop from the Bureta airstrip, this tiny place reopened in 2005 with three fine, new, soaring, breeze-cooled *bure*. An eight-bed dorm has been added, with boys (blue mosquito net) separated from girls (pink mosquito net), and a bar is on its way. All have cold-water shared facilities. There is a fantastic view of sunrise from the beach and sunset from 'The Rock', a five-minute scramble from the resort. Food is traditional Fijian with an emphasis on locally caught fish and seafood.

There is no telephone on the island. Book through either Ovalau Watersports or Ovalau Community Centre in Levuka. Transfers from the airstrip or Levuka are $10 one way. Transfers from Waidalice on Viti Levu (southeast of Korovou) cost $40.

MOTURIKI

The hilly, lush island of Moturiki is just southwest of Ovalau and home to 10 villages. Although it has no accommodation for travellers, both Leleuvia and Caqalai resorts will take guests to the village of **Niubasaga** for typical a Sunday church service. Be prepared: one of your party will have to get up and introduce the group to the congregation.

CAQALAI

The gorgeous coral island of Caqalai lies just south of Moturiki. It's only a 15-minute walk around the island's beautiful **white-sand beaches**, which are fringed with palms and other large trees. If you're lucky you may see **dolphins** and **baby turtles**.

WHAT LIES BENEATH

Don't tempt the spirits of Gavo Passage. If you head out to the islands south from Ovalau, your boat will likely travel through a break in the reef. Many indigenous Fijians believe that beneath the waters of Gavo Passage lies a sunken village inhabited by ancestral spirits. Stories of fishermen hooking newly woven mats are whispered around Levuka. When passing over the *tabu* (sacred) site, Fijians remove their hats and sunglasses and talk in hushed tones. They believe the spirits will avenge any act of disrespect. Stay on the safe side, take off your baseball cap and give your sunnies a rest. Even if there are no spirits to annoy, irreverent behaviour might put the wind up your boatman.

Caqalai Island Resort (☎ 343 0366; www.owlfiji .com/caqalai.htm; camping per person without/with all meals $12/25, dm/bure incl meals per person $35/45) proves that, surprisingly, the Methodist church knows how to run a resort (although it doesn't know how to run a bar: alcohol isn't served here, but you're welcome to bring your own). Caqalai comes close to being the best a backpacker island can get. It's rustic, with cold showers in shared bathrooms, but the food is delicious, the white-sand beach is scrumptious, snorkelling from the shore is spectacular, and the staff are enormously welcoming. At low tide it's possible to walk out to Snake Island (named after the many black-and-white-banded sea snakes here), for even better snorkelling. Diving is available, too. Also on offer are village trips to Moturiki for a Sunday church service and boat trips to tiny Honeymoon Island. At night, there is singing, dancing and *kava* drinking beside a bonfire on the beach. There is a once-a-week day trip to Leleuvia ($10).

Getting There & Away

If you're coming from Levuka, you can book transport and accommodation from Ovalau Watersports. One-way transfers cost $20 per person in a group and $30 for one person. Transfers from Caqalai to Bureta airstrip on Ovalau cost $50 for one person, $25 per person for two or more.

(Continued on page 189)

LOMAIVITI GROUP

Ovalau Club (p179), Levuka, Lomaiviti Group

SIMON CHARLES ROWE

ROBYN JONES

Taking it easy in laid-back Levuka (p174), Lomaiviti Group

Colonial-era buildings, Levuka (p174), Lomaiviti Group

ROBYN JONES

Indio-Fijian dance troupe, Suva (p118), Viti Levu

LIZ T'

Young villagers, Bukuya (p145), Viti Levu

DANIEL BOAG

CHRIS MELLOR

Fijian father and son, Viti Levu (p71)

JOHN BORTHWICK

Sailing the azure sea, Wakaya island (p189), Lomaiviti Group

Buildings in Fiji's old capital, Levuka (p174), Lomaiviti Group

ROBYN JONES

Bishops' Tomb (p176), Cawaci, Lomaiviti Group

ROBYN JONES

PETER HENDRIE

Moored yachts, Savusavu Bay (p195), Vanua Levu

TOM COCKREM

Young Indo-Fijian girl, Labasa (p204), Vanua Levu

Aerial view, Vanua Levu (p191)

DAVID WALL

ROBYN JONES

Shrine featuring Ganesh, Labasa
(p204), Vanua Levu

Women socialising, Savusavu (p193), Vanua Levu

PETER HENDRIE

Toilets built in the style of a *bure* (traditional thatched dwelling), Nukubolu ruins (p202), Vanua Levu

ROBYN JONES

CASEY & ASTRID WITTE MAHANEY

Tropical sunset, Taveuni island (p210)

ROBYN JONES

Children on the beach, Matei (p218), Taveuni island

Sea kayaking, Taveuni island (p210)

LIZ THOMPSON

ROBYN JONES

Woman making pandanus mats, Kadavu island (p224)

Matava Resort (p226), Kadavu island

SIMON CHARLES ROWE

Long stretch of beach, Kadavu island (p224)

ROBYN JONES

CASEY & ASTRID WITTE

Diving off the Bay of Islands (p232), Lau Group

View of offshore island, Vanua Balavu
(p232), Lau Group

CASEY & ASTRID WITTE MAHANEY

CASEY & ASTRID WITTE

Blue-spotted red coral trout, Wailagi Lala Passage
(p232), Lau Group

(Continued from page 180)

From Suva, catch a bus heading down the Kings Road from the main bus terminal and get off at Waidalice. You need to call ahead for a boat from Caqalai to pick you up here ($30 per person).

LELEUVIA

Just south of Caqalai sits Leleuvia, another palm-fringed coral island with golden-sand beaches. At low tide a vast area of sand and rock is exposed – it's a good time to explore the island's tidal pools. It's also possible to swim off the western side or to do some OK snorkelling and great diving.

Things seem to be on the up and up at **Leleuvia Island Resort** (☎ 330 1584; www.owlfiji .com/leleuvia.htm; bungalows per person $42, bungalows with kitchen per person $60) after a muddle of managers had left the resort ramshackle and rundown. But Lena, who used to run the place in 1997, has been reappointed to clear things up. There are some pretty *bure*, but the scrubby resort still feels a bit unkempt, and the flush toilets are dingy. All rates include three meals, tea and coffee. Lena is a qualified pastry chef. Guests take breakfast and lunch in the dining *bure* and dinner on the sand. Cold beer is available from the restaurant; hot snorkelling from the beach.

Getting There & Away

Boat transfers to/from Suva are $30 each way (the boat ride is one hour from Korovou town, which is about a 1½-hour bus ride from Suva). Transfers to/from Levuka (one hour) cost $20 each way. Book through Ovalau Watersports.

WAKAYA

About 20km east of Ovalau, Wakaya is a privately owned island visible from Levuka. It has forests, cliffs, beautiful white-sand beaches, and archaeological sites, including a **stone fish trap**. In some areas you'll find feral horses, pigs and deer roaming freely; in others there are millionaires' houses.

Wakaya Club (☎ 344 8128, www.wakaya.com; garden/ocean view d $2600-12,100) is one of Fiji's most exclusive resorts. Bill Gates honeymooned here with his first wife. Russell Crowe and Nicole Kidman stayed at Wakaya (together!) in 2001. Face it, it could be out of your league. There is a five-night minimum stay.

Getting There & Away

The island is a 20-minute speedboat ride from Levuka; however, as it's private, you'll need an invite to visit. Call ahead to see if you'll be welcome.

KORO

Many villages are nestled in the lush tropical forests of Koro, northwest of Ovalau. Roads over the mountainous interior provide for plenty of thrills and wonderful views. A portion of the island is freehold, so foreigners can build their second, third, fourth or fifth homes; their seasonal neighbours include Lauren Hutton.

At Dere Bay, a wharf allows you to walk out to good swimming and snorkelling; inland is a waterfall and natural pool.

Dere Bay Resort (☎ 331 1075; fijimiller@connect .com.fj; d bure incl meals $400; 🖳) was previously occupied by people who had either bought or were looking to buy land on the island. It should now be operating as a regular resort. The well-designed *bure* have soaring ceilings, delightful furnishings, 360-degree outlooks, and spacious verandas. Sit and watch the sand crabs while you wait to be called for another gourmet meal. There are kayaks, scuba-diving equipment, game-fishing facilities and a resident diving instructor.

Getting There & Away

Air Fiji flies Koro–Suva on Wednesday (adult/child $125/62.50 each way), and **Turtle Airways** (☎ 672 1888; reservations@turtleairways .com) or **Pacific Island** (☎ 672 5644; www.fijiseaplanes .com) sea planes will fly you in from Nadi. Ferries run by **Consort Shipping** (Map p122; ☎ 330 2877; fax 330 3389; Thomson St, Suva) leave Suva twice weekly, stopping at Koro on their way to Savusavu (deck/air-conditioned cabin $35/65, eight hours). You really need to take a cabin. This is not a wholly reliable service. There is a small chance the return boat from Koro might not pick you up. From Savusavu, the Dere Bay boat costs $100 one-way. Enquire about transport when you book your accommodation. Pick-up from the ferry/airport is $20/30.

Terry Grey (☎ 885 0674) of the yacht *Sea Rov* in Savusavu, Vanua Levu, will take you to/from Koro for $600 one-way if you're stuck. This isn't too bad if you have a small group. He'll also do a day trip for a similar price.

NAIGANI

Naigani (Mystery Island) is a mountainous island about 10km offshore from Ovalau. The island has white-sand beaches, lagoons, a fringing coral reef, the remains of a **precolonial hillside fortification** and 'cannibal caves'. According to locals, 1800 villagers were slaughtered in this area by marauding tribes. The place is *tabu* (sacred) and locals keep away; out of respect, you should do the same. There is one village on the island, about 10 minutes' walk from the resort.

Naigani Island Resort (☎ 330 0925; www.naigani resort.com; tw/studios/villas $120/150/180; ☒), a former copra plantation, is a friendly, unpretentious family resort popular with time-sharers, and Suva-based expats at weekends. The spacious cabin-style *bure* are a bit shabby but the white-sand beach is pretty enough and there is good snorkelling about 50m out from the shore. The day trip to Picnic Beach is highly recommended for snorkellers, too. There are good dive sites nearby. Kiwi foot fetishists might be interested to see a pair of slippers once worn by *Shortland Street* star Stephanie Teavehii (Donna) on display in the gift shop.

The food is good, and you can eat à la carte for less than the meal plan. There's a *lovo* every Saturday night, and a free kids' club during Australasian school holidays (and babysitting is always available at $4.50 an hour).

The great mystery of Mystery Island is why the guard turns off the *bure*'s hot-water supply every night. Hint: the power switch is out the back.

Return boat transfers to/from Suva, via Natovi Landing, or to/from Taviya village, near Rukuruku on Ovalau, are $50/25 per adult/child. Transfer to Ovalau takes 90 minutes or less, depending on weather conditions. A taxi from the landing at Taviya is another $20, despite what you may be told at Naigani. Ovalau Watersports can arrange these transfers for only $40 one-way.

NAMENALALA

The volcanic island of Namenalala rests on the Namena Barrier Reef, 25km off the southeastern coast of Vanua Levu and about 40km from Savusavu. Namenalala has lovely **beaches** and the island is a natural sailors' refuge. There is an old **ring fortification**, but the villages disappeared long ago. Today there's just one small, upmarket resort.

Moody's Namena (☎ 881 3764; www.moodysna menafiji.com; all-inclusive packages for 5 nights, incl transfers from Savusavu, s/d $3190/4570, extra night s/d $570/770; ☒ closed March & April) has six bamboo-and-timber *bure* on a forested ridge. Diving here is excellent and costs $85 per tank. (Divers must be certified.) Other activities, which include windsurfing, fishing, snorkelling, reef excursions, barbecues, volleyball, and use of canoes and paddle boards, are included in the rate. The island has a nature reserve for bird-watching and trekking and is home to seabirds, red-footed boobies and a giant clam farm. From November to February, hawksbill and green turtles lay their eggs on Namenalala beaches. There is a five-night minimum stay; no children under 16 years old are allowed.

Vanua Levu

Vanua Levu (Big Island) is lively and exciting – and peaceful and relaxing. The frantic gringo colonisation of Savusavu coexists alongside traditional villages, unspoiled countryside, and a handful of calm, relaxing resorts.

The predominantly indigenous-Fijian southeast of the island has gorgeous landscape brimming with rainforests, coconut plantations and fantastic views of the ocean. The area is popular with yachties and divers. Savusavu, a small town that is growing by the day, is the main tourist destination. The north and the west are virtually untouristed. Indo-Fijians are concentrated around hot, hard-working Labasa in the north, Vanua Levu's largest town. As well as native forest, there are lots of sugar-cane and commercial pine plantations in this area. Much of the western coast is remote and accessible only by boat.

The island has an unfair reputation for poor beaches, and a well-deserved name for diving and snorkelling (Jean-Michel Cousteau himself set up a resort here). Its nearby Rainbow Reef has some of the best dive sites in the South Pacific. The many deep bays are fantastic for kayaking and the lush, rugged interior rainforest provides good bird-watching.

The coastline of Vanua Levu is irregular and deeply indented; the large Tunuloa Peninsula forms the huge Natewa Bay, the longest bay in the South Pacific. It is edged by steep, green mountains and frequented by spinner dolphins.

HIGHLIGHTS

- Rent a 4WD and explore the island, especially the **Tunuloa Peninsula** (p202)
- Drink through happy hour at **Savusavu Yacht Club** (p201)
- Trek the pristine rainforest around **Waisali Rainforest Reserve** (p202)
- Be among the first travellers for decades to visit **Wainunu Bay** (p209)
- Take an adventure cruise with **Tui Tai** (p196)
- Sit on the deck of the **Planters' Club** (p201) in Savusavu, soaking up history
- Kayak **Savusavu Bay** (p195)
- Snorkel **Split Rock** (p195) in Savusavu Bay

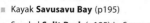

Waisali Rainforest Reserve ★
Tunuloa Peninsula ★
Savusavu Bay ★ Savusavu
Wainunu Bay ★

- POPULATION: 139,510
- AREA: 5587 SQ KM

VANUA LEVU

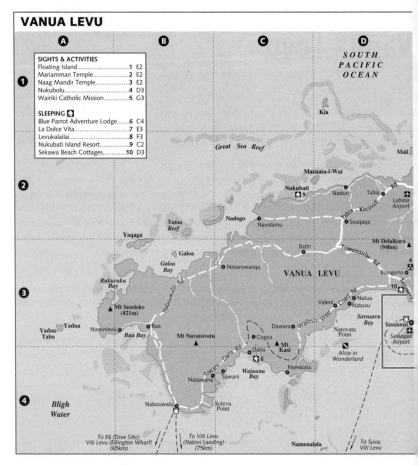

VANUA LEVU

SIGHTS & ACTIVITIES
Floating Island...........................1 E2
Mariamman Temple..................2 E2
Naag Mandir Temple................3 E2
Nukubolu.................................4 D3
Wairiki Catholic Mission.............5 G3

SLEEPING
Blue Parrot Adventure Lodge......6 C4
La Dolce Vita............................7 E3
Levukalailai..............................8 F3
Nukubati Island Resort..............9 C2
Sekawa Beach Cottages...........10 D3

Getting There & Around

Vanua Levu is easily reached by frequent Air Fiji and Sun Air flights from Nadi or Suva. You can fly into Labasa or Savusavu and the flight over the reefs and coconut plantations is superb. Flights also operate between Savusavu and Taveuni. See p259 for details.

Travelling to Vanua Levu by boat takes a great deal longer and often it's not much cheaper than taking a plane trip. Beachcomber Cruises, Consort Shipping, Patterson Brothers Shipping and Suilven Shipping all service Vanua Levu from Viti Levu, Ovalau, Koro and Taveuni. Grace Ferry operates a bus/boat service from Labasa and Savusavu via Buca Bay to Taveuni. See p261 for schedules and ticket prices.

Getting around the island's main routes is possible by bus but it's easier to explore those wild, tropical roads by 4WD. Hire cars are available in Labasa and Savusavu, but given the bumpy terrain, they're not always in top condition. There are unsealed roads around most of the island's perimeter. The sealed road from Labasa to Savusavu is mostly a good, smooth drive. The first 20km of the Hibiscus Hwy from Savusavu along the scenic coast is also paved. Unfortunately, the rest of the highway is very rough. Avoid driving at night as there are lots of wandering animals and there is often fog in the mountains. Petrol stations are scarce and usually closed on Sundays so plan to fill up in Labasa, Savusavu or

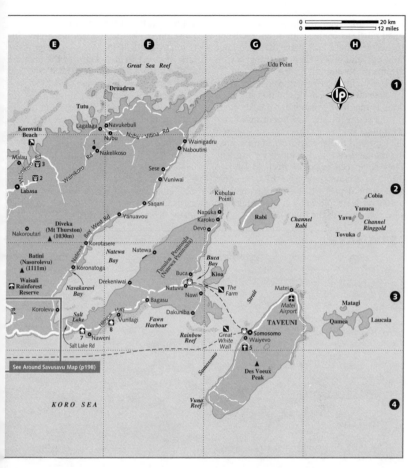

0 — 20 km
0 — 12 miles

Seaqaqa. It's also a good idea to take some food with you on the road.

Just remember, you cannot wander on foot through the countryside without permission from the landowners.

SAVUSAVU

pop 4970

Savusavu is the fastest changing place in Fiji. The town is in the grip of a property boom, fuelled by scores of new residents from the USA and Europe. Good restaurants and lively bars have opened on the main street. Well-stocked shops – including a peerless bottle shop – cater for expats and yachties. While other colonial clubs – such as those in Labasa – have become rather desperate

places, the lovely old Savusavu Planters' Club has built a comfortable new deck.

The Tourism Association has prettied up the town with flowers, had traditional designs painted on the telegraph poles, and planted tall trees for shade around the bus station and the market. There is a new gringo vibrancy about the place.

The first settlers to arrive in Vanua Levu during the colonial era were North American copra planters, and ownership of properties often changed hands in the USA. Today, you can buy land around Savusavu from Hawaii. The local economy grew up around the copra trade in the second half of the 19th century, but the big money went out of copra long ago. The families that

VANUA LEVU

own the big plantations are subdividing small portions of their inheritance, cutting 10 hectares here and there off their huge holdings, and selling them to strangers with dreams of developing resorts.

More yachties arrive here every year. There are 40 to 60 boats in the harbour at any given time. Things have expanded so quickly, there is little room for any new moorings. Some traditional landowners are refusing to renew the leases on Indian sugar-cane farms, hoping the land can be developed for tourism. They have seen prices of freehold land go through the clouds, and have the same hopes for leasehold properties – but anyone who builds on leasehold land in Fiji is taking a wild risk. Just ask the Indo-Fijians.

Orientation & Information

Built along one main road, it's pretty difficult to get lost in Savusavu despite the lack of street names. Maps of the area are available from the **Yacht Shop** (☎ 885 0040; Copra Shed Marina; ☉ 8am-1pm & 2-5pm Mon-Fri).

Savusavu is an official point of entry for yachts, with customs, immigration, health and quarantine services all located here. **Customs** (☎ 885 0727; ☉ 8am-1pm & 2-4pm Mon-Fri) is located west of the marinas.

The ANZ, Colonial National and Westpac banks have branches in the main street. They all change currency and travellers cheques and give cash advances on major credit cards, as well as have ATMs that accept all major debit and credit cards.

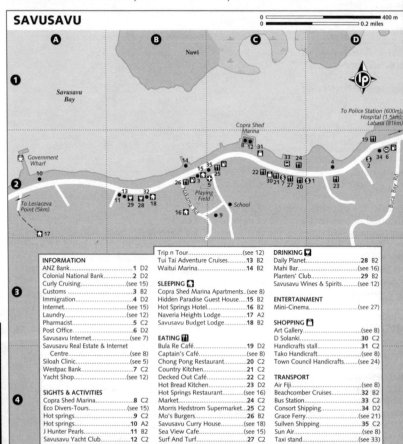

SAVUSAVU

0 ————— 400 m
0 ————— 0.2 miles

INFORMATION	
ANZ Bank	1 D2
Colonial National Bank	2 D2
Curly Cruising	(see 15)
Customs	3 B2
Immigration	4 D2
Internet	(see 15)
Laundry	(see 12)
Pharmacist	5 C2
Post Office	6 D2
Savusavu Internet	(see 7)
Savusavu Real Estate & Internet Centre	(see 8)
Siloah Clinic	(see 5)
Westpac Bank	7 C2
Yacht Shop	(see 12)

SIGHTS & ACTIVITIES	
Copra Shed Marina	8 C2
Eco Divers-Tours	(see 15)
Hot springs	9 C2
Hot springs	10 A2
J Hunter Pearls	11 B2
Savusavu Yacht Club	12 C2

Trip n Tour	(see 12)
Tui Tai Adventure Cruises	13 B2
Waitui Marina	14 B2

SLEEPING	
Copra Shed Marina Apartments	(see 8)
Hidden Paradise Guest House	15 B2
Hot Springs Hotel	16 B2
Naveria Heights Lodge	17 A2
Savusavu Budget Lodge	18 B2

EATING	
Bula Re Café	19 D2
Captain's Café	(see 8)
Chong Pong Restaurant	20 C2
Country Kitchen	21 C2
Decked Out Café	22 C2
Hot Bread Kitchen	23 C2
Hot Springs Restaurant	(see 16)
Market	24 C2
Morris Hedstrom Supermarket	25 C2
Mo's Burgers	26 B2
Savusavu Curry House	(see 18)
Sea View Cafe	(see 15)
Surf And Turf	27 C2

DRINKING	
Daily Planet	28 B2
Mahi Bar	(see 16)
Planters' Club	29 B2
Savusavu Wines & Spirits	(see 12)

ENTERTAINMENT	
Mini-Cinema	(see 27)

SHOPPING	
Art Gallery	(see 8)
D Solanki	30 C2
Handicrafts stall	31 C2
Tako Handicraft	(see 8)
Town Council Handicrafts	(see 24)

TRANSPORT	
Air Fiji	(see 8)
Beachcomber Cruises	32 B2
Bus Station	33 C2
Consort Shipping	34 D2
Grace Ferry	(see 21)
Suilven Shipping	35 C2
Sun Air	(see 8)
Taxi stand	(see 33)

Other places of interest:

Curly Cruising & Internet (☎ 885 0122; Internet per hr $10; ◷ 8am-5.30pm Mon-Fri, till noon Sat) A yachting information centre, tour office that also has a few computers for surfing the Net.

Hospital or ambulance (☎ 885 0444) The hospital is 1.5km east of town on the road to Labasa.

Laundry service (Copra Shed Marina; wash & dry 6/10kg $7/10; ◷ 8am-5pm Mon-Fri, till 1pm Sat)

Pharmacist (◷ 9am-5pm Mon-Fri, till noon Sun) Next door to the Siloah Clinic, the staff in this pharmacy are very helpful.

Police (☎ 885 0222) The police station is 600m past the Buca Bay Rd turn-off.

Post office At the eastern end of town near Buca Bay Rd.

Savusavu Internet (☎ 885 3250; Westpac Building; per hr $9; ◷ 7.30am-5pm Mon-Fri, 8am-2pm Sat)

Savusavu Real Estate & Internet Centre (☎ 885 0929; Copra Shed Marina; per hr $12; ◷ 8am-5pm Mon-Fri, till noon Sat)

Siloah Clinic (☎ 885 0721; ◷ 9am-5pm Mon-Fri) This new private health centre is behind Suilven Shipping on the main road.

Sights & Activities
MARINAS

Dating back to 1880 and originally one of Fiji's first copra mills, the **Copra Shed Marina** (☎ 885 0457; coprashed@connect.com.fj) has been rebuilt into Savusavu's service hub for tourists and expats. In one visit you can book a flight or a boat, check your email, buy postcards, pick up your laundry, swig a beer and devour a pizza. Toilets and hot showers are available for yachties. There is even a small historical display, and a couple of units for rent upstairs. Moorings in the pretty harbour between Savusavu and Nawi Islet cost $10/220 for a day/month in high season, and $7/150 for a day/month in low season.

Close by is **Waitui Marina** (☎ 885 0536; fax 885 0344), based in a beautiful, restored boatshed with showers ($3/free for guests/yachties), laundry ($8 a load) and a private club (see p201). Moorings cost $10 a day. Use channel 16 for assistance in locating moorings on arrival. The marina is closed on Sunday.

HOT SPRINGS

Savusavu Bay once saw a great deal of bubbling volcanic activity; those vents of steam you see along the water's edge are evidence of the geothermal activity that remains. You'll find hot springs near the wharf and behind the playing field. Don't even think about bathing in them as they're literally boiling hot.

DIVING & SNORKELLING

With excellent dive sites in and around Savusavu Bay as well as along the coast towards Taveuni, Savusavu is a diver's dream.

KoroSun Dive (☎ 885 2452; www.korosundive.com; Hibiscus Hwy) is on the jetty opposite Koro Sun Resort. Two-tank dives/PADI Open Water Course, including all gear, cost $208/750; night dives are $130. There are special rates for multiday diving and it also offers day trips to the Somosomo Strait or the Namena Marine Park near Namenalala in the Lomaiviti Group.

L'Aventure Jean-Michel Cousteau (☎ 885 0188; laventurefiji@connect.com.fj; Jean-Michel Cousteau Resort; see p199) has excellent daily dives. Two-tank dives/PADI Open Water Course cost $250/1000 (not including gear).

Split Rock has a deep crevice containing some gorgeous soft coral, which attracts hordes of equally colourful fish. You can easily swim out from the road and snorkel. Ask the locals how to find it.

OTHER ACTIVITIES

A popular kayaking area is Savusavu Bay. **Eco Divers-Tours** (☎ 885 0122) rents kayaks (per hour/day from $15/55), mountain bikes (per hour/day $15/25) and catamarans (per hour $15). See also Tours, following, for details of other activities.

Tours

Eco Divers-Tours (☎ 885 0122) advertises a variety of individually tailored village and hiking tours in the area. Eco Divers also organises guided kayaking tours around Savusavu Bay, ranging from three to 14 nights and staying in Fijian villages. Activities along the way include snorkelling, fishing and swimming.

With **J Hunter Pearls** (☎ 885 0821; www.pearls fiji.com) you can snorkel among black pearls at 9.30am and 1.30pm weekdays on this working farm ($25). Staff members give talks on how pearls are made and afterwards you can head to the shop to buy pearls and shell jewellery. Bring your own snorkel.

Naveria Heights Lodge (☎ 851 0157; justnaveria@ connect.com.fj) runs half-/full-day tours hiking ($35/65) or mountain biking ($45/75), including snacks, lunch and rum punch.

For those looking to charter their own boat, **SeaHawk Yacht Charters** (☎ 885 0787; www .seahawkfiji.com) rents out a beautiful 16m yacht with captain and a cook/crew for $250 to $420 per person per day depending on the season and level of service required. You can go practically anywhere in Fiji and the crew can help you arrange activities such as diving. SeaHawk also offers cruises around Savusavu Bay, including full-day picnic cruises ($85), half-day sail and snorkel trips ($55), sunset cruises ($50) and overnight cruises ($720 per couple).

Trip n Tour (☎ 885 3154; tripntour@connect.com.fj; Copra Shed Marina) offers a range of tours, including the Red Prawn Tour to Naweni village (adult/child $55/22.50) where locals call the unusual prawns, which are so red they look cooked, to the surface by chanting and slapping the water. There are also tours of the copra plantation of Nukutoso, Savusavu and surrounds, Waivunia village and Waisali Waterfall (adult/child $35/17.50 each). Full-day Labasa tours cost $90. Diving, fishing and snorkelling trips can be arranged, as can overnight trips.

A voyage with **Tui Tai Adventure Cruises** (☎ 885 3032; www.tuitai.com) is a fantastic way to see and do a lot in a short time. Sailing between Vanua Levu, Taveuni and the more remote islands of Kioa, Koro and the Ringgolds, you'll get to snorkel, kayak, bike, trek, swim, fish, dive or just lounge on deck to your heart's content. Captivating dolphins and – if you're lucky – majestic whales swimming alongside the boat, star-lit dinners on deck, and welcoming villagers you meet on out-of-the-way islands all make it a great experience. The snorkelling and diving sites are some of the world's best, and the newly refitted sailboat itself is gorgeous. All accommodation is in cabins with private bathroom and air-con. A five-night cruise costs from $2622/3450 for singles/doubles up to $3908/5143 for the Grand Staterooms, including all meals and activities except diving. Cheaper rates are available for singles willing to share a cabin. There are also three- and four-night options. Your itinerary may vary according to the weather. Don't count on going to Koro in rough seas, for instance. Tui Tai is the only way to reach the Ringgolds.

Tui Tai also runs a Nasekawa River kayak day tour ($140 including lunch and snacks) once a week, which combines cruising, snorkelling and kayaking around Savusavu Bay.

Sleeping

Most options are out of town, either on Lesiaceva Point to the southwest or on the Hibiscus Hwy to the east. Buses service both these locations (see p201).

BUDGET
In Town

Hidden Paradise Guest House (☎ 885 0106; s/d $25/50, with air-con $30/60; ✷) This extremely clean hotel, run by the very helpful Elenoa, offers some of the cheapest double rooms in Fiji – and negotiation may bring the prices down even further. The rooms are basic but liveable, breeze-cooled with shared kitchen, bathroom and cold-water showers. There's one room with air-con. Avoid the windowless chamber Elenoa rents out if everything else is full. Breakfast is included in the price. The Sea View Café is here (see p200).

Savusavu Budget Lodge (☎ 885 3127; fax 885 3157; s/d $30/50, s/d/tr with air-con $55/80/105, extra person $20; ✷) The lodge's enterprising Indian owner seems to be trying to turn this place into an unlikely urban resort. Downstairs there's a good curry restaurant (see p200) and a separate, cramped, air-conditioned bar, neither of which have any outside windows. The cheaper rooms are small, but guests can take their restaurant meals on the balcony and watch the street life go by. This is just as well, since the view from your private porch might well be a concrete wall next door. Breakfast is included in the price.

Out of Town

Bayside Backpacker Cottage (☎ 885 3154; tripn tour@connect.com.fj; Lesiaceva Rd; s/d $40/50) A great bargain; travel agent Eddie Bower has a granny *bure* in the grounds of his home. The *bure* (traditional dwelling) has two single beds and a decent kitchen with a gas stove. It's not luxurious, but it's stocked with luxury items including a microwave, TV and DVD. The beach across the road is pebble, but the snorkelling is wonderful at high tide. The cottage is 3km from town, and the friendly Bowers will let you use their mountain bikes to make the journey. Otherwise, it's a $3 taxi ride. There's a minimum two-night stay.

VANUA LEVU

Yau Kolo (☎ 885 3089; yaukolo@yahoo.com; Hibiscus Hwy; tent sites per person $12, s/d onsite tent $20/30) About 13km from Savusavu is this lush, welcoming campground, café and 'beer garden'. You have to walk along a 'bulavard' – one of the many bad *bula* (welcome!) jokes in Fiji – to get to the two excellent, spacious furnished tents, with decent mattresses and bedding. Showers are cold and the toilets compost. There is a lagoon for snorkelling, and a freshwater creek on the property, which backs onto the friendly village of Waivunia. The beer garden is really just a bar in the garden. Breakfast is included. Recommended. Bring mosquito repellent. It's a $12 taxi ride from town or $1 by bus.

Vatukaluvi Holiday House (☎ 885 0561; r $80) This is a fantastic deal if you're looking for a secluded and self-contained place. The Vatukaluvi is 15-minute taxi ride from town on a rocky point overlooking the Koro Sea and a few desert islands. You can snorkel from the small beach, windsurf or visit nearby hot springs. The house is fully furnished, has hot-water showers, Sky TV, and sleeps a maximum of seven people. The owner can arrange for a cook and cleaner ($2.50 an hour). It's best to book ahead; enquiries can be made through the Copra Shed Marina. From town, the journey costs $4 in a taxi.

Mumu's Resort (☎ 885 0416; Hibiscus Hwy, dm $25, bure $60-$150) Balanced on ruggedly beautiful Maravu Point, about 17km east of Savusavu, Mumu's is a bit rundown, but each building is unique, like a typical, ramshackle Fijian village. Ask to see a few *bure* before you choose. There's no guarantee you'll be shown the best first, even if they are all empty. Most have cooking facilities and all have bathrooms. The Dream House (recommended) has the best views, a cold-water shower and toilet. It houses a double room, but you have to walk through the dorm to get there. Many people love it but there have been some complaints about animals at Mumu's.

Simple meals cost $8/$15 for breakfast/dinner. Local buses ($1 to Savusavu) pass Mumu's five times a day, Monday to Saturday, and a taxi to/from Savusavu is $15.

Olivia's Homestay (☎ 885 3099; silina@connect.fj; Nagigi; per person $13) Guests at Olivia's live the village life at Nagigi. They have to, really, because there's nothing else around. Olivia, who has lived in California, tries to educate her guests in the Fijian way of doing everything from cookery to massage. No activity costs more than a few dollars, and both Olivia and the villagers are extremely welcoming. The no-frills homestay is a single cabin with four simple bedrooms and a cold-water shower. Do not expect luxury. Children are adored. Buses from Savusavu to Nagigi ($1.60, 40 minutes) leave about every two hours, or take a taxi (about $20).

MIDRANGE
In Town
Naveria Heights Lodge (☎ 851 0157; justnaveria@connect.com.fj; Naveria Pde; r incl breakfast $140; ✉) Mountain biking is the speciality at Naveria Heights. The owners, a fitness instructor and a massage therapist, will take you up and down moderate-to-difficult trails for a whole week, if you're up to it. Pedestrians can work out on the punching bag, do fitness classes on the deck, eat healthy food from the low-fat, low-carb menu, and go hiking in the hills. The house is lovely, the views are unbeatable and bread is baked daily. The lodge runs speciality programmes including 'activity week' (seven nights, five tours, all meals and transfers from Sevusevu for $1380 per person) and 'weight loss' week (seven nights, six-day fitness programme, all meals and transfers for $1630 per person). Call for a pick up as it is hard to find.

Copra Shed Marina Apartments (☎ 885 0457; coprashed@connect.com.fj; Copra Shed Marina; r $165; ✉ ✉) The marina has two luxury units with good views in the most convenient location in town. They are a bit overpriced, but worth it if you plan to spend a lot of time in the Yacht Club – which you might well end up doing anyway.

Hot Springs Hotel (☎ 885 0195; hotsprings@connect.com.fj; Nakama Rd; r with fan/air-con incl breakfast $80/125; ✉ ✉) Unkind competitors call the Hot Springs 'Fawlty Towers', which is unfair, since it has no towers. All rooms have a great, landscape painter's view of the harbour. The 1st- and 2nd-floor rooms are fan-cooled with run-down hot-water bathrooms that include a bath as well as a shower (good for a baby if you can secure the hotel's precious plug); 3rd- and 4th-floor rooms have air-con (good if you can secure the hotel's precious remote control). Enjoy the most panoramic sundowner in town from the Hot Springs' broad, majestic decking. The pool is great, too. It has a restaurant (see p200).

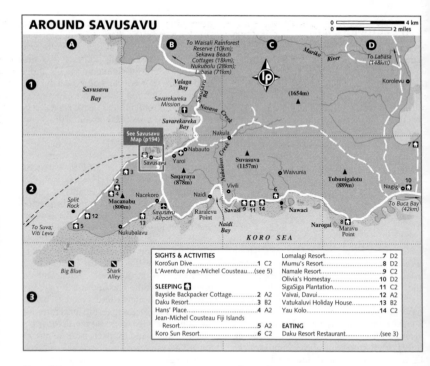

AROUND SAVUSAVU

SIGHTS & ACTIVITIES
KoroSun Dive................................1 C2
L'Aventure Jean-Michel Cousteau....(see 5)

SLEEPING
Bayside Backpacker Cottage.............2 A2
Daku Resort.................................3 B2
Hans' Place.................................4 A2
Jean-Michel Cousteau Fiji Islands
  Resort....................................5 A2
Koro Sun Resort...........................6 C2

Lomalagi Resort...........................7 D2
Mumu's Resort.............................8 D2
Namale Resort.............................9 C2
Olivia's Homestay........................10 D2
SigaSiga Plantation......................11 C2
Vaivai, Davui............................12 A2
Vatukaluvi Holiday House.................13 B2
Yau Kolo.................................14 C2

EATING
Daku Resort Restaurant...............(see 3)

Out of Town

Hans' Place (☎ 885 0621; www.fiji-holiday.com; Lesi-aceva Rd; Yasiyasi studio day/week $80/400; Yaka cottage day/week $100/500) Located about 3km south of town on Lesiaceva Point, Hans' two pretty, self-contained cottages are nestled among lush, beautiful gardens 250m from the ocean. Yasiyasi is a studio built using native hardwoods. Yaka is a one-bedroom cottage, with the bed partitioned off from the room. Each has a kitchenette with a gas stove and fridge, TV and DVD player. They are fan-cooled with hot showers. Long-term guests are preferred. This is great choice for couples, or people looking for a quiet time. Local meals are available on request. It's a $4 taxi ride from town.

Daku Resort (☎ 885 0046; www.dakuresort.com; Lesiaceva Rd; oceanview bure s/d $95/130, 2-bedroom bure $110-195; 4-bedroom pool house $200, 3-bedroom beach house $225; 🖳 🕿) The Daku is a quiet resort with sweeping views of the sea, and smart, well-kept rooms. The beach across the street is mainly pebbles, but there is great snorkelling from the jetty. There's also a beautiful pool, and a decent restaurant and bar.

The Daku runs an intriguing programme of courses, from creative writing to Fijian politics. Breakfast is included in the price. It has a restaurant (see p200). A taxi from town will cost about $3.

Sekawa Beach Cottages (☎ 851 0154; nasekawa@hotmail.com; d day/week $95/650, extra person per night $20; 🗙) Accommodation is in a pretty one-bedroom plantation-style house, about a five-minute walk from a beach and 18km north of Savusavu town. There is everything a family could possibly need here, from a microwave to a DVD player, twin beds in the lounge for the kids, and 2 hectares for them to run amuck in. There's a fishing boat for hire, too and free kayaks. A four-night minimum stay applies.

SigaSiga Plantation (☎ 885 0413; www.theultimate paradise.com; Hibiscus Hwy; d bure $95; 2-bedroom villa $250) This fine oceanfront home, 11km from Savusavu and set back from a 1.6km white-sand beach, sleeps up to six guests. In the grounds are two better-than-basic *bure* with excellent bathrooms and spacious, modern kitchens. It's a $10 taxi ride from town and the bus passes by as well.

THE AUTHOR'S CHOICE

Vaivai & Davui (☎ 885 3154; tripntour@connect
.com.fj; Vaivai per week Nov-Apr/May-Oct
$1320/1495, Davui per week Nov-Apr/May-Oct
$1150/1320; 🔁) These are two magnificent
two-bedroom, two-bathroom homes with
huge decks and extraordinary views over
Savusavu Bay. Both have air-con in the master bedroom. The reef here is as good for
snorkelling as the Cousteau resort a little
further down the road – that is to say, it's
fantastic. Ask the locals how to find 'Split
Rock'. Vaivai is the larger and the pick of
the two, with a lush garden rich in ginger,
haliconias, bananas and golden palms. You
could tug on a frond and pick a pawpaw
from the balcony. Vaivai could comfortably
sleep six: there is another small bedroom
around the back, and a cot for a baby. The
kitchen is amazingly well equipped, including stuff you don't even have at home
such as cheese parers. Extras include a
telescope!

Next door, Davui is much smaller – but
still luxurious – and the bedroom walls don't
quite reach the ceilings.

TOP END

All of Savusavu's top-end accommodation
is a taxi ride from the town centre.

Jean-Michel Cousteau Fiji Islands Resort (☎ 885
0188; www.fijiresort.com; garden-view/oceanview bure
d $915/1140, 2-bedroom bure $1360; 🖥 🔁) This
is a great boutique resort with a fabulous,
educational kids' club. Meals are gourmet
and are included in the rate; *bure* are lavish with large decks and private screened
gardens. About half the guests are divers,
and the snorkelling is as good as you would
expect in a place associated with the family
that brought the undersea world into a million living rooms, without even wetting the
carpet. All activities (except diving) are included in the rate. Cousteau would have to
be the first choice in Vanua Levu for parents
with children. Kids *have to* check into the
Bula Camp. There is no choice. Heh heh.
Parents can spend time with them, but they
are kept away from the lovers' pool and the
rest of the guests. The resort is on Lesiaceva
Point, where Savusavu Bay meets the Koro
Sea. It's a $5 taxi ride from town.

Koro Sun Resort (☎ 885 0262; www.korosunresort
.com; Hibiscus Hwy; s/d bure $500/620, 2-bedroom bure from
$910; 😵 🔁) The Koro Sun is a pretty resort
facing a beautiful lagoon. There are clusters
of plush *bure*, some with bamboo beds and
rock showers. Those on the hillside feel like
tree houses, with sea views and birds singing
outside. The pool, tennis courts, a nine-hole
golf course, kayaks, bikes and snorkelling
gear are all free to guests, plus all meals included. The resort has an excellent children's
programme and a rainforest spa, where you
can make like a Fijian meal and get wrapped
in banana leaf, among other treatments. Diving is available through KoroSun Dive (see
p195), which operates from a jetty across the
road. The resort is 13km east of Savusavu. A
taxi from Savusavu costs about $12.

Namale Resort (☎ 885 0435; www.namalefiji.com;
Hibiscus Hwy; s/d bure from $1350/1640, grand villas from
$3765; 🔁) This is an exclusive, amazingly
expensive resort on the water, 9km east of
Savusavu. Casual callers are not welcome,
day-trippers are not accepted. The price
includes all meals and activities except diving. Dive Namale operates here. Owned by
Anthony Robbins, the American self-help
guru, the resort has several *bure* set aside
for workshop attendees to unleash their giants within.

Lomalagi Resort (☎ 851 0585; www.lomalagi.com;
Salt Lake Rd; d incl meals $750; 🔁) Lomalagi (Heaven)
has views to die for. It is the only resort at the
base of Natewa Bay, the largest deep-water
bay in the South Pacific. The area has barely
been touched. The beach is grey coral but
the snorkelling is great. You can take a two-
person ocean-going kayak to a 10m drop-
off 100m out, tie the kayak onto the reef
marker and swim among sea horses. There
is a 1km white-sand beach about 3km up
the coastline, with four Fijian homes at one
end. Guests have permission to picnic there.
You can visit two resident pods of dolphins
that are a 25-minute trip away in the snorkel
boat. Whales have been sighted December to
February. The villas are spacious with large
kitchens and decks, but some of the décor is
a bit naff. Lomalagi takes infants as long as
they're not mobile – but no other children
under 12 – and can organise a nanny. There's
a swimming pool, a good library, a video library and a reasonably priced wine list. This
is perhaps the only resort in Fiji to encourage
midnight skinny dipping. The walk-in rate

is fantastic value. If you're driving, turn off at the Salt Lake Rd sign, about 24km east of Savusavu, not far from where the Hibiscus Hwy turns south.

About 24km offshore, southwest of Savusavu, is Moody's Namena, on the island of Namenalala (see p190).

Eating

Surf And Turf (☎ 851 0966; lunch/dinner meals from $8/20; ☺ lunch & dinner) The signs on the window still proclaim Charan's Dinning Room (sic), but Surf And Turf is an altogether more upmarket affair. The manager's husband is a chef at the Cousteau resort, and he trained the chef here. He did a great job; this place is highly recommended. Surf and turf (lobster tail and fillet mignon) is $50 at dinner, by the way.

Captain's Café (☎ 885 0511; Copra Shed Marina; pizza from $10, lunch/dinner $8/16; ☺ breakfast, lunch & dinner) The food here is usually good – but forget about Sunday (when the chef takes the day off) – and the views of the harbour are fantastic. There are pizzas, fish and chips and sandwiches, and the daily specials are always worth trying. You can buy drinks – including cheap draught beer – from the Yacht Club next door (see opposite).

Hot Springs Hotel (☎ 885 0195; meals $19; ☺ breakfast & dinner) The breakfast buffet is limp and dull, and dining in this big, often empty room can be a lonely and comparatively expensive experience – but the evening meals are great. There is a choice of two mains every night, generally including an excellent fish dish. Turn up at dusk for sunset drinks at the Mahi Bar (opposite) and play hunt-the-barstaff while you wait.

Mo's Burgers (☎ 885 3231; burgers $6, with chips & drink $8; ☺ lunch & dinner; ✗) The fajitas here are made with baked rotis, and the quesadillas are made with fried rotis, but everything is tasty and fresh in this mutant Tex-Mex joint so very far from home. As well as burgers, Mo's offers pizza, fish and chips, and chicken and chips.

Decked Out Café (☎ 885 2929; mains $6.50; ☺ breakfast, lunch & dinner) A fine place to watch the world go by on a sunny day, this café is a big, open deck on the main street, offering filling breakfasts and a limited menu of tasty and filling burgers and sandwiches. The daily specials are large and cheap. The fresh fruit smoothies ($3) are excellent.

Country Kitchen (☎ 927 1372; breakfast $2, meals $5; ☺ breakfast, lunch & dinner) One step up from a hole in the wall, and popular with local Indians for its sweets, Country Kitchen also does Chinese standards and fresh, tasty, boneless (if you request them) curries in dilapidated surrounds. Worth a try.

Sea View Café (☎ 885 0106; Hidden Paradise Guest House; meals $8; ☺ breakfast daily, lunch & dinner Mon-Sat) Here you'll get cheap, cheerful travellers' food, served by the endlessly helpful Elenoa.

Savusavu Curry House (☎ 885 3127; Savusavu Budget Lodge; meals $5; ☺ lunch & dinner) Unsurprisingly, Savusavu's only real Indian restaurant cooks pretty good curries – albeit in a gloomy backroom. Order one hour before for speciality dishes such as goat and duck.

Daku Resort (☎ 885 0334; lunch/dinner $7/15; ☺ lunch & dinner) Take a taxi out of town ($3) and eat poolside in the dining *bure* at the Daku. Sandwiches, steaks and salads are served for lunch. At night, you can chuck your own prawn (or chicken, meat or fish) on the barbie, or have the chef chuck it on for you. Daku's regular curry night is popular, as is the Sunday evening barbecue.

Chong Pong Restaurant (☎ 885 0588; mains $5; ☺ lunch & dinner) Serves your standard Chinese food such as chow mein, sweet-and-sour pork and noodle soup. Up a long flight of stairs, it's simple but has nice views across the main road to the market and sea beyond.

Savusavu has a few grocery stores including a well-stocked Morris Hedstrom Supermarket. The market has fruit and veggies as well as lots and lots of *kava (yaqona)* root, used to make the narcotic drink of the same name. The **Hot Bread Kitchen** (☺ 6am-8pm Mon-Sat, 6am-1pm Sun) has fresh loaves daily.

Drinking

Savusavu Yacht Club (☎ 885 0685; Copra Shed Marina; ☽ 10am-10pm Sun-Thu, till midnight Fri & Sat) It has a friendly pub feel about it, although it gets a bit rough around the edges on a Saturday night. With picnic tables by the waterside, the Yacht Club is a good place for a drink and to meet local expats. There's cold beer on tap and bar snacks ($5.50) and meals can be ordered from the next-door Captain's Café. Happy hour is 5.30pm to 6.30pm. Tourists are considered temporary members.

Waitui Marina (☎ 885 0536; ☽ 10am-10pm Mon-Sat) There are classic South Pacific views from the balcony bar here: palm trees, yachts, an island beach and ethereal hot springs. The décor is suitably nautical, and merry yachties might find it hard to tell if they're at sea or on land. The club is friendly and comfortable, the bar is well stocked, and you are a temporary member if you are a foreigner on holiday.

Planters' Club (☎ 885 0233; ☽ 10am-10pm Mon-Fri, till 1am Sat, till 8pm Sun) This was traditionally a place for planters to come and drink when they brought in the copra, and some of their descendants can still be found clustered around the bar today. You can taste the history in the air as you taste the beer in your glass. Happy hour is 5.30pm to 6.30pm. Once a month, the club holds a Sunday lunch *lovo*. The bar staff will sign in a tourist.

Mahi Bar (☽ 10am-11pm Mon-Sun) Drink prices at the bar at the Hot Springs Hotel are a little steeper than in the clubs. Fijians seem to get around that by bringing their own *kava*. Still, the views are great.

Daily Planet (☽ 7pm-1am Fri & Sat) Surrounded by barbed wire fortifications, the Daily Planet looks as if it has been built to defend itself from attack, or to keep everyone inside. It's probably best not to stay until closing time, when fights occasionally roll down the main street.

Savusavu Wines & Spirits (☎ 885 3888; ☽ 8am-6pm Mon-Fri, till 1pm-Sat) It's a popular, absurdly well-stocked bottle shop in the Copra Shed Marina. The place to come for imported wines and beers.

Entertainment

Mini-Cinema (admission $2; ☽ noon-10pm) Upstairs next to Surf And Turf restaurant, this cinema plays recent DVDs on a big screen; you can go in halfway through for $1.

Shopping

Art Gallery (☎ 885 3054; Copra Shed Marina) This gallery has paintings, cards, freshwater pearl jewellery, sculptures and other work by local artists.

Tako Handicraft (☎ 885 3956; Copra Shed Marina) Also has local handicrafts and postcards.

D Solanki (☎ 885 0025) Head to this drapers for bargain-priced, beautifully made double-stitched lined saris tailor-made. It also sells traditional Fijian dress and Western clothes.

Next door to the Copra Shed is a handicrafts stall where a local man sells his wooden carvings. At the back of the market is the Town Council Handicrafts, devoted to local woven and wooden handicrafts.

Getting There & Around

For flights, head to the office of **Air Fiji** (☎ 885 0173) or **Sun Air** (☎ 885 0141) in the Copra Shed. Savusavu airstrip is 3km south of town. Local buses pass the airport every so often; however, a taxi there from Savusavu only costs $2. See p259 for more flight information.

For boat travel **Beachcomber Cruises** (☎ 885 0266; fax 885 0499), **Suilven Shipping** (☎ 885 3191; fax 885 3193), **Consort Shipping** (☎ 885 0443; fax 885 0442) and the agent for Grace Ferry, the **Country Kitchen** (☎ 927 1372; ☽ 7.30am-5pm Mon-Sat) restaurant, are all in the main street. See p261 for more details on boats.

The Savusavu bus station and taxi stand are both located in the centre of the town, near the market. Buses travelling the scenic sealed highway from Savusavu over the mountains to Labasa ($6, three hours, five times daily) depart from 7.30am to 3.30pm. Some buses take the longer, scenic route from Savusavu to Labasa along Natewa Bay, and these depart at 9am ($11.50, six hours).

Buses from Savusavu to Napuca ($6.30, 4½ hours), at the tip of the Tunuloa Peninsula, depart at 10.30am, 1pm and 2.30pm daily. The afternoon bus stays there overnight and returns at 7am. A 4pm bus only goes as far as Naweni ($2.25). There is no bus from Savusavu to Nabouwalu; you have to catch a morning bus to Labasa and change buses there.

From Monday to Saturday there are five bus services from Savusavu to Lesiaceva Point ($0.70, 15 minutes) between 6am and 5pm. For confirmation of bus timetables in the south, ring **Vishnu Holdings** (☎ 885 0276).

BÊCHE-DE-MER

European traders flocked to Fiji in the early 19th century to hunt the lucrative *bêche-de-mer* (sea cucumber). It fetched huge profits in Asia, where it's still considered a delicacy and aphrodisiac.

You are likely to see some of these ugly sluglike creatures while snorkelling or diving. They feed on organic matter in the sand and serve an important role as cleaners in the lagoon ecosystem. There are various types: some are smooth and sticky, some prickly, some black and some multicoloured. After being cut open and cleaned, they are boiled to remove the salt, then sun-dried or smoked. Many find the taste revolting, but they are highly nutritious, with 50% to 60% protein.

Bêches-de-mer are depleted in Asian waters but still prevalent in the South Pacific. They make for a lucrative commodity, both for local use and for export, and unscrupulous traders are delivering dive equipment to remote areas and promising high rewards. Villagers of the Bua region are renowned for harvesting the creature. Usually untrained and unaware of the risks, they are encouraged by the traders to dive in deep waters, risking their lives by using dodgy scuba equipment. Many end up with the bends and a stint in the Fiji Recompression Chamber and several have died.

There is an abundance of taxis. They can be hailed on the street or booked. You can also hire small carriers from the bus station; they're really reasonable if you're travelling in a group.

Carpenters Rental Cars can be booked through **Trip n Tour** (☎ 885 3154; tripntour@connect .com.fj; Copra Shed Marina) and prices start at $55 a day for a tiny sedan and $100 a day for a 4WD. Bula Re Café is an agent for **Budget Rent a Car** (☎ 885 0377) where prices start at about $100 a day for a sedan, and $120 for a 4WD.

NORTH OF SAVUSAVU
Waisali Rainforest Reserve
In the verdant mountains north of Savusavu, lies the beautiful, protected **Waisali Rainforest** (☎ 851 0939; Savusavu Rd; adult/child $5/0.50; ◷ 8am-5pm Mon-Sat). While it doesn't offer much of a trek (it's about a 30-minute slow walk each way), the foliage is beautiful, as is the waterfall at the bottom. Take care if it has been raining – the rocks at the foot of the waterfall can be treacherously slippery. You can enter the park 20km north of Savusavu, directly off the road to Labasa. Bus drivers should know where to drop you (ask before you board) as should most carrier and taxi drivers. If you are driving it's at kilometre/culvert 14.4, which is also a good viewpoint at which to stop.

Nukubolu
The remains of the ancient village of Nukubolu are in the mountains north of Savusavu on the banks of a creek, in a fertile volcanic crater with hot springs steaming nearby. There are well-preserved stone building foundations, terraces and carefully constructed thermal pools. Locals dry *kava* roots on corrugated-iron sheets laid over the pools and bathe in the hot springs when sick.

You can visit the ruins by 4WD. They are on the property of the village of Biaugunu, so take a *sevusevu* (gift) for the chief and ask permission first. The turn-off is about 20km northwest of Savusavu. Continue about 8km inland and over a couple of river crossings. You can also rent a carrier from town to take you there and combine it with a trip to Waisali Rainforest Reserve.

TUNULOA PENINSULA
Tunuloa Peninsula, also known as Natewa or Cakaudrove Peninsula, makes up the southeastern section of Vanua Levu. Lush and scenic, it's an excellent area for exploring by 4WD. If you can arrange a guide in Savusavu or from your resort, the area can also offer some great bird-watching and hiking. The bumpy, mostly dirt Hibiscus Hwy runs from Savusavu to the road's end at Napuka, passing copra plantations, old homesteads, waving villagers and thriving forests. The road becomes extremely slippery in the rain; if you've rented a vehicle, check the tyres are good before you set out. There are no restaurants or shops along this route; pack a lunch and bring water.

About 20km east of Savusavu, the Hibiscus Hwy veers right (south); the turn-off to the left (north) follows the western side of Natewa Bay, an alternative 4WD route to Labasa. About 35km further along the highway from this intersection is the turn-off into the village of **Drekeniwai**, where former prime minister Sitiveni Rabuka was born.

Once you hit Buca Bay, the highway turns left (north), becoming more potholed as it heads through the habitat of the rare **silktail bird**. There's a small reserve here. Found only on this peninsula and on Taveuni, the silktail has sadly made it onto the world's endangered-species list with logging being its major threat. The bird is about 8cm high and is black with a white patch on its tail.

If you turn right (south) at Buca Bay, you'll head through Natuva village and then up over the mountain to the next village of **Dakuniba**. The road is one big pothole and the going is slow but you'll be rewarded with dazzling views over the forest and out to sea. In a beautiful forest setting, just outside Dakuniba, **petroglyphs** are inscribed on large boulders. They are thought to be of ceremonial or mystical significance. Be sure to bring a *sevusevu* for the village chief and read up about village etiquette (see p36); the people of Dakuniba are very friendly and may offer to take you to a nearby beach to swim, fish or snorkel. The famous Rainbow Reef (see p61) is offshore from Dakuniba, but is more easily accessible from the island of Taveuni.

Sleeping

Levukalailai (☎ 888 0888; levukalailai@connect.com.fj; Hibiscus Hwy; bure $210, lodges $250; 🏊) This lovely new resort promises to be fantastic when it finally opens. The central lodge (suitable for adults only) has four rooms with bathroom and is made of Australian woods such as western red cedar, and tastefully decorated traditional motifs and *mangi mangi* (traditional weavings). The beach here is incredible: 5.5km of white sand, the best in Vanua Levu. Fishing and snorkelling are great, but vegetarians might be disturbed that the owners slaughter their own beef, and honeymooners should be aware of Cathedral ceilings in the lodge bedrooms; so sound carries. It's highly recommended for everyone else. There's a swimming pool as well as Sky TV, and Levukalailai is run on solar power.

La Dolce Vita Holiday Villas (☎ 851 8023; ladolcevitafiji@connect.com.fj; Hibiscus Hwy; bure $515-600, d house $345) La Dolce has spanking new bunga-

lows with great decking, large, modern bathrooms and fabulous sea views. Rates include all meals. There is a bar and dining room. Compulsive golfers can play six holes, ordinary people can snorkel, or follow horse trails and bush walks through the hills. This place is owned by an Italo-Australian called Lui, and Lui's Italian pizza-oven-in-a-*bure* might be unique in the South Pacific. The resort beach is a little grey but Lui's private island – known as 'Lui's Island' – is fringed with white sand, and La Dolce Vita guests are welcome to take the walkway over. You can also rent out a big, comfortable three-bedroom house, with cane lounges and a huge freezer. A taxi from Savusavu costs about $25.

There are two other accommodation options on the western edge of the Tunuloa Peninsula; budget Olivia's Homestay (see p197) and the top-end Lomalagi Resort (see p199).

Dolphin Bay Divers Retreat is southeast of Buca Bay. Accessible only by boat, it's most easily reached from Taveuni. See p217 for more information.

OFFSHORE ISLANDS
Kioa

The island of Kioa (25 sq km) is inhabited by Polynesians originally from the tiny coral reef island of Vaitupu in Tuvalu. As their home island suffered from poor soils and overcrowding, the community decided to purchase another more fertile island and relocate some families. Kioa was purchased in 1947 for $15,000; the people of Vaitupu had earned the money working for the Americans who had occupied their islands during WWII. When they began to move to Kioa, they knew nothing about the climate or lifestyle and were concerned the Fijians might still be cannibals. About 600 people now live here, in a colourful and immaculately kept village. The people are very warm and friendly; one of the first things you can see from the sea is a giant sign saying '*Talofa*' (the equivalent of Fijian *bula*). The women are known for their woven crafts and fishing is done from small, traditional *drua* (double-hulled canoes). The people of Kioa have a traditional drink called toddy. Made of fermented coconut sap, it's got something more of a kick than *kava*.

You cannot show up at Kioa without an invitation. You can travel there and back on outboards owned by the Island Council ($50 from/to Taveuni, about $35 from/to Buca Bay). If you can find a boatman, that constitutes an invitation. There is no accommodation or facilities for tourists; however, Tui Tai Adventure Cruises (p196) does make a stop here and Taveuni Estate Dive (see p212) does day trips. For snorkellers and divers, the **Farm**, off the most easterly point of the island, has fantastic corals.

Rabi

Rabi (66 sq km), east of the northern tip of the Tunuloa peninsula, is populated by Micronesians originally from Banaba, in Kiribati. At the turn of the 20th century the naive islanders were first tricked and then pressed into selling the phosphate mining rights of Banaba in return for an annual payment, and their tiny island was slowly ruined. WWII brought these people another blow when the Japanese invaded Banaba and massacred many villagers. Following the war, Rabi was purchased for the Banabans by the British Government – with money from the islanders' own Provident Fund – and 2000 survivors were resettled here. Scandalously, they were dropped in the middle of the cyclone season with only army tents and two months rations. They had never been so cold (Banaba is on the equator) and many died. Today the island has four Banaban villages, with a total population of 4500.

If you're interested in visiting Rabi, you must first ask permission from the **Island Council** (☎ 881 2913). If you're extended an invitation, catch a bus from Savusavu to Karoko where small boats wait for passengers to Rabi ($50 one way). The **Rabi Island Council Guesthouse** (☎ 881 2913 ext 30; dm $50; ☯ Mon, Wed & Fri) has beds in basic, four-bed rooms. You'll eat with the villagers.

LABASA

pop 24,100

Labasa is a sugar town, with crushed cane husks fallen from trucks lying like roadkill on the road, and snakes of trucks banked up at the sugar mill. The air smells of molasses, as if the clouds were candy floss, and a sugar train runs up a sugar railway. It is also India town. Labasa's population is predominantly Indo-Fijian, many of whom are descendants of indentured labourers brought to work on the plantations. There are beggars

in the doorways here, some flashing their stumps. The stores sell trinkets, bangles and saris, and blast out Bollywood music. Dozens of shop assistants do nothing identifiable in the shadow of mosques and Sikh and Hindu temples. You're in luck if your watch breaks here, because there are a lot of watchmakers.

Labasa is Vanua Levu's largest town, about 5km inland on the banks of the meandering Labasa River. The fertile riverbanks and reclaimed mangrove swamps have made this area a centre for the sugar industry since colonial days. Sadly, in early 2003, Cyclone Ami all but obliterated the surrounding cane fields. Also, farmers are struggling to restore their livelihoods against fallen world sugar prices. In addition, many Fijian landowners are terminating Fijian-Indian leases, leaving people who have lived on the land for generations without a living or a home.

While hot, serious Labasa is a bustling trade, service and administrative centre for northern Vanua Levu, the town itself doesn't have a lot to offer tourists. If you hire a 4WD, however, the surrounding area is great for exploring.

Information

Labasa's main drag is Nasekula Rd; this is where you'll find the majority of shops and services.

The ANZ, Colonial National and Westpac banks have branches in the main street. They all change currency and travellers cheques and have 24-hour ATMs that accept all major debit and credit cards.

Govinda Internet Café (☎ 881 1364; Nasekula Rd; login $1, per min $0.10; ☯ 8am-8pm Mon-Sat, 5pm-8pm Sun) This air-conditioned café has five computers with cheap Net access.

Hospital/ambulance (☎ 881 1444; Butinikama-Siberia Rd) The hospital is southeast of the river.

Library (Jaduram St; ☯ 9am-1pm & 2-5pm Mon-Fri, 9am-noon Sat) At the Civic Centre, it has a limited collection of books.

My Chemist (☎ 881 4611; Nasekula Rd; ☯ 8am-6pm Mon-Thu, 8am-7pm Fri, 8am-3pm Sat) Fairly well stocked with medicines and vitamins.

Police (☎ 881 1222; Nadawa St)

Post office (Nasekula Rd) Has a row of cardphones outside.

Sights & Activities

Just south of town is the **Wasavula Ceremonial Site** (Vunimoli Rd). At the entrance to the site

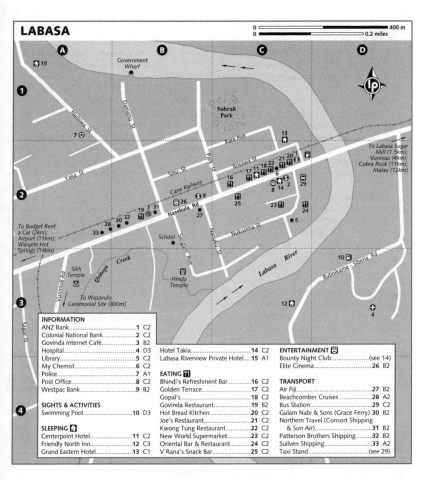

LABASA

To Labasa Sugar
Mill (1.5km);
Vunivau (4km);
Cobra Rock (11km);
Malau (12km)

To Budget Rent
a Car (2km);
Airport (11km);
Waiqele Hot
Springs (14km)

To Wasavulu
Ceremonial Site (800m)

INFORMATION	
ANZ Bank	1 C2
Colonial National Bank	2 C2
Govinda Internet Café	3 B2
Hospital	4 D3
Library	5 C2
My Chemist	6 C2
Police	7 A1
Post Office	8 C2
Westpac Bank	9 B2
SIGHTS & ACTIVITIES	
Swimming Pool	10 D3
SLEEPING	
Centerpoint Hotel	11 C2
Friendly North Inn	12 C3
Grand Eastern Hotel	13 C1

Hotel Takia	14 C2
Labasa Riverview Private Hotel	15 A1
EATING	
Bhindi's Refreshment Bar	16 C2
Golden Terrace	17 C2
Gopal's	18 C2
Govinda Restaurant	19 B2
Hot Bread Kitchen	20 C2
Joe's Restaurant	21 C2
Kwong Tung Restaurant	22 C2
New World Supermarket	23 C2
Oriental Bar & Restaurant	24 C2
V Rana's Snack Bar	25 C2

ENTERTAINMENT	
Bounty Night Club	(see 14)
Elite Cinema	26 B2
TRANSPORT	
Air Fiji	27 B2
Beachcomber Cruises	28 A2
Bus Station	29 C2
Gulam Nabi & Sons (Grace Ferry)	30 B2
Northern Travel (Consort Shipping & Sun Air)	31 B2
Patterson Brothers Shipping	32 B2
Suilven Shipping	33 A2
Taxi Stand	(see 29)

is a sacred monolith that villagers believe grew from the ground. Behind the standing stone is the village cemetery, surrounded by a small garden. Beyond is the area used during cannibalistic ceremonies – a flat *vatu ni bokola* or head-chopping stone, another rock where the severed head was placed, and a bowl-like stone in which the brain was placed for the chief. Unless you are given a guided tour, you could probably walk right past most of these stones without noticing. Tourists have complained about being charged $10 (as well as the obligatory *sevusevu*) to look at nothing much. The site is on the left, about 2km south off Nasekula Rd. For more on the rituals conducted on this site, see the boxed text, p206.

Waiqele hot springs is about 3km beyond the airport; take the Waiqele bus ($0.75). You might like to go there if, for instance, you are on a mission to visit every hot springs in the world.

To cool off from the heat, head to the Grand Eastern Hotel where nonguests can use the pool if they buy lunch in the hotel's restaurant. There is also a public **swimming pool** (☎ 881 6387; Butinikama-Siberia Rd; $1.10; ☺ noon-5pm Mon-Thu, 9am-6pm Fri-Sun) southeast of town.

Sleeping

Labasa Riverview Private Hotel (☎ 881 1367; fax 881 4337; Nadawa St; dm $15, s/d with shared bathroom $20/30, s/d with bathroom $30/45, s/d with air-con & bathroom $50/60;

MONOLITHIC GODS

Although the Wasavula Ceremonial Site (p206) is shrouded in mystery, it is thought to be related to similar sites of the *naga* (snake) cult found in Viti Levu's Sigatoka Valley. In the old religion, those who betrayed ceremonial secrets would face insanity and death by the ancestral spirits and gods, so what is known about such places is mostly based on hearsay and vague memories.

Before the arrival of Christianity, ceremonial sites were venues for communicating with ancestral gods. Rituals performed at the sites provided a spiritual link between the people and the earth, time, crops and fertility. It is believed that this was where chiefs and priests were installed, where male initiation rites took place and where a *bokola*, the dead body of an enemy, was offered to the gods.

Stone monoliths at the sites were seen as actual gods or as the shrines of gods. These stones were often used for refuge; if someone who had committed a crime made it to the monolith before being caught, their life would be spared.

While the rituals of long ago are no longer practiced at Wasavula Ceremonial Site, the ancestral gods haven't been evicted so easily. It is still revered as a sacred place by the village people and is now where they bury their dead. Some people continue to see the monolith as supernatural; it is said that in photos of villagers with the monolith, the villagers have often vanished from the developed pictures.

🗙) Rooms are cosy and comfortable and the five-bed dorm has a clean, well-equipped kitchen. The hotel's bar and veranda overlook the river, and the hotel is probably the best place for a cold beer in Labasa. A five-minute walk north of town, this place is peaceful, relaxed and has a very friendly proprietor.

Grand Eastern Hotel (☎ 881 1022; grest@connect .com.fj; Rosawa St; r standard/deluxe/executive $77/103/128; 🗙 🖭) Labasa's most upmarket hotel has a pleasant colonial atmosphere, a swimming pool and a decent restaurant. Rooms have views of the river, small porches, air-con and private facilities. It's worth paying the extra for the newer deluxe rooms for their river-facing porches. The renovated Grand Eastern was reopened by Sitiveni Rabuka in 1997, which would have been the last time Rabuka did anything for an Indo-Fijian town. It has a restaurant (see opposite).

Friendly North Inn (☎ 881 1555; fni@connect.com .fj; Butinikama-Siberia Rd; s/d with fan $35/45, s/d with air-con $45/55, apt with air-con $65, extra mattress/bed $10/15; 🗙) Opposite the hospital, an easy 15-minute walk from town, the Friendly North is utterly quiet. Follow the rose-lined paths to the motel-like rooms in duplex villas. All come with bathroom and are clean but cramped, and the beds are a bit lumpy. The hotel's large, open *bure* has a TV and beer on tap; meals are available if ordered in advance. A taxi into town will cost $2.

Hotel Takia (☎ 881 1655; hoteltakia@connect.com .fj; Nasekula Rd; s/d with fan $45/55, s/d with air-con $80/90, s/d ste $108/118, extra person $10; 🗙) There is a slightly desperate air to the Takia, although the rooms are large and clean with TV, fridge and kettle. It's $5 extra per night if you pay by credit card. The Tapa Restaurant offers big meals for $13. The bar is open 6pm to 9pm daily, and the drinkers here look pretty serious. The Bounty Night Club operates here (see opposite).

Centerpoint Hotel (☎ 881 1057; cenhotel@connect .com.fj; Nasekula Rd; s/d with fan $45/62, with air-con $55/77, extra person $10; 🗙) At the centre point of town, the rooms at this hotel are big and clean and come with bathrooms. Rates include one free meal.

Eating

Labasa is teeming with hole-in-the-wall places dishing up Indian or Chinese food. Note: most restaurants, although open for dinner, close by 7pm.

Gopal's (Nasekula Rd; thali $9; 🕑 breakfast, lunch & dinner) It serves great Indian vegetarian food: thalis, samosas and sweets.

Oriental Bar & Restaurant (☎ 881 7321; Jaduram St; meals $7; 🕑 lunch & dinner Mon-Sat, dinner Sun; 🗙) Definitely Labasa's most atmospheric restaurant, with a strong Chinese twist to its Fijian décor. Although it feels slightly upmarket, the prices are reasonable. The bar is fairly well stocked and the menu has a good variety of tasty Chinese dishes, including lots of veggie and a few Fijian options. No caps or vests allowed.

Grand Eastern Hotel (☎ 881 1022; Rosawa St; lunch/dinner $15/25; ⓨ breakfast, lunch & dinner) The Grand Eastern serves Western-style food. Decorated with historical photos of Labasa and spilling out onto the deck, it's a pleasant place to dine.

Govinda Restaurant (☎ 881 1364; Nasekula Rd; meals $4, thali $7; ⓨ breakfast, lunch & dinner) Like Gopal's, this is a Hare Krishna vegetarian restaurant. It serves fantastic thalis, samosas and sweets. Its $4 deal is a delicious, healthy combo of curry, dahl, chutney and rice or rotis.

V Rana's Snack Bar (☎ 881 4351; Nasekula Rd; snacks $0.50; ⓨ 7am-6pm Mon-Fri, till 4pm Sat) This place is friendly and has comfortable booths where you can snack on bhajis, samosas and Indian sweets. Ask for the tamarind dipping sauce with your samosa.

Bhindi's Refreshment Bar (☎ 881 3007; Nasekula Rd; snacks $1.40, meals $3.20; ⓨ breakfast, lunch & dinner) Bhindi's serves good homemade Indian snacks and sandwiches.

Kwong Tung Restaurant (☎ 881 1980; Nasekula Rd; mains $5; ⓨ breakfast, lunch & dinner Mon-Fri, lunch Sat) It has a huge dining hall with a range of very good Chinese meals, but no beer.

Golden Terrace Restaurant (☎ 881 8378; Nasekula Rd; meals $3.50; ⓨ breakfast, lunch & dinner) Serves dishes taken from Labasa's three main cuisines: Chinese, Indian and Greasy.

Joe's Restaurant (☎ 881 1766; Nasekula Rd; meals $6, pizza $10; ⓨ lunch & dinner) Joe's is a Chinese restaurant with a large menu including dishes not normally associated with China such as pizza and fish and chips.

Hot Bread Kitchen (Nasekula Rd; ⓨ 5am-8pm Mon-Thu & Sun, till 8.30pm Fri & Sat) Has fresh bread.

For supplies there are several supermarkets near the bus station, including the **New World Supermarket** (☎ 881 2586; Jaduram St; ⓨ 7.45am-6pm Mon-Thu, till 6pm Fri, till 4pm Sat).

Entertainment

There's not much going on in town.

Elite Cinema (☎ 881 1260; Nasekula Rd; adult/child $3/1) It shows older films, the majority of which are in Hindi.

You might try the bar at the Grand Eastern Hotel for a poolside drink, or brave the **Bounty Night Club** (ⓨ 8pm-1am Wed-Sat) at the Takia Hotel. The owners assure us it's safe, but not only is the bar in a cage, the disco mirror ball is in a cage of its own! A night out at the Labasa Club or the Farmers Club is definitely *not* a good idea.

Getting There & Around

For flights head to the office of **Air Fiji** (☎ 881 1188; Nasekula Rd) or **Sun Air** (☎ 881 1454; Northern Travel Service office, Nasekula Rd). The airport is about 11km southwest of Labasa. The turn-off is 4km west of Labasa, just past the Wailevu River. To reach the airport, catch the Waiqele bus from Labasa bus station; it departs between 6am and 4.15pm ($0.55, four services daily Monday to Saturday; as per flight schedule Sunday). A taxi from Labasa costs $8.

For boat tickets **Beachcomber Cruises** (☎ 881 7788), **Consort Shipping** (☎ 881 1454; Northern Travel Service office), **Patterson Brothers Shipping** (☎ 881 2444), **Suilven Shipping** (☎ 881 8471), and the agent for Grace Ferry, **Gulam Nabi & Sons** (☎ 881 1152) are all along Nasekula Rd. It is possible to buy tickets in Labasa for bus/boat combinations to Suva and Lautoka. See p261 for more information on reaching Vanua Levu via boat or plane.

There are regular buses between Labasa and Savusavu ($6, three hours, five times Monday to Saturday, four on Sunday) departing between 7am and 4.15pm. There is also a 9am bus that takes the long route ($11.50, six hours) to Savusavu around the northeast, following Natewa Bay. Buses to Nabouwalu depart three times Monday to Saturday ($8, six hours).

The majority of shops, businesses and hotels in Labasa are within walking distance of the centre. If you are going further afield, there is no shortage of taxis. You'll find the majority of them at the main stand near the bus station. **Budget Rent a Car** (☎ 881 1999; Vakamaisuasua) has an office a little way west of town where you can rent sedans/4WD from $100/120 per day.

AROUND LABASA

The area around Labasa is a great place to explore by 4WD. There are a few points of interest; however, it's definitely the adventure of finding them rather than the sights themselves that make it worthwhile. For all of these sights, you'll need to turn left onto Wainikoro Rd, just past the sugar mill and across from a secondary school. This is the main road out of town to the east.

Cobra Rock

The area's most intriguing attraction is the sacred Cobra Rock inside the **Naag Mandir**

Temple. The 3m-high rock looks (a bit) like a huge cobra poised to strike. Draped with colourful flower and tinsel garlands, the rock looms over offerings of fruit, fire and *lolo* (coconut cream) from people who believe the rock can cure sickness and infertility. Devotees swear that the rock grows and that the roof has had to be raised several times over the years. Remove your shoes outside the beautifully tiled temple; then circle the rock clockwise three or five times, ringing the bell after each round. Several buses pass the temple, including those to Natewa Bay. A taxi costs about $10. If you're driving, the temple is 10km from the turning for Wainikoro Rd; you'll pass two smaller temples before you reach Naag Mandir. The temple is packed on Sunday mornings. On the hill above the temple, there is another growing stone, which might be worth seeking out if you were planning to visit every growing stone in the world.

If you're going to Cobra Rock, you may wish to take a short detour to the **Mariamman Temple** in Vunivau (just east of Labasa), where the Ram Leela festival is held around October.

Korovatu Beach

Down through dense coconut trees and past the lounging cows lies **Korovatu Beach** (admission per car $5). Again, you might want to visit if you were trying to go to every beach in the world. Bring your own water and snacks.

Floating Island

This is definitely to be done for the journey rather than the final spectacle. You'll pass rugged scenery and maybe get lost in a cane field. The Floating Island, 50km northeast of Labasa, is land with trees that bobs on a pond and gets blown around with the wind. As the pond is only about three times the size of the island, it's easy for the island to reach an edge and disguise itself as attached land. If this happens you might not realise you have seen the Floating Island at all.

To reach the island by 4WD, follow the directions to Cobra Rock and continue following Wainikoro Rd. At the roundabout, this road turns left; follow it through the village. Continue on for 19km and take the turning on the right for Nakelikoso. After 6km, take a left onto Lagalaga Rd. Ask permission at the first house on your right and then follow the track up behind it. When you reach a creek, park and trek right through the long grass to the pond. By this point, you will hopefully have been accosted by the children from the village who will gladly show you the way. Be sure to head out on a full tank of fuel and some food and water. The dirt road can be rather treacherous; probably not the best trip to make in the rain.

There is a bus to Lagalaga that departs Labasa at 1.30pm for the 2½ hour journey. This bus returns, often almost immediately, leaving you little hope of finding the island and much hope of getting stranded.

Nukubati

This privately owned island is just off the northern coast of Vanua Levu, about 40km west of Labasa. Actually two small islands linked by mangroves, it's about a 30-minute walk around at low tide. Once occupied by Fijian villagers, in the 19th century a local chief gave the island to a German gunsmith who settled here with his Fijian wife.

Nukubati Island Resort (☎ 881 3901; www.nukubati.com; bure beachfront/honeymoon $1310/1600) is a secluded place far from the usual tourist spots. *Bure* face a white-sand beach. The steep prices include gourmet meals, all drinks (including alcohol) and activities, except game fishing, diving and massages. Included activities are tennis, sailing, windsurfing and fishing. The 4WD/speedboat return transfer from Labasa airport is $290 per couple. There is a maximum of 14 guests and only adult couples are accepted. You can book the whole island for a mere $8100 per night. A minimum five-night stay is required. Two-tank dives are $175, plus equipment hire (one-off $60 fee). Guided surf trips to the Great Sea Reef are possible from November to March.

NABOUWALU & AROUND

Nabouwalu is a small settlement on the island's southwestern point. Early in the 19th century, European traders flocked to nearby **Bua Bay** to exploit *yasi dina* (sandalwood), which grew in the hills. Today, the ferry landing is about the only draw for travellers.

Nabouwalu has administrative offices, a post office, a small market and a store. Offshore to the northwest, the island of **Yadua Tabu** is home to the last sizeable population of the rare and spectacular crested iguana.

It became Fiji's first wildlife reserve in 1980. It might be possible to visit the iguanas with a local guide, weather permitting, but there are no organised tours. Rumour has it that the last time a film crew came over to make a documentary, they were unable to land on Yadua Tabu, and had to make do with a 'stunt iguana' filmed at the Fijian Resort instead.

Sleeping

Boats that arrive here are met by buses heading for Labasa but if you want to stay in Nabouwalu, there is a basic, clean government **guesthouse** (☎ 883 6027; r per person $20). It's an old timber cottage on a steep hill and the view is beautiful. It's often booked out with government workers so be sure to call ahead to the district officer. There is a kitchen but no food and it's a good idea to bring along some of your own supplies as there are no eateries nearby.

Getting There & Away

For ferries, see p261. Nabouwalu can only be reached by bus from Labasa, not from Savusavu. The ferry bus is much quicker than the local bus.

The road from Nabouwalu around the southern coast to Savusavu (127km) is barely passable by 4WD or carrier.

WAINUNU BAY

This is the forgotten Fiji, a place few travellers have ever visited. It's difficult to get here, and the land has never been commercially logged, so the beautiful rainforest, replete with waterfalls, is largely untouched. Wainunu River, the third-largest river in Fiji, flows into Wainunu Bay, the spot where pioneer David Whippy led the whites of Levuka when they were briefly expelled by Cakobau in the mid-19th century. Tea was grown here until the 1920s, on Wainunu Tea Estate, owned by Captain David Robbie, a prominent citizen of Levuka. Robbie kept 200 acres of tea gardens within 1000 acres of volcanic tablelands, managed by George Chapman Barratt, who had experience growing tea in India. This was the longest surviving tea estate in Fiji, worked, predictably, by Indians. After it closed, there were attempts to grow cocoa, vanilla and other crops in the area, but all eventually failed. Today, the factories and plantations lie in ruins, and the locals are mostly Fijian subsistence farmers who make money selling timber and *kava*.

Sleeping

Tiny **Blue Parrot Adventure Lodge** (blueparrot bures@yahoo.com; s/d/tr $145/190/235) It's the first new business to open in Wainunu for a very long time. It is owned and run by Joe Whippy, a third-generation member of the Whippy families. The property is actually an island at the point where two rivers meet to form a creek. Joe and his wife Robin have built two traditional thatched *bure* with bamboo walls, bathrooms, cold-water showers and flush toilets. Each *bure* has its own jetty onto the river. There are also four beds in the dorm-style loft in the main building. Rates include all meals and nonmotorised tours; book via email but be aware that emails are only answered about every two weeks. You could rent the whole island – two *bure* and the Whippy house – for $3500 a week, including a cleaner and a boat, but you would have to bring your own supplies and cook your own food. Local shops are poorly stocked except for the ubiquitous tinned fish. The reefs, though, are teeming with live fish, and Joe will take your out game fishing for $60 an hour. Credit cards are not accepted. Children are accepted only if you book the entire resort.

Getting There & Away

Wainunu is three hours by very, very bad road from Savusavu, and about an hour from Nabouwalu. (It's actually closer to Viti Levu than Savusavu.) You can hire a carrier for $100 in Savusavu, and arrange to have them pick you up again at the end of your stay. A carrier from Nabouwalu is $15. The very slow local bus from Savusavu ($8) stops 10km short of Wainunu, but you could arrange transport from there, or perhaps have Joe pick you up. Explore your options with the Whippys by email before you set out or contact **Trip n Tour** (☎ 885 3154; Copra Shed Marina, Savusavu; tripntour@connect.com.fj), which offers two-/three-/four-night tours to the lodge.

Taveuni

The island of Taveuni is a vast and luscious garden: a tropical flower garden on land and a coral garden beneath the sea. It is easy to get to, relatively small, and far from crowded. Bring an umbrella, though: it rains here.

Taveuni's volcanic past is evident in its many black-sand beaches, but the beaches at Lavena and Matei have some white sand and are good for swimming and snorkelling. The nearby islands of Laucala, Matagi and Qamea have stunning beaches. The eastern side of the island has dramatic waterfalls while the southern coast boasts caves and blowholes.

Indigenous Fijians make up most of Taveuni's population, with a few hundred Indo-Fijians and a growing number of expats, mainly North Americans. Taveuni is the chiefly island for the northern part of Fiji. The Tui Cakau (King of the Reef) is based in Somosomo. It is the third-highest chiefly title in Fiji, and more than one branch of a fractured family would like to claim it as their own. Accordingly, there's a low rumble of traditional politics bubbling below the surface. The current Tui Cakau supported Speight's 2000 coup.

There are no big towns on the island. Taveuni's main income is from agriculture, mostly copra and to a lesser extent *dalo* (taro plant) and *kava* crops. Many of Taveuni's hotels, restaurants and dive shops are in Matei, within walking distance of the airport. The land here was once a single copra plantation, since subdivided and sold.

HIGHLIGHTS

- Dive the Somosomo Strait around the incredible **Rainbow Reef** (p212)
- Snorkel gorgeous **Vuna Reef** (p212)
- Celebrate Mass joyously at **Wairiki Catholic Mission** (p215)
- Trek the lush **Lavena Coastal Walk** (p222) and wash off the sweat in a deep waterfall pool
- Take a guided day hike along the **Vidawa Rainforest Trail** (p221)
- Raft, snorkel and learn about reef conservation at **Waitabu Marine Park** (p222)
- Manage not to kill yourself at **Waitavala Water Slide** (p215)
- Scale the 1195m **Des Voeux Peak** (p215) at dawn, 'twitching' for orange-crested doves

- Wairiki Catholic Mission
- ★ Rainbow Reef
- ★ Waitavala Water Slide
- ★ Waitabu Marine Park
- Vidawa Rainforest Trail
- ★ Des Voeux Peak
- Lavena Coastal Walk
- ★ Vuna Reef

- POPULATION: 12,000
- AREA: 442 SQ KM

Geography & Geology

Much of Taveuni's coastline is rugged, set against some of Fiji's highest peaks. Des Voeux Peak reaches up 1195m and the cloud-shrouded Mt Uluigalau, at 1241m, is the country's second-highest summit. The volcanic soil and abundant rainfall make Taveuni one of Fiji's most fertile areas. While the northeast of Taveuni is fringed by reefs, the southwest has deep water close to shore.

Orientation

Most visitors arrive by air at Matei airport in the north of the island. Heading southeast you eventually reach Bouma National Heritage Park, where the road stops at Lavena.

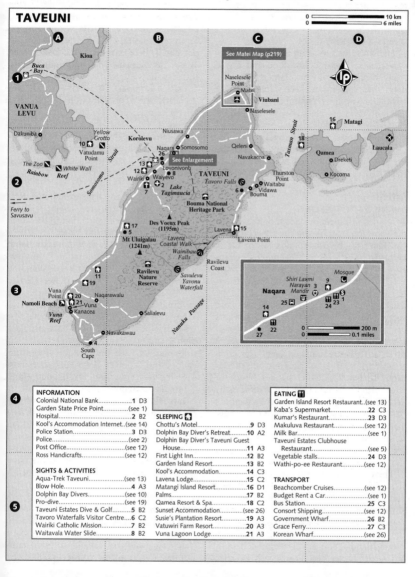

TAVEUNI

INFORMATION
Colonial National Bank..................1 D3
Garden State Price Point.............(see 1)
Hospital.......................................2 B2
Kool's Accommodation Internet..(see 14)
Police Station...............................3 D3
Police.......................................(see 2)
Post Office..............................(see 12)
Ross Handicrafts.....................(see 12)

SIGHTS & ACTIVITIES
Aqua-Trek Taveuni..................(see 13)
Blow Hole....................................4 A3
Dolphin Bay Divers..................(see 10)
Pro-dive..................................(see 19)
Taveuni Estates Dive & Golf.........5 B2
Tavoro Waterfalls Visitor Centre...6 C2
Wairiki Catholic Mission...............7 B2
Waitavala Water Slide.................8 B2

SLEEPING
Chottu's Motel.............................9 D3
Dolphin Bay Diver's Retreat........10 A2
Dolphin Bay Diver's Taveuni Guest
   House...................................11 A3
First Light Inn.............................12 B2
Garden Island Resort..................13 B2
Kool's Accommodation................14 C3
Lavena Lodge..............................15 C2
Matangi Island Resort..................16 D1
Palms.......................................17 B2
Qamea Resort & Spa...................18 C2
Sunset Accommodation............(see 26)
Susie's Plantation Resort.............19 A3
Vatuwiri Farm Resort...................20 A3
Vuna Lagoon Lodge....................21 A3

EATING
Garden Island Resort Restaurant..(see 13)
Kaba's Supermarket....................22 C3
Kumar's Restaurant....................23 D3
Makuluva Restaurant................(see 12)
Milk Bar....................................(see 1)
Taveuni Estates Clubhouse
   Restaurant...........................(see 5)
Vegetable stalls...........................24 D3
Wathi-po-ee Restaurant...........(see 12)

TRANSPORT
Beachcomber Cruises.................(see 12)
Budget Rent a Car.....................(see 12)
Bus Station.................................25 C3
Consort Shipping......................(see 12)
Government Wharf......................26 B2
Grace Ferry.................................27 C3
Korean Wharf...........................(see 26)

Heading southwest from Matei you reach the towns of Somosomo, Naqara and Waiyevo where most of the budget accommodation, shops, services and not much of the beauty of the island are located. If you arrive by boat it will be at one of the three wharfs in the Waiyevo area. In the south of the island you'll find a few low-key resorts around Vuna. The road doesn't go much further than this making the southeast coast almost inaccessible.

Dangers & Annoyances

Theft is a problem – although locals say you're more likely to lose food and booze than laptops and cameras. Always lock your door when sleeping and keep valuables out of sight. Don't wander around alone at night.

All of Taveuni's electricity is supplied by generator. Upmarket resorts have 24-hour power; however, some budget and midrange places only run their generators in the evening, usually between 6pm and 10pm. Keep a torch handy.

Activities

DIVING & SNORKELLING

Taveuni is world-renowned among divers. In the Somosomo Strait, you can expect to see a gazillion fish, the occasional shark or turtle, fantastic coral and, in November, perhaps even pilot whales. The patch reefs are fairly shallow (10m to 22m) while the strait's fringing reef has wall diving (15m to 30m), larger fish, and is more exposed to weather and surge. Novice divers may find the currents challenging, however, a descent line is generally used; the area is not just for experienced divers as there are many different sites.

Colourful soft-coral sites include the famous **Rainbow Reef**, which fringes the southwest corner of Vanua Levu but is most easily accessed from Taveuni. There are a plethora of sites on this reef. See p61 for more details. The island is especially hot and humid in January and February when the water clarity is reduced due to plankton blooms and northerly winds from the equator.

There is plenty for snorkellers, too. Vuna Reef off southern Taveuni boasts dazzling coral and improbable creatures. The three small islands immediately offshore from Naselesele Point in Matei have good snorkelling (the third is known as the local 'Honeymoon Island'). You can also snorkel happily at Prince Charles Beach or Beverly Beach.

There are a number of dive operations on Taveuni, and the upmarket resorts on the offshore islands of Matagi and Qamea have diving for their guests.

Aqua-Trek Taveuni (☎ 888 0286; www.aquatrek .com), based at Garden Island Resort (p216), is a well-equipped dive shop with good boats, Nitrox facilities and a photo centre. It organises dives at Rainbow Reef. Two dives cost $165 and six dives (three days) cost $470 (tanks and belts supplied only). Equipment rental costs $35 per day or $25 per day if three days or more. PADI Open Water Courses cost $660 and one-day dive introductions are $148.

Dolphin Bay Divers (☎ 888 0531, 992 0531; www .dolphinbaydivers.com) operates from Dolphin Bay Divers Retreat (see p217) on Vanua Levu, but is more easily accessed from Taveuni. It offers a two-tank/night/shore dive for $130/80/45. It also has multiday dive packages and offers a number of courses including the PADI Open Water Course ($500), rescue ($450) and dive master ($1100). As well as Vuna Reef, it also does dive trips to Rainbow Reef and other sites in the area. Divers taking a course get free accommodation in the dorm and airport transfers from Matei.

Pro-dive (☎ 888 0125; www.susiesplantationresort .com) is based at Susie's Plantation Resort (see p217). Two-tank dives cost $170, including gear, and the PADI Open Water Course is $495. Rainbow Reef dives are $195 and multiple dive packages are available.

Swiss Fiji Divers (☎ 888 0586; www.swissfijidivers .com), near Beverly Beach in Matei, provides high-quality gear including computer consoles, masks with underwater communication, and scooters. Two-tank dives cost $185 including gear, and PADI Open Water Courses cost $600.

Taveuni Estates Dive (☎ 888 0063; www.taveuni dive.com), located on Taveuni's southwest coast, has an enthusiastic manager and experienced staff who welcome nonguests. A two-tank dive/PADI Open Water Course costs $210/660. It also offers snorkelling trips for $80 to $110 per person, depending on group size.

Vunibokoi Divers (Dive Taveuni; ☎ 888 0560; www .tovutovu.com), Tovu Tovu Resort's dive operation in Matei, is ecstatically recommended by customers. Popular divemaster Tyrone Valentine (scion of an old colonial family) has logged an incredible 14,000 dives, mostly around Taveuni. Dives are in the Rainbow Reef area and a two-tank dive/PADI certification costs $195/650.

HIKING

Taveuni's Lavena Coastal Walk and Tavoro Waterfalls in Bouma National Heritage Park are must-dos. Avid walkers could also consider the guided Vidawa Forest Walk, also in Bouma, or Des Voeux Peak. If you're super keen and don't mind mud, you can also seek out a guide in Somosomo and trek up to Lake Tagimaucia.

WILDLIFE WATCHING

Taveuni is one of Fiji's best areas for bird-watching. Over 100 species of bird can be found here. Try Des Voeux Peak at dawn for a chance to see the rare orange dove (the male is bright orange with a green head, while the female is mostly green) and the silktail. Avid bird-watchers also recommend the Vidawa Rainforest Hike. Another good site is near Qeleni village southeast of Matei. On the Matei side of the village, follow a 4WD track for 3.5km up the mountain. Here you might see parrots and fantails, particularly in August and September when they're nesting. The deep-red feathers of the kula parrot were once an important trade item with the Tongans. The forested Lavena coast is also a good spot to see orange or flame doves, Fiji goshawk, wattled honeyeater, and grey and white heron. Vatuwiri Farm Resort at Vuna Point in the south is a great place for viewing fruit bats. Down south you can also see and hear magpies, introduced to control insects in the copra plantations.

OTHER ACTIVITIES

Raikivi Game Fishing (☎ 888 0371) in Matei will take you near Qamea in search of sailfish, wahu, maimai and skipjack tuna. Half-/full-day trips cost $570/900 for up to six people.

Tango Fishing Adventure (☎ 888 0680; makaira@connect.com.fj) takes you fishing for big game aboard the *Tango* with Captain John Llanes Jr who has over 30 years experience. The boat has GPS, VHF and seven rod holders. A half/full day costs $520/900.

Taveuni Estates (☎ 888 0441), see p218, welcomes visitors to its nine-hole golf course ($40 green fee or there's a $50 lunch-and-golf deal), four tennis courts ($15) and swimming pool.

Getting There & Away
AIR

The flights between Taveuni and Viti Levu are stunning, giving you a chance to peer down at the gorgeous reefs. At Matei airport, both **Sun Air** (☎ 888 0461) and **Air Fiji** (☎ 888 0062) have at least two flights daily to/from Nadi (1½ hours) and also Savusavu, but be aware that both routes are often heavily booked. Air Fiji flies twice daily to Suva as well (45 minutes). See p259 for more details.

BOAT

The Government Wharf for large vessels, including *Spirit of Free Enterprise (SOFE)* and *Adi Savusavu,* is about 1km from Wai-yevo, towards Naqara. Smaller boats depart from the Korean Wharf, a bit further north. **Consort Shipping** (☎ 888 0339; First Light Inn, Wai-yevo), **Beachcomber Cruises** (☎ 888 0036; Wathi-po-ee Restaurant, Naqara) and **Suilven Shipping** (☎ 888 0261) have regular Suva–Savusavu–Taveuni ferries with competitive rates. Suilven is the most comfortable and reliable service. **Grace Ferry** (☎ 888 0320; Naqara) runs a bus/boat trip to Savusavu and Labasa ($20). The boat departs from the Korean Wharf at 8.45am. The booking office is the green building in Naqara – ask locals for directions.

For more information on these ferries see p261.

Getting Around

Taveuni's main road hugs its scenic coast from Lavena in the east, up north and around to Navakawau in the south. At the time of writing it was sealed from Matei to Wairiki. There are also a couple of inland 4WD tracks. Getting around Taveuni involves a bit of planning, the main disadvantage being the length of time between buses. To get around cheaply and quickly you need to combine buses with walking, or take taxis. You can rent 4WDs in Naqara; however, it's far cheaper to hire a taxi for the day.

TO/FROM THE AIRPORT

From Matei airport expect to pay about $18 to Waiyevo, and $50 to Vuna (about one hour) in a taxi. Most upmarket resorts provide transfers for guests.

BUS

Local buses are the best way to meet locals. **Pacific Transport** (☎ 888 0278) has a depot in Naqara, opposite the Taveuni Central Indian School. From Monday to Saturday, buses run from Wairiki to Bouma at 8.30am, 11.30am and 4.20pm. The last bus continues to Lavena where the first bus of each morning starts out at 5.45am. On Tuesday and Thursday, all buses go as far as Lavena. On Sunday there is one bus at 3.30pm from Wairiki to Lavena and one from Lavena to Wairiki at 6.45am.

Going south from Naqara, buses run to Navakawau at 9am, 11.30am and 4.45pm Monday to Saturday, returning at 5.30am and 8.15am. On Sunday a bus departs Navakawau at 6.45am and returns from Naqara at 4pm. From Matei, buses run to Wairiki at 11.30am Monday to Saturday and also at 7am and 3pm, Monday to Friday, during school term times.

The bus schedule is very lax; buses may show up early or an hour late. Be sure to double check the time of the return bus when you board, just to make sure there is one.

CAR
In Naqara, **Budget Rent a Car** (☎ 888 0291; gardenstate@connect.com.fj; Garden State Price Point; ☻ 8am-5pm Mon-Fri, till 1pm Sat & Sun) has 4WDs for $125 to $185 per day.

TAXI
It's easy to find taxis in the Matei and Waiyevo areas. It may be wise to book ahead on Sunday. Hiring a taxi for a negotiated fee and touring most of the island's highlights in a day will work out cheaper than hiring a car. Try **Nand Lal** (☎ 888 0705). You may be able to get one for under $120 for the day; ask a local to negotiate it for you. For destinations such as Lavena you can go one way by bus and have a taxi pick you up at the end at a designated time (but arrange this before you go).

WAIYEVO, SOMOSOMO & AROUND
This part of the island is important but unattractive. Somosomo is the largest village on Taveuni and headquarters for its chiefly leadership. The **Great Council of Chiefs' meeting hall** *(bure bose)* was built here in 1986 for the gathering of chiefs from all over Fiji. Somosomo runs directly into Naqara, the village with the largest shopping area – but don't expect a mall. You'll find a couple of gloomy supermarkets, the island's one bank (no

ATM), transport links and two budget hotels. A short taxi ride or a long, dusty walk away is Waiyevo, the administrative capital of the island, with the hospital, the police station, a budget hotel and resort, and more ferry links. About 2km further south of Waiyevo is Wairiki village, which has a general store and a beautiful old hilltop Catholic Mission.

Information
EMERGENCY
Hospital (☎ 888 0444; Waiyevo)
Police (☎ 888 0222; Waiyevo) The main police station is at the government compound behind the Garden Island Resort in Waiyevo. There is also a police station in Naqara.

INTERNET ACCESS
Garden State Price Point (☎ 888 0291; Naqara; per min $0.50; ☻ 8am-5pm Mon-Fri, till 1pm Sat & Sun) One pricey computer.
Kool's Accommodation (☎ 888 0395; Naqara; per min $0.20; ☻ 4-9pm)
Ross Handicrafts (☎ 330 9872; Waiyevo; per min $0.22; ☻ 8am-5pm Mon-Sat) Next to the post office.

MONEY
Colonial National Bank (☎ 888 0433; Naqara; ☻ 9.30am-4pm Mon, 9am-4pm Tue-Fri) The only bank on the island will exchange currency and travellers cheques but won't do cash advances and doesn't have an ATM.
Kaba's Supermarket (☎ 888 0088; Naqara; ☻ 8am-5pm Mon-Fri, till 1pm Sat & Sun) Offers cash advances on credit cards, up to $500, although it charges 5% commission.

POST
Post office (☎ 888 0027; Waiyevo; ☻ 8am-1pm & 2pm-4pm Mon-Fri) Among the shops beneath the First Light Inn.

TELEPHONE
You'll find a cardphone at the post office as well as outside the supermarkets in Naqara.

Sights
INTERNATIONAL DATELINE
For workability, the International Dateline doglegs around Fiji, but the 180-degree meridian actually cuts straight through Taveuni, about a 10-minute walk south of Waiyevo. Along the side of the road to Wairiki, a small, red survey beacon marks the spot. If you take the road uphill from Waiyevo (towards the hospital) and cross the field on the right, you'll find a big sign with a bit of

local information and a map. Dateline nerds might enjoy the 'half in one day, half in the other' photo.

WAIRIKI CATHOLIC MISSION

This grand mission looks out over the Somosomo Strait. Its beautiful interior has an impressive beam ceiling and, reputedly, French stained glass. In the presbytery, there's a painting of a famous battle in which a Catholic missionary helped Taveuni's warriors develop a strategy to defeat their Tongan attackers. It's worth attending Mass at 7am, 9am or 11am on Sunday; the congregation sits on the floor and belts out tremendous song.

The mission is about 20 minutes' walk south along the coast from Waiyevo. You can't miss it on the hill to the left. A dirt track behind leads up to a huge white cross. The views from here are superb.

WAITAVALA WATER SLIDE

This natural water slide is only for the brave. A bruise or two is unavoidable as you fly down these rock chutes. If there's been rain it can be dangerous; wait until you see locals going down it before you make an attempt.

It's about a 25-minute walk from Waiyevo. With the Garden Island Resort on your left, head north and take the first right at the bus stop. Take another right at the branch in the road, pass a shed and then go left down a hill. You'll see a 'waterfall' sign. The river is on the Waitavala estate, which is private land, so if you pass anyone on your way there, ask if you can visit.

LAKE TAGIMAUCIA

Lake Tagimaucia is in an old volcanic crater, in the mountains above Somosomo. At 823m above sea level, masses of vegetation float on the lake, and the national flower, the rare *tagimaucia* (an epiphytic plant) grows on the lake's shores. This red-and-white flower blooms only at high altitude from late September to late December.

It is a difficult trek around the lake as it is overgrown and often very muddy; you'll need a stick to find firm ground. The track starts from Somosomo where you need to present the Chief with a *sevusevu* and ask permission. Take lunch and allow eight hours for the round trip.

THE LEGEND OF THE TAGIMAUCIA

There once lived a young girl with a wild spirit and a tendency to be disobedient. On one fateful day, her mother lost her patience with the girl and beat her with a bundle of coconut leaves, saying she never wanted to see her face again. The distraught girl ran away until she was deep in the forest. She came upon a large vine-covered *ivi* (Polynesian chestnut) tree and decided to climb it. The higher she climbed, the more entangled she became in the vine and, unable to break free, she began to weep. As giant tears rolled down her face they turned to blood and, where they fell onto the vine, they became beautiful white-and-red *tagimaucia* flowers. Calmed by the sight of the flowers, the girl managed to escape the forest and, upon returning home, was relieved to find an equally calm mother.

DES VOEUX PEAK

At 1195m, Des Voeux Peak is the island's second-highest mountain. On a clear day, the views from its peak are fantastic. It's possible to see Lake Tagimaucia and perhaps even the Lau island group. Allow three to four hours to walk the 6km up, and at least two to return. It's a steep, arduous climb in the heat, so it's best to start out early. Try to make it up there by dawn if you are a keen bird-watcher. To get here, take the inland track just before you reach Wairiki Catholic Mission (coming from Waiyevo). Alternatively, arrange for a lift up and then walk back at your leisure. On weekdays it's sometimes possible to hitch a ride with Telecom or Public Works Department (PWD) workers who go up to service their equipment. (The First Light Inn can sometimes arrange this for guests.) Taxis can be fairly pricey.

Sleeping

BUDGET

Garden Island Resort (☎ 888 0286; www.aquatrek .com; dm $38; ❷) The only top-end hotel in the area (see p216) also has two four-bed dorms, which are good value

First Light Inn (☎ 888 0339; firstlight@connect.com .fj; Waiyevo; r with fan/air-con & bathroom $55/60; ❷) This inn is a clean, friendly hotel with a kitchen for guests. Satellite TV is provided by the

TAVEUNI

enormous satellite dish in the backyard. The reception doubles as the office for Consort Shipping; if you turn up late in the evening or on Saturday (and perhaps Sunday) afternoon, there won't be anyone there.

Kool's Accommodation (☎ 888 0395; kools@connect.com.fj; Naqara; dm/s/d $15/25/35; 🖳) Cheerful Kool's was renovating at the time of writing, and adding a restaurant (breakfast/lunch/dinner $8/10/12) specialising in Indo-Fijian food. Private, fan-cooled hotel rooms have bathrooms. Electricity comes on from 4pm to 9pm, when you can watch satellite TV or borrow videos from Kool's library. Laundry is $5.

Chottu's Motel (☎ 888 0233; Naqara; s/d/tr budget $25/35/55, deluxe $45/55/60) Chottu's has big, deluxe rooms with kitchens, phones, satellite TV and hot showers. The budget rooms share a cold-water bathroom and a kitchen.

Sunset Accommodation (☎ 888 0229; s/d/tr $15/25/40) This place is basic but very cheerful. Two cottages each have a double and single room and a kitchen, and mosquito nets and fans. There's electricity in the evenings. Ask to see both cottages – one has an outside bathroom. The building is very near the Korean Wharf at Lovonivonu. Look for a sign for Bucalevu School at the bend in the road between Naqara and Waiyevo.

TOP END

Garden Island Resort (☎ 888 0286; www.aquatrek.com; dm $38, s/d/tr $166/210/250; 🍴 🖳 🏊) Some guests rave about this apparently unremarkable place. It's the only resort in the area, and it's popular with dive groups. The rooms are clean and comfortable with air-con and sea views. The pool and restaurant-bar area looks out to the Somosomo Strait and Vanua Levu beyond. There is an optional meal plan for $80 per person.

The resort has a children's pool and under-16s stay for free. There is no beach, but you can swim here at high tide. (Watch the current, though, and don't swim near Korean Wharf as sharks are sometimes attracted here by fish-cleaning.) Aqua-Trek (see p212) runs snorkelling trips to the nearby Korolevu Island and the Rainbow Reef. Transfers to and from the airport are $40 per person.

Eating & Drinking

Garden Island Resort Restaurant (☎ 888 0286; Waiyevo; lunch/dinner $17.50/35; 🕙 breakfast, lunch & dinner) It's a pleasant place. The tables have a view of the pool and garden and in the evening there's live local music, which non-guests can attend if they eat there. The bar is well stocked but, unless you're a guest, you'll only be served alcohol if you've ordered food.

Wathi-po-ee Restaurant (☎ 888 0382; Waiyevo; meals $5; 🕙 breakfast, lunch & dinner Mon-Fri, breakfast & lunch Sat & Sun) A basic place with omelettes and sausages for breakfast, and oily Sino-Fijian food for lunch and dinner, this is the de facto restaurant-bar for the First Light Inn. Around the back are a few tables under a corrugated iron roof bearing the restaurant's old name, The Cannibal Café, and its notorious slogan, 'We'd love to have you for dinner'. Not a bad spot for a beer.

Makuluva Restaurant (☎ 994 5394; Waiyevo; breakfast/lunch $3/4; 🕙 8am-4pm Mon-Fri & Sun, dinner by arrangement) This place looks like a fresh-fish shed – and, in fact, it is, but there's a restaurant around the back. Order dinner in advance, before 4pm (you can either drop off your order at the fish shed or call the owner on her mobile). Makuluva is run by Seventh Day Adventists, and may be one of the few places open on Sunday.

Kumar's Restaurant (☎ 888 1005; Naqara; breakfast $2, meals $4; 🕙 breakfast, lunch & dinner before 7pm Mon-Sat) Kumar's is a friendly Indian place with good curries served in a rustic, shedlike atmosphere.

Milk Bar (Naqara; snacks $3; 🕙 7am-5pm Mon-Sat) Disguised behind the Hot Bread Kitchen sign, it has a few tables and serves fresh chop suey, pizza and sandwiches.

For self-caterers, **Kaba's Supermarket** (☎ 888 0088; Naqara; 🕙 8am-5pm Mon-Fri, till 1pm Sat & Sun) is fully stocked. There is also MH Supermarket in Somosomo (which sells alcohol, but not on Saturday afternoon or Sunday) or the Wairiki supermarket which is open on Sundays. It can be difficult to buy fresh fruit and vegetables as the villagers usually grow their own; try the stalls along the main street of Naqara. There are also a couple of bakeries in Naqara.

SOUTHERN TAVEUNI

The main villages on southern Taveuni are Naqarawalu, in the hills, and, on the southern coast near Vuna Reef, Kanacea, Vuna and Navakawau.

Check out the **blow hole** on the dramatic, windswept South Cape. As the water jumps

---

DRUA

For assisting him in a war against the people of Rewa, Ratu Cakobau presented King George of Tonga with a *drua*, a traditional catamaran. Named *Ra Marama*, the *drua* was built in Taveuni in the 1850s. It took seven years to complete, was over 30m long and could carry 150 people. Hewn from giant trees, it could outsail the European ships of the era.

Building *drua* could involve entire communities; some boats could carry up to 300 people. Their construction often involved ceremonial human sacrifices, and the completed vessel was launched over the bodies of slaves, which were used as rollers under the hulls. The last large *drua* was built in 1913 and is on display at the Fiji Museum in Suva. If you visit the island of Kioa, north of Taveuni, you can still see fishermen out in small, one-person *drua*.

---

up through the volcanic rock, it creates rainbows in the air. It's best at low tide when it can reach up to the top of the palm trees on shore. At high tide it can be barely visible. The water here is very changeable and, if conditions turn bad, the waves can quite suddenly pound the shore; be wary of climbing down on the rocks.

Sleeping

BUDGET

Dolphin Bay Divers Retreat (☎ 992 0531, 888 0531; www.dolphinbaydivers.com; Vanaira Bay, Vanua Levu; dm/house tent/bure per person $20/25/45; 🖳) This retreat is an excellent, cheap, friendly place on Vanua Levu, although it's most easily accessible from Taveuni. The *bure* are okay, although there is no hot water and the showers are only curtained off. The house tents – all of which face the sunrise – are fantastic, and include a bright, cheerful, three-bed tent dorm. The mattresses are comfortable but it is bit of a walk from the tents to the shared bathrooms. A resort tent, with tent bathroom, should now be in operation. Most of the guests here are divers, but snorkellers will also enjoy the fantastic undersea scenery. There is no spearfishing. Startlingly, Dolphin Bay has a lovingly tended wine list, with mainly Australian wines priced around $25. Nights here are boozy and companionable, like the owners.

Transfers from Taveuni cost $50 return. Meal plans are $35 per day with snacks. Important: Dolphin Bay connects through Vodaphone and there is no Vodaphone connection and no mobile-phone reception at Buca Bay on Vanua Levu. Do not turn up at Buca Bay and expect to phone Dolphin Bay Divers. You will be stranded, although the locals will put you up for the night.

Dolphin Bay Divers Taveuni Guest House (☎ 888 0531; www.dolphinbaydivers.com; r $35, per person $20) This is a big, spotless house with two double bedrooms with shared bathroom, generally used by guests of Dolphin Bay Divers before or after their stay at the resort. There is a lounge with views to Vanua Levu, and the owners reputedly cook delicious Indian food. Lighting is electric by day, lanterns by night.

Susie's Plantation Resort (☎ 888 0125; www.susiesplantationresort.com; s/d/tr bure $70/120/150; lodge divers/nondivers $20/25; 🖳) Susie's is a former plantation set in a peaceful location with gorgeous sea and sunset views. The double room ($50) with attached hot-water bathroom in the main house is spacious and comfortable and the six garden *bure* (one large enough for four people) are basic but clean. There's *kava* drinking in the evenings and on Friday nights there's a *meke* (traditional dance). An all-meal plan is available for $39. There's excellent snorkelling and diving through Pro-Dive (see p212). Major credit cards are accepted.

Vuna Lagoon Lodge (☎/fax 888 0627; dm/s/d $15/30/50) Visit Vuna if you want contact with Fijian village life in a beautiful setting. There are simple, clean rooms with bathroom (one with four beds), two minutes' walk from Vuna village on the edge of Vuna Lagoon. The house has a kitchen, a laundry with washing machine, a sitting area, and electricity from 6pm to 11pm. Self-caterers can cook for themselves with free fruit and vegetables from the garden; however, bring all other supplies. Otherwise, home-cooked meals are available for $15. There is a sandy beach nearby so bring your own snorkelling gear. To find the lodge, turn down the dirt lane towards the coast at Vuna village; it's the last blue house on the left. It's best to call ahead.

Palms (☎/fax 888 1241; adult/child under 12 $65/32.50) The Palms is a tremendously atmospheric, 120-year-old plantation house with five bedrooms, a big kitchen, a grass tennis court and a beautiful view. There are mangos, avocados, pineapples and pears in the garden, a barbecue and *lovo* (pit oven) outside and a cook available on request. The owner prefers a week's notice but it's worth calling anyway. The house is on the left just before you reach Taveuni Estates. The Palms is the one with, um, all the palms.

TOP END
Vatuwiri Farm Resort (☎ 888 0316; vatuwiriresort@connect.com.fj; cottages d incl meals $340; ☺ closed from mid-Oct–early Jan) Unlike any other resort you'll set foot in, this is one of the last working estates in the South Pacific still in the hands of the founding family. Five generations of Tartes have lived on Vatuwiri, Taveuni's biggest cattle farm and largest single producer of copra. A visit here gives you a chance to experience life on a plantation in one of the two small cottages perched on a lawn on the water's edge. Both have gorgeous views with high tide bringing colourful fish to the doorstep. The Tartes are branching out into horse-riding holidays, and there are loads of activities available, such as swimming and snorkelling, or you can just enjoy the peace and quiet.

Eating & Drinking
Taveuni Estates Clubhouse Restaurant (☎ 888 0441; breakfast/lunch/dinner $8/15/20; ☺ breakfast & lunch daily, dinner Fri-Sun & Mon-Thu only if booked) Taveuni Estates is a development of private, expat housing about 8km south of Waiyevo, but the restaurant, bar and sporting facilities are open to the public. The restaurant serves good breakfasts and claims to make the only true cappuccino on the island. The menu is mainly Western and management plan to install a wood-fired (of course) pizza oven.

Local nightlife in the area tends to centre around the *kava* bowl, but the clubhouse bar at Taveuni Estates is a great place to stop off for a drink in the unlikely event you are in the area.

MATEI
Matei is a residential area on Taveuni's northern point. Much of the freehold land has been bought by foreigners searching for a piece of tropical paradise. Within easy vicinity of the airport, there are a number of

places to stay, some of the island's best dining options, dive shops and a couple of OK beaches. There's also snorkelling nearby.

Information
Matei doesn't have much in the way of services. There are cardphones at the airport and outside the Bhula Bhai & Sons Supermarket and Sonal Shopping Centre. The larger supermarkets and top-end resorts accept credit cards, but you may be charged extra. Some resorts will also change travellers cheques.
Police There is a police post at the airport.
Swiss Fiji Divers (☎ 888 0586; per min $0.25; ☺ 9am-5pm) Get online at this dive shop on Beverly Beach.

Sleeping
BUDGET
Beverly Beach Camping (☎ 888 0684; sites per person $10) One of those magical spots where everybody makes friends easily and camping isn't a chore, this small site is set on a white-sand beach, beneath fantastic, huge, poison-fish trees. The camp has very basic facilities including flush toilets, shower and a sheltered area for cooking and dining. The owner sometimes brings around fresh fruit and vegetables in the morning. He can also provide equipment for snorkelling and fishing, and he'll rent you a kayak for $10 per person. Beverly Beach is about 15 minutes' walk west of the airport.

Tovu Tovu Resort (☎ 888 0560; www.tovutovu.com; bure with/without kitchen $95/75, f bure $125) Built on a subdivided copra estate, and owned by the Petersen family who once ran the plantation, the Tovu Tovu takes pride in its history. There's even a family chapel – still in use – on a hill overlooking the *bure*. The accommodation, good for the price, is fairly comfortable with hot-water bathrooms and fans. The restaurant (see p220) offers a rare pocket of nightlife in sedate Taveuni. The excellent Vunibokoi Divers (p212) is based here. The resort is a 20-minute walk southeast of Matei airport, past the Bhula Bhai & Sons Supermarket. Meal plans cost $45 per person

Bibi's Hideaway (☎ 888 0443; sites per person $15, r $50, 2-bedroom cottage $90, s/d/f bure $60/70/90, villa $110) This cheap (even the low prices are negotiable), relaxed and friendly resort was started by its affable Fijian owners on the suggestion of the author of the first Lonely Planet guide to Fiji. The newest *bure* is very good value,

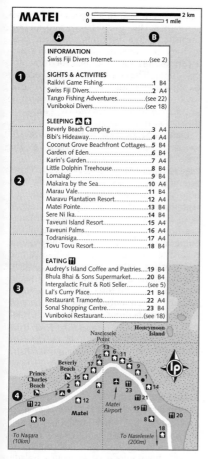

MATEI

INFORMATION
Swiss Fiji Divers Internet...................(see 2)

SIGHTS & ACTIVITIES
Raikivi Game Fishing............................1 B4
Swiss Fiji Divers..................................2 A4
Tango Fishing Adventures................(see 22)
Vunibokoi Divers..............................(see 18)

SLEEPING
Beverly Beach Camping.......................3 A4
Bibi's Hideaway..................................4 A4
Coconut Grove Beachfront Cottages...5 B4
Garden of Eden...................................6 B4
Karin's Garden...................................7 A4
Little Dolphin Treehouse.....................8 B4
Lomalagi..9 B4
Makaira by the Sea...........................10 A4
Marau Vale.......................................11 B4
Maravu Plantation Resort..................12 A4
Matei Pointe.....................................13 B4
Sere Ni Ika.......................................14 B4
Taveuni Island Resort........................15 A4
Taveuni Palms..................................16 A4
Todranisiga......................................17 A4
Tovu Tovu Resort.............................18 B4

EATING
Audrey's Island Coffee and Pastries...19 B4
Bhula Bhai & Sons Supermarket.......20 B4
Intergalactic Fruit & Roti Seller...........(see 5)
Lal's Curry Place...............................21 B4
Restaurant Tramonto.........................22 A4
Sonal Shopping Centre......................23 B4
Vunibokoi Restaurant........................(see 18)

and Bibi has built a free emergency rain shelter *bure* for faint-hearted campers. Rooms vary, but all are clean and well-kept (only the bathrooms in the lodge are a bit rundown). Guests love the vibe at Bibi's – but bring mosquito coils. There's electricity in the evenings but no hot water at any time.

Little Dolphin Treehouse (☎ 888 0130; d cottage $90) This place was built as a sleep-out and looks like a slightly precarious kind of proto-pagoda. The breeze-cooled bedroom is upstairs, with a comfortable queen-size bed and a veranda looking out to the ocean. Downstairs is a kitchen and hot-water bathroom. There are a couple of shelves of books – a big plus in Taveuni, where there is no bookshop.

MIDRANGE

Karin's Garden (☎ 888 0511; www.karinsgardenfiji.com; d/tr/f $195/250/320) A lovingly cared for two-bedroom cottage with a bird's-eye view of the reef, a kitchen, sitting room and veranda, Karin's is only rented out as a single unit. The rooms are big and cosy, the owners affable and relaxed, and there is a two-night minimum stay. There's beach access at the end of the property where, on a clear day, you can see large fish – and, on a lucky day, perhaps even dolphins – swimming past.

Matei Pointe (☎ 888 0422; www.taveuniresort.com; d bure walk-in rate from $120, otherwise per day/week $260/1490, beachhouse per day/week $460/2980; ✉ ▣) There are lovely views, gardens, caretaker family and beach at the closest accommodation to the airport. Just step off the plane and look for the sign. The spacious new Bula House has three bedrooms all with en suite, steps to a pretty pocket of white sand, great views from a big deck, washing machine and phone. The Beach House has 2.5 bedrooms, a kitchen and a huge deck. The three big *bure* with kitchens are better than basic – a bargain at the walk-in rate – but already showing signs of tropical wear.

TOP END

Taveuni Palms (☎ 888 0032; www.taveunipalmsfiji.com; d villa $1580, per extra person/child $375/290; ✉ ▣ ✆) Breathtakingly beautiful, completely tasteful and directly on the beach, Taveuni Palms boasts two villas, each on their own private half-acre with private beach and swimming pool (one has a private spa, the other an infinity pool) and personal chef. The cook will prepare a five-course meal for you every night, but the villas have kitchens anyway. One villa has an attached sleep-out for kids, and the resort provides a free nanny (who may even stay over in the sleep-out). Both villas are fitted with incredible entertainment centres with big TVs, DVD players and stereos. It is hard to imagine a better luxury resort in Fiji. There's a five-night minimum stay.

Taveuni Island Resort (☎ 888 0441; www.taveuniislandresort.com; bure $1500; ▣ ✆) This is a small, opulent resort on a hill over the beach, all polished wood and wicker, with a swimming pool and absolutely gorgeous views. The *bure* are made of rock and wood and are very private. Some have the biggest bathrooms in Taveuni, if not in Fiji; they're the same size as some budget *bure*. The resort is popular with honeymooners. Meals are a gourmet's delight and are included in the price. No children under 15 are allowed.

Maravu Plantation Resort (☎ 888 0555; www .maravu.net; s/d/tr standard bure $310/450/560, deluxe bure $370/570/690, s/d oceanview villa $580/990; ❄ ⬚) You have to cross the road to get to the beach from this tastefully decorated resort, a former copra plantation that nonetheless has ocean views from the lovely, deluxe 'ocean-front' villas. (The cheapest villas have no water views, no air-con, and are a couple of minutes' walk from the beach). Free activities include horse riding, mountain biking and kayaking. Meal plans offer two/three meals per day for $55/85, but the food is disappointing.

Garden of Eden (☎ 888 2344; 2-bedroom house $200; ⬚) This huge, timber home, with shuttered windows, dark-wood furniture, and inexplicable Oriental touches to the décor, is a great choice for families. There's a large empty loft space for kids to hang out in, a great deck, and a private pool that is as big as some resort pools. The ocean view is partly obscured by some authentically Garden of Eden–style lush foliage. There's 10 hours of power a day.

Coconut Grove Beachfront Cottages (☎ 888 0328; www.coconutgrovefiji.com; bure $270-340) It's a pretty little resort with three spacious, comfortable cottages, a good restaurant, and a secluded white-sand beach. The Mango and Banana *bure* have rock showers; all have 24-hour electricity. The Californian owner, Ronna, is friendly, knowledgeable and (praise God!) efficient. She'll paddle you out to a great snorkelling spot in her kayak just for the exercise.

Makaira by the Sea (☎ 888 0680; makaira@connect .com.fj; bure per day/week $230/1400) Makaira by the Sea is really Makaira up a hill, over a road and by the sea, but the sole *bure* has a deck with a panoramic view, and even the bathroom boasts ocean views from the tub. It's clean, compact and very private. Meals are also available (from $15, including vegetarian). Makaira is a $3 taxi ride from Matei airport, but only a three-minute walk from Tramonto's licensed restaurant. The family that runs Makaira also owns Tango Fishing Adventures (p213) across the road.

Todranisiga (www.travelmaxia.com; d $230) This is a well-appointed new fan-cooled *bure*

on the beach side of the road, with a gas stove top outside on the balcony. Inside, it's furnished with a fine timber table and candlesticks for romantic dining. There's also a comfortable king-size bed for romantic postdining. The en suite includes an ocean-facing outdoor hot-water shower. You can walk to the beach through an improbably lush garden. The owner will cook lunch or dinner ($15) on request.

Lomalagi, Sere Ni Ika & Marau Vale (☎ 888 0522; www.fiji-rental-accommodations.com; Lomalagi d per day/ week $270/1700, Sere Ni Ika d per day/week $380/2440, Marau Vale d per day/week $442/2900, extra person $30) Three beautiful, beachfront expat-owned holiday homes are among a number of properties for rent through Matei identity Bob Goddess; rates include a housekeeper. Ideal for families, houses are spacious and fully equipped. Some have beach access, kayaks and outdoor rock showers. Marau Vale is Bob's own fine house with a fantastically equipped kitchen. Lovely Lomalagi has steps that go down to a private cove, and three glass walls give the master bedroom unbelievable views. Sere Ni Ika has three bedrooms, and the whole front of the house can be opened out to the fresh air. These houses all tend to be well stocked with books and videos and, unlike many properties on the island, they have not been allowed to slowly deteriorate.

Eating & Drinking

Coconut Grove Restaurant (☎ 888 0328; meals $15, 3-course dinner $40; ☾ breakfast, lunch & dinner) Coconut Grove has great food made from fresh ingredients. The menu includes vegetarian dishes, home-made pasta, soups, salads, fish and delicious desserts and brownies. Meals are served on the veranda, overlooking the water and nearby islets. Try the best fresh-fruit shakes on Taveuni for $5. Place your dinner order before 4pm; there are usually only three choices, always including one fish and one meat. There is an Island Tunes and buffet night on Saturdays.

Vunibokoi Restaurant (☎ 888 0560; dinner mains $18; ☾ breakfast, lunch & dinner) Tovu Tovu Resort has a friendly, comfortable restaurant with an outdoor deck overlooking the island of Viubani. The food is surprisingly tasty and very good value and, on Friday, there's a popular buffet and music night ($20). It's worth popping in just to have a drink, especially on a Sunday night.

Lal's Curry Place (☎ 888 0705; meals $12; ☖ lunch & dinner Mon-Sat) You know Mrs Lal mixes her own garam masala because there are chillies and cumin drying in the sun on her front lawn. She serves big plates of good, filling curries with roti, rice and dahl. Her husband, Nand, is a knowledgeable, reliable taxi driver.

Restaurant Tramonto (☎ 888 2224; pizza from $18, meals $18; ☖ lunch & dinner) A pretty restaurant on the water, the Tramonto specialises in pizza. There's a menu of other well-prepared dishes, but the ingredients may not always be available. Ring to book ahead, tell them what you'd like, and they'll tell you if you can have it. It's a great spot for a sunset dinner. On Sunday there's a buffet dinner ($25) and on Wednesday there's a barbecue ($20); reservations are required.

Audrey's Island Coffee and Pastries (☎ 888 0039; coffee & cake $7; ☖ 10am-6pm) US-born Audrey serves sweet snacks on the deck of her own home. You can chat to her while you eat naughty pastries and drink even naughtier coffee with a sly shot of Kahlua.

Bhula Bhai & Sons Supermarket (☎ 888 0462; ☖ 7.30am-6pm Mon-Sat, 8am-11am, 3-5pm Sun) It sells a range of groceries (including disposable nappies, not including beer), phonecards, stationery and film, and accepts Visa and MasterCard (10% commission, $90 limit). It has a public phone and a petrol pump (petrol is not served on Sundays). **Sonal Shopping Centre** (☎ 888 0431; ☖ 7.30am-6pm Mon-Sat, 8am-11am Sun), near Matei Point, is another well-stocked supermarket that doesn't sell beer. There are a couple of pool tables outside.

Opposite Coconut Grove there's a guy who will shout, leap around, perhaps even run across the road to get to your attention. He means you no harm. He has come from another planet to sell you fresh fruit or fish roti from his small gate-side stall.

Really good rotis ($1.50) can be bought at Matei airport.

EASTERN TAVEUNI

The local landowners of beautiful eastern Taveuni have rejected logging in favour of ecotourism, under the banner of the Bouma Environmental Tourism Project. Scenes for the 1991 movie, *Return to the Blue Lagoon*, were filmed at Bouma National Heritage Park's Tavoro Waterfalls, and at Lavena Beach.

Bouma National Heritage Park

This **national park** (admission $8) protects over 80% of Taveuni's total area, covering about 150 sq km of rainforest and coastal forest. The park has the three **Tavoro Waterfalls** near the falls' visitor centre, each with natural swimming pools.

The first waterfall is about 24m high and only 10 minutes' walk along a flat cultivated path. There's a change area, picnic tables and barbecue plates. The second waterfall, a further 30 or 40 minutes along, is a bit smaller but also has a good swimming pool. The track is quite steep in places, but has steps, handrails and lookout spots to rest. As you near the second waterfall, deep in the rainforest, you'll have to cross a river; a rope is suspended across the water to balance you as you leap from stone to boulder. Reaching the third fall involves a hike along a less maintained, often muddy path through the forest for another 30 minutes. Smaller than the other two (about 10m high), it has a great swimming pool and rocks for jumping off (check for obstructions first!). If you bring your snorkelling gear, you'll be able to see the hundreds of prawns in the water.

If you are a keen walker, try the **Vidawa Rainforest Trail**, a full-day guided trek led by shamans. Beginning at Vidawa village, it passes through the historic fortified village sites of Navuga and follows trails into the rainforest where you'll see lots of birdlife. The trek then takes you to the Tavoro Waterfalls. You can only do this walk with a guide and need to book in advance. The trip runs Monday to Saturday and can take a maximum of eight people ($60/40 per adult/child). It includes pick-up and drop-off at your hotel, guides, lunch, afternoon tea and park admission fee. Book through **Tavoro Waterfalls Visitor Centre** (☎ 888 0390; ☖ 9am-4pm).

If you are in the mood for a marathon, it is possible to catch the early morning bus to Bouma (45 minutes from Matei, 1½ hours from Naqara), make a flying visit to all three waterfalls, and catch the early afternoon bus at about 1.40pm on to Lavena. In a rush you can also do the coastal walk before dark and either stay overnight at Lavena or be picked up by a pre-arranged taxi. But this is Fiji – you'll be the only one rushing. For transport information see p213.

Waitabu Marine Park

This area is excellent for snorkelling or lounging on the white-sand beach. It is only possible to visit the park with a guide. The village of Waitabu has set up a half-day tour that includes a local guide, guided snorkelling, a *bilibili* (raft) ride, morning and afternoon tea in the village, and transport to and from Matei ($40 per person, or $35 each if a group of four or more). There's also a Backpackers' Tour with guided snorkelling and boat transfers ($20 per person). Bookings are taken on ☎ 888 0451.

Lavena Coastal Walk

The 5km Lavena Coastal Walk is well worth the effort to get to – and the effort it takes to get around. The trail follows the forest edge along a white-sand then volcanic-black beach, passes peaceful villages, and climbs up through the tropical rainforest to a gushing waterfall. There's some good snorkelling and kayaking here and Lavena Point is fine for swimming.

The path is well-maintained and clearly marked. About halfway along the trek, watch for the *vatuni'epa*, bizarre rock pedestals formed by the erosion of the coral base along the coast. Past these, the path seems to disappear at Naba settlement: follow the path onto the beach, then follow the shore past the *bure* and cross the stream to where the path reappears. Further ahead is a suspension bridge and eventually the trail takes you up the valley of Wainibau Creek.

To reach the falls at the end of the trail, you have to walk over rocks and swim a short distance through two deep pools. Two cascades fall at different angles into a deep pool with sheer walls. If you're visiting in the rainy season, the rocks near the falls can be slippery, if not flooded; it can be difficult and dangerous to reach the falls at this time. Ask at Lavena Lodge for current conditions. At any time of year (even if it hasn't been raining), violent flash floods can occur and readers have advised staying to the left of the pool, where you can make an easier getaway.

The park is managed through Lavena Lodge (see right). Entrance to the park is $5, or $15 including a guide. You can also take a guided sea-kayak journey and coastal walk for $40 (including lunch). Usually you can order a meal for when you return to the lodge ($10) but it's a good idea to bring

along some food and definitely bring water. Kayaks can be hired for $40 per day.

Lavena village is about 15 minutes' drive past Bouma, 35 minutes from Matei. However, by local bus it takes about one hour from Matei or just under two from Waiyevo. Expect to pay about $30 for a taxi to/from Matei. See p213 for information on transport services.

Sleeping & Eating

Lavena Lodge (☎ 888 0116; tw per person $15) Run by friendly, informative staff, the lodge has basic, clean rooms, and a shared kitchen and bathroom. Electricity is supplied in the evening. There's a maximum of eight people. Next to a beach, this is a great place to relax after a hard day's hike. Meals are available ($7 breakfast, $10 lunch or dinner). There's a tiny shop in the village, but if you're planning to cook, bring your own supplies.

Tavoro Waterfalls Visitor Centre (☎ 888 0390; sites per person $10; ⏰ 9am-4pm) This place offers simple meals ($5 to $10) in a lovely spot. You can picnic by the river here, too. There's a kitchen, toilets and an open shower for campers, as well as a covered eating area. The generator kicks in at the evening. Staff will let you store your bags here while you hike up to the falls.

OFFSHORE ISLANDS

Qamea, Laucala and Matagi are a group of islands just east of Thurston Point, across the Tasman Strait from northeastern Taveuni. All three of the islands have lovely white-sand beaches. The original inhabitants of Qamea and Laucala were displaced by local chiefs in the mid-19th century for siding with Tongan chief Enele Ma'afu during a war. Today, Laucala and Matagi are privately owned. Generally the only travellers who see these beautiful islands are resort visitors or divers heading for Motualevu Atoll (p62), although the adventure cruise ship *Tui Tai* sometimes stops at Laucala.

Matagi

Stunning horseshoe-shaped Matagi (area: 1 sq km), formed by a submerged volcanic crater, is 10km off Taveuni's coast and just north of Qamea. Its steep rainforest sides rise to 130m. The bay faces north to open sea and there is a fringing reef on the southwest side of the island.

The witches'-hat-style deluxe *bure* at **Matangi Island Resort** (☎ 888 0260; www.matangi island.com; s/d/tr standard bure $470/792/964, deluxe bure $608/1084/1410, d treehouse $1352, child 2-11 $150; 🖳 💹) have more space inside than furnishings. You could turn a cartwheel in one, should you feel so inclined. The high ceilings help the air flow without fans. Each *bure* is surrounded by a neat tropical garden. The beach is lovely, and the 'treehouses' are perched 5m up in the tree canopy with views to the beach through some fairly dense foliage. The pretty restaurant, where all meals are taken, looks over Qamea and out to the ocean. Rates include all meals, most activities and transfers to and from Taveuni. Matangi boasts 30 dive spots within 10 to 30 minutes of the island; a two-tank dive is $225 (including gear) at the resort's dive shop.

Qamea

Qamea (area: 34 sq km) is the closest of the three islands to Taveuni, only 2.5km east of Thurston Point. Its villages came under harsh attack by Cyclone Ami in early 2003. The island's coast has a number of bays with white-sand beaches and a narrow mangrove inlet on the west side. The interior, especially on the north side, is covered with steep green hills and sloping valleys. Qamea is rich in birdlife and is also notable for the *lairo,* the annual migration of land crabs. For a few days from late November to early December, at the start of their breeding season, masses of crabs move together from the mud flats towards the sea.

The magnificently thatched *bure* at **Qamea Resort & Spa** (☎ 888 0220; www.qamea.com; d/tr bure $1250/1540, d premium villa $1910; 🔏 💹) lie on a long stretch of beautiful white-sand beach. The resort is decorated with an eclectic selection of artworks and crafts, most of which seem to be from Papua New Guinea and Irian Jaya. Rates include meals and transfers to and from Taveuni; children under 16 are not accepted unless you book the entire resort! There is excellent snorkelling just offshore as well as windsurfing, sailing, outrigger canoeing, nature walks, village visits and fishing trips. The spa offers 55 different treatments, and there's a dive shop where two two-tank dives/PADI Open Water Courses cost $260/950, including gear. Only Qamea dives the site known as Australian Coconut.

Laucala

Just 500m east across the strait from Qamea, 30-sq-km Laucala was once owned by the estate of the late US millionaire Malcolm Forbes. The upmarket hideaway he built, Fiji Forbes, is now a ghost resort. The fans still turn in the *bures,* as the people from the nearby Forbes-built settlement – which looks more like a midwestern town than a Fijian village – seem never to have turned them off.

During the 2000 Speight Coup, the resort was occupied by opportunists, who beat up the managers.

Kadavu Group

Unspoilt and with positively prehistoric landscapes, this group of islands sits some 100km below Viti Levu's southern coast in a flourish of emerald green. Steep verdant banks rise from the rugged shoreline hinting at an untamed interior. It's more than a hint; a dearth of roads and infrastructure largely confines transport to small boats and maintains the islands' flawless complexion. For visitors, the effort of traversing the perimeter is offset by the promise of a truly secluded stay.

Prevailing southeasterly winds batter the exposed southeastern side of the main island and the group can fall prey to unforgiving weather. But when the sun shines and the seas are calm visitors are rewarded with secluded swimming coves and spectacular trekking. The lush, pristine rainforests, especially on the eastern side, support a rich and diverse birdlife that includes the colourful Kadavu musk parrot. The Great Astrolabe Reef skirts the group and hooks its way around the uppermost islands, providing some of the finest diving in the Pacific.

The group comprises of Kadavu (Fiji's fourth-largest island), oval-shaped Ono, Galoa and a number of smaller islands. The main island is irregular in shape and so deeply indented that it is almost cut in three by deep bays. The impressive Nabukelevu (Mt Washington) is the highest peak at 838m.

Kadavu's 72 villages or settlements rely largely on subsistence agriculture and the export of local produce to the mainland. Each village has its own fishing grounds, and resorts negotiate to use the areas for diving, surfing or fishing.

HIGHLIGHTS

- Dive or snorkel the kaleidoscopic **Great Astrolabe Reef** (opposite)
- **Meet the locals** (opposite); spend an afternoon in one of the 72 villages
- Wait for low tide and **trek** (opposite) a stretch of the coast
- Ignore the tide and take an **inland hike** (opposite)
- Indulge at a **top-end lodge** (p227)
- Surf the breaks off **Cape Washington** (p226)
- Dive with the manta rays and sharks at **Naiqoro Passage** (opposite)
- Get offshore and tour the islands by **kayak** (p226)

Great Astrolabe Reef ★

Naiqoro Passage ★

Cape Washington ★

- POPULATION: 12,000
- AREA: 411 SQ KM

ORIENTATION

The small town of Vunisea is Kadavu's administrative centre, with the island's police station, post office, hospital (all on the top of the hill) and airstrip. It is on an isthmus with Namalata Bay to the west and North Bay to the east. Vunisea is easy to get around on foot, but of little interest to travellers.

INFORMATION

Emergency

Fiji Recompression Chamber Facility (☎ 885 0630; recompression@connect.com.fj; cnr Amy & Brewster Sts, Suva) Divers suffering from the bends can be transferred to Suva by Medivac helicopter service.

Police (☎ 333 6007)

Medical Services

Vunisea's **hospital** (☎ 333 6008) was opened in 1996, with the help of Australian aid, as part of a $7 million project to improve Kadavu's health services. Services are fairly limited though, so if you really feel unwell escape Kadavu.

Money

Most of the resorts in Kadavu are distant from Vunisea. Some resorts accept credit cards but bring cash with you especially if you are staying at the budget resorts.

Post & Telephone

The Vunisea post and telephone offices are on top of the hill, a short walk from the airstrip. This **branch** (☻ 8am-3pm Mon-Fri) also sells some groceries, clothes and stationery. Kavala Bay, at the northeastern end of the island, also has a post office.

Dangers & Annoyances

The ferry trip to Kadavu from Suva can be rough and the timetable is erratic; fly instead. The small boats used by budget resorts for transfers to/from the airstrip often don't have covers, life jackets or radios. The weather can be rough from April to August.

ACTIVITIES

Remote and rugged Kadavu is a great place for nature lovers, divers, hikers and bird-watchers.

Hiking

The mountains have rainforests, numerous waterfalls and hiking trails used mainly by school children. There are good treks into the interior from Tiliva Resort, Papageno Eco-Resort and Nagigia Resort. Staff there often act as guides or you can head off on your own but ask locals if a track is clear beforehand. The strip of coast between Waisalima Beach Resort and Tiliva village makes for a scenic walk at low tide. The isolated villagers are very traditional so when visiting a village, ask to speak to the *turaga-ni-koro* (hereditary chief) first, remove your hat and don't carry things on your shoulders (see p36 for more information on village etiquette).

Diving

Most travellers are attracted to Kadavu for its famous **Great Astrolabe Reef**, which skirts the eastern side of the group, and the nearby Naiqoro Passage. Expect brilliantly coloured soft and hard corals, vertical drop-offs and a wonderful array of marine life, including lots of reef sharks. However, diving on the reef is variable, ranging from disappointing to terrific. The weather quite often dictates which sites are suitable to dive, and visibility can range from 15m to 70m. For more information on Kadavu's diving sites, see p62.

The following three outfits have excellent equipment and instructors:

Matava Resort (☎ 330 5222) offers dives from the Soso Passage to Naiqoro Passage, featuring excellent manta ray, cave and shark dives. One-/two-tank dives cost $105/165 and a PADI Open Water Course costs $590.

Papageno Eco-Resort (☎ 330 3355) has knowledgeable instructors, who will take you to the best sites, taking into account weather conditions and what you want to see. Shark feeding in the Naiqoro Passage is a favourite excursion. A two-tank dive/PADI Open Water Course costs $130/600.

Dive Kadavu (☎ 331 7780; www.divekadavu.com) has fast boats with up to four dives per day. A favourite haunt is the Namalata reefs, which are about 5km from the west coast of the island and more sheltered from the prevailing winds than the Astrolabe Reef. A two-tank dive/PADI Open Water Course costs $170/600.

Two budget resorts that offer diving are **Waisalima Beach Resort** (☎ 331 7281), which charges $155 for a two-tank dive, and **Albert's Sunrise** (☎ 333 7555). The latter runs dives to

KADAVU GROUP

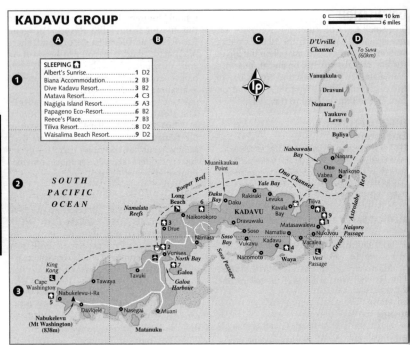

KADAVU GROUP

SLEEPING
Albert's Sunrise.............................1 D2
Biana Accommodation.................2 B3
Dive Kadavu Resort.....................3 B2
Matava Resort...............................4 C3
Nagigia Island Resort..................5 A3
Papageno Eco-Resort..................6 B2
Reece's Place................................7 B3
Tiliva Resort.................................8 D2
Waisalima Beach Resort..............9 D2

the Naiqoro Passage and, during rough weather, sites on the sheltered side of Ono island. A two-tank dive costs $145 but you should check your equipment thoroughly beforehand.

Surfing

The best surfing in Kadavu is found around **Cape Washington**, at the southernmost end of Kadavu. It gets plenty of swell activity year-round. **Vesi Passage**, off Matava, also has powerful surf, but the waves often get blown out.

Sea Kayaking

The season for organised kayaking trips is from May to September – contact **Tamarillo Sea Kayaking** (☎ in New Zealand 04-239 9885; www.tamarillo.co.nz/index.html), which offers interesting and well-organised kayak tours around Kadavu. The seven-day tours cost around $2600 per person. All tours include meals and accommodation in the budget resorts as well as a village stay. It also offers a seven-day family-friendly expedition, which requires less exertion and is designed

with kids in mind. It costs $2600/2100 per adult/child.

All the resorts have two-person ocean kayaks for hire.

Bird-watching

The lush rainforests, especially on Kadavu's eastern side, are home to a wide variety of birdlife, including the indigenous Kadavu honeyeater, Kadavu fantail, velvet fruit dove and the colourful Kadavu musk parrot.

SLEEPING

In Kadavu most of the places to stay are distant from the airport, and the only way to get there is by boat. Consider transportation time and cost when choosing your accommodation.

Budget

Matava Resort (☎ 330 5222; www.matava.com; dm $20, d without/with bathroom $60/110-170; ⊠) The most popular of the budget resorts, Matava has charming traditional thatched *bure* (Fijian dwellings) with timber floors, modest furniture, verandas and plenty of sunlight

THE BATTLE OF THE SHARK & OCTOPUS GODS

Dakuwaqa the Shark God once cruised the Fiji islands challenging other reef guardians. On hearing rumours of a rival monster in Kadavu waters, he sped down to the island to prove his superior strength. Adopting his usual battle strategy he charged at the giant octopus with his mouth wide open and sharp teeth prepared. The octopus, however, anchored itself to the coral reef and swiftly clasped the shark in a death lock. In return for mercy the octopus demanded that the people of Kadavu be forever protected from shark attack. In Kadavu the people now fish without fear and regard the shark as their protector. Most won't eat shark or octopus out of respect for their gods.

The honeymoon and oceanview *bure* are the most expensive and come with wonderful views. The grounds are neat and lush and the eco-friendly owners make the most of solar electricity and water heating. Excellent meals (per adult/child per day $55/20) include vegetables from the organic garden and are served on the veranda of the big restaurant-bar *bure*.

The beach out the front is tidal; a reef links it to a picturesque offshore island, which makes a great snorkelling or kayaking trip. Aside from diving (p225), there is also hiking, village and waterfall visits, kayaking, snorkelling and game fishing. Boat transfers from Vunisea airstrip cost $40 per person one way and take around an hour.

Albert's Sunrise (☎ 333 7555; camping per person $6, dm/s/d $16/37/50) On a beach on the northeastern corner of Kadavu, close to Naiqoro Passage, Albert's is a small, family-run resort offering travellers the flavour of a village visit. Everything's fairly laid-back and more flexible than other resorts – fresh meals (per person per day $37) are served whenever they're cooked and activities are organised if there's interest. Self-caterers can pay $5 to use the kitchen. There is no electricity or hot water, and the rustic *bure* have mosquito nets and woven floor mats. Snorkelling is OK in front of the resort at high tide and gear hire costs $5 per day. One-way transfers to/from Vunisea airstrip

cost $100 for one person and $50 per person for two or more people. The trip takes around 1½ to two hours.

Waisalima Beach Resort (☎ 331 7281; www.waisalimafiji.com; camping per site $8, dm $12, d without/with bathroom $65/130) This rough-hewn budget retreat consists of ageing, thatched *bure*, rudimentary bathrooms, hammocks on the beach and ocean vistas. It's a no-pretensions, no-frills spot but what you're paying for is a backpackers' slice of the island. There's a long stretch of sandy, tidal beach, which is OK for swimming at high tide. The best snorkelling requires a short boat trip ($25 per person). Also on offer are waterfall or village visits ($25 per person) and kayaking. The food (meal plan additional $50 per day) is carb loaded. Return boat transfers from Vunisea airstrip cost $100 per person.

Reece's Place (☎ 333 6097; www.reecesresort.com) One of Kadavu's oldest resorts, Reece's has been operating for more than 30 years as a family-run property, but was bought by new owners in 2005. A major overhaul was in action during research with five new *bure*, a new kitchen/dining area, a dive centre and a bar promised. The resort is based in a nice spot on the northern point of Galoa island, just southeast of Vunisea. Snorkelling right off the island is poor but you can be taken to Soso Passage, which isn't far away.

Staying in Vunisea really defeats the purpose of coming to Kadavu but if you get stuck here **Biana Accommodation** (☎ 333 6010; s/d $40/60), about 2km north of the airport near the wharf, has basic rooms with mosquito nets. Rates include breakfast, and lunch or dinner is $5. There is also a new budget lodge being established virtually outside the airport gates.

Top End

Papageno Eco-Resort (☎ 330 3355; www.papagenoecoresort.com; s from $275, d $400-600; ✗) Papageno is the quintessential island sanctuary and the stuff of comfy castaway dreams. Ecologically friendly, the resort uses solar and micro-hydro energy to complement its generator and the vegetables you eat at dinner will be from the organic garden. The resort itself is small and embedded in a thick tropical garden popular with shining parrots. The connected 'Garden Rooms' include futon-style beds, furniture made from local materials and bark wall hangings. The larger *bure* have a wide berth of space and privacy around them. All digs have plush bathrooms with indulgent products and fluffy beach towels. The food is excellent – a three-course dinner often features catch of the day (which might be lobster). *Kava* (narcotic drink) ceremonies, sea kayaking and hiking are all free; snorkelling, fishing and surfing are extra. Papageno is ideal for couples but singles and families will feel just as welcome.

Tiliva Resort (☎ 333 7127; www.tilivaresortfiji.com; r $400-500; ✗) Spread widely over a soft incline rising from the beach, this tranquil and refined resort has six elevated *bure* with cavernous interiors, high roofs, four-poster beds and lounge chairs to sink into. Each also has a 270-degree timber balcony with just enough high foliage to provide privacy without restricting the view. Hot water and electricity run 24/7. Delicious meals are included in the tariff and served on a fabulous sweeping deck in the central bar/dining area. Tiliva is owned and run by Kim, a retired British Forces Officer who grew up in the village next door, and his wife Barbara. They are exceedingly gracious and Kim cooks a mean fillet of fish.

Dive Kadavu Resort (☎ 331 7780; www.dive kadavu.com; s/d/t/f $320/560/780/980; ✗) This appealing resort has 10 modest *bure* with comfortable beds, verandas, hot water and tidy bathrooms. Many visitors come here to dive but it's a nice place to just hang out for a few days. Sheltered from the prevailing southeasterly winds, it boasts an excellent beach, where the snorkelling and swimming is wonderful regardless of the tide. There's also a sociable, ocean-fronted bar and the management is extremely hospitable. Rates include meals and airport transfers.

Nagigia Island Resort (☎ 333 7774, 600 3051; www.fijisurf.com; dm $115, d from $250; ✗) On the far western side of the island group, this remote resort sits on an unfathomably beautiful island near Cape Washington. Proprietors have made the most of the exquisite landscape, with *bure* and dorms hanging over plots of translucent blue sea and boasting reef, surf and mountain views. Surfing is the main activity, with a choice of five breaks including King Kong lefts just offshore. The surf-breaks produce rideable waves all year-round with bigger swells during midyear. Boat transfers to the breaks are

$35 per person per day, but you can also paddle out to the main break. There are also nice walks nearby, including to Cape Washington lighthouse for a swim in the Nasoso Beach caves. A visit to the village of Nabukelevu-i-Ra, just across the water on Kadavu, is also a must. This is also a great spot for snorkelling and diving, with great cave formations to explore and pristine coral; the resort can arrange trips with Dive Kadavu (p225).

Meal plans are an additional $60 per person. Return boat transfers from Vunisea airstrip are $115 per person.

EATING

The airport has a kiosk selling a few snacks, and there are small stores in Vunisea and Kavala Bay. Most of the resorts are very remote, so even if all your meals are provided it may be an idea to take along snacks, especially to the budget resorts.

GETTING THERE & AWAY
Air

Air Fiji has daily return flights from Suva to Kadavu ($260, 30 minutes). You can sometimes get a discount if you book directly through the Suva office of **Air Fiji** (Map p122; ☎ 331 3666; suvasales@airfiji.com.fj; 185 Victoria Pde).

Sun Air (☎ 0800 672 5725, 572 3016; www.fiji.to) has daily flights to Kadavu from Nadi ($330, 45 minutes). It is advisable to check timetables and always confirm flights the day before departure.

It is a beautiful flight (sometimes turbulent) over stunning reefs to Kadavu from either Nadi or Suva. The approach to Vunisea's Namalata airstrip over Namalata Bay has a spectacular view of Nabukelevu, which rises steeply at the southwestern point of Kadavu. There is talk of another airport being constructed at the eastern end of Kadavu, which would reduce transfer times to nearby resorts considerably. Ideally, have your accommodation and transfers booked in advance, otherwise you could be stranded in Vunisea.

Boat

Suva to Kadavu on the ferry MV *Bulou-ni-Ceva* is $45 per person one way. This service is mostly for cargo and local use, and it is irregular and unreliable, taking anything from four hours to two days! It visits Kavala Bay

Vunisea and also Nabukelevu-i-Ra. The trip can be bearable or terrible, depending on the weather you strike. Contact **Kadavu Shipping** (Map p119; ☎ 331 1766, 339 5000, 339 5788; Rona St, Walu Bay) in Suva for bookings.

GETTING AROUND
Kadavu's few roads are restricted to the Vunisea area, except for one rough, unsealed road to Nabukelevu-i-Ra around the southern end of Kadavu. It's easy to walk around Vunisea or to hitch a ride. Small boats are the island group's principal mode of transport. Each resort has its own boat and will pick up guests from Vunisea airstrip; make sure you make arrangements in advance. Boat trips are expensive due to fuel costs and mark-ups. Most boats don't have life jackets or radios. In rough weather it can be a wet and bone-crunching trip to the more remote resorts.

KADAVU GROUP

Lau & Moala Groups

Strewn across the southwest corner of Fiji's vast archipelago, the Lau Group is a brew of deserted atolls and sparsely populated islands surrounded by thick rims of reef. Within the 57 isles are countless bays, beaches, hilly ascents and seemingly unexplored territory. Although the climate is drier than most parts of Fiji, storms can be fierce and some of the bays are used as hurricane shelters by visiting yachts. Tourism is virtually nonexistent, which is precisely why these islands appeal to hardened and patient explorers.

Lau is subdivided into northern and southern Lau, and the Moala Group lies to the west of southern Lau. Although much closer to the mainland, the Moala Group is even further removed from the reaches of tourists and has no facilities whatsoever.

The group sits about halfway between Viti Levu and Tonga and its proximity to this Pacific neighbour has had a significant influence on the group's cultural development. Historically the southeast trade winds made it easy to sail from Tonga to Fiji, but more difficult to return. Tongan and Samoan canoe builders began settling in these islands in the late 1700s, bringing with them their innovative canoe designs. They intermarried with Fijians, and the Tongan influence is expressed in names, language, food, decoration, architecture and physical features. The islanders of southern Lau are well known for their crafts.

LAU & MOALA GROUPS

HIGHLIGHTS

- Weigh anchor in a kayak, dingy or yacht in the spectacular **Bay of Islands** (p232)

- Dose up on a fusion of Tongan and Fijian culture in the villages of **Vanua Balavu** (p233)

- **Snorkel** (p232) or **kayak** (p232) the smorgasbord of coral reefs and atolls

- Marvel at the limestone walls of **Oso Nabukete** (p234) and **Vale Ni Bose** (p233)

Bay of Islands ★ ★ Vale Ni Bose
★ Vanua Balavu

Oso Nabukete ★

- POPULATION: 11,500 | - AREA: 114,000 SQ KM

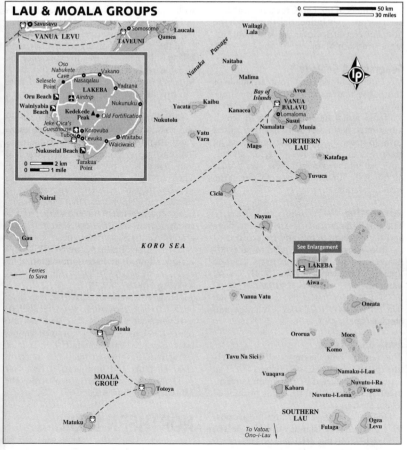

LAU & MOALA GROUPS

History

Lau first came into contact with Europeans in 1800 when the American schooner *Argo* was wrecked on Bukatatanoa Reef east of Lakeba. Fijians from Oneata island looted the wreck for muskets and gunpowder and the sailors lived with the islanders until being killed in disputes.

The greatest visiting influence, though, came from Lau's eastern Pacific neighbour, and by the mid-19th century the whole region was dominated by Tonga. In 1847 Tongan nobleman Enele Ma'afu, cousin of King Taufa'ahau of Tonga, led an armada of war canoes to Vanua Balavu to investigate the killing of a preacher. Six years later the king appointed Ma'afu governor of the

Tongans in Fiji. After the later murder of 17 Wesleyans, Ma'afu took Vanua Balavu by force and subjugated its inhabitants. He then established Sawana village near Lomaloma as his base. The Tongans assisted in local Fijian wars in return for protection by Chief Cakobau of Bau. By 1855 Ma'afu had become a powerful force in the region and influential throughout much of Fiji. He was one of the signatories to the Deed of Cession to Britain and became officially recognised as Roko Tui Lau (Protector of the Tongans of Vanuabalavu). After his death in 1881, Tongan power weakened, the title passed to the Tui Nayau (Traditional Fijian Chief of Lau) and many Tongans returned to their home country.

The chiefs of the Lau Group have always been surprisingly influential; those with the title Tui Nayau include the late Ratu Sukuna and Ratu Mara.

Geography & Geology
Most islands of the Lau Group are made of composite materials; some are pure limestone and a few are volcanic. The group is scattered amid 400km of ocean in which interrupted periods of uplift have permitted coral to grow over the limestone, creating great masses of reefs. Relatively recent volcanic activity is evident by the lava domes on top of the limestone bases of some of the smaller islands.

Information
There is little infrastructure for travellers and there are no banks and no credit card facilities so travellers will need to take sufficient cash for their entire stay. On Lau there is a **Lomaloma post office** (☎ 889 5000) on Vanua Balavu, and a **Tubou post office** (☎ 882 3001) on Lakeba. Tabou also has a **police station** (☎ 882 3043), telephone exchange and **hospital** (☎ 882 3153).

Activities & Tours
The remote Lau Group is still relatively unexplored in terms of diving. The Lau waters are protected by the Fijian Government and commercial fishing is prohibited in the area.

Diving, kayaking and swimming are possible in the Bay of Islands on Vanua Balavu (see right). Diving off Wailagi Lala is for experienced divers only.

Although there are no dive companies based in Lau, there are commercial divers working in the *bêche-de-mer* (sea cucumber) trade who can provide experienced divers

with equipment. Ask for advice and details at Moana's Guesthouse and Nawanawa Estate on Vanua Balavu (see opposite).

In the absence of diving companies, **snorkelling** is the next best way to experience the sizeable reefs and their marine life. Both Moana's Guesthouse and Nawanawa Estate can provide snorkelling equipment but it's also a good idea to bring your own.

Earth River (☎ in the USA 1800-643-2784, 845-626-2665; www.earthriver.com) is an adventure company offering 10-day kayaking expeditions that encompass Pacific Harbour, Beqa and four days of kayaking around Vanua Balavu. There are only about three or four trips a year but they are a fantastic opportunity to snorkel and swim in areas that would be difficult for independent travellers to get to. Accommodation on Viti Levu is in hotels but around Vanua Balavu it's village stays and beach camping. Rates (per person US$2900) include all meals and accommodation.

Getting There & Away
Air Fiji flies Suva–Vanua Balavu (see opposite), Suva–Lakeba (p234) and Suva–Moala (p235).

If you have plenty of time you can also reach the Lau Group by cargo/passenger boats (see p262) and Moala Group (p262).

Yachties wishing to visit Lau need to clear customs and immigration first (see p253) and apply for permission from the Ministry for Fijian Affairs.

NORTHERN LAU

Northern Lau's largest island is Vanua Balavu. It has an airstrip, as does Kaibu. The islands of Naitauba, Kanacea, Mago and Cicia are important for copra production.

VANUA BALAVU
Arguably the most scenic of Lau's islands, Vanua Balavu is enigmatic in shape and substance. Averaging about 2km wide, it resides with eight other smaller islands inside a barrier reef. The islands curl their way around the surrounding water like an inverted S, creating sheltered bays and corridors of calm sea. The interior of Vanua Balavu is scattered with rugged hills and the group's perimeter is ringed by pristine sandy beaches. The celebrated **Bay of Islands**, also known as Qilaqila, sits in the northwest

---

A LOCAL DELICACY

One week after the full moon in November, the people of Vanua Balavu witness the annual rising of the *balolo* (tiny green and brown sea worms). At sunrise the Susui villagers collect worms by the thousands. The catch is first soaked in fresh water, then packed into baskets and cooked overnight in a *lovo* (pit oven). The fishy-tasting baked worms are considered a delicacy.

pocket and is a spectacular site for diving, kayaking and swimming. It's also a lovely place for yachties to draw anchor. Within the rugged limestone hills is **Vale Ni Bose** (literally the Meeting House of the Gods), a gaping cave with limestone walls and a pool of crystalline water. On clear days the hazy green shape of Taveuni is visible across a 115km stretch of open sea.

Vanua Balavu's largest village is **Lomaloma** on the southeast coast. In the mid-19th century Tonga conquered the island and the village of Sawana was built next to Lomaloma. Fifth-generation Tongan descendants still live in **Sawana**, and the houses with rounded ends show the influence of Tongan architecture. The first of Fiji's ports, Lomaloma was regularly visited by ships trading in the Pacific. In its heyday Lomaloma had many hotels and shops as well as Fiji's first botanical gardens, though little remains of its past grandeur. The Fijian inhabitants of Vanua Balavu trace their ancestry to Tailevu (southeastern Viti Levu) and Cakaudrove (eastern Vanua Levu and Taveuni). Today the people of Vanua Balavu rely largely on copra and *bêches-de-mer* for their income.

Curious visitors exploring the island on their own will be welcomed in villages but ask for directions before you head out, and respect village etiquette (see p36).

Sleeping

Moana's Guesthouse (☎ 889 5006; r per person without/with bathroom incl meals $65/85; ✗) Accommodation options may not be rife in Sawana, but Moana's covers all bases, offering beach and village accommodation. Sitting right on the shore about 1km from the village are three unfussy *bure* (traditional dwellings). Two are thatched and share facilities and one has a private bathroom. There is also a Tongan-style cottage within the village with a small dorm, one double room and communal living area. Moana's can arrange boat, snorkelling and fishing trips, but immersing yourself in the village is just as rewarding.

Nawanawa Estate (☎ 889 5144; helenetuwai@hotmail.com; camping per person $10, s/d $40/70; ✗) Less than 5km from the airport, this comfortable homestay is run by the extremely friendly Ratu Joe Tuwai, a Daliconi local, and his New Zealand wife Helene. Accommodation is in their colonial-style home,

---

FATAL ATTRACTION

There is a freshwater lake near the village of Mavana, on the northeast corner of Vanua Balavu, which is considered sacred. The people of Mavana gather here annually for a fun ceremony authorised by their traditional priest. Naked except for a leaf skirt, they jump around in the lake to stir up the muddy waters. This provokes the large fish known as *yawa* (a type of mullet usually only found in the sea) to spring into the air. It is believed that the male fish are attracted to the female villagers and thus easily trapped in the nets. Legend has it that the fish were dropped into the lake by a Tongan princess while flying over the island on her way to visit her lover on Taveuni.

---

which Ratu Joe built. The meals here are an added treat (breakfast/lunch/dinner $5/10/12) and include freshly baked bread and catch of the day bought from local fishermen. Ratu Joe and Helene provide excellent insight into the island's geography and history and can also arrange visits to Vale Ni Bose.

Getting There & Away

Vanua Balavu is 355km east of Nadi, about halfway to Tonga. **Air Fiji** (☎ 331 3666; www.airfiji.com.fj) flies between Suva and Vanua Balavu on Thursday and Sunday ($195 one way, 1½ hours).

Saliabasaga Shipping has fortnightly trips from Suva to the Lau Group, including Vanua Balavu. Expect to spend about a week on board to travel to the far reaches of the southern Lau Group. See p262 for details.

KAIBU

Kaibu (3.5 sq km) is a privately owned island in the northern Lau Group, 55km west of Vanua Balavu. It shares a fringing reef with the larger island of Yacata. The extremely exclusive **Kaimbu Island Resort** (☎ 888 0333; www.fiji-islands.com/kaimbu.html) has been in a state of renovation and sale for several years and rumours of its imminent operation or demise abound. Either way it has been closed indefinitely but if it does reopen, it promises to rival Turtle Island Resort (in the Yasawas) in the opulence stakes.

SOUTHERN LAU

Lakeba, being the hereditary seat of the Tui Nayau (Chief of Lau), is the most important island in southern Lau. There are 16 other islands, mostly within a radius of 100km southeast of Lakeba. Vatoa and Ono-i-Lau are more isolated and much further south.

The islanders of southern Lau are well known for their crafts: Moce, Vatoa, Ono-i-Lau and Namuka produce *masi* (bark cloth) and the artisans of Fulaga are excellent woodcarvers. You may be able purchase crafts from villages on the islands or from handicrafts shops in Suva.

LAKEBA

Lakeba is a roughly circular volcanic island, approximately 9km in diameter, with a small peninsula at its southern end. Its 54-sq-km area is home to about 2000 people. There is a road around its perimeter and several roads across the interior. To the east is a wide **lagoon** enclosed by a barrier reef.

The island has nine villages. Yams, coconuts and *kumala* (sweet potatoes) grow well along the fertile coast and the interior is covered with grasslands, pandanus and pine plantations.

Lakeba was historically a meeting place for Fijians and Tongans; it was also the place where Christian missionaries first entered Fiji via Tonga and Tahiti. Two missionaries, Cross and Cargill, developed a system for written Fijian here and produced the first book in that language. Lakeba was frequently visited by Europeans before the trading settlement was established at Levuka in the Lomaivitis.

The **provincial office** (☎ 882 3164) for the Lau Group is in **Tubou** at the southern end of Lakeba. There is also a guesthouse, post office, police station and hospital here, and some of the nearby **beaches** are good for snorkelling and swimming. Enele Ma'afu, the once-powerful Tongan chief, is buried here, as is Ratu Sir Lala Sukuna, formerly an influential Tui Lau who established the Native Lands Trust Board in 1940.

The island has caves worth visiting, especially **Oso Nabukete**, which translates as 'too narrow for pregnant women'. Adorned with huge pillars of limestone stalactites and inhabited by bats, it's an awesome ex-

---

SHARK CALLING

Traditionally, the villagers of Nasaqalau performed a shark-calling ritual in October or November each year. About a month prior to the ceremony, the spot was marked by a post and a flag of *masi* (bark cloth) and a traditional priest ensured no-one went near the post or fished in the nearby area. On the designated day the caller, standing neck-high in the water, would chant for up to an hour. A school of sharks, led by a white shark, would be drawn to the place. All of the sharks except the white shark would be killed and eaten by the villagers.

Reports on whether shark calling is still performed here vary from village to village, like a wild rural myth. However, the general consensus seems to be that the ritual has not been enacted in earnest for some 100 years.

---

ample of nature's might. Take some *kava* (a narcotic drink pepper shrub) as a *sevusevu* (gift for the chief) to Nasaqalau village, where you can arrange a guide (bring your own torch). There is also an **old fortification** in the middle of the island at Kekekede Peak where the people retreated to during times of war.

Sleeping

Call the **Lau provincial office** (☎ 882 3164) to check if you can visit the island and to book accommodation.

Small **Jeke Qica's Guesthouse** (☎ 882 3035; r incl meals $40) in Tubou offers rooms with a shared bathroom inside 'Jack's house'. Meals are simple but filling and Jack can provide interesting commentary on the area's culture and history.

Getting There & Away

Air Fiji flies between Suva and Lakeba on Monday and Wednesday ($200, 1½ hours). Carriers and buses circle the island.

Saliabasaga Shipping and Kabua Development Corporation each have slow fortnightly trips from Suva to the southern Lau Group, including Lakeba. One-way fares including meals start at $75. See p262 for details.

MOALA GROUP

The three islands of this Group – Moala, Totoya and Matuku – are geographically removed from Lau but administered as part of the Eastern Division. They are about half-way between Kadavu and the southern Lau Group. The islands are the eroded tops of previously submerged volcanic cones that have lifted more than 3km to the sea surface. Totoya's horseshoe shape is the result of a sunken volcano crater forming a land-locked lagoon. The volcano was active 4.9 million years ago. Matuku has rich volcanic soil, steep wooded peaks and a submerged crater on its western side. However, this beautiful island is generally inaccessible to visitors. Each of the islands has villages.

MOALA

Moala (65 sq km) is the largest and most northerly of the group. It is about 160km from Suva. The island is roughly triangular in shape, with a deeply indented coast. The highest peak reaches 460m and has two small **crater lakes**. It has extremely fertile soil and supports nine villages. The villagers produce copra and bananas, which they send to Suva, a night's sail away. The ancestors of Moala's inhabitants came from Viti Levu.

Moala has no tourist infrastructure, and although you don't need to be formally invited as such, your only option for accommodation is with a local family. Consequently, you will need to organise this with a friend or member of the family before you arrive. Additionally you should ask beforehand what kind of *sevusevu* to take with you.

Getting There & Away

Air Fiji (☎ 331 3666; www.airfiji.com.fj) flies between Suva and Moala on Tuesday only ($180, 45 minutes).

Khans Shipping operates cargo/passenger boats that travel to Moala, Matuku and Totoya in the Moala Group once a month. See p262 for details.

Rotuma

Rotuma is an isolated, volcanic island, 450km northwest of Suva. The vast distance between its tiny frame and the mainland is an accident of geography, but the divide nurtures an inimitable culture of which Rotumans are fiercely proud. Ethnically and linguistically distinct from Fiji, the island provides travellers with a unique opportunity to experience a Polynesian outpost and visitors are welcomed as participants rather than spectators.

Physically, Rotuma resembles a whale, with the larger body of land linked to the small tail end to the west by the Motusa isthmus. The island is about 13km long by 5km at its widest point, with extinct volcanic craters rising up to over 250m. The smaller offshore islands of Uea, Hatana and Hofliua, west of Rotuma, are important seabird rookeries. Uea is a high, rocky island and the spectacular Hofliua is also known as 'Split Island' because of its unusual rock formation. The driest and most comfortable months to visit are between July and September, although the best time to visit is during the Fara festival.

Rotuma is administered by Fiji. Most young people leave their remote island home to find work, and about 6500 ethnic Rotumans live elsewhere in Fiji, mostly in Suva on Viti Levu. Rotuma produces copra, which is processed at the mill near Savusavu on Vanua Levu.

ROTUMA

HIGHLIGHTS

- Experience vibrant **Polynesian culture** and **hospitality** (opposite) at its finest
- Dance up a storm – join the locals during **Fara** (opposite)
- Explore beautiful and unique landscapes near **Solroroa Bluff** (opposite)
- Marvel at ancient archaeological sites at **Sisilo** (opposite)

- POPULATION: 3,000
- AREA: 30 SQ KM

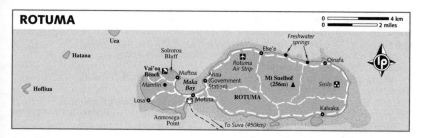

HISTORY

Tongans invaded Rotuma during the 17th century and the Tongan influence is evident in the language and dance. In 1791, Europeans on the HMS *Pandora* stopped here to search for mutineers from the *Bounty*. Rotuma became an important port, and the local people were exposed to traders, runaway sailors and convicts. During the mid-19th century, Tongan Wesleyan and Marist Roman Catholic missionaries introduced their versions of Christianity here. By the 1870s the religious groups were warring and, in response to the unrest, the Rotuman chiefs decided to cede their home to Britain. Rotuma became joined politically to the Fijian colony in 1881.

INFORMATION

There are no banks on Rotuma but there are shops and a **post office** (☎ 889 1003) in Ahau, which also acts as a Western Union agent.

An insightful and informative website designed for Rotumans is www.hawaii.edu /oceanic/rotuma/os/hanua.html.

SIGHTS & ACTIVITIES

Rotuma's volcanic curves offer excellent hiking and there are spectacular views from **Solroroa Bluff** and **Mt Suelhof** (256m). Between Losa and Solroroa Bluff is **Mamfiri**, a volcanic vent which drops around 25m. There are also **archaeological sites** at Sisilo (Graveyard of the Kings), Ki ne he'e and Tafea Point (stone walls). If you're lucky you may spot endemic wildlife including the Rotuman gecko and the red-and-black Rotuman honeyeater.

Rotuma also has some of the loveliest **beaches** in Fiji. The best are at Oinafa, Losa and at Vai'oa, west of Solroroa Bluff. There is also some fine surfing areas around the island; locals will be able to point you in the right direction to best exploit the conditions. Between Else'e and Oinafa are two

fuliu (freshwater springs), which are popular swimming holes.

This beautiful remote island is not just for outdoor addicts, though, and one of the most rewarding experiences is simply staying with villagers. An annual festivities period known as **Fara** begins on 1 December, during which the strong work ethic adopted throughout the year is replaced with six weeks of dancing, parties and general revelry. The festival coincides with Christmas and the emphasis is on hospitality and celebrating friends, family, visitors, life and love. At this time, the population increases by around one-third; it's undoubtedly the best time to be on the island.

SLEEPING & EATING

The easiest way for you to stay on Rotuma is through a Rotuman contact or their family. If you're lucky enough to organise this you should discuss with your contact how best

THE ORIGIN OF ROTUMA

Rotumans believe their ancestors came from Samoa. The spot where the island presently lies was nothing but open sea until the arrival of Samoan chief Raho and his favourite grandchild. The little girl was unhappy in her homeland as her cousin was always annoying her. To escape his torment, she convinced her grandfather to take her away to live on another island. For days and nights their entourage sailed westward in an outrigger canoe, but failed to find land. Eventually the chief threw some Samoan soil overboard. The soil grew to form a beautiful, fertile island, which he named Rotuma. Some of the soil scattered, forming the other small islands. Rotumans commemorate this legend in their dance and song.

to compensate a family during your stay. If staying with friends or family is not an option you should chat to the Fiji Visitor Bureau in either Nadi or Suva (see p252) for updated information and advice. Staff will be able to provide you with the appropriate contact details for the Rotuman Island Council, the body you should approach if you want to visit.

Mojito's Barfly (☎ 889 1144; Motusa) This place has simple rooms with shared facilities but they are generally reserved for government workers. Mojito's will, however, provide meals on request, but you need to give them plenty of notice.

SHOPPING

Mamfiri Oils (☎ 889 1401; www.mamfiri.com) This is a local company that produces healing oils derived from the nuts of hefau trees, which are abundant on Rotuma. The small industry provides a means for women on the island to generate some income. Contact the company beforehand if you want to make a purchase because the company doesn't have a shop.

GETTING THERE & AWAY
Air
Air Fiji (☎ 331 3666; www.airfiji.com.fj) flies from Suva to Rotuma on Wednesday and Friday ($430 one way, two hours).

Boat
Western Shipping (Map p119; ☎ 331 4467) operates the *Cagi Mai Ba* from Suva to Rotuma (deck/cabin $130/150, 36 hours). Call for departure times and dates.

Yachts occasionally visit the island, and must obtain permission to anchor from the Ahau government station in Maka Bay, on the northern side of the island. Note that yachties can't make Rotuma their first port of call; see p253 for details.

ROTUMA

Directory

CONTENTS

Accommodation	239
Activities	242
Business Hours	245
Children	245
Climate Charts	246
Customs	246
Dangers & Annoyances	246
Disabled Travellers	247
Discount Cards	247
Embassies & Consulates	247
Festivals & Events	248
Food	248
Gay & Lesbian Travellers	249
Holidays	249
Insurance	249
Internet Access	250
Legal Matters	250
Maps	250
Money	250
Post	251
Shopping	251
Telephone & Fax	251
Time	252
Tourist Information	252
Visas & Travel Permits	253
Women Travellers	253
Work	253

PRACTICALITIES

■ **Fiji Magic** (☎ 330 0591; www.fijilive.com /fijimagic) and **Fiji Holidays** (☎ 992 8063; promedia@connect.com.fj) are free, monthly publications with details and prices of accommodation, restaurants, activities and tours.

■ The government-sponsored Fiji Broadcasting Commission has stations in English (2Day FM – 100.4 FM), Fijian (Radio Fiji 1 – 558AM) and Fiji-Hindi (Radio Fiji 2 – 620AM and 98 FM).

■ Bula 100 FM plays an eclectic mix of pop, rock, reggae, dance, folk, country and local music.

■ The video and DVD system used in Fiji is PAL, which is the same as in Australia, New Zealand, Europe, the UK and most of Asia and the Pacific. The US video and DVD systems are in NTSC, which is incompatible.

■ Electricity is supplied at 240V, 50Hz AC. Many resorts have universal outlets for 240V or 110V shavers and hairdryers. Outlets use flat two- or three-pin plugs as in Australia or New Zealand.

■ Fiji follows the metric system; kilometres, kilograms, litres, and degrees in Celsius.

ACCOMMODATION

Five-star hotels, B&Bs, hostels, motels, resorts, treehouses, bungalows on the beach, campgrounds and village homestays – there's no shortage of accommodation options in Fiji.

Rates quoted in this book include Fiji's 12.5% value-added tax (VAT). Also they are peak season rates, which tend to be 10% to 20% higher than those for the low season.

Useful accommodation websites:
www.fiji-backpacking.com
www.fijibudget.com
www.4hotels.co.uk/fiji
www.fiji4less.com
www.travelmaxia.com
www.wotif.com

Budget

Budget travellers in Fiji can expect to pay $20 to $30 for a dorm bed, $40 to $80 for a single room and $60 to $90 for a double. Camping is also generally available (see p240). Facilities at budget places are usually shared. Many backpacker resorts in places such as Nadi and the Coral Coast on Viti Levu have their own restaurants, bars, laundries, Internet access and tour desks. On the outer islands amenities become a little simpler and sometimes hot water is a luxury. Budget resorts in the Yasawa and Mamanuca islands often include three meals in their tariffs as there is nowhere else to eat and no self-catering facilities.

When booking offshore budget accommodation get details such as: the safety of the transport (especially if it includes small-boat trips); cleanliness; facilities and equipment available; the type and price of food; and any hidden costs. If possible, quiz other travellers, check Lonely Planet's Thorn Tree (www.lonelyplanet.com) or browse through the comments book of the Fiji Visitors Bureau (FVB) to get the latest picture of a particular place.

If you're making reservations at budget places while you're on the road, don't be completely surprised if you show up and nobody's heard of you. Administration can sometimes be a little less than organised and reservations that are made don't always seem to make it into the book.

Midrange & Top End

The bulk of accommodation in Fiji falls under the midrange banner. Options include hotels, motels and resorts ranging from $80 to $150 for one person and $90 to $170 for two. Guests can expect bathrooms, TVs, bar fridges, and tea and coffee facilities in hotels while many lodges and resorts offer self-contained units with kitchens. Options on some islands such as Taveuni are more costly than at most other destinations.

Top-end options are generally five-star chain resorts and other upmarket resorts, with prices ranging from $170 for a double to sky's-the-limit tariffs. If you're after a short stay in a top-end place, consider prebooking your accommodation as a package deal – you'll almost always get a cheaper price than the quoted 'rack rate'. Moreover, you'll need to book well in advance for popular resorts, particularly during the peak season of May to October. However, it's also often possible to get cheaper walk-in rates, particularly during the very quiet months of February and March.

If you're looking to stay a bit longer and want to move around, avoid paying too much in advance and keep your options open. There are many places to choose from so if you're not happy with the place you booked, you won't be tied by prepaid reservations and can just move on.

Remote islands, such as Kadavu, have few places to stay and the main form of transportation is by small boat. In this case, avoid being left stranded without a vacancy in your price range by prebooking – this will also ensure you'll be met at the airport or ferry.

Types of Accommodation

CAMPING

Don't just set up camp anywhere without permission. Most of Fiji's land, even in seemingly remote areas, is owned by the indigenous population, by *mataqali* (extended families) or villages. If you are invited to camp in villages, avoid setting up next to someone's *bure* (traditional dwelling). Doing so can be misinterpreted as implying that you feel the house is not good enough for you to stay in. Ask where the best place to pitch your tent is and provide a *sevusevu* (gift).

Elsewhere you can pitch your tent at some of the budget lodges in the Yasawa and Kadavu islands as well as Vanua Levu, Taveuni and Viti Levu's Coral Coast. Some resorts in the Yasawas also offer camping in their own tents. Expect to pay $10 to $15 per person per night. For details of the location of camping areas refer to the individual island chapters.

HOSTELS

The Cathay chain has budget accommodation at Lautoka, Saweni Beach, the Coral Coast and Suva. It gives discounts for HI (Hostelling International) and Nomad card holders. There are many cheap hotels with dorm accommodation and some hotels and resorts have converted a room or two into dorms – often a great bargain as you'll have access to all of the resort's facilities.

RENTAL ACCOMMODATION

Most of the long-term rental accommodation is in Suva and Pacific Harbour, and to a lesser extent in Nadi. There are also a number of houses for rent on Taveuni. Renting apartments or rooms with weekly rates may be a cheap option if you are looking for a fixed base from which to take day trips. Normally apartments have cooking facilities, and if you are in a small group, a joint effort to buy groceries, fresh fruit and vegetables from the local market can save a fair bit of money.

RESORTS

The term 'resort' is used loosely in Fiji and refers to accommodation ranging from backpacker-style to exclusive luxury. If you are prepared to put up with rudimentary facilities and services, you can find yourself an inexpensive piece of paradise. There are some beautiful coral islands where you can stay cheaply in simple thatched-roof *bure* in idyllic settings. Most resorts offer meal plans, which are fixed-price packages that generally include breakfast, lunch and dinner. Nonmotorised activities tend to be included in resort rates, but diving, parasailing, water-skiing, jet-skiing, fish-ing and island-hopping excursions generally cost extra.

There are many backpacker resorts on the offshore islands, including the Yasawas, on Mana in the Mamanucas, Kadavu, Nananu-i-Ra, and Leluvia and Caqalai near Ovalau. The standards of many of these places can slide up and down with popularity; normally booking requires a payment up front, so before embarking try to get information from travellers who have just been there. Popular places can become overcrowded and less popular places can feel totally abandoned. Transport is often by small open boat, which can be risky in rough weather.

For those who are happy to spend up to a few hundred dollars per day for extra comfort, services and activities, there are many popular resorts in the Mamanucas, on Viti Levu's Coral Coast, on Taveuni, as well as on more remote islands.

FIJIAN HITCH

Fiancées and honeymooners flock to Fiji like lovesick bees to a honey convention. The tropical beaches, the amber sunsets, the secluded resorts, the island singing – this archipelago smacks of romantic paradise and 'don't it know it'. Many resorts cater to the almost- and newly I-do's with irresistible honeymoon and wedding packages and can provide you with much of the information and planning you need. Regardless of how you go about it there are some fundamentals you'll need in order to tie the knot.

Essentials for a marriage license to be issued in Fiji include; someone of the opposite sex (unfortunately same-sex marriage is not legal in Fiji), birth certificates, passports (it would be tricky getting into the country without one) and, if you're under the age of 21, a document of consent signed by your folks. If (and this is a little prickly) this is your second time round, you'll also need to produce a copy of divorce papers, a Decree Nisi or death certificate.

You'll need to present all of the above documents to a Registry Office prior to your actual marriage in order to obtain a marriage licence. This process only takes around 20 minutes but it's a good idea to make an appointment if you're not getting a resort or travel agent to organise the whole shebang for you. The **Registrar General office** (☎ 331 5280; Ground fl, Suvavou House, ☺ 8.30am-3.30pm) is in Suva, but there are also **Divisional Registrars** (Lautoka ☎ 666 5132; 1st fl, Rogorogoivuda House, Tavewa Ave; ☺ 9am-3pm; Nadi ☎ 670 0101; Korivolu Ave; ☺ 8am-1pm & 2-4pm Mon-Fri). There's a $22 fee involved and you then have 21 days to get hitched.

A less practical but equally important consideration is the weather. Regardless of the wording, your vows will lose some of their romantic impact if you end up reciting them beneath a golf umbrella in gale-force winds (see p17 for more climate information). If you have dreams of you, your betrothed and a priest alone on a secluded beach you may want to check your resort's occupancy before you book.

Lastly, it's a good idea to get some perspective, advice and tips from the romance experts. The following websites can help you plan the perfect Fijian wedding or honeymoon, if not organise it outright:

http://destination-weddings-abroad.com/fiji/
www.fijiweddings.com
www.fijihoneymoon.com
www.holidaysforcouples.com.au/pacificocean-fiji.html
www.weddings-in-fiji.com

DIRECTORY

TOP FIVE RESORTS

Fiji is, unsurprisingly, bursting at the seams with resorts. Fortunately, like travellers, they come in all shapes, sizes and flavours. The following is a selection of the best and each caters to a different guest.

Caqalai Island Resort (p180) Rustic backpacker retreat on a small, gorgeous coral island.

Jean-Michel Cousteau Fiji Islands Resort (p199) Classy boutique resort with superb diving and an excellent (and mandatory!) kids' club.

Octopus Resort (p164) Perfect island resort that manages to appeal to every age and budget. It has friendly staff, fine food and fab rooms.

Tokoriki Island Resort (p154) Pure romance and five-star indulgence for couples.

Treasure Island Resort (p151) One for the families – loads of activities for little and big kids and wallet-friendly rates.

ACTIVITIES

Fiji has plenty to offer the adventurous and active. The archipelago's warm, clear waters and abundance of reef life make it a magnet for divers and snorkellers. Visibility regularly exceeds 30m, though this is reduced on stormy days or when there is a heavy plankton bloom.

Bird-Watching

Fiji features some brilliant members of the feathered family. Taveuni is home to more than 100 species including the rare orange dove. See p213 for information regarding the best sites. Kadavu (p226) is also home to a diversity of birdlife including the Kadavu musk parrot. Taveuni has better infrastructure than Kadavu, and is cheaper and easier to travel around.

On Vanua Levu, the Tunuloa Peninsula (p202) is home to the rare silktail, while the rainforests around Savusavu are popular bird hang-outs. On Viti Levu, Colo-i-Suva Forest Park (p124) near Suva has great birdwatching, as does the area near Waidroka Bay Resort (p111) on the Queens Road. For more about Fiji's birds, see p53 and consider picking up a copy of *Birds of the Fiji Bush*, by Fergus Clunie & Pauline Morse of the Fiji Museum.

Cycling

Cycling is a good way to explore Viti Levu, Vanua Levu (the Hibiscus Hwy) and parts of Ovalau and Taveuni. With the exception of the Kings and Queens Roads, most roads, especially inland, are rough, hilly and unsealed, so mountain bikes are the best option. Some resorts have bikes for hire. Expect to pay around $10 to $15 for half a day. See p79 for information on mountain biking.

Consider taking a carrier (a small truck) up to Abaca and riding down to Lautoka. You could also cycle along Vanua Levu's unsealed roads from Savusavu along Natewa Bay (no accommodation around here) and along the Hibiscus Hwy from Buca Bay, where you can take the ferry over to Taveuni. Ovalau also has a scenic unsealed (mainly flat) coastal road.

There seems to be no official road rule regarding cyclists so the rule of thumb should be to assume all vehicles have right of way. For general information on cycling in Fiji, see p260.

Diving & Snorkelling

The beauty of Fiji is that, with a dive industry that is well-established, you can have great access to diving and snorkelling regardless of whether your funds extend from budget or luxury. For information on diving see p57; for information on diving insurance, see p271.

Snorkelling in Fiji's warm waters is a definite highlight. There are beautiful reefs teeming with amazing life. Snorkelling is often fantastic very close to the coast, making it a relatively inexpensive and easy pastime compared with diving. All you need is a mask, snorkel and fins. Ideally wear a T-shirt and waterproof sunscreen as it is easy to become absorbed by the spectacle, lose sense of time and scorch your back and legs.

If you have not snorkelled before or are not a confident swimmer, familiarise yourself with the equipment in a pool or shallow water. Learn how to clear your snorkel, so that you don't panic and tread over the fragile coral. Keep to the surface if you feel more comfortable there and never dive too deep. It is best to swim with a partner, to always use fins and to ask locals about currents. Some operators who take snorkellers on their dive trips may just dump you overboard with a buoy, on a barrier reef, far from land. If you are not confident, ask for a life jacket. It is common to see reef sharks but don't panic, they're probably more scared of you. The most beautiful creatures can be poisonous so avoid touching anything. Also avoid being washed against the reef as coral cuts can turn into nasty infections.

In Fiji, you are likely to see brilliant soft and hard corals, multitudes of colourful fish of various shapes and sizes, sponges, sea cucumbers, urchins, starfish, Christmas-tree worms and molluscs. Crustaceans are more difficult to spot and many only come out at night. Night snorkelling with a light is a fantastic experience if you can overcome your fear of the unknown!

Most resorts offer snorkelling and have equipment for hire. However, always check first when going to a remote budget resort – it can be frustrating if you are in a gorgeous location without any (or poor) equipment. If you are a keen snorkeller it may be worth having your own equipment – it's relatively cheap and easy to carry. Dive operations usually take snorkellers to outer reefs if there is room on the boat, although some prefer to keep the activities separate.

In many places you can snorkel off the shore; however, often you can only swim at high tide and channels can be dangerous. The best sites on Viti Levu are at Natadola Beach (watch the current here, though), Nananu-i-Ra and Beqa Lagoon. Viti Levu's Coral Coast is not that great for snorkelling as it is usually a fair way to the drop, much of the reef is dead and swimming is mostly tidal.

The best snorkelling sites are on the outer islands. Notable sites include: the Mamanucas and Yasawas (superb reefs with mostly hard coral); Vanua Levu's rocky coastline, especially near Mumu's Resort; Taveuni's Vuna Reef; offshore of the Matava Resort in Kadavu; and the Lomaiviti Group's Caqalai and Leleuvia.

Fishing & Boat Chartering

Villages have rights over the reefs and fishing so you cannot just drop a line anywhere; seek permission first. Many of the more expensive resorts offer game-fishing tours and boat chartering. Taveuni has several companies offering game-fishing expeditions; see p213 for details. On and around Viti Levu, resorts at Pacific Harbour (p113), and Vatulele (p118), and outfits at Nananu-i-Ra (p141) offer fishing trips. There are also fishing and boat chartering possibilities on Vanua Levu – see p195 for more information.

Consider the southeast trade winds when choosing the best spot – the leeward sides of the islands are generally calmer. For boat chartering see p150.

Hiking

It is culturally offensive to simply hike anywhere – you need to ask permission, be invited or take a tour. For information on how to be culturally sensitive in villages, see p36. You should ask local villagers or hotel staff to organise permission and a guide. Good boots are essential for hiking all year-round. Carry plenty of water, good maps, a compass, a warm jumper and a waterproof coat. Be sure to tell others where you are heading in case you get lost or have an accident.

Viti Levu (p142) and Taveuni (p213) are the best islands for hiking and there are some excellent trails on Waya (p163) in the Yasawas. Kadavu is more isolated but equally beautiful. Colo-i-Suva Forest Park (p124) near Suva and the Lavena Coastal Walk (p222) on Taveuni have marked trails. Another good place for hiking is Koroyanitu National Heritage Park in Viti Levu (p143). For an easy but scenic walk, follow the Coral Coast Scenic Railway from the Shangri-La's Fijian Resort to the beautiful Natadola Beach. For more information on the walks and guided tours, see the destination chapters.

If you plan to be in Fiji for a while, consider contacting the Rucksack Club in Suva (contact details available from the FVB). It organises regular walks and excursions.

Horse Riding

There are a few places in Fiji where horse riding is an organised activity. Try the Beachhouse (p111) on Viti Levu's Coral Coast and Vatuwiri Farm in Taveuni (p218).

Kayaking & River Trips

Bilibili (bamboo rafting) and kayaking trips can be made on the Navua River in the Namosi Highlands of Viti Levu; see p113 for details. Many village trips also include a ride on a *bilibili*. Jet Fiji (p87) at Denarau has speed-boat tours through the island's mangroves. See also sea kayaking, p244.

Sailing

Yachties are often looking for extra crew and people to share costs. Approach the marinas, ask around and look on the notice boards.

Fiji's marinas include the Royal Suva Yacht Club (p126); Vuda Point Marina (p89) between Nadi and Lautoka; Levuka Harbour on Ovalau; Musket Cove Marina (p155) on Malololailai in the Mamanucas; and the Copra Shed Marina and Waitui Marina (p195), both at Savusavu on Vanua Levu.

The designated ports of entry for Fiji are Suva, Levuka, Lautoka and Savusavu. Yachties intending to sail to the outer islands, such as the Lau Group, will require a customs permit and a permit to cruise the islands, obtained from the Ministry of Fijian Affairs, or from the commissioner's office in Lautoka, Savusavu or Levuka. Seek advice from a yachting agent or yacht club in Fiji before applying for the permit. Refer to p253 for more details.

The main yachting season is June to August, but there are races and regattas throughout the year. Obviously the Fijian reefs necessitate good charts and crews with sailing experience.

For organised cruises and charters, refer to the individual island chapters. Musket Cove Marina hires out a range of vessels for sailing around the Mamanucas and Yasawas, including some that are fully crewed with skipper and cook. There are also private boats for sail and adventure cruises from Savusavu's marinas. By Fijian law, you must have a local guide on all chartered boats.

Contact individual yacht clubs for further information, and pick up a copy of the *Yacht Help Booklet, Fiji* available from the FVB. *Landfalls of Paradise – The Guide to Pacific Islands* by Earl R Hinz, and Michael Calder's *Yachtsman's Fiji* are also popular references.

Sea & Dive Kayaking

Sea and dive kayaking are becoming increasingly popular in Fiji. Kayaking is a great way of exploring the coast at a gentle pace. Dive kayaks, which can carry lunch, snorkelling gear and scuba gear, can be double the fun.

The islands of Taveuni, Vanua Levu, Yasawa, Nananu-i-Ra and Kadavu are great for kayaking. Some keen kayakers paddle Taveuni's rugged Ravilevu Coast, but generally the western sides of the islands are preferred as they're sheltered from the southeast trade winds.

Many resorts have kayaks for guest use, or for hire at about $20/30 for a half-/full day. There are also special sea-kayaking tours available during the drier months between May and November. Some combine paddling with hiking into rainforests, snorkelling, fishing and village visits, and have support boats that carry camping gear and food. They don't necessarily require that you have previous experience. For more information on kayaking tours, see the destination chapters.

Independent travellers planning extended trips should check weather forecasts, watch the tides and currents, and wear a life jacket, hat and plenty of sunscreen. Ideally, take a signalling device, mobile phone or radio and always let someone know of your plans.

Surfing

It is believed that surfing has existed in Fiji for hundreds of years. Surfing reefs over warm, crystal-clear, turquoise-blue water is a very special experience. The majority of Fiji's rideable breaks are on offshore reefs that require boat trips. When choosing accommodation, also consider the price of getting to the surf. The best surf spots are along Viti Levu's south coast and in the Mamanuca Group. There are also breaks at Kadavu and Taveuni. The dry season (May to October) is the best time to go due to low pressures bringing in big surf. Keen surfers should bring their own board.

You should be aware that Fijian villages usually have fishing rights to, and basically own, adjacent reefs. Some resorts pay the villages for exclusive surfing rights, which has led to disputes between competing surfing and diving operations. If you would like to explore lesser-known areas you will need to respect local traditions and seek permission from the local villagers.

Riding the dangerous southern Mamanuca reef-breaks should only be attempted by experienced surfers. If you want to stay at the popular surf resorts on Tavarua and Namotu, book well in advance. See the boxed text, p117 for a summary of Fiji's major breaks. Some lesser-known spots include: Suva, which has a reef-break at the lighthouse – you need a boat to get there; Kadavu's Cape Washington, which has good surf but no place to stay; and Lavena Point on Taveuni, which also has rideable though inconsistent waves.

Click onto www.globalsurfers.com/fiji .cfm for more useful information.

Visiting Villages

Many tours include a village visit in their activities. Some villages have become affected by busloads of tourists parading through their backyards every other day and the *sevusevu* ceremony and *meke* (traditional dance) can seem somewhat put on. Other village tours, especially those run by the villagers, are smaller in scale with perhaps not so much going on; however, the whole experience can feel much more genuine.

The village tours to Lovoni (p173) on Ovalau are fantastic and Navala (p144), in Viti Levu's highlands, is one of Fiji's most picturesque villages. Avoid visiting villages on Sunday, as it is considered a day for church and rest. Refer to p36 for information on village etiquette.

BUSINESS HOURS

Fijians are not known for their punctuality and usually adhere to 'Fiji time'. Post offices and most shops and cafés open between 8am and 9am and close at around 5pm weekdays, or 1pm on Saturday. Banks are open 9am to 4pm on weekdays, though some close at 3pm on Friday. A few Internet cafés and shops are open for limited hours on Sunday but the general rule is to assume everything will be closed. For indigenous Fijians it is a day for church, rest and spending time with family.

Restaurants generally open for lunch (11am to 2pm) and dinner (6pm to 9pm or 10pm) from Monday to Saturday as well as dinner on Sunday. Many remain open from 11am to 10pm. Bars in Suva and Nadi are open from late afternoon to around midnight on weeknights but extend their hours into early morning from Thursday to Saturday. Resort bars have more flexible schedules and cater to guests' drinking preferences (ie daiquiris at 10am).

Government offices are open from 8am to 4.30pm Monday to Thursday, and 8am to 4pm Friday.

Many places in Fiji close for lunch from 1pm to 2pm.

CHILDREN

Fiji is a major family destination and is very child-friendly. Many resorts cater well for kids, with babysitting, cots and high chairs, organised activities and children's pools. However, smaller exclusive resorts tend not to accept children or at least relegate them to a specific period during the year. Some resorts are on multiple levels and sand paths, which make using prams and strollers difficult.

Lonely Planet's *Travel with Children* has useful advice on family travel, and has a section on Fiji.

Practicalities

Travelling around with kids in Fiji is fairly easy. The large chain car-rental companies can provide baby seats, but local companies and taxis don't. If you intend to take public transport, a backpack for transporting infants is a good idea. Also bear in mind that local buses have bench seating, no seat belts and can be fairly cramped and so may not be particularly conducive to travelling with small children or babies.

Many restaurants in cities and touristed areas such as the Coral Coast on Viti Levu and well-equipped resorts in the Yasawas and Mamanucas have high chairs. Similarly, midrange and top-end resorts in these areas, as well as self-contained accommodation in and around the main cities can provide cots, although the further you get from the beaten track in Fiji the more remote this option will be.

Long-life milk is readily available, as is bottled spring water and fruit juice. Fiji is a fairly conservative and demure society and while breast feeding is common among the local population you'll seldom see it so take their example and find a private place to do so. Nappies, formula and sterilising solution are available in pharmacies and supermarkets in the main cities and towns, but if you are travelling to remote areas or islands, take your own supplies. Consider using cloth nappies wherever you can. Many small boats don't carry enough life jackets and never have child-sized ones; if you're planning to island hop, you might want to consider bringing your own Coast Guard approved inflatable life jackets.

Children are valued in Fiji, and childcare is seen as the responsibility of the extended family and the community. Everyone will want to talk with your kids and invite them to join activities or visit homes. Babies and toddlers are especially popular – they may tire of having their cheeks pinched! Fijian

DIRECTORY

men play a large role in caring for children and babies, so don't be surprised if they pay a lot of attention to your kids. Fijian children are expected to be obedient and spend lots of time playing outdoors. Backtalk and showing off is seen as disruptive to the fabric of the community, so when visiting a village, try to curb any crying, tantrums and noisy behaviour.

For ideas on keeping the kids content, see the boxed text, p80.

CLIMATE CHARTS

Fiji's wet season is from November to April, with the heaviest rains falling between December and mid-April. Fiji has a mild average temperature of 25°C, however it can climb to above 30°C in summer (December and January) and sink to 18°C in winter (July and August). See p17 for information about the best time to visit Fiji.

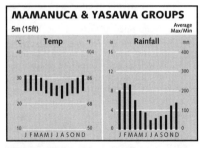

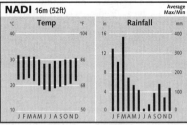

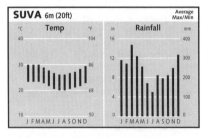

CUSTOMS

If you are travelling with expensive camera or computer equipment, carry a receipt to avoid possible hassles with your customs people when arriving home.

Visitors can leave Fiji without paying VAT on: up to $400 per person of duty-assessed goods; 2L of liqueur or spirits, or 4L of wine or beer; 500 cigarettes or 500g of cigars or tobacco, or all three under a total of 500g; and personal effects.

Pottery shards, turtle shells, coral and trochus shells and giant clamshells cannot be taken out of the country without a permit. You can bring as much currency as you like into the country but you need to declare any amount over $10,000 and you can't take out any more than you brought in.

Importation of vegetable matter, seeds, animals, meat or dairy produce is prohibited without a licence from the Ministry of Agriculture & Fisheries. If you're taking a domestic pet in you need to write to the **Director Quarantine Section** (☎ fax 330 5043; PO Box 18360, Suva) and send them your animal's details including an up-to-date vet report. The department will send you a licence or approval to take your pet into Fiji. Otherwise staff will quarantine your pet on arrival for a few weeks.

DANGERS & ANNOYANCES

Fiji is still a pretty safe place for travellers. When you're in Nadi or Suva, though, do not walk around at night, even in a group, as muggings are common. Locals catch cabs after dark in these cities and you should do the same. Don't hitchhike; while it's commonly done by locals, as a foreigner, you're a sitting duck for muggers. As a precaution, use a moneybelt and keep your valuables in a safe place.

While it's unlikely that you'll be robbed, it does happen, so try to keep all valuables out of sight and lock your door while you're out or sleeping. Most resorts have a safe where you can store your moneybelt. You can also avoid becoming utterly destitute by stashing a small amount of cash or a couple of travellers cheques in a separate place to where the bulk is stored.

As you exit customs at Nadi airport you'll likely be swarmed by touts who will do their best to get you into their shuttle van and on the road to their employer's resort. It's advisable to have at least your first night of accommodation booked, but if you're unsure of where you want to stay and want to avoid these mobs while you consider your options, head to the FVB desk (p77).

Sword sellers are not as common as they used to be, but if anyone becomes overly friendly, wants to know your life story and begins carving your name on a long piece of wood, just walk away, even if they pursue you claiming that you have to pay for the rubbishy item. If you are travelling for an extended period you may tire of being asked where you are staying. While this is often just innocent conversation, it can also be a way of judging how much you're going to be charged for dinner. Male travellers in particular are likely to be approached and asked if they want marijuana (see p250).

If you are unlucky enough to be caught in a natural disaster such as a cyclone or flood, ask locals for advice on where to seek protection from the elements.

If driving there are some road hazards you should be aware of; see p264 for more information.

Contrary to Fiji's image promoted overseas, many beaches, especially on the large islands, aren't great for swimming. The fringing coral reefs often become too shallow at low tide. Avoid swimming or snorkelling alone and be very careful of currents and tidal changes. Always seek local advice on conditions. For safety precautions regarding marine life see p270.

DISABLED TRAVELLERS

In Pacific countries disabled people are simply part of the community, looked after by family where necessary. In some cities there are schools for disabled children but access facilities, such as ramps, lifts and Braille, are rare. Many resorts are designed with multiple levels, lots of stairs and sandy paths, making them difficult for some people to use. Buses do not have wheelchair access and pavements have high kerbs.

Nevertheless, people will go out of their way to give you assistance when you need it. Airports and some hotels and resorts have reasonable access; before booking a particular resort, check if it suits your needs. Access-friendly resorts include Tokatoka Resort Hotel and the Beachside Resort in

Nadi and Treasure Island Resort in the Mamanucas. On the Coral Coast, Hideaway Resort will also cater to special needs.

Organisations

For pretrip planning advice try the Internet and disabled people's associations in your home country. The **Fiji Disabled People's Association** (Map p122; ☎ 331 1203; fax 332 1428; 355 Waimanu Rd, Suva) may also be able to provide advice.

Australian-based **Travelaffare Hove** (☎ in Australia 08-8278 7470; www.e-bility.com/travelaffare) can assist disabled people with information on international holidays, including those to Fiji.

DISCOUNT CARDS

STA Travel and other student-travel agencies give discounts on international airfares to full-time students who have an International Student Identity Card (ISIC). Application forms are available at these travel agencies. Student discounts are occasionally given for entry fees, restaurants and accommodation in Fiji. You can also use the student health service at the University of the South Pacific (USP) in Suva.

Several backpacker resorts also accept VIP cards. Click onto www.vipbackpackers .com to purchase a card and find out about discounts.

We didn't come across any instances where people with seniors' cards received any discounts.

EMBASSIES & CONSULATES

It's important to understand what your own embassy – the embassy of the country of which you are a citizen – can and can't do to help you if you get into trouble. Generally speaking, it won't be much help in emergencies if the trouble you're in is remotely your own fault. Remember that you are bound by the laws of the country you are in. Your embassy will not be sympathetic if you end up in jail after committing a crime locally, even if such actions are legal in your own country.

In genuine emergencies you might get some assistance, but only if other channels have been exhausted. For example, if you need to get home urgently, a free ticket home is exceedingly unlikely – the embassy would expect you to have insurance. If all your money and documents are stolen, the embassy might assist with getting a new

DIRECTORY

passport, but a loan for onward travel is out of the question.

Fijian Embassies & Consulates

Fiji has diplomatic representation in the following countries.

Australia (☎ 02-6260 5115; fhc@cyberone.com.au; 19 Beale Cres, Deakin, Canberra, ACT 2600)

Belgium (☎ 02-736 9050; www.fijiembassy.be; 66 Av de Cortenburg, Boite Postale 7, Brussels 1040)

Canada (☎ 613-233-9252; Suite 750, 130 Slatter St, Ottawa, KIP 6E2)

Japan (☎ 813-3587 2038; www.fijiembassy.jp; 14th fl, Noa Bldg, 3-5, 2 Chome Azabudai, Minato-Ku, Tokyo 106)

New Zealand (☎ 04-473 5401; fax 04-499 1011; 31 Pipitea St, Thorndon, Wellington)

UK (☎ 020-7584 3661; www.fijihighcommission.org.uk; 34 Hyde Park Gate, London SW7 5DN)

USA (☎ 202-337-8320; www.fijiembassy.org; Suite 240, 2233 Wisconsin Ave, NW, Washington, DC 20007)

Embassies & Consulates in Fiji

The following countries have diplomatic representation in Fiji. All embassies are in Suva.

Australia (Map p119; ☎ 338 2211; 37 Princes Rd, Tamavua)

China (Map p119; ☎ 330 0251; 147 Queen Elizabeth Dr)

European Union (Map p122; ☎ 331 3633; 4th fl, Fiji Development Bank Centre, Victoria Pde)

Federated States of Micronesia (Map p122; ☎ 330 4566; 37 Loftus St)

France (Map p122; ☎ 331 2233; 7th fl, Dominion House, Thomson St)

Japan (Map p122; ☎ 330 2122; 2nd fl, Dominion House, Thomson St)

Korea (Map p122; ☎ 330 0977; 8th fl, Vanua House, Victoria Pde)

Malaysia (Map p122; ☎ 331 2166; 5th fl, Air Pacific House, Butt St)

Nauru (Map p122; ☎ 331 3566; 7th fl, Ratu Sukuna House)

New Zealand (Map p122; ☎ 331 1422; 10th fl, Reserve Bank Bldg, Pratt St, Suva)

Tuvalu (Map p122; ☎ 330 1355; 16 Gorrie St)

UK (Map p122; ☎ 322 9100; Victoria House, 47 Gladstone Rd)

USA (Map p122; ☎ 331 4466; 31 Loftus St)

Canadians have access to an Honorary Consul; **Mr Janna Bai Vyas** (Map p76; ☎ 972 2400; Nadi airport, Nadi).

FESTIVALS & EVENTS
February or March

Hindu Holi (Festival of Colours) People squirt coloured water at each other either late in February or early March; mostly in Lautoka.

March or April

Ram Naumi (Birth of Lord Rama) A Hindu religious festival and party on the shores of Suva Bay during late March or early April. Worshippers wade into the water and throw flowers.

Fiji International Jazz Festival Three-day jazz festival showcasing musicians from around the world. Held early to mid-April along the Coral Coast.

July

Bula Festival One of Fiji's biggest festivals – held in Nadi with rides, music, shows and the crowning of 'Miss Bula'.

August

Fiji Ocean Swim (www.manafiji.com/swim2.htm) International swim event attracting athletes from all over the world who race along a 3km course of ocean at Mana island.

Hibiscus Festival Held in Suva, with floats, food stalls, fire-walking, fair rides and the crowning of 'Miss Hibiscus'.

Hindu Ritual Fire Walking Performed by southern Indians in many temples, including Suva's Mariamma Temple (p109).

September

Fiji Regatta Week (www.musketcovefiji.com) Annual regatta luring avid yachties from around the world. Held at Musket Cove.

Lautoka's Sugar Festival Lautoka comes alive with fun fairs, parades and the crowning of the Sugar Queen.

October or November

Diwali (Festival of Lights) Hindus worship Lakshmi (the goddess of wealth and prosperity); houses are decorated and business is settled. Candles and lanterns are set on doorsteps to light the way for the god. Held in late October or early to mid-November.

Ram Leela (Play of Rama) Primarily a Hindu festival, theatrical performances celebrate the life of the god-king Rama and his return from exile. It's held at the Mariamman Temple (in Vunivau, near Labasa) around the first week of October, and has been celebrated here for more than 100 years.

South Pacific World Music Festival Acclaimed Fijian and international musicians treat Savusavu to five days of global harmony. Held in late November.

Armistice Day Also known as Remembrance Day, Suva observes a minute's silence at 11am on 11 November, although sometimes it might actually be at 10.50am, depending on the accuracy of the clocks.

FOOD

Dining options in this book are sometimes listed in order of options; ie Restaurants, Cafés & Quick Eats and Self-Catering. Listings under each category are in order of preference.

Budget travellers can pay around $10 for a meal, although quick-eat options such as bakeries and cheap curry joints are plentiful and with a self-catered meal per day travellers on the cheap can get by on spending $10 to $15 all up. Midrange travellers can expect to pay $10 to $25 for lunch or dinner at a good café or restaurant. In the cities and upmarket resorts fussy palates are catered for with some excellent cuisine (seafood in particular) and meals tend to cost anywhere from $25 to $50.

See p66 for more information about food and drink in Fiji.

GAY & LESBIAN TRAVELLERS

Fiji's constitution states that discrimination must not occur on the basis of sexual orientation and, precoup, Chaudhry's government was all for legalising homosexual activity. However, this sentiment evoked a heated reaction from the present conservative and very Christian government. In 2002 the debate of possibly legalising homosexuality was once again sparked when a new Family Law bill was put forward. Sadly, this stirred greater hostility and two prominent gay men (the Red Cross leader John Scott and his partner) were murdered in July 2002.

There is some indication of changing attitudes in the community, though. A large number of openly gay men work in the hospitality industry, and some nightclubs in Lautoka, Nadi and Suva are gay-tolerant, if not outwardly gay-friendly. Furthermore, in 2005 the Fijian High Court acquitted two gay men who were previously convicted and sentenced for having a sexual relationship. The Judge who gave the ruling also urged the Fijian Law Commission to address reform in legislation regarding homosexuality in Fiji.

It's important to remember, however, that sodomy and other homosexual acts remain illegal in Fiji and as such, the police have the right to arrest and prosecute on these grounds. Public displays of affection are considered offensive in Fiji in general; as a gay or lesbian couple, the risks of receiving unwanted attention for outwardly homosexual behaviour are high. But gay couples who are relatively private are extremely unlikely to have any troubles in Fiji. Gay singles should exercise some caution; don't give anyone an excuse to even think you are paying for sex, and be very careful

not to provide the impression you are after young Fijian men.

Two useful international websites are www.qrd.org and www.planetout.com.

HOLIDAYS

Fijians celebrate a variety of holidays and festivals; for details of the latter, see opposite. New Year's Day is celebrated all over Fiji: in villages, festivities can last a week or even the whole month of January. There is also a day commemorating the man considered Fiji's greatest statesman, Ratu Sir Lala Sukuna.

Public Holidays

Annual public holidays include:

New Year's Day 1 January
Easter (Good Friday & Easter Monday) March/April
Prophet Mohammed's Birthday April
National Youth Day May
Ratu Sir Lala Sukuna Day First Monday in June
Queen's Birthday Mid-June
Constitution Day July
Birth of Lord Krishna August/September
Fiji Day (Independence Day) Early October
Diwali Festival October/November
Christmas Day 25 December
Boxing Day 26 December

School Holidays

School holidays in Fiji, Australia and New Zealand can have an impact on accommodation availability in Fiji. In Fiji they generally last for two weeks from late April to early to mid-May and mid-August to early September. Summer holidays run from early December to late January.

For details on school holidays in Australia and New Zealand, click onto www .school-holidays.com.au and www.minedu .govt.nz.

INSURANCE

Having a travel-insurance policy to cover theft, loss and medical problems is a very good idea. There are many policies available and your travel agent will be able to recommend one. Some policies offer lower and higher medical-expense options but the higher ones are mainly for countries such as the USA, which have extremely high medical costs. Check the small print. You may prefer a policy that pays doctors or hospitals direct rather than you having to pay on the spot and claim later. If you have to claim later make sure you keep all the documentation. See p266 for more information.

Some policies specifically exclude so-called 'dangerous activities', which can include diving, motorcycling and even hiking. If you're planning to dive it's best to purchase either comprehensive cover or pay extra for this activity; see p271. A motorcycle licence acquired in Fiji may not be valid under some policies.

Check that the policy covers ambulances and an emergency flight home. The Australian Department of Foreign Affairs & Trade warns travellers that some insurance companies will not pay claims that arise when travellers have disregarded the government's travel advice.

Worldwide cover to travellers from more than 44 countries is available online at www .lonelyplanet.com/travel_services.

INTERNET ACCESS

Internet cafés are fairly prolific in Suva, Lautoka and Nadi and competition means that you can jump online with broadband access for $0.06 to $0.10 per minute. Budget resorts in Nadi also have Internet access. Outside of the urban centres access is more limited and pricier ($0.10 to $0.20 per minute). Setting up an Internet-based email account is the easiest and most affordable way of keeping in touch while you're on the road.

If you're carrying your own laptop and are in the country for a while you can sign up to a dial-up account with a service provider such as **Connect** (www.connect.com.fj). Many midrange and top-end resorts have phone lines, so you simply need to plug your computer in.

Wireless Internet access (wi-fi) is a recent phenomenon to Fiji thanks to **Unwired Fiji** (☎ 327 5040; www.unwired.com.fj). It enables users to connect to the Internet without the use of a phone line (but you'll need to purchase a special modem from them).

LEGAL MATTERS

The only drug you are likely to come across is marijuana. It's illegal; don't seek it out or buy it as the risk is too high if caught. It is not uncommon for drug users in Fiji to be imprisoned in the psychiatric hospital. It's also illegal to drink and drive. Refer also to p249 for information on gay and lesbian legal restrictions.

Most travellers avoid any run-ins with the local authorities. If you are arrested, though, you have the right to contact your embassy or consulate, which will be allowed to provide you with legal representation but can do little else.

MAPS

The best place to buy maps of the Fiji islands is the **Map Shop** (Map p122; ☎ 321 1395; Rm 10, Department of Lands & Surveys, Government Bldgs) in Suva. It sells big (1:50,000) and detailed topographic maps of each island or island group, as well as maps of Suva.

Bookshops sometimes stock town maps, and some tourist brochures also have simple town maps. At the FVB, or specialist book and map shops overseas, you can usually purchase the latest Hema map of *Fiji*. Specialist marine charts are usually available at Fijian ports but are expensive; try to buy them overseas.

MONEY

The local currency is the Fiji dollar ($); it's fairly stable relative to Australian and New Zealand dollars. See inside front cover for exchange rates. All prices quoted herein are in Fiji dollars unless otherwise specified.

The dollar is broken down into 100 cents. Bank notes come in denominations of $50, $20, $10, $5 and $2. There are coins to the value of $1, $0.50, $0.20, $0.10, $0.05, $0.02 and $0.01. Even though Fiji is now a republic, notes and coins still have a picture of England's Queen Elizabeth II on one side.

It's good to have a few options for accessing money – take a credit card, a debit card, some travellers cheques and a small amount of foreign currency. The best currencies to carry are Australian, New Zealand or US dollars, which can be exchanged at all banks.

Before you head out to remote parts of Fiji, check in the appropriate chapter to make sure you can access money, exchange currency or change travellers cheques.

ATMs

ATMs are common in major urban areas and most accept the main international debit cards including Cirrus and Maestro. The ANZ bank has an ATM at Nadi International Airport and you'll find more in town at Nadi and Suva. There's also one in Savusavu,

DIRECTORY

but have a backup plan (such as travellers cheques) in case it's out of order. Although they are more commonplace, you won't find ATMs in remote areas, so plan ahead.

Credit Cards

Restaurants, shops, midrange to top-end hotels, car-rental agencies, tour and travel agents will usually accept all major credit cards. Visa, Amex and MasterCard are widely used. Some resorts charge an additional 5% for payment by credit card. Cash advances are available through credit cards at most banks in larger towns.

Tipping & Bargaining

Tipping is not expected or encouraged in Fiji; however, if you feel that the service is worth it, tips are always appreciated. At many resorts you can drop a tip in the 'Staff Christmas Fund' jar.

Indigenous Fijians generally do not like to bargain, however it's customary in Indo-Fijian stores, especially in Nadi and Suva. Indo-Fijian shop owners and taxi drivers consider it bad luck to lose their first customer of the day, so you can expect an especially hard sales pitch in the morning.

Travellers Cheques

You can change travellers cheques in most banks and exchange bureaus, and at larger hotels and duty-free shops. It's a good idea to take travellers cheques in both small and large denominations to avoid being stuck with lots of cash when leaving.

The 24-hour ANZ bank at Nadi International Airport charges $2 on each transaction. Other banks and exchange bureaus don't normally charge a fee.

POST

Post Fiji (www.postfiji.com) is generally quick with its actual delivery (if a little slow at the counter) and has offices throughout the country.

To mail a letter within Fiji costs $0.18. Postcards sent internationally cost $0.27, while letters (up to 30g) cost $0.31.

Sending mail is straightforward; by the time you've reached the front of the queue, you'll know the process by heart. Surface mail is cheaper but slow; airmail can usually make it to Australia or New Zealand within three days and Europe or North America within a week. If you're really in a hurry, there's an international express-mail service available through the main post offices.

It's possible to receive mail at poste restante counters in all major post offices. Mail is held for up to two months without a charge. It's also possible to receive faxes at **Fintel** (Fiji International Telecommunications; Map p122; ☎ 331 2933; 158 Victoria Pde) in Suva and major post offices (see p252).

SHOPPING

The main tourist centres of Nadi, the Coral Coast and Suva have lots of handicraft shops. Savusavu (on Vanua Levu) and Lautoka are quieter and the salespeople are less pushy. You can also buy interesting handicrafts direct at villages, particularly woven goods and carvings.

Traditional artefacts, such as war clubs, spears and chiefly cannibal forks, are popular souvenirs. So too are *kava* (*yaqona*; a Fijian narcotic drink) bowls of various sizes (with miniature ones for salt and pepper), woven pandanus mats, baskets from Kioa, sandalwood or coconut soap, and *masi* (bark cloth) cloth in the form of wall hangings, covered books and postcards. Specialties from Taveuni and Ovalau are 'Bula Bears' – stuffed, *masi*-patterned teddies that are quite cute. Pottery can be a good buy – if you can get it home in one piece. Don't buy any products derived from endangered species such as turtle and avoid the temptation of buying sea shells. Also be cautious about buying wooden artefacts. A label reading 'Treated Wood' doesn't guarantee an absence of borers. Inspect items closely for holes or other marks; otherwise you may end up paying more for quarantine in your own country than you did for the actual piece.

Clothing shops in Suva and Nadi have *bula* shirts (a *masi*- or floral-design shirt) and fashion items by local designers. There are also vibrant saris and Indian jewellery on sale. Fijian ceramic jewellery is sold in the Government Crafts Centre in Suva.

The shop at **Fiji Museum** (Map p122; ☎ 331 5944; Ratu Cakobau Rd) in Suva has some interesting books, posters and postcards.

TELEPHONE & FAX

There are no area codes within Fiji. To dial a number in Fiji, dial the country code (☎ 679) followed by the local number. To use

International Direct Dial (IDD), dial ☎ 00 plus the country code.

You'll find a phone in most midrange and top-end hotel rooms. While local calls are often free, hefty surcharges are added onto long-distance calls. **Fintel** (Map p122; ☎ 331 2933; 158 Victoria Pde); in downtown Suva, also provides an international phone service.

Be aware that domestic calls are charged according to time. Rates on public phones are \$0.20 per 10 minutes for a local call; around \$0.20 per 45 seconds between neighbouring towns; and \$0.20 for each 15 seconds for more distant calls (eg Nadi to Suva or between islands). Calls to mobile phones are more expensive (around \$0.80 per minute). Mobile numbers in Fiji generally start with a ☎ 9. Collect calls are also more expensive and, when using operator assistance, there's a minimum charge of three minutes plus a surcharge of \$1.13. Outer islands are linked by cable and satellite to worldwide networks.

You can send and receive faxes from major post offices. If you're faxing internationally, try Fintel in Suva. At post offices, incoming faxes cost \$1.20 per page and sending a local/regional/international fax costs \$1.65/9.65/12.15 per page. Additional pages, though, are usually a little cheaper. Check out the website of **Post Fiji** (www.postfiji .com) for offices offering fax services.

Mobile Phones

Vodaphone (www.vodafone.com.fj) is the only mobile phone company in Fiji. It operates a GSM digital service and has roaming agreements with Vodafone in Australia, New Zealand and the UK as well as Optus in Australia. Ask for rates charged in Fiji for your mobile-phone calls before you leave home – you may end up paying international rates for local calls. Mobile phones can be rented from some car-rental agencies.

Phonecards

The cheapest way to phone home is by direct dial with a public phonecard; as they have a limited credit, it's also a good way to stop your relatives from chatting away your savings. Phonecards can be purchased at post offices, newsagents and some pharmacies and come in denominations of \$3, \$5, \$10, \$20 and \$50. You'll find public phones outside post offices but they're generally just

INTERNATIONAL PHONE CODES	
Country	**Code**
Australia	☎ 61
Canada	☎ 1
France	☎ 33
French Polynesia	☎ 689
Germany	☎ 49
Japan	☎ 81
New Zealand	☎ 64
Tonga	☎ 676
UK	☎ 44
USA	☎ 1
Vanuatu	☎ 678

for décor (they're rarely functioning). You'll also find them at resorts and around town.

For international calls, the cheapest calling cards are 'Call the World For Cheap' cards, available from shops in urban centres.

TIME

Fiji is 12 hours ahead of GMT/UTC. When it's noon in Suva, corresponding times elsewhere are as follows:

City	Time
Same Day	
Sydney	10am
Auckland	noon
Honolulu	2pm
Previous Day	
London	midnight
Los Angeles	5pm
New York	8pm

Subtract one hour from these times if the other country does not have daylight savings in place. See the World Time Zones map (p291) for more information.

TOURIST INFORMATION

The **Fiji Visitors Bureau** (FVB; www.bulafiji.com) is the primary tourist information body in Fiji. The head office in Fiji is in Nadi; **FVB** (Map p76; ☎ 672 2433; www.bulafiji.com; Suite 107, Colonial Plaza, Namaka) and there is also a **Suva office** (Map p122; ☎ 330 2433; www.bulafiji.com; cnr Thomson & Scott Sts).

The **South Pacific Tourism Organisation** (Map p122; ☎ 330 4177; www.spto.org; 3rd fl, Dolphin Plaza, cnr Loftus St & Victoria Pde, Suva) promotes cooperation between the South Pacific island nations for the development of tourism in the region. Check out its website for a Pacific Islands travel directory.

VISAS & TRAVEL PERMITS

You'll need to have an onward ticket and a passport valid for at least three months longer than your intended stay to get a visa. A free tourist visa for four months is granted on arrival to citizens of more than 100 countries, including: most countries belonging to the British Commonwealth, North America, much of South America and Western Europe, India, Indonesia, Israel, Japan, Mexico, Philippines, Russia, Samoa, Solomon Islands, South Korea, Tonga, Tuvalu, Vanuatu and many others. (Check www.fiji.gov .fj/publish/fiji_faqs.shtml for a full list.)

Nationals from countries excluded from the list will have to apply for visas through a Fijian embassy prior to arrival.

Those entering Fiji by boat are subject to the same visa requirements as those arriving by plane. Yachts can only enter through the designated ports of Suva, Lautoka, Savusavu and Levuka. Yachts have to be cleared by immigration and customs, and are prohibited from visiting any outer islands before doing so. Yachties need to apply to the **Ministry for Fijian Affairs** (www.fiji.gov.fj/publish/m_fijian_affairs .shtml) for special written authorisation to visit the Lau Group.

Visitors cannot partake in political activity or study, and work permits are needed if you intend to live and work in Fiji for more than six months. Foreign journalists will require a work visa if they spend more than 14 days in Fiji (see right for more details).

Visa Extensions

Tourist visas can be extended for up to six months by applying through the **Immigration Department** (Map p122; ☎ 331 2672; Government Bldg, Suva). You'll need to show an onward ticket, proof of sufficient funds and your passport must be valid for three months after your proposed departure.

WOMEN TRAVELLERS

Fiji is a fairly male-dominant society, but it is unlikely that solo women travellers will experience any difficulties as a result. Be aware, however, that men in this environment may view the influence of Western women as a threat to their own position and therefore might discourage their wives from talking with you.

If you're travelling alone, you may experience whistles and stares but you're unlikely to feel threatened. Nevertheless, some men will assume lone females are fair game and several female readers have complained of being harassed or ripped off, particularly in touristy areas.

Generally speaking though, women travellers will find Fijian men friendly and helpful, especially if you are travelling with a male partner. You'll be treated with more respect by both men and women if you follow the local dress codes (see p36).

For information on health matters, see p268.

WORK

Those travelling to Fiji for reasons other than a holiday must declare this on their arrival card. They will be given a visa for 14 days and will have to apply for subsequent extensions. Those wishing to live or work in Fiji for more than six months will require a working visa. These can be difficult to get and need to be organised at least two months prior to travelling to Fiji. Application forms can be obtained from any Fijian embassy and must be completed and sent by the applicant to the immigration authorities in Fiji. Your application will normally only be approved if supported by a prospective employer and if a person with your skills cannot be found locally. Unemployment is a problem in Fiji and consequently finding work once you're in the country is difficult. If you want to conduct business in Fiji, contact the **Fiji Trade & Investment Board** (Map p122; ☎ 331 5988; www.ftib.org.fj; 6th fl, Civic Tower, Government Bldgs, Victoria Pde, Suva).

Transport

CONTENTS

Getting There & Away	**254**
Entering the Country	254
Air	254
Sea	258
Getting Around	**259**
Air	259
Bicycle	260
Boat	260
Bus	262
Car & Motorcycle	262
Hitching	264
Local Transport	264
Taxi	264
Tours	264

GETTING THERE & AWAY

Centrally situated in the South Pacific, Fiji is one of the main airline hubs of the Pacific region (Hawaii is the other). Many travellers visit Fiji on round-the-world (RTW) tickets or on a stopover between North America and Australia or New Zealand. Most agents

---

THINGS CHANGE...

The information in this chapter is particularly vulnerable to change. You should check directly with the airline or a travel agent to make sure you understand how a fare (and the ticket you may buy) works. See the airline websites listed for up-to-date fares and information. In addition, the travel industry is highly competitive and there are many lurks and perks.

The upshot of this is that you should get opinions, quotes and advice from as many airlines and travel agents as possible before you part with your hard-earned cash. The details given in this chapter should be regarded as pointers and are not a substitute for your own careful, up-to-date research.

---

will allow those visiting Fiji on a package deal to extend their stay on either side of the accommodation package.

Flights and tours can be booked online at www.lonelyplanet.com/travel_services.

ENTERING THE COUNTRY

Make sure you have a valid passport and, if necessary, an appropriate visa on arrival in Fiji. See p253 for more details. Immigration procedures are straightforward and it's highly unlikely that travellers will experience difficulty.

In general, visitors do not need to show immunisation cards on entry, although it's always wise to check with your local authorities before leaving in case this changes.

AIR
Airports & Airlines

Most visitors to Fiji arrive at Nadi International Airport, situated 9km north of central Nadi. A few international flights land at Nausori airport near Suva.

On arrival you will be greeted by a sea of smiling faces and guitar serenading. Most of these people will be representing local accommodation or the many travel agencies in the airport.

Nadi International Airport has a 24-hour ANZ bank with currency exchange. There are many travel agencies, airline offices and car-rental offices in the arrivals area, as well as a post office, cafeteria, restaurant, duty-free shop, newsagency and luggage storage area. Luggage storage costs $3 to $6 per day.

Nausori International Airport, about 23km northeast of downtown Suva, hosts Air Fiji flights to Tuvalu, and Air Pacific and Qantas flights direct to and from Sydney. Air Pacific also flies to New Zealand. Otherwise the airport is mostly used for domestic flights.

The following international airlines fly to and from Fiji. Phone numbers are those in Fiji unless otherwise stated.

Air Fiji (airline code PC; ☎ 672 2521, 331 3666; www .airfiji.com.fj/index.cfm; hub Nausori & Nadi, Fiji)

Air Nauru (airline code ON; ☎ 672 2795, 331 2377/3731; www.airnauru.com.au; hub Nauru)

Air New Zealand (airline code NZ; ☎ 331 3100; www .airnz.co.nz; hub Auckland, New Zealand)

SPECIAL NEEDS

If you have special needs of any sort – you've broken a leg, are vegetarian, in a wheelchair, taking the baby, terrified of flying – let the airline know as soon as possible so that it can make arrangements accordingly. You should remind staff when you reconfirm your booking (at least 72 hours before departure) and again when you check in at the airport. It may also be worth ringing airlines before you make your booking to find out how they can handle your particular needs.

Children under two travel for 10% of the standard fare (or free, on some airlines) as long as they don't occupy a seat. They don't get a baggage allowance either. 'Skycots' should be provided by the airline if requested in advance; these will take a child weighing up to about 10kg. Children aged two to 12 years can usually occupy a seat for half to two-thirds of the full fare and get a baggage allowance.

You can take bicycles to pieces and put them in a bike bag or box as luggage, but (if it's allowed) it's much easier to wheel your bike to the check-in desk, where it should be treated as a piece of baggage. You may have to remove the pedals and secure the handlebars sideways so that it takes up less space in the aircraft's hold. It's best to check all this with the airline well in advance, preferably before you pay for your ticket.

Many travellers also bring surfboards into Fiji. This is easy enough as long as you have a suitable case or bag. Be prepared to pay a hefty excess baggage fee also.

TRANSPORT

Air Pacific (airline code FJ; ☎ 672 0888, 330 4388; www.airpacific.com.fj; airline hub Nadi, Fiji)

Air Vanuatu (airline code NF; ☎ 672 2521, 331 3666/3055; www.airvanuatu.com; hub Port Vila, Vanuatu)

Aircalin (airline code SB; ☎ 672 2145; www.aircalin.nc; hub Noumea, New Caledonia)

Freedom Air (airline code SJ; ☎ 0800 600 500; www.freedomair.co.nz; hub Auckland, New Zealand)

Korean Air (airline code KE; ☎ 672 1043; www.korean air.com.au; hub Seoul, Korea)

Pacific Blue (Virgin Blue International; www.flypacific blue.com; hub Brisbane, Australia)

Polynesian Airlines (airline code PH; ☎ 672 3822; www.polynesianairlines.com; hub Samoa)

Qantas Airways (airline code QF; ☎ 672 2880, 331 3888/1833; www.qantas.com.au; hub Sydney, Australia)

Royal Tongan Airlines (airline code WR; ☎ 672 4355; rtafiji@connect.com.fj; hub Apia, Tonga)

Solomon Airlines (airline code IE; ☎ 672 2831; www.solomonairlines.com.au; hub Honiara, Solomon Islands)

United Airlines (airline code UA; ☎ in Australia 131 777; www.united.com; hub Chicago, USA)

Tickets

It is always worth putting aside a few hours to research the current travel market. Talk to recent travellers, look at advertisements in newspapers and magazines, search the Internet and watch for special offers. Airlines are useful for supplying information on routes and timetables; however, except at times of airline ticketing wars, they usually do not supply the cheapest tickets. For straightforward return tickets, online booking agencies tend to offer the best deals.

High-season travel to Fiji is between April and October as well as the peak Christmas and New Year period. Airfares peak between April and June and in December and January. If you book well enough in advance, however, it's possible to escape the seasonal price variations.

Fijian departure tax is $30, payable at the airport before passing through immigration. This situation is likely to change, though, and the tax may be incorporated into your ticket by the time you read this.

Recommended websites for bookings:

Cheap Flights (www.cheapflights.com) Informative site with specials, airline information and flight searches from the USA and other regions.

Cheapest Flights (www.cheapestflights.co.uk) Cheap worldwide flights from the UK.

Expedia (www.expedia.msn.com) Mainly US-related travel site.

Flight Centre International (www.flightcentre.com) Respected operator with sites for Australia, New Zealand, the UK, the USA and Canada.

Opodo (www.opodo.com) Reliable company specialising in fares from Europe.

Orbitz (www.orbitz.com) Excellent site for web-only fares.

STA (www.statravel.com) Prominent in international student travel, but you don't have to be a student; site linked to STA sites worldwide.

Travel.com (www.travel.com.au) Good site for Australian travellers.

Travelocity (www.travelocity.com) A US site that allows you to search fares (in US dollars) to/from practically anywhere.

Trip Advisor (www.tripadvisor.com) Good site for flights from the USA.

TRANSPORT

INTERCONTINENTAL (RTW) TICKETS

RTW tickets are often real bargains. One that takes in the Pacific will cost between US$1700 and US$2500, depending on where you want to stop. They are usually put together by a combination of two or more airlines and permit you to fly anywhere on their routes as long as you do not backtrack. Most tickets are valid for up to one year.

The cheaper RTW tickets usually have more restrictions such as fewer choices of where you can stop, large fees to change flight dates and mileage caps. It's also worth checking the minimum and maximum number of stops you can make and how many different airlines you can use. An alternative type of RTW ticket is one put together by a travel agent using a combination of discounted tickets.

Circle Pacific tickets use a combination of airlines to…circle the Pacific – they generally include stops in the USA, South Pacific, Southeast Asia, New Zealand and Australia. As with RTW tickets, there are advance purchase restrictions and limits to how many stopovers you can take. These fares are likely to be about 15% cheaper than RTW tickets.

Online ticket sales for RTW and Circle Pacific fares:

Airbrokers (www.airbrokers.com) A US company.
Just Fares.com (www.justfares.com) A US company.
Roundtheworld.com (www.roundtheworldflights.com) This excellent site allows you to build your own trips from the UK with up to six stops.
Usit (www.usit.ie) Irish company.
Western Air (www.westernair.co.uk) A UK company.
World Travellers' Club (www.around-the-world.com) A US company.

Asia

There are direct flights to Nadi from Japan and South Korea. Low-/high-season return airfares from Tokyo to Nadi are around ¥118,300/414,000 (US$1000/3500); from Seoul to Nadi they are about US$1700/2700. Fares are most expensive between December and January, and June and July.

Most flights to/from Southeast Asia go via Australia or New Zealand. Return airfares from Hong Kong to Nadi are around US$1400/2700 for low/high season. Most countries offer fairly competitive deals – Bangkok, Singapore and Hong Kong are good places to shop around for discount tickets.

Recommended agencies in Japan:
No 1 Travel (☎ 03-3205 6073; www.no1-travel.com)
STA Travel (☎ 03-5391 2922; www.statravel.co.jp)

Australia

Qantas, Air Pacific and Pacific Blue operate between Australia and Fiji. Qantas planes don't actually fly to Fiji but the airline sells tickets and code shares seats on Air Pacific flights. The flight time is about 4/4½ hours from Sydney/Melbourne.

Fares from Sydney or Brisbane are typically A$550/800 return for low/high season. Flights from Melbourne cost A$100 or A$150 more. The further in advance you book the cheaper your ticket is likely to be.

Agencies in Australia with specialist Fiji knowledge:
Essence Tours (☎ 07-3245 7815; info@essencetours .com.au)
Fiji & Pacific Specialist Holidays (☎ 02-9080 1600; www.pacificholidays.com.au)
Hideaway Holidays (☎ 02-8799 2500; www.hide awayholidays.com.au)
South Pacific Holidays (☎ 1300 997 287; www .tropicalfiji.com)
Talpacific Holidays (☎ 1300 137 727; www.talpacific .com)

Canada

Fiji is a popular stopover between Canada and Australia or New Zealand, and for those on RTW tickets. Air Pacific flies between Vancouver and Nadi; fares start at around C$2300 from June to November, peaking at around C$2700 between November and February. Fares from Ottawa or Toronto are C$100 to C$150 more; these generally fly via Chicago and LA.

Toronto's *Globe & Mail*, the *Montreal Gazette*, the *Toronto Sun* and the *Vancouver Sun* are good places to look for cheap fares.

Canadian-based travel agencies:
Pacesetter Travel (☎ 1800 387-8827, 604-687-3083; www.pacesettertravel.com)
Travel Cuts (☎ 866-246-9762; www.travelcuts.com) Canada's national student travel agency with offices in all major cities.

Continental Europe

Generally there is not much variation in airfares for departures from the main European cities, but deals can be had, so shop around. Expect to pay around €1400/2000 for low/high season.

Useful agencies:

Adventure Travel (www.adventure-holidays.com) German agency specialising in South Pacific travel.

BarronTravel (☎ 020-625 8600; www.barron.nl) Dutch agency operating 3 Oceans Travel, which specialises in the South Pacific.

OTU Voyages (☎ 08 20 81 78 17, 01 44 41 38 50; www .otu.fr) French network of student-travel agencies; supplies discount tickets to travellers of all ages.

Nouvelles Frontières (☎ 08 25 00 07 47; www.nouvelles -frontieres.fr)

Voyageurs du Monde (www.vdm.com)

Wereldcontact (☎ 0343-530 530; www.wereldcontact .nl) Dutch agency.

New Zealand

Air Pacific flies from Auckland, Wellington and Christchurch to both Suva and Nadi. Air New Zealand also flies between Nadi and Auckland and has shared services on the other routes. Freedom Air flies from Christchurch, Wellington, Palmerston North and Hamilton to Nadi. From Auckland to Fiji (three hours) costs about NZ$460/730 for low/high season. Flights from Wellington and Christchurch tend to cost around NZ$200 extra with the bigger airlines, but Freedom Air offers some serious bargains on their lesser-flown routes.

Good booking agencies:

Air New Zealand (☎ 0800 737 000; www.airnewzealand.co.nz)

Flight Centre (www.flightcentre.co.nz)

Go Holidays (☎ 0800 464 646; www.goholidays.co.nz) South Pacific specialists for accommodation and packages.

House of Travel (www.houseoftravel.co.nz) Nationwide travel agency.

STA (www.statravel.co.nz)

Talpacific Holidays (☎ 09-914 8728; www.travelarrange.co.nz) South Pacific specialists.

Travel Online (☎ 0800 000 747, 09-920 6000; www .travelonline.co.nz)

Zuji (www.zuji.co.nz) Online booking service.

Pacific Countries

AIR PASSES

Intercountry flights in the Pacific can be expensive. The only really workable way to travel to more than a handful of countries is by using an air pass. Fortunately, there are lots to choose from. New deals are always coming up so it's worth checking with your travel agent or searching the Internet. Conditions apply and seating can be limited, so book early.

Polynesian Airlines (www.polynesianairlines.com) offers a number of air passes through the Pacific that take in cities on the US west coast and Australian east coast, New Zealand, and a number of South Pacific countries including Fiji, Samoa, the Cook Islands, and Tonga. Valid for up to 45 days, a Poly Pass ticket including six stops costs between US$1100 and US$1600. Passes are not valid for travel in December or January.

Air Pacific's Triangle Fare links Fiji, Samoa and Tonga for $670 (Fijian dollars). The fare is only available from North America, and travel must be completed within 60 days. You must stop in each county and can fly on Air Pacific, Polynesian Airlines or Air New Zealand flights. There are also limited offers on other Triangle Fares, such as New Zealand, Fiji and Vanuatu.

The Visit South Pacific Pass allows for travel with lots of different airlines (including Air Pacific, Aircalin and Qantas), with a minimum of two stops and a maximum of eight. Each flight costs between US$220 and US$370. The ticket covers the South Pacific as well as Australia and New Zealand.

The Qantas Boomerang pass is only available in connection with travel to/from Australia, New Zealand or Fiji from outside the region; it is not available to residents of these countries. The pass covers Fiji, Vanuatu, Tonga, Western Samoa and the Solomon Islands with a minimum of two stops and a maximum of 10. Tickets range in price, depending on how many 'zones' you cross. A flight in Zone A (up to 1200km) costs from A$160, in Zone B (1200km to 1840km) costs from A$295 and Zone C (over 1840km) costs from A$360.

UK & Ireland

London is the travel discount capital of Europe. Airline ticket discounters are known as bucket shops in the UK, and many advertise in the travel pages of the weekend broadsheets, such as the *Independent* on Saturday and the *Sunday Times*. Also check the travel section the free magazine *TNT*. A return ticket from London to Nadi costs about £850/1100 in low/high season. Some agencies to check out:

Bridge the World (☎ 0870 444 7474)

Ebookers (☎ 0870 814 0000; www.ebookers.com)

Trailfinders (☎ 0845 058 5858; www.trailfinders.co.uk)

Travel Bag (☎ 0870 814 4441; www.travelbag.co.uk)

TRANSPORT

USA

Fiji is a major stopover between the west coast of the USA and Australia or New Zealand. Fiji is about six/12 hours from Hawaii/west-coast USA. Fares from the USA vary greatly depending on season and ticket restrictions. Los Angeles to Nadi with Air New Zealand is about US$920/1300 for low/high season.

The following agents specialise in travel to Fiji and the South Pacific:

All Travel (☎ 800 300-4567, 310-312-3368; www.all -travel.com)

Fiji Travels (www.fijitravels.com)

Golden Fish Travels (☎ 877-255-7438; http://golden fishtravels.com/fiji.html)

South Pacific Direct (www.southpacificdirect.com)

Sunspots International (☎ 800 334-5623, 503-666-3893; www.sunspotsintl.com)

SEA

Travelling to Fiji by sea is difficult unless you're on a cruise ship or yacht.

Cargo Boats

Few of the shipping companies will take passengers on cargo ships and those that do will usually charge hefty rates. It is virtually impossible to leave Fiji by cargo ship unless passage has been prearranged. A useful American company is **Freighter World Cruises** (☎ 800 531-7774; www.freighterworld.com), which can organise travel on a freighter ship around the South Pacific. You could also try asking your local shipping agents, or go to the docks and personally approach the captains.

Yacht

Fiji's islands are a popular destination and stopover for yachts cruising the Pacific. The best time to sail is in the 'winter' from early November to late April when the southeasterly trade winds are blowing. During the 'summer' months (May to October), winds change direction more often and the chance of finding yourself in a storm or cyclone is greater.

Yachts need to head for the designated ports of entry at Suva, Lautoka, Levuka or Savusavu, to clear customs, immigration and quarantine. Be sure to have a certificate of clearance from the previous port of call, a crew list and passports. Before departing, you'll again need to complete clearance formalities (within 24 hours), providing in-

ISA LEI, A FIJIAN FAREWELL SONG

As your boat departs from the shore or you hike off from the village, Fijians are likely to sing you this farewell song written by a student in the early 20th century for his forbidden love, Isa. While her social standing may have separated Isa from her lovesick suitor, it couldn't keep what became Fiji's No 1 song from reaching her ears. By the time you leave Fiji, you too may well know it by heart.

Isa Isa Vulagi lasa dina
Isa Isa you are my only treasure
Nomu lako au na rarawa kina
Must you leave me so lonely and forsaken
Cava beka ko a mai cakava
As the roses will miss the sun at dawning
Nomu lako au na sega ni lasa
Every moment my heart for you is yearning

Isa lei, na noqu rarawa
Isa Lei, the purple shadows fall
Ni ko sa na gole e na mataka
Sad the morrow will dawn upon my sorrow
Bau nanuma na nodatou lasa
Oh forget not when you are far away
Mai Viti nanuma tiko ga
Precious moments from Fiji

Vanua rogo na nomuni vanua
My heart was filled with pleasure
Kena ca ni levu tu na ua
From the moment I heard your tender greeting
Lomaqu voli me'u bau butuka
Mid the sunshine we spent the hours together
Tovolea ke balavu na bua
Now so swiftly those happy hours are fleeting

bound clearance papers, your vessel's details and your next port of call. Customs must be cleared before immigration, and you must have paid all port dues and health fees. For more information see p253.

Other marinas in Fiji include Vuda Point Marina (between Nadi and Lautoka), Port Denarau (Denarau Marina), and Musket Cove Marina on Malololailai (Plantation Island) in the Mamanucas. Yachties are often looking for extra crew and people to share day-to-day costs. If you are interested, ask around the marinas and look on the noticeboards. For more details on travelling by yacht see p243.

GETTING AROUND

By using local buses, carriers (small trucks) and ferries you can get around Fiji's main islands relatively cheaply and easily. If you'd like more comfort or are short on time you can use air-conditioned express buses, rental vehicles, charter boats and small planes.

AIR

The international airports on Viti Levu, at Nadi and Nausori (near Suva), are also the main domestic hubs. Other domestic airports include Savusavu and Labasa on Vanua Levu; Matei on Taveuni; Vunisea on Kadavu; Bureta on Ovalau and; in the Mamanucas, Malololailai and Mana. Many other small islands also have airstrips. There are flights to some outer islands where there is no accommodation for tourists and an invitation is needed to visit – in some cases

it is illegal to turn up uninvited. Rotuma, Gau, Koro, Moala and Vanua Balavu, and Lakeba in Lau have airstrips but receive few visitors, while other islands such as Vatulele, Yasawa and Wakaya have their own airstrips that serve the upmarket resorts.

Airlines in Fiji

Fiji is well serviced by internal airlines, which have frequent and generally reliable flights. Some may find the light planes scary, especially if it's windy or turbulent, but the views of the islands, coral reefs and lagoons are fantastic.

Air Fiji and Sun Air have regular interisland flights by light plane. Most of Air Fiji's services operate out of Nausori, while Sun Air is based in Nadi. Sun Air often transports passengers' luggage in a separate plane, and arriving before or after your possessions is a common occurrence. Prices on routes shared by the airlines are almost identical.

Air Pacific was planning to re-enter the domestic market by 2006, with a plan to fly to Taveuni, Savusavu and other northern destinations. At the time of writing it was

FIJI AIR FARES

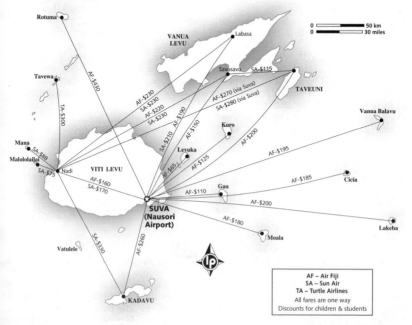

uncertain whether the airline would simply add these destinations to its route map or purchase Sun Air.

Air Fiji (☎ 331 3666; www.airfiji.com.fj) operates flights from Suva to Nadi, Kadavu, Koro, Labasa, Lakeba, Levuka, Moala, Rotuma, Savusavu, Taveuni and Vanua Balavu. From Nadi, there are flights to Suva, Labasa, Malololailai, Mana, Savusavu and Taveuni.

Sun Air (☎ 0800 672 5725, 572 3016; www.fiji.to) flies from Suva to Nadi, Labasa and Taveuni, and from Nadi to Suva, Kadavu, Labasa, Malololailai, Mana, Savusavu and Taveuni.

Air Passes

Air Fiji has a 30-day air pass for $520 (US$270). It is sold only outside Fiji in conjunction with an international air ticket. The pass includes four flights but you can have additional legs for $100 per sector. It's best to book your seats, as the small planes often fill up quickly. Children under 12 get a 25% discount and infants are charged 10%. There is a $100 predeparture cancellation fee, and reimbursement is minimal once in Fiji. If you change your mind it will cost $100 to re-issue your ticket.

Charter Services & Joyflights

Charter services and joyflights are available.

Island Hoppers (☎ 672 0410; info@helicopters.com.fj) offers transfers to most of the Mamanucas island resorts, as well as helicopter flights departing from Denarau island and Nadi airport. A flight to Malololailai by helicopter costs $210 one way per person. A 20-minute flight over the Sabeto mountain range and the gorges of Koroyanitu (Mt Evans), east of Lautoka, costs $170 per seat (four to six passengers). A 25-minute flight over the Mamanuca islands is $200 per seat and a combination of the two – the 'Islands & Highlands' trip, costs is $260 per person and lasts 35 minutes.

Turtle Airways (☎ 672 1888; reservations@turtleairways.com) has a fleet of seaplanes departing from New Town Beach or Denarau, near Nadi. As well as joyflights, it provides transfer services to the Mamanucas, Yasawas, the Fijian Resort (on the Queens Road), Pacific Harbour, Suva, Toberua Island Resort and other islands as required. Turtle Airways also charters a five-seater Cessna and a seven-seater de Havilland Canadian Beaver. Contact them for rates.

Pacific Island Seaplanes (☎ 672 5644; www.fijiseaplanes.com) also offers transfers to islands in the Mamanuca, Yasawa and Lau Groups.

BICYCLE

Fiji's larger islands have good potential for cycling, although some areas are too hilly and rugged. Viti Levu has long, flat stretches of sealed road along the scenic Coral Coast, and it is possible to cycle around the perimeter of the island by the Kings and Queens Roads.

The best time to go is the drier season (May to October), and note that the eastern sides of the larger islands receive higher rainfall. Mountain bikes are best for exploring the interior. If you intend to cycle around Fiji as a main form of transport bring your own bike, helmet, waterproof gear, repair kit and all other equipment. It is difficult to get bike parts in Fiji. Maps are available from the government **Map Shop** (Map p122; ☎ 321 1395; Rm 10, Department of Lands & Surveys) in Suva. If you wish to take a bike on a domestic flight, make sure it is demountable.

The biggest hazard is the unpredictable traffic – Fijian drivers can be pretty manic and are not used to cyclists. Avoid riding in the evening when visibility is low. Travel light but carry plenty of water – it can be hot and dusty or humid. You can usually buy coconuts and bananas from villages along the way. Storage at Nadi airport is relatively expensive; the cheapest place to store bikes is at backpacker hostels. For information on routes, see p242. For information on taking a bike on a plane, see the boxed text, p255.

Hire

Bicycles can be rented in Nadi, the Coral Coast and Ovalau and cost around $25 to $40 per day. A security deposit is not generally necessary. Wacking Stick Adventure Tours near Nadi runs mountain-bike tours (see p79). Rental bikes can be in pretty poor condition, so test the brakes and gears beforehand. Also helmets aren't provided by all operators.

BOAT

With the exception of the Mamanuca and Yasawa groups, and upmarket resort islands, often the only means of transport to and between the islands is by small local boats, especially for the backpacker resorts. Life jackets are rarely provided on the small boats and usually they have no radio-phones as well. If the weather looks ominous or the boat is overcrowded, consider postponing the trip or opting for a flight.

In other areas, it is difficult to explore and hop from island to island unless you have a charter boat or yacht. On Kadavu, for example, transport is mostly by small village or resort-owned boats. Apart from the Suva–Kadavu ferry, there is no organised transport here and most resorts have their own boats.

Ferry

Interisland trips for sightseeing and catamaran transfers are available to the Mamanucas and Yasawas; see this section as well as p150 and p161 for more details.

Regular ferry services link Viti Levu to Vanua Levu and Taveuni, and also Viti Levu to Ovalau. See the map on pp2-3 for ferry routes. The Patterson Brothers, Beachcomber Cruises and Consort Shipping boats are large roll-on, roll-off ferries, carrying passengers, vehicles and cargo. They have canteens where you can buy drinks, snacks and light meals. Ferry timetables are notorious for changing frequently; boats sometimes leave at odd hours and there is often a long waiting period at stopovers. The worst thing about the long trips is that the toilets can become disgusting (take your own toilet paper). There are irregular boats that take passengers from Suva to Lau, Rotuma and Kadavu.

NADI–MAMANUCAS

South Sea Cruises (☎ 675 0500, www.ssc.com.fj) operates two fast catamarans from Denarau Marina to most of the Mamanuca islands, including Malolo, Walu Beach, Castaway Island, Mana, Treasure Island, Beachcomber Island, Bounty Island, South Sea Island, Matamanoa and Tokoriki. See p150 for information on these services.

NADI–YASAWAS

Awesome Adventures (☎ 675 0499, www.awesome fiji.com), which is the same company as South Sea Cruises, operates the lurid yellow *Yasawa Flyer*, a large catamaran that services all the resorts in the Yasawa islands plus some of the Mamanuca resorts daily. It's a large boat with a comfortable interior including a snack shop and toilets but you'll still feel the swell on choppy days. See p161 for more details.

SUVA–SAVUSAVU–TAVEUNI

Consort Shipping (Map p122; ☎ 330 2877; fax 330 3389; Ground fl, Dominion House Arcade, Thomson St, Suva) sails three times a week from Suva to Savusavu ($80/50 for cabin/seat), departing Suva at 6pm on Monday and Friday and noon on Wednesday. It takes 12 hours to reach Savusavu. On Wednesday and Friday it continues for another eight hours on to Taveuni ($90/55 from Suva for cabin/seat). On the way back it departs Taveuni around noon on Friday and Sunday, arriving in Savusavu at around 5pm. This service sometimes stops at Koro – a nine hour trip; see p189 for more information.

Beachcomber Cruises Lautoka (☎ 666 1500; fax 666 4496); Savusavu (☎ 885 0266); Taveuni (☎ 888 0036) has a 500-passenger ship the *Adi Savusavu*, which has good facilities and runs three times a week between Suva and Savusavu ($45/65 for economy/1st class). The journey takes 11 hours and departs Suva at 10am on Tuesday, noon on Thursday and 6pm on Saturday, returning from Savusavu at 8pm on Wednesday and Friday and 7pm on Sunday. The boat also travels between Savusavu and Taveuni ($25/45 for economy/1st class), departing Savusavu at 1am on Wednesday and Friday, returning from Taveuni at noon on Wednesday and Friday. This journey takes five hours.

Grace Ferry Labasa (Gulam Nabi & Sons; ☎ 881 1152; Nasekula Rd); Savusavu (Country Kitchen; ☎ 927 1372) has a bus/boat trip from Taveuni to Savusavu and Labasa ($20). See p213 for more information.

(LAUTOKA)–ELLINGTON WHARF–NABOUWALU (VANUA LEVU)–(LABASA)

Patterson Brothers Shipping Labasa (☎ 881 2444; Nasekula Rd); Lautoka (☎ 666 1173; 15 Tukani St); Levuka (☎ 344 0125; Beach St); Suva (Map p122; ☎ 331 5644; fax 330 1652; Suites 1 & 2, Epworth Arcade, Nina St) travels this route twice a week ($60). It involves a bus ride (3½ hours) from Lautoka, a trip on the Ashika ferry (3¾ hours) and a trip on another bus to Labasa (four hours). Buses depart from outside the Lautoka office at 4am on Friday and Monday, and from Labasa at 6am on Sunday and Wednesday.

(SUVA)–NATOVI–NABOUWALU–(LABASA)

Patterson Brothers Shipping (above) travels this route ($45 one way) on Wednesday, Friday, Saturday and Sunday. Again it involves a bus ride (1½ hours) from Suva, a ferry trip (4½ hours) and another bus to Labasa (four hours). Buses depart the Suva office at 4.30am.

(SUVA)–NATOVI–BURESALA–(LEVUKA)
Patterson Brothers Shipping operates a daily service ($24 one way), which involves a bus ride (1½ hours) from Suva (Western Bus Terminal, Rodwell Rd) to Natovi Landing, followed by a ferry to Buresala Landing (one hour) and another bus to Levuka (one hour). Buses depart Suva at 2pm and Labasa at 5am.

(SUVA)–BAU LANDING–LELEUVIA–LEVUKA
There are services from Suva to Leleuvia via Bau Landing ($30 one way) and from Leleuvia to Levuka ($20 one way). See p189 for more information.

SUVA–KADAVU
Kadavu Shipping (Map p119; ☎ 331 1766, 339 5000, 339 5788; Rona St, Walu Bay, Suva) has irregular passenger services on the MV *Bulou-ni-Ceva* ($45 one way). See p228 for more information.

SUVA–LAU GROUP
Saliabasaga Shipping (Map p119; ☎ 330 3403; Walu Bay, Suva) has fortnightly trips aboard the MV *Tunatuki* to Lakeba, Nayau, Cicia, Tuvuca, Vanua Balavu and occasionally Moce and Oneata. The one way fare to Vanua Balavu is $90/120 for deck/cabin including meals.

Kabua Development Corporation (Map p119; ☎ 330 2258; fax 332 0251; Muaiwalu Complex, Old Millers Wharf, Rona St, Walu Bay, Suva) has fortnightly trips aboard the *Taikabara* to the southern Lau Group. It visits Lakeba, Vanuavatu, Komo, Kabara, Moce, Fulaga, Namuka, Vatoa, Ogea Levu and Ono-i-Lau (deck/cabin including meals $75/85 one way). It costs an extra $10 to visit the far south of the group (Vatoa and Ono-i-Lau). Boats can take up to a week to get to these distant outer islands.

Khans Shipping (Map p119; ☎ /fax 330 8786; Maui-walu Complex, Rona St, Walu Bay, Suva) visits islands in southern Lau about once a month. It's best to talk to them about their itinerary as it varies depending on demand. The journey takes about 10 hours and costs $80 each way.

SUVA–MOALA GROUP
There is no accommodation for visitors on the Moala islands – you would need to be invited to stay by a local. Khans Shipping (see left) has monthly trips to Moala, Matuke and Totoya in the Moala group. The journey takes about eight hours and a one-way fare is $80.

SUVA–ROTUMA
Western Shipping (Map p119; ☎ 331 4467; Naryan Jetty, Suva) operates the *Cagi Mai Ba* to Rotuma (deck/cabin $130/150). The journey takes 36 hours; phone for departure times and dates.

Yacht
Yachting is a great way to explore the Fiji archipelago. It is possible to charter boats or hitch a ride at marinas. See p258 and p243.

BUS
Fiji's larger islands have extensive and inexpensive bus networks. Local buses are cheap and regular and a great way to mix with the locals. While they can be fairly noisy and smoky they are perfect for the tropics, with unglazed windows and pull-down tarpaulins for when it rains. There are bus stops but you can often just hail buses, especially in rural areas.

Air-conditioned express buses run on some major routes such as Nadi to Suva.

Sunbeam Transport and Pacific Transport are the main carriers on Viti Levu; see p75 for more information. Pacific Transport also operates services on Taveuni (see p213). Local companies operate buses on Vanua Levu (see p201 and p207).

Reservations are not necessary for local buses. If you are on a tight schedule or have an appointment, though, it's a good idea to buy your ticket in advance, especially for bus trips and tours over longer distances (eg Suva to Nadi). Pacific Transport and Sunbeam issue timetables (available from the Fiji Visitors Bureau; FVB), but for most local buses just ask around the bus stations.

CAR & MOTORCYCLE
About 90% of Fiji's 5100km of roads are on Viti Levu and Vanua Levu, of which about one-fifth are sealed. Both of these islands are fun to explore by car, 4WD or on motorcycles.

Driving Licence
If you hold a current driving licence from an English-speaking country you are entitled

to drive in Fiji. Otherwise you will need an international driving permit, which should be obtained in your home country before travelling.

Fuel

Petrol stations are common and easy to find on Viti Levu and Vanua Levu. They are most prolific and competitive in the cities. Once you get off the beaten track they become fewer and further between. If you plan to do some driving by 4WD into Viti Levu's interior you should take a full tank with you. If you do run out of fuel, it might be available in village shops (but don't assume so).

Hire

Rental cars are relatively expensive in Fiji. Despite this, it is a good way to explore the larger islands, especially if you can split the cost with others.

Some rental agencies will not allow their cars to be driven on unpaved roads, which greatly limits exploration of the highlands. It is possible to take vehicles on roll-on, roll-off ferries to Vanua Levu or Taveuni, but again, some companies do not allow this. The ferry costs are pretty expensive and vehicles are available to rent on both these islands anyway. If you do take a car on a ferry to Vanua Levu, it's best if it's a 4WD.

The shorter the hire period, the higher the rate. Delivery and collection are often included in the price. Rates for a week or more with an international company start at around $70 per day, excluding tax, but the same car can cost twice as much per day for just one or two days' hire. Some companies will hire at an hourly rate or per half-day, while some have a minimum hire of three days. It's usual to pay a deposit by credit card. If you don't have a credit card you'll need to leave a hefty cash bond.

A valid overseas or international driving licence is required. The minimum-age requirement is 21, or in some cases 25.

Ask the FVB about the various companies. Generally, the larger, well-known companies have better cars and support, but are more expensive. Consider what's appropriate for you, including how inconvenienced you might be if the car breaks down, what support services are provided, the likely distance, insurance to travel, if value-added tax (VAT) is included and the

excess or excess waiver amount. Regardless of where you rent from check brakes, water, and tyre pressure and condition before heading off.

The easiest place to rent vehicles is on Viti Levu. Most rental agencies have offices at Nadi International Airport; the established companies also have offices in other towns and rental desks at larger hotels. Car-rental agencies on Vanua Levu and Taveuni have mostly 4WDs due to the islands' rough roads.

Some of the more reputable car-rental agencies on Viti Levu include:

Avis Rent a Car (www.avis.com) Nadi airport (☎ 672 2233); Nausori airport (☎ 347 8963); Suva (☎ 331 3833)
Budget Rent a Car (www.budget.com.fj) Labasa (☎ 881 1999); Nadi airport (☎ 672 2636); Nausori airport (☎ 347 9299); Suva (☎ 331 5899); Taveuni (☎ 888 0291)
Hertz (www.hertz.com) Nadi airport (☎ 672 3466); Nausori airport (☎ 338 0758); Suva (☎ 338 0981)
Thrifty Car Rental (www.thrifty.com) Nadi airport (☎ 672 2935); Suva (☎ 331 4436)

Although not widely available, motorcycles and scooters are not a bad way to travel in Fiji. Similar traffic rules and rental conditions as mentioned previously for car rental apply to motorcycles and scooters. Rental per day starts at around $35/60 for scooters/125cc motorcycle.

Beat Rentals Nadi (Map p76; ☎ 672 1471; Queens Rd, Martintar); Suva (Map p119; ☎ 338 5355; Grantham Rd, Nabua) have been in the game for a while.

INSURANCE

Third-party insurance is compulsory and all car-rental companies add it onto the daily rental rate (count on $22 to $30 at least). Personal accident insurance is highly recommended if you are not already covered by travel insurance. Renters are liable for the first $500 damage. Common exclusions, or problems that won't be paid for by the insurance company, include tyre damage, underbody and overhead damage, windscreen damage and theft of the vehicle.

Road Conditions

The perimeter of Viti Levu is easy to get to know by car: the Queens Road and most of the Kings Road are sealed, although the section between Korovou and Dama is still unsealed. Roads into the interior are unsealed and a 4WD is generally necessary.

TRANSPORT

There are unsealed roads around most of Vanua Levu's perimeter, but there's a sealed road from Labasa to Savusavu and the first 20km of the Hibiscus Hwy from Savusavu along the scenic coast is also paved. The remainder of the Hibiscus Hwy is quite rough.

Road Hazards

Some locals drive with a fairly heavy foot on the accelerator pedal and many ignore the whole idea of sticking to the left-hand side when navigating bends (particularly along the Coral Coast). Local drivers also tend to stop suddenly and overtake on blind corners, so take care, especially on gravel roads. Buses also stop where and when they please. There are lots of potholes, and sometimes the roads are too narrow for two vehicles to pass, so be aware of oncoming traffic.

Watch for sugar trains in the cane-cutting season, as they have right of way. Dogs wandering onto the road can be a major hazard so observe the speed-hump enforced 20km/ h rule when driving through villages. Avoid driving at night as there are many pedestrians and wandering animals – especially along the southeast coast of Viti Levu, on Vanua Levu and Taveuni.

Road Rules

Driving is on the left-hand side of the road. The speed limit is 80km/h, which drops to 20km/h in villages. Many villages have speed humps to force drivers to slow down. Seat belts are compulsory for front-seat passengers. Should you pick up a parking fine in Suva it's likely to be around $2.

HITCHING

Hitching is never entirely safe in any country, and we don't recommend it. Travellers who decide to hitch should understand that they are taking a small but potentially serious risk.

Hitching in Fiji, however, is common. Locals do it all the time, especially with carriers. It is customary to pay the equivalent of the bus fare to the driver. Hitchhikers will be safer if they travel in pairs and let someone know where they are planning to go. Crime is more prevalent around Suva, although there have been cases of hitchhikers being mugged around Nadi.

LOCAL TRANSPORT

Many locals drive small trucks (known as carriers) with a tarpaulin-covered frame on the back. These often have passenger seating and some run trips between Nadi and Suva. You can pick one up in Nadi's main street; they leave when full and are quicker than taking the bus.

Minivans are also an increasingly common sight on the road. Popular with locals, they're also quicker and more expensive than a bus but much cheaper than a taxi. Your ride won't necessarily be more comfortable, though – it's generally a sardine-type affair. Minivans plough up and down the Queens Road around Nadi.

TAXI

You will find taxis on Viti Levu, Vanua Levu, Taveuni and Ovalau. The bus stations in the main towns usually have taxi depots and there is often an oversupply of taxis, with drivers competing for business. There are some good cabs, but most are rickety old dinosaurs bound for or retrieved from the wrecker. Most taxi drivers are Indo-Fijians keen to discuss life and local issues. They invariably have relatives in Australia, New Zealand or Canada.

Unlike in Suva, the taxi drivers in Nadi, Lautoka and most rural areas don't use their meters. First ask locals what is the acceptable rate for a particular trip. Then, if there is no meter, confirm an approximate price with the driver before you agree to travel. Cabs can be shared for long trips. For touring around areas with limited public transport such as Taveuni, forming a group and negotiating a taxi fee for a half- or full day may be an option.

Always ask if the cab is a return taxi (returning to its base). If so, you can expect to pay $1 per person or less, as long as the taxi doesn't have to go out of its way. To make up for the low fare, the driver will usually pick up extra passengers from bus stops. You can usually recognise a return taxi, as most have the name of their home depot on the bumper bar.

TOURS

Fiji has many companies providing tours within the country, including trekking, cycling, kayaking, diving, bus or 4WD tours. Cruises to the outer islands such as the

Mamanucas (p149) and Yasawas (p159) are popular. There is also a sailing safari on the *Tui Tai* from Savusavu to Taveuni, Kioa and Koro (p196).

Viti Levu has the most tours, including excellent two-, four- or six-day treks with Mount Batilamu Trek (p143) or Adventure Fiji (p81). There are also a few tours on Ovalau (p173) and Vanua Levu (p195).

Feejee Experience (☎ 672 0097; www.feejeeexpe rience.com) offers coach and accommodation packages for budget travellers. It can be a fun and social way to get around, especially if you are short on time. Travel passes allow you to hop-on-and-off as you like within six months; the six-day 'Lei Low' ($600) includes

Natadola Beach, sandboarding down the Sigatoka Dunes, the Coral Coast, highland trekking, tubing on the Navua River, Suva nightclubs, *bilibili* (bamboo raft) trips, kay-aking, snorkelling and a night on Nananu-i-Ra and Beachcomber Island. The four-day 'Hula Loop' ($425) includes slightly less.

Green Turtle Tours (☎ 672 8889; www.greenturtle tours.com/fiji) offers small group tours around Viti Levu that include highland villages, Nananu-i-Ra and islands in the Yasawa and Mamanuca groups. Three-/four-day tours costs $720/1100 including all accommoda-tion, meals and activities.

There are also live-aboard dive boats (see p65).

TRANSPORT

Health Dr Michael Sorokin

CONTENTS

Before You Go	**266**
Insurance	266
Recommended Vaccinations	266
Medical Checklist	267
Internet Resources	267
Further Reading	267
In Transit	**267**
Deep Vein Thrombosis (DVT)	267
Jet Lag & Motion Sickness	267
In Fiji	**268**
Availability & Cost of Health Care	268
Infectious Diseases	268
Traveller's Diarrhoea	269
Environmental Hazards	270

Rabies is no danger in any of the Fijian islands. And there are no crocodiles. There is also no malaria in Fiji, a huge health plus. Mosquitoes do exist, though, and the main danger from them is dengue fever. Health facilities are good in Fiji; however, this is a small country with a limited budget so 'good' does not necessarily equate with the facilities in a well-developed country.

BEFORE YOU GO

Prevention is the key to staying healthy while abroad. A little planning before departure, particularly for pre-existing illnesses, will save trouble later. See your dentist before a long trip, carry a spare pair of contact lenses and glasses, and take your optical prescription with you. Bring medications in their original, clearly labelled, containers. A signed and dated letter from your physician describing your medical conditions and medications, including generic names, is also a good idea. If carrying syringes or needles, be sure to have a physician's letter documenting their medical necessity.

INSURANCE
If your health insurance policy does not cover you for medical expenses abroad, con-

sider taking supplemental insurance. (Check www.lonelyplanet.com/travel_links/ for more details.) Find out in advance if your insurance plan will make payments directly to providers or reimburse you later for overseas health expenditures. (In Fiji most treatment requires payment in cash, though.)

Really serious illness or injury may require evacuation, eg to Auckland or Sydney; make sure that your health insurance has provision for evacuation. Under these circumstances hospitals will accept direct payment from major international insurers.

RECOMMENDED VACCINATIONS
The World Health Organization (WHO) recommends that all travellers be covered for diphtheria, tetanus, measles, mumps, rubella and polio, regardless of their desti-

---

REQUIRED & RECOMMENDED VACCINATIONS

If you have been in a country affected by yellow fever within six days of arriving in Fiji, you will need an International Certificate of Vaccination for yellow fever to be allowed entry into the country. Vaccinations are recommended for hepatitis A, hepatitis B and typhoid fever.

All injected vaccinations can produce slight soreness and redness at the inoculation site, and a mild fever with muscle aches over the first 24 hours. These are least likely with hepatitis A and a little more common with hepatitis B and typhoid inoculations. Typhoid inoculation can cause a sensation of nausea within 24 hours and the hepatitis B vaccine can produce temporary joint pains.

An allergy to eggs or poultry is a condition that makes the yellow-fever vaccination inadvisable; an exemption certificate can be issued. Very rarely, an acute allergic (anaphylactic shock) reaction can occur within minutes of any vaccination. More commonly a flulike illness of varying severity may occur at any time up to 10 days after vaccination. In the elderly, encephalitis has been recorded.

nation. Since most vaccines don't produce immunity until at least two weeks after they're given, visit a physician at least six weeks before departure. A recent influenza vaccination is always a good idea when travelling. If you have not had chicken pox (varicella) consider being vaccinated.

MEDICAL CHECKLIST

It is a very good idea to carry a medical and first-aid kit with you, in case of minor illness or injury. The following is a list of items you should consider packing.

- acetaminophen (paracetamol) or aspirin*
- adhesive or paper tape
- antibacterial ointment, eg Bactroban for cuts and abrasions (prescription only)
- antibiotic plus steroid eardrops (prescription only), eg Sofradex, Kenacort Otic
- antibiotics (prescription only), eg ciprofloxacin (Ciproxin) or norfloxacin (Utinor; Noroxin)
- antidiarrhoeal drugs, eg loperamide
- antigiardia tablets – tinidazole (prescription only)
- antihistamines (for hay fever and allergic reactions)
- anti-inflammatory drugs, eg ibuprofen
- bandages, gauze, gauze rolls, waterproof dressings
- DEET-containing insect repellent for the skin
- iodine tablets (for water purification)
- oral rehydration salts, eg Gastrolyte, Diarolyte, Replyte
- Permethrin-containing insect spray for clothing, tents, and bed nets
- pocket knife[+]
- scissors, safety pins, tweezers[+]
- steroid cream or hydrocortisone cream (for allergic rashes)
- sun block
- syringes and sterile needles (prescription only), and intravenous fluids if travelling in very remote areas
- thermometer

*Aspirin should not be used for fever – it can cause bleeding in sufferers of dengue fever
+ Do not take on planes in carry-on luggage

INTERNET RESOURCES

There is a wealth of travel health advice on the Internet. For further information, www.lonelyplanet.com is a good place to start.

WHO produces a superb free, online text, *International Travel and Health*, which is available at www.who.int/ith/. Other websites of general interest are MD Travel Health at www.mdtravelhealth.com, which provides complete travel health recommendations for every country (updated daily), also at no cost; the Centers for Disease Control and Prevention at www.cdc.gov; and Fit for Travel at www.fitfortravel.scot.nhs.uk, which has up-to-date information about outbreaks and is very user-friendly; and www.traveldoctor.com.au a similar Australasian site.

It's also a good idea to consult your government's travel health website:

Australia (www.dfat.gov.au/travel/)
Canada (www.hc-sc.gc.ca/)
New Zealand (www.mfat.govt.nz/travel)
UK (www.doh.gov.uk) Click on Policy and Guidance, then on Health Advice for Travellers.
USA (www.cdc.gov/travel/)

FURTHER READING

Good options for further reading include: *Travel with Children* by Cathy Lanigan; *Healthy Travel Australia, New Zealand and the Pacific* by Dr Isabelle Young; and *Your Child's Health Abroad: A Manual for Travelling Parents* by Dr Jane Wilson-Howarth and Matthew Ellis.

IN TRANSIT

DEEP VEIN THROMBOSIS (DVT)

Blood clots may form in the legs during plane flights, chiefly because of prolonged immobility. The longer the flight, the greater the risk. The chief symptom of DVT is swelling or pain of the foot, ankle or calf, usually but not always on just one side. When a blood clot travels to the lungs, it may cause chest pain and breathing difficulties. Travellers with any of these symptoms should immediately seek medical attention.

To prevent the development of DVT on long flights you should walk about the cabin, contract the leg muscles while sitting, drink plenty of nonalcoholic fluids and avoid tobacco.

JET LAG & MOTION SICKNESS

To avoid jet lag (common when crossing more than five time zones) try drinking plenty of nonalchoholic fluids and eating light meals. Upon arrival, get exposure to natural sunlight and readjust your schedule (for meals, sleep and so on) as soon as possible.

Antihistamines such as dimenhydrinate (Dramamine) and meclizine (Antivert, Bonine) are usually the first choice for treating motion sickness. A herbal alternative is ginger.

IN FIJI

AVAILABILITY & COST OF HEALTH CARE

Fiji has readily available doctors in private practice, standard hospital and laboratory facilities with consultants in internal medicine, obstetrics/gynaecology, orthopaedics, ophthalmology, paediatrics, pathology, psychiatry and general surgery. Private dentists, opticians and pharmacies are also available. The further you get from main cities the more basic the services.

Private consultation and private hospital fees are approximately equivalent to Australian costs. Fees for government-provided services vary from modest to negligible but waiting times can be very long. Direct payment is required everywhere except where a specific arrangement is made, eg in the case of evacuation or where a prolonged hospital stay is necessary; you will need to contact your insurer. Although hospitals will accept credit cards, there might be difficulty with the more remote small hospitals. If a credit card is not accepted you should be able to arrange cash on credit through local banks.

Except in the remote poorly staffed clinics, the standard of medical and dental care is generally quite good even if facilities are not sophisticated. The overall risk of illness for a normally healthy person is low; the most common problems being diarrhoeal upsets, viral sore throats, and ear and skin infections – all of which can mostly be treated with self-medication. For serious symptoms, eg sustained fever, chest or abdominal pains it is best to go to the nearest clinic or doctor straight away.

Family Health

Tampons and pads are readily available in main centres but do not rely on getting them if you travel to one of the outer islands. Dengue fever, especially in the first three months of pregnancy, poses a hazard because of fever but otherwise there is no reason why a normal pregnancy should prevent travel to the region. However, unless necessary, immunisation in the first three months of pregnancy is not recommended.

For young children, it is again dengue fever that could be a problem. The disease tends to come in epidemics mainly in the hotter, wetter months so it should be possible to plan holidays accordingly.

Medications & Contraception

Most commonly used medications are available. Private pharmacies are not allowed by law to dispense listed drugs without prescription from a locally registered practitioner, but many will do so for travellers if shown the container or a prescription from home. Oral contraceptives are obtainable without prescription in Fiji, as is the 'morning after' pill. Asthma inhalers and most anti-inflammatories are available over the counter. It is best to have a sufficient supply of a regularly taken drug as a particular brand may not be available and sometimes quantities can be limited. This applies particularly to psychotropic drugs such as antidepressants, antipsychotics, anti-epileptics or mood elevators. Insulin is available even in smaller centres, but you cannot guarantee getting a particular brand, combination or preferred administration method. If you have been prescribed 'the very latest' oral antidiabetic or antihypertensive make sure you have enough for the duration of your travel.

INFECTIOUS DISEASES

Despite the long list below, the realistic risks to visitors from infectious diseases are very low with the exception of dengue fever.

Dengue Fever

Dengue fever is a virus spread by the bite of a day-biting mosquito. It causes a feverish illness with headache and severe muscle pains similar to those experienced with a bad, prolonged attack of influenza. Another name for the disease is 'break bone fever' and that's what it feels like. Danger signs include prolonged vomiting, blood in the vomit and a blotchy rash. There is no preventive vaccine and mosquito bites should be avoided whenever possible. Self-treatment involves paracetamol, fluids and rest. Do not use aspirin. Haemorrhagic dengue fever has been reported only occasionally, manifested by signs of bleeding and shock, and requires medical care.

Eosinophilic Meningitis

Eosinophilic meningitis is caused by a microscopic parasite – the rat lungworm – which contaminates raw food. It's a strange illness manifested by scattered abnormal skin sensations, fever and sometimes by the meningitis (headache, vomiting, confusion, neck and spine stiffness), which gives it its name. There is no proven specific treatment, but symptoms may require hospitalisation. For prevention pay strict attention to advice on food and drink.

Hepatitis A

This is a virus disease causing liver inflammation spread by contaminated food or water. Fever, nausea, debility and jaundice (yellow coloration of the skin, eyes and urine) occur and recovery is slow. Most people recover completely but it can be dangerous to people with other forms of liver disease, the elderly and sometimes to pregnant women towards the end of pregnancy. Food is easily contaminated by food preparers, handlers or servers, and by flies. There is no specific treatment. The vaccine is close to 100% protective.

Hepatitis B

Hepatitis B is a virus disease causing liver inflammation but the problem is much more serious than hepatitis A and frequently goes on to cause chronic liver disease and even cancer. It is spread, like HIV, by mixing body fluids, ie sexual intercourse, contaminated needles and accidental blood contamination. Treatment is complex and specialised but preventative vaccination is highly effective.

Hepatitis C

This is a virus similar to hepatitis B that causes liver inflammation, which can progress to chronic liver disease or result in a symptomless carrier state. It is spread almost entirely by blood contamination from shared needles or contaminated needles used for tattooing or body piercing. Treatment is complex and specialised. There is no vaccine available.

HIV/AIDS

The incidence of HIV infection is on the rise in the whole South Pacific and is fast becoming a major problem in Fiji. Safe-sex practise is essential at all times. If an injection is needed in a smaller clinic it is best to provide your own needles. Blood transfusion laboratories do tests for HIV.

Leptospirosis

Also known as Weil's disease, leptospirosis produces fever, headache, jaundice and, later, kidney failure. It is caused by a spirochaete organism found in water contaminated by rat urine. The organism penetrates skin, so swimming in flooded areas is a risky practice. If diagnosed early it is cured with penicillin.

Typhoid Fever

Typhoid is a bacterial infection acquired from contaminated food or water. The germ can be transmitted by food handlers or flies, and can be present in inadequately cooked shellfish. It causes fever, debility and late-onset diarrhoea. Untreated it can produce delirium and is occasionally fatal, but the infection is curable with antibiotics. Vaccination is moderately effective, but care with eating and drinking is equally important.

TRAVELLER'S DIARRHOEA

Diarrhoea – frequent, loose bowel movements – is caused by viruses, bacteria or parasites present in contaminated food or water. In temperate climates the cause is usually viral, but in the tropics bacteria or parasites are more usual. If you develop diarrhoea, be sure to drink plenty of fluids, preferably an oral rehydration solution (eg Diarolyte, Gastrolyte, Replyte). A few loose stools don't require treatment, but if you start having more than four or five stools a day, you should start taking an antibiotic (usually a quinolone drug) and an anti-diarrhoeal agent (such as Loperamide). If diarrhoea is bloody, persists for more than 72 hours or is accompanied by fever, shaking, chills or severe abdominal pain you should seek medical attention. Giardiasis is a particular form of persistent, although not 'explosive', diarrhoea caused by a parasite present in contaminated water. One dose (four tablets) of tinidazole usually cures the infection.

To prevent diarrhoea pay strict attention to the precautions regarding food and water; see opposite for details.

ENVIRONMENTAL HAZARDS

Threats to health from animals and insects are rare indeed but you need to be aware of them.

Bites & Stings

Fiji is blessedly free of dangerous land creatures. There are some land snakes but these are very rarely seen.

JELLYFISH

The notorious box jellyfish (seawasp) has not been recorded, but the blue-coloured Indo-Pacific 'Man o' War' is found in Fijian waters. If you see these floating in the water or stranded on the beach it is wise not to go in. The sting is very painful. Treatment involves ice packs and vinegar; do not use alcohol. Smaller cubo-medusae are abundant and are found particularly on still, overcast days. They usually produce only uncomfortably irritating stings but rarely can cause generalised symptoms, especially in someone with poorly controlled heart disease.

POISONOUS CONE SHELLS

Poisonous cone shells abound along shallow coral reefs. Stings can be avoided by handling the shell at its blunt end only and, preferably, using gloves. Stings mainly cause local reactions but nausea, faintness, palpitations or difficulty breathing are signs flagging the need for medical attention.

OTHER MARINE LIFE

As in all tropical waters, sea snakes may be seen around coral reefs. Unprovoked, sea snakes are extremely unlikely to attack and their fangs will not penetrate a wet suit. First-aid treatment consists of compression bandaging and splinting of the affected limb. Antivenom is effective, but may have to be flown in. Only about 10% of sea-snake bites cause serious poisoning.

Some of the most beautiful sea creatures such as the scorpion fish and lionfish are also highly venomous. Avoid the temptation and keep your hands to yourself! Sea urchins, crown-of-thorns starfish and stonefish can be poisonous or cause infec-

tions. Barracuda eels, which hide in coral crevices, may bite. Sea lice or stingers can also be a nuisance.

Shark attacks on divers and snorkellers are rare in Fiji. Reef sharks don't normally attack humans for food, but they can be territorial. Avoid swimming near waste-water outlets, areas where fish are being cleaned, and the mouths of rivers or murky waters. If you are lucky enough to see a shark, just move away calmly.

Coral Cuts

Cuts and abrasions from dead coral cause no more trouble than similar injuries from any other sort of rock, but live coral can cause prolonged infection. If you injure yourself on live coral don't wait until later to treat it. Get out of the water as soon as possible, cleanse the wound thoroughly (getting out all the little bits of coral), apply an antiseptic and cover with a waterproof dressing. Then get back in the water if you wish.

Coral Ear

This is a commonly used name for inflammation of the ear canal. It has nothing to do with coral but is caused by water entering the canal, activating fungal spores resulting in secondary bacterial infection and inflammation. It usually starts after swimming, but can be reactivated by water dripping into the ear canal after a shower, especially if long, wet hair lies over the ear opening. Apparently trivial, it can be very, very painful and can spoil a holiday. Apart from diarrhoea it is the most common reason for tourists to consult a doctor in Fiji. Self-treatment with an antibiotic-plus-steroid eardrop preparation (eg Sofradex, Kenacort Otic) is very effective. Stay out of the water until the pain and itch have gone.

Diving Decompression

Because Fiji has wonderful opportunities for scuba diving, it is easy to get overexcited and neglect strict depth and time precautions. The temptation to spend longer than safe times at relatively shallow depths is great and a major cause of decompression illness (the 'bends'). Early pains may not be severe and may be attributed to other causes but any muscle or joint pain after scuba diving must be suspect. A privately run compression chamber is available in Suva but transport

---

FISH POISONING

Ciguatera is a form of poisoning that affects otherwise safe and edible fish unpredictably. Poisoning is characterised by stomach upsets, itching, faintness, slow pulse and bizarre inverted sensations, eg cold feeling hot and vice versa. Ciguatera has been reported in many carnivorous reef fish, especially barracuda but also red snapper, Spanish mackerel and moray eels. There is no safe test to determine whether a fish is poisonous or not. Although local knowledge is not entirely reliable, it is reasonable to eat what the locals are eating. However, fish caught after times of reef destruction, eg after a major hurricane, are more likely to be poisonous. Treatment consists of rehydration and if the pulse is very slow, medication may be needed. Healthy adults will make a complete recovery, although disturbed sensation may persist for some weeks.

---

to it can be difficult. Even experienced divers should check with organisations such as **Divers' Alert Network** (DAN; www.diversalertnet work.org) about the current site and status of compression chambers, and insurance to cover costs both for local treatment and evacuation. Novice divers must be especially careful. If you have not taken out insurance before leaving home you may be able to do so online with DAN.

Food & Water

The municipal water supply in Suva, Nadi and other large towns can usually be trusted, but elsewhere avoid untreated tap water, and after heavy rain it's worth boiling the water before you drink. In some areas the only fresh water available may be rain water collected in tanks and this should certainly be boiled. Food in restaurants, particularly resort restaurants, is safe. Be adventurous by all means but expect to suffer the consequences if you succumb to adventurous temptation by trying raw fish or crustaceans as eaten by some locals.

Heat Exhaustion

Fiji lies within the tropics so it is hot and often humid. Heat exhaustion is actually a state of dehydration associated to a greater or lesser extent with salt loss. Natural heat loss is through sweating making it easy to become dehydrated without realising it. Thirst is a late sign. Small children and old people are especially vulnerable. For adults, heat exhaustion is prevented by drinking at least 3L of water per day and more if actively exercising. Children need about 1.5 to 2.5L per day. Salt replacement solutions are useful as

muscle weakness and cramps are due to salt as well as water loss and can be made worse by drinking water alone. The powders used for treating dehydration due to diarrhoea are just as effective for heat exhaustion. Apart from these, a reasonable drink consists of a good pinch of salt to a pint (0.5L) of water. Salt tablets can result in too much salt being taken, causing headaches and confusion.

Heat Stroke

When the cooling effect of sweating fails, heat stroke ensues. This is a dangerous and emergency condition characterised not only by muscle weakness and exhaustion, but by mental confusion. Skin will be hot and dry. If this occurs 'put the fire out' by cooling the body with water on the outside and if possible with cold drinks for the inside. Seek medical help as a follow-up anyway, but urgently if the person can't drink.

Sunburn

It should go without saying that exposure to the ultraviolet (UV) rays of the sun causes burning of the skin with accompanying pain, dehydration and misery (with the long-term danger of skin cancer) but experience shows that reminders are necessary. The time of highest risk is between 11am and 3pm and remember that cloud cover does not block out UV rays. Neither does a pleasant breeze. The Australian *Slip, slop, slap* slogan is a useful 'mantra' – slip on a T-shirt or blouse, slop on a sunscreen lotion (of at least 15-plus rating) and slap on a hat. Treat sunburn like any other burn – cool, wet dressings are best. Severe swelling may respond to a cortisone cream.

HEALTH

Language

CONTENTS

Fijian	**272**
Pronunciation	272
Further Reading	273
Accommodation	273
Conversation & Essentials	274
Directions	274
Health & Emergencies	274
Numbers	274
Shopping & Services	275
Time & Dates	275
Transport	275
Fiji-Hindi	**275**
Pronunciation	275
Conversation & Essentials	276
Directions	277
Health & Emergencies	277
Numbers	277
Time & Dates	277
Transport	277

One of the reasons many visitors from the English-speaking world find Fiji such a congenial place to visit is that they don't have to learn another language – the majority of the local people they come in contact with can speak English, and all signs and official forms are also in English. At the same time, for almost all local people, English is not their mother tongue – at home, indigenous Fijians speak Fijian and Indo-Fijians speak Fiji-Hindi (also known as Fijian Hindi and Fiji Hindustani). If you really wish to develop a better understanding of the Fijian people and their culture, it's important that you know something of the Fijian languages and, no matter how poor your first attempts at communicating, you'll receive plenty of encouragement from Fijians.

FIJIAN

The many regional dialects found in Fiji today all descend, at least partly, from the language spoken by the original inhabitants. They would have come from one of the island groups to the west, either the Solomons or Vanuatu, having left their Southeast Asian homeland at least 1000 years previously and spread eastwards by way of Indonesia, the Philippines and Papua New Guinea. From Fiji, groups left to settle the nearby islands of Rotuma, Tonga and Samoa, and from there they spread out to inhabit the rest of Polynesia, including Hawaii in the north, Rapa Nui (Easter Island) in the east, and Aotearoa (New Zealand) in the south. All the people in this vast area speak related languages belonging to the Austronesian family.

There are some 300 regional varieties (dialects) of Fijian, all belonging to one of two major groupings. All varieties spoken to the west of a line extending north–south, with a couple of kinks, across the centre of Viti Levu belong to the Western Fijian group, while all others are Eastern Fijian.

Fortunately for the language learner there is one variety, based on the eastern varieties of the Bau–Rewa area, which is understood by Fijians throughout the islands. This standard form of Fijian is popularly known as *vosa vakabau* (Bauan), though linguists prefer to call it standard Fijian. It's used in conversation among Fijians from different areas, on the radio and in schools, and is the variety used in this chapter.

In Fijian, there are two ways of saying 'you', 'your', and 'yours'. When speaking to someone who is your superior, or an adult stranger, you should use a longer 'polite' form. This form is easy to remember because it always ends in *-ni*. In all other situations, a shorter 'informal' address is used.

PRONUNCIATION

Fijian pronunciation isn't especially difficult for the English speaker, since most of the sounds found in Fijian have similar counterparts in English. The standard Fijian alphabet uses all the English letters, except 'x'. The letters 'h' and 'z' are used for borrowed words only and occur rarely.

The Fijian alphabet was devised relatively recently (in the 1830s) by missionaries who were also competent linguists. As a result it

---

'FIJINGLISH'

Here are a few English words and phrases used in Fijian but with slightly different meanings:

Fijian English	English
grog	*kava*
bluff	lie, deceive
chow	food, eat
set	OK, ready
step	cut school, wag
Good luck to ...!	It serves ... right!
Not even!	No way!

---

is economical and phonetically consistent – each letter represents only one sound, and each sound is represented by only one letter.

As with all Pacific languages, the five Fijian vowels are pronounced much as they are in languages such as Spanish, German and Italian:

a	as in 'father'
e	as in 'bet'
i	as in 'machine'
o	as in 'more'
u	as in 'flute'

Vowels have both short or long variants, with the long vowel having a significantly longer sound. In this guide a long sound is written as a double vowel, eg **aa**. An approximate English equivalent is the difference between the final vowel sound in 'icy' and 'I see'. To convey the correct meaning of a word it's important that vowel length is taken into account in your pronunciation. For example, *mama* means 'a ring', *mamaa* means 'chew it', and *maamaa* means 'light' (in weight). Note that *maamaa* takes about twice as long to pronounce as *mama*.

Most consonants are pronounced as they are in English, but there are a few differences you need to be aware of:

b	pronounced with a preceding nasal consonant as 'mb'
c	as the 'th' in 'this' (not as in 'thick')
d	pronounced with a preceding nasal consonant as 'nd'
g	as the 'ng' in 'sing' (not as in 'angry')
j	as the 'ch' in 'charm' but without a following puff of breath
k	as in 'kick' but without a following puff of breath
p	as in 'pip' but without a following puff of breath
q	as the 'ng' in 'angry' (not as in 'sing')
r	trilled as in Scottish English
t	as in 'tap' but without a following puff of breath, often pronounced 'ch' before 'i'
v	pronounced with the lower lip against the upper lip (not against the upper teeth as in English) – somewhere between a 'v' and a 'b'

Occasionally on maps and in tourist publications you'll find a variation on the spelling system used in this guide – it's intended to be easier for English speakers to negotiate. In this alternative system, Yanuca is spelt 'Yanutha', Beqa 'Mbengga', and so on.

FURTHER READING

A good introduction to the language is Lonely Planet's *Fijian Phrasebook*, which provides all the essential words and phrases travellers need, along with grammar and cultural points. Lonely Planet's *South Pacific Phrasebook* covers the languages of many South Pacific islands – ideal if you intend visiting a few countries in one trip. Those interested in further studies of Fijian will find George Milner's *Fijian Grammar* (Government Press, Suva, 1956) an excellent introduction to the language. Likewise, Albert Schutz's *Spoken Fijian* (University Press of Hawaii, Honolulu, 1979) is a good primer for more advanced studies.

ACCOMMODATION

Where is a ...?	*I vei ...?*
hotel	*dua na otela*
cheap hotel	*otela saurawarawa*

A note of caution. The term 'guesthouse' and its Fijian equivalent, *dua na bure ni vulagi*, often refer to establishments offering rooms for hire by the hour.

I'm going to stay for...	*Au na ...*
one day	*siga dua*
one week	*maacawa dua*

LANGUAGE

I'm not sure how long I'm staying.
Sega ni macala na dede ni noqu tiko.
Where is the bathroom?
I vei na valenisili?
Where is the toilet?
I vei na valelailai?

CONVERSATION & ESSENTIALS

Hello.	*Bula!*
Hello. (reply)	*Io, bula/Ia, bula.* (more respectful)
Good morning.	*Yadra.*
Goodbye.	*Moce.* (if you don't expect to see them again)
See you later.	*Au saa liu mada.*

You may also hear the following:

Where are you going?
O(ni) lai vei? (used as we ask 'How are you?')
Nowhere special, just wandering around.
Sega, gaade gaa. (as with the response to 'How are you', there's no need to be specific)
Let's shake hands.
Daru lululu mada.

Yes.	*Io.*
No.	*Sega.*
Thank you (very much).	*Vinaka (vakalevu).*
Sorry.	*(Ni) Vosota sara.*
What's your name?	*O cei na yacamu(ni)?*
My name is ...	*O yau o ...*
Pleased to meet you.	*Ia, (ni) bula.*
Where are you from?	*O iko/kemuni mai vei?*
I'm from ...	*O yau mai ...*
How old are you?	*O yabaki vica?*
I'm ... years old.	*Au yabaki ...*
Are you married?	*O(ni) vakawati?*
How many children do you have?	*Le vica na luvemu(ni)?*
I don't have any children.	*E sega na luvequ.*
I have a daughter/ a son.	*E dua na luvequ yalewa/tagane.*
I don't speak Fijian/English.	*Au sega ni kilaa na vosa vakaviti/vakavaalagi.*
Do you speak English?	*O(ni) kilaa na vosa vakavaalagi?*
I understand.	*Saa macala.*
I don't understand.	*E sega ni macala.*
May I take your photo?	*Au tabaki iko mada?*
I'll send you the photo.	*Au na vaakauta yani na itaba.*

DIRECTIONS

I want to go to ...	*Au via lako i ...*
How do I get to ...?	*I vei na sala i ...?*
Is it far?	*E yawa?*
Can I walk there?	*E rawa niu taubale kina?*
Can you show me (on the map)?	*Vakaraitaka mada (ena mape)?*
Go straight ahead.	*Vakadodonu.*
Turn left.	*Gole i na imawi.*
Turn right.	*Gole i na imatau.*

Compass bearings (north, south etc) are never used. Instead you'll hear:

on the sea side of ...	*mai ... i wai*
on the land side of ...	*mai ... i vanua*
the far side of ...	*mai ... i liu*
this side of ...	*mai ... i muri*

HEALTH & EMERGENCIES

Help!	*Oilei!*
Go away!	*Lako tani!*
Call a doctor!	*Qiria na vuniwai!*
Call an ambulance!	*Qiria na lori ni valenibula!*
Call the police!	*Qiria na ovisa!*
I'm lost.	*Au saa sese.*
I need a doctor.	*Au via raici vuniwai.*
Where is the hospital?	*I vei na valenibula?*
I have a stomach-ache.	*E mosi na ketequ.*
I'm diabetic.	*Au tauvi matenisuka.*
I'm allergic to penicillin.	*E dau lako vakacaa vei au na penisilini.*
condoms	*rapa, kodom*
contraceptive	*wai ni yalani*
diarrhoea	*coka*
medicine	*wainimate*
nausea	*lomalomacaa*
sanitary napkin	*qamuqamu*

NUMBERS

0	*saiva*
1	*dua*
2	*rua*
3	*tolu*
4	*vaa*
5	*lima*
6	*ono*
7	*vitu*
8	*walu*
9	*ciwa*
10	*tini*
11	*tinikadua*
12	*tinikarua*

20	ruasagavulu
21	ruasagavulukadua
30	tolusagavulu
100	dua na drau
1000	dua na udolu

SHOPPING & SERVICES

I'm looking for ...	Au vaaqaraa ...
a church	na valenilotu
the market	na maakete
the museum	na vale ni yau maaroroi
the police	na ovisa
the post office	na posi(tovesi)
a public toilet	na valelailai
the tourist office	na valenivolavola ni saravanua
What time does it open/close?	E dola/sogo ina vica?
Where are the toilets?	I vei na valelailai?
How much is it?	E vica?
That's too expensive.	Au sega ni rawata.
I'm just looking.	Sarasara gaa.
bookshop	sitoa ni vola
clothing shop	sitoa ni sulu
laundry	valenisavasava
pharmacy	kemesi

TIME & DATES

What time is it?	Saa vica na kaloko?
today	nikua
tonight	na bogi nikua
tomorrow	nimataka
yesterday	nanoa
Monday	Moniti
Tuesday	Tusiti
Wednesday	Vukelulu
Thursday	Lotulevu
Friday	Vakaraubuka
Saturday	Vakarauwai
Sunday	Sigatabu

TRANSPORT

Where is the ...?	I vei na ...?
airport	raaraa ni waqavuka
(main) bus station	basten
bus stop	ikelekele ni basi
When does the ... leave/arrive?	Vica na kaloko e lako/ kele kina na ...?
bus	basi
plane	waqavuka
boat	waqa

FIJI-HINDI

Fiji-Hindi (also known as Fijian Hindi and Fiji Hindustani) is the language of all Indo-Fijians. It has features of the many regional dialects of Hindi spoken by the Indian indentured labourers who were brought to Fiji from 1879 to 1916. (Some people call Fiji-Hindi 'Bhojpuri', but this is the name of just one of the many dialects that contributed to the language.)

Many words from English are found in Fiji-Hindi (such as room, towel, book and reef), but some of these have slightly different meanings. For example, the word 'book' in Fiji-Hindi includes magazines and pamphlets, and if you refer to a person of the opposite sex as a 'friend', it implies that he/she is your sexual partner.

Fiji-Hindi is used in all informal settings, such as in the family and among friends, but the 'Standard Hindi' of India is considered appropriate for formal contexts, such as in public speaking, radio broadcasting and writing. The Hindu majority write in Standard Hindi using the Devanagari script with a large number of words taken from the ancient Sanskrit language. The Muslims use the Perso-Arabic script and incorporate words from Persian and Arabic. When written this way, it is considered a separate language, Urdu, which is the principal language of Pakistan. Indo-Fijians have to learn Standard Hindi or Urdu in school along with English, so while they all speak Fiji-Hindi informally, not everyone knows the formal varieties.

Some people say that Fiji-Hindi is just a 'broken' or 'corrupted' version of standard Hindi. In fact, it is a legitimate dialect with its own grammatical rules and vocabulary unique to Fiji.

PRONUNCIATION

Fiji-Hindi is normally written only in guides for foreigners, such as this, and transcribed using the English alphabet. Since there are at least 42 different sounds in Fiji-Hindi and only 26 letters in the English alphabet, some adjustments have to be made. The vowels are as follows:

| a | as in 'about' or 'sofa' |
| aa | as in 'father' |

e	as in 'bet'
i	as in 'police'
o	as in 'obey'
u	as in 'rule'
ai	as in 'hail'
aai	as in 'aisle'
au	as the 'o' in 'own'
oi	as in 'boil'

The consonants **b**, **f**, **g** (as in 'go'), **h**, **j**, **k**, **l**, **m**, **n**, **p**, **s**, **v**, **y**, **w**, and **z** are similar to those of English. The symbol **ch** is pronounced as in 'chip' and **sh** is pronounced as in 'ship'.

The pronunciation of the consonants 't' and 'd' in Fiji-Hindi is a bit tricky. In 't' and 'd' in English, the tip of the tongue touches the ridge behind the upper teeth, but in Fiji-Hindi it either touches the back of the front teeth (dental) or is curled back to touch the roof of the mouth (retroflex). There are also two 'r' sounds, both of which differ from English. In the first, the tongue touches the ridge above the upper teeth and is flapped quickly forward, similar to the way we say the 't' sound in 'butter' when speaking quickly. In the second, the tongue is curled back, touching the roof of the mouth (as in the retroflex sounds) and then flapped forward. In this chapter we've used a simplified pronunciation guide and haven't made these distinctions. You can substitute the English 't', 'd' and 'r' for these sounds and still be understood.

Finally, there are 'aspirated' consonants. If you hold your hand in front of your mouth and say 'Peter Piper picked a peck of pickled peppers', you'll feel a puff of air each time you say the 'p' sound – this is called aspiration. When you say 'spade, spill, spit, speak', you don't feel the puff of air, because in these words the 'p' sound is not aspirated. In Fiji-Hindi, aspiration is important in distinguishing meaning. Aspiration is indicated by the use of an 'h' after the consonants – for example:

pul/phul	bridge/flower
kaalaa/khaalaa	black/valley
taali/thaali	clapping/brass plate

Other aspirated consonants are:

bh	as in 'grab him' said quickly
chh	as in 'church hat' said quickly

dh	as in 'mad house'
gh	as in 'slug him'
jh	as in 'bridge house'
th	as in 'out house'

CONVERSATION & ESSENTIALS

There are no exact equivalents for 'hello' and 'goodbye' in Fiji-Hindi. The most common greeting is *kaise* (How are you?). The usual reply is *tik* (fine). In parting, it's common to say *fir milegaa* (We'll meet again).

More formal greetings are: *namaste* (for Hindus), *salaam alaykum* (for Muslims) – the reply to the latter is *alaykum as-salaam*.

There are no equivalents for 'please' and 'thank you'. To be polite in making requests, people use the word *thoraa* (a little) and a special form of the verb ending in *naa*, eg *thoraa nimak denaa* (Please pass the salt). For 'thanks', people often just say *achhaa* (good). English 'please' and 'thank you' are also commonly used. The word *dhanyavaad* is used to thank someone who has done something special for you. It means something like 'blessings be bestowed upon you'.

The polite form of the word 'you', *ap*, should also be used with people you don't know well. The informal mode uses the word *tum*. Polite and informal modes of address are indicated in this guide by the abbreviations 'pol' and 'inf', respectively.

Yes.	*ha*
No.	*nahi*
Maybe.	*saayit*
I'm sorry. (for something serious)	*maaf karnaa*
What's your name?	*aapke naam kaa hai?* (pol)
	tumaar naam kaa hai? (inf)
My name is ...	*hamaar naam ...*
Where are you from?	*aap/tum kaha ke hai?* (pol/inf)
I'm from ...	*ham ... ke hai*
Are you married?	*shaadi ho gayaa?*
How many children do you have?	*kitnaa larkaa hai?*
I don't have any children.	*larkaa nahi hai*
Two boys and three girls.	*dui larkaa aur tin larki*
Do you speak English?	*aap/tum English boltaa?* (pol/inf)
Does anyone here speak English?	*koi English bole?*
I don't understand.	*ham nahi samajhtaa*

DIRECTIONS

Where is the ...?	... kaha hai?
shop	dukaan
airport	eyapot
(main) bus station	basten
market	maaket
temple	mandir
mosque	masjid
church	chech

You can also use the English words hotel, guesthouse, camping ground, toilet, post office, embassy, tourist information office, museum, café, restaurant and telephone.

I want to go to ...	ham ... jaae mangtaa
Is it near/far?	nagich/dur hai?
Can I go by foot?	paidar jaae saktaa?
Go straight ahead.	sidhaa jaao
Please write down the address.	thoraa edres likh denaa

By the ...	... ke paas
coconut tree	nariyal ke per
mango tree	aam ke per
breadfruit tree	belfut ke per
sugar-cane field	gannaa khet

HEALTH & EMERGENCIES

Help me!	hame madad karo!
Call the doctor/police.	doktaa ke/pulis ke bulaao
Go away!	jaao!
Where is the hospital?	aaspataal kaha hai?
I'm diabetic.	hame chini ke bimaari hai
I'm allergic to penicillin.	penesilin se ham bimaar ho jaai
I have a stomach-ache.	hamaar pet piraawe
I feel nauseous.	hame chhaant lage
condom	kondom/raba
contraceptive	pariwaar niyojan ke dawaai

medicine	dawaai
sanitary napkin	ped, nepkin
tampon	tampon

NUMBERS

1	ek
2	dui
3	tin
4	chaar
5	paanch
6	chhe
7	saat
8	aath
9	nau
10	das
100	sau
1000	hazaar

English is normally used for numbers from 20 to 99.

TIME & DATES

What time is it?	kitnaa baje?
It's ... o'clock.	... baje
When?	kab?
today	aaj
tonight	aaj raatke
tomorrow	bihaan
yesterday	kal

English days of the week are generally used.

TRANSPORT

When does the ... leave/arrive?	kitnaa baje ... chale/pahunche?
ship	jahaaj
car	mottar

You can also use the English words bus, plane, boat.

Glossary

See p70 for some useful words and phrases dealing with food. See the Language chapter, p272, for some other useful words and phrases.

(F = Fijian; FH = Fijian-Hindi/Hindi; O = Other)

adi (F) – female chief

balabala (F) – tree fern with the unique property of not igniting over hot stones – good for fire walking rituals
bêche-de-mer (O) – elongated, leathery sea cucumber, with a cluster of tentacles at the mouth – sound appetising? Considered a delicacy in Asia; you may find it on your menu
beka (F) – flying fox
bete (F) – priests of the old Fijian religion
bhindi (FH) – okra
bilibili (F) – bamboo raft
bilo (F) – drinking vessel made from half a coconut shell
bolubolu (F) – traditional custom of apology and reconciliation
breadfruit (O) – It's a fruit…with a breadlike texture; trees are common throughout the Pacific and the (bready) fruit is cooked and eaten
bua (F) – frangipani
bula (F) – cheers! hello! welcome! (literally, 'life')
bula shirt (F) – masi- or floral-design shirt
burau (F) – ceremonial kava-drinking ritual
bure (F) – traditional thatched dwelling or whatever your resort decides it to be
bure bose (F) – meeting house
bure kalou (F) – ancient temple

cibi (F) – death dance
copra (O) – dried coconut kernel, used for making coconut oil

dadakulaci (F) – banded sea krait, Fiji's most common snake
dakua (F) – a tree of the kauri family
dele (F) – a dance where women sexually humiliate enemy corpses and captives; also called wate
drua (F) – double-hulled canoe; traditional catamaran

FVB – Fiji Visitors Bureau

girmitiya (FH) – indentured labourer; the word comes from girmit, the Indian labourers' pronunciation of agreement

ibe (F) – a mat
ibuburau (F) – drinking vessels used in kava rites
ika (F) – fish
io (F) – yes
ivi (F) – Polynesian chestnut tree

kai colo (F) – hill people
kaihidi (F) – Indo-Fijian
kaivalagi (F) – literally, 'people from far away'; Europeans
kaiviti (F) – indigenous Fijian
kanikani (F) – scaly skin from excessive kava use, often accompanied by a tranquil grin
kasou (F) – very drunk
kava (F) – Polynesian pepper shrub; more importantly the mildly narcotic, muddy and odd-tasting drink made from its aromatic roots; also called yaqona
kerekere (F) – custom of shared property; also means please
koro (F) – village headed by a hereditary chief
kumala (F) – sweet potato

liku (F) – traditional skirt of womanhood, made from grasses or strips of pandanus leaves; phased out by the missionaries
lovo (F) – Fijian feast cooked in a pit oven

malo (F) – see masi
mangi mangi (F) – traditional weavings
mangrove (O) – a tropical tree that grows in tidal mud flats, and deserves praise for beautifying wet dirt
masi (F) – bark cloth with designs printed in black and rust; also known as malo or tapa
mataqali (F) – extended family or landowning group
meke (F) – a dance performance that enacts stories and legends

nama (F) – an edible seaweed that looks like miniature green grapes…not so yum
namaste (FH) – hello/goodbye; perhaps the word that got the Beatles all confused
narak (F) – hell
NAUI (O) – National Association of Underwater Instructors

PADI (O) – Professional Association of Diving Instructors
paidar (FH) – on foot
paisa (FH) – money, moola, dosh
pandanus (O) – a plant common to the tropics whose sword-shaped leaves are used to make mats and baskets
pelagics (O) – large predatory fish, or whales
piala (F) – small metal enamelled bowl

rara (F) – ceremonial ground
ratu (F) – male chief

saqa (F) – trevally fish
sega (F) – no
sevusevu (F) – presentation of a gift to a village chief and, consequently the ancestral gods and spirits; the gift is often *kava (yaqona)*; however *tabua* is the most powerful *sevusevu;* acceptance of the gift means the giver will be granted certain privileges or favours
sulu (F) – skirt or wrapped cloth worn to below the knees

tabu (F) – forbidden or sacred, implying a religious sanction
tabua (F) – the teeth of sperm whales, which carry a special ceremonial value for Fijians; they are still used as negotiating tokens to symbolise esteem or atonement
taga yaqona (F) – pounded *kava*
takia (F) – Fijian canoe
talanoa (F) – to chat, to tell stories, to have a yarn
tanoa (F) – *kava* drinking bowl
tapa (F) – see *masi*
tevoro (F) – a god of the old Fijian religion
tikina (F) – a group of Fijian villages linked together
trade winds (O) – the near-constant (and annoying) winds that buffer most of the tropics
tui (F) – king

turaga (F) – chief
turaga-ni-koro (F) – hereditary chief

vale (F) – a family house
vale lailai (F) – toilet
vanua (F) – land, region, place
vasu (F) – a system in which a chiefly woman's sons could claim support and ownership over the property of her brothers from other villages
vatu ni bokola (F) – head-chopping stone used during cannibalistic rituals
veli (F) – a group of little gods
vesi (F) – ironwood, considered a sacred timber
vilavilairevo (F) – fire walking (literally, 'jumping into the oven')
vinaka (F) – thank you
Viti (F) – the name indigenous Fijians used for Fiji before the arrival of Europeans (whose mispronunciation gave Fiji its current name)
vulagi (F) – visitors; also *kaivalagi*

waka (F) – bunch of *kava* roots
wakalou (F) – climbing fern species
wate (F) – see *dele*

yaqona (F) – see *kava*
yasana (F) – a province formed by several *tikina*
yavu (F) – bases for housing

BEHIND THE SCENES

Behind the Scenes

THIS BOOK

Lonely Planet's guide to Fiji was first published in 1986. We've had a small army of authors work on the book since then, with the last edition written by Korina Miller (coordinating author) plus the Fiji-ophile team of Robyn Jones and Leo Pinheiro.

This 7th edition was comprehensively updated by Justine Vaisutis, Mark Dapin, Claire Waddell and Virginia Jealous (Suva-based provider of wine, pasta and inside information to authors and commissioning editors alike). Clement Paligaru called on his family and friends in Fiji once more to update the special chapter on Indo-Fijian History & Culture, while Jean-Bernard Carillet donned flippers and tank to write the new special chapter on Fiji's awesome scuba diving. Andrew Bock provided the boxed text, A Surfer's Guide at a Glance.

Commissioning Editors Errol Hunt, Marg Toohey
Coordinating Editor Evan Jones
Coordinating Cartographer Julie Sheridan
Coordinating Layout Designer Adam Bextream
Managing Editor Suzannah Shwer
Managing Cartographer Corie Waddell
Assisting Editors Kate Evans, Gennifer Ciavarra
Cover Designer Julie Rovis, Jacqui Saunders
Colour Designer Katie Thuy Bui
Project Managers Nancy Ianni, John Shippick
Language Content Coordinator Quentin Frayne

Thanks to Dave Burnett, Sally Darmody, Karen Emmerson, Rebecca Lalor, Adriana Mammarella, Jennifer Mundy-Nordin, Malisa Plesa, Debbie Roller, Wibowo Rusli, Jane Thompson, Lisa Tuckwell, Meagan Williams, Gabrielle Wilson, Celia Wood.

THANKS
JUSTINE VAISUTIS

Many people made this gig an utter joy. Big thanks go to my co-authors, particularly Mark and Virginia for their outstanding work. V your vegetarian lasagne, chilled white, sense of humour and infinite knowledge of Fiji (and seemingly everything else) was a pleasure to experience. Cheers also to Errol Hunt, Marg Toohey, Corie Waddell, Evan Jones and Julie Sheridan in-house.

For invaluable assistance and advice on all things Rotuma I owe many thanks to John Bennett and Dr John Fatiaki. The Fiji Visitors Bureau in Nadi deserves a round of drinks, particularly Tupou for her tireless patience and advice. For making me smile, laugh, relax and generally enjoy myself on the road, big thanks go to Simon H, Adam C, Paul and Vicki for the Sigatoka Dunes trek, Rachael and Scott, my dearly beloved baby seals Mette and Kim, and Manuel 'Manny' for the diving.

At home and always thanks to my beautiful sister Aidy for always propping me up when I need it as well as Simon Sellars, Alan Murphy, my awesome crew at the Australian Conservation Foundation, particularly Anna, Margie, Katie H and Josh, and last but not least mum, dad and Bill.

MARK DAPIN & CLAIRE WADDELL

Thanks to everybody who helped us out on the road – you know who you are, even if you didn't know who we were – but particularly Bobby the Talking Taxi Driver in Savusavu and Nand the Efficient Taxi Driver in Taveuni. Peter Thomson in Sydney helped immeasurably by putting everything into context. Thanks to Virginia for putting us up and helping us out in Suva, and to Justine and Errol. Mark would also like to thank David Smiedt and Jamie Tarabay. They were no help at all, but they thanked him in their books and he did not do anything much to help them either.

VIRGINIA JEALOUS

Thanks to the following locals who cast an expert eye over the chapters and, fortified as necessary with *kava*, coffee or wine, provided comment and input. Lionel Gibson, former USP geographer and current NGO regional governance programme manager, read the History chapter; colleague David Hesaie, of the Foundation of the Peoples of the South Pacific International, guided me through Suva market's aisles-less-travelled in preparation for the Food & Drink chapter; Craig Morley, conservation biologist and USP lecturer, helped tackle the Environment chapter; and writer and film-maker Larry Thomas reviewed the Culture chapter.

OUR READERS

Many thanks to all the travellers who used the last edition and wrote to us with helpful hints, useful advice and interesting anecdotes:

A Connie Adams, Mick Adams, Kevin Arnold, Vinay Arora **B** Oli B, Andrea Barbante, Abbie Bennett, Fiona Bergin, Siri Berman, Clint & Carly Blackbourn, Chris Bluemel, Eleanor Booth-Davey, Cheryl Bowden, Chloe Boyes, Stuart Brandwood, Grant Bridger, Jeffrey Bright, Lyndsay Brodie, Sarah Brown, Rene & Sonja Brutschin, Claudia Busch **C** Kirsty Cambridge, Manuela Campanale, Jennifer Caufield, Chris Cheng, Fiona Chung, Caroline Clark, Ceire Clark, Michael Clark, Jan Cloin, Aporosa Colaudolu, Karen Collins, Phoebe Collyer, John Connell, Cathryn Anne Cordyack-Washington, John Coulson, Margaret Cowan, Michael Cox **D** Martine De Flander, Maximo Diaz, Andrew Dienes, Jane Dobson, Emma Donegan, Allie Doyle, Paul Duckett **E** Roger Paul Edmonds, Roni & Manny Elder **F** Simon Fathers, Nicola Ferris, Christina Finsterer, Chris Fletcher, Steve Ford, Carolyn Fotofili **G** Jason Galea, Stefan Gary, Jean Pierre & Fernande Gigoux, Roger Ginger, Melissa Graovac, Ronalie Green, Andrew Griffiths, Leslie Griffiths, Roy Groom **H** Erika Hahn, Trevor Hancock, Darren Hart, Robert Hart, Martin Hatz, Chris Heighton, Angela Hey, Tony Hickey, Melody Hiew, Klaus Hoeflich, Kate Holden, Quentin & Ann Hunter **I** Tiffany Ingersoll **J** Ann Jagger, Tara Jane, Tom Johnson, Alice Jones, Rowan Jones, Rowan & Anna Jones, Anne Julh **K** Ulf Kalla, Line Kallstad, Bernadette Keeffe, Sarah Dawn Kellett, Jenny Kerr, Carla Kersten, Danielle Klap, Anne-Marie Kleijberg, Viola Koch, Shannon Kozak, Charlotte Kreipke **L** Ross Larsen, J P Leighton-Scott, Michal Levy, Dave Lih, Penny Liu, Erik Locht, Vanessa Lovegrove, Kelsi Luhnow **M** Monica M, Heather Macleod, Claire McConnell, Dan McGanty, Liam McGowan, Louisa McMorris, Gerald Meral, Melina Merryn, Alexander Miller, Hannah Miller, Jim Miller, Kylie Mitten, Joan Moody, Steffi Morgner, Felix Mueller, Ronaldo Müller, Tony Murray **N** Dev Naidu, Ken & Margery Nash, Christopher Neighbours, David Nesbitt, Caoimhe Ní Nualláin, Vanessa Nitsos, Fane Niumataiwalu, Anushe Nizam, Paul Norris, Rob Nouten, Lars Nyman **O** Tim O'Leary, Lizette Oberholster, Paul Ohashi, Stacy Orr, Jack & Nancy Ostheimer **P** Carla Page, Bruce Palmer, Cherie Palmer, Rebecca Palmer, Katerina Pecova, Ruth Perez-Merino, Wesley Petzinger, Hanne Bjoernestad Platz, Dennis Plink, Caroline Powell, John Powell, George Prasad, Michael Pugwash **Q** Antony Quarrell **R** Paul Recher, Vivian Regan, Andrew Riha, Chris Ripke, Jens Rittmann, Sebastian Rockenfeller, Fiona Roscoe, Steve Rose **S** Eleanor Sbogar, Sarah Scarborough, Björn Schiffbauer, Lukas Schmid, Edwin Schuurman, John Self, Tamra Shanly, Steven & Truus Sharp, Robin Shaw, Molly Sinclair, Anna Solotskaya, Rita Squire, Drew Squires, Isabelle Stiegeler, Christian Stuerwald **T** John Terry, Helen Thompson, Laura Totis, Darius Tremtiaczy, Diane Turner, Liz Turner, Max Turner **U** Kalina Unger **V** Wilna van Eyssen, Liz Vinall, Michael Vink **W** Margit Waas, Maria Wahlgren, Rosemary Walsh, Chris Walters, Viliame Waqa, Andy Waterman, Edel Waters, David Watkin, Emily Watts, Mandy Weare, Arlett Weise, Ken Westmoreland, Amy Whiteside, Janie Whyld, Adam Williams, Gerry Willms, Joanne Willms **Y** Rob Yee **Z** Harry Zawacki

ACKNOWLEDGMENTS

Many thanks to the following for the use of their content:

Globe on back cover © Mountain High Maps 1993 Digital Wisdom, Inc.

SEND US YOUR FEEDBACK

We love to hear from travellers – your comments keep us on our toes and help make our books better. Our well-travelled team reads every word on what you loved or loathed about this book. Although we cannot reply individually to postal submissions, we always guarantee that your feedback goes straight to the appropriate authors, in time for the next edition. Each person who sends us information is thanked in the next edition – and the most useful submissions are rewarded with a free book.

To send us your updates – and find out about Lonely Planet events, newsletters and travel news – visit our award-winning website: **www.lonelyplanet.com/feedback**.

Note: We may edit, reproduce and incorporate your comments in Lonely Planet products such as guidebooks, websites and digital products, so let us know if you don't want your comments reproduced or your name acknowledged. For a copy of our privacy policy visit www.lonelyplanet.com/privacy.

Index

A

accommodation 239-41, *see also*
    Nadi, Suva
    camping 240
    hostels 240
    rental 240-1
    resorts 241-2
activities 242-5, *see also individual*
    activities
air travel **259**
    air fares 255-6
    airline offices 254-8, 259-60
    airports 254-8
    scenic flights 81
    to/from Fiji 254-8
    within Fiji 259-60, **259**, **99**
animals 51-4, *see also* birds, fish,
    individual animals
architecture 42
    bure 42, 81
Arovudi 177
art galleries, *see* museums & galleries
arts 39-43, *see also individual arts*
    dance 41-2, **96**
    Internet resources 39
    literature 20, 39-40, 51, *see also*
        books
    masi 43
    music 20, 41, 49
    pottery 42
    woodcarving 42-3
Astrolabe Reef 62-3, 225, **6**
ATMs 250-1

B

Ba 142
Baker, Reverend Thomas 28-9, 120
bargaining 251
Bau 137
Bavadra, Dr Timoci 31, 45, 89
Bay of Islands 232-3, **188**
Beachcomber Island 151
bêche-de-mer trade 28, 40, 202
beer 66
Beqa 115-16
Beqa Lagoon 58, 112, 115
Biausevu 110
Biausevu waterfall 110, **11**
bicycle travel, *see* cycling, mountain
    biking

birds 53, *see also* bird-watching,
    individual birds
    books 53
bird-watching 53, 242
    Kadavu Group 226
    Lomaiviti Group 190
    Taveuni 213, 223
    Vanua Levu 202-3
    Viti Levu 107, 111, 124, 137
blackbirding 29-30
Bligh Water 60, 141
Bligh, Captain William 27
Blue Lagoon 167
boat travel, *see also* kayaking, sailing,
    yachting
    to/from Fiji 258-9
    within Fiji 260-2, **95**
books
    birdlife 53
    crafts 43
    diving 54, 58
    food 69
    health 267
    history 28, 30, 33
    language 273
    literature 20, 39-40, 51
    travel 20
Bouma National Heritage
    Park 221
Bounty Island 150
Bua Bay 208
Bukuya 145, **5**, **182**
bure 42, 81
bus travel 262
bushwalking, *see* hiking
business hours 245, *see also inside*
    front cover

C

Cakobau, Chief 28, 137, 171, 176, 209,
    217, 231
    cession to Great Britain 29, 30, 171
    enslavement of the Lovoni 177
    establishment of Suva 118
camping 240
cannibalism 28-9, 120, 137, 139, 144,
    205, 12
canoeing, *see* kayaking
Cape Washington 226
Caqalai 180-9

car travel 262-4
    driving licence 262-3
    hazards 264
    hire 263
carrier travel 264
Castaway Island 154
Castle Rock 143
cathedrals, *see* churches &
    cathedrals
caves
    Naihehe cave 145-6
    Oso Nabukete 234
    Wailotua Snake God Cave 138
Cawaci 176, **183**
cession to Britain 30, 174
Chaudhry, Mahendra 33, 46, 249
children, travel with 69, 80, 245-6,
    268
Christianity 38, *see also* missionaries
churches & cathedrals, *see also*
    missions
    Centenary Methodist Church 125
    Church of the Holy Redeemer 196
    Holy Trinity Cathedral 125
    Navoka Methodist Church 176
    Roman Catholic Cathedral 125
    Sacred Heart Church 174
cinema 19, 40-1
climate 17-18, 246
Cobra Rock 207-8
Colo-i-Suva Forest Park 124-5, **125**
consulates 247-8
Cook, Captain James 27
coral 53, 54, 62, 161, *see also* diving
Coral Coast 103-18, **72-3**
Coral Coast Scenic Railway 103
costs 18
    diving 64
coups 26, 31-2, 33-4, 119, 223, *see*
    also ethnic tensions
courses, diving 60, **59**
crafts 42-3, 251, **12**, *see also individual*
    crafts
    books 43
    Coral Coast, Viti Levu 105, 110, 113
    Mamanuca Group 153, 155
    Nadi, Viti Levu 86-7, 87
    Suva, Viti Levu 134-5
    Vanua Levu 201, 203
credit cards 251

crested iguana 53, 208
cruises, *see also* tours
   Mamanuca Group 80, 149, **97**
   Vanua Levu 196
   Yasawa Group 80, 102, 159-60
cultural centres
   Arts Village 113
   Ka Levu South Pacific Cultural
     Centre 103
   Oceania Centre for Arts & Culture
     39, 124
culture, *see* Fijian culture, Indo-Fijian
   culture
customs regulations 246
cycling 103, 171, 242, 260, *see also*
   mountain biking

D
Dakuniba 203
dance 41-2, **96**
deep vein thrombosis (DVT) 267
deforestation 56
Denarau island 87-8, **95, 96**
dengue fever 268-9
departure tax 255
Des Voeux Peak 215
Deuba 113
diarrhoea 269-70
disabled travellers 247
diving 57-65, 242-3, 244
   Beqa Lagoon 58
   Bligh Water 60, 141
   books 54, 58
   Coral Coast 58-9, 78, 89, 90, 102,
     107, 110-11, 111, 112, 113,
     115, 118, 126
   costs 64
   courses 60, **59**
   dive centres 63
   E6 60
   Great Astrolabe Reef 62-3, **6**
   Internet resources 63
   Kadavu Group 62-3, 225-6, 228,
     6, 63, 187
   Lau Group 232, **64, 188**
   Lomaiviti Group 60-1, 171-3, 180,
     189, 190, **7, 94**
   Mamanuca Group 59, 148-9,
     150, 151, 152, 153, 154, 156,
     157, **59**
   Nananu-i-Ra 59

   Nigali Passage 60, **6**
   Rainbow Reef 61-2
   responsible diving 56, 64
   safe diving 63, 270-1
   Somosomo Strait 61-2
   Taveuni 61-2, 212-13, 223, **6**
   Vanua Levu 61, 195, 196, 204, **94**
   Viti Levu north & east coasts 58-9,
     137, 138, 140, 141
   Yasawa Group 60, 163, 164, 165,
     166, 169
Diwali 49, 67-8, 248
Drekeniwai 203
drinks 66, *see also* beer, *kava*
driving, *see* car travel
drua 217

E
E6 60
economy 26, 35-6, 128
education 36, 47
electricity 239
Ellington Wharf 139-40
email services 250
embassies 247-8
emergencies, *see inside front cover*
Enadala 167
environment 51-6
environmental issues
   air pollution 55-6
   deforestation 56
   global warming 54
   Internet resources 53, 55, 56
   water pollution 56
ethnic tensions 31-4, 45-6, 48, *see*
   also coups
etiquette 36
European contact 27-8, 28-30, 30-1
exchange rates, *see inside front cover*

F
fauna 51-4
Fara festival 237
fax services 251-2
ferry travel 261-2, **98**
festivals 19, 248, *see also* special
   events
   Bula Festival 248
   Diwali 49, 67-8, 248
   Fara 237
   Festival of Lights 49, 67-8, 248
   Fiji International Jazz Festival 248
   Hibiscus Festival 248
   Hindu Ritual Fire Walking 248
   Lautoka's Sugar Festival 248

   Ram Leela 248
   Ram Naumi 248
   South Pacific World Music Festival
     248
Fiji-Hindi language 47, 275-7
Fiji Museum, Suva 42, 121, **12**
Fiji Visitors Bureau (FVB) 252
Fijian culture 19, 35-43, 133, **9, 95,
   96, 182**, *see also* Fijian language
   Great Council of Chiefs 32
   precolonial culture 29, 38, 39, 40,
     41, 204-5, 206, **12**
   responsible travel 36, 69
   village etiquette 36
Fijian language 272-5
   food 70
films, *see* cinema
fire walking 88, 108, 109, 125
fish 53-4, **7, 94, 188**, *see also* diving,
   fishing, *individual fish*
fishing 243
   Kadavu Group 227, 228
   Lau Group 233
   Lomaiviti Group 173, 190
   Mamanuca Group 151, 152,
     153, 156
   Taveuni 213, 218, 223
   Vanua Levu 196, 198, 203, 208, 209
   Viti Levu 103, 113, 116, 118, 141
   Yasawa Group 169
Floating Island 208
flora 54-5
food 66, 68-70, 248-9
   books 69
   cultural considerations 69
   festivals 67-8
   health 271
   Indo-Fijian 47, 49, 50, **9**
   Internet resources 67, 68
   lovo 67, **96**
   vocabulary 70
football 38, 49, 50
Frigates Pass 117
Frigates Passage 115, 116

G
Garden of the Sleeping Giant 89
Gavo Passage 180
gay travellers 249
geography 26, 51, 52
gold mining 145
golf
   Taveuni 213
   Vanua Levu 199, 203
   Viti Levu 79, 87, 103, 111, 113, 139

Great Astrolabe Reef 62-3, 225, **6**
Great Council of Chiefs 32
Gun Rock 176

H
handicrafts, see crafts
health 266-71
    books 267
    bites & stings 270
    children's health 268
    coral infections 270
    deep vein thrombosis (DVT) 267
    dengue fever 268-9
    diarrhoea 269-70
    diving decompression 270-1
    food 271
    heat exhaustion 271
    hepatitis 269
    HIV/AIDS 269
    insurance 266
    Internet resources 267
    medical services 268
    vaccinations 266-7
    women travellers 268
hiking 243
    itineraries 25
    Kadavu Group 225, 228
    Koroyanitu National Heritage Park
        143, **10**
    Lavena Coastal Walk 222
    Lomaiviti Group 176, 190
    Taveuni 213, 221, 222
    Vanua Levu 195, 203
    Viti Levu 81, 89, 105, 114, 115,
        124, 125, 128, 138, 140, 143,
        144, 145
    Yasawa Group 160, 162, 163-4
Hinduism 38, 79, **93**, **185**
history 27-34
    books 28, 30, 33
    coups 26, 31-2, 33-4, 119, 223
    ethnic tensions 31-4, 45-6, 48
    European explorers 27-8
    European settlement 28-30, 30-1
    indentured labour 30-1, 32, 44
    independence 31
    Levuka 171
    Suva 118-19
    Tongan influence 27, 28, 231, see
        also Ma'afu Enele
    Vitian culture 27
hitching 264
holidays 18, 249
horse riding 102, 111, 144, 218,
    220, 243

I
immunisations 266-7
indentured labour 30-1, 32, 44
independence 31
indigenous Fijians, see Fijian culture
Indo-Fijian culture 19, 44-50, **8**, **10**,
    46, **49**, **93**, **182**, **184**, **185**
Indo-Fijians in Fiji 26, 30-4, 37,
    44-50, 128
    indentured labour 30-1, 32, 44
insurance 249-50, 266
International Dateline 51, 214-15
Internet access 250
Internet resources 20
    culture 20, 35, 39, 40
    diving 63
    environmental issues 53, 55, 56
    food 67, 68
    health 267
    newspapers 20, 31, 37
    sports 20, 38
Islam 38, **46**
itineraries 15, 21-5
    beaches 25
    hiking 25

J
jet-boat trips 87
Joske's Thumb 125

K
Ka Levu South Pacific Cultural Centre
    103
Kadavu Group 224-9, **226**, **5**, **11**
    diving 62-3, 225-6, 228, **6**, **63**, **187**
    travel to/from 228-9
Kaibu 233
kava 36, 67, **9**
Kavu Kavu Reef 115, 117
kayaking 243, 244
    Kadavu Group 226, 227, 228
    Lau Group 232, 233
    Lomaiviti Group 189, 190
    Mamanuca Group 150, 151, 152,
        153, 154, 155, 156
    Taveuni 218, 220, **186**
    Vanua Levu 195, 196, 198, 199
    Viti Levu 79, 112, 113, 114, 115,
        128, 140, 146
    Yasawa Group 160
Kings Road 136-42, **72-3**, **93**
Kingsford Smith, Charles 124
Kioa 203-4
Koro 189
Korolevu 110-12, **110**, **5**

Korolevu hill fortification 176
Koro-ni-O 145
Korotogo 107-10, **106**
Korovatu Beach 208
Korovou 137-8
Koroyanitu National Heritage Park
    143, **10**
Kuata 162
Kula Eco Park 107

L
Labasa 204-7, **205**, **46**, **49**, **184**, **185**
Lake Tagimaucia 215
Lakeba 234, **231**
languages 272-7, see also inside front
    cover
    books 273
    Fijian 272-5
    Fiji-Hindi 47, 275-7
    food vocabulary 70
Lau Group 230-4, **231**
    diving 232, **64**, **188**
Laucala 223
Lautoka 90-101, **88**, **91**, **9**
Lavena Coastal Walk 222
Lawai 105
legal matters 250
Leleuvia 189
lesbian travellers 249
Levuka 171, 174-6, 177-8, **175**,
    181, **183**
Levuka village 176
Likuri 102
literature 20, 39-40, 51, see also
    books
    Internet resources 40
Lomaiviti Group 170-90, **172**
    diving 60-1, 171-3, 180, 189,
        190, **7**, **94**
    tours 173
Lomaloma 233
Lomolomo Guns 89
lovo 67, **96**
Lovoni 176, 177
Luva Gorge 113

M
Ma'afu, Enele 28, 222, 231, 234
magazines 239
Malolo 154-5
Malololailai 155-7, **11**, **97**
Mamanuca Group 147-57, **148**, **6**, **98**
    cruises 80, 149, **97**
    diving 59, 148-9, 150, 151, 152,
        153, 154, 156, 157, **59**

Mamanuca Group *continued*
  tours 80-1, 149
  travel to/from 150
Mana 152-3, **59**
Mangroves 54
Manta Ray Island 164
maps 250
Mara, Ratu Sir Kamisese 33, 45, 232
Mariamma Temple 109, 125
marinas
  Copra Shed Marina 195
  Musket Cove Marina 155, **11**
  Vuda Point Marina 89, 90
  Waitui Marina 195
masi 43
Matacawalevu 168, **166**
Matagi 222-3
Matamanoa 153
Matei 218-21, **219**, **186**
Matuku 235
Mavana 233
measures 239, *see also inside front cover*
medical services 268
metric conversions, *see inside front cover*
missionaries 28-9, 136, 137, 234
missions
  Naililili Catholic Mission 136-7
  Naiserelagi Catholic Mission 138
  Wairiki Catholic Mission 215
Moala Group 230, 235, **231**
Moala island 235
mobile phones 252
Momi Bay 101-2
Momi Guns 101
Monasavu Dam 145
money 18, 247, 250-1, *see also inside
  front cover*
motorcycle travel 262-4
  hire 263
Motualevu Atoll 62, **6**
Moturiki 180
Mt Evans 143
Mt Koroyanitu 143
Mt Lomalagi 145
Mt Suelhof 237
Mt Tova 138
Mt Victoria 145
mountain biking 242, *see also* cycling
  Taveuni 220
  Vanua Levu 195, 199
  Viti Levu 79, 89

museums & galleries
  Fiji Museum, Levuka 174, 177
  Fiji Museum, Suva 42, 121
  Indo-Fijian Gallery 121
  La Galerie 155
music 41, 49
  Internet resources 20
Musket Cove Marina 155, **11**

N
Naag Mandir Temple 207-8
Naboro 162
Nabouwalu 208-9
Nabutautau 29, 120
Nacula 168-9, **166**
Nacula Tikina 166-9, **166**
Nadarivatu 145
Nadi 75-87, **76**, **78**, **88**, **8**
  accommodation 82-4
  attractions 77-8
  diving 78-9
  drinking 86
  emergency services 77
  entertainment 86
  food 84-6
  Internet access 77
  medical services 77
  money 77
  safe travel 77
  shopping 86-7
  tourist offices 77
  tours 79-82
  travel to/from 87
  travel within 87
Nagigi 197
Naigani 190, **94**
Naihehe cave 145-6
Naililili Catholic Mission 136-7
Naisali Island 90
Naiserelagi Catholic Mission 138
Nakabuta 105
Nakauvadra Range 139
Nakavika 113
Namara 162
Namenalala 190
Namosi Highlands 146
Namotu 157
Namuamua 113
Nananu-i-Ra 59, 140-2, **140**
Nanuya Lailai 167
Nanuya Levu 169
Naqara 214, **211**
Nasilai island 128
Nasilai village 136-7
Natadola Beach 102-3

national parks & reserves 55
  Bouma National Heritage Park 221
  Colo-i-Suva Forest Park 124-5, **125**
  Koroyanitu National Heritage Park
    143, **10**
  Kula Eco Park 107
  Waisali Rainforest Reserve 202
  Waitabu Marine Park 222
  Yadua Tabu 208-9
Natovi Landing 138
Nausori Highlands 143-5, **95**
Nausori town 136
Navai 145
Navala 144-5, **95**
Navatu Rock 139
Navatusila 120
Navini 151-2
Naviti 164-5
Navua 112-15
Naweni 196
New Town Beach 82-7
newspapers 37
  Internet resources 20, 31, 37
Niubasaga 180
Nukubati 208
Nukubolu 202, **185**
Nukusere 113

O
Oceania Centre for Arts & Culture
  39, 124
orange dove 53, 213
Oso Nabukete 234
Ovalau 171, 173-4, **172**
  travel to/from 179

P
Pacific Harbour 112-15
passports 254, *see also* visas
people, *see* Fijian culture, Indo-Fijian
  culture
permits 253
planning 17-20, 247, *see
  also* itineraries
  health 266-7
plants 54-5, *see also* tagimaucia
politics 26
pollution 55-6
population 26, 35, 36-7, 48
postal services 251
pottery 42
Promotion of Reconciliation, Tolerance
  and Unity Bill 26, 32, 34
PRTU Bill 26, 32
public holidays 18, 249

Q

Qamea 223
Qarase, Lasenia 33, 34, 46, 48
Qilaqila 232-3

R

Rabi 204
Rabuka, Lieutenant Colonel Sitiveni
    32, 33, 45-6, 203
radio 37, 239
rafting, *see* river rafting
Rainbow Reef 61-2, 212-13
Rakiraki 138-40, **138**
religion 37-8
    Hinduism 79, 109, **93**, **185**
    Islam 38, **46**
resorts 241-2, **5**, **187**
responsible travel
    cultural considerations 36, 69
    diving 56, 64
    environmental issues 56
    village etiquette 36
Rewa Delta 136-7
river rafting 79, 113, 114, 128, 146,
    243
robbery 246
Robinson Crusoe Island 102
Rotuma 236-8, **237**
    travel to/from 238
rugby 20, 38, 134
    Internet resources 38
Rukuruku 176-7

S

Sabeto Mountains 88-9, **10**, **93**
safe travel 162, 246-7
    diving 63
sailing 139, 160, 196, 208, 223, 243-4,
    183, *see also* yachting
    travel permits 253
sandalwood trade 27-8
Savusavu 193-202, **194**, **198**, **9**, **185**
Savusavu Bay 61, 195, **198**, **94**, **184**
Sawa-i-Lau 169, **99**
Sawana 233
scams 246-7
scenic flights 81, 260
sea snakes 53
Shark Reef 58
sharks 54
    Kadavu Group 225
    Lau Group 234
    Lomaiviti Group 60, 61
    Mamanuca Group 59
    Taveuni 62, 212

Vanua Levu 61
Viti Levu 58, 148
Shobna 49-50
shopping 251, *see also* crafts
Sigatoka 103-5, **104**
Sigatoka Sand Dunes 105, **10**
Sigatoka Valley 105-6, 145-6, **106**
Silana 177
Singh, Vijay 39, 48
Sisilo 237
Snake Island 180
snorkelling 242-3
    Kadavu Group 227, 228
    Lau Group 232, 233
    Lomaiviti Group 171-3, 178, 180,
        189, 190
    Mamanuca Group 149, 150, 151,
        152, 153, 154, 155, 156, **6**
    Taveuni 212-13, 218, 220, 222, 223
    Vanua Levu 195, 196, 197, 198,
        199, 203, 204
    Viti Levu 102, 103, 112, 115, 116,
        137, 138, 140, 141
    Yasawa Group 162, 163, 164, 165,
        166, 168
soccer 38, 49, 50
Solroroa Bluff 237
Somosomo 214-16
Somosomo Strait 61-2
South Sea Island 150-1
special events 248, *see also* festivals
    Fiji Ocean Swim 248
sports 38-9, *see also* individual sports
    Internet resources 20, 38
Sri Siva Subramaniya Swami Temple
    77-8, **93**
student cards 247
sugar industry 26, **93**, *see also*
    indentured workers
surfing 117, 244
    Kadavu Group 117, 226, 228
    Lau group 117
    Mamanuca Group 102, 117, 149,
        155, 157
    Rotuma 237
    Vanua Levu 117
    Viti Levu 90, 102, 105, 110, 111,
        112, 113, 115, 116, 117, 126
    Yasawa Group 117
Suva 118-36, **119**, **122**, **95**
    accommodation 128-30
    activities 125-6
    attractions 121-5
    drinking 133-4
    emergency services 120

entertainment 134, **182**
food 130-3, **7**
Internet access 120-1
medical services 121
money 121
safe travel 121
shopping 134-5, **8**, **12**
tourist offices 121
tours 128
travel to/from 135
travel within 135-6
walking tour 126-8, **127**

T

tabua 29, 33
tagimaucia 54, 215
Tavarua 157
Taveuni 210-23, **211**, **186**
    diving 61-2, 212-13, 223, **6**
    travel to/from 213
Tavewa 166-7, **166**
Tavoro waterfalls 221
Tavua 142, 153
Tavuni Hill Fort 106-7
taxi travel 264
telephone services 251-2
temples
    Mariamma Temple 109, 125
    Mariamman Temple 208
    Naag Mandir Temple 207-8
    Shree Laxmi Narayan Temple
        125
    Sri Siva Subramaniya Swami
        Temple 77-8, **93**
textiles 251
theft 246
Thurston Gardens 123
time 252, 291, **291**
tipping 251
Toberua 137
Tokoriki 154
Tomanivi 145
Tongan influence 27, 28, 231, *see also*
    Ma'afu, Enele
tourist information 252-3
tours 264-5
    Lomaiviti Group 173
    Mamanuca Group 80-1, 149
    Nadi area 79-82
    Vanua Levu 195-6
    Viti Levu 80, 102, 107, 113-14,
        128, 139
    Viti Levu Highlands 81-2, 107,
        143-4, 146
    Yasawa Group 80-2, 102, 159-60

traditional culture 29, 38, 39, 40, 41, 204-5, 206, **9**, **12**, **95**, **96**
train travel
Coral Coast Scenic Railway 103
tramping, *see* hiking
travel permits 253
travellers cheques 251
Treasure Island 151
trekking, *see* hiking
Tubou 234
Tunuloa Peninsula 202-3
Turtle Island 169
turtles 53, 107, 190, 212
TV 37

U
Uciwai Landing 90
Udreudre's Tomb 139
Uluisolo 154
University of the South Pacific 124
Uru's Waterfall 137

V
vaccinations 266-7
Vaileka 139-40
Vale Ni Bose 233
Vanua Balavu 232-3, **188**
Vanua Levu 191-209, **192**, **193**, **183**
diving 61, 195, 196, 204, **94**
tours 195-6
travel to/from 192-3
Vatukarasa 110
Vatukoula 142
Vatulele 116-18
vegetarian travellers 69
Vidawa Rainforest Trail 221
video systems 239
village etiquette 36
village visits 36, 245, **9**
visas 253, *see also* passports

Viseisei 89-90
Viti Levu 71-146, **72-3**
children, travel with 80
cruises 80
diving 58-9, 78, 89, 90, 102, 107, 110-11, 111, 112, 113, 115, 118, 126, 137, 138, 140, 141
highlands 81-2, 88-9, 142-6, **5**, **9**, **10**, **11**, **95**, **182**
itineraries 74
tours 79-82, 102, 107, 113-14, 128, 139, 143-4, 146139, 143-4, 146
travel to/from 74-5, 254-8, 259-60
travel within 75
Viti Levu Highlands 81-2, 88-9, 142-6, **5**, **9**, **10**, **11**, **95**, **182**
Viwa 137
Vomo 151
Vuda Point 89-90
Vunisea 225, **11**
Vunivau 208

W
Wadigi 154
Wailagi Lala Passage 232, **188**
Wailoaloa Beach 83-7
Wailotua 138
Wailotua Snake God Cave 138
Wainaloka 173
Wainikoroiluva 113
Wainunu Bay 209
Wairiki Catholic Mission 215
Waisali Rainforest Reserve 202
Waitabu Marine Park 222
Waitavala Water Slide 215
Waitovu waterfall 173
Waiyevo 214-16
Wakaya 189, **96**, **183**

walking, *see* hiking
Wasavula Ceremonial Site 204-5, 206
Waya 163-4, **166**
Wayalailai 162-3
Wayasewa 162-3, **166**
websites, *see* Internet resources
weights & measures 239, *see also* inside front cover
whales 176, 196, 199, 212
white-water rafting, *see* river rafting
wildlife 51-5, *see also* animals, birds
Wilkes, Commandant Charles 29
windsurfing
Lomaiviti Group 190, 197
Mamanuca Group 152, 154, 156, **97**
Taveuni 223
Vanua Levu 208
Viti Levu 102, 112, 141
women in Fiji 38
women travellers 253
health 268
woodcarving 42-3
work 253

Y
yachting 258-9, *see also* sailing
Yadua Tabu 208-9
Yanuca island 116, **4**
Yanuca Lailai 180
Yanuca village 103
yaqona 36, 67, **9**
Yasawa Group 158-69, **159**
cruises 80, 102, 159-60
diving 60, 163, 164, 165, 166, 169
tours 80-2, 102, 159-60
travel to/from 161-2
Yasawa island 169, **96**, **99**, **100**

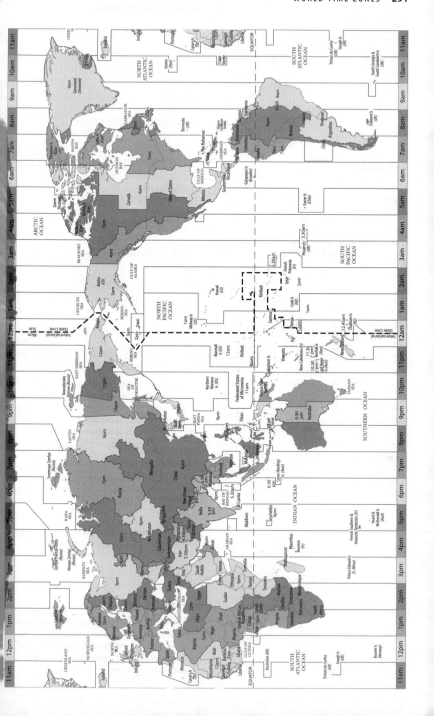

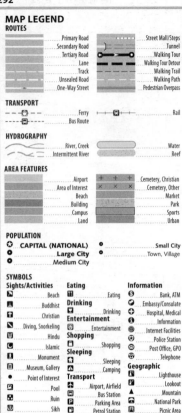

MAP LEGEND

ROUTES
- Primary Road
- Secondary Road
- Tertiary Road
- Lane
- Track
- Unsealed Road
- One-Way Street
- Street Mall/Steps
- Tunnel
- Walking Tour
- Walking Tour Detour
- Walking Trail
- Walking Path
- Pedestrian Overpass

TRANSPORT
- Ferry
- Bus Route
- Rail

HYDROGRAPHY
- River, Creek
- Intermittent River
- Water
- Reef

AREA FEATURES
- Airport
- Area of Interest
- Beach
- Building
- Campus
- Land
- Cemetery, Christian
- Cemetery, Other
- Market
- Park
- Sports
- Urban

POPULATION
- ◉ CAPITAL (NATIONAL)
- ● Large City
- ● Medium City
- ● Small City
- ● Town, Village

SYMBOLS

Sights/Activities
- Beach
- Buddhist
- Christian
- Diving, Snorkeling
- Hindu
- Islamic
- Monument
- Museum, Gallery
- Point of Interest
- Pool
- Ruin
- Sikh
- Surfing, Surf Beach

Eating
- Eating

Drinking
- Drinking

Entertainment
- Entertainment

Shopping
- Shopping

Sleeping
- Sleeping
- Camping

Transport
- Airport, Airfield
- Bus Station
- Parking Area
- Petrol Station
- Taxi Rank

Information
- Bank, ATM
- Embassy/Consulate
- Hospital, Medical
- Information
- Internet Facilities
- Police Station
- Post Office, GPO
- Telephone

Geographic
- Lighthouse
- Lookout
- Mountain
- National Park
- Picnic Area
- Waterfall

LONELY PLANET OFFICES

Australia
Head Office
Locked Bag 1, Footscray, Victoria 3011
☎ 03 8379 8000, fax 03 8379 8111
talk2us@lonelyplanet.com.au

USA
150 Linden St, Oakland, CA 94607
☎ 510 893 8555, toll free 800 275 8555
fax 510 893 8572
info@lonelyplanet.com

UK
72–82 Rosebery Ave,
Clerkenwell, London EC1R 4RW
☎ 020 7841 9000, fax 020 7841 9001
go@lonelyplanet.co.uk

Published by Lonely Planet Publications Pty Ltd
ABN 36 005 607 983

© Lonely Planet Publications Pty Ltd 2006

© photographers as indicated 2006

Cover photographs by Lonely Planet Images: Warriors' dance performer on Robinson Crusoe Island, off Viti Levu, Robyn Jones (front); Riding horses along a palm-fringed beach, Coral Coast, David Wall (back). Many of the images in this guide are available for licensing from Lonely Planet Images: www.lonelyplanetimages.com.

Printed through The Bookmaker International Ltd
Printed in China